IN SEARCH OF CANADA

IN SEARCH

VOLUME 2 *Prentice-Hall of Canada, Ltd., Scarborough, Ontario*

OF CANADA

Ronald C. Kirbyson *assisted by* Elizabeth Peterson

to Cam Shepherd

Canadian Cataloguing in Publication Data

Kirbyson, Ronald C., 1937–
  In search of Canada

Includes index.
ISBN 0-13-453852-8 (v.1). ISBN 0-13-453860-9 (v.2).

1. Canada—History. I. Title.

FC170.K57   971   C77-001060-1
F1026.K57

Prentice-Hall, Inc., Englewood Cliffs, New Jersey
Prentice-Hall International, Inc., London
Prentice-Hall of Australia, Pty., Ltd., Sydney
Prentice-Hall of India, Pvt., Ltd., New Dehli
Prentice-Hall of Japan, Inc., Tokyo
Prentice-Hall of Southeast Asia (PTE.) Ltd., Singapore

Design by John Zehethofer
Maps by James Loates

Printed in Canada
ISBN 0-13-453860-9
      3 4 5 THB 81 80 79 78

Contents

Acknowledgements

The efforts of many people went into *In Search of Canada*. I shall be forever grateful for the support I received over the past three years.

To Elizabeth Peterson I must express special gratitude. She has been my colleague and friend throughout the enterprise. Not only did she contribute substantially to the writing, but she devoted thousands of hours to research, discussion and the myriad of tedious jobs that are involved in building such a book, including the typing of most of the manuscript in several stages.

Prentice-Hall of Canada supported me in the best way a publisher can: by providing talented personnel. As editor, Rob Greenaway has been a constant source of shrewd advice, ideas, helpful criticism and encouragement. His friendship and many kindnesses have been especially important during the difficult times when it seemed *In Search of Canada* would never be completed. Barb Steel has been much more than a production editor. She made countless suggestions for improving the writing. Not only did she supervise the research for pictures and illustrations, but she did much of the actual work. Without Barb's loyalty to the project, her talent for organizing, and her capacity for long hours of work, the preparation of *In Search of Canada* might have continued forever. John Ford, Executive Producer, Media Division, Prentice-Hall of Canada, Ltd., kindly made his extensive picture files available.

Many other people provided help along the way: Paul Hunt, who launched the project in fact; Jim Burant of the Public Archives of Canada who assisted with picture research; Ken Osborne, who read much of the manuscript in its early stages and offered much helpful advice; Cam Shepherd, who freely made his time available and helped me avoid many errors about economics; Janet Warren, who patiently handled many chores like preparing the bibliography; Janice Yeo and the staff of the Elizabeth Dafoe Library, University of Manitoba; Stephen Stankovic, with whom I so often discussed material in preparation; Laurie Hughes and Harvey Herstein, the other authors of *Challenge and Survival: The History of Canada*, who willingly allowed the use of selected material originally researched and developed for that book.

My debt to my family cannot ever be repaid. My parents, Jean and Bill, helped me feel less guilty about spending so little time in their company. Dawn, Geoffrey and Jillian never wavered in their understanding, and they accepted "the book" with humour and patience as part of the household.

RCK

The author and publisher would like to thank the following for permitting illustrations to be used:

The Public Archives of Canada: pp 3, C 19313; 4, C 3758; 46; 48, C 16408, C 56472; 52, C 78604; 53, PA 26435; 54, C 6686B; 55, C 4953; 64, C 10148, C 6536; 69, C 34213; 73, C 3641, C 4522; 75, C 15282, detail, C 1875, C 1873; 77, C 1879; 79, C 22002; 81, C 6460; 85, C 16741; 88, C 5329; 93, C 28727; 98, RD 347, C 8058; 104; 105, C 8893; 109, C 8498; 110, C 81683; 124, C 30624, C 52819; 125, C 61544; 129, C 30953; 135, C 681; 136, PA 38567; 145, C 6648; 162, PA 1123; 164, PA 1654; 165, PA 1689; 166, PA 648; 168, C 23488; 171, PA 8158; 173, C 5110; 176, PA 5904, PA 5909; 178, PA 24438; 179, PA 24640; 181, C 2422; 183, PA 28912; 185, C 9007; 195, C 74971; 204, C 12187, PA 26987, C 694; 206, C 57030; 212, PA 15178; 213, C 31934; 214, C 6595; 215, PA 48394; 216, PA 40459; 220, C 26783; 223, C 34443; 235, C 80901; 237, C 80906; 248, C 7731, PA 33656; 251, C 55451; 254, C 16476; 256, PA 19628; 261, C 20954; 262, C 24834; 263, C 21528; 271, C 29449, C 29447; 285, C 53114; 288, PL 3055; 291, King Coll. Box T 1220; 296; 304, C 26110; 307, C 29464; 308, C 14118; 311, C 47402; 319, King Coll. T 1227; 323; 324; 325; 327, C 20048; 329, C 5337; 332, D. Cameron Coll., C 17646; 344, C 22719; 346, C 22859; 348, D. Cameron Coll.; 376, C 18347; 388, C 58126; 426, C 75818; 434, C 15160; 445; 456, C 20021; 469, PL 4484; 478, C 20074; 480, SF 840.

NEA Ltd.: pp. 31, 35, 39, 379, 401, 412, 420. Miller Services: Cover photo, p. 39. Norris, *The Vancouver Sun*: pp. 39, 451. United Feature Syndicate: p. 39. Ministry of Supply and Services: p. 44. Eaton's Archives: pp. 102, 151. Manitoba Archives: p. 126, 272. Nelvana: p. 303. *Reader's Digest*: pp. 289, 298, 299. Canada Committee: p. 180. Globe and Mail: p. 283. Dr. C. Burton Stewart: p. 288. Canadian Forces Photo Unit: pp. 483, 484. Royal Winnipeg Ballet; p. 388. Stratford Shakespearean Festival: p. 370. The Register and Tribune Syndicate: p. 386. Crawley Films Ltd.: p. 393. *Toronto Star*: pp. 334, 342. National Gallery of Canada: p. 404. Bruce Cole: p. 405. Canadian Opera Company: p. 406. The Pearson Family: pp. 343, 344. UNESCO: p. 357. CBC: p. 382, 384, 409. Regina Leader Post: p. 129. World Health Organization: 489.

Every reasonable effort has been made to find the copyright holders of illustrations and quotations used in this book. The publishers would appreciate having errors or omissions brought to their attention.

Introduction

Nobody reads introductions—well, almost nobody. But since you must be one who does, this introduction has a simple purpose: to point out the kinds of things you can find in *In Search of Canada*.

Not surprisingly, there is basic information in the form of narrative, description and explanation about Canadian history. But there is much more. Take, for example, the features. These appear in blue type in the book. They are designed to let you explore some topics which may be beyond the scope of a straight history course—things like problems in writing and interpreting history; ideas from the other social sciences like archaeology, anthropology and sociology; values analysis and choices; controversial events and people; and Canadian literature and how it reflects changes in society. On occasion, they also try to indicate how historical patterns repeat themselves—in other words, to help you appreciate how studying history can help you to understand what is happening in Canada and the world today.

Throughout the book, as well as within features, there are documents. These are drawn directly from primary sources—they give you the actual words written or spoken by people who played a part in Canadian history—or provide modern comments about people and events in the Canadian story. They have been chosen because they expand the basic narrative of the book, and make it more interesting, and they should help to develop basic inquiry and analytic skills.

Marginal notes explain points, define terms, identify people, raise questions—and introduce the lighter side of things on occasion.

Illustrations in the form of pictures, charts and maps are found in every chapter, of course, to help you get some visual impressions of the topics being discussed. But Chapter 14 in Volume 2 uses these visual materials in a different way. In this chapter, you will not find the usual pages of narrative and explanation. Instead, what you will be given are impressions of the many sides of important issues facing Canada and the world at present. You will not find solutions to problems since they are complicated problems; but you will find questions and ideas to help you clarify your thinking and points of view.

You can think of *In Search of Canada* as a history book. But look again. Included are ideas from economics; there are some from anthropology and sociology and other subjects you may be interested in. From time to time you can even find a poem or an excerpt from a novel or a short story. We hope *In Search of Canada* helps open some doors for you. It is intended to be a beginning, to encourage you to think about Canada and the world—and about yourself.

RCK

A Word to Help You Use This Book

The features, as was noted in the Introduction, appear in blue ink. They also start at the top of a page. Sometimes they may interrupt the text, but it is very easy to find where the narrative carries on, since you simply flip the pages until the black starts again. Then you can go back and pick up the features when you've finished your other reading. Sometimes, you'll notice words in **boldface** in the text; these will be defined in the margin, also in boldface, immediately opposite the spot where they appear. You'll also encounter asterisks (*) within the body of the text, and once again, these refer to specific notes in the margin which also begin with asterisks and can be found right opposite the material they refer to.

1

Canada's political system: what is it based on?

"What holds the provinces together is not the BNA Act but the interlocking schedule of the Western and Eastern Football Leagues."[1]

The year is 1985. Martin Richard is 18 years old and he has just returned to Canada after spending his first year out of high school in a university overseas. His mission: to find out how Canada's government works. While in school he had been exposed to Canadian history and politics, but he had managed to avoid thinking very much about the subject. In the company of students overseas, however, he had frequently been asked questions—even quite basic ones—for which he did not have the answers.

Martin looked up his former teacher and asked for help. The teacher agreed to a series of conversations.

In their first meeting, they began to talk in general about governments, before getting down to discussing Canada's government, and in particular, the constitution.

Question: Any government operates according to a set of laws and practices and within certain institutions. These are often spelled out in a constitution. Can you get me a copy of Canada's constitution?

Answer: Not exactly. The Canadian constitution does not come in a compact volume. Our constitution includes ideas, customs, laws and court decisions that originated with Great Britain in the days when Canada was a colony or Dominion within the Empire. Canadian laws and court decisions, which have accumulated since 1867, are part of the present constitution.

The British North America Act, 1867, is the foundation of the Canadian constitution. So the BNA Act, as it is called, is a good place to start. By examining some of its main parts and how they have worked out, a person can begin to grasp the essentials of Canada's present political system. Here is a copy of the BNA Act.

The Preamble

Question: What is this short part at the beginning?

Answer: The preamble, or introduction, which outlines the general purposes of the BNA Act. The language is complex, but simply worded the preamble states that the purposes were to establish a federal union (which the Fathers of Confederation had agreed to at the Quebec Conference of 1864); to provide a constitution based on British principles (that is, parliamentary government as it had evolved in Britain over several centuries); to provide for the expansion of the Dominion in the expectation of including other provinces and territories.

Union

Question: Here we have the terms of union. Is there anything to explain here?

I. PRELIMINARY

1. This Act may be cited as the *British North America Act, 1867.*

II. UNION

3. It shall be lawful for the Queen, by and with the Advice of Her Majesty's Most Honourable Privy Council, to declare by Proclamation that, on and after a Day herein appointed, not being more than Six Months after the passing of this Act, the Provinces of Canada, Nova Scotia, and New Brunswick shall form and be One Dominion under the Name of Canada; and on and after that Day those Three Provinces shall form and be one Dominion under the Name accordingly.

5. Canada shall be divided into Four Provinces, named Ontario, Quebec, Nova Scotia, and New Brunswick.

6. ... The Part which formerly constituted the Province of Upper Canada shall constitute the Province of Ontario; and the Part which formerly constituted the Province of Lower Canada shall constitute the Province of Quebec.

7. The Provinces of Nova Scotia and New Brunswick shall have the same Limits as at the passing of this Act.

8. In the general Census of the Population of Canada which is hereby required to be taken in the Year One thousand eight hundred and seventy-one, and in every Tenth Year thereafter, the respective Populations of the Four Provinces shall be distinguished.

Answer: While the specific date is not mentioned, in accordance with Section 3 Queen Victoria proclaimed July 1, 1867, as the effective date for Confederation. You may note that the creation of the Dominion is placed first, then come the terms for dividing Canada into provinces and separating the old Province of Canada into Ontario and Quebec.

Executive Power

Question: What is "Executive Power" about? The word "executive" makes me think of someone who gives orders.

Answer: Your impression is partly right, since most countries, including Canada, have one official who has the final say in making decisions. Canada's case is a little confusing at first. Read this passage and tell me who *appears* to hold the executive power in Canada.

Queen Victoria

III. EXECUTIVE POWER

9. The Executive Government and Authority of and over Canada is hereby declared to continue and be vested in the Queen.

10. The Provisions of this Act referring to the Governor General extend and apply to the Governor General for . . . carrying on the Government of Canada on behalf and in the Name of the Queen. . . .

11. There shall be a Council to aid and advise in the Government of Canada, to be styled the Queen's Privy Council for Canada; and the Persons who are to be Members of that Council shall be from Time to Time chosen and summoned by the Governor General and sworn in as Privy Councillors, and Members thereof may be from Time to Time removed by the Governor General.

13. The Provisions of this Act referring to the Governor General in Council shall be construed as referring to the Governor General acting by and with the Advice of the Queen's Privy Council for Canada.

15. The Commander-in-Chief of the Land and Naval Militia, and of all Naval and Military Forces, of and in Canada, is hereby declared to continue and be vested in the Queen.

16. Until the Queen otherwise directs, the Seat of Government of Canada shall be Ottawa.

The fiction that our elected representatives are legally subservient to a master on the other side of the world must be particularly puzzling to immigrants who came to Canada expecting a free country, in form as well as fact.[8]
—*Toronto Star* editorial, 1972

Parliament Buildings, Ottawa, 1867

Question: The Queen appears to have the supreme position. Does the Queen rule Canada?

Answer: It is sometimes said that the Queen, or monarch, "reigns but does not rule." The monarchy symbolizes power but does not exercise it. Even in 1867, when Canada was a colony, it was not the Queen but the Colonial Office, whose head was a member of the British Cabinet, which made decisions about Canada's "external affairs."

THE PLACE OF THE MONARCHY IN THE CANADIAN SYSTEM

A publication of the federal government on the Organization of the Government in Canada [1974] describes the role of the monarchy in these terms.

The monarchy no longer divides Canadians. If to some it seems anachronistic—irrelevant but harmless—to others it is a source of pride—and pleasure. We should let it be for that alone.[2]
—James Eayrs, political scientist, 1972

"The Sovereign, the person on whom the Crown is constitutionally conferred, symbolizes Canada's status as a constitutional monarchy, the Canadian form of responsible government.

"Parliament is composed of the Crown, the Senate and the House of Commons. Formal executive power in Canada is thus vested in The Queen. Her Majesty's authority is, however, in most cases, delegated to her representative who is appointed on the recommendation of the Prime Minister and, since 1952, has been chosen from amongst the nation's most outstanding and respected citizens.

"Her Majesty comes to Canada from time to time to mark events of national significance and to visit various regions of the country. In her absence, the Governor-General carries out most of the Queen's functions and, of course, both act in accordance with Canadian constitutional practice.

4

"The Crown is seen as a symbol of national sovereignty belonging to all Canadians, a link between citizens of every national origin and ancestry. The Queen herself stated in Toronto, in June, 1973, that 'the Crown is an idea more than a person' which should 'represent everything that is best and most admired in the Canadian ideal'.

"In her position at the apex of Canadian state, governmental and judicial functions, the Monarch is the fountain of justice in that all judicial functions are carried on in her name. She is also 'fons honoris', the fountain of honor. In this capacity she is Sovereign of the Order of Canada, and also of the Order of Military Merit, and approves the award of the Canadian Bravery decorations.

"Her Majesty is Colonel-in-Chief of eleven Canadian regiments, Honorary Commissioner of the Royal Canadian Mounted Police, and Patron of numerous associations and organizations.

"The Queen is Head of the Commonwealth and as such is the symbol of the free association of the 32 member countries of this unprecedented, multilingual, international partnership which represents millions, of all races and creeds.

"As Canadian Head of State, but also as Head of the Commonwealth, Her Majesty was in residence at Government House, Ottawa, from 31st July to 4th August, 1973, and received and entertained Commonwealth Heads of Government and delegations during the first Commonwealth Heads of Government meeting to be held in Ottawa.

"The Canadian government does not contribute to The Queen's Privy Purse which is provided by the United Kingdom government. Only when Her Majesty is in Canada do the Canadian Government, and provincial governments involved, assume responsibility for expenses."[3]

Question: What about the Governor General then?
Answer: Taken literally, the terms of the Act appear to assign almost dictatorial powers to the Governor General, in peacetime as well as during war. However, responsible government in Canada's internal matters had already been established before 1867 and was assumed to continue with Confederation. The men who devised the BNA Act thus felt no need to include any written guarantees.

Even so, the position of the Governor General was much different in 1867 from what it is today. Canada was still a colony, subject to the laws which Great Britain applied to the Empire as a whole. The Governor General represented the might and splendour of the Empire, over which the British government remained supreme in matters of defence and foreign affairs. He was also expected to exert influence in Canadian affairs when the occasion arose.

In the years since, as Canada acquired its autonomy,* the position of Governor General decreased in power and took on symbolic value instead. Today, the man filling the office is the monarch's personal representative, in no way an agent of the British government.

In fact, the Canadian cabinet chooses the person who will be Governor General, and since Vincent Massey's appointment in 1952, the office has been held by Canadians.

Question: To any observer of Canadian government today, the prime minister is the central figure. Why is he not even mentioned in the BNA Act? And what about the Cabinet?

Answer: The Privy Council, referred to in Section 11, is the formal term for the cabinet, which includes the prime minister. As I mentioned before, responsible government was already established, at least in Canada's internal affairs, by 1867. In other words, a cabinet, headed by a prime minister was said to be "advising" the Governor General.

You might review the fundamentals of responsible government* before our next discussion, since it is basic to an understanding of modern cabinet government.

Question: Can I get enough of an idea about the modern office of the prime minister by reading up on the situation of a century ago?

Answer: That depends. The prime minister's job today is much more complicated than it was in earlier years. We could have several long discussions about the differences between the world we live in and the world of a century ago, and about how these differences have changed the role of the prime minister. Even then we would only scratch the surface. For example, government plays a much larger part in the lives of Canadians now than it used to.

Many of the essential facts about the prime minister are the same. He is still the member of Parliament who leads the political party with the greatest number of seats in the House of Commons. He still chooses his cabinet mainly, if not entirely, from among the members of Parliament who belong to his party. The prime minister, as the actual head of the executive branch, has great influence over policy and decision-making.

The prime minister has always been a dominant figure in the cabinet, since he is the leader of the government and important decisions inevitably reflect his views. In a very practical sense he has the power to "hire and fire" members of the cabinet.

Since the advent of national television, the prime minister has become more important as a "symbol" of the party. If he has "charisma," that certain magnetic quality which enables him to

During World War II the government of Prime Minister Mackenzie King found itself in extreme difficulty over the issue of conscription. The Minister of Defence, James Ralston, had disagreed with King over the prime minister's refusal to reinforce the Canadian army overseas with conscripts. Ralston went so far as to submit his resignation to King in July, 1942, when the issue first became serious. Although King was able to convince his defence minister to remain in office, he did retain Ralston's letter of resignation.

The conscription issue split the cabinet in 1944, with Ralston leading those in favour of conscription against King and the others who were still opposed.

During a very dramatic cabinet meeting the prime minister was given an ultimatum by Ralston: the prime minister would either support Ralston's position or the minister would resign. Ralston was a very popular minister and did have the support of other cabinet colleagues. The prime minister appeared to be backed into a corner with no room either to manoeuver or to escape. King then informed the astonished cabinet that Ralston had submitted his resignation two years earlier. He would now accept this resignation as final since there was no chance of an agreement. After a few tense moments, Ralston quietly rose and informed the prime minister that he would formally resign on the following day. Although the method employed by King may appear to be somewhat devious, it was certainly effective and illustrates the dominant position that the prime minister maintains within the cabinet.

sway the electorate, he is likely to be even more of a boon to his party's image, especially at election time. The importance of creating the right image on television is best shown by comparing the successful election campaigns of John Diefenbaker in 1958 and Pierre Elliott Trudeau in 1968 with those of Lester B. Pearson. While both Mr. Diefenbaker and Mr. Trudeau were able to generate that charismatic quality when appealing to the electorate, Mr. Pearson's public image was a political handicap.

Of concern to some critics of the federal government in the present day, is the dominance of the prime minister and his cabinet in the legislature. This is partially explained by the fact that under the Canadian parliamentary system, the executive is also part of the legislative branch of the government. This enables the prime minister and his cabinet—depending on whether there is a majority or a minority government and the relative size of each party—to control effectively what takes place in the House of Commons. But what is of greatest concern to these critics is the apparent change in the office of the prime minister which has taken place within the past few years.

Question: What kind of change?

Answer: Those who see a new style of government and politics in the 1970s claim that real control of Canada's government has shifted from Parliament to the offices of the prime minister (the PMO) and the **Privy Council** (PCO). Look at the diagram below which shows the organization of the PMO and PCO.

Privy Council is the formal term which in practice means the Cabinet.

Organization of Prime Minister's Office and Privy Council Office

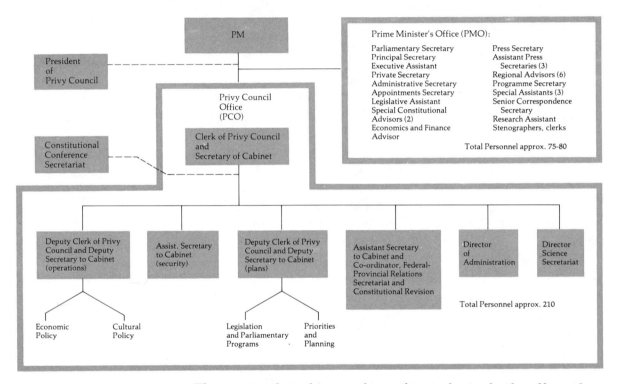

*PMO: in 1967 (Prime Minister Pearson —44 people; in 1969 (Prime Minister Trudeau)—75-80 people; in 1976 (Prime Minister Trudeau)—70-80 people

PCO: 1967-68—150 people in 1969—210 people

They note that the number of people in both offices has increased since 1968* while the distinction between them has become somewhat obscured. The expanded size and influence of the PMO has created suspicion in the minds of many politicians, civil servants and journalists. Furthermore, the tendency for an inner circle of advisers to grow up around the prime minister has raised questions about how government policy may be influenced. While it is true that prime ministers in the past tended to go beyond the cabinet and the civil service to get advice on important issues, it is said that this tendency is increasing.

In summary, the PMO is seen by its critics as the centre of a huge, powerful and often unseen decision-making apparatus.

Question: What caused this change?

Answer: Remember that we are talking about an *issue,* on which there are different points of view. It can be argued that the change is not so great as critics say. Even those who believe that the role of the prime minister is changing may not agree on the reasons, or whether the changes are necessarily good or bad. For example, it may be said that issues facing government today are more complex than those of a few years ago. Solutions may require greater involvement of experts from outside government. Procedures that were once adequate may need to be altered. Government is not the only institution making adjustments in the face of new challenges; look at the churches and the educational system, for example.

Question: Earlier I asked if a person could understand the modern job of the prime minister by studying the way things were when the British North America Act was written. I'm not sure you answered my question.

Answer: Well, you could get many of the basics—I mentioned his leadership of the majority party in the House of Commons, his influence over decision-making procedures and his domination of the Cabinet—and you would get some perspective on how the office has evolved. But there would be many aspects of the position about which you would gain little understanding simply by studying the prime minister's role at the time the BNA Act came into effect. Perhaps the most interesting way would be to compare and contrast the career and role of a recent prime minister with that of Sir John A. Macdonald or one of the earlier prime ministers to see how the functions and requirements have changed.

[The Office of the Prime Minister] has shown an almost magical power to elevate men or to bring out the worst in them.[14]
—Peter C. Newman, journalist

Legislative Power

Question: What is the meaning of "legislative"?

Answer: The word "legislative" refers to law-making. Any time you hear the words "legislative", "legislation", or "legislative assembly", you know that law-making is involved.

Question: I remember something about an MP introducing a bill, and how the bill goes through three readings before it is signed by the Governor General and becomes a law. As I remember, the whole thing seems pretty mechanical.

Answer: Your comment only scratches the surface. Law-making is a process in which decisions are made and implemented. It can get very complicated, although it may *seem* cut-and-dried if studied only in a general way.

   If you really want to learn how Canada's Parliament works,

you will have to be prepared for this fact: you won't achieve your goal overnight, or by taking one course. All we can do in our conversations is to identify some of the *structures*, *general procedures* and *processes* of Parliament. Hopefully you will go on learning and refining your knowledge in future.

For the time being, a person could start with any of the following pieces of information.

Structure of the Canadian legislature

Let's have a look at what the British North America Act has to say about the *structure* of the Canadian legislature. Here is a summary based on the terms of the Act:

GENERAL

Parliament under the Crown consists of two "Houses", the Senate and the House of Commons. Parliament must hold a session at least once a year.

THE SENATE

Representation in the Senate is supposed to provide a balance among the regions of Canada. In the Canada of 1867, the three regions were Ontario, Quebec and the Maritimes. Each was assigned 24 seats in the Senate. A fourth region eventually came into being as the West became a part of Confederation, also with 24 seats.

> Newfoundland received six seats when it joined, to make the total of 102 seats in the present Senate. In the Maritimes and the West, the 24 seats are divided among the provinces.

To become a Senator, one must be at least thirty years of age; be a British subject; possess real and personal property worth at least $4 000; live in the province one represents.

> Senators were intended to be persons of property, representing the *status quo*. In practice, they have also been supporters of the political party in power when they received their appointment.

Appointment of Senators is made officially by the Governor General.

> The Governor General makes the formal appointment. The Prime Minister makes the actual choices.

Senators must retire at the age of seventy-five.

Until 1965, a Senate appointment was for life. The amendment is one of the few changes in this section of the British North America Act, in spite of repeated cries for reform or abolition of the Senate.

The following was written more than fifty years ago, in 1926: Clearly, Senate reform has been one of the most lasting issues in Canadian politics.

The problem of a second chamber recurs annually in Canada.... Of late years it has become the fashion to attack the Senate as the foe of public ownership because it has interfered with several bills for the construction of railways by the Dominion. The Senate as a "Home for the Aged", as a refuge for old warriors, and as a means of rewarding contributors to the party war chest, is the continual butt of newspaper wits. And yet, for all its unpopularity, the Senate continues on its dignified way, little changed from what it was half a century ago.

The reform of the Senate has been in the air almost since the federation of 1867. In 1875 the subject was introduced and debated at length for the first time in Parliament. Since then the debate has been reopened many times in both Houses.... [4]

THE HOUSE OF COMMONS

Representation is related to population and to a ratio between the number of Quebec seats and the number of each of the other provinces. There were 181 seats in the original House of Commons, with Quebec having 65, Ontario 82, Nova Scotia 19 and New Brunswick 15.

As the population of Quebec and Ontario increased in comparison to other provinces, representation in the House of Commons was adjusted. For example, Quebec now has 75 seats, Ontario 88, Nova Scotia 11 and New Brunswick 10—out of a total of 264.

According to the Act, the Governor General has the power to summon the House to hold its sessions and to dissolve the House, at least every five years, in order that elections may be held.

In practice the Prime Minister has these powers. Elections are normally held more often than every five years, either because the Government has been defeated on a vote by the Opposition, or because the Government (the party in power) calls an election hoping to increase its numbers.

Money bills must be approved by the House of Commons. Only the elected representatives have the right to authorize taxes and the spending of the revenue obtained.

Votes are decided by simple majority. For a bill to become a law it must be passed by both the House of Commons and Senate and be signed by the Governor General.

What is not said in the BNA Act

Question: Am I right in thinking that the British North America Act leaves a lot out?

Answer: The British North America Act is not a comprehensive constitution, as is the constitution of the United States, for example. Many interesting and important facts about Canadian government are not included. Here is a summary of information about the legislative branch which you could not discover merely by reading the Act:

INFLUENCE OF THE EXECUTIVE BRANCH

The Cabinet may dominate the legislative branch. This is especially true if the party in power—of which the Cabinet is a part—has a large majority in the House of Commons, or if the Opposition is divided. In modern governments, the Cabinet maintains strict discipline over the other party members. Once a policy has been adopted in caucus, members normally follow the idea of party unity.

THE OPPOSITION

In the House of Commons, the party with the second largest number of members is Her Majesty's Loyal Opposition, or simply, the Opposition. According to custom, the function of the Opposition is to act as a watchdog for the citizens, criticizing the Government and trying to keep the public aware of the Government's actions, policies and general performance. Of course, the Opposition is an alternative government, and one of its objectives is to gain power.

In the Canadian Parliament, at least since World War I, the Opposition has included "third parties". Although they have always been minority parties with little prospect of forming the government, parties like the C.C.F. (now the New Democratic Party) and Social Credit have been active in keeping the government "on its toes". On more than one occasion, a third party has held the "balance of power", i.e. the government depended on it to stay in office.

The life of an MP

What is the life of an MP really like? Is it full of glamour?

Frank Maine, 38, is a new member elected on his first try in 1974, and is the first scientist MP for Canada. There have been engineers, but Maine has his PhD in organic chemistry and has worked in industry, both as a pure science researcher and as a manager of research and development.

He, his wife Mary Eva and their four children aged five to nine years, live in Guelph, Ont.

Guelph accounts for 85% of the Wellington riding population. The balance of the 40-mile long, 20-mile wide riding is farmland.

[Maine] ran because he felt the lack of a national science policy was a serious problem for Canada and that there is a gap in Ottawa's knowledge of the needs of scientists. "There comes a time when a person has to try to do something and stop sitting on the sidelines squawking."

Maine has resisted the common freshman MP urge to rush in with all his ideas. He is visiting every government department and agency concerned with scientific activities (about 10) to find out who is doing what and why.

He is also making a speaking tour of branches of the Chemical Institute of Canada across the country, explaining to scientists why a national policy is important, especially in times of energy and food shortages.

In the meantime, there is always a heavy load of constituency work.

He has a riding office, as do most MPs, and has also established three riding committees to provide him with knowledge of local concerns and to act as contact people on the spot while he is in Ottawa. The committees: agriculture, urban (for the smaller centres outside Guelph), and multi-cultural.

What has happened to his personal life since last summer? A glance at the diary [see typical day, March 18th] gives a fair idea of the pace and the shortage of time with the family. On the financial side, his salary decreased from $26,000 to $18,000 and his expense allowance from $12,000 to $8,000. The latter does not cover all the expenses of being an MP. One example of the hidden costs; the Maines estimate they spend $100 per month on babysitters so that they can both attend events across the riding.

The salary becomes $1,000 a month, after taxes, and Maine says his wife is *just* managing to meet high mortgage payments and increased living costs by reducing their previous level of expenditure wherever possible and cutting out any extras.

Given all those complications in one's life, what makes MPs run? There is obviously a slightly different motivation for each individual but there is a basic feeling common to all: the desire to make things happen—to influence the direction of their country.

TYPICAL DAY IN THE LIFE OF AN MP

Tuesday, March 18

  8:00 Breakfast
  8:30 First of twice weekly 1½ hour French lessons
 10:00 Office: Correspondence and phone calls
 11:00 Agriculture Committee meeting. (Maine is appointed to four committees and is attending the meetings of four more of special interest to him)
 12:00 Meeting of 7-member Liberal Hamilton regional caucus
  1:00 Office: phone calls to riding
  2:00 Question period in House
  3:30 Office: work on speech for evening debate
  5:30 Working dinner with assistants going over speech and constituents' letters
  6:00 Phones home and worked on speech
  8:00 Participated in debate on bill to establish a national petroleum company, Petro-Canada.[5]

Decision-making: the elements of law-making in Canada

Each of us is familiar with decision-making as a "non-political" activity. We all make *personal* decisions all the time. Each of us has had experiences with *group* decisions, such as those of a family or peer group. Also common to most of us are *organizational* decisions, such as those relating to a club, team or school association.

What influences go into the making of a *personal* decision? Depending on its seriousness, one is likely to act according to one's values,* the advice of others, such as parents and friends, and the possible consequences. For example, if you are trying to decide whether or not to quit school before graduating, you are likely to think about such things as the value of schooling to your personal growth or choice of career, the feelings of your family, whether or not there is something else you can do instead.

The decisions of a *group* differ in a significant way, because no decision is likely to satisfy all members equally. An individual in a group must consider the wishes of other people whom he knows, the possible effects on them, their feelings about the decision and toward the others involved. Agreement by the group may depend on

*See Volume 2, Chapter 2.

the **model** they adopt. The simplest procedure is the *authoritarian*, in which one person or faction imposes a choice on the others. At the other extreme is the idea of *consensus*, in which action depends on the agreement of every member of the group. Somewhere in the middle is the idea of *majority*, which is the principle underlying Parliamentary decision-making.

Majority rule is often thought of as the usual way of making decisions in a liberal democracy like Canada. However, even in a democracy, decisions are made in all kinds of ways, depending on what may be appropriate.

Can you not think of examples from everyday life—at home, at school, on your hockey team—where majority rule is not practised? In fact, majority rule may not even be the ideal, let alone the practice, in many situations. Can you imagine a workout of your hockey team or a rehearsal of your school orchestra where every decision had to be put to a vote?

The term "model" is used here to mean plan or set of procedures.

POSSIBLE INFLUENCES ON PARLIAMENTARY DECISION-MAKING

Before and during the passage of a bill through Parliament, a bill may be subjected to many influences. The diagram illustrates some of the possibilities.

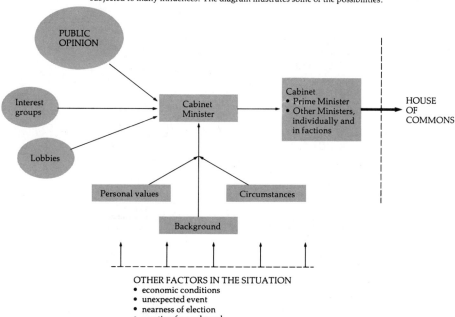

Possible Influences on Parliamentary Decision-Making

Before and during the passage of a bill through Parliament, a bill may be subjected to many influences. The diagram illustrates some of the possibilities.

Some of the basic differences between the manner in which Parliament decides and the way an individual or group decides are that:

15

1. as a representative body, Parliament makes decisions on behalf of the citizens of Canada, not for itself;
2. in a country with as many different groups as Canada has, Parliament must take a great variety of influences into account;
3. the process is much more complex. One person, for example the prime minister, cannot make decisions by himself. Even the decision to propose a certain government bill to Parliament is a decision made by the Cabinet, and it is probably the end result of many other decisions made along the way.

HOW A BILL IS PASSED

Once a bill is introduced to Parliament, it must go through three readings in both the House of Commons and the Senate.

Generally bills are first handled by the House of Commons and then by the Senate, although occasionally bills are introduced to the Senate first.

How a Bill is Passed

Once a bill is introduced to Parliament, it must go through three readings in both the House of Commons and the Senate.

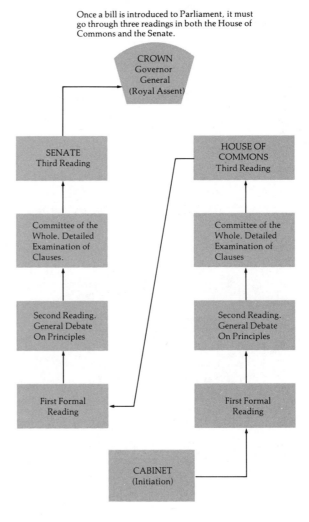

Foreign magazines in Canada: a case study in the complexities of law-making

The proximity of the United States to Canada tends to complicate the problems that Canadians have in their search for national identity and their desire for cultural survival. As the desire for cultural survival becomes more pronounced, attempts have been made to reduce the influence of periodicals from the United States which are sold in Canada, particularly the Canadian editions of *Time* and *Reader's Digest*. Although they had been publishing Canadian editions since the 1940s, *Time* and *Reader's Digest*, came under attack because they attracted so much Canadian advertising revenue, due to tax advantages granted by the Canadian government in the 1950s. They were said to deprive the Canadian magazine industry of much needed income and indirectly to arrest the development of Canadian culture.

The Secretary of State, Hugh Faulkner, proposed a bill to disallow the special tax privileges for advertisers using the Canadian editions of *Time* and *Reader's Digest* unless these magazines met domestic ownership and content requirements. The bill stated that these magazines must be 75% Canadian-owned and contain a certain minimum Canadian content. The figures 60-80% were being quoted at the time. The bill was a very controversial one and served to illustrate the complexity of parliamentary decision-making. It showed us some of the numerous factors and forces that are always in operation during the passage of any important piece of legislation.

What are some of these factors which influence the legislative process? First, the bill is usually a reflection of the personal values of the cabinet minister from whose department it originates, in this case the Secretary of State, Hugh Faulkner. It also reflects the values expressed by various Canadian interest groups such as certain sections of the Canadian magazine industry, Canadian authors' groups and other people who have attempted to put pressure on the government to deal with the problem of the cultural influence of the United States on Canada.

These values must also be shared by the majority of the cabinet, particularly the prime minister, and by a substantial portion of the party's **caucus**. There must also be a climate of opinion throughout the country which is favourable to the passage of this bill. Obviously the bill would not have been introduced if there were very widespread opposition. Yet, this in itself is not always sufficient to explain what takes place during the legislative process.

The *"Time-Reader's Digest* bill" was drawn up early in 1975 and the Government expected it to become part of the law before the end of the year. However, when Parliament recessed in the summer, the bill was still in mid-passage and the issue had touched off arguments

Caucus is the term for the private meetings of a party's members of parliament.

across the country. Even within the Government caucus there was a division of opinion.

Resistance to the bill within the caucus came from MPs who experienced opposition to the bill from certain regions and constituencies within the country. There was the prospect of a loss of voter support, and advertising and campaign contributions for the next election.

Meanwhile, the delay in the passage of the bill gave those opposed to it more time to mobilize their opposition. The presidents of Reader's Digest Association of Canada and Time Canada put pressure on the Government, through government channels and the news media, either to withdraw or modify the bill. Direct pressure from the United States' Government, which had led to the special status of *Time* and *Reader's Digest* in the first place, could not be discounted.

Faced with so much negative reaction, what alternatives were open to the Prime Minister and his cabinet? They could push ahead in the hope that the caucus could be persuaded to give united support; this would mean the bill would be passed by Parliament and become law. Other options would be to insist that the cabinet minister sponsoring the bill either water it down or drop it. If the minister were unable to accept the latter, he would likely have no choice but to resign.

Every piece of legislation involves a number of factors and forces —many of them hidden from the public view—which influence the very nature of the bill. These influences are in operation at every step along the way to the passage of the bill. Even when a bill succeeds in becoming a law, it may differ substantially from the original. One can see, therefore, that the three readings given to every bill in both Houses of Parliament represent only the formal procedure and that the legislative process is a very complex procedure.

1. In the case of what became known as the *"Time-Reader's Digest* bill,"* which of the following would likely be in favour? Opposed?

(a) an employee whose firm has printed one of the magazines
(b) a journalist who has contributed articles to the Canadian edition of *Time* magazine
(c) an average reader
(d) a member of the Liberal Party
(e) the editor of a rival Canadian magazine

2. What reasons might each give for his or her view? What would each stand to gain—or lose—as a result of the bill being passed?
3. How can the values of a particular individual or group affect the lives of others?

OUTCOME

Bill C-58 was passed by the House of Commons in February, 1976. Questions which remained to be answered included: would the Senate pass or defeat the bill; would the bill, if passed by the Senate and signed by the Governor General, be put into effect immediately; would there by any leeway in interpreting the bill, so that certain Canadian editions of foreign magazines would not be affected?

1. Which of these questions have been answered since the bill was passed? How were they answered, if at all?

OPERATION OF PARLIAMENT

Many people think that Parliament is little more than an over-sized debating club. While it is true that debate is a vital part of government, and the daily question period gives the Opposition the opportunity to press the Government for explanations, a considerable part of the operation of Parliament is the work of committees. Representatives of the Government and opposition parties, according to their numerical strength in Parliament, meet in committee, where much of the work of preparing the laws of Canada is carried on.

PRESSURE GROUPS

Lobbies, or pressure groups, may exert considerable pressure behind the scenes or in public to get certain laws changed or new laws made. Very often a law that will please one part of the population will displease another. Thus a Government may choose in favour of a certain group, and the Opposition may espouse the cause of another group to try to swing public opinion against the Government.

ROLE OF THE MEDIA

The media, and particularly the members of the Parliamentary press gallery, exercise great influence on the public's view of Government. Relatively few Canadians are able to attend the debates, public hearings and other activities in Ottawa; nor do they read *Hansard* and other reports. Thus most of the population depends in large measure on the reporting and editorial comments in the newspapers and on television.

Provincial constitutions

Executive Power

58. For each Province there shall be an Officer, styled the Lieutenant Governor, appointed by the Governor General in Council by instrument under the Great Seal of Canada.
60. The Salaries of the Lieutenant Governors shall be fixed and provided by the Parliament of Canada.
66. The Provisions of this Act referring to the Lieutenant Governor in Council shall be construed as referring to the Lieutenant Governor of the Province acting by and with the advice of the Executive Council thereof.
68. Unless and until the Executive Government of any Provinces otherwise directs with respect to that Province, the Seats of Government of the Provinces shall be as follows, namely,— of Ontario, the City of Toronto; of Quebec, the City of Quebec; of Nova Scotia, the City of Halifax; and of New Brunswick, the City of Fredericton.

Legislative Power

69. There shall be a Legislature for Ontario consisting of the Lieutenant Governor and of One House, styled the Legislative Assembly of Ontario.
71. There shall be a Legislature for Quebec consisting of the Lieutenant Governor and of Two Houses, styled the Legislative Council of Quebec and the Legislative Assembly of Quebec.
88. The Constitution of the Legislature of each of the Provinces of Nova Scotia and New Brunswick shall, subject to the Provisions of this Act, continue as it exists at the Union until altered under the Authority of this Act . . .

Question: What are the main points in the Act about the provincial governments?

Answer: The first thing to note is that this part of the Act concerns mainly the *form* of government in the provinces. There is much more about the provinces in the next part, "Distribution of Legislative Powers."

The Parliamentary form established in the federal government was extended to the provincial governments. The Lieutenant Governors corresponded to the Governor General, in that they represented the Crown in the provinces. The Act indicates that they might also be the "agents" of the federal government, which was involved in their appointment and paid their salaries. Like the office of Governor General, that of Lieutenant Governor was never as powerful as the language of the Act would make it appear; today, both are symbolic rather than political.

The Civil Service

The civil service is the work force of the government, the paid employees who are hired for particular jobs and generally not because a certain party is in office. The deputy minister is the senior civil servant in each department of government; he works directly with the Cabinet Minister and supervises the work of his department.

Upper echelon civil servants are likely to be people of considerable training and experience, with responsibility for carrying out their department's policies and making recommendations on which policy is based.

The term civil servant is a very broad one, and includes economists, postal employees, management consultants, clerk-typists, truck drivers, computer analysts—in fact, with the increase in size and function of governments at all levels (federal, provincial and municipal), just about every kind of occupation.

Recently, like provincial civil services, the federal civil service has come under attack for its mammoth growth (the public service now is about 250 000, an increase of 44% since 1966) and excessive expenditure of public funds. In an article in the July/August, 1975, edition of *Saturday Night*, Sandra Gwyn describes "Ottawa's Incredible Bureaucratic Explosion".

> Our bureaucracy grows and grows and grows. Just ten years ago, the Government of Canada telephone directory had a sober grey cover with the Coat of Arms in the top left-hand corner. It filled 200 pages. The current version has a snappy two-tone blue cover with a picture of people skating on the Rideau Canal. There are 818 pages, each almost twice the size of those of a decade ago. (To be fair, half the listings are now in French.)
>
> And the bureaucracy gets richer and richer. "People used to come to Ottawa," said a man who's recently left, "out of a real sense of commitment and idealism. Now they come because salaries are much better here than anywhere else, and there's all kinds of room at the top." Between 1969 and 1975, the number of federal public servants earning $20,000 or more increased by 1,300 per cent from 1,225 to 16,868. In the same period, the number of assistant deputy ministers increased by ninety-five per cent. The department of justice holds the record. It has eleven, plus another five people who have the same rank and salary, but not the title.
>
> The environment has changed, too. In the middle of an interview on a quite different subject, a deputy minister—a puritanical type from the Prairies—said to me: "What the hell is a public servant doing in a place like this?" He pointed round his office. Not so much an office, we agreed, as the kind of penthouse living room that gets onto the covers of the classier decorating magazines.

... it may be speculated that federalism as such has meaning only for politicians and senior civil servants who work with the complex machinery that they have set up, as well as for the scholars who provide a continuing commentary on it, but that it has very little meaning for the bulk of the population.[7]
—John Porter, sociologist, 1965

21

Conversational groupings all over the place. Indirect lighting. Acres of pale broadloom. Cool abstracts from the Art Bank. "Come to think of it," he added, "we don't really have a public service any more."

———————————

From my own worm's-eye memory as a Clerk 2A ($2,280 a year), later as a $4,050 junior information officer, let me add a few footnotes. I came, in 1958, to a capital that was full of low buildings and high principles: a world of sickly-green walls and gooseneck lamps; green baize doors; splintery oak desks; tables full of deputy ministers eating lunch in the basement cafeteria at the Chateau Laurier (it had green-tiled walls and the best thing on the menu was the soup). . . .

The mood was Presbyterian Gothic. I remember a man writing six separate memos to explain why he'd tipped the porter on the overnight train to Toronto a dollar instead of the regulation fifty cents. . . .

It had one luminous virtue: integrity. "It was a bit like joining the Church," says a friend, talking about joining external in the late 1950s. "I remember Norman Robertson pulling all the junior officers together and explaining how it was an honour and a privilege to serve."

No one would dream of saying a thing like that any more. Someone in the audience might laugh. "The real conversational passions of your federal public service," Harry Bruce wrote last winter in the Toronto *Star*, "are raises, promotions, transfers, pensions, re-classifications, bureaucratic boondoggles, raw deals, sweet deals, departmental sweetshops, individual rip-offs, collective indignities and the injustices, extravagances, stupidities and blazing absurdities of the effort to make the public service bilingual."

The look has changed. In the new Ottawa, civil servants literally look down on the politicians from twenty-story steel and glass boxes. The joke used to be that the Parliament Buildings and the Chateau Laurier were Disneyland. Now they look like Fantasyland overtaken by Tomorrowland.

You probably grew up thinking of civil servants as contemporary Bob Cratchits. The 1975 substitutes for wobbly stools and quill pens are open-plan offices with burnt-orange area dividers, AM/FM digital clock radios (they come with the job once you're a director), and forests of split-leaf philodendrons. Consider also the hole in the ground on Bank Street where the public works department is about to put up yet another $67 million office building, with room for another 5,000 workers. When a young reporter timidly asked which department, exactly, it was for, an official replied briskly that he didn't know but that anyway the question was irrelevant because by the time it was finished in 1977, *someone* was sure to need it.[6]

1. Before obtaining an appointment to a civil service job, an applicant generally must write a test in competition with others. Once hired, a civil servant is protected in many ways against being fired. Why are such conditions important in the case of a person who works for the government?

2. The author of the article implies that the larger and more extravagant the civil service becomes, the less responsible it is to the people—the public whom it is supposed to serve. What might be some points to support this argument? To contradict it?

In practice, a premier, with his cabinet selected from the members of his party in the legislature, directs the affairs of his province as does the prime minister for the country as a whole.

Question: Does Quebec have a different kind of legislature?

Answer: That is an interesting point. Quebec did keep a bicameral legislature—one with two "houses", a council and an assembly—until 1969, when the Legislative Council was abolished. Ontario's single-house legislature was the example followed by all the other provinces.

Distribution of legislative powers

POWERS OF THE PARLIAMENT

Question: What is the significance of this part?

Answer: This is one of the most important parts of the Act. Canada is a *federation*, a country in which the power to govern is divided between a national* government and provincial governments. The division of powers was one of the most difficult problems facing the Fathers of Confederation*. In spite of the detailed listing of powers assigned to the two levels of government, no perfect separation was possible.

*The words national, central and federal are used interchangeably to describe this level of government.

*See Volume 1, Chapter 12

Section 91 begins,

"It shall be lawful for the Queen, by and with the Advice and Consent of the Senate and House of Commons, to make Laws for the Peace, Order, and Good Government of Canada, in relation to all Matters not coming within the Classes of Subjects by this Act assigned exclusively to the Legislatures of the Provinces;" And just in case there might be any doubt that certain important powers belonged to the national government, the section listed the following:

1. The Public Debt and Property.
2. The Regulation of Trade and Commerce.
3. The raising of Money by any Mode or System of Taxation.
4. The borrowing of Money on the Public Credit.
5. Postal Service.
6. The Census and Statistics.
7. Militia, Military and Naval Service, and Defence.
8. The fixing of and providing for the Salaries and Allowances of Civil and other Officers of the Government of Canada.
9. Beacons, Buoys, Lighthouses, and Sable Island.
10. Navigation and Shipping.
11. Quarantine and the Establishment and Maintenance of Marine Hospitals.
12. Sea Coast and Inland Fisheries.
13. Ferries between a Province and any British or Foreign Country or between Two Provinces.
14. Currency and Coinage.
15. Banking, Incorporation of Banks, and the Issue of Paper Money.
16. Savings Banks.
17. Weights and Measures.
18. Bills of Exchange and Promissory Notes.
19. Interest.
20. Legal Tender.
21. Bankruptcy and Insolvency.
22. Patents of Invention and Discovery.
23. Copyrights.
24. Indians, and Lands reserved for the Indians.
25. Naturalization and Aliens.
26. Marriage and Divorce.
27. The Criminal Law, except the Constitution of Courts of Criminal Jurisdiction, but including the Procedure in Criminal Matters.
28. The Establishment, Maintenance, and Management of Penitentiaries.
29. Such Classes of Subjects as are expressly excepted in the Enumeration of the Classes of Subjects by this Act assigned exclusively to the Legislatures of the Provinces.

And any Matter coming within any of the Classes of Subjects enumerated in this Section shall not be deemed to come within the Class of Matters of a local or private Nature comprised in the Enumeration of the Classes of Subjects by this Act assigned exclusively to the Legislatures of the Provinces.

Now compare these powers to the ones assigned by Section 92 to the provinces. Which set of powers appear *to you* to be more national in scope?

92. In each Province the Legislature may exclusively make Laws in relation to Matters within the Classes of Subjects next hereinafter enumerated; that is to say,—

1. The Amendment from Time to Time, notwithstanding anything in this Act, of the Constitution of the Province, except as regards the Office of Lieutenant Governor.

2. Direct Taxation within the Province in order to the raising of a Revenue for Provincial Purposes.

3. The Borrowing of Money on the sole Credit of the Province.

4. The Establishment and Tenure of Provincial Offices and the Appointment and Payment of Provincial Officers.

5. The Management and Sale of the Public Lands belonging to the Province and of the Timber and Wood thereon.

6. The Establishment, Maintenance, and Management of Public and Reformatory Prisons in and for the Province.

7. The Establishment, Maintenance, and Management of Hospitals, Asylums, Charities, and Eleemosynary Institutions in and for the Province, other than Marine Hospitals.

8. Municipal Institutions in the Province.

9. Shop, Saloon, Tavern, Auctioneer, and other Licenses in order to the raising of a Revenue for Provincial, Local, or Municipal Purposes.

10. Local Works and Undertakings other than such as are of the following Classes:—

(a) Lines of Steam or other Ships, Railways, Canals, Telegraphs, and other Works and Undertakings connecting the Province with any other or others of the Provinces, or extending beyond the Limits of the Province;

(b) Lines of Steam Ships between the Province and any British or Foreign Country;

(c) Such Works as, although wholly situate within the Province, are before or after their Execution declared by the Parliament of Canada to be for the general Advantage of Canada or for the Advantage of Two or more of the Provinces.

11. The Incorporation of Companies with Provincial Objects.

12. The Solemnization of Marriage in the Province.

13. Property and Civil Rights in the Province.

14. The Administration of Justice in the Province, including the Constitution, Maintenance, and Organization of Provincial Courts, both of Civil and of Criminal Jurisdiction, and including Procedure in Civil Matters in those Courts.

15. The Imposition of Punishment by Fine, Penalty, or Imprisonment for enforcing any Law of the Province made in relation to any Matter coming within any of the Classes of Subjects enumerated in this section.

16. Generally all Matters of a merely local or private Nature in the Province.

Question: They must have spent a long time on this part.

Answer: Sections 91 and 92 were painstakingly prepared. After all, the division of powers between the central government and the province was a key issue in the discussion and debate prior to Confederation. The "centralists" wanted overwhelming powers for the Government of Canada; the "provincial rights" people were opposed. The result was a compromise. Nevertheless, Sections 91 and 92 had to be flexible if they were to remain workable in the unknown future. The language was inevitably general, even vague, about many topics. Phrases such as "peace, order and good government" (Section 91) and "property and civil rights" could be interpreted in many ways.

> The Fathers of Confederation and their legal advisers did try to list as many specific powers as they could. However, in 1867, the wisest of men could not have imagined the ways in which governments would expand their functions and thus, their powers. When the need for new powers came up, there were bound to be problems between levels of government.

Question: What are some of the ways that the division of powers became a problem?

Answer: In 1867 the Fathers of Confederation believed a strong central government was essential to the survival of Confederation. The ink was hardly dry on the British North America Act when the first cases of federal-provincial tension challenged this assumption.

> Sir John A. Macdonald seemed to have one crisis after another, where a province or region was resisting the central government's authority. The trend continued, with the provinces gaining power at the expense of the government in Ottawa, until World War I. Then, and again in World War II, the central government assumed much greater powers, to deal with national emergencies.

> Since World War II, the two levels of government have been locked in ongoing conflict. The size of government at all levels has grown tremendously, as we have discussed before. As "government" in general takes on a larger role in our lives, the number of areas of conflict between levels of government seems to increase.

Question: So the Fathers of Confederation were not very good prophets?

Answer: What do you think?

What changes in Canada have occurred in the last century which they could not have anticipated? Consider the following:

1. the growth in the size of Government;
2. the increased cost of Government;

3. the services which governments now provide which, in 1867, were not thought to be responsibilities of government;
4. the increased diversity of Canadian society.

EDUCATION

For a particular example, think of the changes in the importance, nature and operation of formal schooling. After you have read Section 93, decide what the main concerns about education were in 1867. Why do you think these concerns were the important ones?

93. In and for each Province the Legislature may exclusively make Laws in relation to Education, subject and according to the following Provisions:—
    1. Nothing in any such Law shall prejudicially affect any Right or Privilege with respect to Denominational Schools which any Class of Persons have by Law in the Province at the Union:
    2. All the Powers, Privileges, and Duties at the Union by Law conferred and imposed in Upper Canada on the Separate Schools and School Trustees of the Queen's Roman Catholic Subjects shall be and the same are hereby extended to the Dissentient Schools of the Queen's Protestant and Roman Catholic Subjects in Quebec:
    3. Where in any Province a System of Separate or Dissentient Schools exist by Law at the Union or is thereafter established by the Legislature of the Province, an Appeal shall lie to the Governor General in Council from any Act or Decision of any Provincial Authority affecting any Right or Privilege of the Protestant or Roman Catholic Minority of the Queen's Subjects in relation to Education:
    4. In case any such Provincial Law as from Time to Time seems to the Governor General in Council requisite for the due Execution of the Provisions of this Section is not made, or in case any Decision of the Governor General in Council on any Appeal under this Section is not duly executed by the proper Provincial Authority in that Behalf, then and in every such Case, and as far only as the Circumstances of each Case require, the Parliament of Canada may make remedial Laws for the due Execution of the Provisions of this Section and of any Decision of the Governor General in Council under this Section.

Which of the following issues in education are important today that were not important at the time of Confederation:

1. financing of public universities?
2. differences from province to province concerning school

27

law, curriculum and other matters affecting students whose families move from one province to another?

3. separate schools?

4. availability of facilities, materials and instruction for schooling suitable to life in the 1970s?

5. opportunities for attending post-secondary institutions such as universities, colleges, technical schools?

6. decision-making at the individual school level vs. provincial decision-making for all schools?

AGRICULTURE AND IMMIGRATION

95. In each Province the Legislature may make Laws in relation to Agriculture in the Province, and to Immigration into the Province; and it is hereby declared that the Parliament of Canada may from Time to Time make Laws in relation to Agriculture in all or any of the Provinces, and to Immigration into all or any of the Provinces; and any law of the Legislature of a Province relative to Agriculture or to Immigration shall have effect in and for the Province as long and as far only as it is not repugnant to any Act of the Parliament of Canada.

Question: It seems that agriculture and immigration were placed in the same section.

Answer: Yes, the federal and provincial governments have *concurrent* powers over each. In the case of conflict, the federal authority prevails.

Both agriculture and immigration have become much more complicated areas in recent years, and the federal government has seen a growing need for national policies.

In 1966 a new federal Department of Manpower and Immigration was formed. Immigration was no longer to be a phenomenon which "just happened"; it was to be viewed in the light of the country's manpower needs, other conditions of the economy, and effects on Canadian society.

You often hear it said that Canada is a country which has been built by immigrants. Yet immigration, which has been an issue on frequent occasions in Canadian history, seems likely to be a persistent concern in years to come.*

*See Volume 1, Chapter 8 and Volume 2, Chapter 4, for examples.

The Judiciary

Question: So far we have discussed what the BNA Act *does* say about the parts of government that represent the people and make the laws. We have even talked about many features of government not specifically mentioned in the Act. Who enforces the laws?

Provisions of Sections 91 and 92 reflect a fundamental weakness in Canada's "written constitution"; namely, that they establish no machinery for amending the BNA Act. This is understandable since the BNA Act is an act of the British Parliament for what was, in 1867, one of its colonies. Nevertheless, amendments by the British government have customarily been made upon the request of the Canadian Parliament.

After Canada had achieved the status of an autonomous country, its leaders recognized the need for independent power over the Canadian constitution. In 1949, an amendment to Section 91 provided for the "amendment from time to time of the Constitution of Canada," but with important exceptions:

> provincial rights, as set out in Section 92 or any other act;
> rights affecting schools;
> provisions for the use of either the English or French language;
> the requirements that Parliament meet once a year and that elections to the House of Commons be held at least every five years (unless there is a national emergency and not more than one-third of the MPs are opposed to Parliament being extended).

In spite of efforts in recent years, federal-provincial agreement has not been achieved on an overall formula for amending the Constitution. It is still the practice to make amendments by advising the British government to implement the necessary changes.

The reason for this situation has nothing to do with objections from Britain, nor with any doubt about Canada's independence and power to control its own constitution. What once was a question of Canadian autonomy (Canada's relations with Britain) is now a strictly Canadian affair. However, a solution has not been found, partly because the provinces have been fearful of any change that might threaten their powers. Until the federal government and all the provincial governments *unanimously* agree on a procedure, the British Parliament will remain part of the process of amending Canada's constitution.

The Liberal government in 1964 put forward a formula which resulted from months of work under the previous Conservative government as well as under the Liberals. Since acceptance by all the provinces was needed, the project was discarded when Quebec dissented. Yet the basic issue stayed in the political limelight because of increasing complications in the relations between French-speaking and English-speaking Canadians and between federal and provincial levels of government.

A further effort, culminating in a constitutional conference in Victoria in June, 1971, again resulted in failure. The prime minister commented on the irony:

> One part of our task today is with us because Canada blazed a trail that many former colonies, now independent countries, have since followed. Canada was the first part of the then British Empire that achieved the status that grew into the complete independence of today. The other British colonies that much later achieved independence profited by our experience. They were set up in the world complete—able to manage and to amend their own constitutions. The Fathers of Confederation at Charlottetown and at Quebec, were men of courage, imagination and resource. But neither they nor the British legislators of that day could be expected to have foreseen the way in which complete independence would come to Canada more than half a century later. Because of that they did not include in our constitution a way to amend it in Canada. And so today, a century later, we still cannot change in Canada the fundamental aspects of our constitution. Australia can. New Zealand can. India, Nigeria, Jamaica—all these former British colonies, now independent, can amend their own constitutions in entirety, but we cannot. We Canadians, who led the way, must go to the British Parliament to implement our decision.[9]

BRINGING THE CONSTITUTION HOME

Long after other former British colonies had patriated their constitutions, the British North America Act continued to be a British statute by default. Britain had no interest in obstructing Canada's right to "bring the constitution home." The issue was not Canada's independence or relations with Britain, but disagreement among Canadian governments over what to do with the British North America Act once it had been made Canadian.

For a constitution to remain useful over time, there must be ways of updating it; that is, there must be a procedure for making *amendments* to the constitution. Governments in Canada could only agree to a new procedure, and thus to a change from the present procedure involving Britain, when they were satisfied they would lose none of their former powers in relation to each other.

Thus the provinces had to be convinced that the Government of Canada would not gain substantial powers at their expense. The smaller provinces wanted guarantees against enlarged powers for the bigger provinces; Quebec wanted assurances of its authority to act on behalf of its French-Canadian culture; the Canadian government wished to retain sufficient powers to handle matters of nation-wide importance.

Nevertheless, in the summer of 1976 and in the Speech from the Throne in September, Prime Minister Trudeau declared his government's intention to work out a plan for "bringing the constitution home." He called upon the provincial premiers to resolve their differences and thus to remove major obstacles to the historic change.

Answer: The Judiciary—or as it is called in the Act, the Judicature —administers and enforces the laws of Canada. The BNA Act provides only the general framework for the legal system.

FRANK AND ERNEST   by Bob Thaves

VII. JUDICATURE

96. The Governor General shall appoint the Judges of the Superior, District, and County Courts in each Province. . . .

97. . . . The Judges of the Courts of those Provinces appointed by the Governor General shall be selected from the respective Bars of those Provinces.

98. The Judges of the Courts of Quebec shall be selected from the Bar of that Province.

99. The Judges of the Superior Courts shall hold Office during good Behaviour, but shall be removable by the Governor General on Address of the Senate and House of Commons.

100. The Salaries, Allowances, and Pensions of the Judges of the Superior, District and County Courts (except the Courts of Probate in Nova Scotia and New Brunswick), and of the Admiralty Courts in Cases where the Judges thereof are for the Time being paid by Salary, shall be fixed and provided by the Parliament of Canada.

101. The Parliament of Canada may, notwithstanding anything in this Act, from Time to Time, provide for the Constitution, Maintenance, and Organization of a General Court of Appeal for Canada, and for the Establishment of any additional Courts for the better Administration of the Laws of Canada.

Question: Would you "translate" some of that for me?
Answer: I'll try to explain something about judges. The federal government appoints all judges, except those in certain provin-

Laws are made in two ways in Canada. *Statute laws* are those made by the legislatures; that is, laws resulting from acts of Parliament or of provincial governments. The *common law*, which first came to Canada from England, consists of court decisions, made by judges. which become precedents and are applied to later cases.

cial courts. Parliament pays their salaries, but only in exceptional cases can judges be removed from their positions.*

The judiciary is not, in other words, a branch of Parliament. So that judges can interpret and apply the law impartially, they must be protected against political influence and other pressures. Therefore, judges "shall hold Office during good Behaviour", which, until the amendment of 1961 meant appointment for life. Now superior court judges retire at the age of seventy-five.

A Model of Canada's Court System *

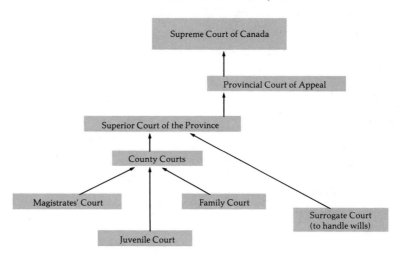

*The names of courts vary from province to province, but the same **types** of courts exist across Canada. A more complete diagram of the **actual** courts in a province would be much more complicated than the one above.

Question: All this talk about the Supreme Court and the legal system seems a little "far away" to me. When I think about the law, I think of lawyers and police, Detective Colombo and jails— things like that.

Answer: Come to think of it, so do I. We could spend hours exploring questions of the type you are raising. Perhaps we can get some impressions, at least, of the legal *process* by looking at some sample cases. Then, if you want to learn more, we will need to contact a law teacher and maybe visit with a lawyer.

THE JUDICIAL PROCESS

Generally speaking, the judicial process consists of two parts: (1) the part that deals with *civil* matters, and (2) the part that deals with *criminal* matters. Civil matters are those that concern disputes involving private citizens in conflict, or private citizens versus the government. Criminal matters involve the police in dealing with actions contrary to society's laws. Which of the following cases are civil? Which are criminal? What could be the main steps in the judicial process with each case?

1. Real Lemon or Sour Grapes?

Barney S. is a citizen who has purchased a car from a dealer named Harry H. The car quickly proves to be a "lemon", and Barney is faced with a bill of $1 000 to keep the car running. What can Barney do to recover his losses, which he is convinced are the fault of the dealer?

If Barney S. approaches Harry for payment and is refused, he can decide to take the dealer to court. The court would then have to decide if the dealer is liable, that is, whether or not he is obliged to provide either a new car or payment for the repairs needed to make the "lemon" roadworthy.

As Barney is not trained in the law, he would be wise to get the services of a lawyer to assist him in pursuing his claim against the car dealership. A lawyer would attempt, on his behalf, to settle the claim by mutual agreement "out of court". If this fails, Barney will likely be advised to take Harry H. to court. As a result of the trial, the judge will determine whether Barney receives compensation, and what form it will take.

2. Take the Money and Run?

Maude M. has been apprehended by the police because she is a prime suspect in the bank robbery which has just taken place. The police will in all likelihood bundle her off to the police station in order to question her, and lay a charge against her, that charge probably being "robbery". If Maude M. is smart, she will refuse to talk to the police until she has an opportunity to discuss her case with a lawyer. Nevertheless, a lawyer usually enters into criminal proceedings at a fairly early stage. With the introduction of legal aid in Canada, everyone is assured of having a lawyer to represent him on the kind of charge that Maude M. is facing.

Maude M. will probably be held overnight in jail and appear in court the next morning. The judge at that time will have to decide whether to release her on bail or whether to keep her in jail until her case is tried. If she is released, she will have to sign an undertaking that she will attend court on the date designated for her hearing. If bail is denied to her, she will have to remain in jail until the matter is settled.

There are two kinds of offences known in Canada—*summary* and *indictable*. Summary offences are of a less serious nature and can include impaired driving, liquor offences and public mischief. These matters are dealt with at the lowest of the court levels, Provincial Judges' Court or Magistrates' Court. Armed robbery is an indictable offence and for a charge such as this Maude M. can elect to have her trial either in Provincial Judges' Court or

Legal aid services

Legal aid is a service to those people who are unable to afford their own lawyers. Although there are variations in the services provided from province to province, legal aid has recently become available across Canada. If a person has an income below a certain level, he or she can request that the court appoint a lawyer to handle the case, at the government's expense.

*A superior court, sometimes
known as the Court of
Queen's Bench, handles more
serious offences.

Magistrates' Court, the High Court or County Court, or before a
judge and jury in superior court.*

Maude M. can either plead guilty or not guilty to the charge
she is facing. In view of the fact that she was arrested emerging
from the bank with $20 000 on her person, it is likely that
Maude M. will be found guilty if she had a trial and may very
well decide to plead guilty to the charge. Her lawyer will represent her in this matter and will speak on her behalf in court. He
will attempt to persuade the judge that Maude M. should be
given as lenient a sentence as possible considering both the
circumstances of the offence and her background. If Maude is
not satisfied with the decision of the court, an appeal can be
made to a higher court for a new hearing or for a more lenient
sentence to be imposed.

3. *To Sell or Not to Sell?*

Quincy Q. decides to sue Gertrude G. for breaking a contract
involving the sale of a house. Both parties will in all likelihood
seek legal advice to assist them with their cases. Without a
lawyer, a person can rarely expect to obtain proper representation in court and in view of the money involved in this matter,
both parties would be well advised to obtain lawyers.

Prior to this matter going to trial, each lawyer will attempt to
get a favourable settlement for his client. If this cannot be done
and a claim is filed in court by Quincy Q., Gertrude G.'s lawyer
will file a reply to the claim. Then the parties engage in what is
known as an Examination for Discovery, a meeting where each is
accompanied by a lawyer and is questioned about the facts
surrounding the case. Quite often this kind of meeting allows a
settlement to be achieved as the facts come out and both parties
can see the strengths and weaknesses of the other's case.

If, however, both parties are adamant and the matter cannot
be settled, it will have to be resolved in the courts by means of a
trial. At this time, both parties will present their cases and
witnesses and, with the assistance of their lawyers, attempt to
persuade the judge that a decision should be given in their
favour.

4. *When Governments Collide*

Mortimer M. is a provincial premier. His province has challenged the federal government's right to require all provinces to
spend money in a certain cost-sharing program.

The problem facing Mortimer M. is one involving *constitutional* law. The British North America Act allots certain law-
making powers to the federal government and others to the

provinces. To test his view that his province has the power to opt out of a federal program, Mortimer will have to take the matter to court. The provincial government will be represented at the court hearing by lawyers from the attorney-general's department; lawyers acting for the department of justice will represent the federal government.

Constitutional cases which are important to the entire country are referred to the Supreme Court of Canada, the highest court of appeal. Before the nine judges of the Supreme Court, Mortimer's lawyers will argue that the British North America Act, in this case, gives power to the province, not the federal government. If they are successful, the cost-sharing legislation will be declared invalid, and Mortimer M. will have the legal right to withdraw his province from the program.

FRANK AND ERNEST   by Bob Thaves

Language rights

Question: One thing surprises me. I don't remember coming across anything so far about the *rights of the individual.* Aren't these important in Canada?

Answer: The topic of individual rights, or civil rights is indeed important. Part of Canada's tradition is that we inherited from British law many liberties established over the centuries. Yet considerable debate has grown up in recent years over the need to establish more specific rights in our constitution.*

*See page 333 regarding Canada's Bill of Rights.

The rights we are examining in this part of the BNA Act concern *bilingualism,* an enduring Canadian issue. Let's look at Section 133:

133. Either the English or the French Language may be used by any Person in the Debates of the Houses of the Parliament of Canada and of the Houses of the Legislature of Quebec; and both those Languages shall be used in the respective Records and Journals of those Houses; and either of those Languages may be used by any Person or in any Pleading or Process in or issuing from any Court of Canada established under this Act, and in or from all or any of the Courts of Quebec.

The Acts of the Parliament of Canada and of the Legislature of Quebec shall be printed and published in both those Languages.

Question: Does this mean that everyone in Canada is supposed to be able to speak French?

Answer: Not at all. For the longest time, the use of French was confined to the Province of Quebec. Even there, where the majority of the population have always been French-speaking, English was the dominant language in the business life of the province.

A century after Confederation, in the mid-1960s, the Royal Commission on Bilingualism and Biculturalism made the following recommendation:

LANGUAGE RIGHTS

416. Section 133 is the only one in the Act specifically referring to the use of the English and French languages. But in this section the guaranteed usage of both languages is limited to debate in the Parliament of Canada and in the legislature of Quebec, official publication of statutes in Ottawa and Quebec, and pleadings and processes of all federal and Quebec courts. . . .

. . . It is our opinion that section 133 should be amended so as to state clearly that English and French are the two official languages of Canada, and to provide rules for the application of the principle of equality at the provincial level and in bilingual districts. . . . [9a]

Then, in the fall of 1969, the Official Languages Act became part of the law of Canada. It states that "the English and French languages are the official languages of Canada" and that they "possess and enjoy equality of status and equal rights and privileges as to their use in all the institutions of the Parliament and Government of Canada."

Other provisions of the Act

FINANCIAL ARRANGEMENTS

Question: This part about money looks too complicated. Can we skip over it?

Answer: The fact of the matter is that financial arrangements were fundamental to the setting up of Confederation. One of the main selling points of the plan was that the Canadian government would assume the debts of each province.

102. All Duties and Revenues over which the respective Legislatures of Canada, Nova Scotia, and New Brunswick before and at the Union had and have Power of Appropriation, except such Portions thereof as are by this Act reserved to the respective Legislatures of the Provinces, or are raised by them in accordance with the special Powers conferred on them by this Act, shall form One Consolidated Revenue Fund, to be appropriated for the Public Service of Canada in the Manner and subject to the Charges in this Act provided.

107. All Stocks, Cash, Banker's Balances, and Securities for Money belonging to each Province at the Time of the Union, except as in this Act mentioned, shall be the property of Canada, and shall be taken in Reduction of the Amount of the respective Debts of the Provinces at the Union.

108. The Public Works and Property of each Province, enumerated in the Third Schedule to this Act, shall be the Property of Canada.

109. All Lands, Mines, Minerals, and Royalties belonging to the several Provinces of Canada, Nova Scotia, and New Brunswick at the Union, and all Sums then due or payable for such Lands, Mines, Minerals, or Royalties, shall belong to the several Provinces of Ontario, Quebec, Nova Scotia, and New Brunswick in which the same are situate or arise, subject to any Trusts existing in respect thereof, and to any Interest other than that of the Province in the same.

111. Canada shall be liable for the Debts and Liabilities of each Province existing at the Union.

121. All articles of the Growth, Produce, or Manufacture of any of the Provinces shall, from and after the Union, be admitted free into each of the other Provinces.

When the federal government took over the provinces' debts, it also took over their assets. These included such public works as canals, railways, customs houses, military establishments, and lighthouses. The *original* four provinces were left in possession of their natural resources.

Tariffs between the colonies were removed, and all government income was to be collected by the federal government. As compensation for giving up such important financial powers as the right to collect taxes on imports, each province was to receive a fixed annual grant, plus an annual grant based on eighty cents per person of its population. A similar formula was to be applied in future years to new provinces joining the Dominion.

The sharing of revenues is closely related to the sharing of power. In later years, as all governments grew in size and power the federal government and the provinces found themselves in frequent conflict over revenue. In the Depression of the 1930s, the provinces were found to have greatly increased powers and responsibilities, but lacked the authority to raise the money necessary to carry them out. A royal commission, the Rowell-Sirois Commission, (1937-40)* investigated the resulting crisis in government. After World War II, the "tug-of-war" over government revenue became an ongoing issue between the two levels of government.

*See page 441.

RAILWAYS

Question: Section 145 is about the Intercolonial Railway. Isn't it strange to find something about railways in a constitution?

Answer: Maybe so, but notice the wording: "the Intercolonial Railway is essential to the Consolidation of the Union of British North America and to the Assent [agreement] . . . of Nova Scotia and New Brunswick [to join].

Question: So railways played a big part in the story of Confederation?

Answer: Yes, it seems that way. Remember that the problems of the Grand Trunk couldn't be solved without Confederation, and, as it turned out, British Columbia was persuaded to join Canada by the promise of a transcontinental railway.

So the Intercolonial was a big attraction to the Maritimes; without the physical link to the rest of Canada, the Maritimes could see little value in a political union.

Once the Intercolonial was completed, from Rivière du Loup to Halifax in 1876, this section of the BNA Act had no purpose. Therefore, Section 145 was repealed in 1893, and is no longer part of the constitution.

THE EXPANSION OF CANADA

Question: Is that the end of the constitution?

Answer: It's not even the end of the BNA Act. Remember the *Preamble*, the introduction to the Act? One of the purposes it stated was to provide for the future expansion of Canada. The original four provinces, united in 1867, were a beginning. Expecting the remaining colonies and territories to join within a short time, the Fathers of Confederation included sections which set out the arrangements.

Question: Where do we go from here? These conversations have been really interesting to me. I think I've learned some important things about our political system. We have talked about many *issues* that seem to have remained all through the life of our country—how to keep government "responsible", the role of the media, federal-provincial cooperation and conflict, bilingualism, regional differences, problems of justice for individuals and groups, and many more.

I'm not sure about the number of *facts* that I've gathered, but I do know much more about the *questions* that I, as a Canadian, need to think about.

Answer: I think you have an attitude that will enable you to carry on from here. If I have been able to help, I'm glad. Good luck. Au revoir.

Turned off by politics?

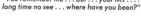

"You remember me . . . but . . . your M.P. . . .
long time no see . . . where have you been?"

"I don't mind telling you that my husband and I are less
indifferent about you than the other leaders."

"Politicians, in general, are crooked."

"My vote won't matter."

"It doesn't matter who wins the election, all politicians are the same."

"Once they're in office, politicians forget who put them there; they don't come around until the next election."

"The little guy doesn't count; politicians only care about those with money and influence."

"Election promises are just a bunch of hot air; we never hear about them after the person wins his seat."

"Even if the candidate has good intentions, when he gets in with the rest of the people in Ottawa, he has no power to make the changes he promised."

If you can agree with one or more of the above statements about our political system, you may be experiencing political alienation. The concept of *alienation* means feeling that things are not going the way you think they should, that you don't understand the way things are and that you feel you have no power to change them. Alienation is not an all-or-nothing thing. People feel more or less alienated at different times in their lives.

Alienation is a very common feeling when people think about politics. For a number of reasons, some being a lack of knowledge about the political system, a feeling of powerlessness, and distance from their elected officials, many Canadians could agree with some or all of the statements quoted above.

What we are concerned with here are the ways people cope with these feelings of alienation. Consider the following examples of politically alienated people:

1. Mr. T. is a plant supervisor in an industrial city. The father of four young boys, Mr. T. has a difficult time spreading his income over a two-week pay period. Mrs. T. must stay at home to take care of the children, so the family has only Mr. T.'s income. When the provincial elections were held a few years ago, several candidates approached Mr. T. with promises of government assistance to lower-income families, lower taxes and other benefits he was not then receiving. Mr. T. was impressed by what one candidate in particular said, and voted for him in the election. Now, several years later, Mr. T. finds that the party for which he voted has not carried through with its election promises and, in fact, has made economic life for his family even more difficult. Mr. T. used to be interested in what politicians said, and he used to read the newspaper carefully. Now, he does not care. All politicians are the same, he says. No one is willing to help the wage earners.

2. Mrs. K. is an intelligent, forthright woman in her early 40s. The mother of two teen-aged children, she has been active in politics at the local level for many years. This year, with the federal election imminent, she decides to try to seek the nomination of her party to run as the candidate for federal election in her riding. She is successful in her bid for the nomination, and is faced with a hard campaign. Much of the opposition she receives while campaigning comes from people who do not think a woman is a serious candidate, but an unfortunate amount of it is focused around the fact that her party is the third party and does not seem to have the power to take enough votes away from the two major political parties. People have told Mrs. K. that they support her, support her party's platform, but will vote for one of the two other parties because she doesn't have a chance of winning. On the day of the

election, Mrs. K. makes a respectable showing, but loses. She doesn't think she'll run again. She says all the power and money are tied up in the two major parties, and no one else has a chance.

3. Bob R. is an 18-year-old high school graduate. He studied history and government in school but couldn't get very interested in what seemed like boring, academic subjects. He wouldn't admit it, but he couldn't tell you who his M.P. is or what the differences are in any of the parties. Monday is election day, and Bob works from 8 a.m. until 4:30 p.m. He thinks about voting before work, but decides that the extra half hour sleep is more important. After work, his friends convince him that cool refreshment is more important than a trip to the polling place. Bob doesn't take much convincing. He wouldn't even know what to do when he walked in to the place, and he isn't going to look stupid. He vows to vote next year.

The fictionalized accounts which you have just read may be more fact than fiction. In each case, the person decided not to try to change the system but rather to opt out. There are those people, however, who do not give up, who try to make the political system and the politicians responsible to those who have elected them. Some of these people run for office, some campaign for candidates, others attend political meetings to voice their opinions on matters of concern. Still others continue to vote as if their one vote *did* matter.

Here is a newspaper editorial which comments upon what it sees as the reality of young people and their political voices:

YOUNG VOTERS

According to a Canadian Press survey this week, some three million young voters will be eligible to vote for the first time in Monday's federal election [July 8, 1972]. This could have a substantial impact on the election results—in the 1968 election there were approximately 11 million Canadians eligible to vote, and of these some 7 million did so.

But will the so-called "youth" vote have that much of an impact? The survey finds that it will not. Of the three million young people who can vote, only half will do so. Here in Manitoba a university student councillor is quoted as saying that the majority of students do not appear to be interested in, or well informed about, the election—this despite the appearance at schools of various party leaders.

If this estimate is accurate, it is regrettable; but it would ill become any older person to point a finger at the young people. Disinterest in, and lack of knowledge about, the election and its issues are not confined to the new voters. . . .

Every one of us in this House [House of Commons] must be committed to the success of involving young Canadians in the political life of this country.[11]
—Pierre Elliott Trudeau, 1969

41

New voters (and old) must accept some of the responsibility. There is an onus on people who are about to elect a government for the next four years to try to learn something about the various parties, their philosophies, as well as something of the candidate. It is all too easy to assume a cynical pose, shrug, sit back and cry "A plague on all your houses." But withholding one's vote isn't going to solve any of this country's problems. It is better, in the words of the old saying, to light one candle than to curse the darkness. And the exercise of one's franchise—even if the person or party to whom the vote is given falls far short of one's ideals—is better than a deliberate evasion of one's responsibilities.[10]

Perhaps in an extreme form of political participation, the heckler plays another role in trying to affect our political system.

THE HECKLER

The heckler is the Official Opposition of the hustings. If he takes his function seriously he persistently questions the statements made by politicians there. When they say the government has done many good things he asks them to "name three". If they say that the present Minister of Finance is the greatest one Canada has ever had, he asks them to "name the Ministers of Finance under Sir John A. Macdonald, Sir Wilfrid Laurier and the first ten years of Mackenzie King".

When they say their party stands for progress he wants to know what they mean by progress. When they promise large welfare payments, he asks whose pocket the money is coming from. When they criticise the activities of other parties, he asks the speaker to name those activities and give the date of any one of them. He is there to take the stuffing out of the stuffed shirts and to make pride lead to a deserved fall.

_____

He is a lively character; he is a dedicated man; he is a pillar of democracy. Salute him and join his ranks.[12]

1. The Heckler is questioning the meaning behind the promises made during political speeches. The next time you listen to a politician speak, try to become a heckler and pick out those phrases which sound appealing to the audience but which really are meaningless unless they are made clearer or more specific.
2. You may also want to listen to the well-known British comedian Peter Sellers' record called "Party Political Speech" on the album, "The Best of Sellers" (Angel Records).

VOTING IN THE FUTURE?

"Franchise," a story by science fiction writer Isaac Asimov explains how an efficient election may be conducted at some time in the future. The excerpts, with a summary in between are the introduction and conclusion of the story:

Linda said, "Grandpa," and stood with her chin down and her hands behind her back until his newspaper lowered itself to the point where shaggy eyebrows and eyes, nested in fine wrinkles, showed themselves. It was Friday, October 31.

He said, "Yes?"

Linda came closer and put both her forearms on one of the old man's knees so that he had to discard his newspaper altogether.

She said, "Grandpa, did you really once vote?"

He said, "You heard me say I did, didn't you? Do you think I tell fibs?"

"N-no, but Mamma says everybody voted then."

"So they did."

"But how could they? How could *everybody* vote?"

Matthew stared at her solemnly, then lifted her and put her on his knee.

He even moderated the tonal qualities of his voice. He said, "You see, Linda, till about forty years ago, everybody always voted. Say we wanted to decide who was to be the new President of the United States. The Democrats and Republicans would both nominate someone, and everybody would say who they wanted. When Election Day was over, they would count how many people wanted the Democrat and how many wanted the Republican. Whoever had more votes was elected. You see?"

Linda nodded and said, "How did all the people know who to vote for? Did Multivac tell them?"

Matthew's eyebrows hunched down and he looked severe. "They just used their own judgment, girl."

In Asimov's story, "Multivac" is the ultimate in computers, able to predict the outcome of a national election from the behaviour of a single voter. Before each election, the computer selects a citizen who is the most representative of the total population at that time. Under tight security, the Voter of the Year —in this case, 2008—is questioned intensively to determine the "bent of his mind," and thus the bent of his fellow citizens. This time Norman Muller, Linda's father, has been given the "honour."

He sat perfectly still and slowly the tension left him. His breathing grew less ragged and he could clasp his hands without being quite so conscious of the trembling of his fingers.

Maybe there would be no questions. Maybe it was all over.

If it *were* over, then the next thing would be torchlight processions and invitations to speak at all sorts of functions. The Voter of the Year!

He, Norman Muller, ordinary clerk of a small department store in Bloomington, Indiana, who had neither been born great nor achieved greatness would be in the extraordinary position of having had greatness thrust upon him.

The historians would speak soberly of the Muller Election of 2008. That would be its name, the Muller Election.

The publicity, the better job, the flash flood of money that interested Sarah so much, occupied only a corner of his mind. It would all be welcome, of course. He couldn't refuse it. But at the moment something else was beginning to concern him.

A latent patriotism was stirring. After all, he was representing the entire electorate. He was the focal point for *them*. He was, in his own person, for this one day, all of America!

The door opened, snapping him to open-eyed attention. For a moment, his stomach constricted. Not more questions!

But Paulson was smiling. "That will be all, Mr. Muller."

"No more questions, sir?"

"None needed. Everything was quite clear-cut. You will be escorted back to your home and then you will be a private citizen once more. Or as much so as the public will allow."

"Thank you. Thank you." Norman flushed and said, "I wonder— who was elected?"

Paulson shook his head. "That will have to wait for the official announcement. The rules are quite strict. We can't even tell you. You understand."

"Of course. Yes." Norman felt embarrassed.

"Secret service will have the necessary papers for you to sign."

"Yes." Suddenly, Norman Muller felt proud. It was on him now in full strength. He was proud.

In this imperfect world, the sovereign citizens of the first and greatest Electronic Democracy had, through Norman Muller (through *him!*), exercised once again its free, untrammelled franchise.[13]

1. Is this how Canadian elections will eventually be decided? Why or why not?

2. Do you think that voting is a citizen's only political responsibility in a democracy? What other responsibilities do citizens have?

---

how to vote
You vote at the **polling station** for your polling division. On **election day**, polls are open between 8 o'clock in the morning and 7 o'clock in the evening (Standard Time). Instructions on how to vote are posted in the polling station and in the polling booth. If you need any help ask the deputy returning officer who gave you your ballot paper.

CANDIDATE A
Political Affiliation

CANDIDATE B

CANDIDATE C
Political Affiliation

The names of the candidates are listed alphabetically. The political affiliation, if any, is printed under the name of each candidate. You vote for only one candidate by making an **"X"** in the circle beside his name.

Who you vote for is YOUR business. The ballot is secret.

Published by the
Chief Electoral Officer of Canada

This pamphlet, explaining voting procedure to voters, was issued by the Chief Electoral Officer.

2

The nation expands: the beginnings of federal-provincial relations

". . . . confederation was not a particularly likely and certainly not an inevitable union. It was anybody's guess whether such an arrangement could last."[1]

The Dominion of Canada was officially born on July 1, 1867. On the first Dominion Day, church bells rang and gun salutes were fired from Ottawa to Halifax. Formal ceremonies like the swearing in of the first Canadian Government, and speeches, parades and picnics marked the beginning of this nation. No doubt most people shared in a vague sort of way the mood of optimism and expectancy that their leaders tried to convey in their proclamations and speeches.

A "Canadian identity" was only an idea in the heads of a few, and the man-in-the-street interviewer asking about it would have drawn blank stares everywhere except in the offices of politicians and editors. Even then he would have received sharply different replies if he moved from Sarnia to Montreal and Quebec to Fredericton. There were fewer than 3.5 million Canadians; three out of every ten were French-speaking and their loyalty was to the family and the local parish; six of every ten came from British origins, and many, like Canada's first prime minister,* had been born in the "Old Country". Diversity of origins, race, culture, church all added to the dis-unifying factor of geography.

Canadians did have things in common. They lived, for the most

*John A. Macdonald was born in Glasgow, Scotland, in 1815.

July 1, 1867, Montreal

In many histories of Canada, the years from 1867 to 1896 are considered a period and referred to as the "Macdonald era". Though this may appear arbitrary, it is not surprising. Sir John A. Macdonald, the first prime minister, held the position, with the exception of one term, until his death in 1891. In that year he won his last political victory, three months before dying at the age of seventy-six, in a successful election that gave his Conservative Party five more years in office.

part, simply and without excitement by modern standards. They worked hard to survive, to "get ahead," to move upward materially from the lower and lower-middle class conditions that so many had escaped overseas. Towns were growing, and the Industrial Revolution was more rapidly bringing changes. With it came the Victorian belief in progress and "survival of the fittest".

DOMINION "FROM SEA TO SEA"

1867: the Dominion of Canada created; Sir John A. Macdonald as first prime minister

1868: Nova Scotia's threat to secede

1869: Canada's purchase of the Northwest from the Hudson's Bay Company

1870: Manitoba as the first new province

1871: British Columbia's entry into Confederation

1873: Prince Edward Island's entry into Confederation; the Pacific Scandal; election of the first Liberal Government

1874: the secret ballot and other reforms of Canada's electoral system

1878: re-election of the Conservatives; the National Policy
1885: the Saskatchewan Rebellion; completion of the Canadian Pacific Railway
1887: the first conference of provincial premiers
1891: death of Sir John A. Macdonald
1896: the Manitoba Schools Question; election of the Liberals led by Wilfrid Laurier

The politics of expansion

Canada began as a political union set up to expand from the original four provinces. In other words, only the first stage of nation-building had been accomplished in 1867. The British North America Act, therefore, provided for the expansion of Canada to include other provinces and territories.

Especially urgent was the acquisition of the West. Without British Columbia, there would be no outlet to the Pacific. And there was not much time to lose. The westward expansion of the United States seemed to threaten a "peaceful invasion" of the Canadian West by American settlers. South of the Red River settlement, the population in the state of Minnesota had swelled to 300 000 by 1865. Trade links with Minneapolis-St. Paul were beginning to draw what is now southern Manitoba into the American orbit. Similarly, British Columbia had many ties with the United States, and thousands of Americans already living in the colony were likely to support annexation of the colony to the United States.

In the "corridors of power" in Britain and in Canada, men had faith in the power of technology to create a nation across a wilderness. Central Canada, that is, Ontario and Quebec, had the money and the expertise or more properly, the hope of attracting it. If a railway could be built to link the far-flung territories, then there would be a chance to create a "new nation".

Three new provinces

MANITOBA

The creation of Manitoba as Canada's first new province was a by-product of a fantastic real estate deal. Nobody in Ottawa or London had plans for a new province out west, at least not in the near future. Sir John A. Macdonald's government had one thing in mind, and that was to acquire the vast Northwest from the Hudson's Bay Company.

Over a period of months in 1868-1869, a three-corner arrangement was worked out. The Bay agreed to give up the control it had exercised for 200 years in the Northwest. In return, the Bay received a payment of £300 000,* ownership of approximately 18 000 hectares of land around its trading posts, and one-twentieth of the total fertile land. Britain was to receive the territory, transfer it to Canada, and guarantee Canada a loan for the purchase.

By December 1, 1869, the official date for the transfer, unexpected events were unfolding. The inhabitants of the Northwest had

Had you been a gambling person in 1867, which trend do you think you would have put your money on— Canadian expansion or United States' absorption of Canadian territory? For what reasons?

*Converting this total to modern value is difficult. Over the years, the purchasing power of the British pound has fluctuated.

Louis Riel

not been consulted, and at Red River, where some 12 000 people lived, young Louis Riel led a resistance movement. The Métis leader headed a provisional (temporary) government that seized control of Fort Garry, the Hudson's Bay Company post strategically located at the junction of the Red and Assiniboine rivers.

The goal was to delay the setting up of Canadian authority in the territory in order to give the settlers a chance to bargain with the Dominion government. The latter was obliged to negotiate with the provisional council, which had drafted a "bill of rights." After several months, agreement was reached for the colony to join Canada as a province. Riel was to hand over his authority to a lieutenant-governor to be appointed by the Canadian government.

The signing of the Manitoba Treaty

A province of Manitoba was created when the federal government passed the Manitoba Act, to be proclaimed on July 15, 1870. The "postage stamp province", a fraction of the size of present-day Manitoba, was to be governed by a Lieutenant Governor, executive council and bicameral legislature.* In accordance with the Bill of Rights drawn up by Riel's provisional government, both French and

*The Legislative Council was disbanded in 1876.

Canada's first federal election

In the 1970s, elections take place on one day, and through the combination of computer predictions and national radio and television, the outcome may be evident minutes after the last polls close. Imagine what our ancestors of a century ago might think of this, considering that Canada's first federal election lasted approximately *six weeks*!

That early election was run very differently from the elections of our time. In effect, each of the four original provinces ran separate elections, with the pro-Confederation groups using a variety of tactics to improve their chances. Since they were in office, they arranged to have the first elections held in particular ridings where victory was likely, then had successful results announced to try to influence the voting in other ridings. Voting was public, too, in the days before the secret ballot; a voter had much more to lose if he "backed the wrong horse".

Of the leading people, supporters and opponents, in the struggle over Confederation, Macdonald, Cartier, and Galt were all successful candidates. Tilley was elected in New Brunswick, and so was Charles Tupper in Nova Scotia, although he was the *only* government supporter among the nineteen members of Parliament from that province. A. A. Dorion, the clever critic of Confederation, was also a member of the first House of Commons. The most conspicuous casualty of the election was George Brown, who had parted company with Sir John A. Macdonald. Running as an opposition candidate in Ontario, Brown was defeated in a campaign in which the government went all-out to back their representative.

On September 18, 1867, the election was finally over. As expected, Sir John A. Macdonald was to be Canada's first prime minister. Members of Parliament were not so clearly divided into Conservatives and Liberals as they would be later, but there was no doubt that Macdonald's cabinet could count on a solid majority in the new House of Commons. The opposition was a collection of groups and individuals, rather than an "opposition party".

Who were the inhabitants of the Northwest? Except for the Red River area, most were Indians who lived semi-nomadically and who belonged to many tribes which were widely dispersed geographically. They moved within loosely defined hunting grounds according to the presence of buffalo and other game and the location of Hudson's Bay Company posts. Few, if any, people in the settled parts of Canada would have thought of Indians as settlers, let alone as citizens with a right to share in decisions about the future of the Northwest.

At the time of Confederation, fewer than 12 000 resided in the vicinity of Red River. Most of these people were of mixed ancestry, descended from Indian and either French or British parentage. The French-speaking mixed bloods, or *Métis*, comprised half the total, and the rest were divided among a large group of English-speaking mixed bloods and small numbers of British, Americans and settlers recently arrived from Ontario. This latter group, who called themselves the Canadian Party, agitated for union with Canada as a means for opening the West for settlers of their own kind.

English were to be official languages in the debates and records of the legislature. Furthermore, the dual school system—denominational Catholic and Protestant schools—which was already in existence, would continue. Settlers were given legal rights to their land, though public land remained the property of the Dominion government.*

*The Dominion government later used grants of land to promote settlement in the West, and to subsidize railway-building.

"Hanging Judge" Begbie

When he arrived to conduct trials in a new district, he is supposed to have checked the area for good gallow-trees.

This is one of the many legends surrounding the name of Matthew Begbie, first judge of the colony of British Columbia and chief justice of the province from the time of its joining Canada until his death in 1894.

Whether or not Judge Begbie actually picked out trees from which to hang people found guilty of capital offences in his courts, he had an image that intimidated juries as well as law-breakers in British Columbia's frontier days.

Standing six feet five inches, Begbie was equipped physically as well as temperamentally to dispense justice in a "rough and ready" society. Colourful, controversial and fearless, Judge Begbie "left behind him a permanent furrow in the history of his province."[2]

In 1867, British Columbia was a Crown colony with a population of less than 40 000, cut off from Canada by the Rockies and the Hudson's Bay Company's territory. The gold rush was over, hard times had set in, and the government was burdened with heavy debts. Annexationists in the colony called for British Columbia to join the United States, which had just purchased Alaska from Russia. The effect would have been to make the entire Pacific coast American.

Public opinion was sharply divided. A British group favoured a continuation of the status quo. The pro-Americans argued that the colony was a natural part of the American Northwest. The pro-Confederationists, however, had many things in their favour. The British government believed that Confederation was the surest way to keep British Columbia "British". And Canada was prepared to "make a deal".

In the summer of 1870, a delegation from British Columbia negotiated the colony's entry into the Dominion. Sir John A. Macdonald promised the construction of a railway to the Pacific to meet the prime condition for British Columbia's entry. Macdonald did so in spite of the fact that few in Canada believed that the Dominion possessed the resources for such an ambitious undertaking. In fact, many dismissed the project of building a railway through the seemingly insurmountable Canadian Rockies as sheer folly.

On July 20th 1871, British Columbia became the sixth province of the Dominion. The Pacific colony entered Confederation on the promise that a railway to the coast would be begun in two years and completed within ten. British Columbia was to receive provincial status, an annual subsidy of $35 000 and a yearly per capita grant of eighty cents until the population reached 400 000. The province retained control of public lands. The federal government also assumed the new province's debt. Canada now stretched from the Atlantic to the Pacific, physically united "from sea to sea."

PRINCE EDWARD ISLAND

Prince Edward Island gave a flat "no" to Confederation in 1867, much to the displeasure of the British government. Even more controversial was the Island's later attempt to make a trade deal with the United States, in the hope of avoiding union with the Canadians. Yet even though many Islanders were fearful of losing their identity in any union with a large country, interest in Confederation remained, in both Prince Edward Island and Canada.

After all, the traditional problem of absentee landlords remained; paying them off was going to be expensive. An over ambitious railway-building program had created an enormous burden of debt and threatened a sharp increase in taxes. The Island government looked for a way out by trying to arrange overseas loans, but bankers in London and New York regarded Prince Edward Island as a bad risk.

Canada, urged on by Britain, made repeated offers, and in 1872, the Island's government reluctantly entered into final negotiations. On July 1, 1873, Prince Edward Island became part of Canada, with full provincial status and annual grants similar to those given to Manitoba and British Columbia. Canada assumed the colony's debts and contributed money for the purchase of land from the absentee landlords. Furthermore, Canada took over the colony's railway lines and guaranteed communication with the mainland through a telegraph system and a year-round ferry service.

Prince Edward Island had thrown in its lot with a "Dominion from sea to sea". The risk was great for a small island, with its particular identity. Yet a century later, the "Garden of the Gulf" remained a distinctive part of Canada.

Within six years after Confederation, the nation included seven of modern Canada's ten provinces. Massive immigration into the Northwest led to the creation, in 1905, of Saskatchewan and Alberta. When Newfoundland finally joined in 1949, only the north—the Yukon and the Northwest Territories—remained as potential sources of new provinces for Canada.

Building the Canadian Pacific Railway

THE PACIFIC SCANDAL

The Canadian promise to start building a railway linking British Columbia to the East within two years of the province's joining the Dominion forced Macdonald's government into hasty action—too hasty, as it turned out.

The resulting "Pacific Scandal" brought about the downfall of the Conservative government, postponed the building of the transcontinental railway, and led to threats in British Columbia of withdrawing from Confederation.

Re-elected in 1872 after a hard campaign, the Conservative Government awarded the railway contract to a group headed by Sir Hugh Allan, owner of the Allan Line of Ocean Steamships. The contract was considered a plum because of the Government's virtual guarantees of long-term profits. However, the Liberal opposition produced evidence that Allan had contributed some $325 000 to the recent Conservative election campaign. Furthermore, it was revealed that Allan had financial backing from American interests. Macdonald admitted that his party, notably such members as Sir George Etienne Cartier, had received the funds. He insisted that contributing to election campaigns was a practice accepted by all parties; and that

Survival of the fittest

In 1859 the British biologist Charles Darwin published a work which was to produce anxiety, doubt, fear and a revolution in thought throughout the world. In the work, *On the Origin of Species by Means of Natural Selection*, Darwin attacked the theory of creation which held that all forms of life appeared on earth at the same time. His theory of evolution explained that complex forms evolved from simpler forms during a struggle for existence in which only the fittest survived.

Darwin's scientific theory was appealing not only to scientists but to sociologists, economists and politicians as well. *Social Darwinism*, as it came to be called, allowed industrialists to use the "survival of the fittest" theory to explain their struggle for existence with members of the working class. In that struggle the rich and hardworking were fit to survive and the poor and lazy were doomed to perish.

"WE IN CANADA SEEM TO HAVE LOST ALL IDEA OF JUSTICE, HONOR AND INTEGRITY."—THE MAIL, 26TH SEPTEMBER.

the railway contract was not a "pay-off". Although there was never any proof that Macdonald received money personally, the talk of bribery was to hurt the government's position badly. The Government therefore resigned and suffered defeat in the ensuing election.

1. Do you believe that politicians can accept campaign contributions from special interest groups without being influenced?
2. Election campaigns are expensive. What alternatives are there to private contributions?

THE DANGERS OF CAUTIOUS PROGRESS

The Liberal Government insisted on a modest railway program, in the light of the difficult economic situation facing the country. The promise to start construction of a railway to British Columbia within two years was not fulfilled. The Intercolonial Railway was completed in 1876 and some track was laid between Fort William and Winnipeg and within British Columbia. A wagon road and telegraph line from the east were being constructed. But British Columbia protested, and when Mackenzie sought to revise the transcontinental railway agreement, the legislature rejected the offer and threatened to secede. The Governor General, Lord Dufferin, felt obliged to make a personal visit to the west coast in 1877 to soothe the irate population.

THE CONTRACT TO BUILD THE C.P.R.

Back in office in 1878 with a substantial majority, Sir John A. Macdonald moved confidently to implement the National Policy upon which he had built his election campaign. One of the main promises was the completion of a transcontinental railway system that would strengthen the political union of Canada and fulfill the agreement with British Columbia. Prosperity was returning, and an "all-Canadian" company, headed by George Stephen, president of the Bank of Montreal, and his cousin, Donald A. Smith, a high official of the Hudson's Bay Company, bid for the contract. This Canadian Pacific Railway Company was offered a partnership with the Canadian Government, in an arrangement between private and public enterprise that would be repeated in kind on various occasions in Canadian history. To encourage the start of construction, the company received generous terms.

In return for building the railway line, the company was to own and operate it. In addition, the company was to be granted $25 000 000, about 10 million hectares of fertile western land, perpetual tax exemption and an assurance that for twenty years, west of Lake Superior, no competing railway line would be built south of the CPR. Also, approximately 1100 km of railway lines that had already been built by the Canadian Government at an estimated cost of $35 000 000 were to be transferred to the Canadian Pacific Railway Company. The company's duty was to complete the transcontinental railway by 1891.

Amor de Cosmos. William Alexander Smith, a native of Nova Scotia, was one of the most aggressive pro-Confederationists in British Columbia. He was a member of the colonial assembly, and he also used his newspaper, The British Colonist, to promote the cause. He wrote under the name of Amor de Cosmos. In September, 1869, he organized a convention at Yale, British Columbia, which passed resolutions for union and responsible government.

1. Define "private enterprise"; "public enterprise". Why have ambitious Canadian projects, such as a transcontinental railway or pipeline (see Chapter 12), been undertaken by a partnership of private and public enterprise?
2. Why was the land grant to the CPR Company so important a term in the contract? Are you surprised at the amount of financial support granted by the Canadian Government to the Canadian Pacific Railway Company?
3. The Liberal opposition attacked the terms as far too generous. What objections do you think they raised?

A railway builder with considerable experience in the United States, the engineer William Van Horne, was given the job of direct-

Chinese labourers at work on the construction of the Canadian Pacific Railway in the mountains of British Columbia.

ing construction. Work proceeded on building the line through the rock, forests and muskeg of the Canadian Shield. By 1882, the section along the rugged north shore of Lake Superior and across the 640 km from Thunder Bay to Winnipeg had been completed. In fact, the Canadian Pacific Railway was well advanced across the prairies, reaching Brandon, Manitoba, before the end of the year.

Financial difficulties plagued the CPR throughout. In 1883, the company declared the need for more money, and the Canadian government obliged with further loans to keep construction going. By 1885, the money had again run out, and opposition was rising against the use of taxpayers' funds to bail out the CPR project.

Ironically, the rebellion of 1885 in Saskatchewan "came to the rescue". The CPR's value was dramatically shown, as troops and supplies moved over the railway to crush the forces of Louis Riel. The government of Sir John A. Macdonald was able to convince Parliament to grant yet another loan. Thus on November 7, 1885, the CPR was completed at Craigellachie, British Columbia.

Alexander Mackenzie: first Liberal prime minister

Another of the many Scots prominent in Ontario's political life, Mackenzie was a believer in the possibility of ordinary men succeeding through hard work and self-sacrifice. He was a stone-mason, a worker, who rose to the highest political office in the country.

Mackenzie's government is remembered mainly as the one that took office by default, when Macdonald was defeated by his own errors of judgment in connection with the "Pacific Scandal". However, such a memory obscures his accomplishments. Even though an economic depression persisted through his term in office, Mackenzie's government completed the Intercolonial Railway between central Canada and Nova Scotia (1876); introduced the secret ballot, voting on one and the same day in all areas, and other election reforms (1874); encouraged settlement in the Northwest, for example, by the Homestead Act which made provisions for the distribution of land held by the Dominion government; established the Supreme Court of Canada (1875); and founded the Royal Military College in Kingston (1874).

Alexander Mackenzie. "Though he had, in his younger days been an incorrigible practical joker, his public image was one of uncompromising sobriety."[3]

Two sides of the CPR: the glory and the tragedy

The construction of the CPR has been usually described in heroic terms, and undoubtedly it deserves recognition as a remarkable achievement. On the other hand, the costs, particularly in human terms, have been downplayed. As you read the following documents, consider the question:

DID THE END JUSTIFY THE MEANS?

THE LAST SPIKE
Sandford Fleming gives this account in the CANADIAN ALPINE JOURNAL, *1899:*

It was indeed no ordinary occasion; the scene was in every respect noteworthy, from the groups which composed it and the circumstances which had brought together so many human beings in this spot in the heart of the mountains, until recently an untracked solitude. Most of the engineers with hundreds of workmen of all nationalities who had been engaged in the mountains were present. Everyone appeared to be deeply impressed by what was taking place....

The blows on the spike were repeated until it was driven home. The silence however continued unbroken.... It seemed as if the

"Sandford Fleming, the original chief engineer of the CPR who left for a time and returned to play a major role in the company, deserves a prominent place in the history of Canadian invention. It was Fleming who came up with the idea of dividing the world into time zones.

Fleming's idea was valuable in the 1880s, when a train might cross one time zone in a day's run, but today, when jet aircraft cruise at seven hundred miles an hour, it is essential."[4]

act now performed had worked a spell on all present. Each one appeared absorbed in his own reflections.... Suddenly a cheer spontaneously burst forth, and it was no ordinary cheer. The subdued enthusiasm, the pent up feelings of men familiar with hard work, now found vent. Cheer upon cheer followed as if it was difficult to satisfy the spirit which had been aroused.... [5]

THE RAILWAY BUILDERS

It was the opening up of the West that changed the whole face of Canadian life, that gave a basis for industrial expansion, that quickened national sentiment and created business optimism. And it was the building of the Canadian Pacific that opened up the West and bound it fast to the distant East. Certainly not least among the makers of Canada were the men who undertook that doubtful enterprise and carried it through every obstacle to success; and not least among the generations whose toil and faith have made possible the nation of to-day were the four millions of the Canada of the eighties who flung a great railway across the vast unpeopled spaces of a continent to the far Pacific.[6]

CONSTRUCTION OF THE C.P.R. IN BRITISH COLUMBIA

Onderdonk [contractor for the BC line of the CPR] found the white labour that he had got from San Francisco—the only source of supply at the moment—consisted for the most part of clerks out of employment, broken-down bartenders and other of that ilk, men who had never handled a shovel before and who often appeared on the scene attired in fashionable garments in a rather tattered state, who might even be seen in the cuttings with patent leather shoes, much the worse for wear and trousers sprung over the foot. So he determined to import a lot of Chinamen... and he got two ship loads, 1,000 men each. They came in very bad weather and had to be kept below hatches most of the way, so as soon as they got upon the work and began to take violent exercise, they developed scurvy and were decimated, fully one-tenth of their number dying. Being fatalists, as soon as a man was stricken with scurvy the others would not wait upon him or even give him a drink, and the government agent at Yale had great difficulty in getting them buried when they died. In fact many of their bodies were so lightly covered with a few rocks and a little earth that one became unpleasantly aware of the fact while walking along the line.[7]

1. Do you think the contractor was justified in importing Chinese labourers?
2. A daily wage of $2.00 was considered good pay in those days. White railway workers usually received $1.50 to $1.75 in British Columbia; Chinese were paid $1.00 a day. Why do you suppose such a discrepancy existed?

THE LAST SUMMER

One railway employee, A. C. Forster Boulton, who came from a notable Toronto family, wrote that the progress of construction was so swift that antelope and other game migrating north were cut off on their return that fall by the lines of rails and telegraph posts, 'and terrified by the sight . . . gathered in hundreds on the north side, afraid to cross it.' It was probably the last summer in which herds of buffalo and antelope freely roamed the prairie.[8]

1. Does the advance of technology always entail destruction of the natural environment? Does man have any responsibility to protect the environment? What specific actions should be taken by the following: (a) governments; (b) businessmen; (c) scientists; (d) environmentalists; (e) youth organizations; (f) religious organizations; (g) media?

2. The buffalo herds of the Northwest were almost wiped out by the combination of railway and rifle. Compare the effects today on the polar bear and the whale of the introduction of the snowmobile and the high powered rifle to Canada's North.

CHANGING THE FACE OF THE WHOLE COUNTRY

Father Albert Lacombe, the voyageur priest who had served his time as chaplain to the railroad navvies of Rat Portage and was now back among his beloved Blackfoot nation, watched the approach of the rails with both sadness and resignation:

'I would look in silence at that road coming on—like a band of wild geese in the sky—cutting its way through the prairies; opening up the great country we thought would be ours for years. Like a vision I could see it driving my poor Indians before it, and spreading out behind it the farms, the towns and cities. . . . No one who has not lived in the west since the Old-Times can realize what is due to that road—that C.P.R. It was Magic—like the mirage on the prairies, changing the face of the whole country.'[9]

1. What benefits, if any, did the coming of the railway bring to the Indians? the Métis?

2. Were the native peoples of the Northwest as helpless before the impact of technology as the antelope?

3. What other examples, past or present, resemble the case of the CPR in the Northwest?

4. Is economic progress for some groups always accompanied by losses for others? Explain.

Canada's moderate tariffs, running at approximately 17%, were important to the government. There was no personal income tax then, and taxes on imported goods were the main source of government income. After the Conservatives took power in 1878, they *doubled* the tariffs. Thus the price of an imported wool garment, formerly priced at $10.00 jumped to at least $13.00. Iron and steel products, so important to the expansion of an industrial economy, were taxed at a similar rate. The same was true of a variety of finished goods, such as shoes and furniture, dishes and clocks.

In the mid-1870s, the Liberal government under Alexander Mackenzie struggled with an economic depression. The early promise of prosperity ushered in by Confederation had failed. Canada lacked foreign markets, especially in the United States; prices on products from farm, fishery and factory were declining. The Canadian government lacked funds to carry out its work. Plans for a transcontinental railway had been interrupted. The Liberals decided to increase tariffs—taxes on exports—enough to meet the government's need for revenue.

But in deciding on only a minimum increase in tariffs the Liberals did not go so far as to protect the Canadian producer against foreign competition. With the Liberals maintaining what was essentially a free trade position, the Conservatives saw their opportunity; they promptly came out with the *National Policy*.

The National Policy capitalized on the mood of frustration in the country. If made part of a larger vision, that of creating a national economy less dependent on "outsiders" like the United States, and even Great Britain, high tariffs could seem very attractive. *Economic nationalism* could appeal to Canadian pride, to the idea of "going it alone".

In the election campaign of 1878, the Conservatives claimed their National Policy would benefit a wide range of Canadians. Manufacturers in the St. Lawrence heartland, where most industries were located, would obviously gain from protection. The expansion of industry would create more jobs for workers. Additional revenue for the national government could be directed into the construction of a transcontinental railway, promoting east-west trade that would benefit farmers and fishermen.

Canadian-based companies whose parent companies have headquarters in the United States.

The election of 1878 gave the Conservatives a strong mandate. Having elected 137 members to the Liberals' 69, the Conservatives wasted little time in announcing tariff rates that were as high as double the former ones. At first, prosperity seemed to follow, even though some of it came from American **branch plants** built in Canada to avoid the effect of Canadian tariffs on imported American-made products. Ontario, where most manufacturing was located, enjoyed a business boom. Canada as a whole, however, was still stagnating economically in 1891, when Sir John A. Macdonald fought his last election after thirteen consecutive years as prime minister. Inter-provincial trade had not grown as expected. Western expansion, in particular, was disappointing; falling prices for farm products and declining immigration interfered with the movement of settlers to the Prairies. Many farmers abandoned their homesteads and joined the exodus from all parts of Canada to the United States.

Proximity to the United States was a dilemma for Canada in

Values and choices: a turning point in Canadian history?

Each of us has opinions and beliefs about many things, and these opinions and beliefs are based on what we consider important in life —our values. For example, you may favour a campaign in your school to increase attendance at basketball games or participation in the music festival. You may expect the result of the campaign to be greater student involvement in the life of the school, which you would like to see because you value school spirit.

Some of our values concern matters that are more vital than school spirit and others that are less vital. But generally speaking, values are important because they influence the choices we make. Therefore you have reason to be interested in the values of those around you, and in the values of those who may be far away but whose decisions may significantly affect your life.

Value choices made in the past have also affected the lives of Canadians today. For example, to the question, "How can we best build a firm foundation for Canadian nationhood?" the Conservatives answered in 1878 with the National Policy, a policy of aggressive economic nationalism. Because the National Policy was adopted and remained a part of Canadian life until the 1930s—that is, for a half century—whether government was in the hands of Conservatives or Liberals, history books tend to assume it was inevitable. But was it? Were there choices other than the National Policy? What influences led to the choice of one policy over another?

The questions that follow are intended to help you analyze values that were held by representatives of three different viewpoints at an important time in Canadian history. It was 1891, an election year, and Canadians were faced with a controversial choice about the future direction of their developing nation. If you can detect values in the extracts from the writings of Sir John A. Macdonald, Goldwin Smith, and George Parkin, you may also sharpen your awareness of values held by people today.

NATIONAL POLICY

In his "Last Address to the People of Canada," Sir John A. Macdonald defended the National Policy:

As in 1878, in 1882, and again in 1887, so in 1891, do questions relating to the trade and commerce of the country occupy a foremost place in the public mind. Our policy in respect thereto is to-day what it has been for the past thirteen years, and is directed by a firm determination to foster and develop the varied resources of the Dominion, by every means in our power, consistent with

Canada's position as an integral part of the British Empire. To that end we have laboured in the past, and we propose to continue in the work to which we have applied ourselves, of building up on this continent, under the flag of England, a great and powerful nation.

When, in 1878, we were called upon to administer the affairs of the Dominion. . . . a profound depression hung like a pall over the whole country. . . . Canadians were fast sinking into the position of being mere hewers of wood and drawers of water for the great nation dwelling to the south of us. . . . So we inaugurated the National Policy. You all know what followed. Almost as if by magic, the whole face of the country underwent a change. Stagnation and apathy and gloom—ay, and want and misery too—gave place to activity and enterprise and prosperity. . . . [10]

1. Can you state two or three values which, according to Macdonald, influenced the policy of his government?
2. What value did Macdonald's Conservative government attach to Canada's ties with the British Empire?
3. What references does Macdonald make to the United States? Does he say anything about the value of Canadian independence from the influence of the United States?

COMMERCIAL UNION

Goldwin Smith, formerly a professor at Oxford and at Cornell in New York, was a noted critic of the National Policy and of closer ties of trade between Canada and Britain. He believed Canada's destiny lay in "unrestricted reciprocity," or commercial union with the United States. The excerpt that follows is taken from his book, Canada and the Canadian Question.

. . . . To force trade into activity between the Provinces and turn it away from the United States, giving the Canadian farmer a home market, and consolidating Canadian nationality at the same time, were the ostensible objects of the adoption in 1879 of a Protective tariff. The real object perhaps was at least as much to capture the manufacturer's vote and his contributions to the election fund of the party in power. . . .

The isolation of the different Canadian markets from each other, and the incompatibility of their interests, add in their case to the evils and absurdities of the protective system. What is meat to one Province is . . . poison to another. . . .

Without commercial intercourse or fusion of population, the unity produced by a mere political arrangement [National Policy] can hardly be strong or deep. It will, for the most part, be confined to the politicians. . . .

That a union of Canada with the American Commonwealth, like that into which Scotland entered with England, would in itself be attended with great advantages cannot be questioned, . . . It would give to the inhabitants of the whole continent as complete a security for peace and immunity from war taxation as is likely to be attained by any community or group of communities on this side of the Millenium. Canadians almost with one voice say that it would greatly raise the value of property in Canada; in other words, that it would bring with it a great increase of prosperity.... [11]

1. In his criticism of the government, what does Goldwin Smith say may have been the actual reason behind the National Policy? What did Macdonald as a political leader value most, according to Smith?

2. As you read Smith's arguments in favour of commercial union between Canada and the United States, can you tell what he values for Canada?

IMPERIAL UNION

In the 1880s in Canada, as well as in Britain and other parts of the Empire, there arose a movement for closer ties within the British Empire. One proposal, that of "imperial federation", was advanced as a means of strengthening British civilization against the dangers posed by Germany, Russia and other nations expanding in the "Age of Imperialism".

The following is an extract from an article published in 1888 by George R. Parkin who, after being principal of Upper Canada College, served for many years as administrator of the Rhodes Scholarship Foundation:

.... the British people seemed for a time to look upon the colonies as burdens which entailed responsibilities without giving any adequate return. All this has now been changed.... The vigor of colonial life, the expansion of colonial trade and power, the greatness of the part which the colonies are manifestly destined to take in affairs, have impressed even the slow British imagination. The integrity of the empire is fast becoming an essential article in the creed of all political parties....

————————

.... Great communities like Australia or Canada would disgrace the traditions of the race if they remained permanently content with anything short of an equal share in the largest possible national [meaning, in this case, *imperial*] life. For both mother land and colonies that largest life will unquestionably be found in organic national unity....

————————

.... Questions of peace and war; the safety of the great ocean routes; the adjustment of international differences; the relations of trade, currency, communication, emigration—in all these their [British colonies such as Canada] concern is already large, and becomes larger from year to year. In dealing with all such questions their voice, as component parts of a great empire, will be far more efficient than as struggling independent nationalities.[12]

1. Why might this policy have appealed to a majority of people living in Canada in 1891?
2. What value is suggested by the phrase "traditions of the race"?
3. What did advocates of Imperial Union value that they believed was dependent on membership in a strong British Empire?

1. On what values did all three policies seem to agree?
2. What was the main difference in values between (a) National Policy and Commercial Union, (b) National Policy and Imperial Union, (c) Commercial Union and Imperial Union?
3. For each of the following, compare and contrast the values of Macdonald's government with those of the present-day government of Canada: (a) economic growth; (b) ties with Great Britain; (c) influence of the United States.

---

many ways. The dynamic republic provided so great a range of opportunities that it attracted the waves of immigration from Europe and drew the discontented from Canada as well. The same was true of investment, which flowed from London and other financial centres to help finance the American industrial revolution. The absence of a Canadian-American reciprocity agreement, which did not seem to interest the United States, meant that Canada was competing with much more advanced countries for American markets. Canadian manufacturers, who had their hopes aroused in the early years of the National Policy, found themselves with limited export trade and slumping markets within the Dominion. Production in such industries as iron-making and textiles slowed down, and many workers were faced with job insecurity.

Response to the troubled conditions of the times took many forms. One was the organization of *lobbies*, to promote the interests of particular groups. The Trades and Labour Congress of Canada, a trade union of skilled workers, was formed in 1886. The next year the Canadian Manufacturers' Association was organized. The Farmers' Protective Union in Manitoba demanded abolition of high tariffs, lower freight rates and a secure market for farm products.

1. How would the attitude toward the National Policy of the Trades and Labour Congress differ from that of the Canadian Manufacturers' Association?
2. Why might the interests of farmers differ from those of either workers or businessmen?
3. How are the conflicting interests of different economic groups

harmonized in a democratic system? Is a government likely to make decisions known to be more favourable to one group than to others?

4. How are decisions about important matters made in your family? Your school? Some organization to which you belong? Your town or city?

OUTCOME

The election of 1891 was hotly contested, as Macdonald's government fought to extend its thirteen consecutive years in office. There were troubles on every side for the Conservatives. In Quebec's provincial elections the Liberals, led by Honoré Mercier, had exploited the Riel affair to gain victory. The Liberals had just won again in Ontario, where the Conservatives were badly divided, with a section of the party accusing Macdonald of being "soft" toward the French Canadians. Clouds of scandal hung over the federal Department of Public Works, whose Minister was accused of accepting "kickbacks"—payment in return for contracts granted to friendly businessmen.

A world-wide depression had undermined Canadian prosperity and made certain that economic issues would dominate the campaign. The National Policy seemed to be a vulnerable target for the Liberals and their new leader, Wilfrid Laurier. Boldly, they launched their program of unrestricted reciprocity, aimed at opening up American markets by removing tariffs between Canada and the United States.

Sir John A. Macdonald knew that an extraordinary campaign would be needed if he were going to lead his party to victory in what was likely, because of his age and health, to be his last election fight. He adopted a dramatic strategy:

> Patriotism and loyalty to a Canada within the Empire—a war cry, not a weapon—would have to be the issue. Canadians would be forced to choose between collective survival as a Britannic community or possible individual betterment as Americans. Macdonald's polarization of the trade issue in terms of loyalty ('A British subject I was born') and treason ('a deliberate conspiracy, by force, by fraud, or by both, to force Canada into the American union') ... had been used to good effect in a by-election. . . . [13]

In other words, the Liberals were condemned for being ready to sell out to the United States, as if their program of unrestricted reciprocity were the first step to severing ties with Great Britain. Macdonald's sentimental plea to the voters was driven home by his declaration, "A British subject I was born, a British subject I will die."

The issues in the election of 1891

It was an effective slogan, and although elections are won and lost for all kinds of reasons, the loyalty cry was one that the Liberals were unable to counter. The Conservatives lost seats in both Ontario and Quebec, but their margin in the West and in the Maritimes enabled them to gain an overall majority of 27 seats, a drop of only 10 since the election in 1887.

1. Although there were public advocates of three alternative policies —the National Policy, a kind of economic union with the United States, and Imperial Union—Imperial Union was not a choice presented to Canadians in the election of 1891. Why not?
2. Consider the statement, "Canadians chose the National Policy over other alternatives when they elected the Conservatives in the election of 1891." What does this statement mean? Try to consider the validity (accuracy) of this statement by thinking about the question: at election time in our country, are Canadians given a choice between policies or between parties and personalities? When you have chosen your answer, try to look at what implications this statement could have for the people's voice in elections. Did, in fact, Canadians choose the National Policy in 1891?

Uprisings in the West: clash of cultures or western alienation?

THE ADVANCE OF THE FRONTIER

To most Canadians, the West 100 years ago was a remote wilderness, habitable only to Indians, fur traders and massive herds of buffalo. To the politicians and railway builders, the territory beyond the Greak Lakes was real estate, over which a railway must pass to reach the Pacific. To the actual occupants, the West was many things —actual or potential—depending on whether a person was an Indian, a Métis, a fur trader or a settler.

Promoting Canada as a nation

Canadians have never been known for boastful national pride. Although there have been exceptional times, such as the two world wars, Canadians generally have not shown strong emotion about their country. Two developments, a hundred years apart, show that at least some Canadians have believed a more aggressive national identity is desirable.

In the 1870s, a group of people led by W. A. Foster, Charles Mair, R. G. Haliburton (son of the author of *Sam Slick*) and G. T. Denison, organized the *Canada First* movement. They published a journal, *The Nation,* in which they printed patriotic essays and poems. Believing that Confederation lacked soul and excitement, they tried to promote a feeling of national pride among Canadians.

The organizers of *Canada First* were not anti-British, but they wished Canada to be less dependent on the mother country. Canada, they believed, was a nation of potential economic power and distinctive culture. In the 1870s, however, most Canadians lacked a vision of nationhood, and the *Canada First* movement collapsed, branded as "disloyal".

A century later, a small group of Canadians believed the time had come for another nationalist movement. Thus the *Committee for an Independent Canada* was launched toward the end of 1969. Journalists, university professors, politicians, writers and other professionals banded together in a non-partisan pressure group. Their stated objective was to promote Canadian nationalism as the basis for Canada's survival as a country. They felt that the need for such action was urgent. Their reason was that foreign influence, mainly that of the United States, was growing rapidly and threatening Canada's independence.

The CIC's program has been active in pressuring governments to limit foreign investment in Canada, promote Canadian content in the media, and encourage Canadian studies in the schools. The founders of the CIC—people like Peter Newman, editor; Abraham Rotstein, economist; and Walter Gordon, businessman and former Liberal cabinet minister—have been joined by many other well-known Canadians in the nationalist campaign. Other new organizations have been formed to carry out particular tasks. For example, the Canada Studies Foundation, an inter-provincial enterprise, has been active since 1970 in promoting the development of Canadian learning materials for schools.

1. What similarities and differences can you find between the *Canada First* movement and the CIC? How do you account for these?

2. Are the CIC and similar organizations likely to be necessary in the foreseeable future to make Canadians aware of their "identity"?

By the 1860s, the West was still essentially the home of the Cree, the Saulteaux, the Sioux, Assiniboine and Blackfoot Indians. Traditionally, most non-natives who spent time there had been transients who were not interested in settling permanently. Yet there were signs that the frontier, the leading edge of white man's society, was beginning to make inroads.

*See page 125.

The Red River colony lay at the eastern entrance to the prairies. There, a nucleus of settlement had slowly grown, since the days of Lord Selkirk, into a mixture of communities.* Newly-arrived outsiders, both Canadian and American, had ideas about the colony's expansion and political future.

Farther west were two types of settlement, and certain ways of life had grown up around them. At Hudson's Bay Company posts, such as Cumberland House, Fort Carlton, Fort Pitt and Fort Edmonton, small numbers of whites resided and Indians and Métis traded. The other settlements were Catholic missions, such as Prince Albert, St. Laurent (near Batoche), and St. Albert.

UPRISING AT RED RIVER

Louis Riel was born in October, 1844, at Red River. His grandfather and father had been employed in the fur trade and his maternal grandmother, Marie-Anne Lagimodière (née Gaboury) had been the first white woman to dwell on the prairies. Educated at St. Boniface until the age of fourteen, Louis was selected by Bishop Taché to study further in Montreal. He returned to Red River in 1868.

On October 11, 1869, a government survey party was stopped from entering property near Red River by a group of Métis, led by twenty-five-year-old Louis Riel. Ten days later, a Métis committee organized by Riel blocked the arrival of William McDougall, the newly appointed lieutenant governor of the Northwest Territory. Fort Garry, the Hudson's Bay Company stronghold, was seized on November 2. What was going on?

Rumours about the future of the Northwest had been circulating at Red River for months, even years. Surveyors had arrived in September, 1868, in connection with the building of the Dawson Road, a roadway from Lake of the Woods to Fort Garry. The Canadian government was known to be negotiating the purchase of the Northwest from the Hudson's Bay Company. Now the government was sending out surveyors to prepare for the expected rush of settlers into the new territory.

The Canadian government assumed that land in the Northwest would be surveyed into townships, six miles square. In the Red River area, this plan conflicted with the pattern of strip farms fronting on the rivers, which was like that of the seigneurial system in Quebec.

The settlers, especially the Métis, became alarmed that their land might be taken away by the Canadian government when the new system of land ownership and legal title was established. There was a general fear of the future. If hordes of new settlers were to come to the Northwest, the Métis way of life would end. In the isolation of the prairies they had developed a separate identity: they were a community that was French-speaking, Catholic and cooperative. They valued an existence that was relatively unconfined, unchanging and unaffected by the "industrial revolution" in the St. Lawrence-Great Lakes area. In their anxiety, the Métis turned to Louis Riel for leadership.

Riel had been instrumental in the resistance at Red River to the Canadian government's unconditional establishment of its authority over the area.* Consequently the province of Manitoba was formed, with some recognition given to the rights claimed by the French-speaking Métis.

*See page 48.

THE IMPACT OF CHANGE IN THE WEST

The days of pre-industrial society in the West were numbered. After Manitoba's creation as a province (1870), a Dominion land office was located in Winnipeg, which was incorporated as a city in 1874. Its population of 5 000 was made up mainly of newcomers. In 1881, the boundaries of Manitoba were enlarged and the Canadian Pacific Railway reached westward, attracting settlers who turned Brandon overnight into a tent city of 3 000. From Ontario came homesteaders in search of cheap land. Expecting a deluge of migrants, the Dominion sent out teams of surveyors, who laid out townships divided into 65-hectare plots, as surveyors had done at Red River a decade or so before.

The Mounties

The North West Mounted Police (NWMP), created by the Dominion government in 1873, were another new influence on the prairies. Headquartered at Fort Macleod, west of the present city of Lethbridge, Alberta, the "red coats" were sent out to bring law and order to the West. With detachments at other strategic posts, such as Calgary and Edmonton, the NWMP had to deal with many problems. One of their first tasks was to drive out the whiskey smugglers who had been distributing American liquor from locations like Fort Whoop-up, and exploiting the Indians. There was the job of discouraging open conflict among Indian bands, and of preventing trouble between Indians and the growing numbers of whites.

Part of the Mounties' challenge was public relations. The Dominion government hoped that the spread of Canadian settlement into the West would be free from the bitter "Indian wars" that had occurred in the United States. The tragic battles to the south—1876 was the year of "Custer's last stand" in Montana—produced another problem for the Mounted Police. Retreating American Indians crossed into Canadian territory, raising the possibility of an international incident and complicating the struggle for survival which Canadian Indians already faced.

At Fort Macleod, where the Mounted Police had their first headquarters in western Canada, the hotel of "Kamoose" Taylor had the following rules posted for its guests:

1. Guests will be provided with breakfast and dinner, but must rustle their own lunch.
2. Spiked boots and spurs must be removed at night before retiring.
3. Dogs not allowed in bunks, but may sleep underneath.
4. Towels changed weekly, Insect Powder for sale at the bar.
5. Special rates to "Gospel Grinders."
6. Assaults against the cook are strictly prohibited.
7. Only registered guests allowed the special privilege of sleeping on the Bar Room floor.
8. To attract attention of waiters, shoot a hole through the door panel. Two shots for ice water, three for a deck of cards.
9. In case of fire the guests are requested to escape without unnecessary delay.
10. Guests are requested to rise at 6 A.M. This is imperative as the sheets are needed for tablecloths.[14]

1. American T.V. and movie westerns depict a certain kind of "uncivilized" or rustic setting. Do you think these hotel rules would be good "ingredients" for a Canadian western?

The Métis

Meanwhile, the Métis in Manitoba had received 97-hectare grants in recognition of their ancestry. However, rather than trying to contend with the growing number of settlers from the East, many of the Métis sold their land to speculators and drifted northwest to the banks of the Saskatchewan. Here they joined other Métis who had occupied strips of land in the pattern of earlier settlements at Red River. Their hope of a life free from outside interference was as futile as it was natural. Once again fearful of being dispossessed, they wanted assurance of clear and official titles to their land.

The Indians

The situation of the Indians differed from that of either the Métis or the white settlers. Starting in 1871, the Dominion government negotiated a series of treaties by which Indian tribes gave up ancestral claims to land from Lake Superior to the Rockies. In return, reservations of land were set aside on the assumption that Indians would adopt a more settled way of life and turn to agriculture. The treaties provided for the distribution of farm implements, oxen and cattle with which Indians might make a start in farming, and there were to

Violence at Red River

The birth of Manitoba was accompanied by tension and violence that had bitter effects far beyond Red River. In the 1860s, the population had grown through the arrival of many Canadians who expected the territory to be annexed to the East. Their aggressive promotion of this step, partly motivated by fear of American expansion, was resented by the majority, of whom the largest number were French-speaking Métis. When Louis Riel and his followers seized control late in 1869, the danger of a confrontation hung over the colony.

In the spring of 1870, a number of the English-speaking settlers were jailed. Among them was Thomas Scott, a militant member of the Canadian group. Even in jail, he showed his contempt for the Métis. Assuming he would escape from Riel's custody, as others had done several times, he screamed insults at his guards and threatened mayhem to them and Louis Riel. The result was a council, presided over by Riel's chief assistant, Ambroise Lepine. Scott was sentenced to death and shot, an action that Riel defended as necessary to protect the authority of the provisional government he headed.

The death of Thomas Scott in the Rebellion of 1870 at Red River.

Whatever the justification for the act, the execution of Scott raised a storm of angry protest in Ontario, where anti-French and anti-Catholic feeling flared up anew. In Quebec, the shooting of Scott was considered to be a necessary part of the Métis struggle for French-Canadian rights. In Ottawa, Sir John A. Macdonald came under considerable pressure to send troops to Red River in order to crush the "rebellion" and protect English Canadians.

Thus the expedition, under Garnet Wolseley, of 1200 soldiers and militia was dispatched to Red River. After a ninety-six-day trek across the rugged terrain of the Canadian Shield, the troops entered the newly created province on August 23. Riel, fearing for his life since an anticipated amnesty had not yet been granted by the federal government, fled to the United States.

Manitoba, the first province to be created by Canada, came into being much sooner than it would have if there had not been an insurrection. Because of Riel's leadership, the federal government was compelled to recognize the existence of a small but flourishing community at Red River. But the tragedy of racial hatred that accompanied the establishment of Manitoba was to have long-lasting repercussions.

---

be small annual money payments. The Indians were to retain hunting and fishing rights on Crown lands; that is, on land not sold to private owners.

The arrangements seemed reasonable enough, and in some cases they worked. By the mid-1880s, however, the system was still faulty in many respects and some Indian bands were becoming desperate. The administration of the treaties, through regional superintendents and agents—called Indian agents, because they were in charge of particular districts of Indians—was often ineffectual, if not corrupt. The attempt to sponsor farming and ranching and to set up schools was largely unsuccessful.

Many Indian bands, like the Crees who were led by Chief Big Bear, had not accepted the new mode of life and refused to settle on reservations. The disappearance of the buffalo, which had been slaughtered in incredible numbers within a few years especially by bounty hunters on the United States' side of the border, deepened the Indians' plight. Famine spread; an ominous restlessness increased among the Indians. There was not sufficient aid available from the authorities; the Dominion government's support for the Indians in a time of difficult transition was lax, both in helping them move toward self-sufficiency and in providing aid in emergencies.

White Settlers

The Métis were not alone in their discontent. White settlers joined in protests against the government's failure to complete the survey and to provide for registration of claims to land. In the early 1880s a political crisis loomed. Besides the land problem, grievances accumulated over crop failures, falling prices for grain, and the high costs of transportation and shipping freight on the railway.

Louis Riel returns

Meetings among both whites and Métis resulted in a series of petitions being sent to the federal government. Ottawa's reaction was indecision and delay. By the spring of 1884, a common feeling of desperation among all groups of settlers led to a meeting in the Prince Albert district, where a resolution was passed to invite the assistance of Louis Riel.

The name "Riel" was magic to the Métis. In their minds, he was still the leader who had forced the government in distant Ottawa to recognize the aspirations of his people at Red River. Why could he not repeat his success, this time for the benefit of Métis on the Saskatchewan? He was living not far away, in Montana. Surely he would answer an invitation to serve once more a cause to which he had proven himself so devoted.

Following the visit by a delegation from the Northwest, Riel agreed to return to Canada. He arrived at Batoche in July, 1884, and soon a petition was dispatched to Ottawa. It outlined the grievances and made requests for such things as self-government, representation for the Northwest in the federal government, guarantees of land titles and a railway linking the region with Hudson Bay.

REBELLION

The federal government showed little sign of having learned from the troubles at Red River fifteen years before. In the face of Ottawa's inaction, the Métis decided to use force to gain their goals. Convinced that he was the "David" who would lead the Métis out of their troubles, Riel established a provisional government at Batoche in March, 1885.

The white settlers, wanting no part in a rebellion, withdrew their support. The clergy opposed Riel's behaviour as extremist and discredited his claim of being God's instrument chosen to lead the Métis nation. Undeterred, Riel prepared his followers for violence. Gabriel Dumont, a skilful buffalo hunter widely known on the prairies, was appointed military commander. The loyalty of the Métis was assured, and several Indian leaders were asked for aid.

In an atmosphere of rising tension, the Northwest Rebellion was ignited by a clash between a force of North West Mounted Police and a band of Métis led by Gabriel Dumont. On their way to retrieve supplies and ammunition stored at Duck Lake, the Mounted Police were intercepted and, after a brief but terrible fight, ten of

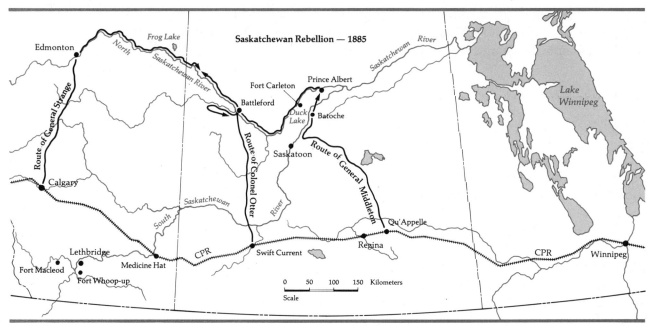

Saskatchewan Rebellion — 1885

them lay dead. The Métis then destroyed Fort Carlton, just after the white inhabitants had fled to Prince Albert.

The Métis success set in motion a number of Indian attacks and raised the fear of a general Indian uprising. The Crees of Chief Poundmaker laid siege to the town of Battleford, a major white settlement.* Within a few days, Big Bear's Indians sacked the hamlet of Frog Lake and killed several of its inhabitants, before burning down Fort Pitt.

The federal government quickly dispatched troups and volunteers to put down the rebellion. More than five thousand troops traveled west on the partially completed Canadian Pacific Railway. Within two weeks, troops from the Maritimes, Ontario, Quebec and Manitoba, as well as volunteers from western settlements, joined the Mounted Police to fight the rebels.

General Middleton, commander of militia in Canada, was in charge of operations. His strategy was to launch a three-pronged attack on the areas of disturbance in order to localize the Indian violence as well as suppress the Métis. Middleton led the main force from his base at Qu'Appelle and, after an initial setback and a stout defence directed by Dumont, he gained control of Batoche. Another column, under Colonel Otter, heading from Swift Current to Battleford, was fortunate to avoid being trapped by Poundmaker's Indian warriors. However, when Chief Poundmaker learned of the Métis defeat at Batoche and the capture of Riel, he surrendered to Middleton within a few days. Colonel Strange moved a third column from Calgary to the vicinity of Frog Lake, where the last Indian resistance was scattered.

*Battleford was the capital of the Northwest until 1883, when the government moved headquarters to Regina.

TOP: *A gun pit in the Saskatchewan Rebellion.* BOTTOM: *Asleep in the trenches, the Saskatchewan Rebellion.*

Outcomes

In the view of the Canadian government, the suppression of the Northwest Rebellion was a triumph for the National Policy. The rebellion had demonstrated, as no publicity campaign could have done, the value of the Canadian Pacific Railway to the Dominion. If the railway could transport thousands of troops in record time, then it could do the same with settlers and freight. Thus the loans which the railway company had been seeking were approved by Parliament, and the transcontinental was completed in November, 1885.

The policy of economic expansion favoured by political and business interests in central Canada could now go forward in the West. The railway was more than steel and ties; it was a pattern along which towns and businesses and industry could grow. Agricultural land, formerly within the domain of Indian bands, was now available in surveyed lots. It seemed to be just a matter of time before the farms of white settlers would dot the landscape.

For the Indians, the rebellion's failure meant the consolidation of the system of Indian reservations. Resistance to the power of the Dominion government, the advance of technology symbolized by the railway, and the influx of white settlers, had been futile.

The Métis—the "New Nation" as Riel described them—were scattered by the rebellion:

THE DEFEAT OF THE METIS NATION

Louis Riel staked the peace of the country and the fate of his people in a gamble that held no chance of success. The metis were not only defeated; as a distinct national and political group they were annihilated. With their homes burned and looted and their property destroyed, many of the metis had no option but to seek entrance into the Indian treaties by virtue of their Indian blood. Others migrated to the Peace River in order to escape the pressure of a merciless civilization. Those who did not join the rebels were granted the scrip and patents which they had demanded—a procedure which admitted the justice of the metis cause and the culpability of the Federal Government for the rebellion. But as had occurred in Manitoba, the metis disposed of their scrip to eager purchasers, often at ridiculous prices, content to live for the present at the sacrifice of the future; and unable to compete with the white men as farmers or artisans, they sank in the social scale, their life, society and national spirit crushed and destroyed.[18]

For Riel the rebellion was followed by a trial in Regina, where he was convicted of treason, in spite of his defence lawyers' efforts to have him found not guilty by reason of insanity. Execution was

Leading figures in the Saskatchewan Rebellion

Gabriel Dumont: "His ingenuity on the trail, his skills (he was the camp 'doctor,' an expert horsebreaker, and, unlike most Metis, a swimmer), but above all his generosity, made him the 'prince of the prairies.' He spoke several Indian tongues and French, but he could not read or write, could not speak English and understood it very little."[15]

When the Rebellion ended, Dumont escaped to the United States, where he performed as a sharpshooter with Annie Oakley in "Buffalo Bill" Cody's travelling Wild West Show. After the amnesty, he returned to Batoche, where he lived until his death in 1906.

Gabriel Dumont

Poundmaker: "The Great Chief himself is a very remarkable-looking man: tall, very handsome and intelligent-looking, and dignified to a degree. He wears a handsome war-cap made of the head of a cinnamon bear, with a long tuft of feathers floating from it, and a leather jacket studded with brass nails and worked with beads, long beaded leggings coming up to his hips, and brightly coloured moccasins, while over his shoulders hangs a very gaily coloured blanket. . . . [He was] elaborately painted."[16]

For his part in the rebellion, Poundmaker was sentenced to three years in penitentiary. Unable to endure confinement, he was released but died shortly thereafter.

Poundmaker

Big Bear: His fate was similar to that of Poundmaker—imprisonment, early release and death soon after. The most feared of the Indian leaders who joined in the Rebellion, he has been described as follows: "Like Crowfoot he recognized that the red man's day of untrammelled freedom was drawing to a close, but unlike Crowfoot, he was unwilling to accept the consequences of the inevitable change. He sought to postpone as long as possible the break with the past; and then to secure better terms for his people than the Government had been willing to grant to other Indian tribes. From the moment of his refusal to accept the Treaty, Big Bear and his small band were joined by the most independent Indians of the plains. His lodge became the rallying point for the 'die hards' of every band. . . . Big Bear was . . . one of the great Indians of Canadian history."[17]

Big Bear

delayed for several months as the case was appealed through the courts. Finally, against a background of public controversy, the Canadian government had to decide whether or not to intervene. The political pressure from Ontario, combined with the belief among cabinet members that Riel deserved the extreme punishment, led the government to choose not to interfere with the conviction. Riel was hanged in Regina on November 16, 1885.

RIEL'S "DEFENCE" AT HIS TRIAL

Riel's address to the court at his trial. His lawyers pleaded insanity but Riel contradicted their defence:

Your Honors, Gentlemen of the Jury: It would be easy for me today to play insanity.... Under the excitement which my trial causes me would justify me not to appear as usual, but with my mind out of its ordinary condition....

————————

....I know that through the grace of God I am the founder of Manitoba; I know that though I have no open road for my influence, I have big influence concentrated, as a big amount of vapour in an engine. I believe by what I suffered for 15 years, by what I have done for Manitoba and the people of the North-West that my words are worth something....

————————

I am glad that the Crown have proved that I am the leader of the Half-breeds in the North-West. I will perhaps be one day acknowledged as more than a leader of the Half-breeds, and if I am I will have an opporunity of being acknowledged as a leader of good in this great country....

....If it is any satisfaction to the doctor to know what kind of insanity I have, if they are going to call my pretensions insanity, I say, humbly, through the grace of God I believe I am the prophet of the New World....[19]

For French-English relations, the rebellion, and especially the emotions aroused by the trial of Riel, produced bitterness that lasted long after the details of events in the Northwest were forgotten.

ONTARIO'S ANTI-FRENCH FEELINGS

Ontario's anti-French feelings are bluntly expressed in an editorial of the Toronto EVENING NEWS of April 20, 1885, while rebellion was raging in Saskatchewan:

Ontario is proud of being loyal to England.

Quebec is proud of being loyal to sixteenth century France.

Ontario pays about three-fifths of Canada's taxes, fights all

Louis Riel on trial in Regina

the battles of provincial rights, sends nine-tenths of the soldiers to fight the rebels [Riel's], and gets sat upon by Quebec for her pains. . . .

Hundreds of thousands of dollars are spent in maintaining the French language in an English country. . . .

An anti-French party is springing up in all the Provinces except Quebec. . . .

If we in Canada are to be confronted with a solid French vote, we must have a solid English vote. . . .

If she is to be a traitor in our wars, a thief in our treasury, a conspirator in our Canadian household, she had better go out.

She is no use in Confederation. . . .

As far as we are concerned, and we are concerned, and we are as much concerned for the good of Canada as any one else, Quebec could go out of the Confederation to-morrow and we would not shed a tear except for joy.

If Ontario were a trifle more loyal to herself she would not stand Quebec's monkey business another minute.[20]

The uprisings in the West associated with Louis Riel were not isolated events in Canadian history. In fact, they contained many issues that would confront generation after generation: relations between French and English Canadians, the place of the native peoples in Canadian life, the impact of technology on the environment—not to mention the conflict between East and West.

In many respects, the Riel uprisings were early examples of "western alienation", the feeling that the interests of westerners are often different from those of Ontario and Quebec. Since Central Canada holds so much political power, westerners often feel that the

Canadian government neglects the West, and forces "Eastern" policies upon it.

A century later, these issues are still very much alive. What examples can you give from recent years that show this to be true?

Federal-provincial relations: a continuing problem

Sectionalism, or regionalism, a major problem of the Fathers of Confederation, remained a big issue in the decades following 1867. Joining the provinces in a political union did not automatically mean that their interests became the same. Thus, the central government in Ottawa was repeatedly challenged to show that the benefits of Confederation were greater than the drawbacks.

THE WEST

The Riel uprisings in 1869-70 and 1884-85, and British Columbia's unrest over the delays in completing the transcontinental railway showed the extent of western alienation from Confederation.

WESTERN ALIENATION CONTINUES

... for more than eighty-five ... years the people of the Prairies have been shouting their discontent....

Nothing has changed, however, in the reception those Prairie grievances receive when they fall on usually unresponsive Eastern ears.... stories of Prairie discontent have generally failed to stir political or fiscal response....

Now [in the 1970s] Prairie people are striving to be themselves, to be Canadians in their own way, and to build a Canada that they will help to design. They see an important future for Canada in the world of tomorrow, but they also see Ottawa playing a share-the-wealth game with Ontario and Quebec instead of aspiring to Canada's national and international potential. The future, they feel, is clouded by a tendency to regard the West as politically impotent, financially unimportant, and culturally bereft—but, luckily enough with natural resources enough to silence complaints....

How do you explain to uninterested Easterners that not every Western farmer has an oil well in his back yard, and that farmers are suffering from inflation and falling wheat sales to a point where their financial position is reminiscent of the 1930s? How do you explain that resource wealth is meaningless if your children must leave to get their share of it? How do you explain that French language rights just don't look all that important in a region where there are more Ukrainian—and more German-speaking people than French-speaking? How do you explain the feeling that you always have been, and probably always will be, left out of the decision-making process?[21]

THE MARITIMES

Nova Scotia, the most vocal of the Maritimes provinces in displaying the feeling of being "railroaded" into Confederation, was actually the first province to challenge the existence of the young Dominion of Canada. Led by the same Joseph Howe who had been prominent in politics for more than 30 years, Nova Scotia showed its feelings by electing 18 opposition members out of the 19 chosen to represent the province in Canada's first House of Commons. It gave Joseph Howe's Liberals 36 of the 38 members elected in the 1868 provincial election. And it passed a resolution in the provincial legislature calling for the repeal of the British North America Act.

Joseph Howe

Sir John A. Macdonald, Canada's first prime minister, countered the discontent in Nova Scotia by increasing the province's annual financial grant. Joseph Howe's agreement to join Macdonald's cabinet left the anti-Confederationists without a leader.

Maritimers remained disappointed with Confederation, however. The profitable days of the sailing ship were passing, and the effect was a decline in the ship-building industry and the carrying of goods to overseas markets. The construction of the Intercolonial Railway neither enabled Maritime producers to compete successfully in the markets of Ontario and Quebec, nor produced a sufficient flow of goods to Halifax and other ports to encourage the development of steamship companies. Failing to fulfill the early promises of promoting trade between the Atlantic provinces and the rest of Canada, Confederation was blamed for the depressed region's persistent economic problems. In 1886, the legislature in Nova Scotia went so far as to pass a resolution favouring secession from Canada. Although nothing came of this action, it did indicate the extent of discontent.

ONTARIO

The case of Nova Scotia was only the beginning. "Separatist" movements arose in region after region. As provincial leaders tested the authority of the central government, the final arbiter (referee) was the highest court in the British Empire, the Judicial Committee of the Privy Council. Generally its decisions favoured the provinces at the expense of the Dominion government, and thus provincial ambitions were encouraged.

Ontario's battle with the federal government was led by Oliver Mowat, the Liberal Premier of the province from 1872 to 1896. Once an articled student in Macdonald's law office in Kingston, Mowat, as the leader of Canada's strongest province, became a formidable opponent of the Prime Minister. To press his claims that Ontario must be a partner, not a satellite, of the government in Ottawa, Mowat carried many cases to the courts. A particular subject of contention was the Dominion's use of disallowances of provincial laws which the federal government thought were detrimental to the welfare of the country as a whole.

Ontario and Manitoba experienced a quarrel over their mutual border, where possession of a large tract of public land, with its timber and mineral rights, was at stake. The Dominion Government fixed a boundary between the two provinces in 1881. Ontario demanded a settlement more favourable to itself, and took its claim to court. The Privy Council ruled in favour of Ontario.

The decisions of the Privy Council seemed to confine the powers of the federal government to those enumerated in Section 91 of the British North America Act, and to limit the residual (general) power to matters of a strictly federal nature. Ontario's campaign on behalf of provincial rights, attacked by Sir John A. Macdonald as destructive of the Dominion's unity, was meeting with success. Other provinces, in the meantime, were finding it in their interest to follow Ontario's lead.

QUEBEC

In Quebec, Macdonald's government had lost a pillar of strength with the death of Sir George Etienne Cartier in 1873. Yet the Conservatives retained the very important loyalty of church leaders, largely because the only alternative was the *Parti Rouge*, an organization of liberals and radicals who often questioned the power of the church in public affairs. Another reason for Conservative strength in Quebec was the party's apparent support for French-Canadian minority rights in the rest of Canada, including Manitoba and the Northwest.

The hanging of Louis Riel, however, was bitterly condemned throughout Quebec as proof that the Conservatives were really the party of English Canada, and particularly of Ontario Protestant bigotry. To exploit this feeling, Honoré Mercier formed the *Parti National*, to which French-speaking Liberals and many Conservatives were drawn. He then led his party to victory in the provincial election of 1886. Once in office, he set out to win acceptance by the clergy and to establish his image as defender of the Catholic religion and French-Canadian rights.

1. How does the Quebec premier's view of his province compare with Mowat's view of Ontario?

THE FIRST CONFERENCE OF PROVINCIAL PREMIERS

As the federal government found itself embroiled in problem after problem with the provinces, Honoré Mercier invited the provincial premiers to meet at Quebec to discuss their grievances. Thus, in October, 1887, five premiers—those from Prince Edward Island and

A cartoonist's impression of Honoré Mercier's dream of Canada

British Columbia did not attend—met in the first inter-provincial conference. The conference echoed with expressions of sectional discontent. Such outstanding issues as federal disallowance, tariffs and freight rates were discussed. What emerged, however, was the fact that the provinces had few specific interests in common. Macdonald dismissed the affair as a Liberal party conspiracy, in spite of the presence of Manitoba's Conservative premier. Yet, in spite of Macdonald's denial, the problem of Canadian unity, after twenty years of Confederation, stood out more vividly than ever.

The Manitoba schools question

AN ISSUE WITH MANY SIDES

In the Canadian election of 1896, the Manitoba schools question became a political issue of nation-wide importance. How could this have happened? On the surface, it concerned only a small fraction of Canada's population far removed from the main centres of the country. Yet the schools question involved several issues affecting people in other provinces, since it raised conflict between Catholics and Protestants, French Canadians and English Canadians, and between advocates of uniformity and diversity. Just as important was the conflict between the wishes of the majority and the wishes of minorities.

BACKGROUND

In 1890 the Manitoba government passed legislation establishing a single public school system under the direction of a department of education. Separate schools, operated by churches of any denomination,* were no longer to receive financial support from the taxes collected by the government. In the same year, Manitoba abolished the official use of French in the Legislative Assembly, the civil service, government publications and the courts.

*Hence the term "denominational schools" was often used interchangeably with the term "separate schools".

The Roman Catholic minority, French-speaking and English-speaking alike, took up the challenge of the public schools act. When Manitoba had become a province of Canada in 1870, the tiny population was fairly evenly divided between Protestants and Catholics, each of whom operated their own schools. The Manitoba Act continued the dual system by allowing the educational rights existing "by law or practice at the union". The French and English languages were both legally recognized in the province. By and large, French-speaking inhabitants were Catholic and the English-speaking were Protestant.

In the intervening twenty years, an influx of English-speaking Protestants destroyed the racial and religious balance in the population. By the late 1880s the feeling was growing among the majority that separate, church-run schools should be replaced by a public school system. Many reasons were given. Public schools would encourage the democratic spirit and foster unity. French Catholic schools were a privilege, not a right, in a pioneer land. The sparsely settled province could not afford to support two school systems. Such was the view of the *Brandon Sun*, which published editorials in May, 1889 calling for the abolition of separate schools. Public meetings brought Protestant pressure to bear on the Manitoba government, and the following year the public schools act was passed.

A CALL FOR ABOLITION OF SEPARATE SCHOOLS IN MANITOBA
From the second of two editorials in the BRANDON SUN, *May, 1889:*

We are glad to know that The Sun's course in opening the attack on the separate school system of this province is meeting with almost universal approval. It is scarcely necessary to point out or even say that the system is a vicious one. The creation of classes by the state is a very grave error that can only result in harm. Particularly in a new country should there be no distinction. We cannot afford to divide our effort: we must husband our resources in every way. Until our population is materially increased, there must be great difficulty in many parts in maintaining our schools with any degree of efficiency. Until our revenues are very considerably increased our schools must suffer for lack of financial support, or an excessive burden of taxation must be imposed. But what seems to us as worse than these considerations is the fact that a separate school system creates and perpetrates class distinctions that should never be known in a well organized state. Why should Catholics be selected out of the body of citizens, and laws enacted that give them a very decided advantage over the other religious bodies. . . . [22]

1. What seem to be the main reasons given in the editorial for abolishing government support for "separate schools"?
2. The editor charges that "a separate school system creates and [perpetrates] class distinctions that should never be known in a well organized state". What does he mean?
3. What does the editor imply should be the purposes of schooling?
4. What do you think the purposes of schooling should be today? To promote Canadian unity? Encourage tolerance? Prepare students for life in society? Prepare students for jobs? Encourage good citizenship? Train students in the "three R's"? Teach critical thinking? Transmit Canadian cultural values?

THE CONSTITUTIONAL ISSUE

The Roman Catholic minority called upon the Dominion government to disallow the public schools act. The government wished to avoid the charge of interfering in provincial affairs, and was able to sidestep the issue as long as it was before the courts. The Catholics, meanwhile, had appealed the public schools act, claiming in the courts that it was contrary to provisions in the British North America Act (Section 93) and the Manitoba Act (Section 22) protecting the rights of separate schools. After several years of legal battles, the imperial court ruled that the Dominion government had reason to pass remedial legislation—in other words, to pass laws remedying the Catholic minority's loss of rights under Manitoba's public schools act. The time for sidestepping had passed.

THE POLITICAL ISSUE

The Conservative government, now under the leadership of Mackenzie Bowell, resolved to intervene in the question of Manitoba schools. The decision, announced in the Speech from the Throne in January, 1896, split the cabinet. French-Canadian members had been demanding a remedial bill. The English-Canadian ministers, however, refused to cooperate with Bowell. The veteran Conservative from Nova Scotia, Sir Charles Tupper, returned from his post as Canada's High Commissioner in London to become Prime Minister.

A remedial bill was introduced in Parliament, but its passage was stalled by prolonged debate. Before a final vote could be taken, the five-year term of Parliament had expired, and the Manitoba schools question became a major issue in the federal election of 1896.

In their campaign, the Conservatives defended their policy of federal intervention in the Manitoba schools question as necessary to the upholding of the constitution. The Liberals denounced remedial legislation as interfering with provincial rights. Their leader, Wilfrid Laurier, argued that the rights of the Roman Catholic minority could more likely be secured through discussion and federal-provincial cooperation than through federal coercion of the Manitoba government.

THE DEBATE OVER THE REMEDIAL BILL

The proposed remedial legislation under Section 93 of the British North America Act aroused heated debate. Several views are presented here.

Father A. Lacombe to Laurier, expresses the Church's position, January 20, 1896:

...It is in the name of our bishops, of the hierarchy and the Catholics of Canada, that we ask the party of which you are the very worthy chief, to assist us in settling this famous question, and to do so by voting with the government on the Remedial Bill....

If, which may God not grant, you do not believe it to be your duty to accede to our just demands, and if the government, which is anxious to give us the promised law, is beaten and overthrown while keeping firm to the end of the struggle, I inform you, with regret, that the episcopacy, like one man, united with the clergy, will rise to support those who may have fallen in defending us....[23]

Laurier's reply, March 3, 1896:

...So long as I have a seat in this House, so long as I occupy the position I do now, whenever it shall become my duty to take a stand on any question whatever, that stand I will take not upon grounds of Roman Catholicism, not upon grounds of Protestantism, but upon grounds which can appeal to the conscience of all men, irrespective of their particular faith, upon grounds which can be occupied by all men who love justice, freedom and toleration....[24]

Sir Charles Tupper states the government's position, March 3, 1896:

...It is not a question of separate schools, it is a question of the constitution of the country. The progress and the prosperity and the future development of Canada depends upon that constitution being sacredly maintained, and that all the rights that are guaranteed under it, whether to the central or the provincial government, shall be sacredly guarded....[25]

Fellow Liberal William Mulock to Laurier, April 3, 1895:

...Manitoba must be left alone....All these fine-spun arguments of legal rights seem to me quite beside the question of public policy....Suppose the Dominion Parliament were to pass a Remedial Act establishing separate schools in Manitoba and the people there were to withhold the necessary machinery for giving effect to such legislation what good would the Catholics of Manitoba take by such legislation? Why it would involve further legislation and agitation the end of which no one can foresee. If we now establish a precedent we shall encourage appeals to Ottawa from every province....[26]

Sir Wilfrid Laurier

The Conservative party, which had held power for eighteen years, went into the election badly divided. Their popularity had been hurt by the faltering economy and other problems besides the Manitoba schools question. The Liberal party was on the rise; under Laurier's leadership it had finally become a party with support in all parts of the country. Laurier's "charisma"* won him a wide personal following. In Quebec, which turned out to be the key to the election, French Canadians responded to the idea of having one of their own become the Prime Minister of Canada. The Roman Catholic bishops had condemned him for his stand on the Manitoba schools controversy. But Laurier's appeal combined with the effective work of Liberal organizers resulted in forty-nine Liberal seats from the province compared to sixteen for the Conservatives.

*See Chapter 10 regarding the "charisma"—or crowd appeal —of such modern prime ministers as Diefenbaker and Trudeau.

COMPROMISE: A SETTLEMENT OF SORTS

Once in power, the Laurier government wasted little time in tending to the case of Manitoba schools. Before the end of the year, discussions with Manitoba representatives, including Premier Greenway, had produced the "Laurier-Greenway compromise". Public financial support for separate schools was denied, but the right of Roman Catholics to religious instruction in school was recognized. Where the number of pupils in a public school was sufficiently large—forty in a town or ten in a rural school—the school could employ a properly qualified Catholic teacher. Religious instruction in public schools by a clergyman was permitted in the last half-hour of each school day. In any school where ten or more pupils spoke French, or any language other than English, instruction could be given in their original language when requested by parents.

These were token concessions, in the eyes of the minority, and the bishops in Quebec were particularly angry. Laurier then arranged for a representative of the Pope to visit Canada as a mediator. This was followed by a letter from the Pope urging the bishops to use more moderate tactics on behalf of Roman Catholic rights. Evidently the Laurier-Greenway compromise was thought to be the best deal possible, for the time being at least.

THE AFTERMATH

The Manitoba schools question was not an isolated issue that troubled one province long ago, gained national focus with the election of 1896, and then disappeared, never again to stir conflict among Canadians. Questions of separate schools, language rights and cultural survival have been raised at various times in one part of Canada or another.

In the twenty years after the Laurier-Greenway compromise, there were several more "school questions", even though circumstances did not make them quite so attention-getting. When Saskatchewan and Alberta became provinces in 1905, separate schools were permitted but only on a limited basis, and French language instruction did not gain acceptance. Ontario was another battleground; in 1913, the Department of Education issued "Regulation 17", stating that French was generally not to be the language of instruction beyond the first two years of school. Then, in Manitoba, in 1916, the earlier provision for teaching in languages other than English was repealed.

The high value placed by the English-speaking majority on "Canadianizing" the minorities, including French Canadians, was accentuated by the arrival of great numbers of immigrants. World War I further emphasized the role of the public schools as an instrument of national unity and uniformity.

In recent years the gradual acceptance of diversity as a characteristic of Canadian culture has been reflected in the policies of many provincial governments toward the public schools. However, as we have seen to be true in the case of Quebec as well, the objectives of the public school system still tend to be those of the majority. Decisions about public education are ultimately political, and the will of the majority generally prevails. So minorities continue to face a struggle to secure or maintain the kinds of schooling they prefer.

A modern schools question

In the Manitoba schools question, several emotional topics were combined, and the mixture of politics, schools, religion and language has remained a problem in Manitoba ever since. Of great national significance eighty years later is the similar dilemma in Quebec.

In 1975, *Bill 22* was passed by the Quebec legislature as the *Official Languages Act*. The Act makes French the official language in the provincial affairs of Quebec, including the schools. Although English-speaking residents of Quebec may still have their children educated in English, non-English immigrants are generally obliged to attend French language schools.

Seeing their position in the province weakened, the Quebec Association of Protestant School Boards petitioned the federal government to take one of two actions: (1) refer the Official Language Act to the Supreme Court, in the hope that the Act would be struck down as unconstitutional (and therefore illegal), or (2) disallow the Act as contrary to the public interest of Canada as a whole.

In a letter to the president of the Association of Protestant School Boards, Prime Minister Trudeau answered that the federal government did not feel that either action was justified. It was too soon to tell whether Quebec's Official Language Act would prove to be unconstitutional, since many parts were generally worded, and the proof would come when they were put into effect. As to disallowance, this had rarely been used in recent Canadian history and it ran the danger of interfering with provincial rights.

An excerpt from Mr. Trudeau's letter, dated July 17, 1975:
Although we are sympathetic to Quebec's desire to promote the use of French, we regret those provisions of the *Official Language Act* of Quebec which are not consistent with contemporary trends toward the expansion of linguistic rights in Canada and which restrict the freedom of parents to choose the language of education for their children. I would add that the Government would equally disagree with restrictions of a similar nature in other provinces. Nevertheless, although the scope and meaning of some sections of the *Official Language Act* of Quebec are unclear, it appears that the Act is generally within the legislative authority accorded by the B.N.A. *Act* to the Province of Quebec.

That is not to say that certain provisions, the interpretation of which is uncertain, might not be open to constitutional challenge if applied in certain ways, but this will only be known when it is seen how the Act is applied in specific situations.[27]

1. What parallels can you see between the schools question in Manitoba in the 1890s and in Quebec in the 1970s? What differences?

2. What effects on the relations between Quebec and the rest of Canada might result from the federal government's reaction to the language act in Quebec? What if the act had been disallowed?

The personal side of Sir John A. Macdonald

Sir John A. Macdonald

SIR JOHN A. MACDONALD'S SENSE OF HUMOUR

Part of Sir John A. Macdonald's charm, to political foes and friends alike, was his ability to look on the light side:

[At the negotiations (1871) leading to the Treaty of Washington during an official excursion on the Potomac to which he had come early and alone, the wife of an American senator fell into conversation with Sir John:]

'I guess you come from Canada?'

'Yes, Ma'am.'

'You've got a very smart man over there, the Honorable John A. Macdonald.'

'Yes, Ma'am, he is.'

'But they say he's a regular rascal.'

'Yes, ma'am, he's a perfect rascal.'

'But why do they keep such a man in power?'

'Well, you see, they cannot get along without him.'

'But how is that? They say he's a real skalawag, and . . .'

Just then her husband, the Senator, stepped up and said:

'My dear, let me introduce the Honorable John A. Macdonald.'

The lady's feelings can be imagined, but Sir John put her at her ease, saying: 'Now don't apologize! All you've said is perfectly true, and it is well known at home'[28]

ANECDOTES ABOUT JOHN A. MACDONALD

. . . .It is related that, many years ago, Sir John was present at a public dinner, at which he was expected to deliver a rather important speech. In the conviviality of the occasion he forgot about the more serious part of the duty of the evening, and when at a late hour he rose, his speech was by no means so luminous or effective as it might have been. The reporter, knowing that it would not do to print his notes as they stood, called on Sir John next day, and told him that he was not quite sure of having secured an accurate report. Sir John received him kindly, and invited him to read over his notes. He had not got far when he interrupted him: 'That is not what I said.' There was a pause, and Sir John continued, 'Let me repeat my remarks.' He then walked up and down the room, and delivered a most impressive speech in the hearing of the delighted reporter, who took down every word as it fell from his lips. Having profusely thanked Sir John for his courtesy, he was taking leave, when he was recalled to receive this admonition: 'Young man, allow me to give you this word of advice. Never again attempt to report a public speaker when you are drunk.'

When the city of Vancouver was in its infancy, or rather, before there was a city there at all, Lady Macdonald one day expressed the wish to purchase two lots on what is now the town site, and asked Sir John's permission to do so.

She said, 'I don't want any money; I have three or four hundred dollars of my own, and the Colonel (her brother) will give me three or four hundred more.'

'No, my dear,' he replied, 'you had better not!'

'Why?' said Lady Macdonald.

'Well, if you were to buy any lots out there, the first thing I should know would be that a post-office or a custom-house was put on them without my knowing anything about it, and I should have it thrown at me in Parliament that you had been paid for them ten cents more than they were worth.'

So the lots were never bought.

Sir John Macdonald always observed his birthday, and liked others to remember it. . . . Among many congratulatory letters he received [on his last birthday] was one from an unknown little maiden, who wrote him a childish note to announce that her birthday was on the same day as his [January 11th]. She added a hope that he would not follow the 'mean' example of a small boy of her acquaintance, who had not answered a letter she had written him. To this youthful epistle Sir John replied:—

'Earnscliffe, Ottawa, January 6, 1891.

'MY DEAR LITTLE FRIEND,

I am glad to get your letter, and to know that next Sunday you and I will be of the same age. I hope and believe, however, that you will see many more birthdays than I shall, and I trust that every birthday may find you strong in health, and prosperous, and happy.

I think it was mean of that young fellow not to answer your letter. You see, I have been longer in the world than he, and know more than he does of what is due to young ladies.

I send you a dollar note, with which pray buy some small keepsake to remember me by, and,

Believe me your sincerely,[29]
John A. Macdonald.'

3

The turn of the century: impressions of Canadian life

In many parts of the world, New Year's Eve is a time for celebration combined with resolutions and expressions of hope for a better year ahead. On New Year's Day, many people reflect on the problems of the past year and hope that somehow those were last year's problems. They remember the happy times and think about new starts in the next twelve months. Imagine January 1, 1900. Even if Canadians of that time were less inclined to excitement over the passing of a year, think of how dramatic the first day of a new century must have been. Consider also that the 1890s for the most part had not been the "Gay Nineties" but a decade of hard times for the majority of Canadians. But there were signs of change, and the new century could bring progress in many forms that would justify the shift from fear of the future to hope.

The prime minister, Sir Wilfrid Laurier, summed up the general mood of Canadians with his statement that the twentieth century would be "Canada's century".* Speaking in 1904, he could find many examples that supported his hopes for economic progress and national unity. The greatest immigration in the history of Canada was opening the West, and farming based on wheat, was booming. The Yukon gold rush had touched off a chain of mineral discoveries. Business corporations were forming to exploit the resources. Two new transcontinental railways were being built. The South African War,

*See Colombo's Canadian Quotations (pp. 331-332) for a discussion of the origins of the statement, other people who made similar assertions, and comments made over the years about it.

which had reopened divisions between French Canadians and English Canadians, was over. And the feeling was growing that Canada was moving toward greater control of its own affairs.

Prosperity, the promise of Confederation and the generally unfulfilled hope of the generation after, now seemed to be within reach. Improved world trading conditions and the expansion of the Canadian economy offered opportunities for "big business". Fortunes were made by entrepreneurs who were in a position to take advantage of them. Small businesses, too, could be started by a tradesman or farmer who moved to one of the expanding towns and cities. Then there was the West, where a man could get a homestead for almost nothing. If farming did not appeal, he could likely find a job, perhaps working on a railway gang or in a shop in one of the new, growing towns and cities.

In the "Macdonald era", the basic framework of the Canadian nation had been created and held together in spite of many challenges. The period from 1896 to 1911—between Sir John A. Macdonald's time and World War I—may be conveniently thought of, at least in political terms, as the "age of Laurier". Wilfrid Laurier served fifteen consecutive years as prime minister, following the election of the Liberals in 1896. In 1900, 1904, and 1908 he returned to office, only to be defeated in 1911. By that time both Canada and the world had changed immeasurably. Canada was more firmly established as a nation "from sea to sea", because of the economic development in which the opening of the West had played a large part. A French Canadian prime minister had led the country through controversies such as the Manitoba schools question and the South African War, where racial and religious differences had threatened to divide Canada. And the Canadian feelings of self-sufficiency and confidence had held firm against Britain's efforts to strengthen the Empire at the expense of colonial autonomy.

1899/WORLDLY PLEASURES

The most serious passage in the charge of the Bishop of Toronto to his synod was that which referred to the spirit of the age in which we live. We quote from the excellent report in the Globe: "This bishop gave it as his opinion that the prevailing and growing spirit of worldliness which seemed to threaten the life of religion today constituted the chief danger to the church's work. Many people were inclined to forget the principle of giving in their passion for spending." Of the seriousness of these statements there can be no question. We wish there could be some doubt of the truth of them. That, however, we dare hardly suggest....

When we speak of the spirit of worldliness as prevailing in this world, we must remember that this spirit may be found among clergy as well as laity—and that it mixes itself up with all the duties and avocations of both. How shall we discover it? One of the most obvious forms is that of Sloth—the neglect of manifest duties brought on by self-indulgence. It is the reverse of that spirit which teaches us:

"To scorn delights and live laborious days."

Then, closely related to this there is self-indulgence—in eating, drinking, smoking, or any other of those lawful sensuous pleasures which, indulged into excess, quench a man's spiritual vitality. It is the same with all kinds of physical, bodily exercise . . .

We fear that, when people speak of worldliness, they seldom go far beneath the surface; and beneath the surface we must go if we are really to grapple with this evil and, in any degree, overcome it. We must be careful how we abandon ourselves. Dancing may be worldly, or it may not. Card-playing is not the most sublime of occupations, and men of great seriousness and devotion will probably abstain from it. Yet, if we remember that recreation is an actual duty, and that many good people find a simple game of cards to be pleasant recreation, we shall hesitate to condemn them altogether. Perhaps one of the most striking forms of what is ordinarily called worldliness is excessive and extravagant dressing. We dare not say that it is wrong for the wealthy to spend more on their attire than the poor. But we do say most emphatically that no man has a moral right to spend much upon himself, who does not also give much to God and to humanity.

Our readers will, by this time, probably feel with us that the definition and description of worldliness are no easy matters. But this at least we can say, that the cure for worldliness in us all is the stirring up of a sense of our responsibilities to God and to man, the serious undertaking of the fulfilment of duties—with these questions in the front of the inquiry: How do we spend our time, our labor, our money? As in the presence of God or not?[3]

1. According to the article, what seemed to be the main signs of "the spirit of worldliness"?
2. Imagine yourself to be someone living in 1899 who reads the article. You hope to find some advice for better living. What suggestions could you find?

Suppose you were going to prepare a time capsule of sample items and pieces of information to be opened seventy-five years from now. Your objective is to illustrate to a later generation of Canadians what life in the Canada of the 1970s is like. Assuming there will be no problem preserving any of the items in the capsule, what would you include?

Which of the following would you consider to be typical of Canada as you know it?

Canada and the "Diamond Jubilee"

Queen Victoria's "Diamond Jubilee", marking her sixty years on the throne, was held in the summer of 1897. London was the gathering place for representatives from British possessions all round the world. Bemedalled dignitaries and brilliantly attired troops from exotic places like India, Hong Kong, and Jamaica, joined in a festive celebration of Empire and of imperial power. Along with the other colonial prime ministers, Laurier was a feted guest.

As prime minister of the leading colony, Laurier was accorded the special favour of a knighthood. He was treated to the splendour of London's aristocratic social life and flattered with personal attention and compliments. For his part, Laurier responded with glowing public speeches in which he paid tribute to the British Empire and counted the blessings for Canada of membership in it. The occasion called for rhetoric, and Laurier disappointed no one.

THE DIAMOND JUBILEE OVERWHELMS LAURIER

John W. Dafoe believed that Laurier was greatly affected by the adulation showered upon him in England:

To be translated from the humdrum life of Ottawa to a foremost place in the vast pageantry of the Diamond Jubilee, there to be showered with a wealth of tactful and complimentary personal attentions was rather too much for Laurier. The oratorical possibilities of the occasion took him into camp; and in a succession of speeches he gave it as his view that the most entrancing future for

Queen Victoria's Diamond Jubilee, London, 1897

93

Canada was one in which she should be represented in the imperial parliament sitting in Westminster. "It would be," he told the National Liberal Club, "the proudest moment of my life if I could see a Canadian of French descent affirming the principles of freedom in the parliament of Great Britain." This, of course, was nothing but the abandonment of the orator to the rhetorical possibilities of the situation. . . . [1]

To British leaders like Joseph Chamberlain, the Colonial Secretary, the Jubilee was much more than a celebration. A colonial conference was held at the same time. British leaders tried to persuade colonial prime ministers to back their expressions of imperial sentiment with concrete support. To requests that political ties within the Empire be strengthened and that colonies give money grants to build up the military, Laurier replied that Canadians could best contribute to the power of the Empire by developing their own country. While this was not the kind of answer the British were looking for, it represented the feeling of many Canadians, who were proud of the British connection but chose to show it in their own way.

A CANADIAN CELEBRATION

Professor Arthur Lower tells of a Canadian celebration of the "Diamond Jubilee":

In the year 1897 youthful minds were dazzled by a grand and spectacular event, the Diamond Jubilee of good Queen Victoria. In one not untypical little town, the approaching apocalypse filled the school days. In church, sermons were preached; even Methodist congregations went to the length of introducing into their services that bit of state church secularism *God Save the Queen.* The streets began to fill with arches, full of loyal mottoes. On the day itself, processions formed, bands played, and the spirits of all children rose. In one little boy's case, a relative arrived from 'the city' and presented to him a 'medal' (probably bought in Eaton's and of American manufacture) with the Queen's head on one side and the British flag on the other. A great float had been built out on the water in front of the town and at night the little row-boats which were so integral a part of that age drifted about it, illuminated with Chinese lanterns. At a given signal, the float burst into flames, which shot to heaven. A band struck up a patriotic air, and a display of fireworks rose from the nearby wharves. To small boys, Queen Victoria, *Rule, Britannia* and Heaven's command seemed all one.[2]

subway token   ballpoint pen   an Olympic coin   saran wrap
a curling rock   a pain killer pill   frozen food   barbecue tools
a beer can   an electric tooth brush   poem by Alden Nowlan
a lobster trap   a recording by Paulien Julien
pictures of the following:

> five o'clock in downtown Toronto
> Trudeau addressing an election rally
> a colour television set
> a professional athlete and his manager signing a contract
> finalists in a Miss Canada contest
> a student seated in a beanbag chair reading a Canadian novel
> a Grey Cup final
> a combine harvesting in a Saskatchewan wheatfield
> a skier going up the lift at Grouse Mountain
> a participant in a Ukrainian festival at Dauphin, Manitoba
> a Klondike girl at a festival in Edmonton, Alberta
> a reveler at a St. Jean Baptiste celebration

Have you thought of enough examples to wonder about the guidelines you are using in your selection? In choosing your items, how many would be associated with the following:

—life in the city/life in a rural area
—politics
—children/adolescents/young adults/middle age/senior citizens
—education
—pleasure-seeking/luxuries/entertainment/outdoor activity
—transportation
—occupations
—technological advances
—clothing/food/appliances
—class differences, in terms of material opportunities?

We often take "history" for granted, assuming that it is cut-and-dried. But there is more than one version of history, and histories vary from general accounts to histories of particular themes —military, economic, political, legal, scientific, social.

To do this exercise at the turn of the century would have been difficult enough for a person living at that time. For you, in the latter part of the 20th century, identifying things that were typical of 1900 is more difficult in some ways, easier in others. Your disadvantages include the lack of first-hand evidence; you cannot experience life in 1900, except indirectly. You might find it difficult to interview anyone who lived at the time, hear any actual voices, view motion pictures of people and events.

On the other hand, you can turn to many kinds of written evidence left by Canadians of that earlier time—speeches, private letters, autobiographies, newspapers, diaries and so on. Photographs, paintings and other visual records remain. Historians and other writers have studied such sources and prepared summaries and interpre-

The raw materials of Canadian history that are most readily available are the records of prominent people—political leaders, powerful businessmen, generals. More difficult to locate and interpret are the records of the "average Canadian". Yet an understanding of a time in history is incomplete without knowledge of everyday life, of events involving the mass of Canadians.

tations. These can give you a wider view of Canada in 1900 than was possible for Canadians who lived at that time.

The documents and pictures which follow are intended to give you impressions of Canada around 1900. What do they tell you about the following:

1. how life in the city differed from life in the country;
2. what difficulties people had in common;
3. Canadian customs;
4. clothing and styles;
5. how people used their leisure time?

As you look at the materials, see if you can identify what turn-of-the-century people might have included in their time capsules.

Life in the city

During the early 1900s Canadian cities generally were growing remarkably in population and in overall prosperity, as well as extending rapidly into the countryside. In line with the general belief of the time, that initiative and drive would make a person successful (rich), increasing numbers of Canadians were "getting ahead". In every city the visitor could note the new businesses, recently paved streets, the expanding railway yards, the jungle of telegraph and telephone wires, fine horse-drawn carriages and some of the first automobiles.

There was another side to the city, just as there is in the case of cities today. For every entrepreneur whose business profits were climbing, there were many employees whose incomes were not. Main streets were often paved; side streets were more likely to be dusty roads that turned to mud every time it rained. Railway yards may have thrilled the hearts of the industrialists who shipped products across the country but they depressed the average citizen who found the river or lake blocked from view.

As you read the passages that follow, try to see "life in the city of 75 years ago" through the eyes of different kinds of people. Do you think the turn of the century was "the good old days"? Why or why not?

TORONTO 1913—WHAT CAN ONE SAY?

Toronto (pronounce *T'ranto*, please) is difficult to describe. . . .

A brisk city of getting on for half a million inhabitants, the largest British city in Canada (in spite of the cheery Italian faces that pop up at you of excavations in the street), liberally endowed with millionaires, not lacking its due share of destitution, misery and slums. It is no mushroom city of the West, it has its history;

Problems of writing history: social history in Canada

"Canadian social history is still in its infancy...."

What is this *social history*, which, though it is still one of the younger branches of Canadian history, has commanded so much attention in the last decade?

"In a nation that has slowly divested itself of the mantle of the motherland, naturally there has been a concentration of interest on constitutional and political issues." (See Volume 1, p. 334)

> "Social history is about people.... It is concerned not only to encompass as much of the sweep of Canadian history as possible ... it is interested in the social history of our native peoples, in immigration and acculturation, in the development of social institutions such as the family, classes, and voluntary organizations, in ideas and attitudes in their social context, in the social dimension of occupations and industries, in community formation and urban growth, in social movements such as the temperance crusade, the movement for prison reform, and that for the liberation of women, in sports and leisure activities."[4]

These words, taken from the general introduction to a series of books on Canadian social history, illustrate the rich variety of topics for historical investigation. But they don't indicate the great difficulties that exist in trying to describe "what life was like", or to analyze the behaviour of groups, organizations and institutions. Professional investigators, whether they be historians, sociologists, journalists or others trying to explain Canadian society, have been faced with serious problems of sources, methods and time.

Very little in the way of organized social history has yet been written. Besides recognizing the difficulties involved in researching social history, historians have been influenced, until recently, by the need to explain Canada's ongoing process of political growth. Themes such as responsible government, Confederation and the growth of autonomy (the gradual achievement of independence from Britain) have preoccupied historians until recent years, and much that has been written has dealt with the decisions and actions of a small number of influential people.

Is history just "his-story" alone? Not so, said a group of five Saskatoon women. In May of 1973, they organized and produced HERSTORY 1974, A Canadian Women's Calendar. Each day in the appointment calendar "records a significant event in the herstory of women in Canada.... the struggle and achievements of women in politics, women in sport, women in the arts, in education and in medicine.... the story of ordinary women, whose lives and work have been ignored in the history of Canada." A similar calendar was produced in subsequent years.

In this chapter, you will find glimpses of social history, selected "bits and pieces" about Canadians—how they lived, worked and played some 75 years ago. You are encouraged to think about those aspects of history that generally have been unavailable in textbooks. In so doing, you can gain insights into the society in which you live today.

1. What sources might students of the future have available for writing a social history of the 1970s?

TOP: *Toronto, 1898.* BOTTOM: *Vancouver, 1904*

but at the same time it has grown immensely of recent years. It is situated on the shores of a lovely lake; but you never see that because the railways have occupied the entire lakefront. So if, at evening, you try to find your way to the edge of the water, you are checked by a region of smoke, sheds, trucks, wharves, storehouses, "depots," railway lines, signals and locomotives, and trains that wander on the tracks up and down and across streets, pushing their way through pedestrians and tolling as they go in the American fashion an immense melancholy bell intent, apparently, on some private and incommunicable grief. . . .

—*what* must one say about Toronto? What can one? What has anybody ever said? It is impossible to give it anything but commendation. . . . The only depressing thing is that it will always be what it is, only larger, and that no Canadian city can ever be anything better or different. If they are good they may become Toronto.[6]

LIVING IN MONTREAL 1897—1929

The typical Montreal family of 1897 was made up of a husband, wife and three children who lived in a five-room, cold water flat located on a narrow, densely populated side street in what is now the inner core of the city. The husband, who hoped to be able to work sixty hours a week, fifty-two weeks a year, was more likely to find himself faced with "short time" if not a layoff, especially during the winter months. Even if regular work was available, the average wage earner could not provide his family with more than a bare subsistence.

———————

. . . the vast majority of families in Montreal in [the years 1897-1929] was unable to reach the minimum income level unless there was relatively full employment and at least two wage earners per family unit. For the two-thirds of the adult male labour force employed as hourly wage earners there was little chance of earning sufficient income, even at maturity, to provide an average family with the minimum standard of living. Certainly if the modern Statistics Canada definition of poverty—"any family or individual spending more than seventy per cent of total income on food, clothing and shelter"—is used, then poverty was the common experience of the majority of the population of Montreal.[7]

THE TWO FACES OF WINNIPEG, 1894

[In August, 1894] Winnipeg was a city of contrasts. A magnificent site for a great city at the confluence of two historic rivers, the Red and the Assiniboine, but apart from the shops and stores of Portage Avenue and Main Street a city of shacks and mud roads. It was the distributing center for the business of the whole West, but the self-confidence of its old-time merchants had been so badly shattered by the experience of the Big Boom that anything like daring

[In 1901] there were in Canada nearly 17,000 persons of "Unsound Mind", over 6,000 deaf and dumb (of whom 2,002 were in Ontario and 2,488 in Quebec), 3,279 blind (Ontario 1,063, Quebec, 1,035) and that of the total of 81,201 reported deaths, 21,328 were of infants under one year of age, about one in four. The principal causes of death were not as accurately defined then as now, but the merest glance at the tables shows the much greater prominence of infectious and contagious diseases (nearly 9,000 of the total from tuberculosis, for example).[5]

enterprise was throttled. However, at the time of my coming the city was on the eve of a new development.[8]

POPULATION OF CANADIAN CITIES, 1891-1921[9]

	1891	1901	1911	1921
Montreal	219 616	328 172	490 504	618 566
Toronto	181 215	209 892	381 833	521 893
Vancouver	13 709	29 432	120 847	163 220
Winnipeg	25 639	42 340	136 035	179 087
Hamilton	48 959	52 634	81 869	114 151
Quebec	63 090	68 840	78 710	95 193
Ottawa	44 154	59 928	87 062	107 843
Calgary	3 876	4 392	43 704	63 305
Edmonton	—	4 176	31 064	58 821
Halifax	38 437	40 832	46 619	58 372
Regina	—	2 249	30 213	34 432
Saskatoon	—	113	12 004	25 739
Saint John	39 179	40 711	42 511	47 166

VANCOUVER AND THE C.P.R. AFTER 1886

The City of Vancouver was incorporated April 6th, 1886. . . .

Naturally, during its first two decades, the Canadian Pacific Railway Company mothered and moulded the new city, which thus had all the inaugural advantages and disadvantages of a place under control of one powerful private company. Among the immediate advantages, apart from those involved in the fact of being made a transcontinental railway terminus, was the establishment of a magnificent fleet of freight and passenger ships to the Orient, Australia and New Zealand; and the erection of a first-class hotel and opera-house, both under the efficent management of the company. The disadvantages need not now be detailed. They were removed when, after much official obstruction, entry was provided in 1906 for the Great Northern and Northern Pacific Railways; and later by the entry of the Canadian National Railways, with new terminals, new steamships, and the promise of a metropolitan hotel on a par with any on the continent.[10]

WAGES AND PRICES

In an introduction to a volume of pictures from Eaton's catalogues, Judith McErvel gives some indication of wages and prices at the turn of the century:

In 1895 a man or woman who could type and take shorthand could command $5 to $8 a week. An experienced coachman might earn $20 per month, possibly with quarters provided, a general servant in the house half that amount. A youth of 17 could make $2 a week packing goods and running errands.

A six-room house could still be rented in Toronto for as little as $6 a month, but a 12-room house, furnished, could run as high as

$35. A butcher shop, with fittings, could be rented for $17 a month. A solid brick house, modern and "in A1 order" in Toronto cost $3,600; a seven-room house in what was then the suburbs sold for $1,600 with a sizeable lot.

In August the Auditorium Meat Market in Toronto advertised a special: round steak, sirloin, and lamb chops, all 10 cents a pound. Rib roasts were 8 cents a pound. Housewives could buy seven pounds of sugar for 25 cents, a loaf of bread for 3 cents, a pound of butter for 10 cents.

In 1905 wages were rising and hours of work were dropping. A very few trades were gaining the eight-hour day. Perhaps the greatest advance was made by workers in seven British Columbia smelters, who had their working hours reduced from 84 to 54 per week. In this year stone masons earned 45 cents an hour. Snow shovellers in Prince Edward Island, after a brief strike, won a raise from $1 to $1.25 per day. Farm hands received $100 to $250 per year according to experience. The chief of police in Saint John, New Brunswick, had his annual salary increased from $1 200 to $1 500. In Toronto, a young lady might earn $3 a week for "light office work", a "smart boy" $2.50 a week for work in a factory. Stenographers started at $8 a week. In Hamilton, workers in a canning factory made $2 or more a day peeling tomatoes. A Toronto artist, in need of a model for a mythological character, offered $12 a week for the right young woman.

Room and board—with the use of a piano—was advertised in Toronto for $3.50 a week. For the enterprising, there were articles on how to build a city cottage for only $750.

Sirloin steak sold for 12½ cents a pound, rib roast for 10 cents, tea for 25 to 60 cents a pound depending on quality and kind. Bread was up to 4 cents a loaf. A "good cigar" cost 5 cents. A man could get a haircut for 20 cents, a shave for 10 cents, and his shoes shined for another nickel.[11]

WHAT THEY WORE: MEN'S AND WOMEN'S CLOTHING

In the business world of the 1890's, women were occupying a greater place as stenographers and sales girls. They wanted smart but practical clothes for daytime wear: the career girl sought to create an impression of trim efficiency. Because she was invading a man's world she adopted mannish styles—the suit with matching jacket and skirt, worn with a neat blouse or shirtwaist with stiff collar and tie. Eaton's advertised this style under the heading of "costumes," which was the older English term, but it was commonly called by the newer American name of "suit." By 1894 the catalogue showed "Ladies' Eton Suits" with waist-length jackets and "Ladies' Blazer Suits" with hip-length jackets.

In the 1890's the suit was accepted outdoor daytime wear even for ladies of leisure. Indoors, the blouse and skirt reigned supreme both at home and at the office. Skirts were already on the ready-

Ladies' Dress Skirts.

Navy, black and brown serge, lined throughout, Empire style as cut, $3.00.
Same style in black cashmere, lined throughout, $3.50.
Same style in tweed, in brown, gray and fawn mixture, $3.50, 4.50.
Same style as cut in navy, black and brown serge, trimmed with three rows black military braid, $3.75.
Same style as cut in navy, black and brown serge, trimmed with two rows each, black military and tracing braid, $4.00.
Fine black henrietta cashmere skirts as cut, lined throughout, $5.00, 6.00.

Ladies' fine navy and black serge skirts, braid trimmed, as cut, $5.00.

When ordering costumes give bust and waist measure, also length of front of skirt.

From every part of this vast Dominion there keeps a-coming by mail orders for this thing and that. We supply thousands of families in just such a way. Why not you?

Ladies' Eton Suits.

Black and navy serge, similar style to cut, $5.50, 6.50, 7.50 and 8.50.
Also a similar style in brown, navy and black, $11.00.
White duck costumes, similar styles, $7.00, 8.00, 9.00, 10.00.

Ladies' Blazer Suits.

In black and navy serge, $7.00, 8.50, 10.00.
Linen costumes, similar style, $8.00, 10.00, 12.00, 14.00.

1614. Striped cotton, washing material, colors navy and white, black and white, and cadet and white, $4.50.

Ladies' Bathing Suits.

This style in all-wool, navy blue estamine serge, trimmed with white braid, $3.00.
Same style in misses' size, $2.50.

to-wear list by this time. Blouses appeared in the catalogues for the first time in the fall winter season of 1890-1. There was quite a selection, though some of the cuts and colours are no longer remembered by the fashionable names then given them. "Cream flannel, tennis blouse...All-wool challi...China sun waists, in cream, black, cardinal, navy, reseda, flame, crushed strawberry, Eiffel, with belt...Ladies' white lawn waists," the entries read: reseda was a pale green named after a plant, the Eiffel Tower had been built only a year before in Paris and was as up-to-date a style name as Bikini would be in the 1950's. Styles, colours and fabrics increased in number as the decade advanced. By 1899 four pages of the catalogue were devoted to shirtwaists, twelve on a page.[12]

Rural life

Canadians living in rural areas were no different than their city cousins in looking forward to a more prosperous existence. Loneliness and feelings of isolation could be a problem, and rural people lacked some of the goods and services available in the city. But new technology was taking some of the hardship out of work and making daily living more convenient and easy.

The Eaton's catalogue brought city-dress to the country, and for the first time, it became economical to buy some "store-bought" items for the whole family.

ELEVATOR, SASK.

There were no other significant variations between this town and the other; brown wooded false fronts on the stores, canned soups, boys' sweaters, calico dresses, Lowney's Nut-Milk Bars, and Fels Naphtha Soap lurking beneath the green partly-drawn blinds; the yellow steeple of the [church] poking skyward at the top of the street; further on, the high board fence guarding the fair grounds and after that the prairie, clean shining snow and winter-blackened poplar bluffs. It was the small town of Saskatchewan, a town much idealized by those who have never lived there, much moved-away-from by those who have, and much mourned by people of both kinds.[13]

DAILY LIFE IN RURAL MANITOBA

The immigration policy of Sir Clifford Sifton and the new technology of the turn of the century brought changes to the Canadian prairies:

It was also the time which marked the first encroachment of the mechanical and scientific age, with all its impatience and future promise, the impact of which definitely began to change the entire economic and social structure of life on the western plains.

Prairie town at the turn of the century

A few of the more quickly-adopted items which reduced physical stress and provided new services may be noted here. One of these was two- or three-furrow gang plows with spring seats on which the rider could sit all day, guide his team of horses and control the operation of the machine by adjusting levers within easy reach. This early attempt at automation did away with most of the fatigue previously brought on by walking behind a single furrow plow, steered by the operator as he grasped two long handles, the while endeavoring to keep his motive power—two horses—pulling the plow ahead in the straightest line possible.

The lady of the house was not forgotten by inventors. Old rub-a-dub-dub washboards, on which the family wash was laboriously scrubbed clean, were replaced by wooden slatted contraptions doing the rubbing through rotating motion of the simple mechanism propelled by human arms, all a great time- and muscle-saver.

Bicycles were becoming common, mostly with young folk. For the reason that no lady would think of wearing slacks (that name was unknown then) a specially designed frame enabled women to ride these bicycles with every-day, full-length skirts.

Binding grain

The first telephones were being installed in towns and villages where demand warranted.

Concrete paving was beginning to replace plank sidewalks, though streets were still to remain unpaved for years.

In Souris [Manitoba], an acetylene gas plant was constructed to provide street, business and household lighting. The coal oil lamp was being replaced. The use of electrical current was still in its infancy, and confined to large cities.[14]

LIFE IN THE NEWLY OPENED PEACE RIVER COUNTRY

There was no lack of friendliness and hospitality when neighbours were in contact with each other, but distances and lack of roads and means of conveyance contributed to isolation and loneliness. The social meeting-places at stores, schools, churches, and homes were spasmodic and infrequent. Yet there were colourful events which broke up the monotony of an isolated existence. In such matters the few women of the area were a God-send. One of these pioneer women writes: 'In 1907 I gave a Christmas dinner to all the white residents of Grande Prairie. I had only eleven guests and I was the only woman present. I made it a Grande Prairie dinner, that is, everything we ate was home-grown as far as possible.[15]

If the Western man is not too busy planting orchards, buying grain, or tunnelling mountains, he may find time to tell you, with the steady, calm egotism indicative of a strong character, how he is a real-estate agent, assessor, pound-keeper, auctioneer, horse-dealer, insurance broker, and undertaker, and that he gets on fairly well in the whole successive list.

Presently, he will be mayor of the town, then Member of Parliament, and, before he knows what has happened, he has prospects for a Senatorship, which means that he does go "back East" permanently, with the Simcoe, Huron, or Bruce thistlegrown plot well in sight.[16]

HOUSES IN THE VILLAGES

The houses in our village are built without the slightest reference to taste. They are stiff and ugly enough to serve as object-lessons for the crude. They are great wooden sarcophagi built solely to furnish shelter.

Our own house is undergoing renovation. It is a hideous, cardboard box that looks like a toy in which, if you lifted the roof, you would find jellies, fruits, or chocolates. I must not forget to mention that it is decorated on the gable with a blue and crimson sunset.

When we came to move in, we found there were no laths or plaster on the walls, because, forsooth, there are no plasterers here. The paper is put on over stretched cheese-cloth, and every time you lean against it, you go through and see daylight in the chinks of the outer shell.

The men are at work doing better things for us. We shall have three bedrooms, a dressing-room, parlour, study, dining-room, kitchen, and servant's room. We have no furnace, bathroom, cellar, or woodshed. Perhaps we shall have these later, for the rule here seems to be to build from the top. The stone foundation is usually built after the house has been standing a year; later a cellar is dug out, and finally, as the family increases in wealth, or as they get leisure, a drain is added.[17]

Recreation

Recreation, too, was becoming more and more popular. As people had more time to relax, leisure became a more important part of their lives. Organized sports were a popular part of community life, and team sports were gaining many new participants.

There were certain characteristics of drama during this period:

The golden era of the legitimate theatrical stage on the western prairies began in the early 1890's when a few companies came in from the United States to appear in public halls in Winnipeg.

———————————

These companies presented every type of stage entertainment.

It was a time when melodrama would rouse audiences to cheer the rescue of the young maiden from the clutches of the leering, black-moustached villain.

[Dramas such as "Uncle Tom's Cabin" were seen over and over again.]

There were comedies with clean humor that old and young might enjoy; black-faced minstrels with their interlocutor and end-men, bones and tambourines, sparkling with snappy wit, glorious male voices and specialty acts; magicians, hypnotists, elocutionists and medicine shows.

The technique of stage performance was less artificial in those days. Performers did not need to adopt mannerisms to win applause, but if they lacked genuine talent they were more likely to be booed.[18]

And certain characters:

Without a doubt, William B. Sherman was the most bizarre individual ever engaged in the theatrical business in the Canadian west. He first came to Canada from the United States on a vaudeville circuit with his own animal act, which consisted of one educated goat! Sherman was not, by any means a headliner with this act. He gained recognition in Canada in an entirely different phase of the business. He parted with the goat and turned to operating theatres and producing his own shows, both drama and musical.

His first venture was management of the Grant Theatre in Calgary, built by a local group of investors.

Bill was an uncouth man with only a meagre education. He was heavily built with a substantial girth. Though attired in the best styled clothing, it always seemed to clash with his personality. His voice was rough and coarse, yet such irritation was forgotten through the cleverness he displayed in business negotiations.[19]

THE SPORTING LIFE

Bowling

It is believed that Tommy Ryan of Toronto invented five-pin bowling in 1905 or 1906.

Tommy's clientele included some very prominent citizens who spent their noon hours bowling the big ball at tenpins. But it was a rather strenuous exercise for sedentary business men, so Tommy experimented with a variety of pin games, including duck and

Bowling

candles. Finally he derived one of his own, with a new scoring value and using only five pins of a small size and a ball that could be grasped more easily. The new game became popular over-night, but it had two big objections. One was that it was too noisy, and the other that the pins occasionally bounced through windows and out to the street below. To save potential customers from injury, Tommy devised a pin with a heavy band of rubber around its middle. In the process, he had invented the universally approved game of fivepins.[20]

Curling

Curling was one of the most popular sports in Canada by the year 1900. Men, women, boys, and girls in countless towns and cities enjoyed the game. Bonspiels were frequently held with enthusiastic competition for trophies and medals. Some devoted curlers felt that the competitive spirit, which had taken a strong hold in curling circles of that period, had a detrimental influence on the game. For instance, the executive committee of the Ontario Curling Association " . . . expressed strongly the view that the practice of playing for trophies and prizes had been now carried to dangerous lengths and was transforming the game of curling from a friendly rivalry, which produced recreation and amusement and promoted friendships and good fellowship, into fierce struggles for victory. Indeed it went so far as to brand the prevalent craze for winning trophies 'as a degrading prostitution of the grand old game and not to be distinguished from professionalism.' "[21]

Skiing

Skiing is today undoubtedly one of the most popular winter activities in Canada. Interest arose in skiing as a recreational pastime at

108

A curling party

the end of the nineteenth century and was further fanned by Scandinavian immigrants during the first years of the twentieth century. These immigrants brought with them their light, narrow skis and soon Hagen skis and bindings from Norway could be obtained in the Montreal area.

February 11th, 1904, marked the formation of the Montreal Ski Club.[22]

Skating

Skating, a sport enjoyed by young and old alike, continued to be popular in the 1900s. Speed skating, in particular, flourished during the period prior to the First World War. Each club conducted its own speed-skating races, cities sponsored events, and some provinces arranged provincial championships.

Canada and the United States met annually to conduct the amateur skating championship of America and these meets were always packed by enthusiastic spectators.

During the early years of the century, professional speed skating attracted top skaters to its ranks. Many skaters, like T. K. McCulloch of Winnipeg, turned professional after winning the Canadian Amateur Championship. There was notable harmony among amateurs and professionals, for they conducted meets and championships together.

The number of tournaments and championship events in skating was so extensive and the number of participants so great that the need was evident to create a governing body for both Canada and the United States. As a result, the International Figure Skating Union of America was established in 1907.[23]

Skating at McGill University

HOW TIMES HAVE CHANGED?

Hockey on ice is played by seven men on each side, all of whom are, necessarily, good skaters. It combines, in a remarkable degree, continuity of movement, individuality of play, and open team work. It has a speed which no other game can approach, and the matches, which are played in covered rinks, usually attract thousands of spectators. These matches and the rules governing them are controlled by a national association, consisting of the representatives from the different clubs interested. The expertness of Canadian skaters makes a well-contested match an extremely graceful and interesting sight.[24]

Now you have some insight into conditions in Canada at about the time your great-grandfather lived. Had you lived at the turn of the century, and been asked to select typical items for a time capsule, what would you have included? What things would best tell a future generation about the actual history of the time?

Development of a Canadian literature: post-Confederation to the "Great War"

BACKGROUND

A generation after Confederation, Canada could boast a literature of considerable volume and variety. We now had authors who were writing and publishing not only descriptions and travel books about the new land, but novels, poetry, magazines, newspapers and encyclopedias. Poets who imitated the style of famous British poets like Tennyson and Browning were writing about their own land and the delights of life in Canada. Novelists, too, wrote vivid descriptions of their homeland—the mountains, valleys, rivers, the prairies, the sea. They told of the fishermen, the farmers, the lumbermen and the small-town people. But added to these descriptions and portraits in the novels of the nineteenth century were now ideas of romance, escape from the toils of everyday life, and happiness for all at the end. Although the times were not easy ones, people wanted to read about the heroism, courage, love, happiness and optimism which the novelists gave them in abundance. Daily living might be difficult, but there was hope that hard work and perseverance would make everyone happy in the end.

Humour, too, was blossoming in the new Canadian nation. The first and foremost humorist of the day was Stephen Leacock. Born in Orillia, Ontario in 1869, Leacock wrote clever, funny stories and novels about the "human side" of all of us. His memorable *Sunshine Sketches of a Small Town* and stories like "My Financial Career", "A, B and C", and "The Yahi-Bahi Oriental Society of Mrs. Rasselyer-Brown", have delighted readers in Canada and abroad for more than half a century.

Literary Time Line

1868	Charles Mair, *Dreamland and Other Poems*
1872-78	*Canadian Monthly and National Review* published
1874	Joseph Howe, *Poems and Essays*
1877	William Kirby, *The Golden Dog*
1880	Charles G. D. Roberts, *Orion*
1887-98	William Kingsford, *History of Canada*
1888	Archibald Lampman, *Among the Millet*
1890	Sara Jeannette Duncan, *A Social Departure*
1893	Bliss Carman, *Low Tide on Grand Pré*
	Archibald Lampman, *Lyrics from the Earth*
1897	W. H. Drummond, *The Habitant*
1897-1900	J. C. Hopkins (ed.) *Canada: An Encyclopedia*

1898	Ralph Connor, *Black Rock*
1899	Ralph Connor, *The Sky Pilot*
1900	Archibald Lampman, *Collected Poems*
1901	Ralph Connor, *The Man from Glengarry*
1905	W. H. Drummond, *The Voyageur*
1907	Robert Service, *Songs of a Sourdough*
1908	Lucy Maude Montgomery, *Anne of Green Gables*
	Nellie McClung, *Sowing Seeds in Danny*
1911	Stephen Leacock, *Nonsense Novels*
	Pauline Johnson, *Legends of Vancouver*
1912	Stephen Leacock, *Sunshine Sketches of a Little Town*
1919	John McCrae, "In Flanders Fields"
	Canadian Bookman established

Highlights

THE "CONFEDERATION POETS"

Charles G. D. Roberts, Bliss Carman, Archibald Lampman and Duncan Campbell Scott were all born in the 1860s; these men became known as the "Confederation Poets". Anxious to "write Canadian", they encouraged one another in the development of a distinctly Canadian literature. Much of their work dwelt on the usual descriptions of the land, nature, life, death and personal relationships.

In 1880, at the age of 20, Charles G. D. Roberts published *Orion and Other Poems*. Archibald Lampman, a friend and contemporary of Roberts, wrote of his tremendous excitement at the thought that the book was Canadian poetry:

> "I sat up all night reading and re-reading Orion in a state of the wildest excitement and when I went to bed I could not sleep. It seemed to me a wonderful thing that such work could be done by a Canadian, by a young man, one of ourselves."[25]

Archibald Lampman and Duncan Campbell Scott both made nature their primary subject and Scott also featured Indians in remote outposts in his poetry.

Bliss Carman, a cousin of Charles G. D. Roberts, is probably most remembered for his poem "Low Tide on Grand Pré", written about the beauty of Nova Scotia.

Grouped together, the "Confederation Poets" make a well-defined mark upon the time line of Canadian literature.

THE "CANADA FIRST" MOVEMENT AND CHARLES MAIR

Although Charles Mair published his first poetry before the "Confederation Poets", it is not necessarily his poetry for which he is remembered. An ardent nationalist, Mair, along with several other men, formed the "Canada First" movement in 1868. Basically a political and intellectual movement to maintain a Canadian identity, the "Canada First" movement was reflected in Mair's poetry. He felt that the incorporation of Canadian history was necessary to the development of a *Canadian* literature. His poetry is not remembered for its art but rather as a first attempt at establishing a unique literature for the nation.

The following brief excerpt is taken from his longer ode, "In Memory of Thomas D'Arcy McGee". McGee, also an avowed nationalist, had been assassinated a month before Mair arrived in Ottawa for a meeting with others of the "Canada First" movement:

" . . . And in his visions true
There came high forms anew—
  Dim outlines of a nation yet to stand,
Knit to the Empire's fate,
In power and virtue great,
  The lords and reapers of a virgin land—
A mighty realm where Liberty
Shall roof the northern climes from sea to sea.
And when 'gainst the emprise
Arose those enemies
  Whose house is hell with chambers full of death,
Who knit their hands and weep,
And curse us in their sleep,
  And drink the wine of madness with their breath,
He wrung the secret from their minds,
And cast their schemes unto the shuddering winds.

———————

For this they slew him! Now
We lift his abusèd brow
  And in our anguish vainly cry to Thee
Who art our God! How long
Shall hellish crime be strong
  And slavish spirits tamper with the free?
  . . . "26

SARA JEANNETTE DUNCAN

Born in Ontario in 1862, Sara Jeannette Duncan wrote nineteen novels, all of which gained international popularity at the turn of the century. Her novels, including *The Imperialist*, were comedies of manners and social relationships.

Sara Jeannette Duncan's own life was very unusual. She was educated to become a teacher, taught for a short time and then became a journalist, writing internationally under the pen name of Garth Grafton. She travelled around the world in 1889 and used this experience for her first novel, *A Social Departure: How Orthodocia and I Went Round the World By Ourselves*.

The female narrator of the story and Orthodocia, her British friend, are preparing to sail around the world. Since they were only young girls, this trip would not win the approval of many of their relatives, since they would be travelling unchaperoned. In this scene, the precocious Orthodocia is not properly hiding her personal garments and thus she receives this scolding:

When I came back to Orthodocia, . . .

I found her kneeling in a secluded corner before her open boxes, surrounded by a sea of fine linen, and wearing a small triumphant expression about the corners of her mouth. A man in brass buttons hovered as near as he dared, looking troubled and unhappy. "I suppose", she said, as I approached, "you thought I didn't know about Customs surveillance in America. Well, you see I did. I have shown this person the inside of my handkerchief-boxes, and taken out all these white skirts and dressing jackets, and collars and cuffs, and things, but he doesn't seem to want to look at them. He said a few minutes ago that I might 'leave it to him!' and I told him that I would do nothing of the kind. As if one would let a *man* go through all this!" And Orthodocia waved her arm to include a quantity of the nearest embroideries. As the same moment she shook out a flannel petticoat at the man in buttons, austerely remarking, "You see there's nothing dutiable in that!" The man fled.[27]

RALPH CONNOR

Ralph Connor was the pen name of Charles William Gordon, the popular turn-of-the-century novelist from Glengarry County in eastern Ontario. A Presbyterian minister who later moved from Ontario to Winnipeg, Gordon wrote over 25 novels, all of which combined excitement, description and romance while at the same time paying heed to the virtues of honesty, humility, kindness and charity. Among his most popular novels are those which recreate the early days of life in Glengarry County.

This excerpt is from *Glengarry School Days: A Story of the Early Days in Glengarry*, which was published in 1902.

THE SPELLING MATCH

It was Friday afternoon, and the long, hot July day was drawing to a weary close. Mischief was in the air, and the master, Archibald Munro, or "Archie Murro," as the boys called him, was holding

114

himself in with a very firm hand. . . . He was the only master who had ever been able to control, without at least one appeal to the trustees, the stormy tempers of the young giants that used to come to school in the winter months.

———————

But now he was holding himself in, and with set teeth keeping back the pain. The week had been long and hot and trying, and this day had been the worst of all. Through the little dirty panes of the uncurtained windows the hot sun had poured itself in a flood of quivering light all the long day. Only an hour remained of the day, but that hour was to the master the hardest of all the week. The big boys were droning lazily over their books, the little boys, in the forms just below his desk, were bubbling over with spirits—spirits of whose origin there was no reasonable ground for doubt.

Suddenly Hughie Murray, the minister's boy, a very special imp, held up his hand.

"Well, Hughie," said the master, for the tenth time within the hour replying to the signal.

"Spelling-match!"

The master hesitated. It would be a vast relief, but it was a little like shirking. On all sides, however, hands went up in support of Hughie's proposal, and having hesitated, he felt he must surrender or become terrifying at once.

"Very well," he said; "Margaret Aird and Thomas Finch will act as captains." At once there was a gleeful hubbub. Slates and books were slung into desks.

"Order! or no spelling-match." The alternative was awful enough to quiet even the impish Hughie, who knew the tone carried no idle threat, and who loved a spelling-match with all the ardor of his little fighting soul.

———————

At length the choosing was over, and the school ranged in two opposing lines, with Margaret and Thomas at the head of their respective forces, and little Jessie MacRae and Johnnie Aird, with a single big curl on the top of his head, at the foot. It was a point of honor that no blood should be drawn at the first round. To Thomas, who had second choice, fell the right of giving the first word. So to little Jessie, at the foot, he gave "Ox."

"O-x, ox," whispered Jessie, shyly dodging behind her neighbor.

"In!" said Margaret to Johnnie Aird.

"I-s, in," said Johnnie stoutly.

"Right!" said the master, silencing the shout of laughter. "Next word."

With like gentle courtesies the battle began; but in the second round the little A, B, C's were ruthlessly swept off the field with second-book words, and retired to their seats in supreme exultation, amid the applause of their fellows still left in the fight. After that there was no mercy. . . .

Steadily, and amid growing excitement, the lines grew less, till there were left on one side, Thomas, with Ranald supporting him, and on the other Margaret, with Hughie beside her, his face pale, and his dark eyes blazing with the light of battle.

Without varying fortune the fight went on. Margaret, still serene, and with only a touch of color in her face, gave out her words with even voice, and spelled her opponent's with calm deliberation. Opposite her Thomas stood, stolid, slow, and wary. He had no nerves to speak of, and the only chance of catching him lay in lulling him off to sleep.

They were now among the deadly words.

"Parallelopiped!" challenged Hughie to Ranald, who met it easily, giving Margaret "hyphen" in return.

"H-y-p-h-e-n," spelled Margaret, and then, with cunning carelessness, gave Thomas "heifer." ("Hypher," she called it.)

Thomas took it lightly.

"H-e-i-p-h-e-r."

Like lightning Hughie was upon him. 'H-e-i-f-e-r."

"F-e-r" shouted Thomas. The two yells came almost together.

There was a deep silence. All the eyes were turned upon the master.

"I think Hughie was first," he said, slowly. A great sigh swept over the school, and then a wave of applause.

The master held up his hand.

"But it was so very nearly a tie, that if Hughie is willing—"

"All right, sir," cried Hughie, eager for more fight.

But Thomas, in sullen rage, strode to his seat muttering, "I was just as soon anyway." Every one heard and waited, looking at the master.

"The match is over," said the master, quietly. Great disappointment showed in every face.

"There is just one thing better than winning, and that is, taking defeat like a man." His voice was grave, and with just a touch of sadness. The children, sensitive to moods, as is the characteristic of children, felt the touch and sat subdued and silent.

There was no improving of the occasion, but with the same sad gravity the school was dismissed; and the children learned that day one of life's golden lessons—that the man who remains master of himself never knows defeat. . . . [28]

NELLIE MCCLUNG

In the early 1900s, feminism and female suffrage were far away from the minds of most Canadian women—most that is, except for the likes of Nellie McClung. Born in 1873 in Ontario, Nellie McClung was an advocate of many aspects of social reform, but particularly the rights of women. She was a vigorous campaigner for female suffrage in Manitoba and Alberta, and eventually became an MLA in Alberta, and a Canadian delegate to the League of Nations. Her novels became vehicles for her campaign on behalf of women's rights. Not a liberationist in the modern sense, Nellie McClung believed instead that women's special temperaments and instincts should be utilized in areas other than just the home. A family and motherhood were certainly part of women's roles, but women could extend their talents to wider concerns including social reform.

In this excerpt from *In Times Like These* (1915), Nellie McClung expresses her ideas on female beauty and politics.

This cruel convention that women must be beautiful accounts for the popularity of face-washes, and beauty parlors, and the languor of university extension lectures. Women cannot be blamed for this. All our civilization has been to the end that women make themselves attractive to men. The attractive woman has hitherto been the successful woman. The pretty girl marries a millionaire, travels in Europe, and is presented at court; her plainer sister, equally intelligent, marries a boy from home, and does her own washing. I am not comparing the two destinies as to which offers the greater opportunities for happiness or usefulness, but rather to show how widely divergent two lives may be. What caused the difference was a wavy strand of hair, a rounder curve on a cheek. Is it any wonder that women capitalize on their good looks, even at the expense of their intelligence? The economic dependence of women is perhaps the greatest injustice that has been done to us, and has worked the greatest injury to the race.

If women would only be content to snip away at the symptoms of poverty and distress, feeding the hungry and clothing the naked, all would be well and they would be much commended for their kindness of heart; but when they begin to inquire into causes, they find themselves in the sacred realm of politics where prejudice says no women must enter.

A woman may take an interest in factory girls, and hold meetings for them, and encourage them to walk in virtue's ways all she likes, but if she begins to advocate more sanitary surroundings for them, with some respect for the common decencies of life, she will find herself again in that sacred realm of politics—confronted by a factory act, on which no profane female hand must be laid.

Now politics simply means public affairs—yours and mine, everybody's—and to say that politics are too corrupt for women is a weak and foolish statement for any man to make. Any man who is actively engaged in politics, and declares that politics are too corrupt for women, admits one of two things, either that he is a party to this corruption, or that he is unable to prevent it—and in either case something should be done. Politics are not inherently vicious. . . .

If politics are too corrupt for women, they are too corrupt for men; for men and women are one—indissolubly joined together for good or ill. Many men have tried to put all their religion and virtue in their wife's name, but it does not work very well. When social conditions are corrupt women cannot escape by shutting their eyes, and taking no interest. It would be far better to give them a chance to clean them up.[29]

STEPHEN LEACOCK

One of the best-known of Canadian humorists is Stephen Leacock. He is famous for his humorous books like *Sunshine Sketches of a Little Town* which is a spoof of small-town living narrated by the village story-teller, and *The Leacock Roundabout*, an anthology of his best works. However, he also wrote books on political science, history, economics and education. In fact, most of his life was spent in various academic pursuits. He did graduate studies in economics and politics, and was the head of the Department of Political Science and Economics at McGill University.

MY FINANCIAL CAREER

WHEN I GO into a bank I get rattled. The clerks rattle me; the wickets rattle me; the sight of the money rattles me; everything rattles me.

The moment I cross the threshold of a bank and attempt to transact business there, I become an irresponsible idiot.

I knew this beforehand, but my salary had been raised to fifty dollars a month and I felt that the bank was the only place for it.

So I shambled in and looked timidly round at the clerks. I had an idea that a person about to open an account must needs consult the manager.

I went up to a wicket marked 'Accountant.' The accountant was a tall, cool devil. The very sight of him rattled me. My voice was sepulchral.

'Can I see the manager?' I said, and added solemnly, 'alone.' I don't know why I said 'alone.'

'Certainly,' said the accountant, and fetched him.

The manager was a grave, calm man. I held my fifty-six dollars clutched in a crumpled ball in my pocket.

'Are you the manager?' I said. God knows I didn't doubt it.

'Yes,' he said.

'Can I see you,' I asked, 'alone?' I didn't want to say 'alone' again, but without it the thing seemed self-evident.

The manager looked at me in some alarm. He felt that I had an awful secret to reveal.

'Come in here,' he said, and led the way to a private room. He turned the key in the lock.

'We are safe from interruption here,' he said: 'sit down.'

We both sat down and looked at each other. I found no voice to speak.

'You are one of Pinkerton's men, I presume,' he said.

He had gathered from my mysterious manner that I was a detective. I knew what he was thinking, and it made me worse.

'No, not from Pinkerton's,' I said, seeming to imply that I came from a rival agency.

'To tell the truth,' I went on, as if I had been prompted to lie about it, 'I am not a detective at all. I have come to open an account. I intend to keep all my money in this bank.'

The manager looked relieved but still serious: he concluded now that I was a son of Baron Rothschild or a young Gould.

'A large account, I suppose,' he said.

'Fairly large,' I whispered. 'I propose to deposit fifty-six dollars now and fifty dollars a month regularly.'

The manager got up and opened the door. He called to the accountant.

'Mr. Montgomery,' he said unkindly loud, 'this gentleman is opening an account, he will deposit fifty-six dollars. Good morning.'

I rose.

A big iron door stood open at the side of the room.

'Good morning,' I said, and stepped into the safe.

'Come out,' said the manager coldly, and showed me the other way.

I went up to the accountant's wicket and poked the ball of money at him with a quick convulsive movement as if I were doing a conjuring trick.

My face was ghastly pale.

'Here,' I said, 'deposit it.' The tone of the words seemed to mean, 'Let us do this painful thing while the fit is on us.'

He took the money and gave it to another clerk.

He made me write the sum on a slip and sign my name in a book. I no longer knew what I was doing. The bank swam before my eyes.

'Is it deposited?' I asked in a hollow, vibrating voice.

'It is,' said the accountant.

'Then I want to draw a cheque.'

My idea was to draw out six dollars of it for present use. Someone gave me a cheque-book through a wicket and someone else began telling me how to write it out. The people in the bank had the impression that I was an invalid millionaire. I wrote something on the cheque and thrust it in at the clerk. He looked at it.

'What! are you drawing it all out again?' he asked in surprise. Then I realized that I had written fifty-six instead of six. I was too far gone to reason now. I had a feeling it was impossible to explain the thing. All the clerks had stopped writing to look at me.

Reckless with misery, I made a plunge.

'Yes, the whole thing.'

'You withdraw your money from the bank?'

'Every cent of it.'

'Are you not going to deposit any more?' said the clerk, astonished.

'Never.'

An idiot hope struck me that they might think something had insulted me while I was writing the cheque and that I had changed my mind. I made a wretched attempt to look like a man with a fearfully quick temper.

The clerk prepared to pay the money.

'How will you have it?' he said.

'What?'

'How will you have it?'

'Oh'—I caught his meaning and answered without even trying to think—'in fifties.'

He gave me a fifty-dollar bill.

'And the six?' he asked dryly.

'In sixes,' I said.

He gave it me and I rushed out.

As the big door swung behind me I caught the echo of a roar of laughter that went up to the ceiling of the bank. Since then I bank no more. I keep my money in cash in my trousers pocket and my savings in silver dollars in a sock.[30]

4

A new age, a new spirit: Canada enters the 20th century

According to a book published in 1905:

Fate holds in store for this young Dominion a golden future. From whatever point of view we regard it, the Canadian prospect is full of promise. It is safe to say that the natural resources of the country, viewed as a whole, are absolutely unequalled. Even the United States does not possess either the extent or variety of resources found in Canada. In her vast forests, her coast and inland fisheries, her exhaustless coal deposits, her gold and silver mines, iron, copper, nickel, and nearly every other known variety of mineral, and, above all, in the tremendous possibilities of her grain fields, Canada holds the promise of such commercial prosperity as the world has seldom seen.[1]

In the 1970s, Canadians were faced with many concerns about the economic development of their country. On the one hand, there was the traditional drive to exploit the country's resources and promote commercial activity in order to maintain one of the highest living standards in the world. Political and financial leaders in all regions spoke of the need to expand. The "have not" provinces* had the added challenge of bringing the living standards of their residents more in line with those of people in Ontario, British Columbia or Alberta.

    In spite of the continued pursuit of "the good life", many Cana-

*Canadian provinces can be described as either "have" (more prosperous) provinces or "have not" (less prosperous) provinces.

121

dians have become convinced that economic growth was neither an automatic, nor unmixed, solution to their problems. The energy crisis, along with other factors like unrelenting inflation, seemed to trigger a re-examination of Canadian values. Were we endangering our future through our rising use of non-renewable resources such as oil and gas? How much longer would our mines and forests and fisheries be able to yield the raw materials on which so much of our prosperity is based? Was our natural environment—the lakes and rivers, the wilderness—suffering irreparable damage through the many forms of pollution? How much of our best agricultural land was falling prey to urban sprawl? Were there drawbacks in the growing concentration of our population in Montreal, Toronto and Vancouver?

At the turn of the century, few of these questions were on the minds of Canadians. They saw the land as a kind of limitless challenge, to be conquered by the plough, or the axe, or the miner's pick and shovel. Every industrial, commercial or agricultural development was a chance for profits or wages, the means to a better material life.

The Laurier era coincided with a number of world developments that worked in Canada's favour. In Europe and the United States, the emphasis on industrial development and the growth of cities created a strong demand for foodstuffs. Competition from grain producers such as the United States and Russia declined. Prices for raw materials, particularly farm products, rose sharply. The reduction in ocean freight rates meant higher profits on exports.

In the campaign to utilize the resources of Canada, the classic partnership of government and business was crucial. To promote economic growth, the Canadian government of Sir Wilfrid Laurier adopted policies that promoted foreign trade, immigration, the opening of the West and the expansion of business.

Promoting the "good life": the Liberals' brand of "National Policy"

During the long years in the role of opposition (1878-1896), the Liberals faced many challenges in trying to make their party a national one, with nation-wide support. Their main following in most of Canada came from rural areas. The Quebec Liberals, the Parti Rouge, had limited support because their reputation for **anti-clericalism** was unpopular with many French Canadians.

The rise to prominence of Wilfrid Laurier in the 1880s began to change the fortunes of the Quebec Liberals. However, the party as a whole was held back by the lack of policies which would appeal to voters as solid alternatives to those of the Conservatives. Sir John A. Macdonald and the "National Policy" seemed to be an unbeatable combination. In the election of 1891, the Liberal platform called for

Victory for tariffs in the U.S.

In the United States' election of 1896, the year Laurier became Prime Minister of Canada, William McKinley was elected president of the United States by a wide margin. His Republican administration, heavily supported by "Big Business", stood for high tariffs, and in 1897, the so-called Dingley tariff raised taxes on imports by as much as 50%. What were the chances that Canada's wishes for reduced tariffs between the two countries would interest the American government?

criticism of the power of the Church; Laurier worked hard to convince French Canadians that one could be a Liberal without being anti-religious.

122

unrestricted reciprocity with the United States. The Conservatives, using Sir John A.'s ringing cry of imperial loyalty, "A British subject I was born, a British subject I will die!", attacked the proposal as a sure step to union with the United States.

Canadian-American tariff-free trade in any, and all, products upon which the two countries could agree.

The election of 1896 was a different story. Questions of tariff and trade were in the background. The Liberals had shifted away from a narrow version of reciprocity, and attacked the National Policy for the size of the tariffs, not on the principles behind it. They agreed that some taxes on imports were needed to provide revenue for the government and to give a certain amount of protection to Canadian manufacturers. On the other hand, they argued that tariffs should be lowered to encourage trade with both Britain and the United States. And they expected that the subsequent lowering of prices for imported goods would win support among farmers, who felt victimized by tariffs. The Conservatives, for the first time since Confederation, did not have Sir John A. to rally them.

Once in office, the Laurier government wasted little time in reassuring Canadians that it planned no major changes in economic policy. Although the Liberals were associated with preference for closer trade relations with the U.S. and with hostility to the Conservatives' National Policy, Laurier was set against any drastic changes. Yet he believed in taking some steps to promote international trade, so vital to Canadian prosperity.

Thus the first budget retained the basic features of the National Policy. But a limited number of reductions in tariff were provided in the hope of promoting trade. Canada offered a 25% reduction in tariffs to any country willing to return the favour. Since Britain was a free trade country, it qualified immediately—thus the label of Imperial Preference for the Liberals' new approach.

The Liberals had acted shrewdly. They had maintained to a large extent the protective tariff on behalf of Canadian manufacturers. Freer trade, at least with Britain, was made possible. To those who wished for increased trade with the United States, the government could say that Canada had provided the opportunity. People who were campaigning for a stronger British Empire saw the new policy as a move toward imperial solidarity.* The old fears that the Liberals would weaken the ties with Britain and pave the way for a flood of American products were not realized.

The ministry of all talents

In July, 1896, Wilfrid Laurier was sworn in as Canada's first French-Canadian prime minister. His cabinet was an impressive team, including Sir Oliver Mowat from Ontario, W. S. Fielding of Nova Scotia and A. G. Blair from New Brunswick, all former provincial premiers. Other notables included Isräel Tarte, the main organizer of the successful Liberal campaign; Sir Richard Cartwright, who had served in Mackenzie's cabinet twenty years before; Clifford Sifton, member from Brandon, Manitoba, who was appointed to the important post as Minister of the Interior, with responsibility for immigration.

*See page 61.

Opening the West

One of the disappointments of the first thirty years of Confederation was the failure to develop the West. Even before 1867, many Canadians recognized the importance of the West in creating a prosperous national economy. Once the CPR was completed, settlers were

123

By no means did all the immigrants arriving in Canada between 1896 and 1914 go West or take up farming. Many thousands looked for jobs in the mines, on railway construction, or in the factories and shops of the expanding cities. Nevertheless, the most dramatic story of immigration in this period was the wave of settlers who populated the prairies and made the region a vital part of the nation.

The United States had always been a magnet for immigrants seeking land, but by the 1890s the agricultural areas had been occupied. Several consecutive years of drought in the Midwestern states like Kansas and Nebraska had, in fact, discouraged many experienced American farmers, who were ready to seek opportunity elsewhere. Western Canada could provide the "new frontier" that no longer existed in the United States.

expected to pour into the prairies. Products from their farms would mean business that would yield profits for the CPR and exports that would bring money into the country. A growing population would provide a market for the manufactured goods of central Canada and the natural products of the Maritime provinces.

Not until the turn of the century, however, were conditions ripe. The general improvement in world trade helped to create a mood of optimism in Canada as a whole, and highlighted the need for an all-out effort to settle the West. The Laurier government responded with a vigorous policy to attract immigrants, with emphasis on those who would make good farmers.

Clifford Sifton, a resourceful businessman from Brandon, Manitoba, had been named to Laurier's cabinet in 1897 as Minister of the Interior. His knowledge of the West made him eminently qualified to take charge of immigration. He set about reorganizing his department and planning a campaign to attract people who would turn hopes for the West into reality. Besides the traditional source of immigrants, Great Britain, Sifton concentrated also on the United States and on the farming populations of central and eastern Europe.

Sifton believed that "hard sell" techniques were needed to stimulate immigration. Not only were advertisements placed in British and American newspapers, but editors from the United States were treated to free trips to the prairies, so they could see the cheap, fertile land available. A flood of literature—pamphlets, handbills and pictorial displays—was circulated in Europe. Besides the govern-

These posters were distributed to encourage immigration at the turn of the century.

Among the first groups of non-English immigrants were the Mennonites, a German Protestant sect who had lived in Russia, and who came to Manitoba in 1874. They left their homeland because the Czarist regime ordered them to serve in the army; bearing arms was contrary to their religious beliefs. The Canadian government, anxious to have these hardy peasants settle in the West, granted them homesteads and in addition guaranteed them exemption from military service and allowed them their own schools. By 1879, 6 000 Mennonites had settled in Manitoba, centred around the town of Steinbach.

The first colony of Mennonites arrive at Winnipeg, 1874

Many of the Icelanders who came from Kinmount, near Toronto, in 1875 were experienced deep-sea fishermen. The abundance of fish in Lake Winnipeg prompted them to relocate on the northwestern shores of the lake. In the same year, a volcanic eruption in Iceland devastated much of its arable land and set the Icelanders in search of a new homeland. In 1876, a large group of these joined the earlier settlers in New Iceland, as the colony on Lake Winnipeg was called. Some 1 500 newcomers settled on farms along the lake with Gimli as the principal town. The word "Gimli" is Icelandic for Paradise, but their early experiences were far from heavenly. They had difficult times — a smallpox epidemic took its toll, poor crops threatened famine, and hostility from neighbours made life unpleasant. But they managed to overcome these early difficulties, and their settlements made steady progress.

Prior to 1880, there were a few Jews in Winnipeg engaged in the purchase and export of furs for the American market in St. Paul,

TOP: *A group of settlers from Iceland arrive at Willow Point, Manitoba, 1874.*
BOTTOM: *A Jewish shop on Main Street, Winnipeg.*

Minnesota. In 1882, 271 Russian Jews who had fled religious persecution reached Winnipeg. Some of these worked on railway construction. Others proceeded farther west to outlying farming districts to start agricultural colonies. The rest remained in Winnipeg where they were housed in the temporary wooden immigration barracks while waiting for land grants.

ment-sponsored promotion, land companies conducted recruitment campaigns, often giving bonuses to agents according to the number of settlers they were able to provide.

Settlers arrived by the hundreds of thousands, either overland in covered wagons from the United States, or by steamship and railway from Europe by way of eastern Canada. To the government official or the officer of a corporation like the CPR or the Hudson's Bay Company, the story was one of spectacular success. At last "the west was won," as farms spread out across the prairies, and towns sprung up almost out of nowhere. The growth of population in the West was nothing short of phenomenal.

THE GROWTH OF POPULATION IN THE WEST[2]

| Province | 1901 | |
	Total Population	Immigration
Manitoba	255,211	11,254
Saskatchewan	91,279	
Alberta	73,022	14,160
British Columbia and Yukon	178,657	2,600
TOTALS	598,169	28,014

| Province | 1911 | |
	Total Population	Immigration
Manitoba	461,394	34,289
Saskatchewan	492,432	40,076
Alberta	374,295	44,091
British Columbia and Yukon	392,480	52,786
TOTALS	1,720,601	171,242

Starting in the 1890s, settlers from central and eastern Europe, mainly from the vast Austro-Hungarian empire, began to arrive.

These Slavic peoples included Poles and Russians but most were Ukrainians*, then called "Galicians". This was a catch-all word used by Canadians to refer to the many different nationalities who came from that unfamiliar part of Europe.

By 1914, more than 100 000 had come, taking up whole districts in areas such as Dauphin, Yorkton and Edmonton. New place names such as Esterhazy, Odessa, Ruthenia, Makaroff, and Bruderheim reflected the ethnic influence. Those without money or support, and there were many, worked on railway construction or took other labouring jobs to raise funds to buy land. Still others crowded into cities, particularly Winnipeg, where they lived in tenements. They found jobs where they could—in the railway yards, in construction and in other jobs that did not require skilled labour—and used the scores of shops that were established on Main Street to cater to the needs of the immigrants.

THEY DIDN'T UNDERSTAND
In his novel, The Foreigner: A Tale of Saskatchewan (1909), *Ralph Connor describes an Anglo-Saxon view of the "Galicians".*

By their non-discriminating Anglo-Saxon fellow-citizens they are called Galicians, or by the unlearned, with an echo of Paul's Epistle in their minds, "Galatians." There they pack together in their little shacks of boards and tar-paper, with pent roofs of old tobacco tins or of slabs or of that same useful but unsightly tar-paper, crowding each other in close irregular groups as if the whole wide prairie were not there inviting them. From the number of their huts they seem a colony of no great size, but the census taker, counting ten or twenty to a hut, is surprised to find them run up into hundreds. During the summer months they are found far away in the colonies of their kinsfolk, here and there planted upon the prairie, or out in gangs where new lines of railway are in construction, the joy of the contractor's heart, glad to exchange their steady, uncomplaining toil for the uncertain, spasmodic labour of their English-speaking rivals. But winter finds them once more crowding back into the little black shacks in the foreign quarter of the city, drawn ... by their ... social instincts, or driven by economic necessities. All they ask is bed space on the floor or, for a higher price, on the home-made bunks that line the walls, and a woman to cook the food they bring to her; or, failing such a happy arrangement, a stove on which they may broil their varied stews of beans or barley, beets or rice or cabbage, with such scraps of pork or beef from the neck or flank as they can beg or buy at low price from the slaughter houses, but ever with the inevitable seasoning of garlic, lacking which no Galician dish is palatable.[3]

128

TOP: *A group of Galacian settlers.* BOTTOM: *Many early immigrants would begin life in a new land living in tenements similar to this one.*

There was thus another side to the immigration picture in the West. The Americans, British and eastern Canadians took their place in western Canada with relative ease. At least there was no language barrier. While adjustment to the severe climate and isolation of the prairies was not easy for the English-speaking settler, at least customs were reasonably familiar. Such was not the case for the immigrants from continental Europe. Recruited because of their hardy qualities and farming backgrounds, the Galicians, the "men in sheepskin coats", came by the thousands to the Canadian West. They added a new element to the population of Canada, not always with happy results. While they struggled to build new lives for themselves and their families, the Europeans met with hostility and fear from others. Though they made their contribution to the economic growth of the West, they were part of a massive social problem. The repercussions were to continue for generations.

SIFTON DENOUNCES PREJUDICE

From a letter by Mr. Sifton, November, 1901:

The cry against the Doukhobors and Galicians is the most absolutely ignorant and absurd thing that I have ever known in my life. There is simply no question in regard to the advantage of these people. The policy of exciting racial prejudice is the most contemptible possible policy, because it is one that does not depend upon reason. You can excite the prejudice of one nationality against another by simply keeping up an agitation. You can excite the French against the English or the English against the French, or the Germans against the English. All you have to do is to keep hammering away and appealing to their prejudices, and in the course of time you will work up an excitement; but a more ignorant and unpatriotic policy could not be imagined.[4]

The resulting influx of settlers was a major cause of the opening of the West. So were other developments that made possible the "wheat economy". To be successful, farming on the prairies required techniques different from those effective, for example, in southern Ontario or Ohio. In particular, the practice of "dry farming", or summer-fallowing, was important in the prairies, where rainfall was often scarce. Ploughing a field early in the summer and leaving it for planting until the next spring would enable it to retain moisture and to be ready for a new crop.

HOMESTEADING IN THE WEST

After the train came the trip to the homestead site; Moosomin, Weyburn, Moose Jaw, Swift Current, Maple Creek, Calgary, were

What it's like to be different

The immigration movement occurring between 1896 and 1914 differed from previous ones in Canada's history because of the large numbers of people who came from very different cultural backgrounds. To residents of Canada, these newcomers spoke harsh-sounding languages, dressed differently, brought strange habits and customs. Thus the interaction between "old" and "new" Canadians proved to be confusing, difficult, and even painful for both sides.

When we do not know what to expect of people, we sometimes fear them. Fear in turn makes us distant or hostile to the newcomer. On his part, the immigrant has to deal not only with feelings toward people of the majority culture, but also his feelings toward himself and his own identity. Should he maintain the customs and traditions of his homeland, or should he discard them while trying to look and act like "a Canadian"?

This is the problem for Sandor Hunyadi in the John Marlyn novel, UNDER THE RIBS OF DEATH. *Young Sandor, the son of a Hungarian immigrant family in Winnipeg, is faced with a family who wish to maintain their European customs in a Canadian society which points fingers at "foreigners".*

This conversation between father and son indicates some of the reasons Sandor wants so desperately to become Canadian:

Above him he heard his father clearing his throat.

"Why did you fight?" he asked gruffly.

Sandor trembled.

The shame he had felt that afternoon standing in front of the class, spelling out his name for the new school nurse, while his teacher smiled and even his friends giggled and grimaced—the hatred he had felt for everybody and everything swept over him again.

"I didn't wanna fight," he cried. "I don't like fightin', but they made me." His voice grew shrill. "They call me ... "

It rang in his ears, the way he heard it sometimes in his dreams before he wakened clammy with sweat and terror. "Hunky, Hunky —Humpy Ya Ya."

"Everywhere I go," he cried, "people laugh when they hear me say our name. They say 'how do you spell it?' The lady in the library made fun of me in fronta all the people yesterday when I took your book back and she hadda make out a new card. And the school nurse ... everybody ... even the postman laughs. If we changed our name I wouldn't hafta fight no more, Pa. We'd be like other people, like everybody else. But we gotta change it soon before too many people find out."

"So?" his father laughed, "and who are all these people?" And there was an indulgence in his voice that caused Sandor to take heart. The subject was an old and bitter one between them but tonight he felt that he might be able to make his father understand.

"The English," he whispered. "Pa, the only people who count are the English. Their fathers got all the best jobs. They're the only ones nobody ever calls foreigners. Nobody ever makes fun of their names or calls them 'bologny-eaters,' or laughs at the way they dress or talk. Nobody," he concluded bitterly, " 'cause when you're English it's the same as bein' Canadian."

His father walked on a few steps before answering. But at his first words Sandor knew that it was hopeless. His father would never understand.

" . . . to the first point," he heard his father saying in German. "You told me the English make you fight. But not once have you told me that you tried to reason with them."

"But, Pa, for God's sake they chase me," he cried. "When they catch me they make me fight. How can I talk to them while they're punching me?" If he continued, he knew that he would start to cry.

He grew silent.

"It is not only stupid," his father said. "It is meaningless to call anyone a foreigner in this country. We are all foreigners here. And what is more I detect a prejudice against the English in what you say. This is wrong, as I have told you many times. Nationality is of no consequence. In the things of the spirit there is no such barrier."[5]

1. In a schoolroom where most names were Anglo-Saxon like Smith, Jones, White and Evans, is it realistic to think that young children would laugh at a "foreign-sounding" name? How might the person with the unusual name feel?

2. Sandor wants to change more than his name; he wants to abandon the customs of his Hungarian heritage because Canadians don't do these things. Do you think he would have a different view of things if he were older? Why or why not?

When we talk of the cultural mosaic, we usually agree that Canada gains from having people of foreign birth add their unique cultural contributions to our country. We probably agree too that immigrants should have some choice in whether to be different from, or similar to us. When we are faced with these differences in our personal lives, though, conflicts may occur. For example, we cannot easily accept differences. If a family next door behaves differently than we have come to expect neighbours to behave, we will not perhaps be as tolerant of cultural differences as we would like to be. What if your immigrant neighbours like privacy and thus allow their shrubs and trees to grow bush-like around their house? What if they decide to allow other relatives to live with them and their house gets

132

overcrowded and noisy? You might think they should adapt to their new culture and act like the other neighbours do. Often we agree with the idea of a Canadian cultural mosaic more in theory than in practice.

When he wrote his book, THE FOREIGNER: A TALE OF SASKATCHEWAN, *Ralph Connor was creating characters the way he imagined them. When we read about the Scottish police sergeant, Cameron, and his obviously stereotyped view of the "foreigners", we must remember that the book was written in 1909. The sergeant brings out some of the views many Anglo-Saxons held about immigrants at that time.*

In this scene, the sergeant is about to walk his beat when he decides to take Elex Murchuk, the railway station interpreter, along because the sergeant has heard a lot of commotion coming from one house:

Sergeant Cameron waited till the crowd had gone, and then turning to Murchuk, he said, "You will be coming along with me, Murchuk. I am going to look after some of your friends."

"My frients?" enquired Murchuk.

"Yes, over at the colony yonder."

"My frients!" repeated Murchuk with some indignation. "Not motch!" Murchuk was proud of his official position as Dominion Government Interpreter. "But I will go wit' you. It is my way."

Away from the noise of the puffing engines and the creaking car wheels, the ears of Sergeant Cameron and his friend were assailed by other and less cheerful sounds.

"Will you listen to that now?" said the Sergeant to his polyglot companion. "What do you think of that for a civilised city?...."

From a house a block and a half away, a confused clamour rose up into the still night air.

"Oh, dat noting," cheerfully said the little Russian, shrugging his shoulders, "dey mak like dat when dey having a good time."

"They do, eh? And how do you think their neighbours will be liking that sort of thing?"

The Sergeant stood still to analyse this confused clamour. Above the thumping and the singing of the dancers could be heard the sound of breaking boards, mingled with yells and curses.

"Murchuk, there is fighting going on."

"Suppose," agreed the Interpreter, "when Galician man get married, he want much joy. He get much beer, much fight."

"I will just be taking a walk round there," said the Sergeant. "These people have got to learn to get married with less fuss about it. I am not going to stand this much longer. What do they want to fight for anyway?"

"Oh," replied Murchuk lightly, "Polak not like Slovak, Slovak not like Galician. Dey drink plenty beer, tink of someting in Old Country, get mad, make noise, fight some."

"Come along with me," replied the Sergeant, and he squared his big shoulders and set off down the street with the quick, light stride that suggested the springing step of his Highland ancestors on the heather hills of Scotland.[6]

1. What does Sergeant Cameron say is the problem with the celebration?
2. What reasons does Murchuk give for the commotion?
3. What might Sergeant Cameron think about the assimilation* of these immigrants into Canadian society?
4. If these people were your neighbours, how might you feel about their celebrations?
5. If you were living at that time, with whom do you think you could most easily empathize* and why? Sandor Hunyadi or Sergeant Cameron?
6. If your parents, grandparents or great-grandparents came to Canada from a foreign land, ask them to tell you about how they solved this conflict.
7. How would you have solved the dilemma of how to become a Canadian while maintaining your foreign heritage if you were an immigrant to Canada in the early 20th century?

*Assimilation is the process by which a distinct racial, cultural or ethnic group assumes the values and customs of a more dominant group.

*To have empathy or to empathize means to try to "put yourself in someone else's shoes", to understand the feelings that person is experiencing in order to better understand why he acts the way he does.

alive with teams of oxen and horses and wagons, loaded with children, pots and pans, supplies, furniture, crated chickens, pigs, covered with a canopy of canvas or oil cloth, often a cow behind, swinging her lowered head. They travelled usually in spring with no road, sometimes over snow laid down by the last of April's blizzards, more likely across sodden prairies mired with rain, gumbo glueing wheels and baling underfoot. With poignant infrequency they passed tents and sod huts and wooden shacks with roof camber so gentle it seemed borrowed from the earth's great curve. Finally, they reached that spot which, with great irony, they must consider their new home.

First there was a tent but as soon as possible, unless they were in bush country, they went to ground like the gopher and the badger and the burrowing owl. Sods were cut and lifted to be piled up against a frame of poles; some might boast a wooden roof with shingles or even a board floor. A sod shack gave superb insulation in winter, but as one pioneer put it, "a three-day rain outside meant a five-day rain inside." One woman's diary explained, "... When it rained for several days at a time the only dry place in the shanty was under the table which had an oil cloth on, and I put sugar, flour, etc., under it to keep dry." Another brought her piano with her, an awkward miscalculation for the chatelaine of a sod hut; her husband built a hay stack over it and two years later when a more permanent house was up the hay came off the piano. In the Wilcox district Mrs. Dave Andrews' two canaries arrived in a raging blizzard February 12th, 1904; they thawed out over the stove and sang the rest of the night while the wind howled.[7]

TOP: *Sod Hut.* BOTTOM: *Instead of using horses these Dukhobour women harnessed themselves to the plough.*

The steel plough: an early advance in farm machinery

Advances in farm machinery proved to be another reason for the success of agriculture on the prairies. Steel ploughs made "sod-busting" practicable in a region where farms had to be large to be profitable. With the short growing season, seeding and harvesting had to be as efficient as possible. Thus the implement dealers brought out better seed-drills, and the giant threshing machines with their "threshing gangs" became a familiar sight on prairie farms.

SECOND THOUGHTS ABOUT TECHNOLOGY

In her autobiography, Nellie McClung tells how the threshing machine changed the lives of farmers:

The first encroachment of the machine came after Will and Jack got the threshing outfit. From then on Sunday changed in its spirit and essence. Sunday had always been to us a day set apart; a day when every activity on the farm ceased. Even the hens were late in getting out on Sunday mornings; the cows knew they would not be milked early, and took their time in coming up to the bars. It was the one morning of the week when we saw patches of sunshine on the floor before we left our beds, or could watch the golden radiance on the walls. Everyone got dressed-up on Sunday with blackened shoes and "other clothes"; even on the Sunday that had no church service in the Schoolhouse, for then there would be visitors. Sunday's work, as much as could be, was done on Saturday, the house was made clean and tidy, vases were filled with flowers, and the pantry shelves with cooking. So Sunday was not only a day it was a feeling of rest, contentment, friendliness, a sense of peace and well-being. Even in harvest time, Sunday held its place, horses were turned into the pasture for their day of rest too, and before we had driving horses, we walked to church rather than drive a tired team!

But after the threshing-machine came Jack and Will lost their day of rest. Sunday was the day the machine had to be overhauled or one of them had to drive to Brandon or Glenboro for repairs. There was always something that must be done. The dominance of the machine had begun and none of us were far-seeing enough to know the end.[8]

1. If Nellie McClung were alive today, what labour-saving devices might she think illustrate the "dominance of the machine"?

Another way in which science and technology came to the aid of prairie farming was in improvements in types of grain. The development of Marquis wheat by the Saunders, father and son, revolutionized the grain business. This variety of wheat, with its hard kernel and high protein content, matured quickly enough to be harvested before the killing frosts of western autumn, and helped to make Canada a world leader in wheat exports.

How the West was changed

The Canadian prairies were transformed, in little more than a decade, from an isolated frontier to an integral part of the Canadian nation. Where there had been endless grasslands almost unchanged from their original state, there were now farms, villages, towns and even cities. The population had jumped from a few thousand to 1 322 709 according to the census of 1911.

Wheat had become Canada's major export, and the results of the grain economy were in view everywhere. The grain elevator was the main landmark of the hundreds of settlements spread out over the prairies from Winnipeg to the Rockies. The farm implement business, the western extension of eastern industry, was a major enterprise in prairie towns.

Socially, the West was virtually an experiment in human relations. The mixture of nationalities—English, American, Ukrainian, German, native peoples and almost every other national group—gave the prairies a multicultural character at the turn of the century. In the years ahead, the question of "ethnic mosaic" or "melting pot" would be ever-present, dormant or active, depending on national and international circumstances.

"We are all immigrants to this place even if we are born here: the country is too big for anyone to inhabit completely, and in the parts unknown to us we move in fear, exiles and invaders."[9]

CANADIANIZING THE IMMIGRANT

Written by J. W. Sparling, Principal of Wesley College, Winnipeg (1909):

Perhaps the largest and most important problem that the North American continent has before it to-day for solution is to show how the incoming tides of immigrants of various nationalities and different degrees of civilization may be assimilated and made worthy citizens.

The United States have been grappling with this question for decades, but have not yet found a solution. Canada is now facing the same problem, but in an aggravated form. A much larger percentage of foreigners, in proportion to our population is coming to us just now, than came at any one period to the United States. . . .

_____

Either we must educate and elevate the incoming multitudes or they will drag us and our children down to a lower level. We must see to it that the civilization and ideals of Southeastern Europe are not transplanted to and perpetuated on our virgin soil.[10]

1. In the present, Canada is said to be a "cultural mosaic"—a society in which newcomers can retain their ethnic identity and still become Canadians. From these statements written early in the 20th century, what do you think would be the attitudes of these authors to the modern idea of "cultural mosaic"?

Politically, two new provinces were created with the admission of Saskatchewan and Alberta to the Dominion in 1905. Previously governed by a Lieutenant Governor and Council from 1875, they had been given an elected Assembly in 1888 and responsible government in 1897. Now Saskatchewan and Alberta became provinces "like the others", with certain limitations. For example, the Dominion Government kept control of public lands, as it had in Manitoba.*

The federal government allowed these new provinces to maintain the separate schools that had existed in the Northwest Territories. Religious minorities had the right to channel their portion of school taxes to support the schools of their denominations.*

*Not until 1930, when most of the arable land had been settled, did the Dominion government turn control of public lands over to the governments of the Prairie Provinces.

*See page 49.

A FARM BOY IN THE CITY

This sketch by Alberta author Jim MacGregor describes the awe with which a prairie boy greeted the city in the early 1900s:

Who can describe a city as seen for the first time by a farm boy? Nothing has prepared him for the many and varied sights. . . . It's not only the crowds but the multitudes of other sights that fascinate, attract or repel him. For there, jammed hard against their neighbours in long rows, the buildings tower over the street two or three storeys high, and even brick and stone buildings of six storeys. Whoever imagined so many buildings, or such variety? And the signs advertising their owners' business, painted in large letters, some illuminated and all overhanging the street in bewildering confusion, why, they make your head swim! And there was the wooden horse, nearly life-size, standing by the door of the saddlery shop. There were the great jars filled with coloured liquids in the windows of the drug stores, and the barbers' revolving poles— fascinating to a boy. Then, down the street, open to the summer day, was the shoe-shine stand, where also hats were cleaned and blocked. . . .

But it was only after dark that the king of the signs stood out in all its glory over the Selkirk Hotel. This one, done in many light-bulbs, showed by successive combinations a man pouring a glass of beer, lifting it to his lips, and then quaffing the liquor. If I had seen nothing else in all the city, this would have been enough.

On nearly every street corner was a red mail-box, a marvellous thing where you could mail letters without having to wait until Tuesday or Friday. . . .

And sounds! . . . the surge of the crowd, the clumping of horses' feet on the pavement, the rattle of street cars, the roar of the riveters as they piled storey after storey on new buildings in every block. But there were other and gentler sounds. For instance, there was the persistent ring of the telephone bell in the hotel lobby when no one attended to it. A marvellous invention it was, by means of which one could talk to someone blocks or miles away.[11]

New transcontinental railways

"There has to be something wrong with a country whose National Dream is a railroad."[12]

What interest or importance does the story of railways hold for us in the Space Age? Spectacular voyages into space, including landings on the moon, have scientific and military significance. But they have little to do with the average earth-bound person's need to get from one place to another.

For most people, mass transit is likely to be a more serious concern in the years ahead than making a reservation on a rocket ship. Railways may seem like a poor cousin to airplanes in terms of speed and convenience. But given the energy crisis, the rising costs of travel and the financial plight of airlines, railway travel may have a function that is not obvious to Canadians now. If you live in an urban area, you may already appreciate the convenience of trains in travelling from one part of your city to another, or to a suburb or nearby city.

Canadians who live on the prairies depend on trains to carry the grain crops to terminals at Vancouver and Thunder Bay. Such long-distance hauling is only one of the many ways which railways serve Canadians today. Though much of the traditional function of carrying mail, freight and passengers has been taken over by trucks, buses and planes, trains still provide such services.

Railways are also an important part of our national heritage. For more than half Canada's history since Confederation, railways were the only form of long-distance mass transportation. In every town and city the railway station was—and often still is—a major landmark. It influenced the location of businesses and residential areas. Seventy-five years ago, in town after town in the newly settled West, "Railway Avenue" was the main thoroughfare.

Settlement in the West had followed the path of the Canadian Pacific Railway. This first transcontinental crossed the prairies to the Pacific in the 1880s and extended a second line through the Rockies, by way of Crow's Nest Pass, just before 1900. The very success of the CPR raised fears of monopoly. Farmers demanded alternative railways to keep down the freight rates and provide more service. Under pressure from the West, swept along by the optimism of the time, and cajoled by aggressive promoters, the Laurier government found itself supporting the construction of two new transcontinental railways.

The most amazing promoters of the time were William Mackenzie and Donald Mann, creators of the Canadian Northern. In the first decade of the century, they bought up railway lines built in the West by other promoters and constructed more sections, with the help of financial aid from provincial governments. Then, successful in securing federal support, they extended the Canadian Northern from Quebec City to Vancouver by the outbreak of World War I. Unfortunately for the Canadian taxpayer, the Mackenzie—Mann railway system, built largely at government expense, would require miraculous profits to continue. A break in the economic boom was likely to leave the Canadian government "holding the bag".

THE TWO-HUNDRED MILLION DOLLAR MANN (AND MACKENZIE)

Mann was a tough, barrel-chested construction boss, while Mackenzie was a small and neat business promoter; the two combined to form one of the most amazing partnerships in Canadian affairs. At the turn of the century they already owned a few short lines in Manitoba which went by the name of the Canadian Northern Railway. The Canadian Northern was a frontier railroad, cheaply constructed, using old steam-engines and box-cars bought second-hand from other railway companies, and depending for revenue on such local traffic as the hauling of firewood into Winnipeg. But

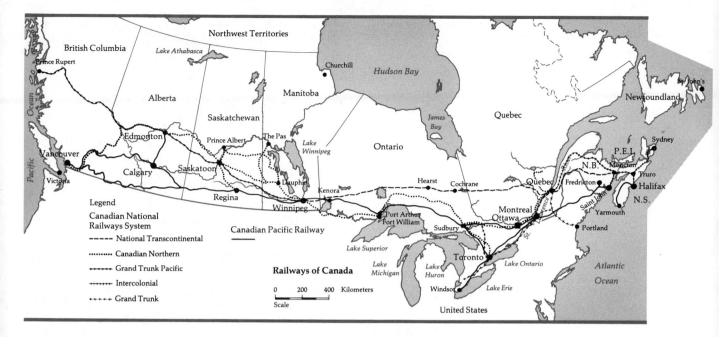

Railways of Canada

Legend
Canadian National
Railways System
- - - - - National Transcontinental
.... Canadian Northern
+++++ Grand Trunk Pacific
+++++ Intercolonial
+++++ Grand Trunk

Canadian Pacific Railway

Scale: 0 — 200 — 400 Kilometers

these two men were ambitious and daring. They applied to the Manitoba government for a subsidy to build a line from Winnipeg to the Great Lakes and so create an alternative outlet to the Canadian Pacific from the prairies. The Manitoba government was more than willing and even subsidized the construction of the section located in the neighbouring province of Ontario. . . .

But for Mackenzie and Mann this was only the beginning. They had visions of a transcontinental railway. Money was no obstacle because federal and provincial governments were generous and private investors had confidence in Canada and in these two men. By 1910 Mackenzie and Mann had borrowed more than two hundred million dollars and their railway consisted of some three thousand miles of track, mainly in western Canada, with construction under way across the Rockies to Vancouver and across the Canadian Shield to eastern Canada. Even in this era of optimism, this was a fantastic achievement. The partnership of Mackenzie and Mann had shown that there was scope for the talents of daring entrepreneurs in the Canada of the twentieth century.[13]

WINNIPEG'S IMPORTANCE IN 1911

In 1911, W. E. Curtis, a reporter for the *Chicago Record Herald*, wrote the following about Winnipeg:

All roads lead to Winnipeg. It is the focal point of the three transcontinental lines of Canada, and nobody . . . can pass from one part of Canada to another without going through Winnipeg. It is a gateway through which all the commerce of the east and the west and the north and the south must flow. No city, in America at least, has such an absolute and complete command over the wholesale trade of so vast an area. It is destined to become one of the greatest distributing commercial centres of the continent as well as a manufacturing community of great importance.

In 1911 Winnipeg had a population of 136,035. . . .

Winnipeg reached the height of its power and influence in the west by 1912. Winnipeg controlled grain marketing for the entire prairie region, wholesaling from the Great Lakes to the Rockies, its financial institutions operated throughout Canada and controlled the prairie region. The manufacturing industry was meeting demands for products in the construction industry. The railway yards and shops were crucial to the operation of the whole western network. Although other cities such as Edmonton and Calgary were beginning to develop into important western cities, Winnipeg by far was the most dominant and the prevailing attitude of its residents was one of optimism and hope for continued expansion.[14]

Yet a third transcontinental involved the government more directly. The Grand Trunk Railway Company, during a half century of existence, had developed a network of railways in central Canada and a number of links with American railways. The Grand Trunk directors convinced the Laurier government to build 2900 km of track across the wilderness of the Canadian Shield, between Winnipeg and Moncton, New Brunswick.* This railway would be leased from the government on bargain terms by the Grand Trunk, which would build the western section of the transcontinental from Winnipeg to Prince Rupert, British Columbia.

*This section was known as the National Transcontinental.

Even before the new transcontinentals were fully in use, the outbreak of World War I stopped the flow of immigration and increased the costs of construction and operation. The Dominion government could not afford to allow the railway companies to collapse. Both the taxpayers' money and the country's reputation were involved. Temporary assistance was given and, in 1916, a royal commission was appointed to look into the problem of transportation and to suggest solutions.

The report of the commission urged that the government take over the troubled companies. The very complicated procedure was begun under Prime Minister Robert Borden and completed in 1923, when Mackenzie King's Liberal party was in power. The Canadian National Railways, as the new combination was called, incorporated almost all the railways in Canada not belonging to the CPR. Manageagement was given a board of directors appointed by Parliament. When taking over the railways, the Canadian government also assumed their debts. The C.N.R. remained a problem in the years to follow.

142

Early Industrial Operation

The pre-World War I "railway boom" resulted in the completion of more than 36 000 km of track, the stimulation of the Canadian economy and the opening of the West. But there had been much unnecessary railway building, involving a huge outlay by the Dominion. The Laurier government has, therefore, often been criticized for catering to the railway promoters and for failing to establish a national policy for transportation.

Rise of big business

The effects of the wheat economy which began on the prairies during the Laurier years were not confined to the West. In fact, the "wheat boom" had stimulated the entire Canadian economy. The resulting railway construction across the prairies had contributed to an expanding steel industry and related manufacturing industries. Investors, especially from Great Britain and the United States, suddenly found Canada attractive. Investment capital flowed in to develop mining, pulp and paper and hydro-electric power. Immigration provided a large and mobile labour force. The expansion of business and industry led to bigger and more complex forms of business organization and to opportunities for Canadian businessmen.

INCREASE IN MANUFACTURING[15]

Net Value of Production

	1900	1910	1923
	($000)	($000)	($000)
Rubber Products	606	3 438	30 178
Tobacco	8 078	13 199	41 889
Boots and Shoes	7 623	16 000	22 958
Textiles and Textile Products	32 874	67 282	157 995
Clothing	19 960	43 657	79 470
Cotton Textiles	6 537	13 032	39 342
Furniture	4 280	8 018	16 582
Iron and Its Products	34 967	106 313	208 821
Agricultural Implements	5 469	10 667	14 434
Boilers, Tanks and Engines	2 842	7 585	2 786
Machinery	831	2 332	19 857
Primary Iron and Steel*	3 111	14 919	17 500
Railway Rolling Stock	5 178	25 221	28 008
Wire and Wire Goods	769	2 239	11 500
Automobiles		2 444	33 462
Chemicals and Chemical Products	3 910	12 167	56 800
Electric Light and Power	1 960	12 892	67 500
Total of above†	94 298	239 309	602 723
Other Manufacturers	120 228	325 158	701 834
GRAND TOTAL, ALL MANUFACTURERS	214 526	564 467	1 304 557

*Excludes iron-smelting in 1900 and 1910.
† Includes totals of textiles and textile products and of iron and its products.

NATURAL RESOURCES

On the west coast, the most spectacular exploitation of natural resources was the Klondike gold rush (approximately 1897–1903). In the remote area of the Klondike River, a tributary of the Yukon, a rich find of gold in the summer of 1896 led to a flood of fortune-seekers. Most reached the area in 1898 after a hard journey.

The vast majority of gold-seekers attempted the shorter, more direct, cheaper routes, and approached the Yukon from its headwaters. They proceeded by ship to ports on the Alaska Panhandle, some to Juneau or Wrangell, from which they worked their way up the Taku or Stikine rivers, then overland to Atlin or Teslin lakes.

Dawson City, 1899

Most made their overland journeys from Pyramid Harbor, Dyea, or Skagway on Lynn Canal. A few travellers, wiser than most, chose the longer but more gradual northwesterly route known as the Dalton Trail, which led them to Dalton Post and the Yukon River above the future settlement of Carmacks. More adopted the route of Schwatka and Ogilvie that led from Dyea by the Chilkoot Pass to the plateau beyond. Within eighteen miles of Dyea, broken by camping areas at "Canyon City" and "Sheep Camp," the route ascended the Taiya River then mounted to the summit of the pass. From the foot of the pass, steps were cut into the steep slope that led to the 3,739-foot summit, beyond which the route descended to Lakes Lindeman and Bennett, the headwaters of Yukon navigation. Most travellers attempted the somewhat easier White Pass route Ogilvie had reported in 1887, a route that began at Skagway, followed the Skagway River a few miles, then started a dizzying six-mile climb to the 2,600-foot summit, followed by an easier descent by various rivers and streams to Lake Bennett. More than 30,000 persons traversed these two passes during the winter of 1898-99 alone. All who attempted this route found the climb up the passes their greatest trial, characterized by unremitting toil as they or their porters moved in ant-like columns up and down the icy slopes, packing their supplies in relays.[16]

By 1903, gold valued at nearly $100 million had been extracted. Then the boom collapsed, and the individual prospectors departed, leaving the field to mining companies. Even the more large-scale approach to mining met with falling profits. The Yukon territory languished. Other more stable mining enterprises were started in southern British Columbia, where silver, lead, zinc and copper were to be found. Trail, where the Cominco Company established its plant, was built as a centre for refining.

The mining frontier of the Canadian Shield showed promise of being the bonanza of the future. Just as the Klondike gold rush was declining, a series of boom towns sprang up where major mineral deposits were located: Cobalt (silver), Porcupine (gold), Kirkland Lake (gold). Meanwhile, the copper-nickel deposits at Sudbury had attracted American investors, who formed the Canadian Copper Company* and acquired mineral rights to vast areas of the Sudbury Basin. The chief rival was Mond Nickel, a British company. Sault Ste. Marie became an important processing centre for minerals of the Ontario northland.

Elsewhere in Canada, mineral production was underway in Alberta (coal), Quebec (asbestos), and Nova Scotia (coal). Encouraged by the willingness of governments to promote the extraction of minerals, and the growing markets both within Canada and abroad, businessmen invested their capital in the mining phase of Canada's national expansion.

*In 1902, this company became part of the newly-formed International Nickel Company (INCO).

146

Forest products were also becoming a major enterprise, as the demand for lumber rose in the construction industry across Canada, and in the growing cities of the United States. The forests of British Columbia, Ontario, Quebec and New Brunswick were "harvested" not only for timber and lumber, but for pulpwood. The rising demand for paper products, especially newsprint, led to heavy investment by Canadian, British and American companies in paper mills.

The expanded mining and forest industries created increased demands for inexpensive power. Consequently, hydro-electric projects began to harness the rivers of Canada and hydro lines carried electrical power to industry and, increasingly, to private homes.

INDUSTRY AND COMMERCE

The development of east-west trade, helped by the Western wheat boom, railway expansion, and the exploitation of natural resources, created an unprecedented opportunity for the rise of "Big Business". No longer was the family business adequate to handle the size of investment and degree of skill required in the major industries.

Consequently a form of business quite new to Canada—the corporation—became a fact of life in Canadian business during the first decade of the twentieth century. Through the corporation, which sold shares to large numbers of investors, a company could raise money from the general public, rather than relying on the resources of the founding partners. As a historian explains:

> ...The modern business corporation was emerging. In the first decade of the new century it assumed the form that was to be familiar and typical for the next forty or fifty years.
>
> Before the short 1907 business recession, in spite of the fact that the great era of giant trust-building was over in the United States, there had been few large industrial mergers in Canada. In the three years after the recovery, the small wave of new corporations turned into a flood. From 1909 to 1911 there were no less than 41 industrial amalgamations in Canada, with a total authorized capital of one-third of a billion dollars. They were formed out of 196 individual companies, and they represented such widely differing fields as flour milling, textiles, paint, coal, lumber, electric power, and machinery.[17]

As well as the tycoons like Sir James Dunn (Algoma Steel) and Sir Edmund Osler (a leading financier in Toronto), a whole new class of financial promoters emerged during this time of almost frantic growth in Canadian business. In the pattern of British and American capitalists, people like Max Aitken (later Lord Beaverbrook) engaged in the formation of mergers. By joining several companies in the same industry into a single operation, the promoters aimed to create huge

The importance of hydro-electric power led to a showdown, initially in Ontario, between private enterprise and the general public. To prevent a business monopoly from securing control over so valuable a resource, politicians such as Adam Beck campaigned for years for government control of hydro. The result was that Ontario, and then other provinces, established electricity as a "public utility". This practical solution was another example of the Canadian tradition that government has an important role, both in encouraging conditions for commercial progress and in protecting the citizen against exploitation.

corporations which could hold their own in the marketplace, where foreign competitors; mainly from Britain and the U.S., were becoming increasingly involved.

A historian summarizes the impact of such entrepreneurs as Max Aitken (Lord Beaverbrook):

1909 and the early part of 1910 were the heyday of Aitken's financial achievements. These brought him great wealth and also some opprobrium. Where previously he had been content with the West Indies and Nova Scotia, all Canada now became his field of operations. His ceaseless travels taught him that Canada could be treated as an economic unit instead of being a collection of separate provinces. Existing concerns of the same kind could be brought together with immediate economies in specialization, purchase of raw materials, and division of markets. Increased profits would follow almost at once. Moreover these new larger concerns would at last be able to face the competition from their greater American rivals, particularly if they were protected by Canadian tariffs. Here was the case for the mergers which Aitken inspired. He ranged wide. He merged the cast-iron trade and said: "Everyone who buys an enamelled iron pan in Canada pays tribute to me". He merged the manufacture of freight cars. He merged grain elevators and hydro-electric stations in the west.[18]

"Cash on the line" purchases were a rarity in these times. Many items were paid for by barter—a farmer trading so much produce, say, for a wooden chest or perhaps some dental work. A big part of buying and selling was "dickering" or the negotiations that took place between buyer and seller. It was assumed by the buyer that retailers over-priced their goods so that they could be talked into giving the buyer "a bargain". Likewise, it was assumed by the seller that the buyer would offer a starting price which was lower than the worth of the goods. In this way, both buyers and sellers could use their skills in dickering for the best deal.

The trend toward bigness, reflected in finance and manufacturing, affected selling as well. Thus the department store made its appearance. Until the turn of the century, families made much of their own clothing and made careful purchases of clothes, supplies, household goods, farm equipment and other necessities from general stores and local markets. Merchants set up stores wherever groups of people settled. With rapid urbanization, however, the chance to open several stores in one—the department store—was irresistible.

One of the first, and most notable, efforts at retailing was the establishment and growth of Eaton's department stores. Beginning with small shops in southern Ontario, Timothy Eaton opened what was to be the forerunner of today's Eaton's in Toronto in 1869. Initially a modest dry goods store, this first "T. Eaton & Co." built its business and its reputation on the unusual practices of one price for all, cash only and money back guarantees. Since "dickering for a price" and credit buying were common practices, no one thought Eaton could make his business work. When he offered "satisfaction guaranteed or money refunded," people thought he would fail indeed. All these policies, however, have contributed to the success of the Eaton corporation.

148

The first Eaton's department store

Among the most notable moves on the part of Timothy Eaton was his introduction in 1884 of the first Eaton's catalogue. What was to become an institution in Canadian life began as a 32-page, black and white booklet without illustrations, but it gave detailed descriptions and prices of goods.

Distributed first at the Canadian Industrial Exhibition (the forerunner of the Canadian National Exhibition), the catalogue was an instant success. It was a welcome boon to settlers far away from an Eaton's store, or in fact to anyone who wished to buy by mail. The catalogue combined convenience with low prices, and became a household feature in thousands of Canadian homes. In fact, in the outlying districts, Eaton's catalogues found many uses. Many a family argument arose over who would be the first to look at the newly-arrived catalogue.

The announcement that Eaton's was abolishing its catalogue operation astounded many Canadians in the winter of 1976. After all, the Eaton's catalogue had been a part of growing up in Canada.

Despite the economics and what certainly must have been a wise financial move on the part of the corporation, many lament the demise of the book which was as important a part of growing up in rural Canada as threshing machines and one-room schools.

"No more Eaton's catalogue," said the headline Wednesday.

No more Eaton's catalogue?

At first, it's unbelievable. For those with any experience of isolated rural life, it's like saying "No more CPR," "No more kerosene for the lamps," "No tomorrow."

I was born in the city, but close to 40 years ago, before the Second World War, I went to teach in an utterly isolated rural school where there was no power, no telephone, and no social worker. Some of the kids in my school had never even seen a train, and there were four motor vehicles in the entire community.

Mail came twice a week, and mail day meant the arrival of more than letters. It brought parcels from Eaton's.

Everybody had an Eaton's catalogue, a volume which was just about the most-thoroughly-read book in the house. And most of the reading was not about the things you were going to buy, but about the things you maybe couldn't afford and maybe would never be able to own.

Days when the new catalogues arrived were large and important ones in such communities. In large families, especially those with several girls, the rivalry was intense over who would get the first chance to open the Wish Book and see all the wild and wonderful things you could—with a few dollars—order from the outside world.

And long after the first frantic forays into its pages in search of affordable clothes and housewares, there were the pleasant, almost euphoric and at the same time frustrated occasions when you could idly leaf through the pages and dream.

Most of the catalogue was in black and white in those days, which only made the scattering of colored pages that much more magical. But even black and white offered a treasure-house of largely-unattainable goods.

From the catalogue, you ordered dresses and stockings (good stout cotton, unglamorous but highly serviceable), shirts and socks, workboots and heavy shoes and that universally-worn long-handled underwear displayed on male models of most unrural appearance and nobility of expression.

You could buy building materials, barbed wire, sheet metal, tools of all sorts, from a simple screwdriver to logging chains and hayforks. A man could get his fencing from Eaton's and, if he had enough money and vision, a wind-propelled electricity generator.

All these things didn't come in the mail, of course. Bulky hardware items had to be picked up at the express office nearest you,

The first Eaton's catalogue, 1884

but masses of parcels—of all shapes and sizes—wrapped in the familiar paper with the universally-recognized labels, came out to our little rural post office every time the courier made it from town.

If the sight of the parcels in the post office was exciting, the opening of them when they arrived at the house created a kind of restrained delirium. The first question, as items were removed, was "Will it fit?" Then "Is the color okay?" and then the thought, sometimes voiced, sometimes not: "Has anyone else ordered one like this?" The anyone else referred of course to the community.

Mail order parcels produced a full gamut of emotions, from elation and pride, through quiet satisfaction and shoulder-shrugging acceptance to heart-breaking despair.

What a coup for the young female members of the family to find that they had, after all their frantic searching the pages, making the choice, scraping together the money and rushing off the order as soon as possible after the new catalogue had arrived—that they had in fact, got something that fitted well, was a most becoming color and design, and was something that no other girl in the district had.

And what a black day when it was discovered that Mary on the next farm had beaten you out by one mail-day on the most wonderful item in the book.

And always, of course, you looked among the items to find, and save, the new order form thoughtfully enclosed to replace the forms from the catalogue you had used.

You could order men's hats and ladies' hats, washing machines and baby carriages, jewelry and books, baby clothes and china and even groceries, canned and packaged, of course, but still a wide variety of foodstuffs which came packed in stout boxes with all sorts of future uses.

Several generations of Canadians grew up considering the Eaton's mail-order catalogue the ultimate in merchandising, and many a farm family felt a close relationship with those nameless, faceless people in Winnipeg who filled their orders for most of the necessities and a few of the luxuries of life.

And several generations of small-town storekeepers grew up with a jaundiced view of that same mail-order catalogue, and the sometimes bitterly-spoken belief that it shouldn't be allowed.

"A lot of these people came in and buy the odd thing they can't get from the catalogue and ask us to give them credit, and then turn around and buy all their other stuff from Eaton's," you might hear them say. For in those days, you sent your cash with the order. No credit, no handy plastic cards with a number, no budget accounts. You paid your money or you got no parcel.

Now it's going.

It was the showcase for millions of people on farms and in tiny settlements. It was the nearest thing to the world of fashion and elegance. It was, after the new catalogue had come out, the source of paper for a variety of uses. It was the fount of necessities and the stuff of dreams. It was, for many a growing lad, as furtively viewed as Playboy magazine, and for many a growing girl, it was the basis for visions of beauty and romance.

Nothing will ever replace it, and I feel sorry for the poor, deprived children of today and of the future, who will miss out on the magnificence of spirit generated by ordering from the catalogue.[19]

Canadians reacted with mixed feelings to the rise of big business. Although the buying public bought the products of large corporations, the traditional fears of monopoly were greater than ever. There was a growing danger that the **monopolies**, should they emerge, would not even be Canadian. American firms were establishing their subsidiaries, or "branch plants" in Canada. Public pressure on the government, both in newspapers and in Parliament, rose sharply. The Combines Investigation Act was passed in 1910, giving the government the authority to inquire into complaints about business combinations that might be against the public interest. However, the effect was small and the trend toward bigger companies, if not monopolies, continued.

The situation in which a small number of companies control the market, and are able to use their power to raise prices—and their own profits.

With governments, both federal and provincial, geared to policies favouring economic development, opposition to the rise of big business began to take the form of farmers' organizations and trade unions.* Up to World War I, however, the prevailing mood in Canada was optimism that the pattern of economic growth was, in the long run, the best thing for Canadians in general.

*See Chapter 7.

1. Is the prevailing mood in Canada today still optimism about the present state of economic growth?

2. The terms "Big Government", "Big Business", and "Big Labour" are common today. How would you explain each of them? Is there such a thing as "Big Agriculture"?

3. What events in our country over the past year have shown the power relationships between government, big business and labour? In each of these issues, did anyone of the three sectors have the upper hand over the others?

4. The consumer movement has been an important economic development of the last ten years. Why? What is the relationship between the growth of the consumer movement and increase in the size and power of government, business and labour?

5

Canada and World War I

The world looks on in a stunned, incredulous way while Europe is rushing forward to a stupendous catastrophe. It has heard much of the restraining powers of diplomacy. . . . We have been told again and again that the financiers of the world . . . would never permit the great nations to impoverish themselves by a general war. . . .

Yet in the present outburst of belligerency all these restraints have been scorned. Diplomacy has accomplished nothing. . . . The protests of the money market have gone unheeded. The staggering cost in life and the vast burden of debt to be imposed both on this generation and its successors weigh as nothing in the balance against race and national animosities and the blind passions of controlling groups which think that they see in war the best means of accomplishing a deep seated political purpose.[1]

Background to the "Great War", 1914–1918

In the early 1900s, Canada as a whole was enjoying a long-awaited prosperity. Business opportunities attracted entrepreneurs to railway building, mining, and manufacturing. Corporations were growing in size and power. Many Canadians opened their own small businesses—grocery stores, hardwares, bakeries, cafes, barbershops. Although workers and farmers often shared less equally in the general prosperity, jobs were plentiful and cheap land beckoned in the

West. The political issues of the day—Canadian or foreign—could be ignored by the average Canadian in his pursuit of a brighter future.

But world affairs were not without effect on the lives of Canadians, who had experienced the bitterness of war in South Africa and British pressure on the Canadian government to contribute money to imperial defence.* Yet developments in Europe were far away. The main effect of the troubles there seemed to be the sharp increase in immigration to Canada, the largest influx in the country's history. Few Canadians could have guessed that a tragedy with roots in Europe would soon carry thousands of their countrymen to their graves.

*See Chapter 6, pp. 182, 185.

Europe was headed for war, however—total war. For several decades, the causes of widespread conflict had been building, as a series of rivalries became connected. Two old enemies, Germany and France, were preparing for the day when their struggle would be renewed. In trying to gain an advantage, each had drawn other major powers into alliances. By 1914, Germany, Austria-Hungary and Italy*—the Triple Alliance—were lined up against the Triple Entente of France, Russia and Great Britain.

*Italy was no longer committed to the Triple Alliance; secretly, Italy had agreed to support the Triple Entente.

Each alliance had its members bound by secret treaties. If one member were attacked, the others were obligated to come to its defence. Thus, any war was likely to involve all members of both alliances. The result was an atmosphere of increasing suspicion and fear. A series of confrontations, which erupted into a number of limited wars in Eastern Europe, added to the tension.

Canadian newspapers did keep a kind of "box score" on their front pages, giving brief accounts of incidents and wars involving Serbia, Greece and other peoples struggling to break away from old European empires, particularly Austria-Hungary, Russia and Turkey. Troubles were so frequent in the decade prior to 1914 that they were almost taken for granted.

While the politicians of the major powers were busy trying to outmanoeuver one another, *nationalism* was becoming the most important influence in European affairs. In the established nations, such as Germany, France or Britain, the belief that one's race and culture were superior to those of another country had been growing for many years. Public opinion in a country could be easily aroused by the disrespectful or threatening action of a rival.

Closely related to nationalism was the rise of *militarism*. This tendency was shown by the "arms race", in which countries increased their budgets for standing armies—that is, full-time professional forces—warships, and bigger and more destructive guns. The increasing influence of military leaders in politics made war more likely as a means of advancing national interests.

Nationalism was creating pressures within the empires of Eastern Europe and the Middle East. Throughout the region known as the Balkans, stretching from the Baltic Sea to the Mediterranean, unrest was brewing among Poles, Czechs, Slovaks, and other nationalist groups. These peoples who had been governed for generations, even centuries, by Austro-Hungarian, Turkish or Russian overlords were struggling for "self-determination"—in a word, independence. As the

The *Panther* incident of 1911 was one of many confrontations on the road to war. In the North African country of Morocco, both France and Germany were trying to increase their influence. Britain, fearful of German ambitions, was strengthening its ties with France as a counterbalance. When riots broke out in Morocco in 1911, France sent in troops, claiming they were needed to restore order and protect Europeans living in the country. Germany reacted by dispatching a gunboat, the *Panther*, to the Moroccan port of Agadir. This action was interpreted as an insult by France and Britain. When Germany demanded that France give up territories elsewhere as compensation for advantages it appeared to be gaining in Morocco, hostility was even greater.

strength of the empires declined, several provinces had already won some form of self-government. In this "powder keg of Europe", a sudden event could ignite a war that would draw in all the major powers.

Meanwhile, in Africa and in many other parts of the globe, European nations had established empires. The competition for colonies, for the resources to be exploited, was another source of conflict. The "old imperialists" like Britain and France were now being challenged by the "new imperialists" like Germany. A series of incidents there threatened to lead to war.

On June 28, 1914, the Archduke Francis Ferdinand, heir to the Austrian throne, was assassinated by a young Serbian, whose country was hostile to Austria and supported by Russia. In retaliation, Austria made demands on Serbia that would have amounted to a takeover, a situation that Russia was not prepared to tolerate.

Germany backed Austria in the crisis; France and Britain prepared to support Russia. Deciding to strike first and hoping to secure a quick conquest of France, Germany unleashed its invasion, through Belgium.

A LULL IN HATE

A British soldier fighting the Germans in France recalls the extraordinary events of Christmas Eve, 1914. Bitter trench warfare suddenly stopped, and rival armies shared a feeling of celebration:

The day had been entirely free from shelling, and somehow we all felt that the Boches, too, wanted to be quiet. There was a kind of an invisible, intangible feeling extending across the frozen swamp between the two lines, which said "This is Christmas Eve for both of us—*something* in common."

About 10 p.m. I made my exit from the convivial dug-out on the left of our line and walked back to my own lair. On arriving at my own bit of trench I found several of the men standing about and all very cheerful. There was a good bit of singing and talking going on, jokes and jibes on our curious Christmas Eve, as contrasted with any former one, were thick in the air. One of my men turned to me and said:

"You can 'ear 'em quite plain, sir!"

"Hear what?" I inquired.

"The Germans over there, sir; you can 'ear 'em singin' and playin' on a band or somethin'."

———————

"Come on," said I, "let's go along the trench to the hedge there on the right—that's the nearest point to them, over there."

So we stumbled along our now hard, frosted ditch, and scrambling up on to the bank above, strode across the field to our next bit of trench on the right. Everyone was listening. An improvised Boche band was playing a precarious version of "Deutsch-land, Deutschland, uber Alles," at the conclusion of which, some of our mouth-organ experts retaliated with snatches of ragtime songs and imitations of the German tune. Suddenly we heard a confused shouting from the other side. We all stopped to listen. The shout came again. A voice in the darkness shouted in English, with a strong German accent, "Come over here!" A ripple of mirth swept along our trench, followed by a rude outburst of mouth organs and laughter. Presently, in a lull, one of our sergeants repeated the re-quest, "Come over here!"

"You come half-way—I come half-way," floated out of the dark-ness.

"Come on then!" shouted the sergeant! "I'm coming along the hedge!"

"Ah! but there are two of you," came back the voice from the other side.

Well, anyway, after much suspicious shouting and jocular deri-sion from both sides, our sergeant went along the hedge which ran at right-angles to the two lines of trenches. He was quickly out of sight; but, as we all listened in breathless silence, we soon heard a spasmodic conversation taking place out there in the darkness.

Presently, the sergeant returned. He had with him a few German cigars and cigarettes which he had exchanged for a couple of Maconochie's and a tin of Capstan, which he had taken with him. The séance was over, but it had given just the requisite touch to our Christmas Eve—something a little human and out of the ordi-nary routine.[2]

The Schlieffen Plan

In 1870-71, Germany had crushed France in a war that left both countries expecting a sequel—France, for revenge; Germany, for defence. In preparation, German military planners continued over the years to build up their armies. The chief of staff in the 1890s, Count von Schlieffen, prepared a detailed plan for invading France by way of Belgium which was the easiest invasion route. Success of the plan depended on the swift movement of German troops through Belgium, the capture of Paris and the surrender of France. Then Germany would be in a position to throw its strength against Russia, topple the declining regime of the Czars, and flushed with victory, confront an isolated Great Britain.

If the Schlieffen Plan were interrupted, Germany could face a prolonged war on both its western and eastern borders.

Canada enters the war

When German troops marched into Belgium, a small country which had nothing to do with causing a war, Great Britain declared war on Germany.* The date was August 4, 1914 . Canada, as a part of the British Empire, was automatically at war.

*Britain was honouring obligations to Belgium first undertaken in a treaty of 1839.

Writing in Le Canada, *August, 1914, L. O. David concurs:*

England being at war, Canada, like all parts of the British Empire, is at war. Our destinies are bound to those of England, our duty and our interest command us to aid her to triumph, to protect ourselves and to protect France. Loyalty, patriotism, our most sacred interests make it a duty for us to contribute in the measure of our strength to the triumph of their arms.[3]

The only question was the extent to which Canada took part. Most Canadians supported a vigorous effort. The government

Ypres, after the battle

wasted little time in mobilizing the country, through such legislation as the *War Measures Act.** This gave the Canadian government the power of censorship over its citizens; the power to arrest, imprison and deport people; the power to take over the nation's resources and use them for an all-out war effort.

At the beginning of the war, Canada had an army of only 3 000. Within weeks, Parliament had authorized $50 000 000 as a war budget. By October, 33 000 volunteers had joined the First Contingent for training at Valcartier, near Quebec City. They were transported in November to England for further training, and by February, 1915, troops from this force were in action in France. By the end of 1915, more than 200 000 had enlisted. All together, more than 600 000 Canadians served in the armed forces, and 425 000 went overseas.

Canadians on the battlefields

The Princess Patricia's Light Infantry Regiment was the first Canadian organized troop to patricipate in the war. Early in 1915, this regiment had joined compatriots from Britain and other parts of the Empire in the trenches. Weeks of struggle followed, leading up to the terrible battles at Ypres, a little Belgian town. There, in May, Canadians were among the first to suffer death by poisonous chlorine gas. Yet the Canadians held their position and stopped the Germans from breaking through to the English Channel.

YPRES—1915

That old man on television last night,
a farmer or fisherman by the sound of him,
revisiting Vimy Ridge, and they asked him
what it was like, and he said,
There was water up to our middles, yes,
and there was rats, and yes,
there was water up to our middles
and rats, all right enough
and to tell you the truth
after the first three or four days
I started to get a little disgusted:
Oh, I know they were mercenaries
in a war that hardly concerned us.
I know all that.
Sometimes I'm not even sure that I have a country.
But I know they stood there at Ypres
the first time the Germans used gas,
that they were almost the only troops
in that section of the front
who did not break and run,
who held the line.

*Compare Canadian attitudes to the War Measures Act when it was reactivated in 1939 and 1970.

Trench warfare became the typical form of battle early in World War I. The German plan of overwhelming France had been stopped by the "Miracle on the Marne". There on the Marne River, French and British soldiers, transported by Paris taxis, had stalled the initial German offensive. Rival armies then dug in for the hideous struggle across mud plains and barbed wire.

159

Perhaps they were too scared to run.
Perhaps they didn't know any better
—that is possible, they were so innocent,
those farmboys and mechanics, you have only to look
at old pictures and see how they smiled.
Perhaps they were too shy
to walk out on anybody, even Death.
Perhaps their only motivation
was a stubborn disinclination.

Private MacNally thinking:
You squareheaded sons of bitches,
you want this God damn trench
you're going to have to take it away
from Billy MacNally
of the South End of Saint John, New Brunswick.
And that's ridiculous, too, and nothing
on which to found a country.
                    Still
it makes me feel good, knowing
that in some obscure, conclusive way
they were connected with me
and me with them.[4]

By January, 1916, the three Canadian divisions were formed into the Canadian Corps. Under the command of the British General, Lord Byng, the Canadians distinguished themselves in the Battle of the Somme. One of the bloodiest battles of the war, this struggle produced close to 50 000 casualties among Canadians alone.

In the spring of 1917, the Canadian Corps distinguished themselves at Vimy Ridge. Where previous allied attacks had failed, the Canadians overcame veteran German troops on April 9, 1917—Easter Monday; but the Canadians suffered thousands of deaths. In recognition of their sacrifices, the Canadian Corps were placed under the command of Sir Arthur Currie, a Canadian. In the fall of 1917, the Canadians took Paschendaele, again after fierce fighting and high casualties.

AFTER THE BATTLE WAS OVER

(A) One of Britain's official war artists visited the area of the Somme in the summer of 1917, the year after the battle. He wrote:

Never shall I forget my first sight of the Somme in summertime. ...No words could express the beauty of it. The dreary, dismal mud was baked white and pure—dazzling white. White daisies, red poppies and a blue flower, great masses of them, stretched for miles and miles. The sky a pure, dark blue, and the whole air...

thick with white butterflies; your clothes were covered with butter-flies. It was an enchanted land: but in place of fairies, there were thousands of little white crosses marked "Unknown British soldier" ... blue dragonflies darted about; high up the larks sang; higher still the aeroplanes droned. Everything shimmered in the heat ... [5]

(B) American author, F. Scott Fitzgerald, in his novel, TENDER IS THE NIGHT *gives a final comment on the futility of the war:*

Dick turned the corner of the traverse and continued along the trench, walking on the duckboard ... Then he got up on the step and peered over the parapet. In front of him, beneath a dingy sky, was Beaumont-Hamel; to his left, the tragic hill of Thiepval ...

'This land here cost twenty lives a foot that summer,' he said to Rosemary ... 'See that little stream? We could walk to it, a whole Empire walking very slowly, dying in front and pushing forward behind. And another Empire walking very slowly backward a few inches a day, leaving the dead like a million bloody rugs. ... '[6]

THE BATTLE OF VIMY RIDGE

An eye-witness account:

Easter Sunday, the eve of the battle, was fine and sunny. ... All was peaceful to the eye, as unit by unit took its way in ordered leisure up the slopes and spurs which are the talons of the claw-like Ridge. ...

Wonderful in their work and in their secrecy had been the Engineers. For months they delved underground. ... The tunnel system ran sheer into and up the Ridge, to open at the very feet of the Germans when "Zero" hour struck. ...

Through these subways ... passed every man of the tens of thou-sands who played a part in the battle. ... Sleep, in the rare moments throughout the hectic week ... was so only if one stood flat against the wall. ...

Meanwhile, as night wore on, the historic Easter Monday was dawning to snow and wind and rain. ... So we caught him [the enemy] napping his soundest, and for this occasion the elements, foul as they were for us, were fouler for him. ...

.... Our barrage which opened at 5.30 a.m., involved a gun to every 25 yards of the Bosche front, and was regular as a clock and as sweet as a sewing-machine. Nothing human could stand against it, and, combined with the gale, it sent the Hun helter-skelter for cover. ...

So, from Monday's dawn till midnight of Friday the battle raged. ... Throughout the week, with us had raged the storm, at times a blizzard strength, so that hourly the toil had become harder, and snow and mud made every step purgatory. But we were masters of our fate, filthy but triumphant, and had scored a signal victory as ever crowned Canadian arms.[7]

In the victory at Vimy Ridge, Canadians suffered 10 602 casualties—3 598 of them fatal—between April 9 and April 14.

King George V sent congratulations: "Canada will be proud that the taking of the coveted Vimy Ridge has fallen to the lot of her troops."

ANOTHER SIDE OF WAR

...The Y.M.C.A. stalls were a blessing almost beyond appreciation. On any night in the forward fighting area ration parties going up to the firing trenches and working parties coming out could be found cursing the blackness, and the wet, and the cold. To the east, flares marked the German line: to the west, unseen in the darkness, were the heights that Canada had won in so much hard fighting. And those who tramped forward or back, be they from batteries or battalions, pioneers or engineers, wore their steel helmets, and their gas masks were at the alert. It was dreary, cheerless work until, in a jog in some communication trench or by some ruined house in a wrecked village, the dimmest of dim lights would make them welcome and they would hasten forward where a subdued chorus of voices told them of hot tea and coffee. It would be one of the advanced posts of the "Y" with its free hot drinks and its biscuits, cigarettes, gum, chocolate, and other things to ease the mind and please the belly....

The air aces

The airplane, invented only a few years before, was an important weapon in World War I. Throughout the war, airplanes were used for reconnaissance; that is, scouting the positions of enemy armies. Bombing and machine gun attacks on enemy trenches became more common as the war progressed. Yet duels in the air became a spectacular part of the conflict in the latter part of the struggle. Among the most famous of the fighter pilots were the German Baron von Richthofen ("the Red Baron") and the Canadian W. A. "Billy" Bishop.

THE RED BARON'S LAST FLIGHT

By April, 1918, Richthofen had shot down 80 Allied planes and his red triplane and the Richthofen "Flying Circus" of fighter planes were a constant menace. On April 21, a "dogfight" over the Somme River between a British patrol and the attacking Germans turned out to be the Red Baron's last fight. A young Canadian pilot, Lieutenant May, was heading away from the fighting when suddenly he found a red triplane on his tail:

May went through every manoeuvre that he could think of in his efforts to get out of the way of Richthofen's fire, but the German kept after him until they were low down over the River Somme itself, and almost over the trenches of our front lines, which were occupied by the Australians. Seeing the fix that May had got into, Brown* dived to the rescue, and the German pilot was caught in the hazardous position of being fired at, low down, by a Camel from above him and by machine-gunners from the ground.

*the patrol leader—also a Canadian

Apparently unaware that Brown was on top of him, Richthofen was concentrating on trying to shoot down May. He had to his credit by then eighty of our aircraft destroyed, the last two of which had been Camels that he had shot down only the day before. Brown opened fire and scored an immediate hit. Richthofen's triplane seemed to falter in the air, and then it fell in a clumsy way to a very rough landing in a field just behind our lines. The close proximity of the crashed aircraft to the lines brought it under artillery fire from the Germans, but the Australians nevertheless managed to get to the wrecked machine, and they found that the pilot was Richthofen. He was already dead when they got his body out of the cockpit: one bullet from Brown's fire had passed clean through his chest, and it must have killed him instantly.[8]

THE FEARLESS CANADIAN

W. A. "Billy" Bishop was so valuable as an instructor for the Royal Air Force that he was frequently away from the actual fighting. Yet his*

*Plans to establish a separate Canadian Air Force were not completed until after the war.

163

Billy Bishop

brilliance as a fighter pilot is shown by his record of 72 enemy planes destroyed, many of them in the most daring fashion. He once singlehandedly attacked a German airdrome (June 2, 1917) and shot down three planes taking off to intercept him. In recognition of his service, Bishop received virtually all possible honours awarded by the British and French governments. The official announcement of one such honour, the Distinguished Flying Cross (April 3, 1918), indicates his accomplishments:

"A most successful and fearless fighter in the air, whose acts of outstanding bravery have already been recognized by the awards of the Victoria Cross, Distinguished Service Order, Bar to the Distinguished Order and Military Cross.

"For the award of the Distinguished Flying Cross now conferred upon him he has rendered signally valuable services in personally destroying twenty-five enemy machines in twelve days—five of which he destroyed on the last day of his service at the front.

"The total number of machines destroyed by this distinguished officer is seventy-two and his value as a moral factor to the Royal Air Force cannot be overestimated."[9]

A visit to one of the divisional training schools would reveal two large sheds marked with the red triangle. The first would contain the canteen, reading-room, library, writing, and lounge rooms. It formed part of the educational system and such large signs as the following were prominent:

SPEND AN HOUR IN THE LIBRARY.
RATIONS FOR THE MIND.
FICTION.
SCIENCE.
CIVICS.
AGRICULTURE.
BUSINESS.

DON'T STARVE MENTALLY.
TAKE IN THE TALKS GIVEN IN THE
CANTEEN LECTURE ROOMS.
AGRICULTURE.
THE HISTORY OF THE WAR.
CURRENT EVENTS.
POLITICAL PROBLEMS.
LITERARY READINGS.
SOMETHING EVERY NIGHT BETWEEN
7:30 AND 8.30.

The YMCA *at the front*

Special lectures were given on various questions. One series dealing with the war [included such topics as]

BLACK 1915—FIGHTING FOR TIME.
TURNING OF THE TIDE.
WAR AIMS AND THE FUTURE.

On an average from two hundred to two hundred and fifty men a night attended these lectures. . . . [10]

THE UNIVERSITY OF VIMY RIDGE

With so many varied duties to relieve the terrible routine of the war, the Canadian Corps, in the winter of 1917-18, also established the University of Vimy Ridge, an educational institution unique, not only in Canadian history, but in the battle history of the world. The establishment of the university was officially sanctioned by the Corps Commander in December and the 3rd Canadian Division was selected to test the educational scheme, with the understanding that if the experiment proved successful, the activities of the university would be extended to other divisions and embrace all ranks and all services.

———————

[The purpose of the university was] "not only to relieve the men from the monotony of the daily routine, but, as well, in some measure, to equip men for greater efficiency in business, the professions, agriculture, and the other great industries of the Dominion."[11]

Over the top at the Somme

The year 1918 was a fateful one. The United States, having finally entered the war officially in 1917, was preparing to throw its weight behind the Allied war effort. Yet Russia, ravaged by revolution, had withdrawn from the war and relieved Germany of pressure on its eastern front. Consequently, Germany planned a powerful offensive, hoping to defeat the Allies before the full strength of the Americans could be effective.

While Canadians were not directly involved in breaking the German offensive, they helped spearhead the Allied counter-offensive. From August, 1918, the Canadian Corps were involved in almost continuous frontline action until the end of the war. The Canadians captured town after town from the Germans, and by November 11—Armistice Day, the day Germany surrendered—they had pushed through northern France and into Belgian territory. Canadian troops then crossed into Germany and shared in the Allied occupation while the peace treaties were being negotiated.

Canadians on the home front

Great changes had taken place. The emotions of the people were deeply stirred. The quiet Victorian life of 1914 had become the turbulent atmosphere of war by the end of 1915, a year that witnessed the extention of the world struggle. A drastic change had also taken place in urban and rural Ontario. The comfortable, satisfying old life had become one of wartime dangers, sorrow and exigencies. The clouds hung low, and while the people hoped against hope

The Russian Revolution, threatening for more than a decade, finally erupted as the country suffered the strains of war. The will of the Russian armies broke under the combined pressure of German armies and the actions at home of anti-government forces—especially the Bolsheviks, led by Vladimir Lenin. The Bolsheviks, or Communists, had organized the overthrow, capture and execution of the Czar and his supporters. Having seized power, the Communists made a deal with Germany in order to strengthen their position at home.

166

Those they left behind

BREAKING THE NEWS

One of the busiest parts of government was the Casualty Branch. It had the grim task of notifying relatives of people wounded, killed or missing in action:

"They have . . . been trained to the necessity of breaking the news gently to the next of kin. The feelings of the relatives of the dead heroes therefore have the first consideration when casualties are being handled by the staff. In almost every instance the cablegrams reporting casualties reach the Record Office after 6 p.m. Every effort is made to send out all notices the same evening, but all telegraph companies have been instructed that no telegram reporting a casualty is to be delivered to a bereaved home after 9 p.m., and that no charge whatever is to be made for delivery of the message. So far as possible no information relating to a casualty is communicated to the public press until the next of kin has received notification of same, or every source of information regarding the whereabouts of the next of kin has been exhausted."[12]

THE WHITE FEATHER

As part of the campaign to raise volunteers, recruiting leagues were formed. Young women were encouraged to present men in civilian clothes with white feathers, and others spoke at public meetings:

"Mrs. Grace McLeod Rogers, the Canadian authoress, was another woman who did her bit in speaking. At St. John on Feb. 28 she deprecated so-called Patriotic dances and referred to the effect these social gatherings had on "the young men who were there in their silk hose and patent slippers, while other boys at the Front were standing on guard all through the night knee deep in water." From the Citizens' Recruiting League of Saskatoon at this time (Mar. 11) went out 10,000 circulars signed by the mothers and wives of local men who had enlisted, urging the social boycott of the slacker—dealing with "the man who prefers to allow others to fight for him so that he may pursue a comfortable occupation, the man who is influenced by the selfish appeal either of mother or wife, the man who claims his business would go to pieces without him, and the others—call them what you may. You entertain these wretched apologies in your homes, you accept their donations, their theatre tickets, their flowers, their ears. You go with them to watch the troops parade. You foully wrong their manhood by encouraging them to perform their parlour tricks while Europe is burning up."[13]

Norman Bethune

Norman Bethune, a Canadian, later became a hero to the Chinese for his medical work during their struggle with invading Japanese armies. In the first weeks of World War I he had joined the Canadian army and served in the medical corps. After being wounded in France, he was sent home to Canada and discharged. Even so, the following anecdote shows how he was affected by the "white feather" technique:

Later that spring [1917], a young girl he did not know stopped him on a Toronto street and asked why he was not serving in the trenches in Europe. Before he could answer, she had pinned the white feather of cowardice to his jacket. Within a month he had applied to and was accepted by the Royal Navy as a Surgeon Lieutenant in Chatham Hospital, England."[14]

FARMING OR FIGHTING?

In his novel, Grain, *Robert J. C. Stead describes the dilemma facing many young Canadian men as the war continued. Gander Stake, the main charac- ter, is torn between what his girl friend, Josephine Burge, wanted him to do and what he thought he wanted to do:*

With the outbreak of war Jo wondered whether Gander would enlist. Nothing was further from her hopes than that anything should happen to Gander, but in those early stages the risk of casualty was considered small. The whole neighbourhood shared . . . [the] opinion that the war would be over in three months, but to wear a uniform and march away with bands playing was an heroic gesture. . . . It was yet too early in the struggle to see any- thing heroic in raising wheat. Jo was proud of Gander, but she was not blind to his defects. He was awkward; he was shy; the bound- ary of his world was little further than his father's farm. Enlistment would change all that. Like any honest girl, she was not satisfied that she alone should be proud of Gander; she wanted other people to be proud of him. She wanted to see the stoop taken out of his back, the hitch out of his gait, the drag out of his legs. Then, when the papers began to glare with reports of atrocities in Belgium, she wanted the heroic in Gander to well up and send him rushing to arms, to the defence of womankind, to the defence of Josephine Burge! Gander's heroism did nothing so spectacular. He went on working fourteen hours a day in the harvest field, associating with his father a little more closely than before, and trying to keep the war out of his mind.

. . . He was not lacking in courage or in a spirit of readiness to defend his home; if an enemy battalion had appeared on the road allowance that skirted his father's farm Gander would have faced them singlehanded with his breech-loading shotgun. He might even have marched into Plainville to resist their landing in his market town. But Belgium? Gander was unable to visualize a dan- ger so remote.[15]

that this dreadful war would soon pass away such was not to be. Ahead were the great battles of 1916, 1917 and 1918 with their massive casualty lists. The times ahead were to be filled with grave perils, difficulties and baffling decisions.[16]

Canadians entered the war with patriotic enthusiasm, prepared to postpone normal living and make sacrifices in order to defeat the enemies of the British Empire, whom they also believed to be the enemies of freedom and decency. But the war did not end in three or four months, as expected. It dragged on for months, then years. The unity that had once prevailed among Canadians began to crack.

The government of Sir Robert Borden found itself under mounting pressure over its handling of the war effort. Charges of corruption and graft in the granting of contracts filled the air. A particular target was Sam Hughes, the minister of militia. Accused of awarding profitable deals to friends, and notorious for quarrels with his colleagues in government, Hughes was forced to resign in 1916.

Wartime production

As a primarily agricultural country, Canada made important contributions to the Allied war effort in the form of food supplies.

FOOD DONATIONS

At the outset of the war, Canadian governments responded to the threat of food shortages in Great Britain. As an initial gift, the Canadian governments sent the following:

Canadian Government: 98,000,000 lbs. of flour.
Alberta: 500,000 bushels of oats.
Nova Scotia: 1,000,000 tons of coal.
Quebec: 4,000,000 lbs. of cheese.
Ontario: 250,000 bags of flour.
Prince Edward Island: 100,000 bushels of oats.
Saskatchewan: 1,500 horses.
New Brunswick: 100,000 bushels of potatoes.
Manitoba: 50,000 bags of flour of 98 lbs. each.
British Columbia: 25,000 cases of canned salmon.[26]

As the months passed, voluntary donations by private organizations continued, but the demands of the war were so great that government efforts had to be coordinated. Thus the Food Control Board was set up to organize the production and shipment of supplies on a massive scale.

More dramatic was Canada's production of hardware for the

The Ross rifle

Canadian soldiers were originally equipped with rifles made in Canada, but not long after the Battle of Ypres they were issued the British-made Lee-Enfield rifles:

There had been many complaints on the part of the troops about the Canadian Ross rifle. Excellent though it was as a target rifle, the Ross was sadly deficient as a service weapon; and on the battlefields of Ypres and Festubert, no less than 3,000 men had thrown away their Ross rifles and armed themselves with British weapons. It was for this reason that the changeover was officially made. A few Ross rifles were, however, retained as snipers' weapons.[17]

The Conscription issue

Yet the most pressing demand of the war would not pass away with the resignation of a minister or any other action within Canada. Because of the terrible casualty rate on the European battlefields, the demand for manpower rose sharply. By late 1916, volunteers were no longer enough.

Conscription, unthinkable to Canadians short years before, began to gain public support, at least among many English Canadians. They identified with Britain. They saw a threat to Britain as equivalent to a threat to Canada itself. Germany was the enemy, to be defeated at whatever cost. French Canadians, though many had enlisted from the first weeks of the war, had a different opinion. Cut off from France for 150 years and lacking sentimental attachment to Great Britain, French Canadians felt somewhat isolated from Europe's tragedy. Influential speakers, like Henri Bourassa* had restrained themselves at first but eventually they were provoked to declare their opposition to Canadian participation in the fighting.

*See Chapter 6, page 184 for Bourassa's long-standing opposition to entanglement in European affairs.

Bourassa and his supporters had plenty of ammunition for their position. In 1913, the Ontario Department of Education laid down Regulation 17, denying the use of French as a language of instruction in the province's primary schools. Manitoba, in 1916, abolished French, which had been provided for in the creation of Manitoba as a province. The campaign to encourage French Canadians to enlist was vigorous, but once they had joined the army, they were scattered among English-speaking units.* That a relatively small number of French Canadians were appointed as officers was seen as discrimination. French-Canadian critics of the war effort could ask: Why fight for a future dominated by English Canadians? To English Canadians, Quebec's feelings of alienation could be interpreted as a failure to carry out obligations, even as disloyalty.

*An exception was the Royal 22nd Battalion—the "Vandoos" (from vingt-deuxième)—which established a reputation for valour under officers like Major George Vanier.

In February, 1917, Borden went to the Imperial Conference in Britain. There he was subjected to considerable pressure to adopt conscription, the only way, it was argued, to replace the heavy losses suffered by the Canadian Corps. In Canada, agitation for conscription increased. In the spring of 1917, Borden invited Laurier and the Liberals to join in a union-coalition-government. However, Laurier would not agree to imposing conscription without a referendum or an election, and thus refused Borden's proposal.

Events moved swiftly in the summer of 1917. Conscription, in the form of the *Military Services Act*, was introduced in June and passed in August. This split the Liberal Party, many of whose English-speaking members voted with the Conservative government.

The Conservatives followed up their advantage with the *Military Voters Act*, giving the vote to all men and women serving in the armed forces, and denying it to **conscientious objectors**. Another measure, the *Wartime Elections Act*, gave the vote to the wives, widows, mothers, sisters and daughters of Canadians serving overseas. Citizens from enemy countries who had been naturalized since 1902 were denied the right to vote in the wartime election. Since the Conservatives now appeared as the patriotic party, they stood to gain in the upcoming election.

Emotions were running high, and the country was split along racial lines. French Canadians denounced conscription as a conspiracy to force their young people into foreign wars. English Canadians, who believed French Canadians were not "pulling their weight", generally backed conscription as a way to equalize Canadian sacrifice in defence of freedom. Though there were exceptions on both sides, these were ignored in the irrational atmosphere of the time, and Canada was deeply divided.

Those who refuse to fight on the grounds that war is contrary to their religious and/or moral principles.

Many Canadians, English as well as French, opposed conscription as an instrument of injustice. Workers believed they were being forced to make sacrifices, even to give their lives, while businessmen made profits from contracts to produce war materials. Farmers often complained that as sons left for war, family farms suffered.

Election propaganda at the front, 1917

Under normal conditions, a federal election would have been required, under the British North America Act, in 1916. Borden secured the agreement of the Liberals to petition Britain for a one-year extension to the life of Canada's Parliament. Yet Sir Wilfrid Laurier, still the Liberal leader, was finding his position increasingly awkward. How much longer could he cooperate with the ruling Conservatives without appearing to support their policies, which increasing numbers of French Canadians believed were anti-French?

The depth of anti-
Conservative feeling was
borne out in Quebec in the
1921 election, the first one
after the war. The new
Conservative leader was
Arthur Meighen who, as a
member of Borden's cabinet,
had been closely identified
with the pro-Conscription
movement. The Conservatives
won only four seats of the
province's sixty-five seats in
the House of Commons.

Sir Wilfrid Laurier tried to occupy a middle ground. He contended that conscription would drive French Canadians into the arms of political extremists, and proposed a nation-wide referendum so that all Canadians could express their views. When the Borden government decided to proceed with conscription, however, it had the support of English-speaking Liberals, who joined the Conservatives in a Union Government. In the election of December, 1917, the "Win the War" slogan of the Union coalition resulted in 153 seats to the 82 elected by the "Laurier Liberals".

Conscription was promptly enforced, and close to 100 000 men were called up. The Conservative party could claim that its policy was a success, in spite of the many who were granted exemptions on medical or other grounds. But the bitterness in Quebec, where anti-draft meetings and riots took place, was to remain long after the war. Although the Liberals would eventually regain English-speaking support, the Conservatives were remembered by French Canadians as the party who forced them to support a hated war against their will.

Whether conscription was worth the price of a divided nation was a debatable question. Canada gained much needed manpower for its war effort, but the feelings of hostility between French and English Canadians were to linger for many years.

THE 1917 CONSCRIPTION ISSUE

Supporters of Conscription

Prime Minister Borden addressed the House of Commons:

We have four Canadian divisions at the front. For the immediate future there are sufficient reinforcements. But four divisions cannot be maintained without thorough provision for future requirements. . . . I think that no true Canadian, realizing all that is at stake in this war, can bring himself to consider . . . any suggestion for the relaxation of our efforts. . . .

All citizens are liable to military service for the defence of their country, and I conceive that the battle for Canadian liberty and autonomy is being fought today on the plains of France and of Belgium. . . . The time has come when the authority of the state should be invoked to provide reinforcements necessary to maintain the gallant men at the front. . . . Therefore it is my duty to announce to the House that early proposals will be made to provide by compulsory military enlistment on a selective basis such reinforcements as may be necessary to maintain the Canadian army in the field. . . . The number of men required will not be less than 50 000 and will probably be 100 000. . . . [18]

J. A. M. Armstrong, Conservative M.P. for North York, June 21, 1917:

Why is conscription necessary at this time? I do not wish to be offensive, and as far as possible I shall avoid any acrimonious remarks, but I believe in calling a spade a spade, and in justice to the rest of Canada, I must say that the reason why conscription faces us today is because French Canada has failed to do its duty.[19]

Rev. S. D. Chown, General Superintendent of the Methodist Church of Canada, wrote in support of the Union Government and conscription a few days before the election of 1917:

To me it is as clear as the day that if we defeat conscription we cannot possibly get the last available man and fulfil our promise to Great Britain. . . .

. . . I believe . . . that under any conditions it [conscription] is the fairest, most democratic, most expeditious and least expensive method of raising an army in this country: and under present conditions it is the only possible way of fulfilling our obligations to Christian civilization. I also believe that socially considered it is the most moral and profoundly religious method of doing our national duty. . . . [20]

Opponents of Conscription

Henri Bourassa's stand against conscription:

It is the exact truth. All Canadians who want to fight conscription . . . must have the courage to say and repeat everywhere: *"no conscription! no enlistment: Canada has done enough."*

Henri Bourassa

Another question arises with regard to the fairness of our allies: *How many soldiers would France, and even England, send to America if Canada were attacked by the United States?*

What England needs most are not soldiers, but bread, meat, and potatoes.

Another measure of conscription, which would be vital long before conscription itself . . . [is conscription] of capital and industry. . . .

It is useless to disguise the truth: *two million French-Canadians are united against conscription. . . .* [21]

Laurier in the House of Commons, June 18, 1917:

. . . The law of the land . . . declares that no man in Canada shall be subjected to compulsory military service except to repel invasion or for the defence of Canada.

The law of the land gives power to the Government to repel invasion— that is what I understand by "the defence of Canada."[22]

Laurier on conscription, from his election address, November 4, 1917:

...It is a fact that cannot be denied that the voluntary system, especially in Quebec, did not get a fair trial...it is no answer to say as is now often said, that we must have Conscription or "quit". ...Australia rejected Conscription and Australia did not "quit". Australia is still in the fight under the voluntary system. . . . [23]

Fernand Villeneuve, a very young man, gave this advice to the crowd at an anti-draft meeting at Lafontaine Park, Montreal, on August 8, 1917:

If a recruiting officer comes to you do not be afraid to give him a threshing, and if you have anything to shoot with don't be afraid to use it.

And on August 9, 1917:

It is not out of fear that the French-Canadian is opposed to Conscription. It is out of love for our country and hatred for England.[24]

Another View on Conscription
Premier Brewster of British Columbia expressed his view in a letter, August 23, 1917:

We may as well face the fact that in this western Province the wealthy classes and the big business interests in the East are perfectly willing to see the poor man put all his capital, that is to say, his blood and sinews on the altar to aid in winning the war, but unquestionably is putting up a strenuous fight to block every organization and legislative procedure that would entail equivalent sacrifices of conscription of wealth and material resources. . . . I am of the opinion that if steps are taken to enforce the conscription of manpower alone, it will be met with resistance and in many parts of Canada we shall see exhibitions of violence and possibly bloodshed, with other consequences too serious to contemplate with any measure of complacency, although I am a firm believer in the principle of selective conscription.[25]

1. Which of the arguments for or against conscription do you find most convincing? Why?
2. What facts would help you to look at the arguments more critically?
3. When people feel very emotional about a situation, should they allow their feelings to determine their actions? Why or why not?
4. What are the advantages of using reason in trying to resolve a conflict? What are the difficulties?

war. Under the direction of the Munitions Board and other agencies, Canada produced guns, shells, ships and other vital supplies. Companies with no experience in producing war products acquired the needed skills and converted their factories, with the result that Canada had a multi-million-dollar war industry by 1918.

Besides the effects on manufacturing,* war-time demands gave a great boost to Canada's natural resource industries. Exports of wheat and flour, already high compared to the decade before, doubled in value. Meat became an important export, as did lumber and wood pulp. Mining expanded, as the manufacture of munitions opened up a new market for nickel and other minerals, and as more advanced processing techniques were invented.

*See the table on page 144 for the difference in value of pre-war and post-war production.

VALUE OF CANADIAN EXPORTS FOR THE YEARS 1910 TO OCTOBER 31, 1918[27]

Years.	Forest Produce	Manufactures	Mineral Produce	Miscellaneous	Grand Total
1906-10	40 929 799	30 224 459	35 943 527	1 197 112	252 160 069
1911	45 597 599	40 432 526	43 078 440	1 988 836	299 000 210
1912	41 104 887	42 508 985	41 510 582	1 101 122	307 716 151
1913	43 679 623	52 525 982	57 583 030	2 108 876	377 968 355
1914	43 386 687	67 602 238	59 233 906	3 052 354	455 437 224
1915	43 136 781	95 068 525	52 066 537	4 045 863	461 442 509
1916	51 698 284	250 052 223	73 919 398	8 314 501	779 300 070
1917	56 395 399	487 312 766	85 836 421	8 170 278	1 179 211 100
1918 (October 31)	148 407 269	519 681 332	145 030 298	525 091 384	1 338 210 271

Financing the war

Money to pay for Canada's war effort was raised in many ways. Private groups included the Canadian Patriotic Fund, a voluntary association dedicated to the relief of soldiers' widows and dependents. Other charitable groups, including the Red Cross, played a major role, especially in the early part of the war.

Yet costs were so high that only large-scale government action could begin to attack the problem. New forms of taxation were introduced. For example, *income tax* was introduced as a "temporary" measure and it has never been abolished. Profits on war contracts were taxed. A sales tax on consumer goods was introduced. Even so, the bulk of the expense had to be met by the sale of government bonds, which left the country with a huge national debt.

The Canadian National Railways (C.N.R.) was one of the by-products of World War I. The Canadian government took over the railways of Canada to provide transportation for goods and personnel. The privately-owned Grand Trunk and Canadian Northern railways were purchased from their owners and integrated with the Intercolonial to form the "people's railway", still government operated to this day.

TRADE UNIONISM AND THE WAR

After a decline in the early stages of the war, the labour movement gained momentum from 1916 on. It was widely believed that "Big Business" was

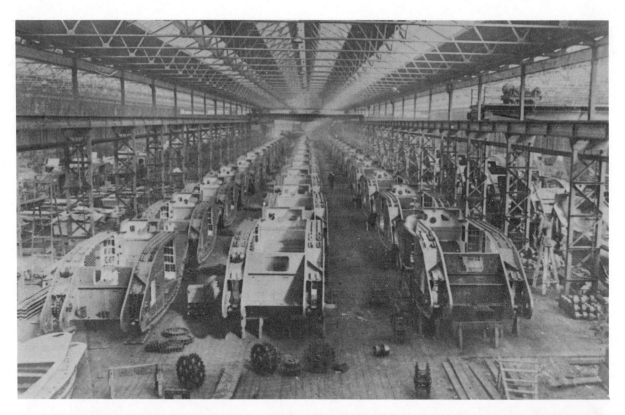

TOP: *Tank production.* BOTTOM: *Airplane production*

176

using the war to reap huge profits while workers were being sent off to die in battle. Thus membership in trade unions rose considerably, and social reform was urgently called for. Labour politicians were active at all levels of government:

One of the most colourful characters in the Canadian labour movement during the first half of this century was James Simpson. He was born in Lancashire in 1873, son of a stone-mason and staunch trade unionist who, angered by a cut in wages, brought his family to Toronto in 1887.

The 14-year-old Jimmy got his first job in a Cabbagetown factory where he worked 12 hours a day dipping bicycle parts in red paint. The turning-point in his career came when his Sunday school teacher had him apprenticed as a printer on the Toronto News. Six weeks later a strike took place and Jimmy was on the picket line. The strikers started their own paper which burgeoned into the Toronto Star.

Simpson worked for the Star for about 25 years, ten of them as City Hall reporter. He spent his evenings working for the labour movement and his Sundays preaching in the People's Church.

His municipal career began with his membership on the Toronto Board of Education from 1905 to 1910. In his final year he was Board chairman and prepared a report for a commission on technical schools. He made an unsuccessful try for Board of Control in 1911 but in 1914 was elected with labour backing on a platform including municipal hospital services, municipal coal and gas distribution and more parks. He was controller again in 1933 and in 1935 became Toronto's first labour mayor. . . .

He had three stretches as vice-president of the Trades and Labour Congress of Canada—1904 to 1909, 1916-1917 and 1924 to 1936. . . . [He was] an eloquent spokesman for the CCF [formed in 1933, a forerunner of the New Democratic Party].[28]

New roles for women

As the men went off to fight in Europe, more and more Canadian women were filling necessary jobs in factories at home. By the end of the war, 30 000 women had worked in munitions factories and thousands more in jobs not previously held by women. Out of necessity, the roles of women were changing, and attitudes were changing with them. Women began to realize that besides being housewives and mothers, they could fill other roles in society, and they began to do something about it. No one, including the most ardent suffragettes, wanted total equality with men, but women were beginning to be vocal about the contributions they could make to Canadian life.

One of the most important and successful areas of reform was

The fight for female suffrage in Manitoba was an "on-again, off-again" battle with Manitoba Premier T. C. Norris. When Norris would not keep his former commitment to female suffrage unless it was "popularly indicated," he got what he was looking for. Forty thousand signatures were his answer, but the most surprising petition was the one with 4,250 names gathered by 94-year-old Mrs. Amelia Burritt of Sturgeon Creek.[29]

Women played a major role in wartime munitions production.

politics, where people like Nellie McClung in Manitoba, Mrs. Gordon Grant in British Columbia, Professor Carrie Derick in Quebec and Mrs. W. F. Hatheway in the Maritimes, campaigned for female suffrage or giving women the right to vote. Manitoba, in 1916, became the first province to grant female suffrage, but other provinces followed suit, and in 1918, Parliament passed a Bill granting all women the right to vote federally.

Changes in Canadian life

*See Chapter 6, page 186.

Horrible as World War I had been, it produced a sense of pride among Canadians about the nation's war effort.* They had not suffered military attack, but they had come through a time of unprecedented challenge and strain. They had known the feelings of vengefulness toward the enemy, and directed some of it at "aliens"

178

On the job in a factory during the war

within the country, but they believed they had helped win "the war to end all wars." They had often been divided among themselves, yet they were confident of Canada's future.

Canada would never be quite the same. Industrialization had increased the nation's manufacturing capacity, contributed to the growth of urban centres, brought women in large numbers into wage-earning positions, and increased the size of the labour movement. The cost of living had nearly doubled since 1913, and there was nostalgia for pre-war days when people saw the future in terms of "Canada's century". The return to peacetime brought a resumption of efforts to achieve a better and more prosperous Canada. Canadians faced the future with hope but were not unaware of tensions in Canadian society which had been sharpened by the war. There would be many problems to be faced in the years ahead.

As part of the campaign to save food for the war effort, restaurant menus carried the following advice: "All persons in ordering their food ought to consider the needs of Great Britain and her Allies, and their armies, for wheat, beef, bacon, and fats, and the Canada Food Board desires the public to do everything in their power to make these commodities available for export by eating as little as possible of them, and by making use of substitutes, and avoiding waste."[30]

6

Canadian autonomy: independence Canadian style

"What is the difference between Dominion Day and Independence Day, between the First of July and the Glorious Fourth? . . . not much —only 48 hours."[1]

In the last few days of June, if you were to take note of news items having to do with the July 1st holiday, you would probably find some confusion over its name. Sometimes it is called Dominion Day, sometimes Canada Day, or sometimes simply "the July 1st holiday". There is even support for the idea of a "Canada Week". In 1969, the Canada Committee, a private organization, was incorporated to encourage Canadians across the country to organize festivities in honour of Canada's "birthday".

Why the confusion? Unlike most countries which were once part of empires, Canada does not celebrate an "independence" day. Canada did not achieve independence through revolution or any other dramatic action which could be associated with a particular day. By a series of steps occurring over several decades, Canada gained the control over her domestic and foreign affairs that resulted in nationhood. This process of evolution toward independence has been described as the achievement of Canadian autonomy.

Though the Centennial celebration of 1967 was considered a celebration of Canada's one hundred years as a nation, Canada was actually a British colony at the time of Confederation and for many decades afterward. While a colony is controlled to a certain extent by its parent country, the relationship between "mother country" and colony is subject to change. In the case of Canada, the powers of self-government were acquired one by one in such a way that eventual independence, either within some loose "family" framework or completely separate from Britain, seemed inevitable.*

Even before Confederation, Canadian colonies were granted responsible government in matters of internal concern. Then, after the formation of the Dominion in 1867, Canadian participation in the handling of its external affairs began to increase. Sir John A. Macdonald was included in the British delegation that made the Treaty of Washington with the United States after the American Civil War. Thereafter, Canadian representatives of both Liberal and Conservative governments had taken the initiative in seeking reciprocal trade agreements with the United States. But an actual treaty still required the official participation of the British foreign office in Washington.

*See, for example, the writings of Chester Martin and many others interpreting Canadian history prior to World War II.

Signing the Washington Treaty

The office of Canadian High Commissioner to London was created in 1880 to make discussion of the mutual interests of Great Britain and Canada easier. In 1887 and 1894, conferences of colonial prime ministers and British cabinet ministers signified that the colonies were "growing up". Their wishes were being considered before the British government introduced policies affecting all parts of the Empire.

Separation from Great Britain was *not* an objective of Canadian leaders. Whether of French or English descent, they professed their attachment to Britain and to British ideals of justice, social progress and liberty. French Canadians looked upon the imperial government,

Dominion Day celebrations in the West, c. 1905.

It was really the opening of the new race track we celebrated, and not Confederation.

From the "Grand" stand the scene was a motley one, but by no means unpicturesque. It presented a queer mix-up of homesteaders "spruced up" in their best things, lumber-jacks with river boots and gay sashes, English chappies in riding leggings and peaked caps, theological students from the East who have come up for the holidays to take our spiritual pulse, long-haired Indians, Doukhobors with flounced jackets and wide-seated trousers and Panama hats.

and such legislation as the British North America Act, as important to their survival on a continent where the overwhelming majority was English-speaking. Yet many Canadians, English as well as those of other backgrounds, expected that their country would keep moving in the direction of nationhood, and that independence would come some day in the future.

The attitudes of the British government for several decades had encouraged greater colonial freedom, which meant the cost to Britain of running and defending the colonies was less. By the 1890s, however, British attitudes began to change. A competition was underway with Germany, France and others for colonies around the world, particularly in Africa. In Britain there was renewed interest in the older, self-governing colonies, such as Canada. Bound more closely to Britain and subject to British control, these colonies would help give the British Empire an image of greater strength and unity in defence and world trade.

The rise of imperialist feeling was not confined to Britain. In Canada and the other colonies, such as Australia, which had large populations of British descent, there was much support for the idea of belonging to a global empire—perhaps the world's most powerful. The idea of Anglo-Saxon superiority appealed to people who preferred to be identified with a glorious empire rather than an obscure colony. Recent British immigrants, numbering in the hundreds of thousands at the turn of the century, and descendants of United Empire Loyalists, had strong feelings for England, the heart of the Empire.

The South African War

British pressure, personified by the Colonial Secretary, Joseph Chamberlain, posed a dilemma for the Laurier government almost from the time of its taking office. Coinciding with the "Diamond Jubilee" in London in 1897, Chamberlain planned a colonial conference. In the private meetings of the conference, Prime Minister Laurier faced for the first of many times, the British proposals for an imperial council which would involve the colonies more closely with the actions of Britain on the international scene, and for Canadian financial contributions to the support of the British navy. Laurier's response was a firm "No". He insisted that Canada had other priorities at home.

The British were not discouraged, however, as was proved by their actions at the time of the South African War (1899-1902). The war, a contest between British imperialism and Boer nationalism, would seem to have been an unlikely problem for Canada. The Boers, descendants of Dutch settlers who had arrived before the

Leaving for the Boer War

British, lived in the northern part of what is now the Republic of South Africa.* They had fallen under British political influence in the 1870s, but had been allowed to keep local self-government. However, fabulous discoveries of diamonds and gold attracted immigrants and huge investments from Great Britain. After a time, British citizens in the Boer territories claimed that the governments there were collecting heavy taxes and fees while refusing to grant any political rights. Empire-builders like Cecil Rhodes,* who was actively promoting British expansion in Africa, saw the opportunity for bringing the Boer territories under British control.

*Areas known as Transvaal and Orange Free State.

*His fortune established the fund for Rhodes scholarships.

Ironically for Canada, when the expected war did erupt in October, 1899, the Canadian government found itself in a difficult position. In the months before, Britain had been working through the Governor General of Canada, Lord Minto, to bring pressure on Laurier to provide Canadian troops in the event of a war in South Africa. A heated debate unfolded in Canada as Conservative leader, Sir Charles Tupper, scolded Laurier for withholding support from the British Empire in its hour of need. Many other English Canadians, especially newspaper editors, joined in. French Canadians, including Laurier's colleague in the cabinet, Israel Tarte, opposed participation in a war which did not involve Canada's interests.*

Laurier and his cabinet proposed a compromise that they hoped would assert Canada's autonomy and minimize the trouble between French- and English-speaking Canadians. Canada would not commit

*The situation was a new one for a Canadian Prime Minister, for never before had a Canadian government needed to make an official decision on the question of military support for Great Britain. There was no question of declaring war, since a colony had no such power. Officially, all parts of the Empire were at war when Britain declared war. But actual participation, and the amount of it, was a decision open to a colony.

Canadian troops in South Africa

Whatever the merits of the war, Canadian troops fought well. The names of Paardeburg, Mafeking and other battles in which they took part became household words among Canadians who were proud of their countrymen's exploits. English-Canadian boys played war games in which the heroes were the RCR's"—the newly formed Royal Canadian Regiment—and the enemy was led by Kruger, the hated symbol of the Boers.

an official force to a British war not directly involving the colony or a threat to Britain itself. However, in view of the number of Canadians who had volunteered for service in South Africa, the government would provide equipment and transportation for those who wanted to join the British army. The Canadian troops—some 8 000 enlisted—were to be organized in units to serve in British regiments, rather than attached individually as the Australians were.

Predictably the compromise did not prevent a division in public opinion. English Canadians charged Laurier with doing too little. French Canadians accused him of doing too much, of submitting to the wishes of the British. Henri Bourassa, the youthful grandson of Louis Joseph Papineau, left the Liberal Party to carry on an anti-Government campaign both in the House of Commons and outside.

BOURASSA ON THE SOUTH AFRICAN WAR

In a letter to Laurier in November, 1899, Bourassa explains his opposition to Canadian participation in the South African War:

.... Note that I am much less ferocious on this question of imperialism than you think. I have never been and I am not now in favour of independence—at least not for the moment and for a long time to come. It seems to me that we can remain in our present state of transition for some time yet. Chamberlain wants to get us out of that stage. That megalomaniac's fixed intention is to go down in history as the *Builder of the Empire*. He could well become the *loosener of the Empire*. . . . However, Chamberlain is not the Empire, nor even England, and I think that we ought to ponder the matter a bit before executing his orders. . . . [3]

LAURIER'S DEFENCE OF HIS ACTIONS IN THE BOER WAR CRISIS

Laurier answers Bourassa's charges that Canadian autonomy had suffered:

I put this question to my honourable friend. What would be the condition of this country today if we had refused to obey the voice of public opinion? It is only too true that if we had refused our imperative duty, the most dangerous agitation would have arisen, an agitation which, according to all human probability, would have ended in a cleavage in the population of this country upon racial lines. . . . [4]

Laurier did what he could to answer critics on both sides. He argued that the Canadian government had decided on its own policy, in response to wishes expressed by Canadian citizens, both those who supported the war as a duty Canada shared with the rest of the Empire and those who wished Canada to make its own choices in overseas affairs.

If the government's policy earned little praise, it was better received in all parts of Canada than its vocal critics predicted. The election of 1900 gave the Liberals an increased majority. Except for a slight drop in support from Ontario, the party had stronger representation from the various regions of the country.

By the end of the war in South Africa the Liberals' balancing act in the imperialist-nationalist debate appeared to have succeeded. The position that seemed acceptable to most Canadians at the time was that of moderate nationalism, and a gradual increase in Canada's autonomy *within* the British Empire. A Canadian could be proud of his country and still support its continuation as a part of the Empire. There were many respectable stations along the road from helpless colony to independent nation.

The naval issue

The naval issue may have started as a problem involving Canadian autonomy, but it ended when Canada and Britain were overtaken by World War I. The immediate questions of survival and mutual support in the face of "total war" took precedence over the long-term question of Canada's status in the Empire.

In the colonial conferences of 1902 and 1907, Laurier could successfully reject British proposals that might draw the colonies into formal obligations in imperial affairs, including financial support for the British navy. But by 1909, Great Britain and Germany were engaged in a naval-building race. A special conference of colonial delegates was called in London. Britain claimed that she needed financial help.

A contemporary cartoon dealing with the Naval issue

Without it, Germany's navy would soon be larger, and the whole Empire would be in danger. Laurier agreed to change his long-standing policy. The question was whether to donate money directly to the British Admiralty or to build a Canadian navy. Laurier chose the latter course.

The naval issue was a major controversy in the election of 1911. As expected, many English Canadians once more accused Laurier of being lukewarm toward Great Britain. They ridiculed his "tin pot navy". His critics in Quebec claimed that Laurier's policy was sacrificing Canadian autonomy, since Parliament would have the power to place the Canadian navy under British control in the event of a war.

Laurier and the Liberals were defeated after fifteen years in power. Their naval plan went down with them. The Conservatives' proposal was that Canada offer a grant of money toward construction of British ships, in return for some voice in imperial decisions about naval policy. But before this plan advanced very far, the Empire was at war, and Canada had other military responsibilities.

1. What are the differences between a colony and a nation?
2. There are limits of one kind or another on the actions a colony can decide to take for itself. What limits on the actions of a nation can you think of?
3. How important to a person's national identity are celebrations of major events in his country's past?
4. Do you think that patriotism is important? Do you think it is more important at some times than at others?

World War I: the birth of Canadian nationhood

One of the many effects of World War I on Canada was to create a feeling that the country had suddenly grown up. A new confidence and sense of destiny had emerged. Had not Canada shown a remarkable capacity for agricultural and industrial production? Had not Canadians felt a new awareness of the vastness of their country? Were not many sectors of society—women in general, wage-earners, western Canadians—thinking differently about their potential roles? And did not the thousands of young Canadians so recently dead and buried in Europe prove that the country had "paid the price in blood" for recognition as a nation?

Canadian political leaders reflected this new mood on two fronts in the country's external relations; first, with respect to Britain and, second, with respect to nations outside the Empire. During the war the British government had acknowledged the right of the Domin-

Two views of Canadian autonomy

The Conservative Party leaders—Sir Robert Borden, who retired in 1920, and his successor, Arthur Meighen—saw Canadian autonomy in terms of a stronger voice within the British Empire, rather than as a growing separation from Britain. They believed that Canada had secure control of its domestic affairs and could best handle its dealings with other countries through the Empire.

William Lyon Mackenzie King, grandson of the leader of rebellion in 1837, was skeptical and suspicious that Great Britain wished to use the Dominions as a continued source of her own power. Furthermore, King had seen the divisive effects of Canada's involvement in British and European affairs, and the damage done to the Liberal Party before and during the war. He saw himself in the image of Laurier, with his first duty being to maintain Canadian unity and his second to defend Canada's "sovereignty". In the election of 1921, his first as Liberal leader, he defeated Meighen and the Conservatives. The 116 seats won by the Liberals included all of Quebec's 65 seats.

On November 4, 1921, Meighen argued that Canada had achieved the ideal —nationhood within the British Empire:

By tradition, by the sense of common inheritance and of common ideals, the dominion of Canada aspires to one destiny, and one only—a destiny than which there is no nobler—nationhood within the British Empire. I am convinced there is no single thing more vital than that the British Empire, as at present constituted, should be maintained. We enjoy the fullest autonomy, and that autonomy is not challenged and never shall be challenged. For the maintenance of the British Empire as a league of autonomous nations there are common burdens that all must share, but these burdens are light and the advantages abundant, in comparison with either the burdens or the advantages of any other destiny that can be conceived. Sentiment and interest are in accord in upholding British connection.[5]

On October 8, 1923, at the Imperial Conference, Mackenzie King delivered his statement on Canada's position:

Canada is not putting forward any new principles.... Canada stands on the old principle of responsible democracy.... For seventy years our most honoured leaders have done what they could to develop the basic principle of responsible government, and to apply it in steadily increasing measure to the whole range of domestic and foreign affairs. . . . We believe that the decision of Great Britain on any important public issue, domestic or foreign, should be made by the people of Britain, their representatives in Parliament, and the Government responsible to that Parliament. So the decision of Canada on any important issue, domestic or foreign, we believe should be made by the people of Canada, their representatives in Parliament, and the Government responsible to that Parliament.[6]

1. With which position do you think you would have agreed had you lived in the 1920s? Why?

---

ions to a voice in imperial war policy. Furthermore, Britain conceded that changes would have to be made which would recognize the Dominions as "autonomous nations" once the war was over.

The Canadian prime minister, Sir Robert Borden, advanced the Canadian cause in this direction. He insisted on Canada's right to take part in the Paris Peace Conference at the close of World War I. Then Canada signed the resulting Treaty of Versailles (1919) as one of the countries which had helped bring about victory over Germany and its allies. When the League of Nations was formed at that same time, Canada joined as a member in its own right, rather than as a part of Britain's representation.

The Statute of Westminster, 1931

Following a decade in which several events led to Canada's taking on greater independence from Britain, the Statute of Westminster legally recognized the existence of the British Commonwealth of Nations in place of the old Empire. The British Crown, in the words of the preamble to the Statute, "is the symbol of the free association of the members of the British Commonwealth of Nations." No act passed by a Dominion Parliament was to be "void or inoperative" because it did not agree with the laws of England. Nor would any act passed by the British Parliament extend to any Dominion unless a Dominion so requested.

Nationhood within the British Commonwealth did not come about solely through the actions of Canada, but the Liberal government of Mackenzie King, which held office from 1921 to 1930, was instrumental. The Halibut Treaty of 1923 between Canada and the United States set a precedent for Dominions to conclude treaties without Britain's involvement. The "King-Byng Affair",* in which Mackenzie King used the election of 1926 to attack the Governor-General for meddling in Canada's political matters, set the stage for

*The names in the "King-Byng Affair" are those of Prime Minister Mackenzie King and the Governor General, Lord Byng. While his active part in Canadian life made Lord Byng memorable to followers of politics, a non-political contribution earned his wife special memory. The trophy awarded annually in the National Hockey League for the player best combining sportsmanship with effective play is the Lady Byng trophy.

188

the imperial conference later that year. One result was the reduction of the office of the Governor General. Thereafter he would be a ceremonial figure, representing the Crown, in no way acting as he had in the past as an agent of the British government.

DECEMBER 11: INDEPENDENCE DAY?

Historian Arthur Lower comments:

The [Imperial] Conference of 1926 solved the great problems of inter-imperial relationships in principle but left a good many details to be worked out. This process was completed at the next Conference, in 1930. . . .

   The Statute of Westminster came as close as was practicable without revolutionary scissors to legislating the independence of the 'Dominions'. There is good ground for holding December 11, 1931 as Canada's Independence Day, for on that day she became a sovereign state. . . . [7]

1. What reasons, historical, constitutional or other, can you think of or discover which may explain why Dec. 11 has not been favoured as "Canada's Independence Day"?

The Statute of Westminster did not grant sovereignty, in the sense of outright independence, to Canada and the other Dominions. The British Parliament could still pass laws on matters which concerned the entire Commonwealth, and, at least theoretically, could repeal the Statute of Westminster itself. Canada was not even given the power to make amendments, or changes, to the British North America Act of 1867, the heart of the Canadian constitution.

Yet the practice of Canadian independence was not in doubt in the years to follow, even though the Canadian government chose to endorse British policies in the late 1930s* and followed Britain's lead in 1939 in declaring war on Germany. Following World War II, legal autonomy was established, when appeals to the Judicial Committee were abolished in 1949 and the Supreme Court of Canada became the final court of appeal for Canada. From 1947, the words "Dominion of" were no longer used as part of the country's name, thus eliminating the reminder of Canada's former subordinate relation to Great Britain. Also in 1947 the Citizenship Act went into effect, defining Canadian citizenship for the first time.

There have been other changes, many of a symbolic nature, such as the proclamation on February 15, 1965 of Canada's national flag. One matter that has remained unresolved until the present is the Canadian constitution. Although in 1949 an amendment* to Section 91 of the British North America Act gave the Canadian Parliament

Canada's first diplomatic office in a foreign country was the legation established in the United States in 1927. Vincent Massey, who in 1953 became the first Canadian-born Governor General, was Canada's first representative in Washington.

*See pp. 197-198.

*See chapter 1, p. 29.

the power to change that Act on matters not affecting federal-provincial relations, an arrangement for making the British North America Act a Canadian statute was not soon in coming. Yet this is no longer a problem of Canadian autonomy, but rather one of federal-provincial relations.

CHRONOLOGY

1758	elected assembly in Nova Scotia
1840s	responsible government in provincial affairs in Nova Scotia, United Province of Canada
1867	Confederation
1879	National Policy
1880	formation of the Canadian High Commission in Britain
1887	the first colonial conference
1897	imperial preference; lower import taxes on British products
1899-1902	South African War (Boer War)
1909	Canada's Department of External Affairs established International Joint Commission set up to facilitate direct Canada—United States relations
1914-1918	World War I
1919	Canada as a member of the League of Nations
1923	Halibut Treaty
1926	King-Byng affair; status of Governor General reduced
1927	Canadian legation in Washington established
1931	Statute of Westminster
1947	Canadian Citizenship Act
1949	Supreme Court recognized as highest court of appeal
1965	Canada's national flag adopted

The Halibut Treaty

The halibut was an unlikely symbol of Canada's continuing struggle for independence from Great Britain. Yet Mackenzie King permitted no opportunity to pass. In the winter of 1923, Canada and the United States were arranging a treaty to regulate the halibut fishery on the Pacific Coast. According to the procedure normally followed at that time, the British Ambassador to the United States would become involved in the last stage of the negotiations. In other words, he would sign the treaty, making it official.

Mackenzie King had decided to eliminate even this last remaining British function in Canada's international trade agreements. The British Government was unaware that something was amiss until the last moment. Two days before March 2, 1923, the date set for the signing, King communicated the Canadian government's wish that its representative *alone* sign for Canada. Britain gave in, and Ernest Lapointe, Canadian minister of fisheries, signed the Halibut Treaty in the absence of British officials. It was the first treaty which Canada handled from start to finish.

Canada in the League of Nations

THE BASIC POLICY

Canada entered the League of Nations as an original member in spite of objections to individual representation for the Dominions. Some British leaders thought it would weaken the Empire by working against a common foreign policy. Other nations, such as France, feared that the Dominions would automatically follow the policy of the mother country and give the British Empire an exaggerated influence in the League.

Whatever the concerns of other countries, Canada soon demonstrated that its participation in the League of Nations would be cautious. There were several reasons for this. First, Canada was far removed from the traditional areas of military conflict, and therefore less likely than most countries to be interested in the "collective

The League of Nations

The League of Nations was created in the hope that the "Great War", as the war of 1914 to 1918 was then called, had truly been "the war to end all wars." Through the untiring efforts of Woodrow Wilson, President of the United States, terms providing for the League were included in the Treaty of Versailles in 1919. Over the objections of skeptical European leaders, an international organization dedicated to preserving world peace was born. Geneva, Switzerland, where the headquarters were to be located, was bound to be the centre of attention during some momentous events.

The League of Nations was based on the principle of collective security. All members were to be responsible for cooperating against the outbreak of war. Should the security of any member be threatened, the others were to assist in preventing armed conflict. Consultation, rather than the application of force, was to be the principal service which the League could provide. The International Court of Justice was set up as a world court for passing judgment on disagreements referred to it by League members. People around the world were hopeful that justice, not force, would prevail in international affairs, and that the League would be successful in achieving its goal of global disarmament.

The Covenant, or charter, of the League, to be realistic, had to provide at least some measures stronger than negotiation and judicial decisions. According to the controversial Article X, League members were called upon "to respect and preserve as against external aggression the territorial integrity and existing political independence of all members." Moreover, Article XVI stated that sanctions could be imposed on a member if it went to war for a reason other than to preserve its own security. This meant that the League had the authority to isolate a belligerent member from trade with the others in order to bring it to its senses.

The weaknesses of the League were evident to many from the beginning. There was little sign that nations would cooperate any more effectively than they had in the past. Old selfish ambitions had not died in the war just fought. In fact, the war had created new problems. Traditional powers such as France and Great Britain were still anxious to maintain world leadership. Not all nations were willing to join the new organization. No special military force was created to back up decisions made by the League.

1. Before 1914, a "balance of power" among the major nations was the basis of world order. Were the creators of the League being

unrealistic in assuming "collective security" to be a workable alternative? Why?

2. If you read p. 477 about the organization of the United Nations, what differences do you find between it and the League?

---

security" which the League was supposed to represent. Second, the United States' decision not to join the League was disturbing; Canada was watchful of any pressure to serve as a North American representative in commitments to the League. Third, successive Canadian governments recognized that their foreign policy would likely carry little weight without the backing of both Great Britain and the United States.

Canadian leaders, in other words, saw the League of Nations as an organization through which autonomy could be advanced, rather than as protection against aggression. As the prosperous years of the 1920s passed, Canadians seemed to enjoy the best of all possible worlds. While not as obviously following the path of "isolationism" chosen by the United States, Canada was content with its "fireproof house". Problems elsewhere in the world were not Canada's concern.

THE THREAT OF TOTALITARIAN AGGRESSION

Suffering in the grip of economic depression, the world was faced in the 1930s with another form of threat—aggression by totalitarian dictatorships. In countries where military groups gained control of government, they played on the nationalistic feelings of their citizens in preparing for the conquest of weaker neighbours. Wars of aggression, first by Japan and then by Italy and Germany, caught other major powers unprepared. As a result of their initial failure to respond, the democracies and the rest of the world were faced with the second global war in twenty years.

CANADA AND THE MANCHURIAN CRISIS

Japan opened the fateful decade of the 1930s with the invasion of Manchuria in northern China. This act of aggression in 1931 started a drawn-out conflict between Japan and China that eventually became part of World War II.

The League of Nations was caught in an embarrassing dilemma. The Asian rivals were both League members. The League waffled; it carried out investigations and invited Japan to accept some form of settlement. When Japan refused to cooperate, League members declined to step in or to cut off trade, although both were possible under the League's charter.

Canada was one of the original League members, and its right to act independently was recognized by Britain in the Statute of Westminster in 1931, the year of Japan's invasion of Manchuria. Yet Canada still followed Britain's lead in matters of foreign policy. Thus the Conservative government of R. B. Bennett went along with the hope of Britain and other major powers that Japan would halt its aggression when the League expressed its disapproval. It is debatable whether Canada was in a position to do otherwise.

By 1933, Japan had gone ahead with its takeover of Manchuria and created a "puppet state". Criticism of this action by the League led to Japan's decision to withdraw from the international organization. As did the major powers, Canada stood helplessly by.

Japan's defiance of the League of Nations was a bad omen. So was the failure of the world conferences on disarmament between 1932 and 1935. Through the League of Nations, peace-loving nations were trying to establish a workable set of rules and guidelines to encourage international cooperation and to settle conflicts without war. Some nations were making up their own rules, without regard for other nations.

CANADA AND THE ETHIOPIAN CRISIS

The spotlight in 1935 was not on Adolf Hitler, the dictator who was actively rebuilding Germany's military power, but on another European **despot**, Benito Mussolini. The Italian leader had become convinced that his country's future was best served by re-enacting the imperialist ambitions of ancient Rome. In the spring of 1935, from Italian colonies in North Africa, Mussolini launched his plan against the weak African nation of Ethiopia.

dictator

The subjects of Emperor Haile Selassie fought vainly to repel the conquest. The League of Nations moved to condemn yet another aggression by one member against another. Limitations on trade, which had not been applied against the more powerful nation of Japan, were voted in the hope of reducing Italy's ability to complete its plan. But the League did not go far enough in implementing a boycott of trade with Italy, and soon had to consider more drastic action if it wanted results.

Mussolini's war machine was dependent on supplies of imported oil. A total ban by the League on trade with Italy would very likely have forced its halt. Even Great Britain and France held back from so forceful a decision. But the Canadian representative, W. A. Riddell, proposed that oil be added to the list of economic sanctions against Italy. The Canadian government was in the process of changing hands, as Mackenzie King had just defeated R. B. Bennett in the election of October, 1935. Forced by circumstances to act on his own initiative, Riddell believed that his strong recommendation was a logical result of Canada's stand up to that point on the question of Ethiopia.

News of the "Canadian proposal", as the overseas press described it, ignited furious controversy in Canada. The most pointed opposition arose in Quebec, where sympathy for Italy, the home of the Pope, was very strong and where some charged that the League's pressure on Italy was a manoeuvre by Protestant, imperial Britain. Canadian public opinion was divided, and Mackenzie King's government feared taking a stand that might not be supported by the people. Neither Great Britain within the League nor the United States outside seemed likely to take the risks associated with real preventative steps against Italy. The Canadian prime minister, therefore, refused a leadership role for his country. Although insisting that Canada would co-operate in whatever decisions the League might reach, he declared that Riddell's proposal was not the policy of the Canadian government.

The major powers seemed to take their cue from Canada. Although it is likely they would have come to the same conclusions regardless, the proposed sanctions on oil were dropped. Whatever the explanation, the League of Nations had failed at its moment of greatest challenge. If a "paper tiger" like Mussolini could flout world opinion and feel confident in the act of forfeiting League membership, what might be the attitude of men heading a government equally militant but commanding far more power?

CANADA AND THE DISPUTE OVER ITALY'S AGGRESSION AGAINST ETHIOPIA

When the proposal of sanctions at the League of Nations was widely interpreted as a Canadian initiative, Mackenzie King promptly dismissed Riddell's action as a personal decision, and not the policy of Canada:

... What was my amazement when on reading a morning paper I found that Doctor Riddell at Geneva was reported to have proposed to add oil, coal, and steel to the list of commodities which by sanctions were to be prohibited from export to Italy. No instructions whatever had been sent to him authorizing anything of the kind ... word was immediately to be sent that no action of any kind was to be taken by Doctor Riddell without specific instructions from the government. I asked whether that communication had been sent, and was informed that it had been sent within an hour after receipt of the communication from Doctor Riddell. So that so far as the present administration is concerned I say we gave specific direction to Doctor Riddell that he was to do nothing in the matter of extending sanctions without express direction from the government itself.[8]

Members of the Mackenzie-Papineau battalion who fought in the Spanish Civil War

CANADA AND NAZI AGGRESSION

The nation with "far more power" was Nazi Germany. Defying the restrictive terms of the Treaty of Versailles (1919), Adolf Hitler had set about re-arming Germany. The year 1936 was fateful. After occupying the Rhineland, forfeited in 1919, Hitler made a treaty with Mussolini that established the "Rome–Berlin axis." The disapproval of the League of Nations seemed to have no effect in discouraging the ambitions of power-mad dictators.

Through 1937, the Nazis supported the Nationalists in the Spanish Civil War (1936-1939), perfected brutality as an instrument of power within Germany, and plotted territorial expansion. Early in 1938, Austria succumbed to Nazi terror and was ruthlessly annexed by Germany. Hitler had satisfied himself that, with Italy as an ally and Great Britain and France standing back ostrich-like from the sorry proceedings, he had virtually a free hand in central Europe. Next he turned his attention to Czechoslovakia, where the population included a large German minority. The pretext he gave to the rest of Europe was his desire to unite the German-speaking peoples and to obtain *Lebensraum*—living space—for the growing population of Germany.

Germany's desire for expansion seems, looking back, to have been so clearly exposed by the fall of 1938 that no one could have failed to

TOP: *Adolph Hitler.* BOTTOM: *Neville Chamberlain returns from Munich proclaiming "peace in our time."*

recognize it. Great Britain and others did, in fact, begin to increase spending for rearmament. But the fear of war and its consequences was so deeply embedded in the thinking of most men that the most acceptable policy for a government to adopt was *appeasement*, to grant Hitler his demands and hope that his ambitions would soon be satisfied. Consequently, Great Britain and France signed an agreement at Munich in September, 1938. Germany could occupy the part of Czechoslovakia known as Sudetenland provided that the rest of the country remained free.

Neville Chamberlain, Prime Minister of Great Britain, returned home from Munich to receive the acclaim of his citizens for having won "peace in our time". The relief which people felt in the democracies was short-lived, however, as Hitler followed up his success by seizing the remainder of Czechoslovakia early in 1939. The hopeless policy of appeasement was finally abandoned as the rest of Europe scrambled to prepare for the war that most men had refused even to contemplate. Following the signing of a non-aggression pact with the Soviet Union in August, Hitler sent his armies rolling into Poland on September, 1, 1939. Two days later Great Britain and France declared war on Germany.

Since regaining office in 1935, Mackenzie King had done little to arouse Canadians to serious thinking about foreign affairs. As crisis followed crisis in Europe, King remained evasive about the government's plans in the event of a major war. With a regularity that struck his critics as monotonous, the prime minister repeated his round-about replies that Canada was a peace-loving nation and could contribute little to resolving foreign disputes by pronouncing judgments on them. Canada would approach each situation on its merits and, should a case arise where the country was confronted with the choice of peace or war, "Parliament would decide."

The nearest the Canadian government came to a declaration of policy was the support given at the Imperial Conference in 1937 to Great Britain's strategy of appeasement. Following the Conference, King made a trip to meet Adolf Hitler and came away convinced that the German leader was not a man to fear as an aggressor. Even when Hitler's behaviour clearly became a menace, King clung desperately to the notion that peace could still be preserved.

King's dilemma was a product, in large part, of his fear that a clear-cut policy might cause a serious division in Canadian public opinion. Remembering the tragic conflict between French-speaking and English-speaking Canadians during World War I over conscription and other issues, King was wary of making any commitments that might lead to another domestic feud. Preserving national unity was the responsibility the prime minister placed above all others. Canada's best hope for continued peace within the country was to avoid involvement in an overseas war. If a war did erupt and Canada's future was clearly at stake, Canadians would forget their differences and meet the challenge in a common spirit of determination.

KING'S STATEMENT TO THE HOUSE OF COMMONS ON CANADIAN FOREIGN POLICY
On January 25, 1937, Mackenzie King stated Canada's foreign policy and praised Great Britain's appeasement policy:

What Britain has done to appease antagonisms in the last few years is something that the rest of the world hardly begins to appreciate. What, I wonder, would be the condition of Europe to-day if Britain had not endeavoured, as she has at every moment, to avert or circumscribe conflict? She has been the great pacifier.[9]

KING CONGRATULATES CHAMBERLAIN ON THE MUNICH AGREEMENT
Mackenzie King showed the false optimism shared by many in the Western world when he congratulated the British Prime Minister on concluding the ill-fated Munich agreement with Adolf Hitler in September, 1938:

The heart of Canada is rejoicing tonight at the success which has crowned your unremitting efforts for peace. May I convey to you the warm congratulations of the Canadian people and with them an expression of their gratitude that is felt from one end of the Dominion to the other? My colleagues in the government join with me in unbounded admiration at the service you have rendered mankind. Your achievements in the past month alone will ensure you an illustrious and abiding place among the great conciliators which the United Kingdom, the British Commonwealth, and the whole world will continue to honour.[10]

Independence, whether it is achieved suddenly by dramatic events or gradually through a series of steps, can bring heavy responsibilities to a nation. Matters of trade, peace and war, human rights and other issues can involve life and death decisions affecting great numbers of people. Of course, becoming a nation is unlikely to mean the freedom to act on the world scene as if other nations did not exist.

In the 1930s, as in our own time, Canada belonged to a family of nations. Then, the family was clearly the British Commonwealth, the successor to the British Empire in which Canada had "grown up". New family ties, like those with the United States, were starting to form. But Canada remained identified with Britain, especially in the hazardous 1930s, as if independence had not been won. Within Canada, the British connection left little doubt about Canada's identity as a British Dominion. A royal tour, such as the one in 1939, was still likely to be a cause for more celebration than any national holiday. Canadians were reassured by belonging to the British family. The Royal Family symbolized the bonds among the members and a sense of solidarity in a dangerous world.

Families serve that kind of function for nations as well as for individual people. For children and adults alike, families can provide support, a sense of belonging, a feeling of worth and identity. Nations, like individuals, may have two kinds of families: the one they are born into and others they choose through marriage, friendship or other forms of association.

In the 1970s, what kinds of families does Canada belong to? The traditional family, the Commonwealth, links us to the past, to the British part of our heritage, and to other nations that made the change from British colony to self-governing nation. When Canadians refer to their American "cousins," they often are talking about the close ties with the United States. Along with the United States, Canada is a member of the North Atlantic Treaty Organization, formed after World War II primarily as a military alliance for the mutual defence of its members. In the United Nations, which includes almost all the nations of the world, Canada has been an active member. There are many more families, or international organizations, of which Canada is also a part.*

*See Chapter 13 for a more detailed account of Canada's relations with other countries.

As the circumstances of a person or nation change, needs may change as well. The value of one family may decrease, of another, grow. One of the characteristics of the modern world is the rapid rate and widespread nature of change. The Canadian nation, along with nations everywhere, can expect changes to continue in their family relationships. Perhaps the number one question is: Will the *family of man* become the most important one for all nations? Will the most important celebration in Canada and other nations in the future be "Spaceship Earth Day"?

1. Is it unrealistic to hope for a "family of man"?
2. Is there more hope in trying to improve relations among the different world "families"?

Developments in Canadian literature: 1920-1945

The period from World War I until 1945 was marked by Canada's direct involvement in international affairs and vast changes within the country itself. The literature of that period reflected the broadened Canadian experience. The effects of two world wars, the prosperous twenties and the terrible depression of the 1930s all made their mark on the short stories, poems and novels of our country.

Canadian literature mirrored both the personal and public triumphs and setbacks of its people. Poets like E. J. Pratt, A. J. M. Smith and Dorothy Livesay and novelists such as Frederick Philip Grove, Morley Callaghan, Mazo de la Roche and Martha Ostenso, wrote about the real world of wars, depression and hardship. Unlike their predecessors, the heroes and heroines of these works were not genteel, "larger-than-life", one-dimensional characters. Rather they were real people—priests, ex-convicts, farmers, mothers, fathers and children—normal people faced with the central social and moral problems of the times. Whether faced with temperance, prohibition and the jazz age of the 1920s or the winds, despair and collapse of dreams wrought by the Depression of the 1930s, the characters of Canadian literature showed a remarkable tenacity—a kind of "stick-to-itiveness" which would lift them out of this darkness to better times ahead. Whether they were writing about personal crises or social ones, Canadian authors handled this new material in an increasingly mature style and gave to their readers both pleasure and insight into Canadian life.

Literary Time Line

1921	Canadian Authors' Association established
1922	F. P. Grove, *Over Prairie Trails*
1923	Laura Salverson, *The Viking Heart*
1923	Mazo de la Roche, *Possession*
1924	F. P. Grove, *Settlers of the Marsh*
1927	Mazo de la Roche, *Jalna*
1934	Morley Callaghan, *Such Is My Beloved*
1936	F. R. Scott (ed.) *New Provinces*
1937	M. Callaghan, *More Joy in Heaven*
1939	Anne Marriott, *The Wind Our Enemy*
1941	Hugh MacLennan, *Barometer Rising*
1941	Sinclair Ross, *As For Me and My House*
1942	Earle Birney, *David and Other Poems*
1944	Hugh Garner, *The Storm Below*
1944	Dorothy Livesay, *Day and Night*

1945   F. R. Scott, *Overture*
1945   Irving Layton, *Here and Now*
1945   Hugh MacLennan, *Two Solitudes*

from THE WIND OUR ENEMY
The prairies in the 1930s suffered a double disaster depression and drought.
In this poem, the poet vividly describes the effects of the wind and drought on
both the physical environment and on the people's spirits.

IX
The sun goes down. Earth like a thick black coin
Leans its round rim against the yellowed sky.
The air cools. Kerosene lamps are filled and lit
In dusty windows. Tired bodies crave to lie
In bed forever. Chores are done at last.
A thin horse neighs drearily. The chickens drowse,
Replete with grasshoppers that have gnawed and scraped
Shrivelled garden-leaves. No sound from the gaunt cows.
Poverty, hand in hand with fear, two great
Shrill-jointed skeletons stride loudly out
Across the pitiful fields, none to oppose.
Courage is roped with hunger, chained with doubt.
Only against the yellow sky, a part
Of the jetty silhouette of barn and house
Two figures stand, heads close, arms locked,
And suddenly some spirit seems to rouse
And gleam, like a thin sword, tarnished, bent,
But still shining in the spared beauty of moon,
As his strained voice says to her, 'We're not licked yet!
It must rain again—it *will*!! Maybe—soon—'. . . . [11]

from BAROMETER RISING
Halifax, Nova Scotia, is the setting for this novel, and the atmosphere of the
city is an important influence on the story. The time is World War I, and a
central incident in the plot is the explosion which results from the collision of
two ships in Halifax harbour. This passage talks of some of the effects.

Three forces were simultaneously created by the energy of the exploding ship, an earthquake, an air concussion, and a tidal wave. . . .

When the shock struck the earth, the rigid ironstone and granite
base of Halifax peninsula rocked and reverberated, pavements split
and houses swayed as the earth trembled. Sixty miles away in the
town of Truro windows broke and glass fell to the ground, tinkling
in the stillness of the streets. . . .

The pressure of the exploding chemicals smashed against the
town with the rigidity and force of driving steel. Solid and un-
breathable, the forced wall of air struck against Fort Needham and
Richmond Bluff and shaved them clean, smashed with one gigantic

blow the North End of Halifax and destroyed it, telescoping houses or lifting them from their foundations, snapping trees and lampposts, and twisting iron rails into writhing, metal snakes; breaking buildings and sweeping the fragments of their wreckage for hundreds of yards in its course. It advanced two miles southward, shattering every flimsy house in its path.[12]

7

Canada in the twenties

The Diamond Jubilee in 1927, the year of Canada's sixtieth birthday, was a time for celebration.

"The country was alive with strawberry festivals; ice-cream festivals, fowl suppers, three-legged races, egg-and-spoon races, baseball games between the fat men and the thin men; historical pageants featuring weirdly made-up and costumed Iroquois and fur traders, hymns, sermons, oratorical contests, millions of Union Jacks, tens of thousands of lithographed portraits of King George and Queen Mary."

"Perhaps Canada will never know another occasion when all the circumstances—an unclouded world horizon, a good and reassuring place within the Empire, an honest and rising pride in itself—will make for such a happy celebration."[1]

The 1920s are often viewed in North America as years of prosperity and fun, the "Roaring Twenties"—the joyful interval between World War I and the Great Depression. Books, movies and television often convey the image of happy, carefree days when just about everyone had money and spent it freely.

Does this image apply to Canada? To what extent is it accurate for some parts of Canada, and some groups of Canadians, but not for others? Had life returned to normal after the terrible interruption of global war? Was life pretty much as it had been before, or had changes been unleashed that set the country, and the lives of the

Mackenzie King
*See chapter 6

Arthur Meighen

Robert Borden

people, on a new and different course? Hopefully these questions will help you to look critically at the information in this chapter and form some impressions about the decade and some of the leading issues.

New leaders, a new age

The armistice of November 11, 1918 finally ended the war. Canadians entered a period of readjustment as the nation resumed peacetime living. The first order of business for the Canadian government was participation in the peace treaty negotiations in France.* This occupied the full attention of Prime Minister Borden for several months. The Union Government remained in office, but the wartime coalition was in the process of breaking down. A return to "party politics" was underway.

The Liberals were the first to move. The death of Sir Wilfrid Laurier on February 17, 1919, opened the way for a leadership convention, where the successful candidate was William Lyon Mackenzie King. He had strong support in Quebec, but he faced the task of rebuilding a political party shattered by the conscription crisis. King's strategy, which he followed throughout his career, was to placate the French Canadians, carefully extend Liberal influence in English Canada, and strive for policies which would maintain a balance between the races.

While the Liberals had a rebuilding job on their hands, the Conservatives were no better off. Sir Robert Borden was weary after a difficult decade in office, and retired. In July, 1920, the Conservative leadership fell to Arthur Meighen, the brilliant cabinet minister who had been the workhorse of the government during the war. Unfortunately for the Conservatives, Meighen was closely identified with some of the most unpopular actions of the government, particularly conscription.

Both "old" parties were challenged by a new political movement represented by the Progressive Party. The Progressives, organized in the winter of 1919-1920, were led by Thomas Crerar, who had resigned his cabinet post in the Union Government. In various provinces, including Ontario, farmers were suddenly active and successful in politics, and the Progressives could count on growing support.

The federal election of 1921 predictably left Canada with a minority government. Mackenzie King became prime minister as the Liberals gained the largest number of seats (116). The Conservatives had been reduced to a mere 50. The surprise of the election was the 65 seats, including the one held by Agnes McPhail, Canada's first female M.P., won by the Progressive Party.

Meanwhile, the end of the war had brought emotional relief to Canadians, but it also brought an economic slump that lasted well into the twenties. The loss of wartime markets, the cutbacks in production, and the return of servicemen from overseas made unemployment a national problem. The rising cost of living, nearly double the pre-war level in most parts of Canada, caused hardship even for those who had jobs. As a result, the trade unions and politically active farmers' organizations enjoyed a period of growth that, while short-lived, gave hints of what strength they could acquire in later years.

A social byproduct of the war had been the introduction of prohibition. Under the War Measures Act, the Canadian government in 1917 had forbidden the manufacture and sale of intoxicating beverages. Federal prohibition ended when the War Measures Act lapsed at the end of 1919, but provincial governments had previously passed their own anti-alcohol laws. Gradually prohibition gave way, however, to government-controlled sale.*

Eventually the postwar instability in Canada leveled off. Issues giving rise to serious conflict, such as the farmers' and workers' grievances and tension between French and English, passed into the background. Most regions of Canada began to experience a period of prosperity.

Major economic developments

MINING

An important advance in the twenties was the development of the great mineral wealth of the Canadian Shield. This vast region of rock and tundra stretched from Labrador across the northern reaches of Quebec and Ontario, around Hudson Bay over northern Manitoba and Saskatchewan to the Arctic Ocean. At the turn of the century, prospectors travelling on foot and by canoe had begun the task of rolling back the mining frontier. In the twenties the stage was set for Canada to become one of the world's leading mineral producers.

Some important new conditions made this possible. World War I and the resulting industrial expansion had created a demand for minerals, including such base metals as nickel, copper and zinc. So *demand* was on the rise. That the *supply* could also rise was due, in part, to an improving technology. Discovering minerals, estimating the potential of these discoveries and mapping the areas was far easier with the use of airplanes. "Bush pilots", the men who flew the float-planes into once-inaccessible regions, were valuable allies of the prospector and entrepreneur. The latter, of course, was a key figure in mining development, for the expenses are extraordinarily high and so are the risks.

Historically, "risk capital" in large quantites has not been avail-

During prohibition, a person wanting an alcoholic drink was not necessarily out of luck. If he was so inclined, he could seek out a bootlegger and buy liquor illegally. Even legal supplies were available, on doctor's prescription, if a person needed whiskey for "medicinal purposes".

*When prohibition was replaced by government-controlled sales, the distillery business was legal in Canada; but prohibition shut down the industry in the United States throughout the 1920s. Thus American liquor dealers, who had a market in spite of prohibition, were eager to buy Canadian supplies and smuggle them south of the border.

How not to win votes

For all his talents and experience, Arthur Meighen had some drawbacks as a political leader. He was unpopular in Quebec because of his role in putting conscription into effect. Many in the labour movement resented his part in the government's handling of the Winnipeg General Strike. Farmers opposed his strong stand in favour of tariffs. Even businessmen were critical, since Meighen had been in charge of the government's takeover of the privately-owned railways that became the C.N.R. Meighen's blunt manner and aggressive way of tackling problems also detracted from his popular support.

International Nickel Company of Canada, set up in 1902 by the J. P. Morgan banking firm of New York, expanded its operations in the Sudbury nickel mines so successfully as to dominate world markets by 1930. Falconbridge Nickel, also financed by New York capitalists, rose as a rival to INCO in the 1930s. In Quebec, Noranda copper mines were discovered in 1927 and the region became the centre of Quebec's base metal industry. The Hudson Bay Mining and Smelting Company, incorporated in 1926 by New York entrepreneurs, had its mines at Flin Flon producing copper by 1930.

Mining in Canada in the twenties

able in Canada. In the 1920s, a Canadian seeking to get ahead in the mining industry was likely to contact investors on New York's Wall Street. American businessmen were active in their own right in forming companies to buy up claims to Canadian mineral discoveries. In this way, American "branch plants"—subsidiaries of companies with headquarters in the United States—began to acquire direct ownership of Canadian resource industries.*

*See later, Chapter 13, for a more detailed treatment of the issue of foreign ownership.

FOREIGN CONTROL AND OWNERSHIP: A CANADIAN DILEMMA

Prominent Canadian economist, O. J. Firestone, observes that foreign ownership, involving Americans in particular, has been growing in Canada for a long time. Why would he refer to this phenomenon as a "Canadian dilemma"? What benefits of foreign ownership does he note? What disadvantages? Why do you suppose the Canadian public's "uneasiness" about foreign ownership did not come to the surface until the mid-1950s?

The inflow of foreign capital has brought many benefits to domestic industry and to Canadians generally. American industries in particular, in sending capital to Canada, were not only desirous of obtaining an adequate return on their investment but they were also interested in acquiring a long term stake in the economic growth of the host country—whether this included access to raw materials, access to energy sources, or access to markets. American investors thus took the long term point of view in placing judiciously their direct investments in Canada, particularly in the field of natural resources development and manufacturing industries.

They were primarily interested in the continuing success of their subsidiaries operating in Canada and not in quick profits. They reinvested large amounts of their earnings in the country and sent additional capital to Canada as and when this was required to finance further expansion and integration of operations. With this capital came American management, American skill, and American know-how, as well as, in a number of instances, assurances of markets either in the United States or overseas.

Canadians were able to expand their manufacturing industries more rapidly than they could have done had they to rely on their own savings and their own initiative. And further, Canadians were able to increase the productivity of their manufacturing operations, in many instances either up to the level of performance achieved in the United States or close to it—sometimes even exceeding it— because they were able to draw freely on American scientific and technological progress and managerial experience. This applies to some extent also to foreign investment coming from overseas though its impact and non-financial contributions to Canadian industrial development were in the last half century less than the contributions made by American investors.

While the benefits brought to Canadian industrial development from foreign investment were fairly readily observable, the disadvantages were less apparent, though in the views of some just as real. While some complaints were being voiced about American controlled industries in Canada not behaving as "good" Canadian corporate citizens—there were fewer complaints about foreign control from other countries—what concrete evidence was presented to substantiate such claims was hotly debated.

The public's uneasiness about growing foreign control over Canadian industry and natural resources development became more pronounced, particularly in the decade commencing with the mid-1950's, when figures released indicated that foreign investors had achieved majority control over most of Canada's key economic sectors, particularly manufacturing and mining. It represented a concern not so much about the lack or the inadequacy of opportunities for Canadians to participate in foreign controlled businesses operating in Canada—though this was one factor—but rather an innate aversion against economic control that could lead to political control and interference in Canadian national affairs.[2]

A HISTORIAN REMARKS ON THE PROSPERITY OF THE TWENTIES
D. G. Creighton regards the unequal distribution of prosperity in Canada as a cause for sectional grievances:

.... Without any question, Canada was in many ways a more favoured and stronger country in an age of electricity, alloys, and airways than she had been in the era of steam, steel, and rail. And yet, though the economic life of the whole country unquestionably grew richer and more varied, the bounty of the post-war period

By the 1920s, child labour which had been a popular and cheap form of getting work done in earlier years, had been made illegal, and situations like this were no longer seen.

Ideas from the social sciences: what is economics?

How is it that a certain product becomes important? Is it because the product, or what it is made of, just happens to be handy? Is it because some group of people expresses a need? The answer is that both the *supply* and the *demand* are necessary; yet, to explain how the combination of supply and demand lead to the making of a product, we need to dig deeper into other questions.

THE BLUEBERRY STAND

It is a summer day, and two nine-year-old sisters, Jill and Jenny, decide to set up a stand to sell wild blueberries. They think they can make some *money* picking the berries on the edge of town, washing them and selling them to passersby. Their mother gives them a table and helps them make a sign advertising blueberries for sale.

After two hours they make 90¢ and decide to continue their business the next day. However, the *supply* of blueberries on the edge of town is nearly exhausted, and the other places where they know wild blueberries grow are too far for the children to reach by bicycle. They ask their mother if she will drive them to pick more berries, and she agrees. However, in order to teach the girls something about money, she suggests that they spend some of their *profits* on the gas it will take to operate the car. The girls agree to pay part of the *costs* for gas, and they drive to the new berry patch where blueberries are plentiful. They return, thinking their "business" will now prosper.

However, down the street, a brother and sister have set up a rival blueberry stand, selling their berries for two cents less.

Jill and Jenny find they must become more enterprising if they are going to stay in business. They decide to do two things. First, they hire their neighbour, seven-year-old Geoff, to run the blueberry stand for two hours a day (he is thrilled by their offer of 25¢ a day). Rather than reduce prices, they prepare several posters, *advertising* their blueberries as "the largest, juiciest and best tasting in town", and display them on several trees in the neighbourhood. Cousin Waldo, who often visits on Saturday afternoon, agrees to ride up and down the street with a poster attached to the back of his tricycle.

The girls then get the idea of *manufacturing* blueberry pies. Since their father enjoys baking, they ask him for assistance and he agrees to help them get started. Father suggests a *division of labour*, so that Jenny learns to bake the pies and Jill, with the aid of her mother, will look after shopping for sugar and other supplies and start an accounts' book to keep track of costs and income. Before many weeks go by, sales have increased to the point where Jenny and her father can no longer produce pies fast enough in their spare time to meet the *demand*.

Jill then thinks of a way to increase their supply. Their unemployed uncle, Slade Barnaway, used to operate a bakery. Why not invite him over on Fridays to bake pies, in return for a free meal and a pie to take home for the weekend?

Meanwhile, the girls decide that they should be getting more work out of Geoff and thereby increasing their profits. Instead of handling the sale of pies themselves, Jenny and Jill reason that Geoff could sell pies at the same time as he sells the berries. Since longer "store hours" could mean more sales, they increase his daily hours of work to three. Geoff is unhappy with his new conditions of employment, and would like to quit. His employers have him over a barrel, however; he had used his first week's pay as a down payment on a used scooter which his older brother, Silas, had sold him.

1. Would you say Jenny and Jill were good "businesswomen"? Why or why not?
2. What problems did they encounter when they branched into manufacturing? How did they solve them? Would you have acted the same way, or differently? Explain.
3. If you were Geoff, the "labour" part of the "labour-management" dilemma, what would you have done? What protection should Geoff have against being "exploited"? How might protection be provided?

BASIC IDEAS OF ECONOMICS

Economics is the study of how a society organizes the making of goods and services and their distribution to consumers. In every society people have needs and choices to make about using their resources to satisfy those needs. Though the ways of making decisions about "what, how, and for whom" vary from one society to the next, certain things are basic to them all.

"The Blueberry Stand" illustrates some of the basic ideas of economics:

money:	anything generally accepted in exchange for other things —a medium of exchange
supply:	the quantity of an economic good that will be offered at a certain value at a particular time
profits:	the return on the sale of goods or services above and beyond all operating costs
costs:	total amount of overhead or outlay for equipment, labour and other expenses involved in production

competition: the situation where there is more than one seller dealing in the same product or service, and no one is able to dominate the market.

resources: wealth, or the means of producing it—natural resources, human resources and capital resources (equipment, financing)

scarcity: the idea that there is never enough of an economic good (resource, product) to satisfy all who want it

price: an item's money value

demand: the quantity of an economic good that will be bought at a given price at a given time

efficiency: increasing the amount of output from a given amount of input; eliminating waste, improving procedures

monopoly: the situation where a single seller controls the market and may determine supply and prices

advertising: publicity about a product to give information and persuade consumers to buy

manufacturing: the conversion of raw materials into finished products

division of labour: the assignment of specific tasks to different people in order to improve efficiency

labour: workers who carry out tasks, often under the direction and supervision of a manager. *Organized labour* refers to unions, by which workers improve the strength of their position with respect to employers.

Miners' strike, South Porcupine, 1910

seemed unequal in its distribution ... the new staples almost seemed to encourage the unfortunate process of regional division. In the pre-war age, wheat had been the one great export staple, round which the whole economic life of the country had centred; but now there were half a dozen distinct staple-producing regions, each with its own important export specialty or specialties, each with its regional interests in markets outside Canada, each with its individual successes and misfortunes. While some provinces ... profited superlatively from the new enterprises, others ... benefited only moderately, and still others ... gained little advantage at all.... [3]

HYDRO-ELECTRIC POWER

The pulp and paper industry had been growing steadily for more than 50 years, but its first "boom" came in the 1920s. The reason was the demands of the American market. The depletion of softwood forests in the United States, combined with the growth of the newspaper industry, helped to make Canada the world's leading exporter of newsprint.

Coal from the mines of Nova Scotia and Alberta, as well as from the United States, was still the main energy source for Canadians. The doubling of hydro-electric power output in the 1920s was nevertheless one of the most significant economic developments of the decade. Particularly in Ontario and Quebec, where the rivers of the Canadian Shield were close to major centres, the harnessing of water power was a boon to mining, the pulp and paper industry and manufacturing.

Inexpensive power was an important factor in the rise of Canadian manufacturing, but so was the availability of materials, such as those developed from nickel and other base metals. A grow-

Hydro-electric development

212

ing market, not just among Canada's population of 9 000 000 but throughout the British Commonwealth, attracted American investors. Money poured into electrical industries, chemicals, farm machinery and automobile manufacturing.

TRANSPORTATION

The formation of the Canadian National Railways (CNR) early in the 1920s as a **public corporation** meant that Canada had two giant railway systems. The CNR was plagued from the beginning by inherited debts, as a result of the costs involved in taking over the bankrupt Canadian Northern, Grand Trunk and other railways that were once privately owned. Hundreds of miles of its track followed parallel routes. They had been built by companies in competition with one another and were unprofitable. Roadbeds and equipment had been allowed to deteriorate. Yet the CNR, which employed nearly 100 000 people, improved its facilities and service. During the prosperous years of the twenties, the CNR entered into vigorous competition with the privately-owned system, the traditionally successful CPR.

Both railways expended large sums to build new branch lines, modernize rolling stock and equip their passenger trains with luxurious parlour cars. In major cities across the country, railway hotels—like the Royal York, opened in Toronto by the CPR in 1928—became familiar landmarks. As long as east-west trade in wheat and other

Owned and operated on behalf of the public by the government.

Canada's first radio network

On July 1, 1923, the Canadian National Railways Radio Department was formed. In the following month, a party of American tourists en route across Canada received a program especially prepared for them. Before the end of that year, Canadian National Railways were the outstanding broadcasters of Canada: parlor cars sold tickets for special events. The first network went into operation in December 1923; a year later Canadian National Railways possessed three broadcasting stations and eleven outlets in addition to its train services. In March 1924, it inaugurated a program that endures to this day—Hockey Night in Canada. Early in 1925, its Moncton station broadcast the first program from Canada to Great Britain. On this occasion both Canadian and American stations gave Canadian National Railways a monopoly of the air.[4]

Model-T ford

goods expanded, railways seemed assured of central importance in the nation's transportation industry.

But the "age of the automobile" had arrived. At the beginning of World War I there were approximately 60 000 cars registered in Canada; by 1920, the total was up to 251 945, and it rose to 1 061 500 by 1929.* Of course, there was a corresponding expansion of road building, although paved roads were a thing of the future for most Canadians outside the urban centres. In their Ford "Model T"s, Chevrolet 490s—or perhaps Hupmobiles in the case of the wealthy—Canadians found a new kind of mobility and freedom.

When gasoline-powered automobiles were first manufactured in Canada, as early as 1900, there was still competition from steam-driven cars. Variety was, in fact, a characteristic of the early automobile industry, as a host of companies experimented with innovations in equipment and design. So was the high cost of cars. By the 1920s, mass production meant more standardized models and cars that sold for well under a thousand dollars.

By the 1920s, the pattern of consolidation so evident in other areas of business and manufacturing was also clear in automobile production. A sign of the times was the formation in 1918, of General Motors of Canada, Ltd., through a merger of the Canadian-owned McLaughlin Motor Company and Chevrolet Motor Company of Canada Ltd. General Motors, and the other two emerging giants of the industry, Ford and Chrysler, then absorbed company after company.

Thus the Canadian car industry came to be served by companies which were "branch plants" of businesses based in the United States. Although some parts were made in Canada, major components were imported from the American plants. Cars were assembled in Canada,

*See James Dykes. *Canada's Automotive Industry*, Toronto: McGraw-Hill, 1970, p. 31.

Canada on wheels

"Early motorists were despised by lawmakers, editors and farmers alike. . . . In Newcastle, Ont, the *Independent* raged, 'We can compare (motorists) to nothing but a lawless gang of hoodlums and stop they must . . . we must make an example of a few of them before a call to arms is given.' The "example" took such drastic forms that the OML [Ontario Motor League] had to engage detectives to apprehend those who spread tacks or glass on the roads or strung wires across at neck-level, hoping to decapitate passengers in open cars.[5]

The last of the Canadian cars

"The last of the Canadian cars was the Frontenac. It was made by Dominion Motors of Toronto. . . . The Frontenac was introduced in 1931 and lasted for just two years. It had an American-built motor and came in four- and six-cylinder models. . . . since the middle Thirties all so-called Canadian cars have been built . . . by branch plants of the great American corporations.[6]

The Lark, one of the first bush planes in Canada

214

A CPR dining car

An early combine

*In other words, by locating in Canada, American manufacturers were able to take advantage of lower tariff arrangements among members of the British Commonwealth.

and sold to customers in Canada and throughout the British Commonwealth as well.*

AGRICULTURE

Following the postwar decline of agriculture, a time of depression when compared with conditions during the war, came the "wheat boom" of the twenties. Again the reasons included a sharp improvement in world economic conditions. Europe was well on the road to recovery from the devastation of the war, and the demands for foodstuffs were rising. Helped by American loans, European countries had the money to buy Canadian wheat, and they lowered tariffs to make their markets more accessible.

Wheat prices shot up, and farmers' costs came down; for example, railway freight rates were reduced, and lower tariffs made imported farm machinery cheaper. By 1928, Canada had a record wheat crop of 567 million bushels and the lion's share of world wheat markets.

216

As long as world conditions were stable, agriculture could continue to expand; so could the rest of the economy. The dangers of overdependence on a staple like wheat were not apparent to many in the boom years of 1926—1929.

THE ORGANIZATION OF LABOUR

The situation

Following the conclusion of World War I, the transition from a wartime economy proved to be a troubled one. The demobilization, the return of soldiers to civilian life, was accomplished quickly and the country was anxious to get back to normal. Unfortunately, in the months after the war, international trade was in a slump and inflation persisted. As prices shot up, wages did not rise correspondingly. Unemployment, made worse by the large number of men released from the armed forces, increased sharply. Men who did have jobs worked long hours, often for employers believed to have been **profiteering** during the war. Labour union membership, though small by today's standards, showed that organized labour was becoming a force in Canadian life.

Unfair profits from the sale of products needed for the war effort.

In 1919, the labour movement blasted its way onto the front pages of the nation's newspapers. The Winnipeg General Strike, Canada's first general strike, drew much of the attention.

Background

Unions were by no means new in 1919. About the time of Confederation, the growth of industry had resulted in the beginnings of organized labour. In 1872, after a successful strike of the Toronto Typographical Society against George Brown's Toronto *Globe*, the Dominion government passed legislation which recognized unions as legal.

The union movement spread mainly in the industrial sections of central Canada. In Quebec, however, unionization was hindered by the influence of the Roman Catholic Church and by French Canadian sentiments against Anglo-Saxon domination and American affiliation of the existing unions. French Canadians organized Catholic unions, closely tied to the French Canadian scene and to the Church. On the west coast a radical American union, the Industrial Workers of the World (IWW), or "Wobblies" as they were called, gained members among the lumber workers.

In the early 1880s, the Knights of Labour, which had gained considerable success in the United States, moved into Canada. This organization aimed to attract all kinds of labourers, both skilled and unskilled. Although the Knights flourished, many of its locals joined the Trades and Labour Congress of Canada (TLC) when it was organized in 1886. The TLC affiliated itself with the American Federation of Labour (AF of L), a federation of craft unions. Both worked to obtain better wages and improved working conditions. In 1902, the remnants of the Knights of Labour were excluded from the TLC and formed the Canadian Federation of Labour, a Canadian-based craft union.

THE CANADIAN WORKING CLASS

View of a European in 1907:

The workers have begun the work of organizing themselves according to American methods, but have been retarded greatly by all their differences of race, religion, etc. In imitation of what has been done in the United States, they have established in most of the towns special Trade Unions for each trade; the different Trade Unions in each locality take part frequently in Trade and Labour Councils. . . .

These Unions have until now devoted themselves principally to professional ends—the securing of higher wages, the reduction of the hours of labour, the improving of the conditions of employment either through their own action or by means of amicable negotiations with employers or through the mediation of the State. . . . The tendency of the Trades and Labour Congress is undoubtedly to exercise influence over the social legislation of the country. Some of the Unions, chiefly in British Columbia, are of a distinctly Socialistic character, but these are the exception. . . .

———————

Coming now to the political side of the matter, we find that the Canadian workers, in spite of some isolated victories at the polls, have not yet succeeded in constituting themselves a Third Party. . . . In a new country, prospering and developing rapidly, the general interests of all classes are too interlaced and interdependent for it to be easy to organize a class policy; the policy of national prosperity comes before all else.[7]

At the beginning of the twentieth century, unions were fairly well established but they represented only a small proportion of Canadian labour. With the growth of population and industrial expansion, the labour force grew and, with it, union membership. The period between 1900 and 1914 was a time of considerable industrial strife; strikes, lockouts by employers, work stoppages and violence were common.

Slow growth

But the growth of unions was slowed by several factors. Business and industry were generally hostile and had the support from the general

Department of Labour formed

The Department of Labour was organized in 1900 under the Postmaster-General, and established as a separate department in 1909. William Lyon Mackenzie King, formerly the deputy minister, was named minister of labour.

public. Many people saw unions as a form of interference with individual freedom and enterprise. Since most of the unions were affiliates of American organizations, the cry of "foreign influence" was raised against labour unions generally and against those on strike particularly. The anti-foreign cry, more credible because many union supporters were immigrants, was raised to divert attention from real issues, like poor wages and bad working conditions. Splits in the ranks of labour such as those between skilled and unskilled workers, and between immigrants and Canadian-born workers, prevented the rise of any sense of "worker solidarity".

Winnipeg General Strike

At the end of World War I the labour movement, like many other areas of Canadian life, was in a state of flux. The Trades and Labour Congress, with which most unions were affiliated, had grown considerably with the industrial expansion of the war years. However, the appearance of harmony was shattered in 1919. A split developed between the more conservative unions, located mainly in the East, and the more radical unions of the West.

Feeling that the TLC was not responsive to their wishes, labour delegates from the prairie provinces and British Columbia met in Calgary in March, 1919, with the intention of forming the One Big Union (OBU). The convention, heavily influenced by men with experience in the British labour movement, adopted a program based on the Marxist doctrine of class struggle. By creating a large-scale organization of workers and using the sympathetic strike as a means of confronting business and industry with mass interruptions of the economy, OBU organizers aimed to secure better conditions for wage-earners.

At the time of this upsurge in militancy on the part of labour organizers in the West, the most dramatic episode in Canada's labour history unfolded—the Winnipeg General Strike.

On May 15, 1919, Canada's first general strike began in Winnipeg. In sympathy with the metal workers who were striking for a shorter work week and higher wages, some 30 000 men had left their jobs. Only the railway workers refused to strike. Almost all other services were withdrawn. Factories, stores and warehouses closed. Milkmen, bakers, streetcar operators, postal workers, garbage collectors, meat processors, firemen and hydro workers were all on strike. Policemen expressed their support. R. B. Russell, Ernest Robinson and Reverend William Ivens were prominent members of the Strike Committee. In opposition was the Citizens' Committee of One Thousand, which included well known business and professional people.

The situation was explosive. Mounted police, including the "specials" hired because of the uncertain loyalty of the regular police,

What is Marxist doctrine?

Marxist doctrine originated with Karl Marx (1818-1883), a German who lived most of his adult life in England. In collaboration with Friedrich Engels, he wrote the *Communist Manifesto* (1848) and *Das Kapital* (1867) which predicted the eventual collapse of capitalism. His observations of conditions in industrial England convinced Marx that capitalism was a transitional stage between feudalism and a worker-controlled economic system. He believed that, under capitalism, "big businessmen" exploited the working class with the result that the "rich got rich and the poor got poorer." Wage-earners could only end their enslavement by gaining control of the "means of production"; that is, by owning and operating factories and businesses. One of the crucial differences among followers of Marx has been the *method* by which the "class struggle", ending in the replacement of capitalism, should proceed. Communists have advocated the use of revolution, assuming the violent seizure of power. Socialists have sought power via the ballot box, believing that workers can organize themselves to win elections —or put pressure on government—and thus bring about changes in the economic and political systems.

219

TOP: *Swearing in specials.* BOTTOM: *The Winnipeg Strike*

220

patrolled the streets lined with striking workers. The attention of the nation was focused on Winnipeg, where the newspapers—the *Citizen*, the *Telegram* and the *Free Press*—decried the strike as "plain ugly revolution," the work of aliens and Bolsheviks.* But the people of Winnipeg refused to panic. The Strike Committee, in the interests of the public well-being, agreed to have some essential public service employees return to their jobs. Violence broke out late in the strike, when a crowd smashed and burned a streetcar. The mounted police "specials" fired on the crowd; several were wounded and two died. Yet for the most part the city remained tense but peaceful.

*The Bolsheviks, or Communists, had seized power in Russia in the Russian Revolution of 1917. Many workers in other parts of the world, without knowing very much about the methods of the Bolsheviks, hailed the Russian Revolution as a victory for workers everywhere.

THE METHODIST "SOCIAL GOSPEL"

In 1918, the Methodist Church adopted these rather radical resolutions to reform society:

1. *Special Privilege Condemned:* We declare all special privileges, not based on useful services to the community, to be a violation of the principle of justice, which is the foundation of democracy.
2. *Democratic Commercial Organization:* . . . labor to have a voice in the management and a share in the profits and risks of business. . . .
3. *Profits of Labour and Capital:* We declare it to be un-Christian to accept profits when laborers do not receive a living wage, or when capital receives disproportionate returns as compared with labor.
4. *Old Age Insurance:* We recommend Old Age Insurance on a national scale. . . . This would protect all citizens from the fear of penury in old age. . . .
5. *Unearned Wealth:* We condemn speculation in land, grain, foodstuffs, and natural resources. . . .
7. *Nationalization of Natural Resources:* We are in favor of the nationalization of our natural resources . . . the means of communication and transportation, and public utilities on which all the people depend. . . . [8]

1. Can you see why methodist ministers, like J. S. Woodsworth, were involved in such actions as the Winnipeg General Strike?

STRIKER SCHNEIDERMAN

The two-act play, "Striker Schneiderman", by Jack Gray is set in Winnipeg in June, 1919, five weeks after the beginning of the Winnipeg General Strike. In this first excerpt Mayor Harold White, Police Inspector Walter Holmes and Magistrate August Hutchison are discussing their strategy for dealing with the strikers:

(At the railway station, the Mayor, Inspector Holmes, and Magistrate Hutchison are examining a platform hand cart on which are piled boxes of various sizes and shapes, many of which could obviously hold guns, and all of which are plainly marked Tinned Goods)

Hutchison: The Free Press has put a wireless right on top of their building, so there's no chance of our being cut off again.

White: I don't like the guns.

Holmes: The 'tinned goods' are to be used only in case of need.

White: Well there is no need . . .

Hutchison: Some of our friends in the South End are keeping rifles at their doors.

White: Some of our friends in the South End are insane. One of them said to me yesterday, 'What we should do is line a few of these boneheads up against the wall and shoot them.'

Hutchison: I trust it won't come to that.

Holmes: It'll be enough to send one or two to jail, perhaps deport some of the aliens. Separate a few from the herd, hunt 'em down, make an example. Then the rest will come to heel.

White: You still don't see what's happening. Here are people who, for the first time, are beginning to understand their condition, and who think they know how to better it. You won't stop that with jails, or deportations—or tinned goods!

Hutchison: I sometimes wonder whose side you're on, Harold.

White: I am *elected* to my office, Angus.

Hutchison: A man of the people?

White: What would *you* do if you're a machinist in the North End, your pay suddenly won't feed your family any more, the boss refuses to talk money, and you slowly begin to realize that there are more machinists than there are bosses, that they can't operate without you, and that if you just stick together maybe you can have a better slice of the pie? What would *you* do?

Hutchison: I'd fight. . . .

The second excerpt from the play is a conversation among Tom Evans, Chairman of the Strike Committee, Moishe Schneiderman, protagonist of the play and who is against general strikes but who supports workers like himself, and other members of the Strike Committee. The non-militancy of the strikers is shown in this scene where Tom refuses to cooperate with those strikers who wish to march in protest:

Tom: What parade is that?

Sam: The protest parade. We've already discussed it.

Tom: I hate to do you out of a job, Moishe [Moishe was elected parade marshall], just when you've begun . . .

Moishe: Please do.

Tom: But there'll be no protest parade. Or any other kind, for that matter.

Sam: We have voted . . .

Tom: I thought you understood. How Hutchison and his friends would love this group. We can't have a parade. If they once get us marching it will be child's play to make an incident. There will be violence for sure.

John: If they start it, what's wrong with a little violence?

Sam: Something's got to happen.

Moishe: A little violence is like a little love—tempting.

Tom: A little violence is all they want—or need. Then they can drop the whole crushing weight of established law and order on our backs. But—and this is our trump card—we must make the first move. And we're not going to. There will be no parade. No parade, and no violence.[9]

Civic and industrial leaders refused to yield; after six weeks of tension, workers began to drift back to their jobs when it appeared that further resistance was futile. The strike was breaking up by the time the federal government stepped in and arrested ten of the strike leaders. This action brought great public protest.

Of the ten arrested, seven were sentenced to a year in jail. J. S. Woodsworth, one of the acquitted, later became the leader of Canada's first socialist party. Professor W. L. Morton, in his book *The Kingdom of Canada*, says of him: "More than any other Canadian public man he helped transform Canadian politics from the politics of special and sectional interests to the politics of collective concern for the welfare of the individual in a society collectively organized."[10] Three of those sent to prison—John Queen, George Armstrong and William Ivens—were elected to the Manitoba Legislature while they were still serving their prison sentences.

J. S. Woodsworth

THE ORGANIZATION OF AGRICULTURE

The situation

In the Canadian election of 1921, the first of the post-war years, the new Liberal leader, Mackenzie King, led his party to victory over the Conservatives and their new leader, Arthur Meighen. However, not only did the Conservatives lose the power which they had held for a decade, but they fell to third place in the party standings.* The Progressive Party—the farmers' party—finished with 65 seats and seemed to be challenging the traditional two-party system. After decades of trying to advance their interests through non-political forms of organization, farmers appeared to have found direct political action to be the answer.

*Liberals, 116; Progressives, 65; Conservatives, 50.

Background

Self-help was the aim of the early agricultural societies, such as the Grange. A fraternal organization brought into Canada from the United States in the 1870s, the Grange was primarily interested in raising the cultural level of farmers and improving agricultural practices. In 1889 the **Patrons of Husbandry** started in Ontario. Similar to the Grange but more aggressive, the Patrons encouraged the

Husbandry is a term meaning farm management.

formation of co-ops and political action; some of its members were elected to the Ontario legislature in 1894.

After 1900 more powerful and broadly supported organizations evolved as farmers began to see themselves as an economic group exploited by big business and neglected by governments. The Grain Growers' Grain Company (G.G.G. CO.) became an influential pressure group on the prairies. In 1908, through pressure of the Manitoba government, the G.G.G. CO. gained a seat on the Winnipeg Grain Exchange which handled the sale of the farmers' grain. Pressure for an equitable and accurate grain grading system resulted in the establishment of the federal Board of Grain Commissioners. In the same year, the GGG CO. began to publish the *Grain Growers' Guide* to express the views of the farm organization and its members.

WHAT DID THE FARMERS WANT?

The Canadian Council of Agriculture, formed in 1909, organized a delegation of almost a thousand, representing the farmers of the prairie provinces and Ontario. The delegation went to Ottawa to present the Laurier government with their requests. Excerpts are presented below:

We come, asking no favors at your hands. We bear with us no feeling of antipathy towards any other line of industrial life . . . but in view of the fact that the further progress and development of the agricultural industry is of such vital importance to the general welfare of the state that all other Canadian industries are so dependent upon its success, that its constant condition forms the great barometer of trade, we consider its operations should no longer be hampered by tariff restriction. . . .

. . . we strongly favor reciprocal Free Trade between Canada and the United States. . . .

. . . it is the opinion of this convention that the Hudson's Bay Railway and all terminal facilities connected therewith should be constructed, owned and operated in perpetuity by the Dominion government. . . .

. . . we . . . request that the Dominion government acquire and operate . . . the elevators of Fort William and Port Arthur, and immediately establish similar terminal facilities . . . at the Pacific Coast. . . .

. . . that the new Bank Act be so worded as to permit the act to be amended at any time and in any particular.

. . . it is desirable that cheap and efficient machinery for the incorporation of co-operative societies should be provided by Federal legislation during the present session of parliament.

The government be urgently requested to erect the necessary works and operate a modern and up-to-date method of exporting our meat animals.

Problems in writing history: interpretation

A. DIFFERING VIEWS

J. S. Woodsworth, a Methodist minister, was a prominent strike leader who would later help organize the C.C.F. Party (forerunner of the New Democratic Party). In the Western Labour News *of June 12,1919, he wrote:*

The general public is up in arms. They have suffered inconvenience and loss. 'Why should innocent non-combatants suffer?' The general public has not been innocent. It has been guilty of the greatest sin—the sin of indifference. Thousands have suffered through the years under the industrial system. The general public have not realized. It did not touch them. They blame the strikers. Why not blame the employers whose arrogant determination has provoked the strike? Why not, rather, quit the unprofitable business of trying to place blame and attempt to discover and remove causes that have produced the strike and will produce, if not removed, further and more disastrous stikes?[11]

Two days later, in a letter to a relative, he wrote:

That strike has been entirely misrepresented. I know the details intimately. Without hesitation I say that there was not a single foreigner in a position of leadership, though foreigners were falsely arrested to give colour to this charge.... There was absolutely no attempt to set up a Soviet government....

In short, it was the biggest hoax that was ever put over any people! Government officials and the press were largely responsible. Of course, some of them were quite sincere, but absolutely hysterical.[12]

Rev. John Maclean, also a Methodist minister, had a different view, which he noted in his diary in May, 1919:

"The labour men have the upper hand, and so far as they can are showing Bolshevik methods.... Mounted Police have come to the city, several thousand men are drilling and in readiness for any riots...."

"We are under the sway of Bolshevism in the city. Everything is quiet, but there are some ugly rumours floating around, and the Home Defence Guards are all ready for action at a given signal...."[13]

1. From the information you have so far, which of the two Methodist ministers seems to have the truest view of the Strike?
2. How was it possible that people in Winnipeg in 1919 could have such opposite views?

B. NEWSPAPER COMMENTS

Newspaper comment, in Winnipeg as well as elsewhere, was generally hostile to the strikers. The Winnipeg Citizen, *which backed the employers against the Strike, wrote on May 19, 1919:*

This newspaper is issued because of the unquestionable necessity for placing before the great body of the citizens of Winnipeg the actual facts of the strike situation from the standpoint of the citizens themselves and in order adequately to inform them of the issue that faces Winnipeg in this, the most serious hour of her history.

It is to the general public of Winnipeg that we speak, in stating without equivocation that this is not a strike at all, in the ordinary sense of the term—it is Revolution.

It is a serious attempt to overturn British institutions in this Western country and to supplant them with the Russian Bolshevik system of Soviet rule.[14]

The Toronto Star, *as reflected in the comment of May 23, 1919, took a more moderate view:*

It is becoming more and more clear that the issue is not Bolshevism or any attempt to usurp the government of Canada, but a dispute between employers and employed on the questions of wages, hours, recognition of unions, and collective bargaining. A strike covering a wide range of industries of course causes great public inconvenience. But what is the remedy? If it is lawful for one set of workers to strike shall it be made unlawful for two or a dozen to strike? The difference of course is that when a strike is general or of very wide range the matter becomes one of national importance, and the Dominion Government may be warranted and even in duty bound to take strong measures to effect a settlement.[15]

1. Which of the accounts is the most objective? Why?
2. On which page of a newspaper would you expect to find such interpretations of events?
3. Watch your local newspapers for an editorial about a present-day strike. Find the news story on pages 1-5 which gives the facts of the situation. How objective is the news story? How does it compare to the editorial as far as fairness? In each story do the writers recommend action by any person or group? If so, by whom?
4. If a newspaper takes a certain editorial viewpoint, would you expect the reporting on the front page to reflect this viewpoint? Why or why not?

C. AN OFFICIAL EXPLANATION

Justice H. C. Robson, who headed the provincial royal commission which investigated the strike, concluded:

It is too much for me to say that the vast number of intelligent residents who went on strike were seditious or that they were either dull enough or weak enough to be led by seditionaries. The men referred to may have dangerously influenced certain minds, but the cause of the strike, and of the exercise of mass action, was the specific grievance above referred to [the refusal of collective bargaining] and the dissatisfied and unsettled condition of Labour at and long before the beginning of the strike.[16]

It is more likely . . . that the cause of the strike is to be found under the other heads [other than unemployment], namely, the high cost of living, inadequate wages . . . , profiteering. [Great inequalities of wealth exist in Canada, and] Winnipeg unfortunately presents a prominent example of these extremes. . . . It is the affair of Government to see that these two important factors maintain proper regard for each other. If Capital does not provide enough to assure Labour a contented existence with a full enjoyment of the opportunities of the time for human improvement, then the Government might find it necessary [to step] in and let the state do these things at the expense of Capital.[17]

1. What is "collective bargaining"?
2. According to the royal commission, how was collective bargaining a factor in the strike?

D. HISTORIANS' COMMENT

Two historians, who themselves have conducted detailed research on the subject, note what historians have written on the subject of the Winnipeg General Strike:

Masters' [D. C. Masters. *The Winnipeg General Strike*, 1950] study was the first specialized account of the events of 1919 which used true historical methodology, and combined documentary evidence with interviews with key persons still alive in the late nineteen forties. His conclusions, therefore, lent considerable support to those who had maintained that the strike was basically an industrial dispute writ large, embittered by irrational and immoderate rhetoric combined with intransigence on all sides. For the most part, Professor Masters' generalizations have been accepted by those who have subsequently studied the subject. . . . [18]

THE FUTURE OF THE WINNIPEG GENERAL STRIKE

In the 1970s, more than 50 years since the event, the Winnipeg General Strike is the subject of intense study. New facts have come to light and the controversy continues about what actually happened during the Strike, and more important, about its effects and significance on the lives of Canadians.

For the strike, as for other crucial passages in Canadian history, the search for evidence continues. But the ground rules for judging the old and the new "facts" shift almost year by year, as they have been doing ever since the spring of 1919. Most historians in the post-Red Scare years of the 1920's and the uneasy years of the depression found it tempting to stress the triumph of constituted authority in the face of a country-wide Bolshevik revolutionary conspiracy—and the temptation . . . was seldom resisted. In the post-depression years of the forties, under the impact of a newly vigourous labour unionism, the growing appeal of some form of social democracy and a healthy wish to escape the dangers of authoritarian repression of progressive social movements, the strike acquired a very different quality. The old orthodoxy collapsed under a barrage composed of newly researched evidence and of new purposes.

The new purposes, of course, included the principal end of "understanding" the strike. But, as always, to understand meant to make comprehensible to the present—in the sense that the present grew out of the past and would govern the future. Thus the strike in the forties and fifties became a legitimate, almost inevitable response to industrialism and to the domination of the West by the East. It was discovered, happily, that the strike had not been led by alien Bohunks and "Ukerainians" but by British-born Canadian citizens; that its organization had been almost spontaneous (against a background of general unrest occasioned by severe resistance to Labour's efforts to organize industrially) and that its immediate goals of higher wages and the right to collective bargaining were its "real" causes. Bolshevik conspiracy as a part of the strike's causation was rejected and evidence that had always been readily available (in response to the questions when they were asked) was used with telling effect. The official Robson Report, issued as part of the agreement by which the strike was ended, had spelled out the essentials of the revised version twenty years before but did not become a part of our "history" until the interpretative assumptions and questions were changed.[19]

1. What events involving the actions of organized labour in recent years are likely to be reinterpreted in the future?

That the Board of Railway Commissioners be given complete jurisdiction in ... matters of dispute between the railways and the people, and to enable them to do this that the law be more clearly defined.[20]

The government took no concrete immediate action. But it could not help but be impressed by the growing influence of Canadian agriculture. To get the farm vote, the Laurier government recognized the farmers' demands in the Liberal party's election platform of 1911. But many farmers were convinced that their organizations, as mere pressure groups, were not effective enough to wring concessions from the government; only political action could achieve their goals.

Farmers' parties

Discontent among farmers grew into political revolt at the end of World War I. Wheat prices declined, while the costs of manufactured goods went up with the removal of wartime price controls. The high tariffs meant that farmers had to pay more for imported goods and machinery. Farmers were also dissatisfied with costly freight rates and high fixed rates of interest on bank loans and mortgages.

More than ever, farmers felt they were being sacrificed to the business and industrial interests of central Canada. Both the Liberals and the Conservatives talked at length about the tariff but neither did very much about lowering it. The feeling among farmers was that they would not find solutions to their problems in the old parties that were wedded to big business.

In 1918, the Canadian Council of Agriculture issued a blueprint for political action in a document that came to be known as the "New National Policy." It expressed some of the exciting new political ideas of the times, such as public ownership of essential utilities and social legislation in the form of old age pensions and widows' allowances. Understandably, it attacked the high tariff and the power of the wealthy financial interests. Farmers quickly organized themselves and translated the new program into political action.

The farmers' program had widespread appeal. In 1919, the United Farmers of Ontario (UFO) won a majority of seats in the provincial election and formed a government with E. C. Drury as Premier. The United Farmers of Alberta (UFA) won the election in that province two years later. In 1922, the United Farmers of Manitoba (UFM) also came to power. Although the initial success of the farm revolt occurred in eastern Canada, Progressivism was to have more lasting effects in the West. The UFO was defeated in the election of 1923; the

United Farmers of Alberta were able to remain in office until 1935. United Farmers' parties sprang up in every western province and, to a lesser extent, in the Maritimes.

In 1920, the Canadian Council of Agriculture called a convention in Winnipeg at which a new party, the National Progressive Party, came into existence. Having the New National Policy as its platform, the support of the United Farmers' groups, and T. A. Crerar as its leader, the National Progressive Party rose to challenge the Liberals and the Conservatives in the federal election of 1921.

Fate of the Progressives

The Progressives failed to develop any cohesion in Parliament. Before their numbers dwindled to two in the 1930 election, many of their members, including Crerar, were absorbed by the Liberal party. In the meantime, however, Mackenzie King persuaded the Progressives and the two Labour members from Winnipeg to support his minority government. The combination of Liberals, Progressives and Labour brought about a modest old age pension and slight reductions in the tariff on farm implements.

In some measure, the unbridled prosperity between 1923 and 1929 was responsible for the decline of Progressivism just as it accounted for the momentary eclipse of the labour movement as a force in Canadian politics. Nevertheless, the spirit of Progressivism never really died in western Canada. It enjoyed renewed activity during the depression years of the 1930s when the democratic and social ideas that Progressivism propounded took on a new meaning. These were advocated with new vigour by the CCF and Social Credit parties.

The people of prosperity

The decade following World War I has been stereotyped with such labels as the "Roaring Twenties", "The Aspirin Age", "The Lost Generation" and "The Era of Wonderful Nonsense". By and large these images originated in the United States, where a social revolution went hand-in-hand with the unprecedented technological and material changes of the time. Recovering from the trauma of the war, Americans were intent on resuming a national life free from foreign entanglements* and based on the solid foundations of the work ethic, family life and the church. However, pre-war values were being challenged by the new prosperity. Material wealth and pleasure, once the privilege of the dominant few, now seemed within the grasp of the majority.

*See Chapter 6.

Ralph Allen, in his book Ordeal by Fire, *speaks of the influence of the United States on Canadian life in the twenties:*

To say that Canada, at this period, had a conscious desire to ape the United States would be rather like saying that the tides ape the moon when they are only yielding to its pull. . . .

Thus, in the immediate aftermath of the war, the United States had a deflationary depression and Canada had a deflationary depression too. Coal strikes broke out in the United States; coal strikes broke out in Canada. The United States embarked on prohibition; so—usually a little before, sometimes a little later—did most all the provinces of Canada. The United States spawned the prohibition gangsters; Canada spawned the prohibition rumrunners to keep him supplied. The American female developed invisible busts and hips, the boyish bob, bells on her garters, and a taste for cigarettes and gin; the Canadian female sought to do the same. . . . [21]

Canada was also affected by the post-war changes, although on a less spectacular scale. Nevertheless, American influence reached into the lives of Canadians as never before. With more money to spend, they had more on which to spend it, including new forms of leisure and entertainment, like radios and motion pictures and organized sports. There was more mobility, too, thanks to the availability of the automobile, which could mean both greater freedom for the individual and a weakening of traditional family and community ties.

Arthur R. M. Lower, in his book Canadians in the Making, *devotes a section to "The great god* CAR *and his associates":*

That inventive society known in Canada as "the country to the south," could make a new goddess as quickly as it made a new car. But in making new cars, it made a new god. For the god, no better name could be found than simply—CAR!

. . . . CAR's devotees increased with the years. And no wonder. A patient, obedient god who takes you where you want to go, faster than any magic carpet. A comfortable, well-upholstered god. . . . And above all, the god of power, who multiplied man's ego manifold. Yet a ruthless god, sometimes, too, who could turn on his idolater and rend him.

CAR brought in his company a whole host of lesser godlets (most of them born of Electra), which their worshippers called 'modern conveniences' or more simply 'progress'. . . .

Meanwhile, CAR and his associates changed our society out of recognition. They scattered our homesteads far beyond the cities, so that many of us became once more, after a fashion, country dwellers. . . . CAR threatened to turn us all into nomads. . . . They invaded every urban space and threatened to destroy every blade of grass. They knocked down houses. They called imperiously for straight, wide roads to be carved out of the diminishing fertile fields. They tore up our precious peach orchards and ordained that factories for making new parts of CAR should be erected in their place.[22]

STYLES AND MANNERS

The social revolution was indicated by the changes in the circumstances, and to some extent the status, of women. Such advances as the refrigerator, the vacuum cleaner, the washing machine and the electric iron freed women from much of their daily drudgery. They enabled many to become more active outside the home and family.

Social barriers between the sexes began to break down. In prewar days, teaching and nursing were often the only forms of employment open to women. In the new era, the number of working women increased greatly as occupations in retail stores, business and even politics opened to them.

Fashions changed dramatically. Petticoats and bustles became old fashioned as hemlines rose and new fabrics, like rayon, became popular. The form-fitting bathing suit, exposing enough skin to make suntanning a possible hobby, replaced the "long johns" of earlier, more modest years. The widespread use of cosmetics created an enormous industry. Hair styles also changed, as bobbed cuts replaced elaborate coiffures; beauty parlours sprang up all over the country.

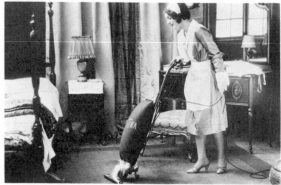

In The Goblin, *a magazine started in the 1920s by some students at the University of Toronto, one observer commented on the new female fashions:*

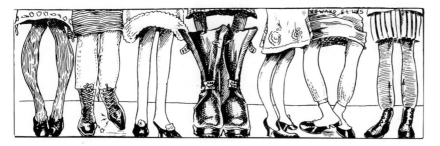

LEGS

—*by Mississippi —Dedicated to Mr. Hippy.*

Legs to the right of us
Legs to the left of us
Legs in front of us
How they display them.
On they go trippingly
Dainty and skippingly
Frost that bites nippingly
Does not dismay them.

Straight legs and bandy ones
Poor legs and dandy ones
Awkward and handy ones
Flirt with the breezes.
Round legs and flatter ones
Thin legs and fatter ones
Especially the latter ones
Showing their kneeses.

Knock-kneed and bony ones
Real legs and phony ones
Silk-covered tony ones
Second to none.
Straight and distorted ones
Mates and ill-sorted ones
Home and imported ones
Ain't we got fun.[23]

Manners and habits were also changing. As long as pipes, cigars and chewing tobacco were the vogue, women were less likely to take up the tobacco habit; however, cigarettes became popular in the twenties and smoking in public became socially acceptable for women. Mixed drinking at parties, especially the consumption of bootlegged whiskey, was thought to be *avant-garde*. Generally women were less confined by "Victorian" notions of propriety; the image of the ideal woman as "shrinking violet" was passing.

MOVIES

Hollywood gained world-wide fame as the centre of the motion picture industry. The public flocked to movie houses to see Mary Pickford, Douglas Fairbanks, Gloria Swanson, Rudolph Valentino or John Barrymore. Torrid love scenes between women of great beauty and men who epitomized masculinity and charm were regular fare on the silent screen. So were lavish scenes in which the luxury of "high society" living tantalized audiences everywhere. The eternal struggle between good and evil, sweet innocence pitted against dark passion—these were familiar themes.

Audiences laughed at the wonderful antics of slapstick comedians like Charlie Chaplin, Mack Sennett's Keystone Cops, Harold Lloyd, W. C. Fields and Laurel and Hardy. On Saturday afternoons, children filled the theatres to see Tom Mix, William S. Hart or Hoot Gibson outwit, outride and outshoot the most villainous of outlaws.

"The Jazz Singer" of 1927 starring Al Jolson marked the beginning of "talking pictures" and signalled the end of the silent picture era. The use of sound with film opened up new possibilities for film-makers. In the 1930s, the dramas starring performers from the Broadway stage and lavish musicals gave North Americans a form of escape from the Depression.

The first Canadian feature film was "Evangeline", produced in 1913 and based on the poem by Longfellow about the expulsion of the Acadians. As late as the 1920s Canadian films were still capitalizing on Canadian themes drawn from history or novels, with the Mounties being a natural favorite. There were too many problems, however. American companies, such as Famous Players, controlled most of the theatres. Costs of production were rising. Canadian talent continued to move south where Hollywood offered fame and fortune. Not until the government set up the National Film Board in the late 1930s was the stable existence of any Canadian film industry assured, and then efforts would be concentrated on short films and documentaries.

BOYHOOD REMINISCENCES

Canadian novelist Harry J. Boyle writes about his boyhood in the 1920s on a farm in southern Ontario:

(a) The Railroad
One never knew where that train was going to stop. People appeared at crossings with baskets of eggs or crocks of butter on

An early movie set

their way to the city market, and the train stopped for them, before ambling along to the next station.

I can remember one day when the train sped along I asked Ed what the hurry was all about. He grinned and said that Jim was trying to get a little ahead so he could stop and try his hand for a big trout that he had spotted under the bridge over the river outside one of the small towns.

For twelve years that train never failed to blow its whistle at a place not marked in the railroad manuals, and for twelve years on the day before Christmas, Ed Patterson, Jim Blake and the brakeman stopped the train and went in to see Willy Jenkins, the crippled son of the section foreman. Not a soul complained.

(b) Radio

The radio came also to our home. One Saturday in late fall, a man in a shiny Gray Dort Touring drove in with a smile on his face. Earlier I had noticed my father hanging around the woodshed and looking down the concession a great deal, as if he expected someone. There was a hint of something in the air, and it wasn't snow.

It was our radio, delivered by Al Walker, the local furniture dealer and undertaker, who had added radios to his inventory. . . .

That was a day of great excitement. The aerial was strung out to the old pine tree. The radio was a long, narrow, brown box with three knobs on the front. The loudspeaker was a large, black horn. We took the wet battery out of the car, attached the "B" batteries and waited. Nothing happened. Al Walker fussed, grew progressively redder of face and began to perspire heavily. At supper-time he was still working on the radio.

That "wireless" changed our lives. Just as it took the regulars away from my uncle's store, it brought the members of our family together. We listened to hockey games, Saturday-night barn dances, and the humour of Amos 'n' Andy. We heard news almost as soon as it happened. Days of isolation, even in the dead of winter, were gone forever from our valley.[24]

RADIO

The advent of radio brought entertainment and "instant" news of the world into homes, at least those within range of the broadcasting stations. A home could be without electricity, but a battery-operated radio could bring in broadcasts of sports events, like Foster Hewitt's "Hockey Night in Canada". First broadcast in 1923, it became a Canadian tradition and Hewitt's exclamation "He shoots, he scores!" became part of the Canadian vernacular. Of course, commercials were a regular part of programming.

The first commercial radio station in North America, KDKA in

An early radio studio

Pittsburgh, Pennsylvania, had been opened in 1920. Listening to radio became a fad in the United States, and to a lesser extent in Canada as well. Into Canada, powerful American stations beamed music by Rudy Vallee, Paul Whiteman's jazz band and the National Barn Dance. Amos 'n' Andy were popular comedians of the day, and the afternoon "soap operas" offered their never-ending dramas.

By 1929, there were nearly 300 000 radios in Canada, and more than 75 broadcasting stations, operated by a variety of owners: corporations, radio clubs, newspapers, universities, and the Canadian National Railways. The nearest thing to a radio network was the hookup among the CNR's stations and private affiliates. However, these stations reached only a minority of Canadians, and while the CNR offered Canadian content in its programming, most stations carried recordings and programs from the United States.

In fact, the popularity of American programming among Canadian listeners prompted a Royal Commission in 1928. The result was the creation, in the 1930s, of the Canadian Broadcasting Corporation to encourage Canadian talent and offset the flow of American cultural influence.

MUSIC

The twenties was a decade in which jazz music and popular songs became part of the culture on both sides of the Canadian-American border. George Gershwin's "Rhapsody in Blue" became a classic and light-hearted, even nonsensical songs—"Happy Days Are Here

Again," "Bye, Bye Blackbird," "Yes, We Have No Bananas"—were hits. And dance crazes, like the Charleston, spread across the border into Canada as readily as the fast-paced music.

CHAUTAUQUAS

To Canadians born after 1930, the name "Chautauqua" will mean very little; yet for ten to fifteen years previous to that date the Chautauqua was a commercialized movement bringing entertainment of a high standard, with a degree of "culture" placing it in a distinctive role.

Usually the afternoon program featured a lecturer. For the evening there would be instrumental or vocal numbers, elocutionists, and sometimes a good dramatic company presenting a wholesome play.[25]

SPECTATOR SPORTS

The public thirst for entertainment gave rise to a phenomenal increase in spectator sports. The National Hockey League, founded in 1917 as a three-team league, expanded to include as many as ten teams from Canada and the United States. In newly-built arenas, crowds up to 10 000 watched teams like the Montreal Maroons, the Ottawa Senators and the Detroit Cougars as well as clubs with names more familiar to present-day fans—the Toronto Maple Leafs and the Montreal Canadiens. It was the hey-day of King Clancy and George Vezina, Eddie Shore, Howie Morenz and "Ace" Bailey, and lines like Cook, Boucher and Cook. Amateur hockey flourished across Canada, and people living in the smaller centres had no lack of entertaining hockey.

Baseball, long popular in Canada as well as in the United States, had a large following. While Canada had no major league teams, Canadians flocked to baseball tournaments and exhibitions by touring teams. They thrilled to newspaper accounts of the exploits of the .400 hitters like George Sisler and Rogers Hornsby and the power hitters, especially Babe Ruth and Lou Gehrig of the New York Yankees. Professional wrestling, with its emphasis on showmanship, became popular in the twenties, and boxing had an almost fanatical following in that decade of the Jack Dempsey—Gene Tunney matches.

AN UNUSUAL STANLEY CUP VICTORY

Early in the second game of the 1928 Stanley Cup playoffs between the Montreal Maroons and the New York Rangers, the Rangers' goalie, Lorne Chabot was injured and taken to hospital. When the Maroons refused to

*allow a substitute from another team, Lester Patrick, the Rangers' coach,
went into the action:*

Patrick, fuming, then decided to put on the pads and play in the
nets himself. He had done the same thing on two or three occasions before, but never with so much at stake. The silver-haired
Patrick was forty-four years old, and the fans alternately hooted
and cheered when he shuffled onto the ice to take his warmup
shots.

When play began, Patrick amazed the fans with his agility.
Throughout the rest of the game and into overtime he handled 18
shots and was beaten only once, when Stewart scored on Smith's
rebound.

At 7:05 of the first overtime period the Rangers broke through
and scored. The exhausted Patrick, dripping with perspiration, was
mobbed by his players and escorted to the dressing room. It is
strange but fitting that Patrick, who spent his whole life in hockey
and made many outstanding contributions to the game, will always
be remembered more for his play as a substitute Stanley-Cup
goaltender than for anything else he ever did. It was one of hockey's most electrifying occasions.[26]

TOUGH MEN PLAYED HOCKEY THEN

*Frank Boucher, star centre, and later coach and general manager of the New
York Rangers, recalls the violence of professional hockey in the early 1920s:*

Tough men played hockey then. Modern purists point to a debilitat-
ing American influence on the game these days, which encourages
bloodlust in the loose interpretation of rules that condone fights and
rough play. The charge does not survive scrutiny, however; games
were tougher and blood flowed even more freely in the years preceding hockey's invasion of the big cities in the U.S. in the mid-
1920's. Jack Adams, coach and general manager of the Detroit Red
Wings for more than thirty years, once recalled a game in the pre-
American era between the Toronto Arenas, for whom he played,
and the Montreal Wanderers, who preceded Hamilton in that
league. The Wanderers carved him up so freely that he came out
looking like the loser of a saber duel. . . . [27]

RELIGION AND MORALITY

It would be incorrect to think of the twenties as a decade of unre-
strained licence and indulgence. Against the desire to break loose
from traditional values and take part in the pursuit of pleasure was
the concern for the spiritual side of life. Church membership and
attendance increased. In 1925 a move to strengthen organized religion was taken by Protestant leaders, when several denominations
joined to form the United Church of Canada. Although a separate

Rumrunning in the twenties

From the Maritimes to the Rockies, rumrunning became a lucrative enterprise. Prohibition in the United States forbade the manufacture, importation and sale of alcohol.

Many Canadians made fortunes by manufacturing whisky and exporting it to clients in the United States. Supplying the large and thirsty American market, without being subject to the high tariffs affecting exporters in legal products, meant high profits. While there were risks involved, the only real hindrance to this lucrative north-south trade was the United States Customs Service. The customs service was less than efficient, however, and the thousands of miles of common border enabled smuggling to proceed almost without interruption.

In a discussion in the House of Commons about liquor smuggling across the border, the Canadian Minister of National Revenue, W. D. Euler, spoke of his own experience:

I was offered safe conduct by a liquor exporter and went out on a launch on the Detroit River. I could see the United States customs office on the other shore and I could see it was not very difficult to detect any boats that left the Canadian shore to go to the American side. While in Windsor I got into conversation with a man engaged in the business of exporting liquor. I asked him 'Do you cross in the daytime?' He answered, 'Yes, quite often.' I said, 'How is it they do not get you?' He replied with a smile, 'It just happens that they are not there when we go across.'[28]

James Gray in his book, Booze, *gives an indication of the amount of money involved in the smuggling:*

Smuggling, the Toronto *Saturday Night* had written, had reached such proportions as to be a national menace. At least fifty million dollars' worth of goods were being smuggled into the country annually, putting Canadian factories out of business and Canadians out of employment.

In the early days of the agitation the spotlight had been focused on the chief enforcement officer of the customs department in Montreal, J. E. A. Bisaillon ... Among other things Bisaillon ran a customs brokerage business on the side and was a prominent landowner in Rock Island, the smuggler's-cove village astride the U.S.—Canadian border. Bisaillon owned one house on each side of the line, both of which, gossip had it, were used extensively for two-way smuggling. He had been the centre of several notorious cases involving smuggled whisky and narcotics, but held onto his job nevertheless. Bisaillon's activities triggered a parliamentary committee investigation into the department. That investigation directed public attention to another and even more serious flaw in the enforcement structure, one which had cost the Government of Canada fifty-two million dollars in lost revenue during the three years ending in 1925. In the 1920's it was no trick at all to blow fifty-two million dollars into a major scandal, which, save for the adroit footwork of Prime Minister Mackenzie King, would have destroyed the Liberal government.[29]

Presbyterian Church remained, many of their members joined with Methodists and Congregationalists in the new and distinctively Canadian Church, which claimed a membership of 50 000 by 1929.

The term "social gospel" has been used to describe the attitudes of those who believed that the churches should be active in social reform as well as in the salvation of individual souls. Since the social gospel was a phenomenon that included many different types of people and groups, it is difficult to describe. It influenced those involved in church reorganization, including the founding of the United Church and new organizations like the Labour Church. Activists within the traditional churches worked on behalf of the less advantaged, like the wage-earner in the Winnipeg General Strike.* Others had channeled their energies into the prohibition movement, attacking the evils of "booze".

*See pp. 219 ff.

The prohibition movement had been a significant force in Canadian life since the turn of the century. By the end of World War I most provinces had limited the sale of liquor in one way or another, on the assumption that "booze" was a root cause of social problems. Unlike the case in the United States, where prohibition was enforced by the national government which forbade the manufacture as well as the sale of alcohol, Canada had wide variation from province to province. Distillers had their Canadian customers, the most notable of whom were the rumrunners.

Business and businessmen

Admiration for the affluent businessman was general in North America in the 1920s. In the spirit of free enterprise, the tycoon had achieved what most people dreamed of achieving—wealth, power and prestige. The habits of the very rich, though most such people guarded their privacy and ignored their critics, were part of the common gossip.

In the hope of "striking it rich," Canadians in growing numbers

A man of power

He was the president of twenty-seven major business enterprises and a director of about three hundred companies. They ranged from the giant Montreal Light, Heat & Power Consolidated, which he founded, to a railroad through the Peruvian Andes that he had surveyed on mule back. Montrealers in the late 1920's complained: 'We get up in the morning and switch on one of Holt's lights, cook breakfast on Holt's gas, smoke one of Holt's cigarettes, read the morning news printed on Holt's paper, ride to work on one of Holt's streetcars, sit in an office heated by Holt's coal, then at night go to a film in one of Holt's theatres.' "[30]

The stock ticker, a symbol of the Depression

began to play the stock markets. Almost everyone could afford a few "penny stocks". Since prices of stocks always seemed to be going up, people were not risking very much if they borrowed money to buy "on margin." Once a stock had risen to a value whereby it could pay off a debt, it could be cashed in. Or it could be used to buy more stocks. The brokers, the financial papers and the tales of sudden fortunes all fed a public confidence that prosperity would never end.

DABBLING IN THE STOCK MARKET
The prospects of profits and quick riches prompted many Canadians to "play" the stock market:

The middle twenties were the days of 'Coolidge Prosperity'.... Signs of disaster were plain to be seen, but neither the people nor the government heeded the signs.

Canada followed in the trail of its big neighbour like a wobbly-kneed puppy after a Great Dane. Canadian stock-exchanges did proportionately as much business as those in the United States. Most of the issues traded in were those favoured by speculators across the line. As an instance of this aberration, one of the favourites of the time was a taxicab company! One day, it was this stock, the next, it was something else. Everybody made money, on paper, because stocks always went up.[31]

8

The Great Depression of the 1930s

More often than not, we signify the importance of the depression by calling it
great. And then, to make sure that no one will misunderstand, we capitalize the
whole thing: The Great Depression.

If there have been other depressions, there has never been one quite like this.
There are those who have never gotten over it, who believe still that a job will
not last or that new bed linen has an absurd priority in the household budget in
memory of fleas and bugs crushed in the sheets of rickety beds in impoverished
dwellings or that Government is the salvation of men or the damnation. Our
lives and our dreams have been conditioned by The Great Depression as they
have not been conditioned by any other recent event, not war, not nuclear power,
not population growth. We search for affluence with neurotic intensity "so that
our children will not have to go through what we went through." And if we are
better protected by economic regulations than were our equally ambitious ances-
tors in the 1920s, still the intervening tragedy has not taught us a great deal
about frugality, abstinence and discipline.[1]

The Great Depression, which occurred between the "crash of 1929"
and the outbreak of World War II in 1939, is perhaps the most
clearly defined period in Canadian history. The poverty, distress and
disruption of that decade scarred a generation. People faced the
future with mixed feelings: the hope that such a depression would
never happen again, and the fear that it might.

What was it like to live during the Depression? Did Canadians generally suffer from poverty and hard times, or did some people bear the brunt? How did those who suffered respond? Were they angry or resigned? What actions were taken by governments, business leaders, organized labour? How did people spend their leisure time? Were the 1930s a decade of total despair, or was progress made on some fronts?

What does the Depression mean to Canadians in the 1970s? Those who lived through it have their memories and their views. Canadians of later generations have learned something about the decade through stories from their elders and from occasional accounts in the media. As conditions throughout the world invite comparisons with the 1930s, and as writers and television producers respond to audiences' nostalgia for the past, the search for a fuller picture and deeper understanding of the time continues.

The economics of the Depression

How did the Great Depression begin? The stock market crash of October, 1929, was the signal that the rising economic prosperity of the twenties had ended. Canada was in for "hard times."

Underlying the collapse of the stock market was a general decline in the world's economic stability. In the United States, the prosperity of the "Roaring Twenties" had sputtered to a stop; economic chaos had taken its place. A chain reaction followed in other countries. Attempting to protect their crumbling economies, nations began dumping exports on the world market at bargain prices. At the same time, they were increasing tariffs to keep out foreign products.

Canada's economy was highly vulnerable to a decline in world trade and falling prices. Rising levels of prosperity, dating back to the turn of the century, had been built on exports. Assuming that demand for their goods would continue to increase, Canadian producers, large and small, had expanded their facilities and accumulated heavy debts. The overdependence on primary products, such as wheat, forest products and minerals, made Canada as a whole, and the West and the Maritimes in particular, open to financial trouble.

The Depression was the economic catastrophe that Canadians had never dreamed would happen. When it began, the United States raised its tariffs to the highest levels ever, and Britain abandoned its traditional policy of free trade. The flow of Canadian exports was stifled by tariff barriers and intense competition from other exporting nations. Wheat was a dramatic example. Competition from Australia, Argentina and the Soviet Union, and a decline in sales to traditional customers, drove prices down. A bushel of wheat sold for $1.60 in 1929, but the price had collapsed to 38 cents by 1933.

244

How does the stock market work?

Basically there are three types of businesses: those owned by individuals, those owned by partners, and those owned by shareholders or stockholders. The latter is called a corporation. A corporation's ownership is divided into a number of equal shares, and a shareholder can own one or more of these shares.

Shareholders in a public company are free to buy and sell shares in the corporation once the original purchase price has been paid in full. Most stockholders sell their stocks through a person called a broker; a broker is the middleman in the buying and selling of stocks. He recommends stocks that look promising. He may advise selling stocks that seem to have reached their peak and are likely to diminish in value rather than earn more profit.

In large cities, brokers combine to operate stock exchanges where they meet daily to conduct their business. Brokers also maintain connections with other brokerage firms and exchanges in other cities in order to carry out the orders of their clients as quickly as possible. Stock exchanges bring buyers and sellers from all parts of the world together via telegraphic communication. This enables a seller to find the best buyer and get the best possible price for his stock. Brokers earn commissions on sales of stocks; the higher the selling price, the larger the commission.

In the 1920s the popular thing to do was to buy on margin, that is, to pay a small amount as down payment and hope that profits would take care of the rest. If a person heard that stock "x" was expected to jump in value, he might even take out a bank loan to make the down payment. People and companies who bought stocks this way made profits "on paper" as long as prices kept rising. When the depression struck, creditors demanded payment, and people in debt rushed to sell their stocks. Panic selling depressed stock values and the downward spiral left stockholders unable to pay their debts.

Jokes from the 1930s

Man: "I'd like a room, please." Hotel clerk: "Yes, sir. Do you want it for sleepin' or jumpin'?"

The collapse of the "wheat economy" was felt throughout the Canadian economy. Railroads, accustomed to transporting the bumper crops from west to east, fell on hard times. The farm machinery business collapsed. Manufacturers faced reduced markets both at home and abroad. Production slumped, and unemployment soared to twenty per cent.

If the Depression was a national problem, it was a tragedy in the regions most dependent on primary production. The Maritimes had little to fall back on with the loss of markets for fish, timber and coal. British Columbia and the northern regions of Ontario and Quebec were similarly vulnerable. But the prairies suffered a double disaster: besides the loss of markets, the prairie provinces were hit by drought. Year after year, the lack of rain and scorching summer wind turned the once-rich farmland into desert. Farmers simply packed up and left, rather than wait for the banks to foreclose on unpaid mortgages.

FALLING WAGES

People who were able to find jobs during the depression often worked for pennies:

. . . in union shops wage reductions and short time had cut weekly earnings for most of the men and women to no more than $10.00 to $20.00 in August of this year [1935]; and in non-union shops the situation was much worse, with some men and women earning as little as $6.00 or $7.00 per week for full time, or 15 cents per hour or less, and with full-time rates of $10.00 to $15.00 for men and $8.00 to $11.00 for women very common. In Montreal we found men working for as little as 10 cents per hour, and women for eight and nine cents. . . .

. . . what the wage figures mean in terms of living standards may be imagined when it is recognized that the most modest minimum health and decency' budgets for a man and wife and two or three children call for expenditures of at least $1,300 or so per annum at present prices, in Toronto and Montreal; and that the Minimum Wage Boards of both Ontario and Quebec state that $12.50 per week, or $625 per year is required, at a minimum, for independent self-support by a working woman living in these cities . . . [2]

THE DECLINE IN PROVINCIAL PER CAPITA INCOMES[3]

	1928-29 average $ per capita	1933 $ per capita	Per-centage Decrease
Saskatchewan	478	135	72
Alberta	548	212	61
Manitoba	466	240	49
British Columbia	594	314	47
Prince Edward Island	278	154	45
Ontario	549	310	44
Quebec	391	220	44
New Brunswick	292	180	39
Nova Scotia	322	207	36
Canada	471	247	48

1. What can you tell from the table about incomes in Canada before and during the Depression? What region appeared to suffer the most? The least?

Prices of goods fell, so people with jobs or other sources of income were able to get along. Yet a great part of the Canadian population lacked the money to buy even the barest necessities, including food. Ironically, Canada's wheat surpluses sat in grain terminals at a time when thousands hovered on the brink of starvation.

In the early years, people hoped that this Depression, like the ones that Canada had experienced before, would soon end. It was said that the business cycle was in a downturn, soon to correct itself; the "bust" would give way to a "boom". Such claims proved to be hollow as the Depression dragged on year after year.

DIG IN YOUR HEELS

Sir Henry Thornton, President of the C.N.R., like so many public figures of the times, tried to get people to look on the bright side:

In many respects, business is like an Alpinist. It has years of high altitudes, when it scales peaks hitherto unthought of, then, like the climber, misses its footing and slips back toward the valley.

Just as at present, after having attained the higher altitudes in 1928 and 1929, it is reorganizing its footing after having slipped from the crest. It is 'digging in' and getting a new toe hold....

The year 1931 has been, for most of us, a period of tightening our belts; ... of digging in our toes that we might advance in the face of greater difficulties than we had previously been called upon to surmount.[4]

Thousands of businesses went bankrupt, and in the case of those that survived, employees were faced with reduced wages, or unemployment. The rate of unemployment, which reached more than 20% in 1933, produced a huge problem of relief, especially for municipal and city governments. Under the constitution, they lacked the wide powers of the federal government to raise money through taxes, but they had the constitutional responsibility to provide social assistance. Consequently, with revenues declining, many local governments were caught between helping the distressed and fighting off bankruptcy.

The federal election of July, 1930, had resulted in a Conservative victory over the Liberals and the replacement of Mackenzie King as prime minister by R. B. Bennett.* The new leader had impressed

*Bennett, who had succeeded Arthur Meighen as Conservative leader in 1927, was a Calgary lawyer and millionaire, although he was originally from New Brunswick.

247

R. B. Bennett

Canadian voters with his energy and conviction, a sharp contrast to Mackenzie King's caution. Bennett declared he would use tariffs, not just to protect manufacturers but to "blast a way" into world markets, increase trade and create jobs.

THE DEPRESSION HITS THE N.H.L.

A headline in the May 11, 1932 issue of the Toronto Daily Star *indicated "$7,500 Wage Limit Set By the N.H.L. Moguls":*

The times being what they are, the National Hockey League has set a limit of $7,500 on individual player salaries and reduced the player limit to 14.

Action to reduce expenses was deemed necessary at the semi-annual meeting yesterday after it was revealed that only three of the eight clubs had not finished 'in the red.' Figures for each club were not made public, but it was understood that the New York Rangers, Boston Bruins and Montreal Canadiens did make money.

Not only was the individual salary limit cut to $7,500, but it was decided each club should be limited to a total expenditure of $70,000 for player salaries next season. To help in this latter respect, the player limit was fixed at 14. Some clubs last season carried as many as 20 players on the payroll, although the league rules provide that not more than 16 may be used in any one game.[5]

The Bennett government did act quickly by calling a special session of Parliament. Twenty million dollars was approved for relief, and tariffs on manufactured goods were raised. These emergency measures had little effect. The Depression had generally deepened by the summer of 1932 when the Ottawa Conference brought together representatives from British Commonwealth countries. After many

At work in a relief camp

248

Accomplishments during the Depression

Neither depressions nor periods of prosperity are total. There are always groups of people or regions that suffer even during times of prosperity; on the other hand, during a depression, good things can happen. The following developments, some resulting from private enterprise and the majority coming from public enterprise—or government—held promise for Canada's future:

the Hudson's Bay Railway was finally completed to the northern port of Churchill, Manitoba;

the oil industry expanded in southern Alberta and at Fort Norman on the Mackenzie River;

mining at Flin Flon and other northern points expanded;

in 1932, the Canadian Radio Broadcasting Commission, renamed the Canadian Broadcasting Corporation in 1936, was created as a government-owned and operated network;

in 1934, the Bank of Canada was founded to give stability to the country's banking system;

in 1935, the Canadian Wheat Board was established to coordinate the sale of Canadian wheat overseas and improve the price paid to farmers;

in 1935, the Prairie Farm Rehabilitation Act was passed to assist with the recovery of agriculture;

in 1937, Trans-Canada Airlines, the forerunner of Air Canada, was established.

---

hours of hard bargaining, some agreements were reached on lowered duties among Commonwealth members. But once again, the effects were minimal.

Meanwhile, the federal government increased its direct aid to the provinces on an emergency basis. But governments declined to undertake any large-scale programs, such as building roads, bridges and other public works. Relief was doled out grudgingly, on the theory that handouts might weaken the initiative of recipients. One of the few nation-wide programs was the *relief camps*, operated by the Department of Defence. These camps, where men were housed, fed and paid 20 cents a day, were located mainly in remote areas, away from the cities and the propaganda of Communists and other radicals.

In 1934, the Conservative minister of trade and commerce, H. H. Stevens, was responsible for an investigation of price-fixing by large companies. Some startling abuses were revealed, but Stevens resigned in protest against the government's slowness to act. He formed the shortlived Reconstruction Party which entered the 1935 election, then passed from the scene when he was the lone member elected.

All the piecemeal actions by government had produced few results by 1935, when a federal election was unavoidable. R. B. Bennett then startled the nation, and the members of his own cabinet whom he had not bothered to inform, with a series of radio speeches. He announced that the government planned to step into the business life of the nation to direct, regulate and control as never before.

What did Bennett promise in the way of government action? To people of our day, his "New Deal", patterned after President F. D. Roosevelt's New Deal in the United States, may seem rather mild. He announced plans to bring in unemployment insurance, a minimum wage law, social security, and a shorter work week. To Canadians in the 1930s, these were dramatic changes. Coming from a Conservative champion of free enterprise, they were incredible.

BENNETT'S "NEW DEAL"

Excerpts from his radio addresses, January, 1935:

In the last five years, great changes have taken place in the world. The old order is gone. It will not return. . . .

. . . in my mind, reform means Government intervention. It means Government control and regulation. . . .

. . . . The dole is a condemnation, final and complete, of our economic system. If we cannot abolish the dole, we should abolish the system. . . .

Selfish men, and this country is not without them . . . fearful that this Government might impinge on what they have grown to regard as their immemorial right of exploitation, will whisper against us. They will call us radicals. They will say that this is the first step on the road to socialism. We fear them not. . . . We invite their cooperation . . . all the parts of the capitalist system, have only one purpose and that is to work for the welfare of the people. And when any of those instruments in any way fails, it is the plain duty of government which represents the people, to remove the cause of failure. . . . The lives and the happiness and the welfare of too many people depend upon our success to allow the selfishness of a few individuals to endanger it. . . . [6]

Once in office, the Liberals referred the so-called New Deal to the courts, where it was declared "unconstitutional". The following year, 1938, Mr. Bennett resigned as Conservative leader. He was replaced by R. J. Manion. Bennett retired to England, where he obtained a seat in the House of Lords. He remained in England until his death in 1947.

Why had Bennett waited so long? People suspected an election gimmick, a ploy to gain votes. The Liberals had only to wait and to raise doubts about Bennett's sincerity. Without putting forward any constructive alternative, Mackenzie King swept back into office in October, 1935.

The politics of protest

The Depression had the effect of increasing the economic disparities and so increasing the tensions and divisions within Canadian society. It acted as a catalyst, accelerating the process of social adjustment.

It was . . . a pre-eminently political decade. Politics was seen as the means by which society would be changed; political leaders were seen as the natural agents of social reform.[7]

The economic and social pressures of the 1930s gave rise to movements of political protest and reform. Many people in the established political parties, the Conservatives and Liberals, were most fearful of Communist agitation in the cities. However, the protests which had significant impact on Canadian life were regional—in the West and in Quebec.

J. S. Woodsworth at work

The Co-operative Commonwealth Federation (CCF) was born in 1933 in Saskatchewan, perhaps the province most severely hit by the Depression. The leader of this new alliance of labour, farmers and intellectuals was James S. Woodsworth, the Labour M.P. from north Winnipeg. The CCF's program, adopted in Regina at the party's first national convention, was set forth in the "Regina Manifesto".

The following are excerpts from the main statements given:

THE C.C.F. is a federation of organizations whose purpose is the establishment in Canada of a Co-operative Commonwealth in which the principle regulating production, distribution and exchange will be the supplying of human needs and not the making of profits. . . . We do not believe in change by violence. We consider that both the old parties in Canada are the instruments of capitalist interests and cannot serve as agents of social reconstruction, and that whatever the superficial differences between them, they are bound to carry on government in accordance with the dictates of the big business interests who finance them. The CCF aims at political power in order to put an end to this capitalist domination of our political life. It is a democratic movement, a federation of farmer, labor and socialist organizations, financed by its own members and seeking to achieve its ends solely by constitutional methods.

1. PLANNING

   The establishment of a planned socialized economic order, in order to make possible the most efficient development of the national resources and the most equitable distribution of the national income.

2. SOCIALIZATION OF FINANCE

   Socialization of all financial machinery—banking, currency, credit, and insurance, to make possible the effective control of currency, credit and prices, and the supplying of new productive equipment for socially desirable purposes.

3. SOCIAL OWNERSHIP

   Socialization (Dominion, Provincial or Municipal) of transportation, communications, electric power and all other industries and services essential to social planning, and their operation under the general direction of the Planning Commission by competent managements freed from day to day political interference.

4. AGRICULTURE

   Security of tenure for the farmer upon his farm on conditions to be laid down by individual provinces; insurance against unavoidable crop failure; removal of the tariff burden from the operations of agriculture:

5. EXTERNAL TRADE

   The regulation in accordance with the National plan of external trade through import and export boards.

6. CO-OPERATIVE INSTITUTIONS
   The encouragement by the public authority of both producers' and consumers' co-operative institutions.

7. LABOR CODE
   A National Labor Code to secure for the worker maximum income and leisure, insurance covering illness, accident, old age, and unemployment, freedom of association and effective participation in the management of his industry or profession.

8. SOCIALIZED HEALTH SERVICES
   Publicly organized health, hospital and medical services.

9. B.N.A. ACT
   The amendment of the Canadian Constitution; the abolition of the Canadian Senate.

11. TAXATION AND PUBLIC FINANCE
   A new taxation policy designed not only to raise public revenues but also to lessen the glaring inequalities of income and to provide funds for social services and the socialization of industry.[8]

1. Which of these "radical demands" of 1933 have since become "rights" which Canadians have come to take for granted?
2. Why are words like "capitalist" and "socialist" often misleading?

The Winnipeg General Strike of 1919 had first made Woodsworth a national figure. He was arrested as one of the strike leaders, although charges against him were eventually dropped. Elected to Parliament as a Labour M.P. in 1921, he acted throughout the 1920s as a spokesman for the underprivileged. A former Methodist minister turned Christian socialist, Woodsworth had come to believe, long before the 1930s, that inequality was an inevitable part of the capitalist system. Only by changing the system could reformers bring about a situation where people were more important than profits.

The CCF elected seven members in 1935 in its first effort in a federal election, and eight members in 1940.* But the party's divided stand on Canada's participation in World War II hampered efforts to make its ideas more appealing to the general public. While the CCF remained a protest movement rather than a major party in federal politics, it gained considerable strength in individual provinces from Ontario westward. In 1943, it became the Official Opposition in Ontario, and the following year gained power in Saskatchewan under Premier T. C. "Tommy" Douglas.

*Its percentage of the popular vote was just under 10%, each time.

By the time of the 1945 federal election, the CCF's popularity was on the rise. More and more groups of Canadians began to think about the postwar future, and to consider ways of making society free from war and economic depression. The Liberal government responded to the pressure by introducing family allowances in 1944, and promising to bring in unemployment insurance and other forms of social security.

Thus Mackenzie King set the pattern for "out socializing the socialists". In the years after World War II, the C.C.F. continued in the role of advocating social legislation, while their ideas were adopted and frequently put into effect by other parties.

In the election of July, 1974, the Conservatives proposed price

In 1961 the C.C.F. became the New Democratic Party (N.D.P.). The first leader was T. C. Douglas, former premier of Saskatchewan.

William Aberhart

In achieving power, Aberhart defeated the United Farmers of Alberta (U.F.A.) which had held office since 1921. In other words, Alberta was already accustomed to a government run by a party other than the Liberals and Conservatives.

and wage controls. The Liberals attacked the idea, yet put it into effect in October, 1975. Can you find other examples of governments "borrowing" from opposition parties?

A second protest party originating in the West was Social Credit. In the Alberta provincial election of 1935, Social Credit gained 56 of the 63 seats in the assembly. Later in the year, the party took 15 of Alberta's 17 seats in the Canadian House of Commons. Albertans had evidently rejected the Liberals and Conservatives and the political system they stood for. But rather than look to the CCF's vision of a new society, they turned to Social Credit, and William "Bible Bill" Aberhart.

Aberhart combined political and religious appeal with a genius for campaigning and organization. The Calgary high school principal was also an evangelical radio preacher. He had wide following throughout the province. When he entered politics at the darkest point of the depression, he adopted a second "gospel", a simplified version of theories advanced by an English engineer named Major Douglas.

According to the Aberhart version of Social Credit, the Depression was the fault of international bankers, with whom Canadian bankers in "the East" (Toronto and Montreal) were in league. This conspiracy of financial interests was tied to an outdated system of money. This monetary system allowed less money to circulate than would buy the supply of goods produced. The solution, Aberhart claimed, was to create enough new money in the form of dividends —or "social credit"—so that people could buy what they needed. By so doing, they would stimulate production, create jobs and generally revive a stagnant economy.

Although dismissed by economists as a "funny money" theory, Social Credit as promoted by William Aberhart looked very attractive to the voters of Alberta. In their condition of poverty and low morale, they could well believe they were victims of a faulty system. Since they seemed to have nothing to lose, they grasped at the promise of $25 monthly dividends.

The Aberhart government actually did nothing radical until 1937, after two years in office. Then a series of acts were proposed to put Social Credit theory into practice. Since these acts dealt with money and banking which were the responsibility of the federal government, the latter either disallowed them or referred them to the courts, which declared them unconstitutional. The results, Aberhart could claim, showed once again that Eastern financial interests were getting in the way of improvements in the lives of the people of Alberta.

Thus the Social Credit Party, without Social Credit policies, kept its lease on life, and Aberhart remained premier until his death in

A Social Credit dividend

1943. Under his successor, Ernest C. Manning, the reputation for careful, honest government sustained the Social Credit Party in office. Although a minor force in federal politics, in spite of some eventual support in Quebec,* Social Credit continued to be influential in the politics of Alberta and, from 1952, in British Columbia.

*See Chapter 10.

In Quebec, Maurice Duplessis headed a new French-Canadian nationalist party, the Union Nationale, that won the 1936 provincial election. Since World War I Quebec had been largely ignored by the rest of Canada. Yet the tension between the "two solitudes", the French- and English-speaking Canadians, was very much a reality. When the Depression struck, cultural and economic tension merged, presenting an opportunity for political change. *Les Anglais*—whether English-speaking Canadian or American—were the targets, since the rich were usually English-speaking and the growing ranks of the poor, town workers and farmers, were generally French-speaking.

Maurice Duplessis

Duplessis gained power by appealing to French Canadians' feelings of exploitation by the English minority. Once in office, however, he identified the federal government as the villain from whom French Canada needed protection. He went so far as to challenge Ottawa in the early months of World War II, and when the federal Liberals threw their efforts against him in the Quebec election late in 1939, he was defeated. However, Duplessis returned to power in 1944 and remained there until his death in 1959.

Ironically, Duplessis proved to be no threat to English-Canadian domination of Quebec's economic life. Foreign investors continued to be attracted to Quebec, with its natural resources, large labour force and a government friendly to business, and hostile to unions. French-Canadian nationalism in the 1930s and until the 1960s, was still based on the traditional image of a rural, church-led culture protected from the mainstream of North American life.

People of the Depression

Jokes from the 1930s

There's nothing to beat some of those rural telephone lines for service. Just give one ring and you get every person in the township.

Who were the people of the Depression, and how did they respond to the extraordinary conditions in which they lived? The following documents give you impressions, through which you meet the prairie farmer, the city dweller, the relief camp worker, politicians and government officials, hoboes and parents desperately trying to provide for their children. You will see how people found escape, how reality continually overwhelmed them, and how they survived in spite of difficulties which most Canadians in our day can scarcely imagine.

Coping with the Depression was a challenge. . . .

ONLY WIND—NO RAIN

Poet Anne Marriott describes what life was like on prairie farms in this excerpt from her poem THE WIND OUR ENEMY:

Wind
in a lonely laughterless shrill game
with broken wash-boiler, bucket without
a handle, Russian thistle, throwing up
sections of soil.
God, will it never rain again? What about
those clouds out west? No, that's just dust, as
thick and stifling now as winter underwear.
No rain, no crop, no feed, no faith, only
wind.[10]

Drought on the prairies

Ideas from the social sciences: history as vicarious experience

That we can "learn from experience" is common knowledge, but the error we sometimes make is thinking that we can learn *only* from personal experience. In fact, time and circumstances tend to limit the number of things in which a person can be directly involved. All of us broaden our knowledge of the world by sharing—through conversation, television, books, newspapers and so on—the experiences of others. Just as we can understand the joy, excitement or sadness of a character in a novel or on a stage, we can learn from the experiences of actual people who lived before us.

On the other hand, the exposure to others' experiences is no guarantee we will benefit in the way of personal growth, knowledge or appreciation. The events of their lives may strike us as obscure, uninteresting, odd or simply irrelevant. If other people are very different—in age, nationality, income, social background—we are even more inclined to say, "It couldn't happen to us." Consider the following statement by a mother who tries to explain the Depression to her children:

THEY JUST DON'T UNDERSTAND

"When I try to tell my children what it was like out there in the Ontario bush without more than a couple of dollars from one month's end to another, and my folks and us kids living worse than any Negroes in the South, my kids pretend they each have a violin and they play all together, the Hearts and Flowers bit, and it's just Mom going into her Depression act again.

"I mean, I used to try to tell them, because I felt they should know, that everyone should know, *everyone*, but it was no use.

"I told them about my little brother, their Uncle Donald, going to school his first year and the teacher enrolling him as Donalda, as a girl, and thinking he was a girl for months because the only clothes he had to wear were the hand-me-downs from my sisters and me. When I told them that, they laughed so hard they rolled on the floor, so I said, 'Never again.' There is just no way to make them understand."[9]

The feeling of being able to "put yourself in someone else's shoes" is a concept psychologists call *empathy*. That is, the ability we have to feel compassion and understanding for another person. Whereas sympathy may only involve feeling sorry for someone, empathy involves sharing as fully as possible that person's emotions. Obviously, we do not scientifically analyze or objectively observe a friend's feelings when we listen to what he is saying; we can empathize with him when he explains how happy or sad he is upon a particular occasion.

1. Why might the mother want to tell her children about the Depression?
2. How does she describe their reactions to her stories? What might account for their reactions?

257

3. To what extent do you think the children can understand, vicariously, their relatives' experiences during the Depression?
4. What benefits might there be for members of a younger generation to hear or read about the history of the "Great Depression"?

IT'S GOTTA RAIN SOMETIME

In this excerpt from a story written by R. Ross Annett, the characters speak about the hopelessness of drought on the prairies:

Big Joe remembered the day the machine-company men came after the tractors that he could not pay for. That was in 1933.

"Where's the other tractor?" they had demanded.

"Buried," said Big Joe.

"Buried!" cried the machine agent. "What the hell for?"

"For eternity, brother," said Big Joe. " 'Nless you bring a steam shovel to dig her out."

The men had gone with him across the road to Uncle Pete's half-section. He showed them the big sand dune that had accumulated in one of the worst blows—and grown considerably since—completely burying tractor and granary.

The men had gone away then, and they never came back. They never expected to see that tractor again. . . .

Everybody thought that the country would never come back, that it ought to be abandoned. Most people, indeed, had moved out.

But not Big Joe. He would not abandon the section of land that had brought him more than one ten-thousand-dollar crop of wheat. True, during the past six years his farm had often not produced feed enough for one cow and a scrawny team of horses, let alone a crop. But Big Joe stuck.

"It's gotta rain sometime," he kept saying.[11]

ENTERTAINMENT AT NO COST

How did people spend their leisure time if they had no money to spend on entertainment? These Canadians recall how they spent some of their time:

Jokes from the 1930s

When people ask you to sing, don't be coaxed—go ahead and do it. It'll be their own fault.

In those days everybody had a piano. Well, nearly everybody.

You could walk down any street in any town or city about 4:30 any afternoon, after school was out, and hear children practising on the piano. It was the thing to do. . . . I remember I took piano, for about four years, from a Mrs. Pearse and for the first two years she charged 15 cents a half hour and then 25 cents a half hour.

Lord, there must have been tens of thousands of pianos in those days. It seemed every house had one and most people could play. Maybe not play well, but play enough for Sunday evening sing-songs.

Others took part in hockey scrimmages:

What good was education? We found that out soon enough, no jobs at all. But there was a lot of fun to be had. The city (of Winnipeg) had skating and hockey rinks around the city, green wooden shacks and boarding, and a caretaker to keep the fire going and all that. We'd hang around there . . . and we had nothing to do but play hockey. Scrimmage. . . . [12]

Author James Gray describes other places where people gathered:

The library . . . was a special haven for the homeless and ageing single unemployed, some of whom might spend eight hours a day, six days a week, in its warm, friendly quiet. Some of them read, some of them just sat and looked at books and magazines until they fell asleep. The librarians frowned on sleepers and would occasionally clear them out of the reading-rooms. . . .

The pool-rooms and brokerage offices were all crowded throughout the depression, though seldom with customers. The brokerage offices supplied free newspapers and the pool-room furnished both recreation and heat . . . the unemployed congregated in such numbers that the players often had to complain to the management in order to get elbow room for their cues. [13]

RADIO NOSTALGIA

Soap operas, comedy and music were the mainstay of radio in the 1930s:

(a) Most of the dramas were, of course, the daytime "soaps"—so called because they were listened to mostly by women while doing their washing and cleaning, who were thus presumably vulnerable to sales pitches by the soap company sponsors. The essential ingredients of these shows were nicely contained in James Thurber's definition of a soap opera:

An early radio

> "A kind of sandwich, whose recipe is simple enough, although it took years to compound. Between thick slices of advertising spread twelve minutes of dialogue, add predicament, villainy, and female suffering in equal measure, throw in a dash of nobility, sprinkle with tears, season with organ music, cover with a rich announcer sauce, and serve five times a week."

(b) Laughter is lifeblood to a comedian, and many [ex-vaudeville comedians] found it difficult telling jokes to a microphone that wouldn't laugh. The first stage show ever broadcast featured Ed Wynn in *The Perfect Fool*, over station WIZ [New York] February 19, 1922. He was appalled at the silence after he told his first, time-tested jokes. He asked the announcer to quickly round up anyone he could find around the studio. A short while later he regained his

Jokes from the 1930s

Short Waves

The day is done.
I seek repose.
I take my glasses
Off my nose.
Then snuggle in
A cushioned chair,
And wonder what
Is "on the air."
I'm weary from
The busy din.
'T will soothe my nerves
To "listen in."
I touch a switch,
Then turn a dial,
And get this programme
In a while;

" . . . this make of car."
" . . . will fit your feet."
" . . . a good cigar."
" . . . is made of wheat."
" . . . no other watch."
" . . . will stop decay."
" . . . so brush your teeth."
" . . . with beauty clay."
" . . . our motor oil."
" . . . will suit your taste."
" . . . this famous soap."
" . . . is nickel faced."
" . . . our kennel food."
" . . . will give you style."
And so it goes
All round the dial.

I place my glasses
On my nose,
And seek elsewhere
A night's repose.

confidence as an audience of maintenance men, telephone operators, electricians, and cleaning women giggled and howled at his silly sallies and facial expressions. Studio audiences became a must for comedy shows.

There was also a kind of humor indigenous to radio. Mock insults and feuds between two leading comedians would boost each other's ratings, and sometimes could be kept running for months, such as the one between Jack Benny and Fred Allen, in which Allen kept finding new ways to describe Benny's stinginess. One evening a sketch had Benny being held up by a thief who snarled, "Money or your life!" The long, long period of dead air that followed became hilarious, and was topped by Benny finally saying petulantly, "I'm thinking it over." This just couldn't be as funny in any other medium. And there was Allen's classic retort to an insult by Benny: "If I had my writers here you wouldn't talk to me like that and get away with it!"

(c) *The National Barn Dance* was a Saturday night fling for millions of farm folk and lovers of country music. Some of the popular big band leaders were Paul Whiteman, Fred Waring and his Pennsylvanians, and Ben Bernie (The Old Maestro—"Yowsah, yowsah . . ."), and some of the top variety shows were *Your Hit Parade, Show Boat, and Kraft Music Hall.*

Outstanding female vocalists of the period were Dinah Shore, Jessica Dragonette, Ruth Etting and outsized Kate Smith. . . .

Among the popular male singers there was a handful of strong, lyric voices like those of James Melton, Morton Downey, and Arthur Tracy. . . . And then there were the crooners—Bing Crosby and Whispering Jack Smith, who probably started it all. Or was Rudy Vallee to blame?[14]

ALL THROUGH THE 'THIRTIES

All through the 'thirties, south of Saskatoon,
A farmer farmed a farm without a crop.
Dust filled the air, the lamp was lit at noon,
And never blade of wheat that formed a top.
One New Year's to the hired man he said,
"I have no money. You must take the deeds.
And I will be the hired man instead,
To shovel snow and fork the tumbleweeds."
So it was done. And when the next year came,
"Take back the farm," the other had to say.
And year by year, alternate, just the same
Till the War came and took them both away.
With such superb resource and self-possession
Canada made it through the long depression.[15]

Some turned to government relief, others took to the rails. . . .

(a) Life in relief camps as described by James Gray:

. . . . In addition to twenty cents per day, the men also got a tobacco allowance—based on 1.45 cents per day for each day in camp. Thus, before a new-comer was able to get a ten-cent package of tobacco, he had to get seven days of camp life behind him. . . . There was little reading material and no means of pursuing an education or a hobby. Nobody was allowed to have a camera in camp.

So they griped about the food, the clothing, the bed bugs, the overcrowding in the dormitories, the martinetish regime, the latrines, and any other grievance they could conjure up. . . . All the investigators who roamed the camp—social workers, preachers, Members of Parliament, and Royal Commissioners—were unanimous on this point: the single unemployed regarded themselves as Canada's forgotten men. They had been filed and forgotten and nobody cared if they lived or died.[16]

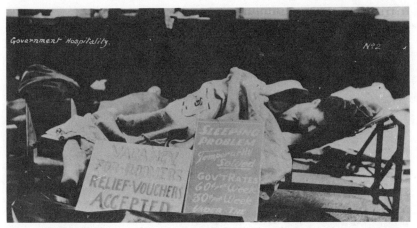

Government hostel

(b) One person's reasoning about what went on in the camps:

If people were to get relief, then a lot of people in official places— mayors, councillors, administrators—felt they should work. . . . You did work for your few dollars and it came out in funny ways. . . .
[One way] was to let the machinery stand idle. Let the men do it, for their 90 cents a day, so you had the crazy situation of a $3,000 bulldozer and a steam roller sitting by the side of the road while 50 men went at the dirt and rock with shovels and picks. Now, under any conditions, those men weren't going to make the dirt fly all that much, and it took many times, say ten times as long, for 20 men to dig away a clay bank on a municipal road than for the bulldozer man to drop his blade and clear the whole thing out, once and for all. So good machinery stood idle, costing the taxpayer money as you'll understand, but by the Great Balls of Fire, those 20 or 30 guys who were accepting relief would be doing some work. . . .

...the municipality was getting its pound of flesh so everything was just fine.[17]

RIDING THE RAILS

Young men without work found "free" transportation. They were always on the move and almost never found work:

Most of the time, the transients weren't really going anywhere. At first they moved out of the West in great numbers looking for work in the factory towns of Ontario, and found a welcome as cold as a Manitoba winter.... By 1933, the idea of getting a job had been abandoned and the legions of single unemployed moved back and forth across the country because they had nothing else to do. The railway towns of the West were overrun in the summers by young transients, who dropped off freight trains to try to exchange a day's work in a garden for a square meal or two....

Riding the rails

They had left home in Glace Bay or Kitchener or Nelson to look for work because their families were on relief. They were often homesick but were resolutely heading in the opposite direction. They had been on the road long enough to have lost any hesitancy about asking for a meal.... [18]

Some blamed the government....

A biographer comments about Bennett's lack of contact with the members of his own party:

One [secretary] employed by Bennett dictated, for Bennett to sign, a very moving letter of condolence to the lady he assumed to be the suddenly bereaved wife of a Conservative M.P. Bennett signed this letter without reading it, and was exceedingly vexed when he received from the M.P. himself a chiding letter saying that he was in fact alive, but saddened to feel that his leader had not noticed his still regular attendance at Party caucus meetings.[19]

Many people blamed Premier Bennett personally for their troubles:

I'll never forget a picture of him, it was in the newspapers when he was prime minister. Here he is, on a luxury liner sailing to England and he is wearing this fine coat with the fur collar and one of those hats they used to call a bowler, but it is his face. A fat, sleek, contented toad of face. Just the way he is standing, well, I know it infuriated a hell of a lot of Canadians, maybe thousands. Beside him is his sister, just as tall and smug and well-fed as R. B. Bennett was. He was a corporation lawyer, you know. A lawyer, God knows, is bad enough, but a corporation lawyer is pure dynamite. Steal the cents off a dead man's eyes and swear because they weren't quarters. Oh, yes, everything I remember bad about the Depression was right there in that picture.

Mr. Bennett was pompous, smug, and rich. He had the most prestigious law firm in Calgary, and could pick and choose his clients.

Hon. R. B. Bennett and his sister

The sole decision-maker?

His cabinet ministers were rarely consulted on major policies and their opinions carried little weight. One of the stories going the rounds in the 1930s was of the tourist who saw R. B. Bennett walking alone towards Parliament Hill from his suite in the Chateau Laurier, talking to himself. He asked a bystander who it was and got the reply that it was the Prime Minister holding a cabinet meeting.[20]

A popular image?

"Bennett, the loud, ebullient one who barked and blasted at the depression in the name of sound money and self-help, of high tariffs and a happier bygone age. . . ."[21]

No, he was not a man of the people. I could never say that. I don't think he knew a thing about the Canadian people. No, even after four years in office, as prime minister, I don't think he knew anything about the people.

I'll tell you a story which might tell you something about him. He bought a new car, the jazziest in Calgary and while he was learning to drive it he ran it up a pole. He walked away from it, and as far as I know he never got behind the wheel of a car again.

Nobody could talk to him at any time and he had a secretary named Miss Miller and you needed eight master keys to get by her.[22]

Others took their own action in the struggle for survival . . .

THE REGINA RIOT—A SNOW JOB?

An eye-witness says:

I always thought the Regina Riot was what you would today call a snow job. A police riot, and against us, the trekkers, and believe you me when I say an awful lot of those smashed windows and stolen goods were the work of good Regina citizens. I know. I saw them. Men in good clothes who weren't with our bunch who came out from Vancouver and so I can say, those guys that did the looting were a lot of Regina people. Well, mostly.

Look, look at it this way. We were disciplined. Art Evans told us it had to be this way, that being polite and organized and neat even in our old duds was the way to gain public support, and we'd got it all along the line. Suppose a trekker was found with a pen and pencil set or a wrist watch or something in his pocket. Well, they

The Regina Riot

Alienation during the Depression

Alienation is the term used to explain negative feelings that people have about their situation in life and their inability to do anything about it. You may also remember that alienated people feel one or more of the following characteristics: *social isolation*, feeling separated from others; *meaninglessness*, feeling that one's life is futile; *normlessness*, feeling there are no standards or rules by which a person can judge things; *estrangement*, feeling out of step with society's accepted standards or rules; and *powerlessness*, feeling that one has no power to change anything.

The Depression of the 1930s was a time when large numbers of people experienced conditions that would seem to be tailormade for mass alienation. Many did in fact feel alienated; many others, including people who suffered extreme poverty and hardship, did not. Why was it that some Canadians were able to cope with potential feelings of hopelessness or powerlessness, while others succumbed? One of the ways of understanding the different reactions to the Depression is to look at the *values* people held.

You may remember that values are standards which influence, or even determine, behaviour. Some values are more strongly held than others, but generally speaking, there are some things which many Canadians probably value at the same time, e.g. freedom, honesty, charity and so forth. Values are also, however, somewhat determined by environment and circumstances, and value change is not necessarily a bad thing. One person's value regarding the sanctity of human life might be quite different in wartime than it would be in peace. Material goods, other than food, shelter and clothing, might be less valued in times of economic depression than during periods of prosperity.

In the prosperous 1920s Canadians were caught up in the spiral of increased wages and increased purchasing power. Rapid technological advances and increased opportunity to acquire material goods overwhelmed men and women alike. No longer were they as concerned with the pre-war values of family, church, hard work and thrift. Instead, people turned to the pursuit of material wealth and pleasure.

However, when the economic tide turned so suddenly with the financial crash of 1929, those people who depended upon money as their comfort and hope, were soon faced with a desperate situation. Whereas in the 1920s, they had optimism and the money upon which to build a better life, in the 1930s, hope had to come from other sources.

Jokes from the 1930s

Snooty
A very self-satisfied man arrived at the gates of heaven and asked for admission.
"Where are you from?"
"Toronto."
"Well, you can come in, but you won't like it."

265

Some people simply could not cope. Hopelessness and human suffering were pervasive. People, who only a few years before were saving for the future were forced to live day-to-day existences. Those who couldn't feed themselves or their families sometimes became thieves; those who saw no alternative sometimes swallowed their pride and stood in long lines for free soup and sandwiches.

Suddenly, without the prospect of obtaining a better life through economic gains, people were forced to re-examine their goals and values. Since families could not depend upon entertainment outside the home, the family took on renewed importance. Once again, sharing and brotherhood were looked upon as important. Value systems were in many cases reversed, and concern for others became more important than getting ahead of others. Thus, during the Depression decade, values became supremely important to the ability one had to survive the Depression or to become alienated to the degree that some of the people in these excerpts did.

Ex-journalist Barry Broadfoot travelled 27000 km across Canada recording statements made by people who survived the Great Depression. In his book, Ten Lost Years, *he records their experiences. The following excerpts show some of the feelings of alienation these Canadians endured:*

HARD TIMES KILLED MY MAN

"The coal killed my man. Just as sure as if he'd been on the field of battle, through shot and shell. He worked for a coal company, first in Winnipeg and then we came to Toronto where my relatives were. . . .

Home after dark, maybe seven or eight loads on an ordinary day, and he got $2.50 a day. His pay packet on Saturday night was $15. About sixty a month for the hardest work one man ever ordered another man to do. . . .

How many's the time, oh hundreds, that he has just lain down on the kitchen floor and I'd be taking off his wool jacket and pants and one of the kids would be working away on his boots. The dinner would be steaming on the table and the dear man would say, 'Eat, it'll get cold.' Sometimes he'd have a bowl of vegetable soup and some bread and then go to bed and sleep right through, not a movement, not a whisper until next morning. Ten, eleven hours of the sleep of the dead.

How could there be a man-wife relationship that way? The man never saw his children. He slept all day Sunday, or just stared out the window. He never cursed. By God, I did though. I used to go to church and I'd curse Mr. Bennett, the prime minister, and then when he was out, I'd curse King, the new one.

In 1939 my man fell and with this load of coal on his back

Depression soup line

something snapped. The doctor said he couldn't do hard work again, so the company hemmed and hawed and finally put him in as a checker . . . he was only 33 . . . He died next year. That's how the hard times destroyed my man. And me."[24]

GO DROWN YOURSELF [about an employee of a relief office]
"It was the way these men had lost their spirit, almost their will to survive, and they'd come shuffling into that office and ask for something more and I'd sometimes scream at them. 'Get the hell out of here. Go down to False Creek and drown yourself. There's the way, right down the hill, and now, beat it.' They'd just stand there and take it and then say something like, 'My kids need shoes to go to school,' or 'My wife has pleurisy and I can't get no doctor to come and see her,' and you'd just have to grit your teeth and reach for a form.

I know what it was doing to these fellows, and I know that even without a Depression, most of them had been in a pretty lousy economic box even before. Talk about your Roaring Twenties! Roaring in New York, maybe, or roaring in the slick magazines, but in Canada it was just a lot of wimpering.

But back to me. I didn't like what was happening to me. In that office I could see the rottenness of the relief system, what it did to people, the graft, and oh yes, there was plenty of that, and the phoney contracts and the phoney people and especially the politicians. You know, there is something about politics that brings out the very worst in people. But to me. I couldn't do much, I was just the guy who was checking forms and okaying extra relief and initialing forms. . . .

So I'd blow up at these people who would come in, and after, I'd apologize, and they would usually just look at me with those goddamned eyes they had. They didn't hate me. Can't even give them that much credit. I found myself turning into a hateful person, spiteful, taking it out on some person when it really couldn't have been his fault. Yelling at my wife, cuffing my kids, snarling at my neighbors, and why? Why? Because I knew that I was part of a system which was wrong, and it was turning me wrong, and to protect my wife and kids I had to keep going wrong, and more wrong. . . . [25]

1. In the excerpt, "Hard Times Killed My Man," what behaviours of the husband and wife show they feel alienated?
2. In "Go Drown Yourself," at whom (or what) is the relief office employee really angry? On whom does he take out his anger? Why?

As a last resort during these difficult times, many Canadians turned to the federal government for help. Despite their feelings of pride and a belief that they should be able to make it on their own, hundreds wrote pleading letters to Prime Minister R. B. Bennett asking for assistance in the form of money, job assistance or even clothing from Eaton's catalogue to help a family survive a Canadian winter. In their book, The Wretched of Canada, *Grayson and Bliss reprint many of these letters. The following are typical:*

Kent Ont.
December 15, 1931

Hon. R. B. Bennett
Royal York, Toronto

Dear Mr. Bennett,—I hope you will pardon my writing to you today.

I saw in the Toronto Star where you were going to be the speaker on Wednesday night at the Royal York so have taken the liberty to write to you and I hope you will regard this as strictly confidential.

I am glad you arrived home safely from your trip abroad and hope it has done you good.

Would like to hear your talk but have no radio.

You will wonder what in the world I have written to you about.

Well, we are farmers. We came out to this place about five years ago to try our hand at farming.

My man has a trade at carpentering but he developed rheumatism in the shoulders, caused I believe by the constant use of hammer and saw, so we thought a change of work, using other muscles might be good for him.

We traded our home, equity 2300. on this farm but found after moving here that the place had been terribly neglected and was in a very run down condition. We have worked very hard and it shows a marked improvement but we seem unable to get far ahead.

There are several buildings which could be renovated but the folks who hold the mortgages will not let us tear them away to improve the rest and we feel it is not fair for us to put on improvements, not having the privilege of using what could be used here as well.

———————————

Please Mr. Bennett, forgive me for sending this letter but somehow it eases my mind to send it.

I hope you have a very Merry Christmas.

Respectfully yours,
Dorothy Franklin[26]

Burton, Alta.
February 19/35

Dear Mr. Bennet:—
I suppose I am silly to write this letter but I haven't any one else to write to so am going to hope and pray that you will read this yourself and help me or us, rather.

We are just one of many on relief and trying to keep our place without been starved out. Have a good 1/2 section not bad buildings and trying to get a start without any money and 5 children all small. Have been trying to send 3 to school and live on $10.00 a month relief for everything, medicine meat flour butter scribblers. Haven't had any milk for 3 months but will have 2 cows fresh in March some time. Am nursing a 10 months old baby and doing all the work cooking washing mending on bread and potatoes some days. This is our worst winter as my husband has had to be home to look after the outside chores. Other winters he always made some money as we lived in town and I could manage alone.

Am so worried on account of the children as we never have any vegetables except potatoes and almost no fruit and baby hasn't any shoes have kept him in old socks instead but now he is getting so he creeps and pulls them off so often. I would like to get a couple of little pigs this spring I am sure we can make a go of this place as its good land and doesn't blow if we would just manage until next fall. Just had 70 acres in last year and the dry spell just caught it right along with the grasshoppers although we poisoned most of them there were hardly any left by fall. I cant hardly sleep for worrying about it. Please help me by lending me some money and I will send you my engagement ring & wedding ring as security. I know I could pay you next fall because I like this place and we have a good deal on it no interest for 10 years.

Yours sincerley
Mrs. R. Paddy[27]

1. (a) Dorothy Franklin asks pardon for writing, and hopes that Mr. Bennett had a safe trip home from abroad. Mrs. Paddy hopes Bennett will not think her silly for writing. Despite the fact they seem desperate, they make only small requests for help. Do you find it surprising that the letters to Prime Minister Bennett are not more hostile?

(b) How typical of Canadians were people who wrote to the Prime Minister likely to be?

(c) Was a person seeking help likely to try masking his or her true feelings in a letter?

(d) Are these letters likely to reflect the general reaction of Canadians toward the role of government during the Depression?

2. If people today were to write their M.P. or the Prime Minister about inflation or taxation, do you think the letters would be as mild? What might be some reasons for the difference?

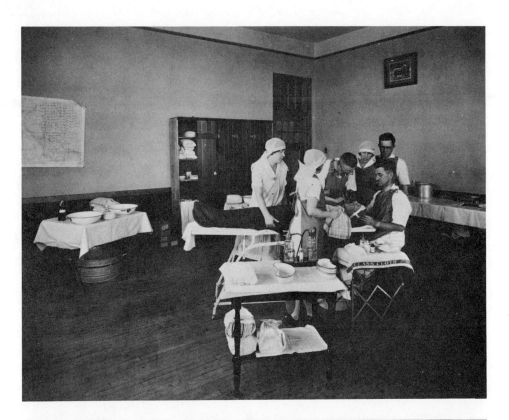

TOP: *A travelling medical clinic in Alberta*. BOTTOM: *Chateau Lake Louise during the Depression*

271

However low in the mind a jobless man might get, trudging from one shabby employment office to another —and I can testify to the lowness—he did not have to feel that, thanks to some inherent inferiority, he was an exile in his own country, forever fixed in a second- or third-class status. And everywhere he turned there were vivid reminders that the Depression was as bad or worse for others: . . . [28]

Canadian novelist, Hugh Garner, in his autobiography, One Damn Thing After Another! *would seem to agree that the Depression did not only mean hard times:*

One summer day in 1935 my friend Howard "Skinny" Moore and I set out for the United States with a package of makin's, a dime in cash, and a bag of my mother's cucumber sandwiches. We slept the first night on somebody's lawn in Oakville, Ontario, and made it to Niagara Falls the following day, hitching rides. We split the dime between us to cross one of the bridges to Niagara Falls, New York; I made it past the US Immigration, Skinny didn't. I went on to New York and Washington and ended up in California. And that's how it was done.

We were two of the many boys and young men who became bums, hoboes, migrant workers, or temporary tramps, call us what you will, who were part of the phenomenon of the Great Depression. During the years between 1930 and 1939 I travelled across Canada from Montreal to Vancouver and from Massachusetts to Mexico, with shorter serendipity trips here and there through the Canadian West, the US South, and the damndest places you ever heard of in search of work—"They're taking on tomato pickers in Santa Barbara"—in search of change, for adventure, or just for the fun of it. . . .

I lived one summer in New York on 60¢ a day, and stocked wheat along the Soo Line and Assiniboine Line in southern Saskatchewan for a buck a day and board, which was the going wage that year. When I'm asked why I rode the freights and beat my way through much of Canada and the United States instead of working at the terrible little jobs I had in Toronto between trips, my best answer is that when I was home I was poor, but when I was on the road I was merely broke. And there's a lot of difference between the two.

Generally speaking the guys on the road were not political at all, although in the American Northwest the older hoboes still carried the old red Wobbly card of the I.W.W. (Industrial Workers of the World) anarcho-syndicalist movement. The Communists tried to organize the hoboes with very little success. Here in Canada we had the Regina riots, when the Mounties tried to stop several hundred hoboes from riding the freights to Ottawa. The American government under Franklin D. Roosevelt was much smarter than its Canadian counterpart, and it set up several administrations such as the Works Projects Administration and the Civilian Conservation Corps, which gave jobs to thousands of young men.

Young people today are either indifferent to the Great Depression or have an exaggerated view of it. It was tough, but it wasn't all hunger and sadness. There were picnics, corn roasts, and cheap dances. People still hadn't been divided one from the other by status and the family car, and we did things communally. Young people fell in love and married. After all, a married relief cheque was better than two single people getting nothing at all. People learned to cope with constant unemployment and penury, and many of them rose to heights of bravery and unselfishness they never would have reached in normal times. Babies were born, whether their fathers were employed or not, and their young mothers made do with handmade or hand-me-down layettes. A wicker laundry basket is just as good a bassinet as a store-bought one.

Do you want to know something? I don't think I'd have wanted to miss the Great Depression for the world.[29]

1. Hugh Garner writes about the Depression with a certain nostalgia. Garner's account was written in approximately the same year and is about the same time period as the accounts of people interviewed by Barry Broadfoot. What was there about Garner's personality and circumstances that might explain why he has more positive memories of the Depression than those people do?

2. Why do you think Hugh Garner said, "I don't think I'd have wanted to miss the Great Depression for the world"?

---

would have thrown the key away. Five, eight, ten years. Looting was the worst crime against property....

There were a lot of store windows bashed in.... There was a lot of damage but two days later, after Dominion Day, you couldn't tell the difference.

I'm sorry the policeman was killed and some of our boys got arrested and it made a lot of noise across the country but as I said, it was a snow job. Old R. B. Bennett wanted a showdown and he got it, piling all those cops into vans and banging them into the square. Guns were firing. Guess who had the guns? He wanted to discredit the trek and he did. Oh, yes, he succeeded.... [23]

Postscript to the Depression

The "Great Depression" left its mark on Canada and Canadians at every level, from the individual to the institution. An entire generation, including those who escaped financial suffering, were affected by the long years of uncertainty and fear that "it could happen again —and to me!" The following statements indicate a feeling about the impact of the Depression.

NOT A HOBO, JUST A WANDERER

One of the hundreds of people interviewed by Barry Broadfoot for his book Ten Lost Years *shows how he kept his self-respect in spite of what he endured:*

Jokes from the 1930s

The Days That Are No More— And yet one cannot refrain from sighing sometimes for the good old days when men were men, but women weren't.

The Bennett buggy

I was not a hobo. A hobo, by definition, is a regular bum, a professional bum, and there probably were hoboes in the time of the Crusades and there are hoboes now. There always have been that kind of people, whether they are on the highways or in the slums, in the Skid Roads or sitting beside a fire sipping Scotch whiskey in Rosedale (a fashionable part of Toronto) and living off their wife's inherited wealth. Hoboism is a state of mind.

I was, you could say, a wanderer. One of the unfortunates. A victim of the economic system? Perhaps. Certainly, most certainly a casualty in the battle between ignorant men who were running this country. There are two places in Ontario, in the fair city of Toronto and down at the even fairer city of London, where ancient records will show that I am a criminal. A criminal in that I violated the Criminal Code of Canada and thereby gained a criminal record for begging. Jail. . . .

. . . I do have a criminal record, and to me, as one who survived what we call The Great Canadian Depression, that is a badge of honor.[30]

"PLAIN AND SIMPLE"—NO MORE

"Anyway, they were good times and bad times and I think the Canadian nation came out of it with a tougher layer of skin. We aren't so naive. My God, but we were naive. Just plain and simple country folk, really, before all that. Fight the King's wars, trust our politicians, believe that big wheat crops were the economic cornerstone of the nation, and go to church every Sunday. The Thirties sure as hell changed all that."[31]

9

Canada and World War II

World War II was a war that our soldiers, sailors and airmen believed in —that people at home supported to the full. The issue was black and white, with no grey areas. Hitler's Nazi regime was a tyranny that had to be destroyed or we would be engulfed by it . . . this Canadian volunteer army that swelled from one division to five was bound together out of a conviction that it was a war that had to be waged and had to be won. . . . [1]

The hope that the 1930s would end in "peace with honour"* was smashed at dawn on September 1, 1939. German armies raced into Poland and bombers began the attacks that would reduce Warsaw and other cities to rubble in a matter of days. The Polish air force was demolished on the ground; the army of 2 500 000 men and 250 000 horses was no match for Germany's **panzer** divisions equipped with armoured cars and tanks. Then on September 17 the Soviet Union invaded Poland from the east and Polish resistance collapsed. Before the end of the month, German armies occupied the bombed-out remains of Warsaw, the capital. The country was then partitioned between Germany and the Soviet Union, who were co-operating under a non-aggression pact which they had arranged in late August.

*The famous phrase uttered by the then British prime minister, Neville Chamberlain, following the Munich agreement of September, 1938. Britain and France had consented to Germany's takeover of part of Czechoslovakia, in the vain hope of "appeasing" Hitler.

armoured

The Poles had little conception of what was about to hit them. On paper their thirty-one infantry divisions, plus six in reserve, might have been a match for the invader, had it not been for the invention of this entirely new form of warfare. The fact that they possessed eleven cavalry brigades and only two armoured brigades was in itself bad enough, but what was worse was that it meant their strategists had no conception of the new role of the tank. Many of them felt that the tank was an overrated weapon, not so mobile or manoeuvrable as the horse, and always liable to break down or get bogged down in the mud. Fuel for the horse is easy to find, they thought, it does not run out of petrol. They would not face the fact that central Poland, with hardly a hill, forest or river between Poznan and Warsaw, is ideal tank country, very difficult to defend. And while a horse can be stopped by a machine-gun bullet, a tank can not.

Psychologically too the Polish leaders were prejudiced in favour of the horse. It was with cavalry that they had fought in the First World War, as a result of which their country regained independence after a hundred years of foreign occupation. . . . The horse had served them well, and in their September 1939 army there were a quarter of a million of them.

The Stuka dive-bombers were from the start particularly effective against infantry in the field, against Polish communications and generally at spreading confusion and panic among the population. Some came hunting in packs against specific military objectives, but others roamed the skies on their own, apparently with orders to shoot at anything that moved—trains, cars, horses or even pedestrians. General Wladyslaw Anders, who commanded the Polish forces in Italy later in the war, wrote of the war's beginning:

> Once I saw a group of small children being led by their teacher to the shelter of the woods. Suddenly there was the roar of an aeroplane. The pilot circled round, descending to a height of fifty metres. As he dropped his bombs and fired his machine guns, the children scattered like sparrows. The aeroplane disappeared as quickly as it had come, but on the field some crumpled and lifeless bundles of bright clothing remained. The nature of the new war was already clear.[2]

THE CONQUEST OF WESTERN EUROPE

Through the winter of 1939-1940, the period called the "phony war", Western Europe wondered what Germany's next move would be. France appeared to be secure behind the Maginot Line, a system of fortifications stretching from Switzerland to the Belgian border. The French army was large, well-equipped, and supported by British troops. But the illusion of security was smashed by events in the spring of 1940.

How does technology affect warfare?

Almost since the last world war ended in 1945 there have been fears of a "Third World War", in which terrible new weapons would produce destruction and death on a scale too horrible to imagine. One side, and probably both sides, would be devastated in a few hours, even minutes. Movies like *Fail Safe* and *Dr. Strangelove*, and books such as *The Last Canadian*, *On the Beach* and *Alas, Babylon*, have given us scenarios depicting "instant" war and its aftermath. Distinguishing between the fantasies of science fiction and reality grows more difficult, as military strategists and other experts use simulated war games to estimate the numbers who would die in the first minutes of a nuclear war.

> The historic pattern of weaponry is epitomized in the TV Western. The bad man draws first; the good man starts late but finishes first. The bad man is finished. Now comes the surprise. The range has been so increased, and the dueling has become so sophisticated, that both sides can get their effective shots in, and nobody wins.
>
> Today's warhead travels at fifteen thousand miles per hour. With five thousand miles to go, it takes twenty minutes to reach its target. Man's eyes, augmented by radar, penetrate around the world at a velocity of six hundred million miles per hour. As he spots the warhead's takeoff in his direction, he has more than nineteen minutes in which to get his own warhead under way. There is ample time for each side to obliterate the other. Both 'good' and 'bad' man lose. Even the world political leaders realize that the pursuit of weaponry has reached absurdity.[3]

It is not just the amount of destruction, but the speed with which an attack could be mounted that distinguishes modern warfare from wars just a few years ago. Even the so-called "conventional" wars, such as the "Six Day" war of June, 1967, in the Middle East or the India-Pakistan war of 1971, were comparatively short.

Thus it might be difficult for a modern student to appreciate the shocked reaction in September, 1939, to the German conquest of Poland which took less than a month. Yet for people of that time who remembered World War I and the years of trench warfare on the "Western Front", the speed and fury of Germany's *Blitzkrieg*— "lightning war"—was astonishing.

In April, Germany moved without warning to invade and occupy Norway and Denmark. Then in May, German armies unleashed the blitzkrieg against Holland, Belgium and France. The Maginot Line left France vulnerable to an encircling movement from the north; furthermore, its fixed positions did not allow for a flexible response to unexpected German strategy. Before the end of the month, Allied defences had crumbled. Some 400 000 British and French troops had been driven back to the English Channel. Further disaster seemed imminent.

Then came the "miracle of Dunkirk". Between May 26 and June 4 almost 350 000 people, including the bulk of the British expeditionary force, were evacuated to England by the navy and a flotilla of small ships. The near disaster brought on by the lack of leadership from the generals was averted by the courage of thousands of lesser officers and civilian boat operators. A major retreat was turned into a legend that bolstered the morale of the British people.

While the evacuation from Dunkirk was in progress, German armies were converging on Paris. The French were stunned; resistance to the rapid German advance seemed futile. Then Mussolini, the Italian dictator who had thrown in his lot with Hitler, attacked a dying France on the Mediterranean front. Suddenly France surrendered, accepting Nazi domination and leaving Britain alone to face the greatest totalitarian threat in modern times.

THE BATTLE OF BRITAIN

In the summer of 1940, Hitler extended his military effort in an attempt to conquer Britain. In the memorable Battle of Britain, the Royal Air Force (RAF) withstood the ferocious air attacks of the *Luftwaffe* (German air force), and the British civilian population endured the Blitz—more than two months of German bombing. It was a grim battle with terrible losses on both sides, but the invasion failed and Hitler called off his plan to "wring the neck of the British chicken".*

*One of Churchill's many memorable remarks was made after the Battle of Britain when, commenting on Hitler's remark, he said, "Some chicken. Some neck."

Sir Winston Churchill, prime minister of Britain from May, 1940, paid tribute to the RAF for the heroic air defence with the words, "Never in the field of human conflict was so much owed by so many to so few."

PROPAGANDA IN WARTIME: A NECESSARY EVIL?

"The first casualty when war comes is truth."[4]

In his history of war correspondents, a British journalist gives one example of how the news was "managed" at the time of the Battle of Britain:

As far as the daily tally of comparative losses [of British and German planes] was concerned, the correspondents had little choice but to accept the figures in the official communiques, and these turned out to be hopelessly wrong and—as the pilots themselves knew—exaggerated to maintain civilian morale. On September 9, for example, *The Times*, in a long story about a raid on London two days earlier, said that 107 German planes had been shot down. In fact the figure was forty-one. On September 15, the Air Ministry [of the British Government] announced 185 German planes destroyed, the 'greatest day' in the whole battle: 185 DOWN AND WE'RE STILL BATTING, the billboards said. The real German loss was only sixty. The Air Ministry's total for the period July 10 to October 31, 1940, was 2,698. Actually the Germans lost 1,733. At the end of the war, the Air Ministry admitted, with a touch of British humour, that it had exaggerated its score by only 55 per cent, whereas the Germans had done so by 224 per cent.[5]

1. What reason is given for the British government's exaggerated announcements of the number of German planes shot down?
2. Do you think the British government was right to make these claims? Why or why not?
3. Is propaganda "a necessary evil" in wartime? In peacetime? What kinds of propaganda?

WAR ON THE EASTERN FRONT

On June 22, 1941, the war entered a new phase. On that day, Hitler's armies invaded the U.S.S.R., Germany's partner in the seizure of Poland. Thus the Soviet Union became an ally of Great Britain and the other countries resisting German plans for conquest.

Germany's objectives included the takeover of the Ukraine with its fertile wheat fields, and of the oil-rich Caucasus. Altogether, Hitler sent in almost three million troops, supported by tanks and airplanes. Initially German forces scored spectacular victories which brought them in sight of Moscow and Leningrad. Hitler was so sure of a Soviet collapse that on October 3, in an address to the German people, he said,

> I declare today, and I declare without reservation, that the enemy in the East has been struck down and will never rise again ... Behind our troops there already lies a territory twice the size of the German Reich when I came to power in 1933.

Hitler's declaration was premature. The beleaguered cities withstood repeated attacks, and the determined Soviet troops barred the road to the Caucasus. Death and devastation descended upon the German-occupied areas, and what the Nazis failed to destroy, the Soviets did. They adopted a "scorched earth" policy of burning and destroying everything of possible use to the enemy. Soon the

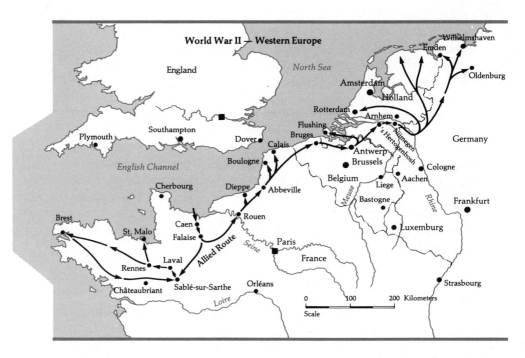

World War II — Western Europe

autumn rains and the fields of mud slowed down the German advance. The early winter, which set in at the beginning of November, together with the stiff resistance by the Red Army, brought the Nazi offensive to a halt. In the winter blizzards the German armies were soon to meet the same fate that had befallen Napoleon's armies in 1812.

During the winter of 1941—1942, on the Soviet fronts, the German armies suffered reverses. By the end of the winter, their casualties reached almost one and one-quarter million. The spring mud slowed the fighting almost to a halt. Towards the end of August, Hitler ordered an offensive against Stalingrad, the key to the Crimea and the Caucasus. German troops, reinforced by armies from Germany's satellites and allies—Rumania, Hungary, Slovakia, Italy and Spain—pursued the retreating Red Army to Stalingrad.

In October, there was bitter house-to-house fighting within Stalingrad. Axis soldiers, who were rushed into the city, were decimated in the fierce, suicidal resistance of the Soviet troops. To all entreaties by his field commanders to withdraw from Stalingrad, Hitler had one answer, "No retreat," and he insisted that "Where the German soldier sets foot there he remains." In November, in a blinding blizzard, the Soviet armies opened an offensive in which the Germans surrendered in the thousands. Fierce fighting continued through January, 1943. At Stalingrad, Germany suffered a shattering defeat. The Soviet victory in the snows of the Ukraine indicated that the tide of battle was turning.

WAR IN AFRICA

The war had been spreading to the south as well as to the east. In September, 1940, while the *Luftwaffe* was bombing Britain, Italian troops from Libya, an Italian colony, invaded Egypt, then a British colony. This threat to the Suez Canal and the route to the oilfields of the Middle East was turned back by British armies. However, in the spring of 1941, in the first of several rescues of its Italian ally, Germany sent in forces which restored the threat to the Suez.

Mussolini's other venture, his attack on Greece, fared no better. When the Italians invaded Greece in October, 1940, Mussolini expected an easy victory, but within a week the Italians were routed and forced to retreat. Again, German forces, in spite of British efforts to defend the Greeks, moved in and occupied the country by April, 1941. As the Germans followed up this victory with a lightning airborne assault on the island of Crete, Hitler had not only saved Mussolini but also gained full control of the Balkans.

Nevertheless, in the spring of 1941, Britain still maintained its hold on the Mediterranean, still kept the Strait of Gibraltar open to shipping, still held the strategically located island of Malta and still hung on to Suez.

Yet the situation in North Africa was ominous. After months of battle in the winter of 1941 – 42 without victory for either side, Rommel, the brilliant German general, directed a successful offensive by the *Afrika Korps*. The Axis powers were in a controlling position in North Africa, and the Suez appeared to be within their grasp. Then, in the fall of 1942, the new British commander, Sir Bernard Law "Monty" Montgomery, led a counter-offensive which smashed the vaunted *Afrika Korps* at El-Alamein.

At the beginning of November 1942 while warfare still flared on the deserts of Libya and the frozen fields of the Ukraine, a combined Anglo-American force under the command of General Dwight Eisenhower was landing on the beaches of French Morocco and Algeria. Over a quarter of a million German and Italian troops were rushed to Tunisia to prevent Eisenhower from seizing it. By the following May most of the Axis troops had become prisoners of the Allies. North Africa, from Gibraltar to Suez, was in Allied hands. The next step seemed obvious: an Allied invasion of Italy, the "soft under-belly" of Europe.

WAR IN THE PACIFIC

On the other side of the world, the surprise Japanese attack on Pearl Harbor on December 7, 1941, turned the European war into a global conflict. The might of the United States was now added to the Allied cause. On the same day, Canada declared war on Japan and the next day, Canadian troops were trapped in a hopeless battle with Japanese.

In October, responding to a request from Britain, Canada had sent two infantry battalions, drawn from the Winnipeg Grenadiers and the Royal Rifles of Canada, to reinforce the British garrison in the colony of Hong Kong. According to army headquarters, the battalions were "in need of refresher training or insufficiently trained and not recommended for operations." On December 8, battle-hardened Japanese forces, experienced in Japan's war with China, attacked Hong Kong. The outnumbered garrison put up a stubborn but futile resistance and was forced to surrender on Christmas Day. Of some 2 000 Canadians in Hong Kong, more than 500 lost their lives, either in battle or in prisoner-of-war camps.

For Canada the war in the Pacific meant the real beginning of Canadian-American cooperation for North American defence. Within a few months the construction of the "Alaskan Highway" and a communications network between the United States and Alaska gave indications of the much more elaborate arrangements of later years.*

*See page 468 for other examples of Canadian-American military cooperation.

Canadians on the battlefield

CANADA DECLARES WAR

In 1914 as a colony, Canada had automatically been at war alongside Great Britain. Technically, Canada had a choice in 1939, but there was little doubt it would support the mother country. Parliament was called into special session where the government of Mackenzie King recommended that Canada face up to its responsibility. On September 10, following three days of debate, King George VI, on the advice of the Canadian cabinet, announced that Canada had declared war.

VIEWS ON CANADA'S WAR DECLARATION

In the House of Commons on September 8 and 9, 1939, Canadian leaders expressed their views on Canada's entry into the war:
Prime Minister Mackenzie King, for the Liberal Party:

I have never doubted that when the fatal moment came, the free spirit of the Canadian people would assert itself in the preservation and defence of freedom, as it did a quarter of a century ago. I have, however, been anxious that when the inevitable hour came, our people should be as one from coast to coast in recognizing the magnitude of the issue which was presenting itself, and as one in their determination to meet it with all the strength and power at their command. I have made it, therefore, the supreme endeavour

282

Metropolitan Edition

The Globe and Mail

Forecast: Cloudy; Cool

VOL. XCVI. NUMBER 27,996. ★★★★ TORONTO, MONDAY, SEPTEMBER 11, 1939. 3 Cents Per Copy 26 PAGES

CANADA DECLARES WAR!

Proclamation Issued Following Solid Vote in Parliament; Warsaw Defenders Hurl Enemy Back on City's Fringes; Germans Raid French Positions Under Heavy Barrage

Counter-Offensive By Nazis Believed Under Preparation

Germans Claim Five Planes Shot Down; Admit 'Activity'

VEIL EXTENT

Berlin. Sept. 10 (CP).—The first German Government admission that there is armed activity on the Franco-German border came tonight when it was claimed five French planes had been shot down and one forced to land at a German airport. Three French officers were made prisoners, it was said.

In addition, officials said, there

POLES HOLD UNDER NAZI ONSLAUGHT

Launch Series of Night Attacks With 'Varying Success'

FIGHTING WIDER

(By CHARLES FOLTZ, JR.)
(Associated Press Staff Writer.)

Basel, Switzerland, Sept. 11 (Monday) (AP).—Shock troops of Germany's Siegfried Line, operating under a heavy curtain of fire from their own forts, launched a series of night raids for the second time on newly captured French positions in the German frontier last night.

City Pounded From Dawn to Dusk by Shells and Bombs

FORM NEW LINE

(By ROBERT RIEFFEL)
(Havas Staff Writer.)

Lublin, Poland, Sept. 10 (CP-Havas).—The Polish high command announced tonight that German troops had been thrown back in the Warsaw outskirts and that still fighting was under way at a number of other points.

Reports reaching here said a

Proclamation of War

OTTAWA, Sept. 10 (CP).—*Following is the text of the proclamation published today in an extra edition of the Canada Gazette declaring a state of war exists between Canada and Germany:*

TWEEDSMUIR,
(L.S.),
CANADA:

George the Sixth, by the Grace of God, of Great Britain, Ireland and the British Dominions beyond the Seas, King, Defender of the Faith, Emperor of India.

To all to whom these presents shall come or whom the same may in anywise concern,

Greeting:

Dominion Committed To Stand With Britain In Fight Against Hitler

Will Fight Here if War Lost on Rhine, Meighen's Warning

BUT ONE COURSE

Ottawa, Sept. 10 (Staff).—"If we do not win this war on the banks of the Rhine, we are going to have to fight it on the banks of the St. Lawrence."

Lapointe Stakes Political Life on Nation's Participation, Declaring Policy of Neutrality Would Mean Siding With Enemies of Empire

TWO QUEBEC DISSENTERS STAND ALONE

(By HAROLD DINGMAN.)
(Staff Writer, The Globe and Mail.)

OTTAWA, Sept. 10.—The Dominion of Canada marching now toward the goal from which there can be of my leadership of my party, and my leadership of the government of this country, to let no hasty or premature threat or pronouncement create mistrust and divisions between the different elements that compose the population of our vast dominion, so that when the moment of decision came all should so see the issue itself that our national effort might be marked by unity of purpose, of heart and of endeavour.[6]

R. J. Manion, for the Conservative Party:

...we are bound to participate in this war. We are British subjects, we are part of the British empire....

...we are fighting in a war for justice, for honour and for liberty. We in Canada...have no selfish motives and no desire for profit. ...We are fighting, or will be fighting, against policies and principles which are anti-christian and anti-democratic...barbarous and brutal....[7]

M. J. Coldwell, for the C.C.F. Party:

...the Co-operative Commonwealth Federation recognizes that Canada is now implicated in a struggle which may involve the survival of democratic institutions....
...Canada should be prepared to defend her own shores, but her assistance overseas should be limited to economic aid and must not include conscription of man power or the sending of any expeditionary force.[8]

J. S. Woodsworth's opposition to the war:

I would ask, did the last war settle anything? I venture to say that it settled nothing; and the next war into which we are asked to enter, however big and bloody it may be, is not going to settle anything either....
...personally I cannot give any consent to anything that will drag us into another war....I have every respect for the man who, with a sincere conviction, goes out to give his life if necessary in a cause which he believes to be right; but I have just as much respect for the man who refuses to enlist to kill his fellowmen and, as under modern conditions, to kill women and children as well, as must be done on every front....[9]

1. What seems to be the main concern of each speaker?
2. What arguments *in favour* of Canada's entering World War II are given? What arguments *against*?
3. Which speaker is the most idealistic? realistic? political?
4. With which speaker would you agree?
5. Would you change your mind if the war were being fought on the North American continent?

6. Mackenzie King, the prime minister, seems very concerned about national unity. What reasons, historical and otherwise, did he have?

CANADIAN-AMERICAN RELATIONS

The plight of Britain in the first two years of the war drove Canada and the United States into closer relations, which included military agreements before the United States entered the war. Even while the Americans were officially neutral, they were prepared to assist the Allies by giving "aid short of war". Alarmed by Germany's initial successes, the United States began sending arms and used destroyers to Britain. With Canada, the United States shared many problems, but one that was unique was the defence of North America.

The Ogdensburg Agreement of August, 1940, was a signal of things to come, as Canada and the United States established a Permanent Joint Defence Board.* A few months later in April, 1941, Prime Minister King and President Franklin D. Roosevelt met again on what they regarded as a matter of mutual interest. The production of war materials was creating financial hardships for Canada, which was purchasing large quantities of supplies and machine tools from the United States. Canada's lack of American currency threatened to curtail such purchases and slow down production. The

*See Chapter 13 regarding NORAD and present-day Canada-U.S. cooperation in matters of North American defence.

An American air force base in Newfoundland

285

resulting Hyde Park agreement provided for an interchange of supplies between the two countries to ease Canada's shortage of American dollars. To her southern neighbour Canada would sell war supplies, such as small arms, ammunition, airplane parts and explosives which Canada was producing in large quantities. Such sales would offset some of the purchases made in the United States and would help Canada's economy.

The immediate objective, up to the autumn of 1941, was to assist Britain in its lonely resistance to Hitler's aggression. Pearl Harbor added a new concern, one that has remained ever since. The sudden Japanese attack of December 7, 1941, on Pearl Harbor in the Hawaiian Islands opened up the very real possibility that North America might suffer direct attack. Consequently, plans for American involvement in continental defence—on both Pacific and Atlantic coasts—were implemented. The Alaskan Highway from Edmonton to Skagway was built in 1942. Air bases where American troops were stationed were established along the Rockies and in Newfoundland. By the end of the war, Canada and the United States were partners, unequal ones, in a continental defence system.

CANADA BUILDS ITS ARMED FORCES

Canada is an unmilitary community. Warlike her people have often been forced to be; military they have never been. . . .

For generations, Canadian governments and parliaments, and certainly also the public at large, appeared to be convinced that it was time enough to begin preparing for war after war had broken out. . . .

It is a remarkable fact that the First World War, which affected Canadian development so fundamentally in so many ways, had almost no long-term influence upon the country's military policy. . . . [10]

Between 1939 and 1945, 730 000 Canadians, including the 21 624 volunteers in the Women's Army Corps (WAC), saw military service. As in World War I, almost all were civilians when the war began. In fact, Canada started the war with less than 10 000 men in its regular armed forces: 4 000 in the army, 1 800 in the navy and approximately 3 000 in the air force. Volunteers in the first month of the war raised the total to nearly 60 000, and the Canadian First Division was dispatched to England in December, 1939. But there was little apparent urgency for Canada to launch a recruitment campaign. During the period of the "phony war", following Germany's conquest of Poland, Britain and France appeared capable of containing Germany. Canada's role was to provide support in the form of limited manpower, specialized personnel and war supplies. The situation changed dramatically in the spring of 1940 with Germany's rapid conquest of Western Europe and

The WRENS on review

particularly of France. Suddenly Canada was a major participant in the war, and the drive to expand the armed forces began.

New Canadian army divisions were mobilized and sent to Britain as part of the defence against a possible invasion of the British Isles. For the most part the army was destined to "play a waiting game" until the time came for Allied campaigns to liberate the European continent. Meanwhile, the air force and the navy expanded in spectacular fashion, as Germany and its allies continued their offensive in the air and on the high seas.

From the early months of the war, Canada's contribution to the Allied air war was crucial. Canadian pilots served in the Royal Air Force during the terrifying weeks of the Battle of Britain. Their role increased steadily throughout the war, due to the British Commonwealth Air Training Plan. At training bases established all over the country, airmen from Britain, other Commonwealth countries, France, Norway and Poland were prepared for combat. Of the more than 130 000 graduated, more than half were Canadians. By the end of the war, Canada's air force numbered more than 200 000. It had taken part in operations in every major theatre of the war.

Canada was also obliged to increase the strength of the Royal Canadian Navy in order to protect Britain's "lifeline" across the Atlantic Ocean. Following the stalemate resulting from the Battle of Britain, Hitler ordered an intensive campaign to isolate Britain from vital supplies—armaments, food, oil—provided by Canada, the United States and South American countries. In the prolonged Battle of the Atlantic, German submarines, the infamous "U-boats", har-

One of the legendary units during the "Battle of Britain" was the R.A.F. 242 "Canadian" Squadron. Almost all the pilots were Canadians, but the leader was Douglas Bader, the British pilot who had lost both legs in an accident before the war. Fitted with artificial limbs, Bader had managed to enlist and proved that his handicap would not prevent him from leading his "unruly Canadian" squadron through some of the most perilous action of the war.

TOP: *Hurricanes used in the Battle of Britain.* BOTTOM: *Many Canadian pilots trained in the Tiger Moth. This restored model in Winnipeg is one of the few in existence.*

288

assed Allied shipping. Canadian patrol boats, especially the speedy corvettes, provided escort service to the convoys of ships that kept supplies moving. In spite of huge losses, the Canadian navy had much to do with preventing a victory for Hitler on the storm-tossed expanse of the Atlantic.

TYPE IIB: the training U-Boat

When Germany began re-arming in the mid-'30s she aimed at building 300 U-boats by 1943. Hitler pushed her into war faster than the navy anticipated, and in 1939 she had only some 60 submarines, about the same as the British. Half were Type IIs, small coastal U-boats used mainly for training. Type IIB: displacement, 279 tons, length, 140 feet; speed, 13 knots (7 knots submerged); six 21-inch torpedoes fired from three tubes forward; one 20-mm. gun; crew 25.[12]

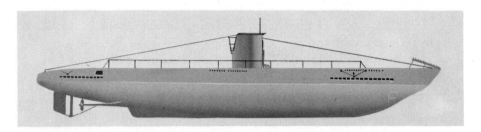

DIEPPE

Until the summer of 1942, Canadians in the army saw little action compared to their counterparts in the air force and the navy. Consequently, army casualties had been few in number. So when Canadians suffered heavy casualties in the raid on Dieppe, for the sake of Allied strategy, the effect was all the more shocking.

The year before, as a consequence of Germany's invasion of Soviet territory, the Soviet Union had become an ally of Great Britain. Month after month the relentless German war machine pushed into the U.S.S.R. Russia's leaders pressured the Allies to open a second front to divert some of Germany's firepower. At the same time, the United States having formally joined the Allies following the Japanese attack on Pearl Harbor, was anxious to launch a full-scale attack on the German-held coast of France. The British judged that the Allies were not yet prepared for such an attack; the alternative agreed upon was a large raid on the French port of Dieppe.

The mission was assigned to a force of 6 000, of whom 5 000 were members of the Canadian Second Division. When the infantry landed on the beaches, the Germans were waiting in concrete fortifications on the high ground. Intense enemy artillery fire pinned the troops and their inadequate tank support on the shore; many soldiers never got off their landing craft. Although naval gunfire and RAF air cover enabled more than 2 000 Canadians, many of them seriously wounded, to return to England, there were 3 367 Canadian casualties.

The Dieppe raid of August 19, 1942 is a bitter memory for Canadians and the subject of continuing debate. Defenders of the raid have claimed that it provided valuable information about the nature of German fortifications and that it was an important "trial run" for the later Allied invasion of the continent. Others have claimed that the military lessons of Dieppe were far outweighed by the slaughter of troops who never had a chance.

A PRIVATE VIEW AND A PUBLIC STATEMENT

Mackenzie King made the following entries in his diary (August 21, September 19) about the Dieppe raid:

... still not too sure of the wisdom of what was attempted. ... I still have a feeling that the part of wisdom would have been to conserve that especially trained life for the decisive moment. It may, in the long run, prove to be for the best but such is war. It makes me sad at heart.

... I question if the information gained could begin to equal the heavy losses. Moreover the enemy themselves are able effectively to represent the whole episode as a gain for themselves between the numbers taken prisoners and those who have been killed. It is a very serious blow to the Canadian forces.[13]

Minister of Defence, J. L. Ralston, defended the Dieppe raid in the House of Commons on May 14, 1943:

The practical experiences of Dieppe have already been translated into training principles, and, as I said last night, have literally become a handbook for the guidance of those who will take part in future landing operations.

Dieppe demonstrated the difficulties and revealed the possibilities of landing on the continent. It established confidence between officers and men which stands to the everlasting credit of both. It destroyed enemy installations and took a heavy toll of Hitler's air force. It proved that there could be superior coordination and cooperation between the four different national contingents comprising the ground force and between the navy, the army and the air force. It gained information and experience and lessons of incalculable value to the allied forces which could have been acquired in no other way. The losses were heavy; but although the price was great, when history comes to be written I believe it will be recorded that Dieppe did a service of untold benefit.

TOP: *The ruins near Dieppe.* BOTTOM: *Mackenzie King at a memorial service in Dieppe after the war.*

291

Some day it may well be considered as having sown the seeds of our final victory. We are proud of the men who planned it; we glory in the heroism of the men who fought it and we revere the memory of the men who died in it.[14]

THIS WAS MY BROTHER

This was my brother
At Dieppe,
Quietly a hero
Who gave his life
Like a gift,
Withholding nothing.

His youth . . . his love . . .
His enjoyment of being alive . . .
His future, like a book
With half the pages still uncut—

This was my brother
At Dieppe . . .
The one who built me a doll house
When I was seven,
Complete to the last small picture frame,
Nothing forgotten.

He was awfully good at fixing things,
At stepping into the breach when he was needed.

That's what he did at Dieppe;
He was needed,
And even death must have been a little ashamed
At his eagerness![15]

THE ITALIAN CAMPAIGN

When the Allies, including large numbers of Canadians, crossed from Sicily to the Italian mainland in September, 1943, Italian armies were not the main obstacle. Since the fall of Mussolini in July, the government of Italy had been secretly negotiating an armistice with the Allies. Hitler had decided to occupy the territory of his former supporter, and German forces prepared to defend against the Allied advance.

CANADIANS CROSS THE STRAITS OF MESSINA TO THE ITALIAN
MAINLAND
Matthew Halton, a Canadian war correspondent, described the landing of the Canadians on the Italian mainland, September 3, 1943:

We are in Italy. The First Canadian Division, with brother forma-
tions of the Eighth Army, is in Italy, unopposed. We made an
assault landing at dawn today, and made the first breach in the
walls of Nazi Europe and it cost us not one single man. As I speak,
a few German shells are landing on our positions, but at dawn
today, when we crashed the gates of Europe, not one machine-gun
bullet broke the silence, not one enemy shell fell among our landing craft, not one mine exploded in our faces. . . . We sailed just after
three o'clock, our three batallions of Canadians, and at "H minus
60", that is the hour before we were to go ashore, our artillery split
the night with one of the most enormous barrages of this war.
Hundreds and hundreds of our guns were pouring tens of thousands
of shells onto the beaches where we were to land, and onto the
enemy gun positions overlooking them. The horizon behind us was
a staggering rippling and flashing fire and flame and the night was
one enormous roar, and the Italian mainland was occasionally vom-
iting explosions. One hour before dawn, the pandemonium died
away into the most complete silence. We were going ashore. It was
our hour.[16]

The Royal Canadian Regiment on reconnaissance in Italy

At first the Canadians had more trouble with the mountainous
terrain and bad weather than with enemy opposition. But once the
Germans had been decisively defeated at Naples by combined British-American forces, they retreated grudgingly. Units of the Canadian First Division fought their way along the Adriatic Sea to the port
of Ortona by December. After a week of bloody, hand-to-hand fighting, the German force was finally dislodged, and the name of Ortona

was added to those which symbolize courage and sacrifice in Canada's military tradition.

THE STORY OF ORTONA

Historian George Stanley describes the situation at Ortona:

The story of the battle of Ortona is one of blaze and blood; of courage and heroism; of seven vicious days of hand-to-hand fighting in the cold, and the damp, and the snow. The town of Ortona was situated on a ledge overlooking the blue waters of the Adriatic. It was a medieval town, with an old castle, strong stone buildings and narrow thoroughfares, many of them too narrow to permit even the passage of tanks. It was a good place to defend.... The enemy knew that artillery and tanks would be of limited use against them. ... To struggle through the streets and over the rocks and rubble was only to fight the battle the way the enemy wanted to fight it; and so the Canadians took to smashing their way through walls and buildings, "mouseholing" it was called. For days and nights the fighting went on.... When, on the morning of the 28th a cautious Canadian reconnaissance patrol moved slowly forward, it found only the enemy dead keeping ghostly watch over the ruins of the city.[17]

CHRISTMAS AMIDST THE RUBBLE

As the battle raged with undiminished fury through the last week of 1943, the two battalions in Ortona insisted on remembering Christmas Day. Both ate their Christmas dinners in relays in whatever shelter they could find, a company at a time, and then crept back into the blackened broken streets to resume the war. The Seaforths were particularly fortunate to find a reasonable suitable hall in the

Christmas at Ortona, 1943

church of Santa Maria di Constantinopoli; there, with their officers serving, as officers always serve the men at Christmas, they ate from white tablecloths. There was no turkey, but the ration parties had arrived with roast pork, apple sauce, four kinds of vegetables, plum pudding, mince pie, candies, nuts and fruit, and a bottle of beer per man, and the church organ played Christmas carols.[18]

Rome was the prize toward which the next Allied drive was aimed. Aside from strategic considerations, the psychological value of the capital of Catholic Christianity was recognized by both sides. In January, 1944 American marines and paratroopers landed at Anzio, some 180 km from Rome. By June, a combined Allied force, including Canadians under General E. L. M. Burns, broke the German defence in a series of battles and entered Rome.

The Canadian Corps, after Rome's capture, had been diverted to the Adriatic for an assault on the Gothic Line, the last German defensive position in northern Italy. Following their hard fought victories, the Canadians were transferred to the Western front, where the liberation of Western Europe was underway.

D-DAY AND THE LIBERATION OF WESTERN EUROPE

On June 6, 1944, the long-awaited Allied invasion of Western Europe was finally launched. At several key points along the 90-km coast of Normandy, France, massive land, sea and air attacks gave the Allies the footholds they needed to challenge Germany's four-year control. Offshore, battleships hammered away at the German defences, and in the air, British, American and Canadian bombers dropped hundreds of tons of bombs. Then the troops, both airborne and carried ashore in a flotilla of landing craft, poured onto the beaches. In spite of the power of technology hurled at the Germans' "Atlantic Wall", the Allies suffered losses in the thousands as the Germans answered back with their shore batteries, smashing landing craft and tanks, and trapping soldiers in deadly crossfire. Yet the Allies captured every beach.

Canadian and British troops fought their way through to Caen, then battled German panzer divisions for several weeks on the way to Falaise. Meanwhile, the Americans had broken through on the peninsula from Cherbourg, trapping several German divisions. As the British headed toward Brussels and the Americans struck for the Seine liberating Paris on August 25,* the Canadians pushed toward the coastal ports. At Dieppe, the scene of the tragedy two years earlier, they were greeted by a celebrating populace. By the end of September, the channel ports had been virtually cleared of enemy resistance and the flying-bomb sites destroyed.

The Canadians were then given the task of clearing the Scheldt

The Atlantic Wall was "a series of formidable casemates, the largest about thirty or forty feet square, with walls four and five feet thick—all reinforced concrete. Between these casemates were lines of concrete pillboxes, dug deep into the ground with just the top above the earth. Trench systems and tunnels also linked each strongpoint and there was not a yard of the beach that the cross-fire from machine-guns and rifles could not cover. There were three or four lines of pillboxes at more vulnerable spots and for five or six hundred yards inland this belt of bristling positions extended from the shore.[19]

*Troops of the "Free French", led by General Charles de Gaulle, were also involved in the march into Paris.

D-Day

estuary so that the Belgian port of Antwerp would be available to the Allies as a supply base. Only then would they be able to obtain the arms, ammunition, reinforcements and other support necessary for an advance on the "Siegfried Line" of German defences and the Rhine River. In some of the most savage fighting of the war, the Canadians slogged across the flooded countryside of Holland, routing Germans from dikes and canals. By November, Allied convoys were delivering supplies to Antwerp.

While Canadian forces were clearing the Germans out of Holland, the First Canadian Army joined the Allied offensive, the final campaign to conquer Germany and impose unconditional surrender.

WAR'S END

By April, 1945, the retreating German forces were engaged in a hopeless fight to the death, their depleted ranks filled with untrained young boys and old men. As the British, Americans, Canadians and other Allies converged on German cities from the West, millions of Soviet troops were driving the German armies out of Poland and other countries on the East. In the race for Berlin, the Soviets arrived first and occupied the ruined German capital. Hitler had committed suicide in his underground bunker. The final German surrender, a total acceptance of Allied victory, came on May 7, 1945.

The war in the Pacific, where Canada had played a limited role, raged on, but the Americans had decided to use a weapon that would end the war suddenly. The dropping of atomic bombs on the cities of Hiroshima (August 6) and Nagasaki (August 9) knocked Japan out of the war, and brought an end to the "hot war"* — World War II.

Canadians on the home front

World War II brought many changes to life in Canada. Some of these passed with the end of the war; others remained to make Canada a different place than it had been before. Much of the country's energy was channeled into the war effort, but not forgotten were long-standing issues, like relations between French-speaking and English-speaking Canadians. Other questions, having to do with conditions when peace returned, caused concern to at least some Canadians.

CANADA — ARSENAL OF DEMOCRACY

At the beginning of the war, it was assumed that Britain's factories would produce the needed war material. In fact, British manufacturers withheld plans, blueprints and processes from Canada. At the time, Canada had neither the skilled workers nor the factories for extensive production of war supplies. The existing factories, many of which had been idle throughout the Great Depression, had to be

the wide mouth of a river, where the ocean tide affects the current and water level.

By the summer of 1944, German scientists had developed the V-1 and V-2 rockets ("V" standing for "Vengeance") that were launched against the civilian population of London following the D-Day landings. The combined efforts of secret agents like "Intrepid" (the British agent, Sir William Stephenson), resistance fighters who operated under the noses of the enemy in German-occupied countries, and Allied scientists managed to counteract the German rocket program until Allied victories shut it down. At a research station called Peenemunde on the Baltic coast, where the research team led by Wernher von Braun developed the V-2, the Germans had come dangerously close to developing intercontinental ballistic missiles.

*See p. 470 concerning the "Cold War" that began between the Soviet Union and the other Allies even before World War II had ended.

converted to war industries. As a consequence, Canada's productive capacity was only partially utilized and industry proceeded at a rather leisurely pace.

But Germany's *Blitzkrieg* in Western Europe altered the whole situation. A desperate Britain, reeling from her disaster at Dunkirk and facing constant aerial attack from the *Luftwaffe*, turned to Canada for both military aid and war material. A sense of urgency pervaded the whole country and Canada geared her manufacturing capacity for war production.

Canada manufactured much of the equipment used by its forces.

Lee Enfield rifle, No. 4, Mark 1

The simple bolt-action rifle was probably *the* standard weapon of the war. Canadian infantrymen used it wherever they fought. Their rifle was the British Lee Enfield whose basic design dated from the 1890s. Until November 1942—after Hong Kong and Dieppe but before Sicily—they carried the Short Magazine Lee Enfield No. 1, a refinement of the rifle their fathers had used in World War I.

Canada manufactured almost a million Lee Enfields during the war. Various sights could be fitted. A superior locking system and easy field maintenance helped make the Lee Enfield superior to most other bolt-action rifles.[20]

Bren .303 light machine gun

The Bren, a basic infantry weapon and one of the finest light machine guns ever made, originated in Czechoslovakia as the Brno ZB and was adopted by Britain in 1932. The British improved it, modified it to take .303 rifle ammunition and called it the Bren, a combination of Brno and Enfield, the British arsenal. Canada made many thousands of these air-cooled, gas-operated weapons.[21]

Flower Class corvette

The rugged little corvette bore the brunt of Canada's war with the U-boats, and of the 122 that served with the RCN ten were lost in action. The original Flower Class ships had an open deck between the forecastle and the bridge superstructure. This was a man-killer in bad weather and in later ships the forecastle deck was extended to abreast of the funnel (as here). Canada built 106 Flower Class corvettes, many of them in shipyards along the Great Lakes.[22]

The federal government assumed sweeping control over Canada's resources—natural, manufacturing and human. By the National Resources Mobilization Act (NRMA), passed in June, 1940, it was authorized to make orders or regulations "requiring persons to place themselves, their services and their property at the disposal of His Majesty in the right of Canada, as may be deemed necessary or expedient for securing the public safety, the defence of Canada, the maintenance of public order, or the efficient prosecution of the war, or for maintaining supplies or services essential to the life of the community."* The newly-created Department of Munitions and Supply began a massive program of industrial expansion.

*Except for conscription into the armed forces for overseas service. See p. 315 concerning the change in 1944.

Since Canada had virtually no armaments industry when the war began, the government had to decide whether to build government-owned factories or to engage privately-owned firms. Although a number of government, or Crown, corporations were eventually set up for specialized purposes, the bulk of production was carried out by private companies, under government supervision. Companies received credit, tax benefits and guaranteed profits as incentives to expand their production.

C. D. Howe, the cabinet minister in charge of the Department of Munitions and Supply, was a kind of "czar" of wartime production. He dismissed criticisms of his powers and of the profits made by manufacturers as he organized Canada's contribution to the war supplies of the Allies.

HERE'S HOWE: WAR PRODUCTION IN CANADA

In his speech of June 17, 1940 in the House of Commons, C. D. Howe explains his procedure and shows his style:

Where a peace-time operation can efficiently carry on war-time work, we believe it is in the best interests of the country to develop that peace-time industry for the purposes of the war rather than start a new enterprise, government-owned, for the same purpose.

We have used the powers indicated in the bill to dictate the prices at which people shall undertake work. We have gone into a plant and said, "We want this article. The price is so much. You must manufacture that article. If you are not satisfied with that price you can take your case to the exchequer court." We have done that on a few occasions; as the need grows more urgent, we will use this power very extensively. We are getting to the point where, if a manufacturer has a thing which the government needs, we pre-empt it; we pay him what we think is a fair price, and if he does not think so he has, as I have said, an appeal to the courts. In many instances we have imposed our price.

In the last week, of course, the situation has reached proportions which none of us could reasonably have been expected to contemplate as likely to come so soon. With this in view, our whole plans are being reorganized, and reorganized very rapidly. I do not think, circumstances being what they are, I care to state what we may be doing next week or next month, but I do say that the powers we have taken under this act were put there because we believed they were necessary. We believe they will be increasingly necessary. Whether they will be sufficient for all time, I cannot say at this moment.[23]

A steady stream of war supplies was pouring out of Canadian factories. Canada built merchant vessels, corvettes, minesweepers, aircraft and armoured vehicles, and produced small arms, machine guns, artillery pieces, ammunition, synthetic rubber, aviation fuel—all vital to the conduct of the war. Over one million workers were employed directly or indirectly by the Department of Munitions and Supply.

To offset the loss of sources of strategic supplies such as rubber and tin resulting from the Japanese occupation of the Dutch East Indies, factories which produced synthetic rubber and plastics were hurriedly constructed. The War Time Bureau of Technical Personnel, a government agency, called upon the talents of Canadian scientists and technicians to build and operate the new industries. The National Research Council was actively engaged in developing new processes and products.

To assure a steady supply of war materials, production of non-essential consumer goods was curtailed. Products of mine, forest and farm were appropriated for the war industries in order to channel maximum supplies into war production. To direct the gigantic war industries, the government drew on the most capable individuals, all experts in their respective fields, and appointed them as advisers to cabinet members to assist them in the operation of their departments. In fact, the experts became part of the civil service, and they synchronized manpower, supplies and production for maximum output of war supplies.

EFFECTS OF THE WAR ON CANADIAN INDUSTRY

In his report of November 19, 1946 to the House of Commons, C. D. Howe reviewed in detail the wartime production carried out under the direction of the Department of Munitions and Supply. Here is an excerpt:

This unprecedented expansion of productive capacity has resulted in manufacturing becoming the leading industry of the country, and what is perhaps more significant, Canadian manufacturing for the first time has been placed on a production rather than on an assembly basis. Products hitherto partly or wholly imported, or never produced at all, have been made in Canada. These include automobile, ship and aircraft components, radio and radar equipment, machine tools and many other items of industrial equipment. At peak production, there were one million, one hundred and eighty-six thousand employed in direct and indirect war industry, or one in every twelve persons of our population.[24]

WOMEN DURING THE WAR

During World War II Canadian women were employed in more diverse occupations than ever before. In government service at both the federal and provincial levels women were assuming positions of power. People like Mrs. Rex Eaton, Director of the Women's Division of National Selective Service and Miss Byrne Hope Sanders, Director of the Consumers' Branch of the Wartime Prices and Trade Board proved that women were capable of holding high administrative posts.

Thousands of other women were able either to find employment for the first time or to find better paying jobs. The number of women in industry during the war years was greatly accelerated. For example in October of 1939, there were 689 000 women employed in non-agricultural industries, and by October of 1945, there were 1 015 000. It became common to see women operating riveting hammers in shipyards, welding in airplane factories or driving trucks and buses on city streets. Moreover, for the first time, women enlisted in the armed forces, and in 1944 they numbered over 35 000.

A rise in salaries was another outcome of the war. Industries like aircraft manufacturing paid women an average weekly wage of $31.81, more than double the highest average weekly wage for women before the war.

Although after V-J Day ("Victory in Japan") many women lost their jobs to returning servicemen, the war did open avenues of employment and power to women on a scale which they had never before attained.

WHEN COMICS WERE CANADIAN

Johnny Canuck was one of the popular Canadian-made comics during World War II.

"Johnny ... and a legion of comic heroes ... populated an extraordinarily successful series of books (more than 20000000 were sold). But the main reason Canadian kids bought them was that they couldn't buy any others—the government had placed a wartime embargo on 'non-essential imports,' including U.S. comic books full of Batman, Captain Marvel and The Human Torch. When restrictions against U.S. books were lifted at war's end, Johnny Canuck and his fantastic colleagues couldn't stand the competition."[25]

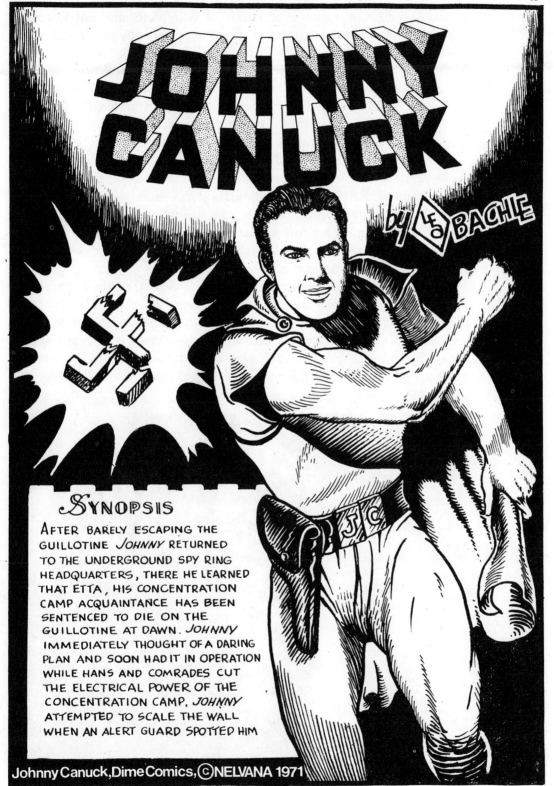

JOHNNY CANUCK

by LEO BACHLE

SYNOPSIS

AFTER BARELY ESCAPING THE GUILLOTINE *JOHNNY* RETURNED TO THE UNDERGROUND SPY RING HEADQUARTERS, THERE HE LEARNED THAT ETTA, HIS CONCENTRATION CAMP ACQUAINTANCE HAS BEEN SENTENCED TO DIE ON THE GUILLOTINE AT DAWN. *JOHNNY* IMMEDIATELY THOUGHT OF A DARING PLAN AND SOON HAD IT IN OPERATION WHILE HANS AND COMRADES CUT THE ELECTRICAL POWER OF THE CONCENTRATION CAMP. *JOHNNY* ATTEMPTED TO SCALE THE WALL WHEN AN ALERT GUARD SPOTTED HIM

GOVERNMENT CONTROLS

It was not just over the production of war materials that Canada's federal government assumed a great deal of power. In October, 1941, the War Time Prices and Trade Board (WTPTB) was established to look after *price and wage controls*.* In addition to price ceilings on consumer goods, the Board froze rents and wages. These steps, the Board claimed, were necessary to prevent a wild spiralling in the cost of living (inflation). But the freezing of wages proved a major cause of labour unrest and industrial disputes.

Rationing of certain foods and strategic supplies was introduced in 1942. This was done to make more food and supplies available for Britain, which Germany hoped to starve into submission. Canadians were issued ration books containing coupons for gasoline, meat, butter, sugar and coffee. Rationing was more a cause of inconvenience than hardship, but shortages of such consumer goods led to the problem of **black markets**.

In financing the enormous cost of the war, Canada attempted a pay-as-you-go policy—raising as much revenue as possible by taxation and less by borrowing. The result was increased direct taxes on individuals and corporations and high sales taxes on luxury goods. Nevertheless, the government was forced to resort to borrowing, through sales of Victory Bonds. Of these, less than half were pur-

*See Chapter 12 about the introduction of Wage and Price controls in 1975.

The term black market refers to illegal sales.

Issuing ration books

chased by individual Canadians, the rest by large corporations, banks, insurance and trust companies. Canadians were thus saddled with an enormous war debt to repay the loans and interest on them.

The CCF regarded Victory Bonds as another example of war profiteering, since the major portion of the interest would go to the already wealthy corporations. As an alternative, the CCF advocated interest-free bonds as a means by which "Big Business" as well as small investors could participate in the nation's wartime sacrifice. This proposal was judged to be impractical for large-scale fund raising, and the sale of Victory Bonds continued through the war.

HELPING THE WAR EFFORT

The rubber rings off sealer jars, they even wanted us to save them. Tin cans. I can remember flattening them and putting them in sacks, and a truck would come around and pick them up. Lead. Oh yes, lead. They wanted every kid to melt down his lead soldiers or at least turn them in, and for a kid of ten or twelve to give his lead soldiers to the war effort, that was a sacrifice.

That's what they called it. "Helping the War Effort!" In capital letters and an exclamation point. It was as well known as "Zap the Jap" or "Loose Lips Sink Ships."

There was a certain day once a month or twice a month when everybody brought in their finds to the schoolyard. Oh, it was such a big deal. On Saturdays we'd go out in the country on our bikes and look for old cars, old abandoned trucks, machinery, and if you found a vehicle with a battery in it, that was a double find, because a battery had a lot of lead plates in it. It wasn't too long before the whole countryside was cleared up. They'd even take old steam engines and cultivators that were just about rusted into pieces.

And, oh yes, the elastic in women's underclothes, men's clothes. When the garment wore out they asked you to take out the elastic and throw that on the pile. Even worn-out elastic! You wonder, you know. Was it all necessary, or was it some bureaucrat or deep thinker in Ottawa trying to justify his existence? At that point, you began to suspect it was all just a game with some people back in Ottawa—but, you know, everybody turned over this worn-out elastic with a straight face.

In those days, you—well, we all did what we were told. I see that now.[26]

CONSCRIPTION

Canada's entry into World War II was much more cautious and free from illusion than its entry into World War I.* The grim memories *See p. 169. of trench warfare and 60 000 countrymen dead in battle were fresh in the minds of older Canadians. Many of the young enlisted in the

Individual liberties in wartime

Because of wartime conditions, the federal government found it advisable to curb certain liberties of individual Canadian citizens. At the beginning of the war, the War Measures Act of 1914, on the statute books but not used over the years, was revived. This Act gave the Dominion government almost unlimited power to pass Orders-in-Council imposing controls deemed necessary for the prosecution of the war.

In September, 1939, an Order-in-Council set up the Defence of Canada Regulations, a series of wartime emergency measures. For the sake of national security, the government was empowered to institute censorship, allow search without warrant and impose other restrictions on individual liberties. The majority of Canadians generally accepted limitations on their individual freedom in the interests of national security, and found them temporary inconveniences rather than dangers to their future.

"Enemy aliens" found themselves affected differently. Those identified as Nazi sympathizers were rounded up and placed in detention camps. Before the Soviet Union entered the war, Canadian Communists, who had openly opposed the war as yet another "imperialist war", were also interned and their meeting places were closed and often disposed of by the government.

1. "A government should place limits on freedom in times of crisis, in order to preserve democratic ideals." Do you agree with this statement? Why or why not? How do you think Canadians might have felt about it during World War II?

Case study: the Japanese Canadians

THE SITUATION

By 1941, some 23 000 Japanese lived in Canada, all but a few hundred in British Columbia. The majority were Canadian-born, as immigration had been restricted since before World War I. Most lived in particular districts in the Vancouver area, although several hundred were scattered in coastal villages from which they worked as fishermen.

For several years before World War II broke out in Europe in 1939, the Japanese Canadians had been the objects of suspicion. The military government of imperial Japan had been conducting a war of aggression on the Chinese mainland since 1931, and had taken over the area known as Manchuria. Japan had avoided any hostility in its relations with the British Empire and Commonwealth, of which Canada was a part. However, many Canadians on the West Coast felt threatened by the growing sea power of Japan and the increasing investment by Japanese corporations in British Columbia. Rumours persisted that some Japanese Canadians, especially among the fishermen, were loyal to, and agents of, the Japanese Emperor.

On December 7, 1941, Japan launched its surprise attack on Pearl Harbor in the Hawaiian Islands, then a possession of the United States. The next day, Canada and other members of the Allies joined the United States in declaring war on Japan.

The Canadian government was subjected to mounting pressure to do something about the Japanese Canadians. Within three months, in February, 1942, all Japanese Canadians were forcibly evacuated from the coastal area. Many of them were taken to internment camps in the British Columbia interior.

1. Do you agree with the Canadian government's decision to evacuate the Japanese Canadians? Why or why not?
2. If not, what should the Canadian government have done?

BACKGROUND

British Columbia had a long history of prejudice and discrimination toward Orientals. When the Canadian Pacific Railway was built through the Rockies in the 1880s, Chinese labourers were imported, given some of the most difficult and dangerous "pick and shovel"

An internment camp at Slocan, B.C.

The Asiatic riots in Vancouver, 1905

jobs, and paid much less than non-Orientals. In the decade before World War I, the Canadian government, under pressure from British Columbia, negotiated directly with the Government of Japan to restrict Japanese emigration to Canada. At that time, a hysterical fear of the "Yellow Peril" threatened Japanese, Chinese and Indian immigrants. They were accused of being willing to work for low wages, thus depressing the living standards of non-Oriental workers and even taking jobs from them. When Japanese went into business they were often thought to be part of an organized movement with overseas backing. Furthermore, they frequently sent their wages to families in the homeland.

A common belief among Canadians was that Orientals could not, or would not, be assimilated into Canadian society. The Japanese, for example, seemed to prefer their Old World values and customs to Canadian ones. Because they were so easily identifiable, both in terms of physical appearance and location, they were vulnerable to hostile treatment, including violence, from the community at large. From time to time, pressure groups had petitioned both provincial and federal governments to "get rid of the Japanese".

1. Does this additional information change your opinion? Why or why not?

A JAPANESE CANADIAN REMEMBERS

Japanese Canadian artist, Shizuye Takashima ("Shichan"), was a child in a "relocation camp" in the Rocky Mountains. Here she dramatizes a child's confusion about the experience and the effects on family relations. (Excerpt from A CHILD IN PRISON CAMP © *1971, Shizuye Takashima published by Tundra Books Inc. in Canada and by William Morrow in the United States.)*

A TERRIBLE DECISION

I often wonder about this war. The Japanese are my father's and mother's people. Strange to be fighting them. My father's nephews are all in the army. We do not receive any letters from our uncles and aunts in Japan and we do not know if they are alive or not. Father does not speak of them much. I ask father, "Why are we fighting?" "For land and other things," father replies. "This is why we are here." But I'm not Japanese, like you. I was born here. So were you." I look at Yuki. She says, "That's nothing—a Jap is a Jap, whether you're born here or not!" "Even if I change my name?" "Yes, you look oriental, you're a threat." "A threat? Why?" "God only knows!" Yuki replies. "It's mostly racial prejudice, and jealousy. Remember we had cleared the best land all along the Fraser Valley. Good fisherman. This causes envy, so better to kick us out.

The damn war is just an excuse. Dad knows. The West Coast people never liked the orientals. 'Yellow Peril' is what they call us."

I look at father. "Yuki is speaking the truth," he says. "This is why we had better return to Japan when we can." Yuki looks surprised. "Return to Japan? I don't want to go. What would I do there?"

Father looks at us. "Would you rather stay in camps? Be treated like dogs? You know you could never get a decent job in Vancouver. Look at cousin Robert, a university graduate, an honors student. No one would hire him. So he's a gardener, just like me. Is this what you want? To be always a third-class citizen? I mind. I didn't come to this country for this kind of treatment. Democracy! I'm a Canadian. I have to pay all the taxes, but I have never been allowed to vote. Even now, here, they took our land, our houses, our children, everything. We are their enemies. Don't you understand? I have no desire to be part of this country. There is no future for you here either."

1. What does Yuki, the eldest sister, say are the real reasons for the evacuation of the Japanese?
2. Given the circumstances, the father's decision is to return to Japan after the war. Is he making the right decision or is he looking for a way out—an escape? Why do you feel as you do?
3. How would you explain Shichan's statement, "But I'm not Japanese, like you. I was born here"?
4. Has this statement influenced your attitude toward the evacuation; that is, has it strengthened your earlier opinion, or caused it to change in any way?

DETAILS ABOUT THE EVACUATION

The evacuation of the Japanese Canadians was carried out under the authority of the War Measures Act. All Canadians were subject to the loss of democratic freedoms which were taken for granted at other times. The Japanese Canadians, however, were particularly vulnerable, since they had never enjoyed such basic Canadian rights as the franchise and the opportunity to hold public office.

The evacuation dramatized the weakness of the Japanese Canadian position. They were not only forcibly relocated, but they were denied any compensation for loss of homes and businesses. Their property was auctioned to others, and even after the war was over, they were powerless to recover their losses. In fact, the Canadian government proposed, in 1945, to ship the Japanese Canadians, including those born in Canada, to Japan.

When news of the government's intention reached the public, the conscience of Canadians was finally aroused and a national protest

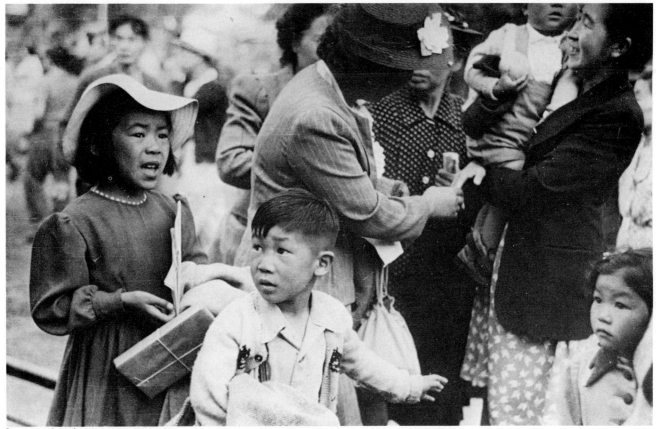

Leaving for the internment camp

developed. The government's decision was revoked, and the Japanese Canadians were granted the right to vote in 1946.

The harm to the Japanese Canadians was not easily undone, however. In spite of efforts through the courts, they were not able to recover their material losses resulting from the evacuation.

1. Has your initial reaction to the evacuation been influenced any further by the additional information?

2. What other issues, besides the rightness or wrongness of the evacuation, can you identify?

3. With these controversial issues, you are likely to find that facts by themselves do not necessarily determine your conclusion. To what extent are you influenced by your *values*?

4. Civil liberties are those rights to which citizens in a democracy believe they are entitled. In your view, were the Japanese Canadians denied civil liberties (a) at the time of the evacuation (b) after the war had ended? If so, what are some examples?

5. What protection, in custom and in law, do Canadians have against the loss of their civil liberties?

6. Are there situations in which the government is justified in suspending civil liberties? Are there any rights which a government should never be able to touch?

Ideas from the social sciences: you've seen one, you've seen them all. The sociology of stereotypes

---

Jake and Slim are two men who meet regularly in Central Park. They pass their time sitting on a park bench, reminiscing about "the good old days."

Today, Jake sees a younger man, probably in his late thirties, and of a nationality different from theirs, across the park.

"Wonder what he's doin' here at this time of the day," Jake exclaims.

"Probably on the way to get his welfare cheque. They don't work," replies Slim.

"Naw! If he was goin' there he'd take a taxi," concluded Jake, and the two men grumbled on about all the people of a certain nationality cheating the honest, law-abiding taxpayers.

The only thing that ends this part of their conversation is the inflated rubber ball which hits Slim on the back on the head. When he turns to look for the cause, he sees a toddler running toward him. The child is about to run in front of another child on a swing when, through pure luck, the ball veers left, and the youngster turns away from the dangerous swing.

"Look at that, will ya," screams Jake. "The kid nearly kills you and then nearly kills himself while the mother—if you can call her that—buries her nose in that stupid book. She's not even paying any attention to her kids."

Slim still surprised from the blow to his head, mutters something incomprehensible.

"Ya know," Jake goes on, "since we've been coming to this park I've been noticing that woman with all those books. She must read two or three a day while her kids run wild. I'll bet she'd rather they weren't around. I don't think women and books go together. Women should stick to what they're cut out for. Take her, if she'd a been watchin' her kid, like a good mother, that kid wouldn't a hit you on the head, Slim. That's the trouble with women who think they were made to be as smart as their husbands, Slim, they're all alike."

Slim absent-mindedly kept rubbing his head, even after the conversation turned to other things. After awhile, Slim remembered he had an errand to do, and he said goodbye to his friend, Jake.

As he roused himself from the bench, Jake was approached by a teen-aged boy with long hair and a guitar. The boy decided Jake looked like the right person to ask for any spare change. This was all Jake needed today after the kind of day he'd had, and he promptly gave the boy a five-minute lecture on the virtues of cleanliness, honesty and hard work—and no spare change.

As though Slim were walking with him, Jake "talked" all the way home.

"Do you believe these kids today? I sure don't. They look like they haven't had a bath in weeks, their hair is as long as a girl's, for heaven sakes, and worst of all, they all want somethin' for nothin'. I worked hard all my life, and these kids today will never go through what I've been through. All they're interested in is freeloadin' offa somebody else. They're already lazy bums, and they'll grow up to be lazy welfare bums! What's this ol' world comin' to anyhow?"

1. What did Jake do that was similar in all three situations?
2. What considerations involved in each situation may Jake be ignoring?
3. What do you suppose would happen the next time Jake met (a) a person of the same nationality as the man they first saw in the park? (b) a woman running for political office? (c) a teenager hitch-hiking?
4. To what extent would his reactions to these people differ if he saw (a) a person of that other nationality as a respected church leader? (b) a woman professor with two children on their school's honour roll?
(c) a long-haired teenager helping a blind man across a busy interesection?

Sociologists, those social scientists who study people in groups, define *stereotyping* as mentally putting all members of one group together and defining them as types rather than as individuals. When Jake judged that all long-haired teenagers were lazy bums because of the behaviour of one teenager, he was stereotyping a group based on his perception of one member of that group.

During, and even for a time after, World War II many Japanese were victims of stereotyping both by the general population and by governments. An individual Japanese was not judged on his own behaviour or traits but rather by his nationality. If people feared, resented or distrusted Japanese, they tended to treat all Japanese alike. For example, many Japanese Canadians, *i.e.*, those people born in Canada but of Japanese ancestry, were treated just the same as Japanese immigrants.

1. We have seen how stereotyping by individuals can be harmful. In what ways can stereotyping by governments be even more damaging?

2. How can stereotyping eliminate individual rights, or "civil liberties"?

3. Why might laws protecting civil liberties be even more important to minority groups than to members of the majority population?

---

armed forces to escape the dreariness and deprivation of the "Great Depression". And the Government of Canada was haunted by fears that another conscription issue would arise to disrupt, or even destroy, national unity.

The warning signs came early. In the debates of September, 1939, the ministers from Quebec in Mackenzie King's cabinet declared their refusal to support conscription for overseas service. Weeks later, Premier Maurice Duplessis of Quebec challenged Canada's declaration of war, and called an election in which involvement in the war was the main issue. The Canadian government strenuously supported the Quebec Liberal Party in its campaign to unseat the Duplessis administration, and the election results of October 26, 1939 rewarded their efforts. But the federal Liberal cabinet ministers from Quebec, including Ernest Lapointe and C. G. "Chubby" Power, left no doubts about their position on conscription. To maintain Canadian unity they had devoted their energies to defeating Duples-

Vote "Yes" to conscription

sis' anti-war threat; they would oppose conscription for the same reason.

On the other hand, Mackenzie King's government was under attack for lack of vigour in leading the nation into war. Premier Mitchell Hepburn of Ontario, though a Liberal, was a political foe of Mackenzie King. The boisterous Hepburn heaped abuse on the Prime Minister, and accused him of taking a weak-kneed approach to the war effort. There was talk among Conservatives of the need for a coalition government, as there had been in World War I. King responded by calling an election for March 26, 1940 and the Liberals set out to defend their record to the people of Canada. Their landslide victory convinced King that his way of doing things, while unspectacular, had wide popular support.

Nevertheless, as World War II went badly for the Allies, demands for conscription arose, particularly among English-speaking Canadians. Mackenzie King found himself in a corner; even some of his cabinet members believed that the non-conscription pledge of 1939 was no longer relevant in the face of a deteriorating military situation. King's strategy was to hold a national plebiscite, held on April 27, 1942, in which the Canadian people were asked to answer "Yes" or "No" to the question:

> Are you in favour of releasing the Government from any obligation arising out of any past commitments restricting the methods of raising men for military service?

The overall vote was 64 percent "Yes", but while the rest of Canada voted 79 percent "Yes", Quebec recorded a "No" vote of 72 percent. Mackenzie King quickly ensured the government's constitutional freedom for the authority to decide on conscription by getting the approval of Parliament to delete the clause in the National Resources Mobilization Act which prevented conscription of people for overseas service. One of his Quebec cabinet ministers, P. J. A. Cardin, promptly resigned, but King allayed the fears of many with the explanation that his government's policy was "not necessarily conscription but conscription if necessary."

So the matter rested until October, 1944, following the Allied "D-Day" landings and the vicious warfare involved in trying to break the German stranglehold on Western Europe. The Minister of Defence, J. L. Ralston, returned from visits to Canadian forces in Britain and on the continent. He was convinced that conscription was now unavoidable to replace the casualties being suffered by the Canadian army. Ralston proposed that people conscripted for home defence now be sent overseas. Mackenzie King heeded the advice of those who believed such an action was not necessary and

Conservative leader R. J. Manion resigned shortly after the 1940 election and Arthur Meighen reluctantly accepted the party's request that he resume the leadership which he had given up nearly 15 years before. Meighen was subsequently defeated in a by-election, and the Conservatives held a leadership convention in Winnipeg in December, 1942. Their choice for a new leader was John Bracken, Premier of Manitoba since he had come to power in 1920 during the hey-day of the Progressive Party*. One of Bracken's conditions was that the Conservative Party be renamed the *Progressive Conservative* Party.

*See p. 204.

The nickname "Zombies" was given to those conscripted for home defence only. They were subjected to a good deal of hostility and pressure from volunteer recruits, and to public criticism. Do you believe that the "Zombies" should have been sent overseas? Why or why not? Do you accept the principle of conscription? Why or why not?

*See Chapter 1, p. 7.

would run the risk of dividing the country at a time when the war was almost over. Ralston's resignation was accepted* and he was replaced as Minister of Defence by General G. L. McNaughton.

McNaughton's appeal for volunteers and efforts to persuade home defence conscripts to volunteer for overseas service was a failure. The Prime Minister was cornered again, under intense pressure from public opinion and senior officers in the army. Searching for still another compromise, he rejected total conscription but agreed to send to Europe some 16 000 conscripts who had completed army training. There were protests: many of the conscripts deserted; scattered violence occurred; "Chubby" Power honoured his pledge to his Quebec constituents by resigning from the cabinet.

Yet conscription during World War II never became the divisive issue it had been in 1917. The Canadian government had learned from experience. The manpower problem did not reach the proportions it had in World War I, and the series of compromises had managed to defuse the issue time after time.

FRENCH-CANADIAN VIEWS ON CONSCRIPTION, 1944

P. J. A. Cardin—anti-conscriptionist:

... For a moment, if you wish to understand me and the French Canadians, reverse the picture if you please. Try to imagine Canada as part of a French empire, with the descendants of British citizens in the minority. Can you tell me that if that French empire, of which you would be part, were in danger you would be as enthusiastic in defending that empire as would be the Canadians of French descent? To any man who would say that he would have the same views and sentiments I would reply that he is not sincere.[27]

Louis St. Laurent:

... believing as I do that whenever the majority, after full consultation and mature deliberation, reaches a conclusion of that kind, it is proper the minority should accept it and loyally assist in carrying it out, I appeal to all the members of this house ... to unite and to assert to the men overseas that this nation, from one ocean to the other, stands pledged to a victory that will be decisive and that will endure.[28]

"IF THEY ONLY KNEW"

We landed in Montreal and they issued us summer khaki dress and paid us off, and for a couple of days I just wandered around Montreal with my eyes hanging out. Honestly, for those first hours in Montreal I had the horrible feeling that those people had not been in a war.

I can't be unique. I'm sure every soldier, sailor and airman had the same feeling when he got back home, and I don't care what country the guy came from.

Here was a city all lit up, and thousands of cars and traffic lights and store windows lit up at night, and windows piled full of stuff, candies, chocolates, clothes, everything anybody could ever want and far more than anybody could ever buy. Once when two other guys and myself drank a 40-ouncer, I felt like standing at the corner by Peel Street and yelling at everybody: "Goddamn it, don't you know that over there are cities that will take years to build up again, and millions and millions of men and women and children dead, by bullets and grenades and bombs, and an awful lot of people over there are eating mud to keep from starving?" Well, something like that, and then I thought, well, they'll just look at me like I'm crazy and call a cop.

Because less than two weeks before, I had seen Manchester and the great piles of rubble and the empty spaces brought on by the bombs, and the port of Liverpool with broken wharves, shattered buildings, and that was just a tiny part of England. You should have seen London, and France, Germany. My God, you just wouldn't believe it, and I don't think I have the imagination to think what a lot of Russia was like.

I remember thinking, as drunk as I was, "God, if these people only knew. If they only knew one percent of it."[29]

10

Politics and politicians: leadership in modern Canada

"Jones is a natural leader."
"Brown was the right person in the right place at the right time."

What do each of these statements mean? Do they appear to be contradictory? Why or why not?

The statements are about leadership and leadership is a complicated subject. Even defining the term is a problem. What does it mean? What characteristics do you think a leader should possess? If you are uncertain, you are in good company, since people have debated such questions throughout history.

Part of the problem is that leadership cannot be discussed apart from its setting. Leaders do not act in a vacuum. Their success depends very much on the circumstances in which they find themselves. In trying to assess a person's leadership qualities, we must look at the situation as well as the person involved.

When we speak of leaders, we are often referring to people in politics. In this chapter, we will look at some of the most highly placed leaders in recent Canadian history, particularly the prime ministers from Mackenzie King to Pierre Trudeau. All displayed leadership qualities, although not necessarily the same ones. Try to observe which qualities each prime minister was noted for, as well as the ones each appeared to lack.

The prime minister is only one of the leaders in the country at any given time. Provincial premiers and mayors are other examples of political leaders. But do leaders in business, religion, labour unions, science, sports, the arts and other areas of Canadian life require qualities expected of political leaders? In what ways might leaders in any of these areas differ from leaders in politics?

The end of the Mackenzie King era

Mackenzie King and the Liberals survived the election of June 11, 1945, a month after the end of World War II. As Canada turned from the emergencies of war to the challenges of peace, the federal government had a large role to play.

Mackenzie King, however, was more than seventy years old and tired from the long years as prime minister. He relied increasingly on members of his cabinet to carry the burdens. When King retired in November, 1948, he had completed twenty-five years as prime minister, longer than anyone in the history of the Commonwealth. Leader of the Liberal Party for almost thirty years, King had held high office over a period that spanned two world wars, the worst depression ever, and Canada's evolution from British colony to sovereign nation.

The Liberals stayed in power in 1945 with 125 seats of a possible 245. They held 72 seats east of the Ottawa River, including 19 of a possible 26 in the Maritimes (not including Newfoundland, which had not yet joined Canada) and 53 of 65 in Quebec. West of Manitoba, the Liberals were very weak, winning only 9 of a possible 54.

How does the distribution of seats in 1945 compare with that of the present Canadian government?

The quiet politics of Louis St. Laurent

In 1948 Louis St. Laurent, the personal preference of Mackenzie King, was chosen as leader by a Liberal convention and he thus

Mackenzie King retires after twenty-five years as prime minister

319

Would you want to be prime minister of Canada?

*Pierre Elliott Trudeau was the fifteenth person to be prime minister of Canada

What kind of person wishes to be the leader of our country? Judging from the people* who have held the office since Confederation, and especially the recent ones, the person who wants this position has a better chance of getting it with a certain combination of qualities and training:

1.	Male sex	all prime ministers have been men;
2.	Irish, Scottish or French ancestry (the latter if you join the Liberal Party)	all have been born into families that were either English or French in ethnic origin;
3.	Central Canadian upbringing	R. B. Bennett, who held office from 1930 to 1935, was the last person raised in the Maritimes to be prime minister. Except for John Diefenbaker, no prime minister has come from west of Ontario;
4.	Fluency in both English and French	this has become increasingly important in recent years;
5.	University graduate	not since Mackenzie Bowell in 1896 has a prime minister not been a university graduate;
6.	Training as a lawyer	ten prime ministers have been lawyers;
7.	Upwardly mobile family background	all prime ministers have come from families that were either financially secure or improving their chances of becoming so.

Which of these do you think is likely to be most important in the future? Are there other characteristics necessary for becoming prime minister?Perhaps a more crucial question is, "What personal qualities will be required of the people who are to be successful in office? Should they be:

—charismatic leaders, able to unite Canadians emotionally?
—youthful, not only to be attractive to voters, but to be able to withstand the workload and pressure?

—humanistic, to set an example for Canadians of concern for other people and for non-material values?

—trained as a technocrat, able to appreciate and apply modern science and technology to the operation of government?

—statesmanlike, willing to give leadership and make decisions, however unpopular, without regard for their personal political futures?

The office of prime minister, we can be sure, will continue to be the most important political position in the country. Whatever the character of the person who fills it, and whatever the style of exercising power, the job is likely to be increasingly demanding. Probably it is safe to say that the job of any politician will be more difficult in the future.

Leadership: William Lyon Mackenzie King

King was widely remembered as the little bachelor who had somehow stayed in office all those years in spite of his dullness. Bland-faced and pudgy, he had the movements, someone said, of one who was walking on eggs. When he spoke, people struggled to find some meaning in his woolly statements. Cautious in his decisions, colourless in his manner, he had antagonized very few Canadians, inspired even fewer.

Yet 25 years after his death in 1950, King remained a subject of interest and controversy. He was a spiritualist and visited a medium for purposes of communicating with his mother and others long deceased. He shared his innermost secrets with his dog, Pat. His personal views of people, events and his own daily experiences were made public as portions of his daily diary, which he began to keep at age eighteen in 1893, were published.

The following documents can scarcely begin to reveal the "real" Mackenzie King, but do raise questions about the man and the office he held for so long.

W.L.M.K.

. . .

He blunted us.

We had no shape
Because he never took sides,
And no sides
Because he never allowed them to take shape.

He skilfully avoided what was wrong
Without saying what was right,
And never let his on the one hand
Know what his on the other hand was doing.

The height of his ambition
Was to pile a Parliamentary Committee on a Royal Commission,
To have "conscription if necessary
But not necessarily conscription",
To let Parliament decide—
Later.

Postpone, postpone, abstain. . . . [1]

A SENSE OF OCCASION

In a speech to the National Liberal Federation on January 20, 1948, Mackenzie King announced his intention to retire before the next election. Writing in his diary afterward, he noted:

I could not but help thinking of how the scene was changing and of the significance of tonight's meeting as marking one of the milestones which bring one nearer to the end of life's journey. . . . My father and mother, ... Lapointe [Ernest] and others and my grandfather Mackenzie, in particular, were much in my thoughts tonight. They would have been more so had I not been so completely absorbed in the task of the speech itself. I am convinced that I have been helped and inspired in its preparation. What pleases me most is to see how it has all worked out and the way I more or less foresaw and believed it would. I thanked God for the guidance that has been vouchsafed to me along the way. . . . It was one of the historic occasions and scenes in Canadian history.[2]

KING'S POLITICAL STYLE

Mackenzie King reacts in his diary to criticism that he is colourless and old-fashioned:

Tonight I read an editorial from the Washington Post written evidently by some editor who had been loaded up on Tory propaganda and prejudices over the past years, making out that I was not suited for our times, etc., being a Victorian Liberal; not enough colour, etc., as though what the policies of today demanded was something in the nature of a cross between a monkey and a jackass to make one sufficiently interesting to hold the attention of the public. It has been because of Mussolini, Hitler and other exhibitionists that the world has gone through agony which it has suffered of late. The theory of these writers is that a political leader must accord with what the times demand, rather than having the quality which helps to get the times out of their difficulties into paths that are helpful and enduring.[3]

1. Do you think Mackenzie King, if he had been born 50 years later, would have been more or less successful in politics today? Why?

2. For additional information about Mackenzie King, see Chapters 6 and 9. Does this new information change your impression of him? If so, how?

3. Is a politician's private life anyone's business but his own? Why or why not?

Women leaders throughout Canadian history

"The future historian of the nineteenth century will find no more prominent or distinguishing feature stamped on it than the enlarged opportunity of labour and usefulness afforded to women and the marvellous march of women to the front in almost every field of human activity."[4]

In the early years of the 20th century, women's rights, especially **suffrage**, were starting to become topics of conversation throughout Canada,* the United States and Great Britain. By 1920 most Canadian women were granted equal voting rights with men. Women such as Dr. Emily Howard Stowe, Dr. Grace Richie-England, Mrs. Irene Parlby and Mrs. Nellie McClung, led the women's struggle in early Canada.

the right to vote

*In Canadian newspapers, although the suffragettes had more letters and more arguments than their male counterparts, the argument was confined to the women's pages next to household hints, fashions and medicines.

Dr. Stowe, Canada's first female medical doctor, founded the first suffragists' group. It was disguised as "The Toronto Woman's Literary Club." Female doctors, teachers, novelists and journalists led the suffrage movement. Married, middle-class women also became leaders in the movement, but more frequently they chose to become involved as participants rather than leaders. Many of these women channeled their efforts into social and charitable work with church groups, and in the late 1870s, the Woman's Christian Temperance Union (W.C.T.U.).

Women's clubs became very popular. They were organized for religious, charitable, literary and social purposes. In 1893, Lady Aberdeen, the wife of Canada's governor-general, organized the National Council of Women of Canada. The interests of members of this group were certainly public affairs, especially suffrage, but no one would dispute that the home and family remained every woman's primary pre-occupation.

The emergence of this new feminism was uneven across the country. In the Maritimes where women were granted suffrage in the early 1920s, the feminist movement was never as active as in central Canada and the West. In Quebec, especially among French-speaking

Helen Gregory Macgill

TOP: *Campaigning for women's suffrage.* BOTTOM: *Nellie McClung, Agnes McPhail and Emily Murphy*

324

women, feminism was even less significant a force for women. However, notable French-Canadian women such as Josephine Dandurand and Mme Gerin-Lajoie actively sought changes in Quebec laws in the interests of women. In the West, women like Irene Parlby, Cora Hind and Nellie McClung were successful in helping the movement grow rapidly. Farm women had an advantage because they had to be equal partners with their husbands in the pioneer settlements; equality in certain spheres was more evident and accepted.

After most provinces had introduced female suffrage, many suffragettes felt that their major goal had been reached and left the movement. Others remained to work for equality of the sexes in other areas. But although women's organizations have been unevenly effective in different geographical areas and at different times, women, either individually or in groups, have made numerous contributions in every sphere of Canadian society.

Jean Sutherland Boggs

JEAN SUTHERLAND BOGGS, Director of the National Gallery in Ottawa until 1976, was the only woman in the world to head a major arts institution. In January, 1977, another woman, DR. HSIO-YEN SHIH, became the new director.

EMILY HOWARD STOWE, born in 1831, was the first Canadian woman doctor.

FRANCES BROOKE, SUSANNA MOODIE and NELLIE McCLUNG were among our first successful Canadian authors.

ANNA LEONOWENS founded the first art school in Halifax, Nova Scotia in 1887 (now the Nova Scotia College of Art and Design).

HELEN GREGORY MACGILL, born in 1864, was the first female judge in British Columbia.

Judy La Marsh

CAIRINE MacKAY WILSON was Canada's first woman senator.

AGNES MACPHAIL, elected in 1921, was Canada's first woman M.P.

ETHEL CATHERWOOD was the first woman to win an Olympic gold medal for Canada (high jump, 1928).

JUDY LaMARSH was Minister of National Health and Welfare (1960s) and a Member of the Privy Council, a lawyer and a journalist.

THERESE COSGRAIN, leader of the Quebec Social Democratic Party (1951), was the first and only woman party leader anywhere in Canada.

EMILY MURPHY, appointed police magistrate in Edmonton in 1916, was the first woman in the British Empire to hold the post.

ALYS McKEY BRYANT was the first woman to pilot an airplane in Canada (1913).

YOLANDE WILSON was the first woman on the executive of a labour organization (1952).

MARGARET MEAGHER, Ambassador to Japan and Israel, was the first woman to hold an ambassadorial post, 1964.

Therese Cosgrain

Charlotte Whitton

CELIA FRANCA, GWENETH LLOYD, BETTY OLIPHANT, JEANNE RANAUD, RACHEL BROWNE and ANNA WYMAN were instrumental in creating most of the existing professional dance companies in Canada.

CHARLOTTE WHITTON was the first woman mayor of Ottawa (1951), and was re-elected to that position in 1952 and 1954.

1. In recent years there has been an effort to emphasize the study of women in history. Why do you think this is so?

2. Who are some of the female leaders in your community today? Have there been any notable female leaders from your community (province, region) in the past?

Leadership: Louis St. Laurent

When Louis St. Laurent was "recruited" for politics during World War II, he told Mackenzie King that he intended to stay only until the war was over. Then he wished to return to his Quebec City residence, his family and his law practice. However, by 1948, St. Laurent was the Liberal Party's choice for leader. During most of his nine years as prime minister, he presided over a powerful Liberal majority with a quiet dignity and business-like manner.

ST. LAURENT'S POLITICAL METHOD

While prime minister, St. Laurent was respected and admired even by his opponents. His method of solving problems was:

... to search for a workable solution of every problem and then, without fanfare or exultation, to make his policy appear not as a dubious innovation but as mere common sense, hardly worth argument. Until he abandoned that method in old age and weariness, St. Laurent not only forestalled divisive controversy but gave his opponents no issue that they could successfully exploit against him.[6]

THEY CALLED HIM "UNCLE LOUIS"

[In the spring of 1949, on a western tour, St. Laurent] made a point of speaking to the children present, and again received an enthusiastic response, both from them and their proud parents. Deep in the Rocky Mountains ... one reporter from a Conservative newspaper remarked ruefully to another: 'Uncle Louis is going to be hard to beat.' The nickname stuck, and St. Laurent had found his feet as a politician.[7]

assumed the office of prime minister. A fluently bilingual and distinguished lawyer from Quebec, St. Laurent had only entered politics at the age of sixty-one. At that time, in the dark days of World War II, the Canadian government needed strong French Canadian representation. He had become Prime Minister King's closest colleague and a key figure in retaining the Quebec support upon which the Liberals depended to stay in office.

In the election of 1949, St. Laurent showed that his appeal was nation-wide. The Liberals won 193 seats, including a majority in every province except Alberta. Opposed by a run-down Conservative Party and a listless CCF, the Liberals made the most of the general prosperity and their record of a smooth transition from war to peace to swamp the opposition.

Louis St. Laurent

Only the Liberals could claim to be a truly national party, as they showed again in 1953, when the results were practically a re-run of 1949. The Conservatives, who had changed leaders several times since losing office in 1935, offered no real alternative. But if the Conservatives were a spent force, neither the CCF nor Social Credit showed any sign of becoming more than a "splinter" party. No wonder the Liberals seemed to develop the attitude that they were the "party of destiny".

A CONFIDENT CANADA MATURES AND EXPANDS

Beyond her borders, the storm clouds were gathering, but within Canada a firmly established government was putting the finishing touches on Canada's long path to independence and expansion from "sea to sea". When Queen Elizabeth was crowned in June, 1953, her role as far as Canada was concerned was clearly that of a *symbolic* head of a sovereign, or independent, country. In 1949 the Supreme Court of Canada had become the final court of appeal for Canadians, when the practice of appeals to the Privy Council in England was terminated. Also in 1949, an act was passed authorizing Parliament to amend the constitution in matters not involving federal-provincial concerns. In 1952, Vincent Massey became the first Canadian-born Governor General.

The entry of Newfoundland into Confederation was one of the first accomplishments of the St. Laurent government. Deciding to "go it alone" in 1867, Newfoundland had remained a colony of Great Britain through the years. However, the island suffered severely during the depression of the 1930s. The war brought a measure of recovery, especially when the United States located important air bases there. But after the war, the people of Newfoundland faced a historic choice: to remain under the commission government set up a few years before, revert to the status of a self-governing British colony, or become the tenth province of Canada.

Provincial Politics

Although the Liberals appeared to have a firm grip on the federal government, there were signs of change in provincial politics. In 1952, the Conservatives gained power in New Brunswick and Social Credit, led by W.A.C. Bennett, nearly eliminated both of the old parties in British Columbia. Robert Stanfield's success in 1956 ended long years of Liberal power in Nova Scotia. Manitoba joined the trend two years later when the Conservatives, under Duff Roblin, took office.

The main negotiations were handled by St. Laurent, J. W. Pickersgill, adviser to the then prime minister, Mackenzie King, and the irrepressible Joseph "Joey" Smallwood. Not all Newfoundlanders were as keen as Smallwood was; in fact, two referendums were needed before the decision was made. The narrow majority was enough, however, to prepare the way for Newfoundland's union with Canada in 1949.

THE SMALLWOOD TOUCH

From a pro-Confederation speech in 1946:

Our danger, so it seems to me, is that of nursing delusions of grandeur. We are not a nation. We are a medium-sized municipality. There was a time indeed when tiny states lived gloriously. That time is now ancient European history. We are trying to live in the mid-twentieth century, post-Hitler New World.

   We can, of course, persist in isolation, a dot on the shore of North America. Reminded continually by radio, visitors, and movies of the incredibly higher standards of living across the Gulf, we can shrug incredulously or dope ourselves into the hopeless belief that such things are not for us. By our isolation from the throbbing vitality and expansion of the continent, we have been left far behind in the march of time, 'the sport of historic misfortune,' 'the Cinderella of Empire.'[5]

The Diefenbaker phenomenon

The election of 1957 produced one of the most stunning upsets in Canadian history and ended twenty-two years of Liberal government. The Liberals were reduced to 105 seats; their defeated candidates included nine cabinet ministers. Although the Conservatives, with 112 seats, also lacked a majority, Prime Minister St. Laurent took the election results as proof that Canadians had lost confidence in his government. He promptly resigned and a new prime minister was sworn into office in June, 1957. His name was John Diefenbaker.

   Few Canadians have inspired such partisan feeling or aroused such controversy as the "man from Prince Albert". Whatever his success as the leader of Canada, Mr. Diefenbaker injected colour into the nation's political life. In the fall of 1956, when he was elected leader of the Progressive Conservative Party, the talented defence lawyer from Saskatchewan launched stinging attacks on the Liberal government that helped send it to electoral defeat. What the nation would come to know as the "Diefenbaker phenomenon" had begun.

The pipeline debate: many issues in one

Just when the Liberal government of Louis St. Laurent seemed most unbeatable, it stumbled into a political crisis from which it did not recover. The 'pipeline debate' of 1956 threw Canadian politics into a turmoil. The Liberals played into the hands of the opposition in Parliament and a newly established form of mass medium, television.

The issue was the proposal to construct a trans-Canada pipeline to carry natural gas from its source in Alberta, to the growing markets in eastern Canada (Ontario and Quebec). The minister of trade and commerce, C. D. Howe, compared the pipeline project to the Canadian Pacific Railway in terms of the potential benefit to Canada's unity and prosperity.

C. D. Howe

In terms of engineering and technology, a trans-Canada pipeline was a real possibility at this time. Such lines had already been built in the United States and American involvement in the Alberta petroleum industry would ensure that Canada benefited from the most up-to-date technology. But there were other critical questions: who would pay for the pipeline's construction? What arrangements would be made between the American-owned natural gas suppliers and the company that operated the pipeline? How much of the natural gas should be exported to the lucrative American market?

The Trans-Canada Pipeline Company, as it was eventually formed, involved a great deal of American capital. High initial investment was required, but the participants certainly expected to make a profit. So the Canadian government agreed to supply a large portion of the needed money, on the condition that it could be recovered once the pipeline became profitable.

C. D. Howe spent many months negotiating the proposal and then defending it in the face of opposition from both opposing interests and a wide range of critics. One of his biggest problems was to convince the members of the cabinet and his party.

By the spring of 1956, the pipeline project was a hot issue in Parliament, and clashes between government and opposition spokesmen added to the rising tension. When the actual pipeline bill was introduced to Parliament, the government was impatient to get the project under way. The opposition was equally determined to examine the proposal thoroughly, and saw the opportunity to shake the government's power. The crisis came suddenly: in order to ensure the passage of the laws necessary for the project to proceed on schedule, the government proposed a parliamentary device known as *closure*. The opposition would have only a few days to examine the bill before debate would end and the government use its majority to pass the legislation.

The result was probably the most violent episode in the history of the Canadian Parliament. The opposition hurled charges of arrogance, even dictatorship, at the government; members insulted one another and defied the procedures of Parliament. Finally, almost the entire opposition walked out before the vote was called. The pipeline bill was passed in the absence of the Conservative and C.C.F. parties.

The following excerpt from HANSARD *(the official record) gives some idea of the atmosphere. The day is June 1, 1956, the day Mr. Bell, a member of the Conservative opposition, called "black Friday":*

MR. FLEMING: Mr. Speaker, it should be placed on the record that when an hon. member rose on a question of privilege you sat down and refused to hear him and the Liberals instigated such an outburst of disorder that no one could be heard. That ought to be on the record. This is the lowest moment in Canadian parliamentary history; the lowest moment. There has never been anything like it.

MR. PEARSON: I thought that was last night.

MR. BELL: This is black Friday, boy.

MR. LESAGE: You brought it on; you did it yourself.

MR. FLEMING: How absurd can you get?

MR. MARTIN: The minority is not running this parliament.

MR. ROWE: The majority isn't running it either; nobody is running it. The majority cannot run it, let alone the minority.

MR. HODGSON: Hitlerism.

SOME HON. MEMBERS [Liberals]

There will always be a pipe line,
The pipe line shall be free;
The gas shall flow from west to east in each locality.
There'll always be a pipe line,
The pipe line shall be free—

MR. FLEMING: Not parliament.

SOME HON. MEMBERS:

—for Fulton means no more to you than Fulton means to me.
There'll always be a pipe line, the pipe line shall be free—

MR. FLEMING: Free to American investors.

SOME HON. MEMBERS:

I've been working on the pipe line all the
day through,
I've been working on the pipe line just to
make the Tories blue.
Can't you hear the Tories moaning, getting
up so early in the morn';
Hear the C.C.F.'ers groaning, for the pipe
line's getting warm.

MR. ROWE: He laughs best who laughs last; go to the country and find out.

AN HON. MEMBER: You laughed yourself.

MR. ROWE: No, I am ashamed of you; that is why I cannot laugh.[8]

The Liberals counted on Canadian apathy and hoped that the affair would soon be forgotten. They expected that Canadians would not be much affected by Parliamentary wrangling over such technical matters as procedure and high finance.

But there were many signs to the contrary, and had the Liberals been more in touch with public opinion, they would probably have noticed them. The highly critical coverage of the government's action in the newspapers, and the dramatic impact of television news convinced the nation that the government was insensitive to the will of the people.

In one sense, an oil pipeline is different—rather more like an endless series of railway tank cars than like a pipeline for natural gas. If necessary it can be moved in sections and used again elsewhere, as was Canol's line from Norman Wells, N.W.T., after World War II. The commitment of gas to a certain route, however, is, because the attached consumer market depends on it, similar to the commitment of hydro-electric power, and hence permanent. Its export has long been treated similarly by Canadian law.[9]

As the Conservatives adapted themselves to the unaccustomed role of exercising political power, the Liberal Party turned to the job of replacing the retired Louis St. Laurent. The almost inevitable choice of the convention, early in 1958, was Lester Bowles Pearson. An internationally known diplomat with many years' experience in the department of external affairs, Pearson was best known to Canadians as their chief representative at the United Nations. For his work in helping to settle the Suez crisis in 1956, he had been awarded the Nobel Prize for Peace. But he had little experience in Canada's internal politics, and was almost a stranger in the House of Commons.

Within days of becoming party leader, Pearson, acting on bad advice from his colleagues, called upon the Conservatives to resign and return the reins of government to the Liberals. In this first of many encounters between the two, Diefenbaker was at his best. In a thundering, scorn-filled denunciation of the new opposition, he set the tone for the election he was about to call. With the Liberals in disarray under a new, and as yet unprepared leader, the Conservatives plunged into the campaign with vigour and high hopes of winning a substantial majority.

What followed was the incredible Conservative landslide of March 31, 1958, in which Mr. Diefenbaker's party won 208 seats out of 265—a record by far—and the Liberals survived with a mere 49. The C.C.F. held the remaining eight seats. The Diefenbaker "vision" of Canadian greatness, expounded by the master campaigner over television and at massive rallies across Canada, captured the imag-

TOP: *Mr. Diefenbaker on the hustings.* BOTTOM: *A formal portrait of John Diefenbaker.*

ination of Canadians in every part of the land. In Quebec the Conservatives won a majority of seats for the first time since Sir John A. Macdonald had done so in 1891. Elsewhere, candidates who normally would have had little chance of victory, were swept into office on the coat tails of their leader.

PROGRESS AND PROBLEMS

Canadians had high hopes for their forceful prime minister, backed by his huge majority in Parliament. To great numbers of Canadians, Diefenbaker was a man of the people, someone with whom they could identify. Born on a Saskatchewan homestead, he had risen from humble beginnings to reach the pinnacle of power. Descended from "new" immigrants as well as from Scottish pioneers, he repeatedly declared his belief in a united Canada where all people were equal. The Bill of Rights, passed in the summer of 1960, was a step in the direction of a more just society.*

In spite of the promising beginnings, however, the magic of the name Diefenbaker soon began to fade. The long postwar boom had given way to economic recession, and unemployment reached the highest levels since the Depression. Mr. Diefenbaker was criticized for failing to delegate authority to his cabinet ministers and for conflicts with senior government officials. His defenders praised his refusal to be dominated by big business; other people feared that hostility between government and the business community was damaging the economy. A brilliant leader of the opposition, Diefenbaker did not show the same talent for leading a government.

French Canadians had joined the Diefenbaker bandwagon, but their enthusiasm was short-lived. Although General Georges Vanier was appointed Governor General in 1959, French Canadians played minor roles in Ottawa during these years. Few of the Conservative M.P.s from Quebec were chosen for the cabinet and those who were were assigned to lesser portfolios. The prairie provinces and the Maritimes remained faithful to Diefenbaker, but declining support in Quebec and other regions revealed growing divisions within the Conservative Party and Canada as a whole.

FROM MAJORITY TO MINORITY

On June 18, 1962, the election results for the Conservatives were almost the reverse of 1958. They lost 92 seats, and were thus reduced to 118, less than the majority usually required to stay in office. However the Liberals, while doubling their numbers, still had only 100 M.P.s. Their victory had been prevented by Social Credit's surprising total of 26 seats in Quebec. The reorganized New Democratic Party succeeded in electing 19 members.

John Diefenbaker clung to office, but he was now clearly a man

*Among lawyers and judges, the Bill of Rights was received with less enthusiasm than it was by Canadians in general. Since it applied only to rights affected by the federal government and not to those under the jurisdiction of the province, the Bill of Rights had little bearing on the civil rights of Canadians.

"SOMEBODY UP THERE DOESN'T LIKE US"

with little authority. Besides his troubles within Canada, the difficulties he had been having with the United States over North American defence were dramatized by the Cuban missile crisis. The result was further dissension in the ranks of the Conservative Party and declining confidence in the government on the part of many Canadians.

Early in 1963, divisions within the Conservative Party were clearly exposed by the resignation of Douglas Harkness, the Minister of Defence. Convinced that the prime minister was not going to equip Canada's Bomarc missiles with the nuclear warheads for which they were designed, and thereby would renege on obligations to the United States and the North Atlantic Treaty Organization,* Harkness chose to leave the cabinet. Then a non-confidence motion in the House of Commons was supported by the combined opposition. The Diefenbaker government had fallen, and an election was called for April 18. A movement by anti-Diefenbaker cabinet ministers to replace the leader failed, but the resignation of two more ministers added to the confusion among Conservatives on the eve of the election.

*See p. 475

Lester B. Pearson and a Liberal minority government

In the 1963 election—"round 2" of the Pearson-Diefenbaker struggle —the Liberals gained the greatest number of seats. But Mr. Pearson,

Leadership: John Diefenbaker

Though the years 1957-1958 were the years of the Diefenbaker phenomenon, John Diefenbaker was no meteor flashing across the political sky. Originally elected to the House of Commons after several unsuccessful attempts in 1940, he remained an M.P. continuously after that. Though defeated as Conservative leader in 1967, he remained in the House of Commons throughout Robert Stanfield's more than eight years as leader and after the choice of Joe Clark as Stanfield's successor, in 1976.

DIEFENBAKER'S "VISION" FOR CANADA

In the election campaign of 1958, John Diefenbaker expounded a "vision" of Canadian greatness that helped the Conservatives elect 208 members. The following excerpts from his speech at the Civic auditorium in Winnipeg, on February 12, may only suggest the force of his oratory:

This national development policy will create a new sense of national purpose and national destiny. One Canada. One Canada, wherein Canadians will have preserved to them the control of their own economic and political destiny. Sir John A. Macdonald gave his life to this party. He opened the West. He saw Canada from East to West. I see a new Canada—a Canada of the North.

Canadians, realize your opportunities! This is only the beginning. The future programme for the next five to seven years under a Progressive Conservative Government is one that is calculated to give young Canadians, motivated by a desire to serve, a lift in the heart, faith in Canada's future, faith in her destiny.

This is the message I give to you my fellow Canadians, not one of defeatism. Jobs! Jobs for hundreds of thousands of Canadian people. A new vision! A new hope! A new soul for Canada. . . . [15]

EXCITING THE PEOPLE

There was little doubt that the Vision had struck a response in the national subconsciousness. Having inadvertently elected John Diefenbaker as their prime minister eight months before, most of the voters now seemed determined to commit themselves to him. 'A country starved of leadership for nearly half a century,' wrote Hugh MacLennan, 'had reached the point where it craved leadership more than anything else.'

It was as if the people had come to identify John Diefenbaker with their own individual desires for a trouble-free future. . . . Diefenbaker transformed . . . [the election] into a secular passion play, with himself as its quasi-divine hero. In that campaign, Diefenbaker possessed that rare quality of leadership, known as 'charisma'.[16]

In 1957, after Diefenbaker first came to power, Canada concluded an agreement with the United States whereby Bomarc missiles would be located on Canadian territory. To be effective, these missiles required nuclear warheads, but the Diefenbaker government was reluctant to permit this step. In the Cuban missile crisis of October 1962, the American president, John F. Kennedy, engaged in a war of nerves with Nikita Khrushchev, before the Russians backed down, rather than try to run the American blockade of Cuba. This crisis, although Canada was not directly involved, brought home the urgency of secure defence for North America.

[His twenty-fifty anniversary in the House]
"The Prime Minister today epitomized the finest traditions of parliament when he added the query, what would the House of Commons be without me. I was reminded of an occasion when that question was asked by a former prime minister, Right Hon. Arthur Meighen, some years after he had been in the House of Commons but before he went to the Senate. He had met with that great wit of parliament S. W. Jacobs, K.C., in Toronto, and asked him, 'What is it like in parliament without me?', to which Mr. Jacobs replied, 'It is like Hades would be without Satan.' "[11]

Diefenbaker's record represented not only his own private confusion but the confusion of society at large and the unnecessary chaos of the whole political apparatus which this radical lamb in conservative wolf's clothing stood on its head.

Above all, despite his bewildered humanitarianism and his genuine feeling for the average man, Diefenbaker represented a strange Canadian illusion but, for the moment, fulfilled a vain Canadian hope.

The illusion was a nation's attempt to do more than its means permitted, to consume more than it produced, to build a society for which neither it nor its leader was ready. The hope of doing these things was nurtured by Diefenbaker's oratory, never by his mind, and was hopeless by definition.

In short, Diefenbaker both represented and blindly fomented Canada's refusal to face the facts of its life.[17]

"Mr. Howe determines what is to be done. Mr. St. Laurent agrees. The rest of the cabinet says 'me too' and the 187 other Liberals add 'amen.' "[14]

A FOOTNOTE TO THE ELECTION
For John Diefenbaker

Once more into the confusion
of ballots and placards and slogans
that fly around my head like mad birds,
comes, ominous and insistent, the voice
of the man that no cartoonist
could have invented,
Zeus with tin thunder
the mad old man of the West
predicting storms.

In 1958 I was too young to vote
but walked the streets of Toronto
on election day for a candidate who lost
(like everyone else that year)
to the words of the visionary huckster.

I have never voted for him or his party
but tonight stare into the blur of television
and marvel again at his inevitable survival,
at the voice that can rejoice more in defeat
than most others in victory.

I will remember him
whether I want to or not,
as if he were a nightmare
or the kind of tune
that you can't get out of your head.

There are worse ways to go down
than as a bad old man

"To the young members (of parliament) who have just come I would say that for the first six months after you are here you will wonder how you got here. Then after you will wonder how the rest of the members ever got here."[10]

"Now they decide to alter the name 'Dominion day' to make it 'Canada day.' It is not a fearful thing but it is indicative."[13]

proud in his righteousness
and refusing everything but homage.

(And in a dozen years, in school
one of my children will probably be bored
with details of his years,
while out on the prairies
a thousand old tin cans
will lie in the stiff grass
behind a thousand empty shacks

and from the mouth of each
to the made ears of withered men
will sometimes come the voice of an old thunder).[18]

"I'm disturbed because the doctors tell me I'm sound as a dollar."[12]

---

leading a government with 129 seats, was still a minority prime minister, facing an opposition of 95 Conservative, 17 N.D.P. and 24 Social Credit MPS. Yet the Pearson government pushed forward with a program of reform, including fuller recognition of the rights of French Canadians, a national flag, expanded social security, and changes in Canadian defence.

A NEW ERA FOR THE CANADIAN ARMED FORCES

The "arms race" between the super powers like the United States and the Soviet Union was bringing many changes to the military situation in the world. In the nuclear age, what roles could a middle power like Canada possibly play? Of course Canada was involved in the United States' provisions for defence of North America, as well as in NATO. Assuming Canada's obligations to its allies would continue, and even expand, however, there was the problem of how Canada could best carry out these obligations.

Following the Liberal government's decision in 1964 to integrate the armed forces, the opposition parties, newspaper editors, military spokesmen and others engaged in an explosive debate that lasted for many months. Some career officers, notably in the navy, denounced integration, saying it would undermine the traditional pride of the separate services and reduce Canada's military strength. Nevertheless, under the direction of the Minister of Defence, Paul Hellyer, the government went ahead with unification of the three services—army, air force and navy. The object was to eliminate duplication of functions while creating a new kind of mobile force capable of limited, but effective, action in non-nuclear warfare.

THE CANADIAN FLAG DEBATE

The Canadian flag debate proved to be one of the most emotional issues of the Pearson years. As they had promised in the election campaign, the Liberals introduced a design for a new and distinctive Canadian flag. The problem was that many Canadians, particularly war veterans, were fiercely attached to the Red Ensign. Months of controversy followed, as the Diefenbaker Conservatives fought against the adoption of a new flag, especially a design they sarcastically called the "Pearson pennant". Finally, a parliamentary committee, representing all parties, recommended a flag design with a single red maple leaf and red borders at either end on a white ground. Prolonged debate in the House of Commons ended in December, 1964, and the new flag was adopted on February 15, 1965.

THE CONSERVATIVE PLAN BACKFIRES

During the parliamentary committee's proceedings, the Conservative members were determined to stick to their position. Their plan, however, did not work out the way they wished it to.

After weeks of study, and testimony . . . the committee got down to the task of voting. The Red Ensign was soon disposed of—defeated by a vote of ten to four. . . . This left the 'Pearson Pennant' and a new design, a single red maple leaf on a white ground with bands of red on either side. The decisive vote was the one taken between these two, and it presented the Conservatives with a problem in gamesmanship.

They assumed that the Liberals would still feel themselves committed to the 'Pearson Pennant'. . . . They assumed that the NDP and perhaps the two Social Credit MPs would prefer the new, one-leaf design, and they knew their own French-Canadian member would vote for it. There was a chance, therefore, that an Opposition majority might deal a nominal defeat to the Liberals by rejecting the 'Pearson Pennant' by a vote of eight to six. . . .

What the Conservatives did not know was that the Liberals had changed their minds. Convinced at last that the 'Pearson Pennant' had too much political flavor to become an acceptable flag for all Canadians, they too decided to vote for the new, single-leaf design.

The result, to the Conservatives' horror, was a unanimous vote of fourteen to zero.

. . . The reasons for their horror were plain enough. The Opposition had no intention of letting the new design, or any design, go through Parliament without a filibuster. The fact that they had actually voted with the Liberals and the minor parties for the new design was bound to be embarrassing to them. They did what they could by putting a new motion, and voting that this new design should *not* become the national flag of Canada, but their faces remained red for some time.[19]

"Now we'll never hear the end of it!"

During the course of the flag debate, newspapers across the country carried stories and letters to the editors which sometimes became quite angry. Arthur Deacon, retired literary critic of the Toronto *Globe and Mail*, however, tried to put things in their proper perspective with his comment about the choice of a national symbol for Canada: "Industrious and ubiquitous, the beaver alone represents us all. The visual objection to this overgrown rat is that its shape is ugly. The bull moose, weighing up to 1800 pounds, is also ugly but is a creature that inhabits all regions except the civilized south. As farms and towns move north there will be fewer moose, but choosing this beast now would postpone the flag controversy for a century, and I am all for us getting back to our regular jobs."[20]

CELEBRATING CANADA'S NEW FLAG

The official acceptance of Canada's new flag on February 15, 1965 was celebrated by Canadians around the world:

In Ottawa a large crowd gathered on Parliament Hill to see the new flag hoisted for the first time. A Conservative secretary was detected in the act of applauding; she was threatened with dismissal for this act of disloyalty, but saved her job by the counter-threat of making public the reasons why she was being fired. In London a handful of Canadians gathered on the sidewalk beside Trafalgar Square while Lionel Chevrier, the High Commissioner, made a brief speech into a microphone, which was audible to the radio audience if any, but not to those standing five feet away. To a NATO base in Germany the Canadian ambassador to the North Atlantic Council came all the way from Paris for a flag-raising ceremony, which was marred when someone let go the halyard so that the flag couldn't be raised until a corporal had shinnied up the flagpole to recover its loose end. In Jamaica, High Commissioner Graham McInnes introduced a little originality and style. Instead of holding the ceremony in the blazing heat of high noon he called it for 5 p.m., not too early for cocktails; the whole Canadian colony was invited, and sang 'Auld Lang Syne' as the Red Ensign was struck for the last time and then 'O Canada' while the new flag went up. There was not a dry eye on the lawn, they say.[21]

MUD-SLINGING AND SCANDAL

The years 1965 and 1966 were dark ones for both Liberals and Conservatives. In a series of disclosures about corruption and scandal, several people associated with government were implicated. The most serious situation involving the Liberals concerned a suspected gangster and narcotics smuggler, Lucien Rivard, who was trying to avoid extradition to the United States where he was wanted for trial. A royal commission in 1965 indicated that the only help he was offered came from a cabinet minister's assistant, but the whole government's image was tarnished.

The Conservatives came in for their share of trouble in March, 1966. The Liberals accused several former ministers in the Diefenbaker government of associating with a certain Gerda Munsinger, a woman from eastern Europe who had been under investigation by the RCMP as a possible spy. Diefenbaker as prime minister was said to have failed to take enough care in handling a potential threat to Canada's military security.

Mud-slinging, rumour-mongering and personal quarrels seemed to dominate Parliament. The Canadian people, growing weary of the spectacle in Ottawa, appeared reluctant to entrust their affairs to any one party. Thus, the election of November, 1965, resulted in another minority Liberal government.

THE HAPPIER SIDE

The troubles of the time all but hid the fact that the Liberal Party was carrying on an ambitious program of legislation. Besides the Canadian flag and the integration of the armed forces, there were the vastly expanded welfare programs, manpower training schemes, assistance to universities and technical schools, aid to regional development, a procedure for non-partisan redistribution of seats in the House of Commons and a trade agreement with the United States designed to encourage the Canadian automobile industry.*

*See pp. 460 ff for additional information

While these and other projects were afoot, Canadians were excitedly preparing for the celebration of Canada's centennial in 1967. Communities large and small put the finishing touches on commemorative projects. These ranged from long-needed public facilities such as libraries in smaller communities to the man-made islands at Montreal, where the magic of Expo would draw Canadians from all over the nation. Countless words were written and spoken about the time-honoured subject of the Canadian identity. An awakened interest in Canadian history was stimulated by the flow of centennial publications. As they toured the travelling centennial caravans, or thrilled to the sight of the canoe pageant retracing the routes of the fur traders, or revelled in the wonders of the World's Fair in Montreal, Canadians came to know their country as never before. For many, the new awareness which came out of the centennial celebrations gave at least a partial answer to the question, "What is a Canadian?"

In other parts of the world, the interest in Canada reached new levels. The death of Georges Vanier was deeply mourned. But Canadians took pride in the way that the new Governor General, Roland Michener, played host to state visitors. The Expo site with its pavilions from nearly seventy nations was an international meeting place. World tensions seemed generally far removed. The only exception was the controversy aroused by the visiting French President Charles de Gaulle's remarks which seemed intended to encourage separatist feeling among French Canadians.

CO-OPERATIVE FEDERALISM: OUTCOME OF THE "QUIET REVOLUTION"

As Canada's centennial celebrations drew closer, the government wanted to be sure that our 100th birthday would be a happy occasion. A major cause for concern was the "Quiet Revolution" that had been unleashed in Quebec. Unless the federal system could be made more flexible to allow for the changes in French Canada, Pearson's government believed that Confederation was in danger.

The election of Jean Lesage's Liberal government in June, 1960 is often taken as the beginning of the "Quiet Revolution". The effect was to open the door to the sweeping changes that had been developing during the long Duplessis regime,* changes which Duplessis had not understood and had struggled to restrain. English Canada's image of Quebec as a rural, backward, priest-controlled society of *habitants*, a society that never really changed, was suddenly challenged.

*See page 255.

While rural life was still important to many people in Quebec, the province has been affected, along with the rest of Canada, by the postwar trends of industrialization and urbanization. Montreal, by far Canada's largest city, and other cities and towns like Quebec City, Trois-Rivières, Sherbrooke and Chicoutimi, attracted a flood of job-seekers to factories, shops and offices. Television brought images of other lifestyles into the homes of families who had lived in traditional ways for generations. Politicians, now replacing the clergy as the champions of French-Canadian language and culture, could reach larger audiences than ever before.

Under the Lesage government, which included such able cabinet ministers as Pierre Laporte, Eric Kierans, Paul Gerin-Lajoie and René Levesque, *Québécois* at last had the opportunity to join the "mainstream" of North American life. The government organized eco-

"HOW DO YOU SPELL ANN LANDERS?"

A provincial royal commission, the Parent Commission, recommended drastic reform of education in Quebec. It advised a new emphasis on training students for a modern industrial society. In 1964, a Ministry of Education was created to reform and supervise the several existing school systems. The task ahead was enormous, but education was clearly a top priority in a changing Quebec.

nomic planning on a wide scale, financed industrial development, permitted the free operation of trade unions, launched a program of road building and began to reform the province's educational system and social services.

To the surprise of many, the Quebec Liberals were defeated in the election of 1966. It was said they had tried "to go too far too fast." Although change had brought excitement and a new spirit of confidence to French Canadians, it also brought rising costs, higher taxes and political turbulence, including the "separatist movement" which called for an independent Quebec. Yet the Union Nationale government of Daniel Johnson continued the trend begun by the Liberals, to make *Québécois* "maîtres chez nous."

Because of the "Quiet Revolution", the Pearson government believed it had no choice but to reconsider the relations between French and English Canadians, between Quebec and the rest of Canada. In 1963, the Royal Commission on Bilingualism and Biculturalism (the "Bi & Bi Commission") was appointed. The results of the investigation, which became known in a series of reports over the next several years, focused attention on the possible alternatives facing the Canadian nation.

1. Make a list of important occasions in Canadian history since Confederation when tensions arose between French Canada and English Canada.

342

Leadership: Lester B. Pearson

As a public figure, Lester Bowles "Mike" Pearson (1897-1972) has been regarded as both a brilliant success and a disappointment. His accomplishments as a diplomat have been recognized internationally; as prime minister, he never quite succeeded in convincing Canadians that he was an effective leader. A biographer comments: "Whatever the assessment of his accomplishments and failures, it is undeniable that he was one of the most likeable public figures in Canadian history. Many of his diplomatic triumphs were due to his unique ability to set people at ease and to win their trust; even when he was later under severe attack as Prime Minister, reporters said privately that they hated to write anything bad about a person as nice as Mike Pearson. . . . It will be some time before a final judgement can be reached about the diplomat and politician, but an assessment of Pearson the man has already been silently made by those who knew him."[22]

A GREAT SPORTS ENTHUSIAST

Even the busy schedule of a prime minister did not prevent Mr. Pearson from attending sports events, especially hockey games involving his favourite team, the Toronto Maple Leafs. He was also an avid baseball fan.

The interest in sports came naturally to him. At Oxford he played on the varsity teams in hockey and lacrosse, and took part in international competition with both. While teaching history at the University of Toronto, he served as head coach of the hockey team.

Lester Pearson playing hockey for Oxford University

Lester Pearson in the Royal Flying Corps

THE MAN'S CHARACTER

The political deeds and misdeeds that account for a prime minister's legacy to history flow as much from luck as from his character. Lester Pearson came to office at a perilous moment in his country's history. A good man in a wicked time, he refused to subvert his decent instincts or abandon his quest for world peace and Canadian unity. A slightly different turn of events might have marked him for greatness. He was not a politician corrupted by power, if only because he so seldom used it.

The reason Lester Pearson stirred so little mass emotion at election time was due to a basic shyness. There was about him an air of reserve, a feeling that he should not be drawn into situations where his prestige would be risked in routine encounters. He confessed to close friends that he just couldn't walk up to strangers and pump their hands without being afraid of either invading their privacy or compromising his own dignity. He acted always within the consciousness of his own limitations and of the voters' awareness of them. The simple fact was that he didn't like people in large groups, because he thought they didn't like him.

Lester Pearson was probably the first man to serve as Prime Minister of Canada whose public and private personalities were one and the same. Unlike most of his thirteen predecessors, he wasn't noticeably enlarged by his arrival at the peak of Canada's political system.

By treating the prime ministership like a job that he was trying to do rather than an urgent mission he longed to fulfill, Pearson inspired familiarity without the undercurrent of mystery and excitement that people yearn for in their leaders. . . . [23]

Lester Pearson conferring with Mackenzie King and Louis St. Laurent

Academic

After graduating from Oxford, Mr. Pearson was appointed lecturer in history at the University of Toronto in 1923. There he met Maryon Moody whom he married in 1925. After he retired as prime minister, Mr. Pearson gave a course in international affairs at Carleton University.

Diplomatic and Political

1928	Joined the Department of External Affairs
1935	Represented Canada at the League of Nations
1935-1941	Deputy High Commissioner to Great Britain
1943	Canadian Ambassador to the United States
1945	In San Francisco at the founding of the United Nations With the U.N.'s relief agency in Europe to assist with aid to refugees
1946	Top civil servant in the Department of External Affairs
1948-1957	Secretary of State for External Affairs
1956	During the Suez crisis he proposed a United Nations Emergency Force
1957	Received the Nobel Peace Prize
1958-1968	Leader of the Liberal Party
1963-1968	Prime Minister
1968-1972	Chairman of the Commission on International Development (World Bank); Chairman, International Development Research Centre author, lecturer

---

2. In what ways has the "Quiet Revolution" been different from previous efforts by Quebec to protect the interests of French Canada?

One of the immediate concessions made to Quebec during the Pearson years was a larger share of the government income granted by the federal government to the provinces. A common practice was the "shared cost" program, in which the federal government paid part of the cost of projects in the provinces. An "opting out" procedure enabled a province to receive money for a project of its own, rather than participate in a federal scheme.

The Canada Pension Plan proved to be a turning point in the financial relations between the federal government and the provinces. A plan worked out by the federal government was presented to a conference of provincial premiers in 1964. Both Ontario and Quebec seemed determined to use the occasion to obtain increased revenues for themselves. Premier Lesage of Quebec, whose govern-

Jean Lesage

A front page story prior to the 1965 federal election was that of the "three wise men", three prominent *Québécois* who had been persuaded to run as Liberals. Pierre Elliott Trudeau was a journalist and law professor; Jean Marchand was a prominent labour leader; Gerard Pelletier was editor of *La Presse*. All would soon become powerful figures in the Canadian government.

ment's reforms involved spending on a scale previously unimagined in Quebec, demanded that the federal government get out of the expanding field of social security. He recommended that money be turned over instead to the provinces, so that each could operate its individual program.

The government of Canada had no intention of going so far, but was prepared to compromise in the interests of harmony. To all the provinces, the federal government agreed to provide additional funds. The Quebec Pension Plan was approved, on condition that it be identical and interchangeable with the Canada Pension Plan. Though he was accused of giving in to Quebec, Lester Pearson insisted that Canadian unity had benefited as a result of the compromise.

The Pearson years concluded with biculturalism more a theory than a reality, more a direction than an accomplished fact. The practical implications of biculturalism would be tested under Pierre Elliott Trudeau.

The Trudeau years

INTO THE NEW CENTURY

As Canada embarked on its second century, many changes had occurred or were anticipated in the national political parties. Robert Thompson left the declining Social Credit Party to become a successful Progressive Conservative candidate in the 1968 federal election. Following his defeat in that election, T. C. "Tommy" Douglas decided to step down from the leadership of the New Democratic Party, and at a convention in April, 1971, David Lewis was chosen as successor. Both the Liberals and Conservatives chose new leaders as well, leaving the Creditistes as the only party to continue under the same management.

The Progressive Conservative Party held its national leadership convention in September, 1967. The meeting was called despite the resistance of Diefenbaker supporters, who regarded it as a deliberate move by such prominent Ontario Conservatives as national party president Dalton Camp to remove "the Chief" from the leadership. Mr. Diefenbaker did stand as a candidate, unsuccessfully, but even in defeat he provided the occasion with much of its drama by keeping the nation guessing about his intentions until the last possible moment. Then he went down fighting with his declaration in support of "one, united Canada" and his denunciation of the "deux nations" concept of Confederation which had recently found favour with Conservative policy makers.

Robert Stanfield, eminently successful as Premier of Nova Scotia, emerged as the new leader of the Conservatives. The quiet-spoken politician from Halifax had defeated eight other candidates, of whom the leading challenger was the former Premier of Manitoba, Duff Roblin.

The governing Liberal party changed leaders at the request of Prime Minister Pearson following his announcement in December, 1967, of his intention to retire. The choice of the convention in April was the dynamic Pierre Elliott Trudeau, an intellectual from Montreal who had entered the Liberal Party and the House of Commons less than three years earlier. Mr. Trudeau's election as Liberal leader was startling in many respects. Little known outside his native province of Quebec, where he had long been identified with the socialists, an unorthodox individual of wide interests, he had been elected in preference to candidates with long experience and power within the Liberal party.

ROBERT STANFIELD

Robert Stanfield, leader of the Progressive Conservative Party from 1967 to 1976, won the respect of fellow politicians and of Canadians from coast to coast during his long years as "leader of the opposition." He never succeeded in becoming prime minister, although he came within a whisker in the election of 1974, and Canadians may debate the reasons for years to come. A biographer calls him "the most improbable of politicians" and quotes two observers about the Stanfield enigma:

He is the most improbable of politicians. In 1969, shortly after stepping down as Prime Minister of Northern Ireland, Terence O'Neill met Robert Stanfield for the first time. This is his impression, as he wrote it in his autobiography: "If ever one of nature's gentlemen strayed into politics, the name of that man is Stanfield."

The Stanfield enigma was succinctly stated by John Aitken in an article in *Maclean's Magazine* in May of 1972:

"Stanfield . . . is in many ways a more interesting politician than Trudeau. He bristles with paradox. He invokes trust in an age that prefers excitement and acceleration. He is humble and we consider humility to be embarrassing. He is diffident and that quality, in this political decade, is catastrophic. . . . Stanfield has failed the public, simply by being what he is—an insuperably reticent man who holds office in which reticence is no virtue."[24]

TRUDEAUMANIA: THE ELECTION OF 1968

In the election of June, 1968, Mr. Trudeau proved to be as appealing to the Canadian voters as he had been to the Liberal delegates a few weeks before. In a skilfully organized campaign of television and radio appearances, rallies of the party faithful, and whirlwind visits to shopping centres and other public locations, Mr. Trudeau aroused

Trudeaumania, 1968

enthusiasm in all parts of the country. "Trudeaumania" was added to the Canadian vocabulary to describe the effect. The almost hypnotic quality, sometimes referred to as charisma, which Trudeau projected was too much for the opposition parties. With 155 members elected, the Liberals had achieved the first majority government in Canada since 1962.

COMMENT ON THE CANADIAN ELECTION OF 1968

A well-known journalist considers the extent to which television contributed to "Trudeaumania":

.... His [Trudeau's] victory at the leadership convention was great television, and paved the way for Trudeaumania.

Trudeaumania, however, depended on his personal appearances, a technique as old as humanity itself. There is no record of outbursts of Trudeaumania around TV sets.

Trudeau used TV as a channel to the people—an instrument of communications superbly suited to his talents and his style....

But television didn't make Trudeau. What made him was the over-all impact on the public of his ideas, and the general impression created by what people saw of him, what they read about him, and what they heard about him.[25]

Political scientist J. Murray Beck examines the variety of support attracted by Pierre Elliott Trudeau in the election of 1968:

Some expected Trudeau to establish clear-cut differences between the Liberals and Conservatives, but in this election he was, if

348

anything, further to the right than Stanfield. However, it would be naïve to believe that Trudeau—pragmatic on everything but the constitution—would normally differ on fundamentals from the equally pragmatic Stanfield. Crucial to Trudeau's success will be his ability to satisfy the demands of the rational exponents of Trudeauism for a new kind of politics. In the election of 1968 he employed his own contradictory qualities to attract conflicting interests and groups; will he appear equally attractive to them when the chips are down?[26]

PLANNING FOR A "JUST SOCIETY"

Elected on the strength of Trudeaumania, the Liberals had managed to avoid making many specific promises that would commit them to any "crash program". The need to create a "just society" and "participatory democracy" was a theme of Mr. Trudeau's campaign speeches, but he repeatedly stated that he was offering no miracles. After a year in office, he faced sharp criticism from the opposition parties for the alleged inaction of his administration. Yet he concentrated on completing business left over from the previous government, including the amendment of the criminal code, for which he had been responsible as Minister of Justice.

Reorganizing the day-to-day operation of the government was another job that Trudeau believed to be important. In the previous decade, the size and responsibilities of government had grown considerably, with the result that efficiency had declined. Cabinet ministers and their staffs found their workloads mounting; at the same time, there was more and more duplication of effort as programs expanded in different departments. Under Trudeau, therefore, new advisers were brought in to increase over-all planning; coordinating committees were set up; cabinet committees assumed some of the workload of government. The new emphasis on efficiency was extended to Parliament itself, where new procedures were introduced to speed up decision-making and the passing of laws.

The opposition parties and many journalists were skeptical of the changes, which could be seen as strengthening the power of the prime minister and the executive branch generally, at the expense of the House of Commons.* The dilemma seemed to be a continuing one: if efficiency tends to concentrate power of government in the hands of a few, at what point does efficiency begin to threaten democracy?

*See Chapter 1, Volume 2.

Another unsettling development was the major review of existing policies and practices that the Trudeau administration set in motion. It seemed that everything was being questioned: federal-provincial relations, the constitution, welfare, the status of women, foreign affairs, to name a few. Canadians in general may have felt let down from the high expectations aroused by Trudeaumania; their lives had not been affected very much by the new government. However, particular groups of Canadians were worried about changes that appeared to be in the offing.

CANADA: A BILINGUAL COUNTRY?

Of the many challenges facing Canadians in the 1970s, one of the most fundamental was the relationship between English-speaking (Anglophone) and French-speaking (Francophone) Canadians. During the 1960s, the "Quiet Revolution" had generated an atmosphere of questioning, debate and conflict.

Meanwhile, the federal government under Lester Pearson endeavoured to improve its image in the eyes of French Canadians. Many able French-speaking people from Quebec were attracted to its service. As we have seen, the government followed a policy of "cooperative federalism", working out a freer arrangement with the provinces. Quebec, a province "not like the others," thus acquired more of the flexibility which its leaders claimed was necessary to preserve the culture of the French-Canadian majority.

Within Quebec, the achievements associated with the "Quiet Revolution" contributed to a rising spirit of French-Canadian *nationalism*. No longer was French-Canadian nationalism expressed merely in terms of survival ("la survivance"), as it had been for generations. Now there was a feeling of confidence, a pride in being French Canadian, and a desire to live in a fully Francophone environment.

Even the main political parties in Quebec, which supported the continuation of Quebec within Canada, seemed to assume that their province would gain increasing autonomy within Confederation in the years ahead. Thus the election of the Quebec Liberals, led by the young economist, Robert Bourassa, in April, 1970, was no guarantee of a relaxation in relations between Quebec and the rest of the country.

Nevertheless, for some French Canadians nothing less than independence, and the establishment of Quebec as a separate nation, was the goal.

Several separatist organizations were founded, varying from moderate groups such as the RIN (Rassemblement Pour L'Indépendance Nationale) to the extremist FLQ (Front de Libération du Québec). Then in 1968, the Parti Québécois was formed as a political party under the leadership of René Levesque. The former Quebec Liberal cabinet minister led the party into the provincial election in 1970 and gained a surprising 24% of the popular vote. By the mid-1970s, the Parti Québécois was the main opposition party in the province of Quebec.

Vive le Québec libre

The late Charles de Gaulle surprised Canadians during his official visit to Canada in July, 1967, during Canada's Centennial Year celebration. From the steps of Montreal's city hall, the President of France exclaimed "Vive le Quebec Libre". By echoing the slogan of Quebec's active and vocal separatist groups, he shocked the Canadian government. Prime Minister Pearson declared the action to be "unacceptable" and Mr. de Gaulle cut short his stay in Canada. The anger of many and the excitement of others remained long after.

The October crisis

The month of October, 1970 was one of the most shocking in the history of Canada. The kidnapping of James Cross, British trade commissioner, on October 5, appeared to be the climax of nearly a decade of activities by the FLQ. Associated with bombings, robberies and other activities which its spokesmen declared to be part of a revolution in Quebec, the FLQ quickly forwarded a series of communiques. In exchange for the life of Mr. Cross, they presented a list of demands, which they insisted be made public, including the release of FLQ members in prison.

On October 10, as the tension grew, the news broke of the kidnapping of Pierre Laporte, Quebec's Minister of Labour and Immigration. Identifying themselves as the Chenier* cell of the FLQ, the captors of Mr. Laporte appeared to be more demanding in their conditions for the release of their hostage. Rumour upon rumour added to the fear of a widespread conspiracy to seize the government of Quebec and declare Quebec separate from Canada.

*Named after Dr. Chenier, who died in the Rebellion of 1837.

The governments of Canada and Quebec coordinated a response to the apparent threat. On October 16, the government of Canada announced that the War Measures Act was in effect, for the first time in peace time.* The usual democratic freedoms were suspended, and a series of raids by the Canadian army led to the arrest and detention of several hundred "suspects". Meanwhile, the day after the announcement, the body of Pierre Laporte was found in the trunk of an abandoned car.

*The War Measures Act was originally passed near the beginning of World War I.

The hunt for the killers of Laporte was intensified as the army and police acted to round up all persons who could be associated in any way with the FLQ. The Canadian Parliament met in emergency debate, and political leaders arrived on Parliament Hill with armed soldiers at their sides. Meanwhile the police located James Cross and arranged for his release by granting his captors safe passage to Cuba. With the Cross ordeal over, police concentrated on tracking down the kidnappers of Pierre Laporte, and in January 1971, they were apprehended.

Fears of a massive conspiracy to seize the government of Quebec proved to be unfounded. The terrorists turned out to be a handful of people who were frustrated because the "Quiet Revolution" was not going the way they thought it should. However, the October crisis raised many issues that were likely to be debated for a long time.

1. Was the Canadian government over-reacting by invoking the War Measures Act?

2. Did the October crisis increase feelings of separatism in Quebec?
3. Were anti-Quebec feelings increased in other parts of Canada?
4. Was Canada a "police state" during the existence of the War Measures Act? Should there be other ways of handling domestic threats to the country's law and order?

THE OFFICIAL LANGUAGES ACT

As a follow-up to the report of the Royal Commission on Bilingualism and Biculturalism, which had been appointed by the government of Lester B. Pearson, the government introduced a bill which became the Official Languages Act. Put into effect in September 1969, the Act declared both English and French to be the official languages of Canada. This meant that both languages could now legally be used in all business of Parliament and the government of Canada.

There were further provisions. A Commissioner was to ensure that people complied with the Act, and to take action on complaints. All documents—reports, speeches, pamphlets—issued to the public were now to be published in both English and French. "Bilingual districts" were to be established in parts of Canada where there was a sizeable minority; in these districts, government services were to be available in both official languages.

Several government departments and agencies were involved in implementing the Official Languages Act. One program promoted bilingualism in the federal civil service, so that Canadians could deal with the government in either English or French. Civil servants were encouraged to become bilingual, especially for certain positions, and language training programs were provided.

Other programs included the Federal-Provincial Program for Bilingualism in Education, which provided funds to each of the provinces to promote bilingualism. Facilities for French-language radio and television in provinces outside Quebec were expanded. Regulations required bilingual labelling on products sold across Canada.

The Official Languages Act was a bold and ambitious undertaking. Prime Minister Trudeau described bilingualism as the most important issue facing Canada since the conscription crisis of World War II. However, widespread criticism and misunderstanding hampered the program every step of the way. Outside Quebec, and particularly in the West, many Canadians felt that the federal government was trying "to ram French down people's throats."

The following account by a journalist in 1976 attempts to give a factual summary of the Official Languages Act and its implications.

The Official Languages Act provides only that where there is a reasonable demand, every citizen has the right to deal with the federal government in either English or French. Other initiatives, such as regulations requiring bilingual labelling and efforts to provide French-language radio and TV outside Quebec, extend people's right to be served in their own language without diminishing anyone else's rights.

Federal language policies add, not subtract, rights. There is no attempt, under the Official Languages Act, to force any citizen to speak the other language or to prevent him from speaking his own.

The only exception is in the case of federal civil servants and here, too, no right is being infringed. There is no basic right to work for the government or any other employer without having the proper qualifications; in a country with two principal language groups, knowledge of both languages is a reasonable qualification to require for certain government jobs.

Even at that, the government has gone to considerable—and very expensive—lengths to avoid injustice to incumbent unilingual employees or to prospective employees willing to learn the second language. Fewer than one-fifth of all federal jobs, moreover, are classified as bilingual.[27]

If the intentions of the federal policy of bilingualism are positive, and intended to benefit Canada as a whole, why has there been so much negative reaction? One reason given was the government's failure to explain the policy fully enough and to communicate adequately with the Canadian people. Another was that the unpopularity of other policies of the Trudeau administration—notably the "war on inflation"—carried over to its program of bilingualism.

Within Quebec, the controversial "Bill 22"* appeared to be contrary to bilingualism. The Quebec government's new laws aimed at making French the working language of the province and restricting the growth of education in English were resented by Anglophones in Quebec as well as outside the province.

*See p. 87.

The attitude of the English majority, nevertheless, seemed to be the key to the bilingualism issue. If French Canadians could see no hope for the French language outside Quebec, they would be more inclined than ever to stress the "French fact" within Quebec. To the extent that language is a vital part of culture, French Canadians would continue to be alienated from Confederation. A growing sense of apartness, combined with a sense of nationalism based on self-confidence, would increase the odds that a majority of Québécois might see an independent Quebec as an alternative.

ELECTION OF 1972

The election of 1972 was contested in a political climate very different from the one of 1968. The October crisis had sharpened French-English tension. Separatists in Quebec were more convinced than ever that a separate state must be created; in much of English

Canada, which had supported the tough stand taken by the Trudeau government in October 1970, anti-Quebec sentiment seemed stronger. Yet the Liberal government under Mr. Trudeau retained its electoral grip on the province of Quebec, where none of the opposition parties offered much of an alternative. Elsewhere, much of the country was alienated by the government's apparent policy of "French power"; the Official Languages Act was the favourite target of critics.

Besides bilingualism, issues in the campaign were primarily concerned with economic problems. The New Democratic Party attacked the advantages of the corporations, labeling them the "corporate welfare bums". Inflation, an underlying problem, especially since World War II, emerged as an enduring issue, in spite of the prime minister's claim that the government was going to "fight inflation to a standstill."

A general issue was the government's failure to live up to the expectations aroused in 1968. Even members of government admitted their frustration at the slow pace with which improvements could be brought about. Not that the government had stood still. The "just society" and "participatory democracy" still seemed far in the future, but extra funds had been pumped into less prosperous regions, like the Maritimes, under such schemes as DREE (Department of Regional Economic Expansion). Incentives were available to young people and other groups in the form of LIP (Local Initiatives Projects) and OFY (Opportunities for Youth) grants. Improved Medicare coverage and income supplements benefited the country's older citizens. The voting age had been lowered to eighteen for federal elections. Yet these moves did not seem to offset the impression that the government had failed to provide strong leadership, and —ironically, since much had been made of the drive for efficiency—businesslike government.

In contrast to 1968, Mr. Trudeau conducted a low-key campaign. The Liberals relied on the slogan "The Land is Strong." The Conservatives replied, "It had to be to Withstand Nine Years of Liberal Rule," and appeared to have a good chance of winning the election.

The results were a stand-off. The Liberals stayed in office with a minority, retaining 109 seats while the Progressive Conservatives improved their standings to 107. The Trudeau government now depended on the support of one of the opposition parties, generally the New Democratic Party whose 30 seats gave it the "balance of power".

THE CONSTITUTION—AGAIN!

A new constitution for Canada was one of Prime Minister Trudeau's top priorities when he came to power. To ensure a united Canada, he believed that the country needed a "made in Canada" constitution that would provide for both English and French Canadians. He also believed in the need for a strong central government, where French Canadians would play an important role—rather than in a decentralized federalism, with French Canadians expressing their aspirations through the government of Quebec. In other words, he felt that if French Canadians could be convinced that they belonged on the larger stage of Canada, they would not wish to confine themselves to a French province.

In Quebec, the Liberal government of Prime Minister Robert Bourassa was moving toward the position that Quebec was the true homeland of French Canadians. Therefore, the policy was to increase the power of the Quebec government at the expense of the Canadian government, especially in matters relating to "social policy"—language, family allowance and other forms of social security, manpower programs, immigration, television and other matters affecting a distinctive cultural identity.

After years of preparation, a constitutional conference was held in Victoria, B.C. in June, 1971. A formula for changing the constitution was proposed by the federal government. It included a procedure for amending the constitution without the involvement of Great Britain. The conference broke down, however, when the government of Quebec decided that the "Victoria charter" failed to allow it sufficient power.

After the failure of the Victoria conference, the Trudeau government downplayed the idea of a new constitution. However, events of the 1970s seemed to point to the need for patriation of the British North America Act and a system of amending laws affecting federal-provincial relations. The "have" provinces were seeking greater autonomy; Alberta, for example, wanted more control over the pricing and sale of petroleum and other natural resources. Quebec was seeking firm guarantees for its French language and culture. The "have not" provinces were concerned that the central government retain sufficient powers to protect their interests. Faced with such conflicts, the federal government had to try to convince Canadians in all provinces of the goals they held in common.

The Canadian government, therefore, took the initiative once more to try to establish an effective, equitable and distinctly Canadian constitution. In the summer of 1976, Prime Minister Trudeau called upon the provincial premiers to resolve, at their annual meeting, their differences over such basic issues as control of natural resources, provincial rights and procedures for amending the constitution. Should the provinces be unable to reach agreement, the federal government could at least use its authority to "bring the constitution home" from Britain.

In 1967, after being pressured by national women's organizations, the Pearson government appointed a Royal Commission to investigate the problems of women in Canadian society. The *Royal Commission on the Status of Women* brought forth its recommendations in 1970. These recommendations called for sweeping legislation in areas such as justice, labour, manpower and immigration, health and welfare, civil service and education. By 1975, the governments had implemented about one-third of the recommendations, but for the most part these were minor improvements. Action Committees set up in many provinces worked for the major changes recommended by the Royal Commission, but these are still being debated by both provincial and federal politicians.

Meanwhile, women's groups are being organized at all levels to act on the special problems women face. Whether it is a group formed to get provincial funding for day-care centres, to lobby the federal government to remove the abortion laws from the criminal code, or to discuss the special problems for mature women re-entering the work world, women are finding that the world outside the home is not the exclusive domain of their male counterparts.

"Consciousness-raising"* on the part of Canadian women, however, was not done in isolation from women across the globe. In fact, the United Nations, through urging by its Commission on the Status of Women, gave its approval to a plan designating 1975 as *International Women's Year*. The U.N. Commission felt that this step would mobilize action on behalf of women throughout the world. Most importantly, the Commission wanted the year to determine the progress made on rights and responsibilities of women and also to plan new programs and ideas which would be set in motion but would carry on well beyond 1975.

Canada set out its program for International Women's Year in the June 1974, bulletin of the Canadian commission for Unesco.

*The term coined by feminists to mean making women aware of the possibilities open to them and also making them aware of their potential to be successful in a *variety* of roles and situations.

WHAT IS CANADA DOING?

Internationally, Canada is officially supporting the proposal for a UN Conference on Women during 1975 and the activities recommended for the Year. Domestically, the Government has decided that Canada should take advantage of the United Nations proclamation of 1975 as International Women's Year to concentrate on the promotion of equality for women in all aspects of life and, in particular, to inform and educate the general public of the changing attitudes concerning women's role in society.... The programme includes such items as:

1) A series of regional and national conferences.
2) A national educational and informational programme involv-

INTERNATIONAL WOMEN'S YEAR

ANNÉE INTERNATIONALE DE LA FEMME

ing the public media aimed at influencing the attitudes of society towards equality for women.

3) Increased financial assistance for voluntary organizations.

4) The removal of remaining provisions in federal legislation which discriminate against women. . . .

5) The implementation by departments and agencies of the Federal Government of special programs for 1975 to promote equal opportunity for women. . . .

6) The hosting of an International Seminar in September 1974, in Ottawa. . . .

[Finally,] an increase in the number of women representing Canada at international conferences of all kinds and on all subjects.[28]

In practice, however, Canadian women had reservations about the idea of a "women's year."

Writing in February of 1975, Doris Anderson, the editor of the Canadian magazine, Chatelaine *said:*

INTERNATIONAL WOMEN'S YEAR: WILL CANADIAN WOMEN GET THEIR $5 MILLIONS' WORTH?

1975 has been declared International Women's Year by the United Nations. It could be a rare opportunity to make a great leap forward for women. Or it could be like Mother's Day or Boy Scout's Apple Day. A tribute. A patronizing gesture. And at this stage it looks a lot more like the latter than the former. Some international covenants will be signed regarding women at United Nations. But meanwhile what's going on here in Canada?

To begin with, the federal government has committed five million dollars to International Women's Year and each province has some program varying from vague plans to honor outstanding females to spending up to half a million dollars.

But when January 1976 rolls around, I'd like to feel some real accomplishments had been achieved with all that money.

The Royal Commission on the Status of Women was set up in February 1967 and it brought in its recommendations—all 167 of them—over four years ago. Only about one third of them have been half-heartedly implemented—and they were the easy ones.

There are still pension plans all across this country where women have to retire five years earlier than men and get less money than men at the end of their working careers, even though they've contributed as much to the plan. A woman working in the home can't contribute to the Canada pension scheme. And, no matter how hard she works in her home, or in her husband's business, has no assurance that she has any real legal claims on the family assets.

There are nearly two million married women working outside the home and an estimated 600,000 children in need of day care. We've been talking about this neglect of our children for 30 years, but is any of the five million dollars going to be used to do anything concrete? . . .

What is the federal government going to do with the five million dollars they've tagged for International Women's Year? Half of it is in the Secretary of State's office. Some of that money will be given to projects in connection with women's year, including a cultural program and an animated film. Half of it is administered by the Privy Council. A good portion of this will be used to stage five conferences—the first one a federal one to be held in Ottawa in April.

But do we really need any more conferences—hundreds of women traipsing off to Ottawa or to regional conferences to hash over the same old problems—that we all know are there but haven't been solved? . . .

Do Canadian women really need to be "sensitized?" I think they know what their problems are. The woman who is working on either an assembly line or in a university department and getting two thousand or three thousand dollars a year less than a man beside her doing the same job, and being passed over for promotion, knows what her problems are—she needs legislative clout to correct that kind of discrimination.

The woman in the home needs to know she has the dignity and right to contribute to her own pension plan and financial future— and is not at the mercy of a husband who can cut her off with a pauper's pittance after 20 or 30 years of work. The working mother who worries about her child left with a neighbor, or left with a key around its neck, knows what she needs to help her. . . .

International Women's Year is a time to get things moving. Enough talk.[29]

CHATELAINE *once again devoted space to I.W.Y. in its November, 1975 edition where Michele Landsberg looked at the year at its close:*

That was the Year that almost was: the year when government ballyhoo in honor of women fell flat, when official funds were dribbled away, and when only the grass-roots efforts of women themselves saved the whole idea from becoming ludicrous.

. . . The federal government produced a tiny nest egg of $5 million (about 62 cents for each Canadian woman) and proceeded to parcel it out in such confusion that halfway through IWY, most women still had no idea where to apply for a grant.

Did anything happen? Did IWY change anything for Canadian women? The benchmark of change still has to be the weary old *Report of the Royal Commission On the Status of Women in Canada*. . . . This year, the government blew the dust off a few of the recommendations (mostly minor) and set them on the path to legislative action. The Canadian Pension Plan will no longer discriminate against women . . . except that housewives can't be part of the plan. An omnibus bill will remove some legal irritants, putting men and women on equal footing in the Citizenship Act . . . though discrimination against native women remains. Married women won't have to call themselves "Mrs." on the voters' list. Working women will have more flexibility in choosing when they want to use their 15 weeks of paid maternity leave under the Unemployment Insurance Act. Girls will be allowed to join military cadets. . . .

Of course, nobody expected that all injustices would be magically erased by a public relations campaign like IWY. The best that could be hoped, according to top IWY officials, was that the public should become more aware of women's struggles, and possibly more sympathetic. . . .

When IWY is over, the onus . . . still . . . will be on the women, probably the same five percent of Canadian women who are actively involved and who achieved IWY's scattered successes. Their struggle for actual change, which might make the lives of all of us better in a concrete way, will go on without the grants and the glossy ads and the government speeches. Their continuing hope will be that IWY reached enough women to swell the ranks of those who are committed to fighting politically for human betterment.[30]

1. What further recommendations from the Status of Women report have been implemented? Which recommendations do you feel should have the highest priority?
2. What is the attitude in your school concerning the roles that girls should have? For example, are girls given equal opportunities in your school to take "tough" courses? To serve on the student council? To represent the school on committees or in other activities involving the community? Are they encouraged to do these things? Why or why not?

THE ELECTION OF 1974

For twenty months after the 1972 election, the Liberals clung to power. It was a difficult period of declining world trade made worse by the "energy crisis", of high unemployment and galloping inflation.

These economic issues dominated the election of July 8, 1974. Robert Stanfield and the Conservatives, sensing that the primary concern of Canadians was inflation, proposed a 90-day freeze on wages and prices to give Canada time to develop a coherent anti-inflation program. The Liberals vigorously opposed such a freeze, and instead stressed the need for experienced leadership in handling the country's economic problems.

The life of a politician's wife

The wives of politicians in Canada have been traditionally known to the public in their role as wife and, sometimes, mother. They have engaged in social activities and given support to their husbands. Few politicans' wives have taken stands on issues or entered into political debate. Whatever their significance within the family circle, they have generally served as little more than decorations in the political arena.

Margaret Trudeau has been that rare kind of political wife, one who has declared herself to the public as a person in her own right. When she married Pierre Trudeau in 1969, Margaret Sinclair appeared to be just what the public wanted in a modern prime minister's wife—young, attractive, personable. The birth of her first two sons, both on Christmas day of different years, added to her mystique.

However, Margaret Trudeau eventually proved that she was no stereotype. In the election of 1974, she plunged into the campaign to get the Liberals re-elected. At that time and on many occasions since, she has held press conferences and given interviews. Although her behaviour has been at once severely criticized and highly praised, Margaret Trudeau was one of the first women to become known as more than "the wife of the honourable. . . . "

1. What benefits or harm to her husband could an outspoken political wife cause? Should these wives consider the effect upon their husbands' careers when they think about their own behaviour? Why or why not?
2. Lack of privacy is one of the biggest problems facing public figures. Do you think every part of a politician's life is public, or do you think a politician should be able to have some privacy? If you opted for privacy, which matters should not be "fair game" for media people?
3. Do you suppose there are the same problems for husbands of female politicians? Why?/Why not? What should be the role of political husbands?

What if the separatists were elected?

In the summer of 1976, René Levesque, the leader of the Parti Québécois (PQ), wrote an article in which he looked into the future. He "supposed" a question about a situation that probably seemed far away to most Canadians:

So, all in all, there is quite a serious possibility that an independentist government will soon be elected in Québec. At first sight, this looks like a dramatically rapid development, this burgeoning and flowering over a very few years of a political emancipation movement in a population which, until recently, was commonly referred to as quiet old Québec. But in fact, its success would mean, very simply, the normal healthy end result of a long and laborious national evolution. . . .

Let us suppose it does happen, and Québec peacefully elects such a government. What then?

The way we see it, it would have to go somewhat like this. There is a new Québec government which is totally dedicated to political independence. But this same Québec, for the time being, is still very much a component of federal Canada, with its quite legitimate body of elected representatives in Ottawa. This calls, first of all, for at least a try at negotiation. But fruitful talk between two equally legitimate and diametrically opposed levels of government, without any further pressure from the population—that would be a real first in Canadian political history! Obviously, there would have to be the referendum which the Parti Québécois proposes in order to get the decisive yes-or-no answer to the tired question: What *does* Québec want? (This was precisely the procedure by which the only new province to join Confederation during our recent democratic past, Newfoundland, was consulted in 1948-49 about whether or not to opt in. So why not about opting out?) If the answer should be no, then there's nothing to do but wait for the momentum of change to keep on working until we all find out whether or not there is finally to be a nation here. If the answer is yes, then the pressure is on Ottawa, along with a rather dramatic surge of outside attention.[31]

To the surprise of everyone, it seemed, the impossible suddenly happened. The Québec premier, Robert Bourassa, called an early election for November 15, 1976. His government's huge majority elected in 1973—102 of a possible 110 seats—was expected to decrease. But instead of merely decreasing, the Liberals fell to 27 seats, and the Parti Québécois swept into power with a strong majority (70 seats), and 40% of the popular vote. To what extent did the election of a separatist party in Quebec raise new alternatives for Canada?*

*See Volume 2, Chapter 14, "Biculturalism".

The results of the elections gave the Liberals a majority in the House of Commons. Political analysts would argue that the Liberal victory was to some extent a vote of confidence in the Trudeau administration and a backlash against the NDP's victories in the western provinces, as well as a rejection of the Conservatives' policy of wage and price controls.

LEADERSHIP CHANGES

In the demanding world of federal politics, the leaders of political parties in opposition have many responsibilities. Canadians expect them to "keep the government on its toes"; the people of their constituencies expect them to represent their interests; and the members of their parties expect them to lead their parties to victory at election time. However effective they may be as MPs and as critics of the government, if they fail to prove winners, their parties sooner or later will seek to replace them.

After the election of 1974, and the clear Liberal victory, Canadians anticipated changes in the unsuccessful parties.* David Lewis retired as leader of the New Democratic Party, and was replaced by Ed Broadbent in the summer of 1975. In February, 1976, Joe Clark took over the leadership of the Progressive Conservatives, as Robert Stanfield stepped down.

*Réal Caouette, however, continued as the head of Social Credit, until his replacement in the fall of 1976 by André Fortin.

POLITICS, PRINCIPLES AND POPULARITY

During the next two years, a wide variety of social concerns such as language rights, consumer protection, crime control and capital punishment* were important. However, the economic situation still demanded the nation's attention. Unemployment remained at the highest levels since the 1930s. Unions and businesses tried to protect themselves with demands for higher wages and increased prices. Inflation was the central fact of life; in response, the Trudeau government introduced its own program of wage and price controls in October 1975.

*Parliament voted to abolish capital punishment in the summer of 1976.

Opinion polls in October, 1975, indicated that most Canadians felt wage and price controls were necessary. However, setting up an equitable program proved a problem. The Anti-Inflation Review Board (AIB) rolled back wage increases granted by employers and resistance to the government's policy became widespread. The Canadian Labour Congress called for a nation-wide "day of protest" on October 14, 1976, urging members of unions to take the day off work to protest government anti-inflation measures. Furthermore, businessmen argued that income restrictions effectively limited profits and decreased the availability of investment capital which was so necessary to stimulate economic growth and create new jobs.

Even Canadians who admired Trudeau and recognized him as an

able leader were capable of extremely negative views of his political style and the principles of his administration. His persistent stand in favour of a bilingual Canada and his unpopular economic policies— particularly his "war on inflation"—cost him considerable support. In the fall of 1976, public opinion polls showed that the Liberal government's popularity had fallen to the lowest level since Trudeau had become prime minister in 1968.

The case of Pierre Trudeau is a perfect example of the difficulty people face in sizing up a political leader. Introduced to the nation as the "gifted newcomer" in 1965, Mr. Trudeau was a controversial "elder statesman" a decade later. The youthful leader on whom so many Canadians had pinned their hopes in 1968 had become the scapegoat in the 1970s, the person they blamed for their problems.

In a democratic country, the policies of a government are generally those of the political party holding office. To continue its policies over an extended period of time, the governing party must stay in office. Concern for winning elections, held at least once every five years, is therefore a fact of political life. Of course, victory at election time depends on attracting votes, on popularity. Every major decision by a government must be made with the recognition that this decision may cost the party votes in the next election.

Although politicians aim to avoid "either-or" choices, if political leaders are faced with choices between "matters of principle" and popularity, they are confronted by such questions as: Do I do what I think and feel is right for the country at large—and what may make my party unpopular with the electorate? Or do I take what appears to be the most popular course of action? When is a political compromise justifiable? When is it not?

Developments in Canadian literature: post World War II

The period after the end of the second world war in Canadian literature is probably most significant for the increase in numbers of its poets, novelists, short story writers, critics and journalists. Never before has Canadian literature been able to produce the volume of work in every literary genre. Through cooperation between private enterprise (publishers such as McClelland and Stewart, Hurtig, House of Anansi as well as Canadian subsidiaries of American publishing houses) and the public domain (the CBC, Canada Council and provincial governments, to name a few), authors have been encouraged to "write Canadian". Whether they are regionalists writing about the Maritimes landscape, nationalists writing about keeping Canada for the Canadians, or realists commenting on issues such as biculturalism, poverty, politics, life and death, Canadian authors seem to find the subject which suits their style or the medium which suits their subject, and they use it with remarkable skill. Canadian authors are helping us realize who we are and what our place is in society.

Although it is impossible to trace the entire course of Canadian literature since 1945, several issues stood out in the minds of our authors. At the end of the war, technology seemed to signal a real hope for people. No longer troubled by the immediate problems of war, Canadians could once again look forward to consumer goods, from scented soap to automobiles, to improve their day-to-day lives. The early 1950s promised startling improvements and the theme seemed to be "the bigger the better". Canadians, perhaps more than ever before, looked for an increasingly higher standard of living, aiming to enjoy the "good life" as they saw people doing in the United States.

With the concern over the pipeline debate in 1956, though, Canadians began to show some concern over increasing American control of Canada's economy. Poets such as Margaret Atwood, Irving Layton, and F. R. Scott are only a few of the writers who have used the theme of Canadian-American relations in their works. In the 1960s and 1970s, when this issue became much more apparent, other writers used the theme for works both favouring and disapproving of our present relationship with foreign nations—the U.S. in particular. Richard Rohmer has proved just how popular this theme can be with such novels as *Ultimatum* and *Exxoneration*.

Another continuing Canadian theme—that of biculturalism has provided material over the years for Canadian authors. Mordecai Richler, Hugh MacLennan, and F. R. Scott are a few of the English

Canadians interested in this theme. There have been many Franco-phone authors whose works are based on the theme of biculturalism.

Perhaps the largest number of works published in this period deal with private, individual matters which are universal in their appeal. Personal conflicts over family relationships, neighbourhood tensions, generation gaps, living, loving and dying are immensely suitable themes around which authors can build successful poems and stories. Their approach to character development, too, puts Canadian authors on a par with other, more established authors. The memorable characters such as Hagar, in Margaret Laurence's *The Stone Angel*, Duddy Kravitz in Mordecai Richler's, *The Apprenticeship of Duddy Kravitz*, Samuel Marchbanks in Robertson Davies' *The Diary of Samuel Marchbanks*, and innumerable others will be remembered throughout time.

What is perhaps one of the most noteworthy facts in the emergence of a Canadian literature is our interest in poetry as an art form. In the past, poetry used to be thought of only as a pursuit of academics or literary critics. Now it is one of the most popular forms of Canadian literature. Michael Ondaatje, Margaret Atwood, Alden Nowlan, Jay Macpherson, James Reaney, Milton Acorn, Raymond Souster, Al Purdy, Miriam Waddington, Irving Layton and Dorothy Livesay have made significant contributions to the poetry of Canada. The lyrics of the songs of Joni Mitchell and Gordon Lightfoot, and the poems of Leonard Cohen set to music, have introduced many young people to Canadian poetry.

The literature of Canada, just as is her history, is marked by change. There is no doubt, though, that Canadian literature is truly a mirror of Canadian society.

"CANADA: CASE HISTORY: 1945"

This is the case of a high-school land,
dead-set in adolescence;
loud treble laughs and sudden fists,
bright cheeks, the gangling presence.
This boy is wonderful at sports
and physically quite healthy;
he's taken to church on Sunday still
and keeps his prurience stealthy.
He doesn't like books, except about bears,
collects new coins and model planes,
and never refuses a dare.
His Uncle spoils him with candy, of course,
yet shouts him down when he talks at table.
You will note he's got some of his French mother's looks,
though he's not so witty and no more stable.

Earle Birney

He's really much more like his father and yet
if you say so he'll pull a great face.
He wants to be different from everyone else
and daydreams of winning the global race.
Parents unmarried and living abroad,
relatives keen to bag the estate,
schizophrenia not excluded,
will he learn to grow up before it's too late?[32]
Ottawa

"A LITTLE-TRAVELLED ROAD"

A trailer, a sign
reading *Bill's Eats*, somewhere
on the road between
Campbellton and
St Leonard.
                Everything except
                the music stops
                when I open the
                screen door:
                Hank Williams singing,
                'Your Cheatin' Heart'.
The locals,
country boys and their
girls drop everything
and wait. I have the irrational
feeling there's something
I'm expected to do or
say and that I won't
realize what it is
until too late. Then
I have the even more
absurd feeling that
they somehow knew
I was going to
stop here, that they've
been waiting for me.
I can imagine them
saying to each other
on the steps of the
church or at the
filling station
this morning:
Did you know a funny
thing is going to
happen at Bill's
this afternoon?
Better be there.

You wouldn't want to miss it.
One thing I know for certain
if I'm still here when
the song ends nobody
will play another.
There'll be no sounds then
except the electric
fan humming, vegetable
oil sizzling, the
Niagara roar of
root beer in the
throat of the stranger.[33]

"THE WELL-WROUGHT URN"

"What would you do
if I suddenly died?"

"Write a poem to you."

"Would you mourn for me?"

"Certainly," I sighed.

"For a long time?"

"That depends."

"On what?"

"The poem's excellence," I replied.[34]

"TRAPPER"

I'm thinking how the cabin was
the wicker chair
still soft for dozing
before the logs I left full
fired to keep the room
and bed warm as a woman.
I set my boots to dry
a cup of hot rum
and sorted the traps for one more line trip
three silver fox would bring
enough for new sled
runners and good strong harnesses
for the team.
God   the wind cuts deep tonight but
it pushed me on
across the frozen lake.[35]

"ACROSS CANADA", WEST FROM TORONTO

Before Winnipeg, only the familar well-travelled
road, weaving in and out of the ageless
evergreen bush. . . .

Across the top of Saskatchewan we ate
Sweet Marie chocolate bars and counted
everything that moved: the new birds, the
hitchhikers, gophers. We formed alliances
with the car ahead and the car behind,
travelling this way for fifty miles, like
partners in a dance. Ahead of us, a country
forever too large for one man's mind; behind us,
more of the same.

Edmonton looked like Winnipeg, and
Winnipeg had looked like something else. . . .

Moving west, the world rises and the horizon
peaks, a mile above the timberline. We roar
through rock cuts between valleys, across valleys
filled with mist and swollen rivers, places
pioneers never went or went at twenty miles a day.
Split Peak, Wild Horse Lake, Glacier: names
for the untamed and places enough to convince you
these mountains will never change, that of all things
they have come the closest to lasting forever.

There is always as much road ahead as
there is behind: this is a fact of continents.
We stop for a moment, beside this road
the length of the country, to check our maps
and then move on, dreaming of the Pacific.[36]

"CANADIANS"

Here are
our signatures:
geese, fish, eskimo
faces, girl-guide
cookies, ink-drawings
tree-plantings, summer
storms and winter
emanations.

We look
like a geography but
just scratch us
and we bleed
history, are full

Miriam Waddington

of modest misery
are sensitive
to double-talk double-take
(and double-cross)
in a country
too wide
to be single in.

Are we real or
did someone invent
us, was it Henry
Hudson Etienne Brûlé
or a carnival
of village girls?
Was it
a flock of nuns
a pity of indians
a gravyboat of
fur-traders, professional
explorers or those
amateur map-makers
our Fathers
of Confederation?

Wherever you are
Charles Tupper Alexander
Galt Darcy McGee George
Cartier Ambrose Shea
Henry Crout Father
Ragueneau Lord Selkirk
and John A.—however
far into northness
you have walked—
when we call you
turn around please and
don't look so
surprised.[37]

from WHO HAS SEEN THE WIND

WHO HAS SEEN THE WIND *tells the story of a boy growing up in a Saskatche-wan town. Early in the story, the boy, Brian O'Connal, is four years old. Typical of children that age, he is fascinated by the idea of God, and believes that God can come to the rescue over two problems he is having—his cranky grandmother and an aggressive playmate, Artie. In this excerpt, Brian is having a conversation with "God":*

He [God as Brian imagined Him] wore a hat like Uncle Sean's, uncreased just as it had come from the store shelf—a blue gum-drop hat. He wore white rubber boots, and He held a very small, very white lamb in His arms. Brian said:—

'I am pleased to meet you.'

The man wiggled the black string that hung down from his glasses. 'You are welcome,' He said. 'I am God. I am Mr. R. W. God, B.V.D. You call me R.W.'

'I knew you were. What did you leave heaven for?'

'I am going to get after Artie Sherry for you,' God said. 'And I will get after your grandmother too.'

'No,' Brian said. 'You can let her alone now. She isn't so bossy now the baby is better.'

'Has the baby been sick?'

'Oh, yes, but he has had his Crissmuss, so he is almost all right again. What will you do to him?'

'It will be awful,' said God. 'I will get Artie to look through a hole in a fence, and then I will kick him real hard.'

'Thank you very much for what you will do to Artie. When?'

'Soon. I am busy now. I will fix up Artie later on.'

'You won't kick him a little?' said Brian anxiously.

'I will give him thousands of kicks. I will give him hundreds.'

Brian heard the sound of footsteps behind him.

'Good-bye, God,' he said.

W. O. Mitchell

Later in the novel, Brian exchanges lines of a verse about the wind with some of his friends. True to form, Art invents a line of his own*:

The wind could be heard in a more persistent song now, and out along the road separating the town from the prairie it fluted gently along the wires that ran down the highway. Brian and Fat and Art descended and went through the barrow pit filled with loose dust. Art shied a rock at a meadow lark. He missed it. Ahead of the boys, the long grass bent to the bidding of the wind, lay a moment, then sprang up again.

'Who has seen the wind?' Fat chanted.

'Neither you nor I,' returned Brian.

'But when the trees bow down their heads—'

'Nobody gives a damn,' Art finished up. Fat laughed.[38]

*The actual line is "The wind is passing by."[36]

from THE STONE ANGEL

Hagar, the 80-year-old heroine of this novel, is spending her final days in the local hospital. She has been a strong, independent woman throughout her life, and she detests being a burden to anyone.

In this poignant scene, she helps her young hospital roommate, Sandra, who has treated Hagar condescendingly up until this point. Hagar desperately wants to be useful for perhaps the last time.

"Sandra—"

"Yes?" Her voice is thin, fearful. "What is it?"

"What's the matter?"

"I need to go to the bathroom," she says. "I've called the nurse, but she doesn't hear me."

"Have you put your light on? The little light above your bed. That's how you're supposed to call the nurse."

"I can't reach it. I can't move up by myself. It hurts."

"I'll put my light on, then."

"Oh, would you? Gee, thanks a million."

The faint glow appears, and we wait. No one comes.

"I'm going to get you a bedpan."

"No—" she says alarmed. "I'm okay, really. You mustn't, Mrs. Shipley."

"I will so. I won't stand for this sort of thing another minute. They keep them in the bathroom, right here. It's only a step."

"Do you think you oughta?"

"Certainly. You just wait. I'll get it for you, you'll see."

Heaving, I pull myself up. As I slide my legs out of bed, one foot cramps and I'm helpless for a second. I grasp the bed, put my toes on the icy floor, work the cramp out, and then I'm standing, the weight of my flesh heavy and ponderous, my hair undone now and slithering lengthily around my bare and chilly shoulders, like snakes on a Gorgon's head. My satin nightgown, rumpled and twisted, hampers and hobbles me. I seem to be rather shaky. The idiotic quivering of my flesh won't stop. My separate muscles prance and jerk. I'm cold. It's unusually cold tonight, it seems to me. I'll wait a moment. There. I'm better now. It's only a few steps, that I do know.

I shuffle slowly, thinking how peculiar it is to walk like this, not to be able to command my legs to pace and stride. One foot and then another. Only a little way now, Hagar. Come on.

There now. I've reached the bathroom and gained the shiny steel grail. That wasn't so difficult after all. But the way back is longer. I miss my footing, lurch, almost topple. I snatch for something, and my hand finds a window sill. It steadies me. I go on.

"You okay, Mrs. Shipley?"

"Quite—okay."

I have to smile at myself. I've never used that word before in my life. *Okay—guy*—such slangy words. I used to tell John. They mark a person.

All at once I have to stop and try to catch the breath that seems to have escaped me. My ribs are hot with pain. Then it ebbs, but I'm left reeling with weakness. I'll reach my destination, though. Easy does it. Come along, now.

There. I'm there. I knew I could. And now I wonder if I've done it for her or for myself. No matter I'm here, and carrying what she needs.

"Oh, thanks," she says. "Am I ever glad . . ."

At that moment the ceiling light is switched peremptorily on, and a nurse is standing there in the doorway, a plump and middle-aged nurse, looking horrified.

"Mrs. Shipley! What on earth are you doing out of bed? Didn't you have the restraint put on tonight?"

"They forgot it," I say, "and a good job they did, too."

"My heavens," the nurse says. "What if you'd fallen?"

"What if I had?" I retort. "What if I had?"

She doesn't reply. She leads me back to bed. When she has settled us both, she goes and we're alone, the girl and I. Then I hear a sound in the dark room. The girl is laughing.[39]

from THE EDIBLE WOMAN

Margaret Atwood is one of Canada's most successful authors. Besides poetry and literary criticism—her book SURVIVAL *is an important commentary on Canadian literature—she is known for such novels as* SURFACING *and* LADY ORACLE.

In her novel THE EDIBLE WOMAN, *from which this excerpt has been taken, Marian is a young woman who finds her conventional lifestyle stifling. She is engaged to Peter, a young man pursuing a career in law. However, the relationship turns sour, as she rebels against his attempts to mould her into the kind of woman he thinks she should be. In this passage, she is baking "an edible woman" which becomes a symbol of her independence.*

She took the cake off the sill, felt it to see if it was cool enough, and put it on the kitchen table. Then she began to operate. With the two forks she pulled it in half through the middle. One half she placed flat side down on the platter. She scooped out part of it and made a head with the section she had taken out. Then she nipped in a waist at the sides. The other half she pulled into strips for the arms and legs. The spongy cake was pliable, easy to mould. She stuck all the separate members together with white icing, and used the rest of the icing to cover the shape she had constructed. It was bumpy in places and had too many crumbs in the skin, but it would do. She reinforced the feet and ankles with tooth-picks.

Now she had a blank white body. It looked slightly obscene, lying there soft and sugary and featureless on the platter. She set about clothing it, filling the cake-decorator with bright pink icing. First she gave it a bikini, but that was too sparse. She filled in the midriff. Now it had an ordinary bathing-suit, but that still wasn't exactly what she wanted. She kept extending, adding to top and bottom, until she had a dress of sorts. In a burst of exuberance she added a row of ruffles around the neckline, and more ruffles at the hem of the dress. She made a smiling lush-lipped pink mouth and pink shoes to match. Finally she put five pink fingernails on each of the amorphous hands.

The cake looked peculiar with only a mouth and no hair or eyes. She rinsed out the cake-decorator and filled it with chocolate icing.

She drew a nose, and two large eyes, to which she appended many eyelashes and two eyebrows, one above each eye. For emphasis she made a line demarcating one leg from the other, and similar lines to separate the arms from the body. The hair took longer. It involved masses of intricate baroque scrolls and swirls, piled high on the head and spilling down over the shoulders.

The eyes were still blank. She decided on green—the only other possibilities were red and yellow, since they were the only other colours she had—and with a toothpick applied two irises of green food-colouring.

Now there were only the globular silver decorations to add. One went in each eye, for a pupil. With the others she made a floral design on the pink dress, and stuck a few in the hair. Now the woman looked like an elegant antique china figurine. For an instant she wished she had bought some birthday candles; but where could they be put? There was really no room for them. The image was complete.

Her creation gazed up at her, its face doll-like and vacant except for the small silver glitter of intelligence in each green eye. While making it she had been almost gleeful, but now, contemplating it, she was pensive. All that work had gone into the lady and now what would happen to her?

"You look delicious," she told her. "Very appetizing. And that's what will happen to you; that's what you get for being food." . . .

Marian had a swift vision of her own monumental silliness, of how infantile and undignified she would seem in the eyes of any rational observer. What kind of game did she think she was playing? But that wasn't the point, she told herself nervously, pushing back a strand of hair. Though if Peter found her silly she would believe it, she would accept his version of herself, he would laugh and they would sit down and have a quiet cup of tea. . . .

———————————

[After Peter arrived] she went into the kitchen and returned, bearing the platter in front of her, carefully and with reverence, as though she was carrying something sacred in a procession, an icon or the crown on a cushion in a play. She knelt, setting the platter on the coffee-table in front of Peter.

"You've been trying to destroy me, haven't you," she said. "You've been trying to assimilate me. But I've made you a substitute, something you'll like much better. This is what you really wanted all along, isn't it? I'll get you a fork," she added somewhat prosaically.

Peter stared from the cake to her face and back again. She wasn't smiling.

His eyes widened in alarm. Apparently he didn't find her silly.[40]

from THE APPRENTICESHIP OF DUDDY KRAVITZ

The setting of this novel is the city of Montreal about the year 1947. Duddy Kravitz, the fifteen-year-old main character, goes through a series of incidents all of which cause him problems in one way or another. Duddy believed his grandfather who always said, "A man without land is nothing," and his goal throughout the novel is to get some land so that his father and grandfather would be proud of him.

Many of the ways Duddy chooses to get money or land, however, are unscrupulous. This excerpt describes one of them.

Mordecai Richler

At the age of twelve Duddy discovered that smiling boys with autograph books could get in to hockey practises at the Forum. Getting in to see minor league teams like the Royals was a cinch; and, if you were quick or smart enough to hide in the toilet after the Royals had left the ice you could also get to see the Canadiens practise, and those were the years of Lach, Blake, and the great Maurice Richard. While they were on the ice the players' spare sticks, kept in a rack against the wall in a gangway leading into the passages out, were guarded by a thirteen-year-old stick boy. Duddy guessed that these sticks, each with a star player's name stencilled on it, would be treasured by many a fan. So he worked out a system. Getting another boy . . . to come along with him and talk to the stick boy, leading him gently away from the rack, Duddy would then emerge from under a seat, grab as many sticks as he could manage, and run like hell. The sticks netted him a tidy profit. But, even though the stick boy was changed from time to time, making further forays possible, the business was a risky one. It was only seasonal, too.[41]

from LIVES OF GIRLS AND WOMEN

LIVES OF GIRLS AND WOMEN *is a story of a young girl's experiences as she grows up in a small Canadian town. This passage describes the relationship she had with Jerry, a male classmate.*

Jerry Storey and I drifted together. We talked in the halls. We developed, gradually, a banter, vocabulary, range of subject matter that was not shared with anybody else. Our names appeared together in the tiny, mimeographed, nearly illegible school paper. Everyone seemed to think that we were perfectly suited to each other; we were called "The Brains Trust" or "The Quiz Kids" with a certain amount of semitolerant contempt, which Jerry knew how to bear better than I. We were depressed at being paired off like the only members of some outlandish species in a zoo, and we resented people thinking we were alike, for we did not think so. I thought that Jerry was a thousand times more freakish, less attractive than I was, and it was plain that he thought putting my brains and his in the same category showed no appreciation of categories;

it was like saying Toscanini and the local bandmaster were both talented. What I possessed, he told me frankly when we discussed the future, was a first-rate memory, a not unusual feminine gift for language, fairly weak reasoning powers, and almost no capacity for abstract thought. That I was immeasurably smarter than most people in Jubilee should not blind me, he said, to the fact that I would soon reach my limits in the intellectually competitive world outside ("The same goes for myself," he added severely. "I always try to keep a perspective. I look pretty good at Jubilee High School. How would I look at M.I.T.?" In talking of his future he was full of grand ambitions, but was careful to express them sarcastically, and fence them round with sober self-admonitions.)

I took his judgment like a soldier, because I did not believe it. That is, I knew it was all true, but I still felt powerful enough, in areas that I thought he could not see, where his ways of judging could not reach. The gymnastics of his mind I did not admire, for people only admire abilities similar to, though greater than, their own. His mind to me was like a circus tent full of dim apparatus on which, when I was not there, he performed stunts which were spectacular and boring. I was careful not to let him see I thought this. He was truthful in telling me what he thought about me, apparently: I had no intention of being so with him. Why not? Because I felt in him what women feel in men, something so tender, swollen, tyrannical, absurd; I would never take the consequences of interfering with it: I had an indifference, a contempt almost, that I concealed from him. I thought that I was tactful, even kind; I never thought that I was proud.[42]

from THE TIN FLUTE,

THE TIN FLUTE, *the translation of Gabrielle Roy's novel originally published in French, is both a moving story and an exposé of urban poverty. Rose-Anna is a long-suffering French-Canadian mother who struggles to raise a large family in a poverty-ridden suburb of Montreal. Her daughter Florentine yearns desperately to escape from the dismal life her mother has always known. In this episode, Rose-Anna decides against buying a tin flute for her son, who is slowly dying of leukemia.*

At the other end of the store, Rose-Anna had stopped at the toy counter, and picked up a little tin flute. As a salesgirl approached, however, she put it down hastily, and Florentine knew that Daniel's desire for the flute would never be any closer to realization than this. Her mother's good intention was quickly suppressed. Likewise between her desire to help Rose-Anne and the peace of mind her mother would probably never have, nothing would be left but the aching memory of a good intention. If she alone could escape from their narrow life, that would be a great achievement, but even for her it was very hard. She would have been happy to

Gabrielle Roy

take her family with her and raise them also to a position of ease and comfort, but she knew that it was useless to think of it.

She forced herself to smile at her mother, who seemed to be asking her advice: "Should I buy the flute, the pretty little toy flute, or should I buy stockings, underwear, food? Which is more important? A flute like a ray of sunshine for a sick child, a happy flute to make sounds of joy, or food on the table? Tell me which is more important, Florentine?"

Florentine brought herself to smile once more as Rose-Anne, deciding at length to leave the store, waved goodbye, but by that time she was ready to rip all her good intentions to shreds, like a useless rag.[43]

11

Canadian leisure: 20th and 21st centuries

Suppose it is a Friday night and you have just completed dinner. You know much of your time will be free during the next two days, and now you have to decide how to use your leisure time. In Canada you may have the choice of going to the theatre, movies, or sporting events; visiting an art gallery, museum, exhibition; or watching television, listening to the radio or working on a hobby.

Which of these things you do depends on many factors, not the least of which is availability. Many facilities for leisure are available only in the larger cities. Yet 75% of Canadians now live in urban areas and the percentage is expected to rise to about 90% by the year 2000. Therefore a very large majority of the population, in theory at least, has access to many leisure activities. However, there is a growing concern in Canada about the necessity of expanding facilities and making more people aware of the possibilities for using their free time. Research data have shown that if a greater number of people were made aware of the activities now available to them, more might participate in a greater variety of activities.

WHY THE CONCERN OVER LEISURE?

With machines taking over more of our workload and with labour bargaining for shorter working hours, Canadians now and in the future will have an increased amount of leisure time. How we spend it may well determine what kinds of new activities will be made available to us. With this increased opportunity to participate in activities, Canadians may well become more relaxed and happy.

FRANK AND ERNEST by Bob Thaves

THE TROUBLE WITH DOING NOTHING IS THAT I'M NEVER SURE WHEN I'M THROUGH.

1. How would you describe Frank and Ernest's attitude toward leisure?
2. Would you agree with them? Why or why not?
3. What leisure activity occupies most of your free time?
4. Do you think Canadians should become participators rather than spectators in their leisure?
5. What kinds of leisure activities do you think will be available in the 21st century? Which, if any, of our current pastimes will no longer be enjoyed or participated in?
6. How might leisure activities benefit our nation as a whole?

GOVERNMENT'S ROLE

The Canadian government has investigated the question of leisure time. In both 1969 and 1971, a Conference on Leisure was held at Montmorency, Quebec. With the support of the Department of Health and Welfare, delegates from many spheres of Canadian society met to try to find ways to encourage Canadians to make better use of their leisure time. In addition, in 1972, the Arts and Culture Branch of the Federal Department of Secretary of State authorized *A Leisure Study—Canada 1972* in which they surveyed 50 000 Canadians about use of leisure time. The report gives the following background to its study:

In a research study done by the Arts and Culture Branch of the Federal Department of the Secretary of State in 1974, researchers found that of the 7230 people surveyed, 97% preferred an "at home" kind of leisure activity such as watching television, while "participation" activities such as participating in or attending a sporting event or working on a hobby were enjoyed by about 70% of those surveyed.

We have reached the threshold of a major and rapid expansion in leisure-time activities. In light of the expanding labour force and rising productivity, the entire issue of work and leisure needs to be re-examined thoroughly. Former standards are likely to undergo significant changes, with much less emphasis on work than was once the case. The altered work week of four and three days, and floating work hours, are two ideas already being tried and there is every indication that some form of condensed work week will soon be generally accepted. In addition, retirement age will continue to decline, and sabbatical leaves and four week vacations will become more frequent. In short, within a decade there will be an unprecedented growth in the amount of non-work, or leisure time available to the average Canadian, accompanied by an increasing personal disposable income, a growing portion of which will be available for expenditure on what have up to now been classed as non-essentials.

As new leisure-related markets develop for business, industry, institutions and government services, it is likely that there will be significant changes in thinking about luxury versus necessary goods, approaches to education, rehabilitation, and social services, and allocation of public funds. Many new types of decisions about expenditures on leisure-time activities—expenditures of time, money, and attention—will, therefore, become necessary.[1]

However you spend your leisure time now, in the future you may have more time and/or different leisure-time needs. You may be interested in other activities which are available in Canada. Whether you wish to *participate in* an activity or choose to be a *spectator*, the following are descriptions of types of leisure which may open new avenues of enjoyment.

Modern Canadian media

Media such as radio, television, magazines and newspapers play an important role in Canadian society. Canadians use these media to communicate ideas from coast to coast and around the world. Canadian identity can be expressed through the media, both to enhance our own understanding of ourselves and to convey a Canadian image to others.

Mass media, especially radio and television, consume a great deal of our leisure time. It is reported that by the time a child reaches the age of 17, he or she has watched 12 000 to 15 000 hours of television. How we use these media, therefore, is very important.

RADIO

Turn the dial on your radio slowly from one end to the other. Along the band you are likely to encounter rock shows, programs for shut-ins, "open-line" talk shows, home-improvement programs, hockey games and broadcasts of classical or country and western music. Whatever your taste, there is probably a radio program which interests you. In fact, the key to the enduring popularity of radio is its diversity.

Since its beginnings in the 1920s, radio has always had a large audience. In the early days, the radio (which resembled today's cabinet model televisions rather than the trim clock-radios or portables we are so familiar with) was the centre of entertainment for the entire family. Everyone gathered around the radio to listen to their favourite shows. Responding to performers' voices and sound effects, they experienced suspense, excitement, fantasy, tears or laughter.

With the advent of television, many people thought that radio would lose its popularity. If this expectation was true at first, it is not so today. Several important changes have occurred, however. One is that radio became individualized. Instead of the family radio, there are now likely to be several types of radio in a house, and each family member may have a favourite station. Secondly, radio stations appeal to particular audiences, and no one station tries to entertain or inform all groups of people. Finally, listening to the radio is the kind of leisure-time activity that can be enjoyed along with some other—driving a car, washing the dishes, sun-tanning on the beach or even doing homework!

1. What changes, if any, can you suggest to make listening to the radio a better leisure-time activity for you?
2. How many of the following CBC radio programs have you listened to:

"This Country in the Morning"
"The Royal Canadian Air Farce"
"Our Native Land"
"Concern"
"Newsmagazine"
"Cross-Country Check Up"
"As It Happens"

As you probably know, there is no national network in the United States comparable to our CBC. What benefits can you see for Canadians in a national network?
3. What role should radio play in the communications field in the 1970s and 1980s?

TELEVISION

Do you remember what it was like *not* to have a television set? Most people your age were born after their family owned a television set and grew up with television as part of the environment. But watching television was not always such a familiar way to spend leisure time. In fact, television was not generally available across Canada until the 1950s and in less populated regions until years later.

When television made its debut in North America in the early 1950s, its promoters were exuberant in their descriptions of it. The potential for television was unlimited, we were told. For the first time we would have easy access to entertainment, information and education.

Wayne and Shuster on CBC

Since those first glorious days, television has been severely criticized not only for falling short of these expectations, but also for having a mass levelling effect on the people who watch it. In other words, television programming, instead of stimulating us intellectually, has brought our appreciation of shows to such a low level that we will spend hours watching almost any program, as long as it is "packaged" effectively. Instead of offering us a chance to think critically about an issue, most television dulls our senses and places us in the position of spectator rather than participant. This has been argued most effectively by using examples of children's shows. Watching them, children don't need to take an active part by thinking, but simply take everything in, and are overwhelmed by the quickly moving images and lively music.

Opponents of this theory argue that television cannot be all things to all people, that it must, in fact, appeal to a mass audience. Others say that people who watch TV, by and large, want to be entertained with comedy, drama or music. They do not want to have to think deeply during their leisure time.

There may not be an answer to the question of television's function in our society. However, television has a vast audience and most people would agree that it perhaps has some obligations to be more than a mediocre medium. If the people surveyed for the Davey

Report* are typical, then Canadians feel that television is the most believed and the most important medium for international news and Canadian news of national importance. It is, they say, the medium for the whole family. It could, if put to better use, offer more programming which would give the family access to ideas and people it would otherwise not have. The CBC tries to make television more than an "idiot box" to Canadians, but it and the private stations could be doing even more. For example, educational programs produced for the Ontario Educational Communications Authority (OECA) could be broadcast on other stations, and public service broadcasting similar to that in the United States could be introduced to all stations thus making such programs accessible to all viewers.

Questions like the following are matters for serious investigation:

1. What is it we want to see and hear on Canadian television?
2. How much are we willing to pay for it?
3. How can we get the programming schedules we want?

How would you answer?

THE CBC TODAY

The Canadian Broadcasting Corporation, according to Pierre Juneau the former Chairman of the CRTC*, is the "central nervous system of Canadian nationhood". It must attempt to be all things to all people —a cultural clearing house and a creator of Canadian identity, which is at the same time entertaining, informative and competitive. The challenge is enormous and it is one which the CBC will always face. The methods it uses to meet that challenge are subject to questions and criticisms from politicians, media personnel, advertisers and average Canadians.

Quality of programming is another subject guaranteed to cause arguments about the CBC. But officials of the Corporation can point to the fine English- and French-language radio programs offered by the CBC.

Critics, however, ask about CBC-TV. The fact that most network shows in the top 10 of CBC's own ratings list are American, and that the only Canadian program that consistently makes the top 10 is *Hockey Night in Canada*, allows people to criticize the CBC's mandate to develop a *Canadian* cultural identity. But the Corporation has enjoyed success with television shows such as the French network's *Appelez-moi Lise*, the English network's *Singalong Jubilee, The Irish Rovers* and *The Nature of Things*. Other well-received programming has included several drama series, the Wayne and Shuster comedy specials, sporting events and consumer shows like *Marketplace*.

*A Royal Commission on the mass media in Canada, 1970.

Canadian content problems

*Today the Canadian Radio-Television Commission keeps a watch on Canadian content in radio, but this is not a new problem. In December of 1928, the Aird Commission was set up to investigate inclusion of Canadian content, advertising regulations, American programming and Canadian cultural unity on Canadian stations. The Commission agreed that "Canadian listeners want Canadian broadcasting," and recommended nationalization of radio stations.

After many problems, Parliament passed the Broadcasting Act of 1932 which established the Canadian Radio Broadcasting Commission. This Commission was also beset with problems, and yet it was able to start a national broadcasting system.

It was not until Parliament passed a new Canadian Broadcasting Act in 1936, that the CRTC was replaced by the Canadian Broadcasting Corporation (CBC).

384

Regulating television in Canada

As had been the case with radio, decisions had to be made about the respective roles of public (government) and private enterprise. Initially the Canadian Broadcasting Corporation (CBC) was given the authority to supervise the television industry. The effect was unsatisfactory, however, since the privately owned stations resented being regulated by a government-financed organization that was also their competitor. Several private stations formed their own network, Canadian Television (CTV), in 1961 and the CBC was recognized as a parallel, public network. The problem of overall regulation was the subject of study and experiment until 1968, when the Broadcasting Act set out a single broadcasting system comprising both public and private sectors. Both the CBC and CTV networks came under the Canadian Radio-Television Commission (CRTC). The CRTC was to be an independent, public authority with wide powers, including the issuing of licenses and the supervising of television stations. In the past decade, the CRTC has dealt with license renewals and applications, FM broadcasting, cable television and Canadian content regulations in both programs and advertising.

In 1951 the Massey Commission* reported on a two-year study which included television. The Commission stressed the need for centralized supervision. Its recommendations included the need for the CBC to exercise strict control over all television stations in Canada in order to prevent the pursuit of profit at the expense of quality programming and to encourage Canadian talent. The Commission also considered the possibility of an independent television authority.

*Royal Commission on National Development in the Arts, Letters and Sciences, headed by Vincent Massey.

ABOUT THE CRTC

In the April, 1972, issue of SATURDAY NIGHT *Jack Batten comments on Pierre Juneau and the work of the CRTC. About the Commission he says:*

What the CRTC is against is *big, old* and *other*. What it's for is *small, innovative* (a favourite word around the commission offices), *local* and *Canadian*.

Many of its rulings, the ones, for instance, that got rid of the other (for which read British and American), were strictly a matter of carrying out the law of the land. The federal government said that broadcasting must be run by Canadians, and the CRTC went to work. In 1968, there were $150 millions worth of Canadian broadcasting companies controlled by foreign outfits. By the end of 1971, the commission had cut the figure to $25 millions. . . .

But in many other decisions, out on its own, the CRTC has acted with a kind of aggressiveness and independence that Canadians have rarely encountered in public commissions. It really has championed *Canadian* and *innovative* over *other* and *old*. It has operated on the assumption that Canadians, buried in imported TV and music, care about doing a little home-grown creating. . . . Forbidding the use of microwave transmission to beam American TV into the North and West and establishing Canadian content rules (though there were loopholes and sliding concessions in both decisions) showed that the commission has been thinking and enforcing *Canadian.*[2]

*See also Chapter 13.

1. How far do you think the CRTC should go in making Canadian content rulings for Canadian broadcasting?*

When a corporation as large as the CBC tries to accomplish so much, there are bound to be problems. It is true that CBC executives must face problems about money, ratings, personnel and many other things. It is also true, however, that the CBC is working on these problems and as long as it does, it will remain Canada's most significant voice in the media.

THE FUTURE OF TV

Choice of the programs you wish to see when you want to see them.

Popular movies currently playing at a local theatre shown on your television receiver.

Wide-screen receivers with stereophonic sound.

3-D TV

Smell-o-vision or Taste-o-vision

Private video cassette libraries

School-at-home via television lectures

Phone-o-vision (video telephone conversation)

All of these advances may be within the realm of our technology within the next decade. It may be possible for television to be a far

© 1974 Gahan Wilson
9/2 The Register and Tribune Syndicate, Inc.

"I DO MISS TWO DIMENSIONAL TELEVISION!"

more influential or popular leisure-time pursuit than ever before dreamed. We must decide now on the role we wish television to play in the Canadian future, or this Gahan Wilson interpretation of future television may become a reality without our consent.

Dance

When you think about "the dance", you no doubt have in mind an activity which you and your friends attend in order to participate. Yet are there not times when, rather than dancing yourself, you take a little time to watch others—because of their style, rhythm and skill?

Dancing that is a pleasure to watch can take many forms and can vary in terms of the training and talent required of the performers. In Canada we can find popular dancing, folk dance, contemporary dance and ballet.

BALLET

Although ballet is one of the arts that the majority of Canadians are not too familiar with, there are several companies in Canada which have received international acclaim.

In the 1930s, amateur ballet groups were formed from ballet schools in Toronto, Winnipeg and Vancouver. It wasn't until the 1950s, however, that the now famous Winnipeg Ballet became fully professional. After a command performance for Queen Elizabeth, its name was changed to the Royal Winnipeg Ballet. Founded by Gweneth Lloyd and Betty Farrally, the Royal Winnipeg Ballet has become known around the world. Under the artistic direction of Arnold Spohr, it has given widely acclaimed performances across Canada, in Russia, and in the United States.* Notably the company explores the use of multi-media and dance. Out of this exploration came the adaptation of George Ryga's play, "The Ecstasy of Rita Joe" with a filmed background featuring Chief Dan George.

*One notable occasion was the U.S. Bicentennial celebration.

The National Ballet Company of Canada celebrated its 25th anniversary in 1976-77. Founded in 1951 by a group of interested citizens, the company grew and now includes chapters in several Canadian cities. One of the highlights of the National Ballet's season is the annual performances at Toronto's Ontario Place. On the outdoor stage, the company presents adaptations of several of the world's best loved ballets. In this way, because the Forum and the grass surrounding it seat several thousand and admission to the Forum itself is free, people who might never be exposed to ballet have an opportunity to see it.

Like the National Ballet Company, Les Grands Ballets Canadiens in Montreal emphasizes classical works. But with the success of its

TOP: *The Royal Winnipeg Ballet dances* The Nutcracker, *December, 1976*. BOTTOM: *Ukrainian dancers*

388

production of the rock opera "Tommy", the company decided to include more modern dance in its repertoire.

FOLK DANCE

Folk dancing is a type of dance perhaps better known to Canadians, especially those with the rich cultural heritage of a foreign land. The Scottish Highland dancers, Ukrainian folk troupes, and many other ethnic groups have entertained people at folk festivals and gatherings across Canada.

CONTEMPORARY DANCE

Much newer to the Canadian dance world is the art of contemporary dancers. Combining the appeal of ballet and modern dance, contemporary dance troups perform in several cities: Toronto has the Toronto Dance Theatre; Montreal, Le Group de la Place Royale; Winnipeg, the Winnipeg Contemporary Dancers.

1. Ballet or contemporary dance attempts to tell a story through movement and music. How does this form of dance differ from the waltz or popular forms of dancing that people your age do?
2. Would you say that dancing to rock music is artistic? Why or why not?

Theatre

Theatre-goers insist that live theatre cannot be matched for excitement by television or movies. Being present in the same room with actors and actresses means sharing their interaction with each other and with the audience.

The growing popularity of theatre, and Canadians' willingness to support it, is shown by the fact that there were active theatre companies in every province during the 1974-1975 season. Canadians spend part of their leisure time watching professional performances of all types of drama in cities across the country: in Stratford, Ontario at the Stratford Shakespearean Festival Theatre; in Winnipeg at the Manitoba Theatre Centre; in Halifax at the Neptune Theatre; in Vancouver at the New Play Centre; in Fredericton at the Theatre New Brunswick; in Montreal at the Théâtre du Rideau Vert, and in many other cities.

In fact, theatre has had a long history in Canada. The first production was a verse play, "Le Theatre du Neptune", written by Marc Lescarbot and performed by a cast of Indians and voyageurs in 1606. Since then, live theatre has been immensely popular. In the 18th century, touring companies of English and American actors performed in Canada, and by the 19th century Canadian playwrights

The Canada Council is an independent agency created by the federal government in 1957 to "foster and promote the study and enjoyment of, and the production of works in the arts, humanities and social sciences," though a broad program of fellowships and grants. Many of Canada's symphonies, ballet companies and theatres and well as individual artists have received grants from the Canada Council.

Nicholas Pennell in Hamlet, *Stratford, Ontario, 1976.*

In Toronto the first theatre to come into being was called "Frank's Hotel" or "Assembly Room". The year was 1820 and the location was the corner of West Market and Colborne Streets; the theatre was "the loft of a 'mean two-storey house of wood . . . the orchestra being a single fiddler named Maxwell who wore a green shade over one eye.' Soldiers from the town garrison sometimes acted as supernumeraries ["extras"] in the various dramatic presentations."[3]

were beginning to emerge. Also by the early part of the 19th century the first theatres were being built; the Theatre Royal in Montreal was built with the help of John Molson and opened in 1825; Toronto's first theatre was built before 1830—over Frank's Hotel. In fact, most cities at that time could boast some kind of theatre.

The fare of these theatres was amateur drama, usually using local talent and local playwrights, and amateur theatre thus became a distinctive part of Canadian culture. Universities, too, joined the "Little Theatre Movement", and companies like the University of British Columbia Players and the University of Toronto Players (later Hart House Theatre) grew in popularity.

By 1933 it was evident that there should be a meeting of amateur theatre groups on a national scale and the Dominion Drama Festival emerged. Known and enjoyed coast to coast, the Dominion Drama Festival is the climax of a series of regional competitive festivals.

In recent years, Canadian actors and playwrights have become known internationally. Actors and actresses like Jackie Burroughs, Kate Reid, Barbara Chilcott, Jessica Tandy, Heath Lamberts, William Hutt, Gordon Pinsent and Donald Davis have left their marks on Canadian theatre productions. But their struggles have been uphill, and many have found that it is frequently more profitable to establish themselves abroad. Canadian playwrights have encountered similar difficulties in having their work recognized. But names like David

Freeman, George Ryga, and Gratien Gelinas have been gaining prominence recently.

1. What theatres are available in your area? What plays are being performed?
2. What limitations are placed on actors in live theatre which would not apply to actors on television?

MOVIES

Dateline: Ottawa, 1894
Andrew M. Holland presents film entertainment *in his Kinetoscope Parlor!*
Admission: 25¢ per person
Opening Night Revenue: $120.

The film industry has come a long way since that earliest commercial film showing in 1894. Almost every town in Canada has a movie theatre, and "going to a show" has become routine entertainment for millions of Canadians.

But what movies do people see? In the "Silent Film" era audiences saw stars like Broncho Billy Anderson, Mary Pickford, Charlie Chaplin and Rudolph Valentino; later there were Greta Garbo, Helen Hayes, Clark Gable, Spencer Tracy and Katherine Hepburn; today they watch Sidney Poitier, Cloris Leachman, Dustin Hoffman, Elliott Gould, Robert Redford and Elizabeth Taylor. For the most part, the movies (along with their directors, producers, actors, actresses and crews) were and still are American.* Hollywood was America's film capital, and the United States took the lead in all aspects of filmmaking.

What about Canadian films? The interest in the film medium here in Canada followed closely that of the United States. There were films made in Canada even before the First World War, but no "home-grown" film industry was established.

*Of course, there will always be international audiences for the films of European filmmakers like Fellini, Bergman and Godard.

MOVIES IN THE BEGINNING

In his book, INNER VIEWS, *film critic John Hofsess talks about Canadian films:*

In [a] large advertisement, *Glengarry School Days* boasts in bold type that it is "Another Wonderful All-Canadian Picture!" Beneath an ink drawing of a boy, a girl and a dog, readers are urged to see such marvels as "Scenes in and around the Parliament buildings, the bear fight at Rockcliffe, the thrilling rescue from the Gatineau river, the picnic with hundreds of Ottawa children taking part, and many other thrilling scenes." Four times daily at the Imperial theatre hundreds of people oohed and ahhed (which is all that film criticism consisted of in those early, dazzling days of moving pictures) at melodramatic perils and sentimental triumphs.

Everything that one could desire for Canadian films existed for a few years half a century ago. They played in major theatres (which were, with few exceptions, Canadian owned), were promoted with substantial advertising budgets, and held their own against all competitors for a sizeable share of the market. *Glengarry School Days* was a sequel to another popular Canadian film, *The Man From Glengarry*, based on Ralph Connor's best-selling novel. It was an immense success and then forgotten—in one era and out another. With the advent of sound, colour and other technological changes, Canadian films developed an unfortunate lag. They lost ground and never recovered it. The spread of American culture (or more precisely, Hollywood's international culture, since many of its best stars and directors came from England and Europe, with Canada contributing such film personalities as Louis B. Mayer, Marie Dressler, Norma Shearer, Mary Pickford, Boris Karloff, Walter Huston, Deanna Durbin, Glenn Ford, Walter Pidgeon, Raymond Massey, among others) was unopposed and as it became more entrenched it was increasingly difficult to displace.[4]

In recent years several new film production companies have been set up in central Canada. They have concentrated on producing documentaries for industry and commercials for television, rather than producing feature-length entertainment films. Theatres themselves are not Canadian owned, but are usually "branch plants" of large, American-owned chains. Thus the question of American domination in entertainment arises.

But, once again, there have been Canadians who "made it" in the motion picture industry. Mary Pickford was one of the first. She has been followed by people like Raymond Massey, Lorne Green, Donald Sutherland, Genevieve Bujold; their problem has been that the lack of a successful and profitable film industry in Canada has necessitated a move south if their careers were to grow.

There are those who say that film, like television and to a lesser extent radio, is a reflection of a nation's values, beliefs and culture, and that Canadians need and deserve films which are Canadian. To this end, the federal government has attempted to legislate Canadian content rulings for our mass media. Then too, the federal government established the Canadian Film Development Corporation (CFDC) in 1967 to foster and promote the development of a feature film industry in Canada. It encourages filmmakers and film technicians to take part in competitions for which it awards grants to winners to help them increase their skills.

Yuichiro Miura
THE MAN WHO SKIED DOWN EVEREST

A Crawley Films Production

A publicity photograph for the Canadian film, The Man Who Skied Down Everest

On the other hand, there are many who equate "Canadian films" with mediocrity and who feel it is not a government's function to legislate entertainment. These people say that a *good* film is a good film, whether it is Canada's, America's or any other nation's film, and that if theatres are forced to show mediocre films simply because they are Canadian, the Canadian film industry will be the long-term loser.

WHY WE CAN'T HAVE A CANADIAN HOLLYWOOD

John Hofsess, movie critic, speaks about American domination of the film industry:

Today, there are many Canadians who object to having so many of our theatres owned and operated by American chains, and to the practices of American film distributors who control where and when new films will open, frequently assigning a Canadian feature a poor theatre or playdate. And they object especially to the fact that all of us are better acquainted with American stars, values and social problems than we are with our own. But these results are due more to inevitability than error. For much the same reasons that Canada does not have a manned space program, or has not developed its own defensive system of nuclear weapons, it has not had a film industry. The cost was prohibitive. It's particularly expensive during a period of rapid technological change—developing systems of sound recording, perfecting colour film stocks and experimenting with different film gauges, screen widths and film image ratios, optical printing techniques and special effects; until such time as the hardware becomes standardized and available in low-cost versions of the prototype, or until copyrights have lapsed and more manufacturers develop competitive models in cameras, projectors and editing equipment, a film industry is beyond the reach of all countries except the largest and wealthiest. Thus while Canada, and virtually any country, could afford to produce black and white silent films, it could not afford the next stages of development.[5]

HOW NOT TO MAKE A CANADIAN FILM

1. Choose an uncommercial subject, so intimate as to be indecent, uninteresting, futile, immoral, sordid, etc. . . .
2. Make yourself the big star, and crowd the screen with old pals.
3. Don't write a line of script, but improvise day by day, not too seriously, but convincing yourself the result will be coherent and significant.
4. Shoot everything in 16mm black and white, with makeshift equipment.
5. Have your best friends participate, call them to meetings with only a few minutes' notice at any hour of the day or night; make

them understand they're working for the sake of Art, and not at all for vile pecuniary considerations.

6. For the inevitable expenditures, borrow from the bank and have the loan endorsed by members of your family and their friends; get what you need as credit, and if that isn't enough, find a friend who's rich enough and idiotic enough to invest a few thousand dollars of his own in the doubtful enterprise.

7. Most of all, don't worry about getting distribution guarantees.

If you take good care not to commit any of these horrible mistakes, you'll avoid the following vexations:

  a) wasting many years of your precious life;
  b) being in debt for many years to come;
  c) looking desperately for someone to whom to "sell" your film;
  d) suffering shame from the critics, or what's worse, humiliation from an indifferent public;

Nevertheless . . .

  a) if these drawbacks are overcome by your passion for cinema;
  b) if creative freedom gives you an inexpressible joy;
  c) . . . and if succeeding in an enterprise that common sense had already condemned gives you an exquisite enjoyment;
  d) if you are willing to put your friendships to the test in the hope of making them closer at the end;
  e) if modesty is not one of your handicaps;
  f) or if you simply want to make a Canadian film . . .

here is my advice:

1. Choose an uncommercial subject, so intimate as to be indecent, etc., etc., etc. . . . [6]

1. What is the author's attitude toward the following: (a) potential Canadian filmmakers, (b) Canadian investors, (c) the Canadian viewing audiences and (d) the actual making of a Canadian film?

Reading

Read a good book lately? How many of your classmates would give the same answer? Do students today read more or less than students of a generation ago? It is a common belief among adults that reading has declined among young people, and it is easy to find educators who agree.

One explanation is that we are in the midst of a communications revolution, in which the media of sight and sound—television, radio and film—are taking over. According to the theory made popular by the electronic media "guru" and University of Toronto professor,

One of Canada's fastest selling paperback series is the Harlequin romances. Harlequin's romantic fiction is pure Cinderella fantasy of the "happily ever after" variety. Fourteen of every hundred paperbacks sold in Canada are Harlequins.

Some Canadian films

Title	Director
Goin' Down the Road	Don Shebib
Mon Oncle Antoine	Claude Jutra
The Apprenticeship of Duddy Kravitz	based on the novel of the same name by Mordecai Richler starring Gordon Pinsent
The Rowdyman	William Fruet
Wedding in White	Paul Almond
Act of the Heart	Paul Almond
Journey	Claude Jutra's film starring Genevieve Bujold
Kamouraska	
La vraie nature de Bernadette	Gilles Carle
Why Rock the Boat?	John Howe

1. How many of these films have you seen?
2. If you saw any of them, would you be able to say that they were distinctively *Canadian* films? Why or why not?
3. *The Apprenticeship of Duddy Kravitz* had runs in American theatres. If you saw it, what do you think it had which made it enjoyable for people in other cultures?
4. Can you name any Canadian film now playing in your city or town? Do you plan to see it?

National Film Board

One initiative in film-making that the Canadian government did take in the past was the creation of the National Film Board (NFB). Unique as a national film production and distribution agency, the NFB was established in May, 1939. Its primary purpose at that time was the planning and production of documentary films illustrating Canadian life and culture, not only for Canadian audiences but for international audiences as well. Then, too, with the Canadian entry into the Second World War, government departments needed films to train airmen, to explain rationing, to sell war bonds.

John Grierson, a producer of documentary films and director of a government film unit in Great Britain, was named Canada's first Government Film Commissioner (and thus head of the NFB) in 1939. He remained in the position until 1945.

Documentaries and innovative short films have proven to be the mainstays of the NFB. Many of these have won international awards.

In particular, the animation techniques of Norman McLaren have gained world renown. In fact, two NFB films have won Oscars at the American Academy Awards presentations. They were "Churchill's Island" in 1940 and the McLaren film "Neighbours" in 1952.

Furthermore, the NFB has played an increasingly important role in the distribution of its films for use in educational institutions and public gatherings. It maintains offices across Canada and in many cities abroad.

Marshall McLuhan, reading is becoming less of a pastime with the development of technological improvements in the media. Perhaps the idea of "curling up with a good book" has given way to the idea of "stretching out with a transistorized portable colour TV".

Marshall McLuhan is a name many people have heard of but a man whom fewer understand. Most famous for coining phrases such as "the global village" and "hot and cool media", McLuhan has tried to theorize about what the technological and media revolution of the 1960s has and will mean for mankind. Although his books such as *The Gutenberg Galaxy: The Making of Typographic Man* and *Understanding Media: The Extensions of Man* have sold extremely well around the world, many people grasp only a fraction of what McLuhan is saying. His name, however, has come to be synonymous with the electronic media

"CANLIT"

The Centennial celebration of 1967 was the occasion for an outpouring of publications, both fiction and non-fiction, on Canadian topics. One problem which plagued the promoters of "Canlit", however, was the lack of Canadian content in school curricula.

To change this situation seemed to require a real campaign. There was a need to increase awareness of the potential value of studying Canadian literature in the schools. Educators had to be persuaded to open the curriculum to Canadian Studies. One of the noteworthy examples of a "Canlit" campaigner was Jim Foley, a teacher in Port Colborne High School, and the originator of Canada Day.

The idea of Canada Day *soon broadened to include other forms of Canadian Studies, especially history and geography, and spread to many other centres. Mr. Foley explains how he went about gathering support for the first* Canada Day, *in 1971:*

We had to gain the co-operation of those who wrote and published books, and our experiment gained a new dimension and a new impetus on our first Canada Day, February 28th, 1971. Hugh Garner, Max Braithwaite, Miriam Waddington, John Newlove, Jeann Beattie and Elizabeth Kimball were present, as well as Premier William Davis and representatives of three publishing companies. Between them they opened up what to most of the teachers and students who participated was an entirely new literary world. Even the sceptics were converted, and, among those who attended, the old negative attitudes to Canadian literature evaporated. Teachers and students came from as far away as North Bay and Manitoulin Island, and they were to return on each succeeding Canada Day. A strong sense of pride in our Canadian writers and affection for them was created on that day, and in many minds a new interest was engendered.[7]

According to the Davey Report, the result of a Royal Commission on the mass media, in 1970 there were 116 daily newspapers in Canada and fourteen million Canadians spent an average of 40 minutes reading them.

*For an account of the demise of *Time's* Canadian edition, see pages 17-19.

Whether or not reading books is one of your hobbies, chances are that you enjoy many other forms of reading. How many different kinds of magazines and newspapers can you find around your home? Whether bought by subscription or from a newsstand, magazines and newspapers have substantial markets in Canada. The daily newspaper is a familiar item in Canadian homes, even though we have come to rely more and more on radio and television. The latter bring us instant information and certain kinds of entertainment; newspapers can not only give us the news in depth, but provide feature stories, photographs, classified advertising and comic strips. These we can enjoy or ponder at our leisure. We may want to know immediately the highlights of the latest federal budget, but we need time to look over particular items and think about their possible effects on our lives.

Among the magazines read by Canadians, *Chatelaine, Maclean's, Saturday Night, Time, Seventeen* and *Sports Illustrated* are among the most familiar. Yet few Canadians are aware that some 1 200 magazines are published in this country. There seems to be a magazine for every imaginable special interest group. Three large-circulation Canadian magazines are *Chatelaine, Saturday Night* and *Maclean's.*

Chatelaine, a Maclean-Hunter publication with a circulation well over one million, is a women's magazine published both in English and French. *Saturday Night,* after closing its doors and admitting financial disaster in the mid-1970s, re-appeared with a substantial grant from Imperial Oil and a guaranteed subscriber's list to provide readers with a larger magazine, more staff, more articles by well-known Canadians, and, of course, increased advertising. Canadians appeared to welcome back a magazine that had been part of the country's life since 1887.

Finally, *Maclean's* (another Maclean-Hunter publication), which enjoyed unrivalled success as Canada's National Magazine, changed its format in 1975 to become a newsmagazine. By publishing *Maclean's* twenty-three times a year (bi-weekly), and by having separate sections on Canadian news, world news, business news, sports news, medicine, science and so forth, Maclean-Hunter is attempting to expand circulation in order to establish its magazine as a competitor for lucrative advertising budgets. Editor Peter C. Newman took the position that Canada needed more than what foreign newsmagazines could offer.

Magazines and newspapers provide Canadians with information, entertainment and opinion—all of which can be digested in less time than it takes to finish a lengthy book. They may prove that reading at one's leisure will be around for a long time to come.

How objective is your newspaper?

Everyone knows that the editorial page is the place in a newspaper for the expression of opinion. Whether the commentary on an election in British Columbia is written by a reporter whose name appears with the story or by a staff reporter after a conference with the senior editors, opinion and interpretation will emerge. We expect explanation and analysis, but we also expect writers to take sides.

Do we expect reporters to take sides on the news stories on the front page as well? Probably not. In fact, newspapers in Canada have traditionally striven to be as objective as possible in reporting on the day's events. Whether the subject was atrocities in some far away war or the strike activities in a local plant, reporters were expected to suppress their own biases and write as objectively as possible. Today, however, the "new journalism" recognizes that opinions and values inevitably influence the most "objective" reporters—especially on subjects about which they have strong feelings. Writers who advocate the "new journalism" say that reporters, as responsible professionals, can and should take a stand on issues of social concern.

Whether a particular newspaper appears to separate its editorial comment from its news reporting or encourages its writers to speak their minds, the reader should be critical in his approach to a newspaper's contents. Otherwise, the individual is in danger of forfeiting the responsibility of forming his own opinion.

1. How objective is your daily newspaper?
2. Proponents of the "new journalism" say that it is unwise to report all events objectively, and that with a *responsible interpretation* of news events comes a clearer view of the situation. Do you agree or disagree? Why?
3. In each of the following pairs of statements, which one is a *fact statement* and which is a *value statement*? Remember that a value statement is one in which the writer indicates a preference or point of view.

> Silas Steele plays lead zither with the "Pink Slippers" rock group.
> Silas Steele, lead zither player with the "Pink Slippers" rock group, should be named to the rock hall of fame.

> Slade Barnaway, the controversial Member of Parliament from Hackney Hollow, should refrain from public speaking, if his remarks at yesterday's meeting of the Flying Eagle Lodge are any indication of his intelligence.

From this list of well-known magazines, which ones are familiar to you? How many on the list are Canadian?

Time
Newsweek
Chatelaine
Good Housekeeping
Popular Photography
The New Yorker
Saturday Review
Mad Magazine
Motorcycling
The Canadian Forum
Reader's Digest
Maclean's
Miss Chatelaine
Woman's Day
Photoplay
Saturday Night
National Lampoon
Kar Kraft
People
Harper's

Is there a need for Canadian magazines which do for Canadians what their American counterparts do for Americans—for example, *Maclean's* as a newsmagazine to do what *Time* or *Newsweek* do; a Canadian sports magazine to compete with *Sports Illustrated*? Why or why not?

Slade Barnaway, the Member of Parliament from Hackney Hollow, was the guest speaker at yesterday's meeting of the Flying Eagle Lodge.

Sadie Swipe, shapely president of the local chapter of D.A.M. (Don't Anger Men), had good advice for the women of this city today when she urged them to recognize the natural superiority of men.

Sadie Swipe, president of the local chapter of D.A.M. (Don't Anger Men), urged women of this city to join her campaign to restore men to their rightful places.

4. Examine a news story from a daily paper for evidence of *value statements*. If your city has two daily papers, you may wish to compare coverage of the same event in both papers.

Art

If you immediately think of painting and sculpture when someone mentions the word "art", you may not think of art as a leisure-time activity available to you. If, however, you've tried to crochet, to do pottery, ceramics or macramé, or even woodworking or photography, then you have shared the experience of the artist. Today the field of art includes all those crafts and many more which allow people to be creative with something other than paint and canvas.

Canada had to wait until the latter half of the 19th century to see any permanent public art museums or galleries. Before this time, although there were a few displays of paintings, Canadians were too busy with the necessities of survival to have time to think about cultural life and displays of art for education and enlightenment.

Once exhibitions were set up, however, they became places where artists could have works displayed along with those of European artists when these were available. Most of the exhibitions were temporary and were moved from one city or town to the next after each exhibition. This high turn-over encouraged people to visit the galleries because each time they went, they could see new displays.

The organization of the Montreal Art Association in 1860 is significant, for it is with the founding of this Association that galleries began to set up art schools for the development and encouragement of Canadian artists. In addition to their schools, galleries in many cities now have a variety of classes for people who wish to learn drawing, painting, and so forth in their leisure.

The establishment of the National Gallery of Canada, with its more than 13 000 works of art, was linked with the founding of the Royal Canadian Academy of Arts in 1880. In 1913 the National Gallery was incorporated by an Act of Parliament and placed under the administration of a board of trustees appointed by the Governor General. Its stated function was to encourage public interest in the arts throughout Canada. The Gallery's collections include both international and Canadian art, and the Gallery's services in Ottawa include a reference library on art history, as well as exhibitions, lectures, films and guided tours. Circulating exhibitions, lecture tours, publications, reproductions and films are all available for distribution both across Canada and internationally. The National Gallery also brings to Canada important exhibitions from abroad.

SCULPTURE

Do you remember the days when you built a sand castle or a snowman? Have you ever made a snow sculpture for your school's winter carnival? You may not think of yourself as a Michelangelo, but if you have known the feeling of creating form out of shapeless material, you have experienced the thrill of the sculptor. If you think about it, you are more likely to appreciate sculpture in the world around you. Whether they be Inuit soapstone carvings, war memorials, life-sized bronze statues or façades on buildings, these works are important representations of our culture.

People such as Emmanuel Hahn, Frances Loring and later Anne Kahane, Donald Stewart, and Louis Archambault are among our best-known sculptors.

Notable Canadian painters include Alex Colville, Jean-Paul Lemieux, Alfred Pellan, Jack Shadbolt, Ronald Bloore, Ivan Eyre, Jack Bush, Jack Chambers, Guido Molinari, Joyce Weiland and Dorothy Knowles.

FRANK AND ERNEST   by Bob Thaves

Music

Participating in a school choir, listening to a song on a local radio station, an opera on CBC radio, a rock concert or a piano recital—these and many other forms of musical entertainment are examples of the leisure-time pursuits of many Canadians. Whether one is a participant or spectator, music is available for pleasure and relaxation. People's musical tastes vary, and a person may prefer different music at different times. More Canadians than ever before now have access to the types of music that match their individual tastes.

In Canada, music, like other expressions of art, is trying to find its Canadian identity. We have had forms of music as long as we have had people, but much of it has been patterned after music of other countries. The first music in Canada was the native melodies and rhythms of Indians and Inuit. When settlers began to arrive in the new land, they brought with them the folk music of their homelands. People sang songs while farming, while doing the endless household chores and during the long winter evenings. French Canadians in particular were very fond of singing, dancing and fiddling, and the songs of the voyageurs became an important part of the culture of early French Canada.

Thus music in the Canadas was as varied as the people who settled here. Some early Canadian songs such as Thomas Moore's "Canadian Boat Song" (1804) and "The Canada Union Waltz" (published in England in 1841 by "A Canadian lady") were among the first examples of truly Canadian music. The first European music in Canada was church music introduced by priests and explorers.

Also of significance was the secular music provided by British regimental bands stationed in garrison towns such as Halifax, Quebec and Montreal. In addition to military performances, regimental bands played at garden parties, in public squares or at subscription concerts.

As the cities grew and people had more time for leisure, participation in the study of music increased. However, music became a pursuit that catered to the vanity of the newly rich.

Musical societies were responsible for concerts which brought the music of Handel, Haydn, Mozart and Beethoven to Canada, and the invention of the steamship and railway made possible visits by world-famous artists. Thus it was that music added to the cultural life of Canadians.

The music most Canadians experienced was that of the fiddle and the piano, familiar melodies that one may call folk or traditional. Radio expanded musical experience, but mainly played popular music, American in origin. The same was true with the introduction of television. Efforts to encourage what may be called "serious" music were made by individuals and groups, but not until after World War II did government make a contribution.

1. What purpose do you feel your school orchestra, band or choir serves? Would you say they are creating music for themselves or for others?
2. Look in the entertainment section of your local newspaper to determine what kinds of musicians are appearing in your town or city. Are they local, national or international talent? What types of music are being offered most regularly? Would you like to have more choice in the kinds of entertainment available to you?

SYMPHONY ORCHESTRAS

To most people, orchestras are probably synonymous with symphonies, and the relationship is in part valid. By 1975, Canada had ten professional symphonies whose members were full-time musicians. Among the most notable of these are the National Arts Centre Orchestra, the Toronto Symphony and the Montreal Symphony, but there are also orchestras in Vancouver, Quebec, Ottawa, Hamilton, Winnipeg, Calgary and Edmonton.

Most of the conductors of our symphonies are Europeans or Americans, but three are native Canadians. They are Mario Bernardi

Indian and Inuit art

Before the influence of white people, the art of both Indian and Inuit was very personal and functional. Both peoples painted and sculpted symbols and pictures which represented life forces and events in their lives or the lives of those close to them. They decorated their clothing and utensils in a personally meaningful way—to call or pacify a spirit, to ask for help with the hunt, to mourn the death of a tribesman, or to celebrate the birth of children.

In the 20th century, however, the beauty of Indian and Inuit arts and crafts was recognized by white people who acted as middlemen in selling native art in southern Canada. Inuit carvings, now so popular as "Canadiana", were first sold on a large scale in 1949 as a project of the Canadian Handicrafts' Guild to help better the economic position of our Arctic peoples. Recently, however, the system by which the Inuit sell their art to white people has come under some criticism.

In 1974, Canadian-born artist Les Levine visited Cape Dorset, N.W.T. What he discovered there has some disturbing implications.

Inuit drawing

Levine found that 'Eskimos make art not because they want to make art, but because they don't have any other means of living.' Cape Dorset, he concluded, is a 'cultural chain gang'.... 'Most of the art that is produced in this community is based by its nature on the producer of it not understanding what he's doing.' Nor do the Eskimos value their sculptures, hewn painfully from soapstone with ordinary hatchets and files, as anything but potential cash. They keep none in their own ramshackle clapboard homes.... For the most part, the artists live in squalor, despite their success ... and filled with deep resentment against the South and the system that exploits them. The fact that the Inuit will not work without guarantee of payment leads to ludicrous dodges in the white-dominated effort to meet the demands of the marketplace. In some cases a person is retained at Cape Dorset, for example, to sign the names of individual artists to editions of graphic prints; if the artists were asked to do so, they would demand payment again.... [8]

Inuit [Eskimo] art has become so representative of Canada that carvings were awarded during the Canada Cup hockey series of September, 1976. A carving was given to the player selected as the most valuable in each game of the series.

The Group of Seven

Most notable in the area of Canadian painting were the group of Toronto commercial artists who decided to get together to share their love of painting Canadian landscapes. Known as the Group of Seven (Frank Carmichael, Lawren Harris, A. Y. Jackson, Frank John-

Lawren Harris, North Shore, Lake Superior, 1926.

ston, Arthur Lismer, J. E. H. MacDonald, F. H. Varley), the Group held their first joint exhibition in Toronto in 1920. Their devotion to the land and the Canadian people gave them a new way of looking at landscape painting, and they successfully interpreted the spirit of the country. At first rejected at home as art revolutionaries because of their artistic interpretations, the Group of Seven had to win international acclaim before they were accepted in Canada. Now, however, the decade of the Group of Seven is considered a landmark in Canadian art history.

1. Do you have any hobbies which allow you to create something? If so, what are they? Do you consider this creating to be artistic?
2. Would you ever go to an art gallery "just to browse" or do you feel that you must know a great deal about art and artists before you could appreciate the collections in a gallery?

Ivan Romanoff conducting his ensemble

of the National Arts Centre Orchestra, Boris Brott of the Hamilton Philharmonic, and Pierre Hétu of the Edmonton Symphony. If Canadian conductors are scarce, so is Canadian classical music—at least in the concert hall. Conductors and musicians have been slow to introduce Canadian works to orchestral audiences, and tend to stay with the more accepted, traditional works.

OPERA

If you are unfamiliar with opera or think that it only appeals to a small percentage of "cultured" people, it may surprise you to know that in 1975, the four performances of Mozart's "The Magic Flute" at Ottawa's National Arts Centre were sold out and that in 1976, the Centre increased its operatic performances to 14.

The National Arts Centre is not the only place where opera (a play in which the dialogue is sung) is popular. Opera companies can be found in many of our cities, and CBC radio has done an exceptional job in promoting this kind of music on its "Opera Series" programs.

Canadian opera lovers have long enjoyed American or British companies performing serious European works. Nevertheless, several Canadian opera companies have existed over the years. The Canadian Opera Company, formed in 1958, was the first to take opera on

Toronto has always loved the opera, and has been the site for many performances of great touring opera companies. When the famous Metropolitan Opera of New York visited Toronto, however, it seemed to meet with less than success. During its first visit in 1899, it failed to attract large audiences even though it brought with it legendary performers and highly-acclaimed operas. The *Toronto Globe* attributed the small attendance at performances of *The Barber of Seville* to the fact that it was not well known and was sung in Italian.

Two years later, the MET's tour encountered more problems. The company was honoured to take part in the prestigious State Concert honouring Their Royal Highnesses, the Duke and Duchess of Cornwall and York, later George V and Queen Mary, but the MET's star performer, Emma Calve, had difficulty making herself heard above the noise of the celebrations outside.

The next time the MET visited Toronto, in 1952, it had an even less suitable theatre—Maple Leaf Gardens![10]

The Canadian Opera Company performs Aida

"Most Canadians would be surprised to learn that a fellow countryman, a contemporary of Mozart, Joseph Quesnel (1749-1809), produced a three-act comic opera, *Colas et Colinette* (1788). It was first performed in Montreal in 1790 . . . [and] is one of only two Canadian operas ever to appear on commercial recordings. . . . The second is Harry Somer's *The Fool* (1953). . . ."[9]

tour to towns and cities outside the major centres of central Canada.

Although the Canadian Opera Company includes native Canadian works in its repertoire, it also performs works by the more traditional composers. Most notable among its accomplishments has been its performance of "Louis Riel", an opera by Canadian composer Harry Somers, written in honour of the Métis leader Louis Riel.

JAZZ

Jazz is a type of music most often associated with the music and dance of the American Negro or the Mardi Gras in New Orleans, Louisiana. As with all other art forms, however, American jazz had almost as big an impact in Canada as it did in the United States in the pre-war years. Canadians could hear concerts by Benny Goodman, Tommy Dorsey, Harry James, Louis Armstrong, Duke Ellington and singer Billie Holiday in most major Canadian cities, and Canadian hotel dance bands were quick to pick up the popular jazz numbers.

Imported jazz was Canada's only choice until the mid-1940s

when a few jazz musicians came to prominence here. Wally Gurd and Oscar Peterson were two talented pianists whose forte was jazz, and Maynard Ferguson became a highly acclaimed jazz trumpeter.

Another Canadian contribution to the jazz field is the Canadian-produced jazz magazine *Coda Magazine*, which, after 18 years of publication, is recognized as one of the most important English-language jazz publications in the world.

Finally, the CBC radio network through its jazz programming has helped jazz get a firm foothold in Canada.

LES CHANSONNIERS OF FRENCH CANADA

French Canadian culture is easily transmitted by the popular music of such chansonniers as Gilles Vigneault, Pauline Julien, and Monique Leyrac. The music of the chansonnier is distinctively Francophone—about Québécois traditions, lifestyle, people. As representatives of the French Canadian culture, these musicians do not depend on what is popular in English Canada or the United States, but rather have a following among French-speaking Canadians.

On the other hand, some chansonniers have been influenced by the musical styles in English Canada and the United States. At the same time, the popularity outside Quebec of French Canadian performers has increased in recent years. Robert Charlebois, René Simard and Ginette Reno are but three notable examples of French Canadians who first achieved fame in Quebec before being recognized elsewhere.

POPULAR MUSIC

Anne Murray, Gordon Lightfoot, Stompin' Tom Connors, Ian and Sylvia Tyson, Murray McLauchlan, the Guess Who, Bachman-Turner Overdrive—all popular performers, all Canadians. Although some of them can be identified as a particular kind of performer—folk, rock, country and western, blues—they are all popular in that they have made recordings which are played over radio for mass audiences and purchased by large numbers of Canadians.

Folk music has always been one of our most popular forms of music. Whether one is singing the folk music of the Maritimes, of French Canada, of the early days in Ontario, of the West or the North, folk represents the music of ordinary people and their everyday lives. The "protest songs" of the 1960s drew attention to political and social issues of the times. Performers like Gordon Lightfoot, Edith Butler, Buffy Ste. Marie, Joni Mitchell and Bruce Cockburn sang songs about the need for social change, songs which often became hits and led to commercial success for those involved.

Perhaps even more than other types of popular music, rock music in Canada is part of an international phenomenon. Since the

Until the early 1970s, Canadian performers had little chance for success at home until they had achieved prominence in the United States. When the CRTC introduced regulations requiring radio stations in Canada to carry a larger proportion of Canadian content, the opportunity for Canadian performers was increased.

Have You Heard René Simard?

Child vocalists have always caught the attention of audiences around the world. René Simard, a Francophone child prodigy, enjoyed phenomenal success in his home province of Quebec. In addition to his single records and albums, he has starred in television productions (in both French and English), in Quebec, the CBC national network and in the United States, as well as in films. Thus René—and his older brother, Regis, who composes some of René's songs— has become an international celebrity.

Famous folk-singers in the United States at this time were people like Joan Baez, Bob Dylan, Judy Collins, Peter, Paul and Mary, the Chad Mitchell Trio, the Kingston Trio—and the "dean" of American folk music, Pete Seeger.

Juno Awards

The Juno Awards are annual awards given in a ceremony recognizing achievement in Canadian music. Founded in 1963 by Walt Graalis, publisher of *RPM* magazine, the Juno Awards are the top honours of the Canadian recording industry.

Winners of Juno Awards over the years have included groups such as The Guess Who, Rush, and Bachmen-Turner Overdrive as well as individual performers like Gordon Lightfoot, Stompin' Tom Connors, Joni Mitchell, Anne Murray and Murray McLaughlin.

1950s, young people, in Canada no less than in the United States and elsewhere, have been fans of Elvis Presley, Bill Haley and the Comets, Little Richard, Fats Domino, Chubby Checker, the Beatles, the Rolling Stones, and others.

Yet Canada has produced a great many performers, both individuals and groups, who have "made a name" for themselves. These have included the Guess Who, David Clayton-Thomas, The Band, Three Dog Night, Steppenwolf, the Stampeders, and Bachman-Turner Overdrive.

Sports

With Canadians' recent interest in physical fitness encouraged especially by Participaction, a non-profit organization largely funded by the federal government, participant sports are gaining in popularity as leisure-time activities for many of us. Although sports at the professional level are enjoyed by most Canadians only as spectator activities, sports on an amateur level—varying from bicycling to tennis to cross-country skiing—are enjoyed throughout the land. Whether they are individual or team activities, these sports can not only improve our physical fitness but give us recreation and enjoyment as well.

Although the first people to inhabit Canada are known to have engaged in sporting activities and games, organized games matching one team against another became popular about one hundred years ago. Lacrosse is one example of a game developed in Canada; others, like cricket and lawn tennis, were imported from England. By the turn of the century, ice hockey, baseball and a kind of football were on their way to becoming the most popular team sports.

In Canada, sports naturally varied with the seasons, and in one sense this is still true today. Like their ancestors, Canadians still skate and ski in the winter and swim and play tennis in summer. However, a characteristic of sports in our day is the extent of professional, highly organized play with full-time, highly paid athletes performing before large crowds of spectators. Even more typical nowadays is televised sport, which enables the "typical" Canadian to be entertained by everything from golf to auto racing. As one season overlaps with another, the spectator may "participate" without any more effort than moving the dial on his television set and positioning himself in his favourite easy chair.

Many Canadians, then, have become accustomed to escapism through viewing the exertions of others. The impact of television has turned sport into one of the biggest parts of the expanding entertainment business. Since the 1960s, "expansion" has become a familiar word. The National Hockey League increased the number of teams from six to eighteen; the World Hockey Association was formed in

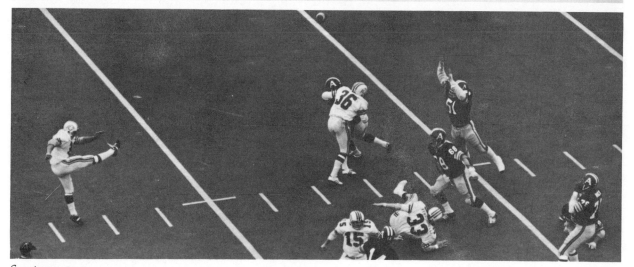

Sports on CBC

Ideas from the social sciences: The psychology of basic needs: when is a sport not a sport?

Every fall, Canadians spend huge sums of money on warm outdoor clothing, camping gear and guns in order to enjoy their favourite sport of hunting. A goose or a moose is a prized catch and sure to be the talk of one's friends. In the spring, Canadians spend as much money or more on boats and fishing gear to enjoy another favourite Canadian pastime—fishing. "Roughing it" has gained a new popularity, and thousands of Canadians take pride in doing without the usual conveniences—generally for very short periods of time.

These same Canadians buy meat, poultry and fish from their local supermarkets and look with interest at the latest model of snow-blower to save them the work of shovelling their sidewalks and driveways. Why are some activities considered "work" and others "sport"?

Sport as *amusement* or diversion is likely to be found in some form in any culture. In less complex cultures, sport is likely to be closely related to everyday activities. The person who must use snowshoes to get around in winter may take part in a snowshoe race during a festival or celebration. Similarly, some activities become sport when they are no longer necessary to survival. For example, hunting, fishing and canoeing were once jobs that people had to do in order to obtain food and other basic needs.

Now that we have supermarkets and department stores where we can buy food, we can look upon hunting as a sport. Similarly, if we do not have to fish for a living, sport fishing is fun. Living in cities, as most Canadians now do, people are even more inclined to "get back to the countryside" and enjoy activities that their forbears did only because they had to.

Psychologist Abraham Maslow has explained this idea in terms of a *theory of basic needs*. Maslow, after much research, experimentation and clinical experience, described a sequence of basic needs which we all try to fulfill. Once the "first level" needs are met, we seek to meet the next order of needs in the hierarchy. Although the categories or levels are not clearcut, that is there are no firm divisions separating each level, most psychologists agree that our most basic, first order needs are physiological—survival needs such as food. Once gratification of these is assured, we attempt to fulfill higher needs such as safety needs, belongingness and love needs, status or esteem needs, and self-actualization or self-fulfillment needs. In other words, no one will worry about who loves him or what others think about his behaviour if he is starving to death or is in some physical danger. Similarly, only when his food needs are met can a person think about hunting a bear to make a bearskin rug.

Considering this hierarchy of basic needs, and our growing number of work-saving devices, what changes may the future bring in what we will consider sport? Can you imagine any activities you now do out of necessity that may, through technological advances, in the future become unnecessary as work? Might they continue to exist as sport?

The poet as taxi driver: support for the arts in Canada

How does an amateur dancer, cellist or painter get to be a respected professional? The easy answer is that the person receives money for the expression of his talent, and that makes him a professional. But the question of who pays is of primary importance here.

Many countries, including Canada, recognize talent and give monetary support to that talent. The Canada Council, The Canadian Film Development Corporation, provincial governments and private patrons all support Canada's potential artists. And yet, the media frequently carry stories about a ballet company being in financial difficulty, a symphony season being curtailed because of money, or a lack of financial encouragement for up-coming Canadian filmmakers. Should we be putting more emphasis on the development of Canadian artists? Look at what noted Canadian composer Louis Applebaum has to say:

In an interview in the Jan. 1974 issue of CANADIAN COMPOSER *Applebaum gives his views on Canadian society's lack of support for the arts:*

Considering the amounts of money being spent on the arts, and your own involvement with this spending, we were a bit surprised when *Charles Wilson,* in a recently published interview (*The Canadian Composer,* November '73) said he heard you state something to the effect that "society in Canada says to the creative artist, 'Don't create! Go out and get a job that's respectable socially, go drive a cab, do anything, but don't create!' "

That's right, let me explain. What I was trying to say was that our Western kind of society is not yet ready to accept poets, composers, painters and other creative artists. We don't give them a place in our society and say, "Go ahead, spend your life composing or painting or writing poetry. We can accept an accountant or a teacher and pay them two, three, four hundred a week and we can justify that economically, but we can't justify a poet. "Sell your poetry", we say. So he writes his poetry and he gets into print and he earns four dollars and eight cents in royalties. Therefore, what we're really saying is, "If you want to be a poet, do it on weekends, as a hobby. Meanwhile, do something useful. Drive a taxi."[11]

YOU HAVE TO UNDERSTAND, MARGARET, THAT BEING IN THE SYMPHONY IS MORE THAN JUST A JOB TO US...IT'S A WAY OF LIFE!

1-24 THAVES

1. What might each of the characters in the cartoon say about Mr. Applebaum's comment?

1. Where do you think the major support for the arts should come from—government, private donations, self-support (fund-raising activities, ticket sales, etc.)? Why?

It is easy to say that we should allow our artists the time to mature professionally and that we should support them while they do so, but how many of us qualify that support in actual fact?

WHAT VALUE CULTURE?

No one would deny that artistic development is a necessity for any country. Furthermore, we have seen throughout this chapter that Canadians do support the arts and, in fact, that governments have passed laws ensuring continuation of support for a variety of Canadian leisure-time activities.

The question to be raised in this section is a value question, that is, there are no rights and wrongs. Rather you are asked to make value judgments which can influence the future of our country.

Consider the following situation after which you will be asked some questions:

Bill and Trudy Matheson were married in June of 1975. Both in their early twenties, Bill and Trudy are devoted to each other. Before they were married, Trudy held a job as head secretary to the president of a large insurance company. She always worked hard in school even though some courses were difficult for her. She met Bill while at business college and dated him on and off for three years. When she met Bill, he had just quit university in order to devote more time to painting which he someday hoped would be his vocation.

After many lengthy discussions, Trudy and Bill agreed that after they were married, she would be willing to keep her job at the insurance company to support them while Bill spent all his time painting. Although their parents and friends were less than pleased with this idea, both Bill and Trudy decided to try it.

1. Should Bill and Trudy have made this arrangement? Would your answer change if:

(a) Bill wanted Trudy to finance his education through medical school?
(b) Bill had already sold many of his paintings?
(c) the Canada Council gave Bill a $2500 grant?
(d) Trudy hated her job at the insurance company?
(e) Bill and Trudy found it necessary to borrow money from Bill's parents to pay their rent?
(f) after five years Bill feels he needs "just one more year" to become a successful artist?

Which of the following may have influenced your decision?

(a) talent?
(b) length of time Trudy would support the two of them?
(c) type of vocation Bill wished to pursue?
(d) contribution Bill could make to the pleasure of others?
(e) individual rights?
(f) scale on which this would be done (i.e. how many people would want to do this)?

Regardless of your answers to these questions, they say something about certain values that you hold, and they are probably very close to the values your parents and other Canadians hold.

The dilemma then becomes one of priorities. If we wish to make it possible for Canadians to be "good" or "successful" at something, how far are we willing to go in terms of support or backing? Where do we draw the line? Should a promising amateur pianist, for example, be supported for a period of time so that he or she could devote all time available to practice? If so, for how long, and who should be responsible for providing support for that person? What if many Canadians decided they would like the opportunity to develop their talents while being supported by others? Should this be a privilege for a few Canadians or a right for all? Do these questions force you to look at your definitions of concepts like "work", "leisure" and "talent"? What, if any, conclusions can you draw?

1971 with some ten teams. Similar changes in professional sport in the United States involved Canadian cities like Montreal, which obtained a National League baseball franchise, and Toronto which fielded a team in the American League in 1977. Television coverage has expanded, not only for sports such as hockey and football, but also for tennis, golf, skiing and many others.

Whether as participant or spectator, more and more Canadians are coming to see sports as at least one pleasurable way to spend their leisure.

What *is* leisure?

Throughout this chapter you looked at some of the possible leisure-time activities available to Canadians. It was assumed that you had just completed a school week and thus that your leisure time would be those two days before your next school week.

Given the social and technological changes we are experiencing, there are some researchers who are investigating a different way of viewing the idea of leisure. Consider the following points of view:

> Traditionally man's time has been for working, interrupted only by still work-related essentials of eating, sleeping, maintenance chores and a Spartan-spent Sabbath. The 'leisure' for the few was supported by the sweat of slaves or exploitation of the many gave that word a historically bad name; and 'leisure' has since been abused into all manner of shapeless and usually invidious meanings. Nor are we overly accomplished at the 'arts' of leisure. Many tackle the expenditure of leisure more strenuously than they work.
>
> For some time now we moderns have theoretically had a lot of 'new' leisure, from our shortening work days. That we have turned this into a new kind of 'rat race' is due in no small part to the fact that our new non-work time comes to us *fragmented*—in bits and pieces strung through the week; most of these fragments of free time are too short to do much with uninterruptedly.
>
> From the human point of view, this free time fragmentation is the prime self-defeating aspect of the five-day week. Its total work time on the job is short, but the gross time it takes out of the day and week is long. Forty hours or less it may well be, but it is a *work week*. Except for some work-night televiewing, most functional 'leisure' of today's typical job holder is crowded into the two end-of-week days.[12]

On the contrary:

> There is a group, however, which tends to ignore this time framework and views life as existence; their whole behaviour is recreationally oriented. At least, we perceive it to be a life of freedom,

the state of being which the philosophers refer to as leisure. Of course, I'm speaking of the Hippies and our inherent dislike for what they represent. We consider them irresponsible, ignoring the basic values of organization and interdependency. We say if all were to enjoy the life of the Hippie, then who will tend the shop, uphold the structures of society? The potentials of a leisure-oriented society trouble us for the freedom we hold to be the essence of the recreational experience can only exist when someone else or some thing is allowing us to act independently of necessity.[13]

What these viewpoints lead to is the fact that we view leisure as the *reward* for *work*. However, some changes in our society may call for us to change our perceptions. Consider:

reduction in the five-day work week;
machines replacing people on jobs;
labour-saving devices in the home;
labour unions' demands for more benefits for workers, especially in on-the-job time;
large numbers of people retiring earlier.

With some or all of these changes may come changed perceptions of everything we do during our waking hours. For example, do we now consider "work" to be only what we do out of the house and for which we are paid? What about the "work" of housekeeping and childcare? Do we feel that we are somehow "cheating" if we are given time off from our "regular jobs" to attend meetings, conventions or even up-grading classes? Do some of us wonder what kind of "job" a businessman has if his hours of work do not conform to the usual 8:30 to 5:00 work period? On the other hand, do we admire or look down upon the person who never seems to have any "free time"—the person who is always "working"—whatever that "work" may be?

Answers to these questions indicate attitudes and values which we now hold but which may need to be re-thought in light of the changes in our future lifestyles. Depending upon the way a person views himself, the people around him and his life goals, what he does during his waking hours may differ radically from what he is "supposed" to do.

Given the choice of lifestyle, Harry Homebody may prefer to centre his whole life around family activities. His "work" may be that of househusband while his wife spends daytime hours in an office or factory; his "leisure" may be spending time with his children, coaching soccer, camping, skiing and so on. At the other extreme, Timothy Tycoon may get satisfaction from the business where he "works" and from the "leisure" hours in which he reads financial papers, dines with clients and counts his money.

Neither Harry nor Timothy makes a separation between "work" and "leisure". For both of them, leisure is more an attitude than a particular time of the day or week or period of the year. Whether or not we have as much choice as Harry and Timothy in deciding how we spend our time, the possibilities for many Canadians are increasing. Could it be that the more leisure-conscious we become, the more creatively we can deal with both "leisure" and "work"?

1. If trends continue so that more Canadians have more leisure time, what kinds of pressures could this put on other Canadians? For example on parks and recreation supervisors, theatre owners, policemen?
2. What kinds of things could people do during leisure time which could benefit more than just the individual? For example, how could this different way of looking at leisure benefit Canadian culture?

12

What is progress? Canadian economic issues

What is an economic system and where does it come from?

In the land of Ob, the people have a problem. One of the country's main resources is the ork tree, from which the Obvians make their houses. Until now the supply has been abundant. However, an inventor named Alexander Graham Gong has just designed a skipper, which resembles a pogo stick. The skipper, useful for rapid travel or just for fun, is made of ork wood. The idea has caught on, and Gong is advertising skippers which he and his family are carving in an extra room in their home. Meanwhile, thousands of Obvians are rushing out, cutting down ork trees and making their own skippers. Gong is angry that his idea is being used by everybody, just as he is beginning to sell the skippers he has manufactured. More seriously, a citizen's group calling themselves S.O.S. (Stamp Out Skippers) is worried that soon there will not be enough ork wood to build the new houses that are always needed. An editorial appears in the leading newspaper:

OB'S CURE

Concern is growing among thinking Obvians about the confusion in our community with respect to ork, the very foundation of our economy. Of all things that may be said, one point is obvious: no longer can we live under the illusion that we will always have all the ork we need. Obvians are faced with some important decisions. There is not enough ork for all the uses we now have, let alone the ones we may discover.

An immediate session of the Council of Ob should be called to consider ways of ending the present state of economic disorganization.

The Council of Ob did meet and, after what seemed like endless discussion, compiled a list of questions that would have to be answered in setting up some economic system. Here are some of the questions:

1. Of the products that could be made from ork, which ones will be made?
2. Who will have the right to use the ork for making products?
3. How will the decisions about the quantites of ork products be made?
4. What means of production will be used?
5. How will the prices be set? Should Gong be allowed to set his own? What factors would he have to consider?
6. For what groups will ork products be made? Will ork be available to all or to certain groups?
7. To what extent should the Council plan and control the allocation, production and distribution? What alternatives are there to control by Council?

Ob is a mythical land, and the situation described is fictional. However, every real-life community faces the same economic issues. Even a modern industrial country like Canada, with its complex economic system, must answer many of the same fundamental questions.

Canada's economy today

Canadians tended to take prosperity, or the hope of prosperity, for granted after World War II. Media, governments, schools, financial institutions and the general public seemed to hold the belief that Canada was uniquely blessed, enjoying a good life now, and expecting a better one in the future. However, the assumptions about unlimited growth and prosperity are now being examined carefully. More and more people—economists, journalists, legislators, homemakers—are asking questions about our economic system and the promise of prosperity. Many of the questions being asked are about everyday concerns like: What will I do if the cost of food keeps rising? Can I afford to buy a new car or should I repair the old one? How can I put away money for the children's education? Can I expect a raise this year? Will I be more economically secure next year?

How well individuals can deal with such questions depends in part on how the whole economic system of the nation is functioning. Therefore, we must consider larger, fundamental questions common to all economic systems. Then we need to relate such fundamental questions to Canada's economic system.

1. What things will be produced?

What products, what services, will be provided—and in what quantities—and which ones will not? Canada cannot produce all things that all Canadians may want. In other words, Canadians are no different from other people in having to make decisions about the use of scarce resources. Consequently, an economic system has evolved to decide whether there are to be full-size automobiles, sugar-coated breakfast cereals, indoor skating rinks, mink coats, snowmobiles, hamburger stands, factory equipment for making tractors, libraries, movie houses, bicycle paths, free medical care, "slick" magazines, public legal services, workers' compensation, whiskey, concert halls, massage parlours, office buildings, and so on.

We can find all of these things in Canada, of course. Yet no one would claim that they exist in quantities which satisfy the needs and wants of all Canadians.

1. Which of the items listed above are goods? Which are services?
2. Which may be considered as basic needs, or serving basic needs?
3. Which of the items is likely to be profitable? Who will profit?
4. Which are likely to be provided by private enterprise? By public enterprise, or government? Why?

The expression *supply and demand* is helpful in understanding what an economic system produces. If there is a *demand* among consumers for pocket calculators or permanent press clothing, manufacturers can take the opportunity to provide the *supply*. At least, this is true of a **free enterprise** system.

Also known as private enterprise, or capitalism.

Free enterprise means that an individual or business is "free" to make a product or offer a service, the main purpose being to earn a profit. If the consumer chooses not to buy or use a certain item or service, say an electric back scratcher or a drive-in poodle wash, such things are not likely to be produced for very long. In this way, the consumer influences what is produced.

There are many other influences too. As well as the consumer demand, or *market*,* a business must take into account the costs and availability of materials, equipment, labour, advertising, distribution. The costs of these "ingredients" are important, as are the costs of loans and other ways of financing a business.

1. A familiar expression in free enterprise systems is "the consumer is king." What do you think this means?

2. To what extent do consumers freely decide what they need? Do you think that advertising, for example on television, is powerful enough to create consumer "needs"?

3. Consumer goods and services are not the only forms of production in an economy. Social services such as schools and hospitals, and public works like highways and bridges, are important examples of what will be produced. What others can you think of?

FRANK AND ERNEST   by Bob Thaves

2. How are goods and services produced?

How goods and services are produced depends on what resources are available; what means are available for making efficient use of resources; forms of business organization; actions by governments.

Production obviously requires natural and human resources, and facilities. If the resources necessary to a certain industry are available within Canada, companies, and sometimes governments, will compete for those resources. Normally the highest bidder, the one that can pay the price, obtains the wood, iron, petroleum, fabric or whatever resources are necessary to the particular industry, as well as the needed financial and human resources.

1. Long before discoveries of major deposits of iron, which is a necessary element in the production of steel, Canada had a steel industry. How was a supply of iron obtained?

2. Historically, Canada has had a small population in relation to her abundant natural resources. How has Canada overcome her human resource limitations to produce a wide variety of services?

The economy of a country benefits if it makes efficient use of resources. In an industrialized country like Canada, efficiency can be increased by mass production, which is made easier by improvements in equipment. Industrial research can develop better ways of producing goods. A more specialized staff can improve efficiency, especially if employees are provided with incentives like opportunities for higher pay, better working conditions and other benefits.

As a vehicle for more efficient use of resources, the *corporation* has developed as a form of business organization. The corporation has advantages over the individual producer or partnership, because it can sell shares to raise money and therefore can generally operate on a larger scale. Another advantage is that the investor in a corporation has "limited liability", which means he can lose only the amount he has invested; if the corporation goes bankrupt, he is not responsible for its debts.

One of the problems with corporations is that they can become so large, either through expansion or mergers, that they can gain a *monopoly*. In the absence of competition this can mean higher prices to the consumer and poorer quality products. These problems, which can grow worse when large corporations make arrangements with each other, create the need for arrangements to protect the customer. The result has been the increased involvement of governments, both federal and provincial, in the economy.

Not all goods and services needed by society are provided by private business. In the Canadian experience, public enterprise has played an important role in providing those goods and services from which profits, at least on a large scale, are unlikely. The CBC, a Crown corporation, which includes among its services the CBC Northern Service and shortwave broadcasting, is one example of public enterprise.

The role of government in the economy has increased dramatically in the twentieth century, especially in recent years. This is particularly true in the realm of social services, such as medical care, educational facilities, manpower and job retraining centres.

3. For whom are goods and services produced?

In a free enterprise system, goods and services are most readily available to the people who are willing and able to pay for them. This ability and willingness, in turn, depends on the success people have in gaining financial security from their land, business or wages. The more financial power people or groups hold, the more they are able to command their share of the "economic pie".

A few hundred years ago, in medieval Europe, a person with a large parcel of land and a castle had a distinct advantage over the

Different economic systems

In direct contrast to the *free enterprise* system is the *command*, or *planned*, economy. In the Soviet Union, for example, the basic economic questions are answered quite differently from the way they are in Canada. The state (government) decides what goods and services should be made available to the citizens. Since the government owns and controls the means of production, it also decides "how" and "for whom" goods and services are to be produced. Many countries, in fact, have "mixed economies", in which the government is an active participant with private enterprise. Even in so-called "free enterprise" societies such as Canada, governments increasingly control business and other sectors of the economy.

Public enterprise means production and services provided by government. In a large country with a small population and limited capital resources (technology), private business often cannot afford the risk that goes with national projects. Therefore, if a country like Canada is to have a nation-wide transportation system or a large power project, the government often acts on behalf of the total population. It can either provide the service itself or act in conjunction with one or more companies. The CPR was built by a company which was given financial support by Sir John A. Macdonald's government (1880s). In the 1970s, PetroCanada, a crown corporation, works in various ways with the petroleum companies.

serf. A hundred years ago in North America, the head of a corporation had probably an even greater advantage over the factory worker. Historically, workers, whether peasants or wage-earners, have been at a disadvantage in the marketplace. All the worker had to sell was his labour; its value depended on many conditions and events over which he had no control, including the power of employers.

The labour movement was the eventual outcome of workers' desires to be less vulnerable and to mobilize their power. In the twentieth century, especially since World War II, labour unions have become increasingly important. Their objectives have included better wages and working conditions, paid vacations and even a better status in society.

Governments, too, have more responsibility now than they used to in increasing the *equity* or fairness of the system by making goods and services available to larger numbers of the population. The *graduated income tax*, by which those with higher incomes pay more taxes, is one way that governments try to reduce the advantages of the more wealthy; unemployment insurance cushions the shock for those who find themselves without jobs.

EVALUATING CANADA'S ECONOMY

We have seen that every society must have an economic system to deal with certain basic questions: *what* should be produced from its resources; *how* should these goods and services be produced; and *to whom* will they be available. Canada's economy is characterized to a large degree by private ownership. Producers compete with one another both in purchasing materials and labour to make products and in selling products or services to consumers. Because of these features, the Canadian economy has commonly been described as a free enterprise system. It is also true, however, that our economy has been changing in recent years. Governments have assumed a greater role in producing goods and services for general public use and in acting to control such things as monopolies and misleading advertising practices. It is therefore more apt to describe Canada's economy today as a *mixed economic system*—a "mix" of free enterprise and government enterprise and regulation.

There are other aspects of an economic system which must be examined if we are going to increase our understanding of how—and how well—it works. For example, every economic system seeks to achieve the broad goals of *growth*, *stability* and *equity*. Growth means basically increased production, or output, of goods and services. Economists measure economic growth in various ways, but the most familiar is *gross national product* (GNP). The GNP is the total money value of all the goods and services produced in a country in a year.

Quality of life: more than economic growth

The Gross National Product (GNP) is a frequently used index of a country's economic growth. However, the GNP does not take into account changes in the level of prices or population, and as a result it can be misleading. Economists often calculate the *real* GNP (GNP minus price increases caused by inflation) per capita (per person), as a more meaningful indicator of economic growth.

Even the real GNP tends to indicate growth in general. Therefore, it says little about the prosperity, or lack of prosperity, of particular groups. In other words, a rising GNP suggests that a country's economic situation is improving, even though the rich may be getting richer while the majority remain as poor as ever. Furthermore, the GNP excludes the value of work performed by those who are not paid directly, like family workers on a farm and homemakers.

Another weakness of the GNP as a measurement of progress is that it does not include the negative effects of economic growth such as the environmental damage caused by huge factories, social problems resulting from urbanization and the effects of organized crime. Nor does the GNP measure the social or cultural "wealth" of a country in terms of the benefits people derive from cultural and recreational activities.

In trying to assess the improvement in the quality of life the government of Canada has begun to develop scales other than the GNP. An explanation is suggested by the following:

QUALITY OF LIFE IN CANADA

As the 1960s drew to a close, commitment to the single-minded pursuit of economic growth began to lessen in western societies. Policymakers and social scientists, as well as the media, commented increasingly on the "quality of life". The gist of this commentary was that there are several dimensions of individual and social well-being that need more attention by decision-makers and statisticians. As we move through the 1970s, the demands grow for a broad conception of the non-economic aspects of our life. Statistics Canada is moving on several fronts to make its statistical system increasingly responsive to these new demands.[1]

In other words, areas of concern other than those easily measured by their monetary value are now being analyzed from year to year in much the same way as the GNP is. In *Perspective Canada*, the Department of Industry, Trade and Commerce published charts and tables on population and family, health, schooling, the use of time, work, income, consumption, quality of the environment, housing, bilingualism, the native peoples, cultural diversity, and criminal justice.

Not all social problems are included in the analysis. The publication explains: "The areas of concern selected . . . are those that focus on the individual, are social rather than economic in content, and can be at least minimally quantified [measured in numbers]. Excluded, therefore, are such problems as national identity, constitutional issues, alienation, inflation, or foreign control of industry." Obviously excluded are "the truly fundamental problems of personal being such as the spiritual life, love, and friendship."

1. Choose one of the areas of concern listed in *Perspective Canada*. To analyze its importance to the "quality of life" in your part of Canada, make a list of questions about the kinds of things which should be measured. For example, under housing, you might want to know how many single-family dwellings are for sale in different areas of your city.

Stability refers to a balance in the economy, to which the main threats are inflation—sharp rises in the cost of living—and unemployment. An economy which is making progress towards these two goals is no doubt doing very well by some of its citizens. However, there is at least a third important goal, equity, which is concerned with a fair distribution of a country's resources among different groups of its citizens.

In examining these goals, we must look at developments relating to these goals, and what problems there have been. But there is still more. We must think about the goals themselves, whether any of them need to be changed, and whether there are other goals of greater importance for the future.

Economic growth

Prosperity has often been taken for granted by Canadians in recent years. Though people in other countries may be trapped in poverty, Canadians have come to expect rising incomes and a wider variety of things to buy. This attitude is not surprising, since Canada has enjoyed tremendous economic *growth* in the years since World War II. That growth has brought material benefits to many Canadians. Yet there have been negative effects as well.

To illustrate this economic growth in terms of both benefits and problems, we can look at the example of *energy*. The development of

424

cheap energy was a major factor in the expansion of other resource industries and manufacturing. Eventually, relying on cheap energy posed some serious problems.

ENERGY: NEW RICHES, NEW PROBLEMS

Oil and natural gas became leading sources of energy in postwar Canada. With the discovery at Leduc near Edmonton in 1947, the oil fields of Alberta* became the basis of an expanding petroleum industry. The "have not" province of Alberta, once known as "next year country" because of its unfulfilled hope of prosperity, was suddenly changed to a "have" province.*

*Much smaller fields are also discovered in western Manitoba, Saskatchewan and British Columbia.

*Historically some regions of Canada have been less well-off than others.

Western Canada in general assumed a stronger position in the nation's economy. With the rise of new industries and increasing population, western Canadians could hope for more broadly-based economic growth.

AN OIL TOWN IN ALBERTA

Shortly after the discovery of oil at Leduc in 1947, a magazine writer noted some of the changes in the town:

Six months ago a traveller always could get a room in the two-storey brick hotel at Leduc, 19 miles south of Edmonton on the highway to Calgary.... The only day in the week when many people were around was Saturday. If a traveller visited Leduc often he probably knew by sight or name many of Leduc's 864 citizens and some of the farmers, too.

Today he'd be lucky to find anyone he knew. Citizens and farmers alike are almost lost in the dozens of men in plaid and khaki shirts, high boots, wide-brimmed hats and oil-stained over-alls—wildcatters, the men who search for new oil fields.

The pool room is full of oilmen off shift, drillers and cathead men and lead tong men and derrick men. Upstairs in the hotel, past the deserted desk with its "No Rooms Vacant" sign, oilmen sit around a blanket-covered table and play quiet, dollar-limit poker. In the beer parlor below some oilmen drink beer and others drink a mixture of beer and tomato juice. The mid-European accents of the Ukrainian and Polish farmers and the clear prairie speech of the townspeople mix with the more precise English of Easterners and occasionally with the drawls of Texas and Oklahoma.

And among oilmen and farmers alike the talk is not of crops but of ... the $130,000 Pete Hairysh got for his half section, or the $41,000 the widow Kate Malchak got for her quarter.... [2]

Serious development of Alberta's newfound source of wealth was made possible by the construction of a trans-Canada pipeline. In one of the great national projects of the 1950s, pipelines were com-

The rig at the first oil well near Leduc, Alberta

pleted to transport crude oil and natural gas to markets both on the west coast and in eastern Canada and the United States. Through the combination of government assistance and private enterprise, largely American in origin, the petroleum and natural gas industry became one of Canada's leading industries.

In the 1960s, the growth of the oil industry, mainly in Alberta, continued and places like Calgary and Edmonton virtually doubled in size in the wake of the new prosperity. The skylines of tall, modern buildings reflected the unprecedented wealth that concentrated in the cities of the West.

The 1970s brought a dramatic change in attitude. The "energy crisis", especially from 1973 on, forced North America, especially the United States at first, to realize that petroleum was a diminishing, non-renewable resource. Canada was not supplying all of her own petroleum needs; provinces east of Ontario imported their oil from Venezuela. Nevertheless, oil from Alberta was being exported to markets in the United States.

Facing the energy crisis

In the 1970s, the phrase "energy crisis" entered the Canadian vocabulary, perhaps permanently. To the surprise of Canadians, proven supplies of oil and natural gas were found to be much smaller than believed. Experts explained that hydro, solar energy and nuclear power would be hard-pressed to "fill the gap" even with the support of massive investment in research and development. Moreover, years would pass before such alternative energy sources would be readily available.

The challenge of maintaining a supply of energy equal to the rising demand was a challenge to the nation as a whole. Everyone was likely to be affected. The unavoidable question seemed to be: How can we use our available energy more *efficiently*?

The answer to this question "depends upon the interaction of energy prices, economic institutions and social attitudes. Of these, only the price effect is clear in direction: the higher the price, the more energy conservation practices will appeal to the consumer."[4] However, our economic practices and our values have tended to be based on pre-"energy-crisis" assumptions: Canada has plenty of energy; and it is economically sensible and socially acceptable to use energy generously.

The calculation of energy supplies and patterns of consumption is a complicated affair. The following chart is only a simple repre-

In the summer of 1973, the world price of oil increased from $2.20 per barrel in the Persian Gulf to $11.50 per barrel.

Domestic Demand and Availability: Total Energy (Two Scenarios) [3]

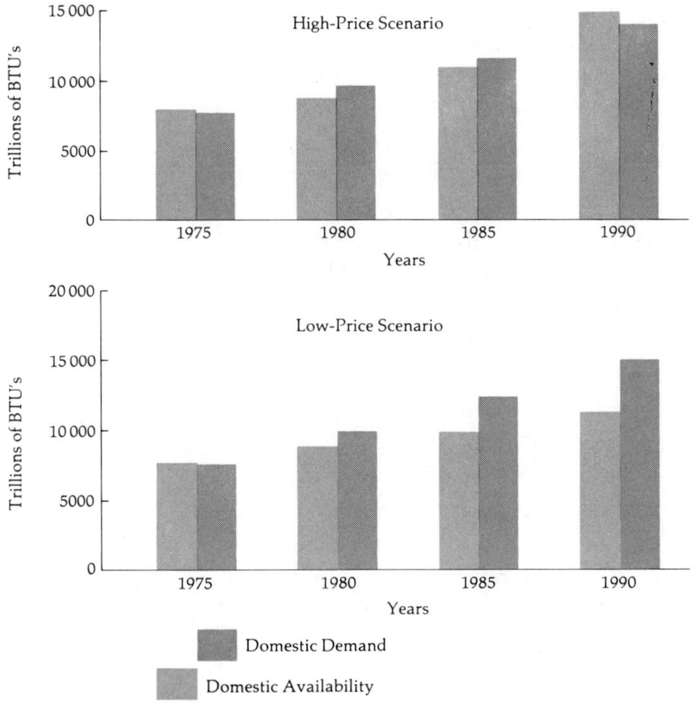

427

sentation of the federal Department of Energy's attempts to show what alternatives we face in the future.

Estimating that present trends will produce a certain rate of increase in future demand for energy, government experts prepared two scenarios. According to the "high-price **scenario**", the supply of energy could keep up with demand—but only at great cost. The "low-price scenario" suggests that supply will fall far behind demand if present levels of investment in energy development are maintained.

If increasing the supply of energy is so costly and likely to require time, the other choice is to reduce the demand. The following example from *An Energy Strategy for Canada* illustrates the possible benefits of energy conservation in the case of home heating:

> The greatest potential for energy savings in the residential sector lies in the more efficient use of energy for space heating. This can be attained by revising standards for new buildings, by modifying existing houses (retrofitting) and by improving the efficiency of oil furnaces, which account for over 60% of all residential heating units. Economically justified revisions in construction standards could result in energy savings in new residences of up to 50% of the energy used in similar-size residences constructed to 1970 standards. Similarly, the existing stock of houses can be improved through retrofitting to yield reductions in energy use, by 1990, on the order of 25% per unit. Oil furnaces could be improved by 20% over current efficiency levels with careful twice-a-year maintenance. Although many aspects of such programs would involve an initial capital expenditure, calculations suggest that—even at current energy prices—this increased investment would pay for itself in the form of reduced fuel costs in about five years.
>
> [The graph] indicates the potential savings that could be achieved in 1990 through revised construction standards, retrofitting and increases in the efficiency of oil-burning furnaces. In 1975, total energy use in the residential sector is estimated at about 1 250 trillion Btu's. Of this, approximately 850 trillion Btu's (about 68%) were used for space heating. If the potential savings through energy conservation that are both technically feasible and economically justified were, in fact, to be realized by 1990, then the use of energy for residential space-heating in that year would amount to only 70% of use in 1975, even allowing for growth in the number of housing units. Housing units built to these energy standards would have somewhat less window area, but still more than minimum standards. Otherwise, they would be no different in appearance from those typical of current construction. Major differences would be in the increased insulation of walls and ceilings, improved vapour barriers, better weather stripping, etc. Such changes could add from $200 to $1 000 to the initial cost of new housing.[5]

Scenario: a short passage or diagram which tells a story or depicts a scene. Futurists (those people who study the possible, probable and preferable alternative futures available to us) use scenarios to describe possible future situations in order to determine what might be preferable. They feel that only if we begin to plan for the future will we be able to control it.

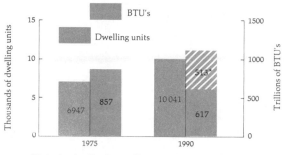

Energy Use for Residential Space Heating

* 'Savings' attributable to improved furnace servicing (20%), new construction standards (31%) and retrofitting (49%),

The Mackenzie Valley pipeline issue

Of the many issues involved in the development of Canada's North in the 1970s, none was more complicated than the transportation of natural gas from the Arctic to population centres in the south. By the mid-1970s, most attention was still focused on proposals to construct a Mackenzie Valley pipeline.

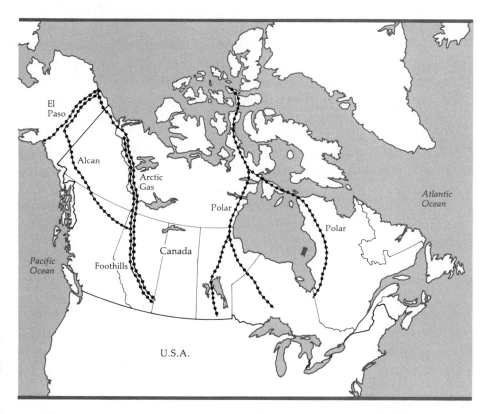

1. This complex issue has many effects, some beneficial and some harmful. How might the following be affected?

	Benefits	*Drawbacks*
Canadian consumers of natural gas		
United States consumers of natural gas		
native residents of the north		
the Canadian environment		

2. Which of these concerns should have the highest priority in deciding whether or not to go ahead with the Mackenzie Valley pipeline? Why?

According to forecasts about Canada's oil reserves, she appeared to have only enough assured supplies to last until the mid-1980s, even if she exported no more oil. Stopping oil exports would, therefore, be only a temporary solution and would risk alienating the United States. Meanwhile, the price of oil imported from OPEC* (Organization of Petroleum Exporting Countries) quadrupled, and further price increases seemed certain.

*An alliance of oil-producing countries, of which the majority are in the Middle East.

This was not all. The Canadian government was faced with the problem of decreasing the regional disparity in oil and gas prices. In addition, Alberta was demanding a larger share of the revenue from the sale of its oil. The main reason was the need to develop new industries for a time when it no longer had such abundant oil resources.

Hydro-electric power is a second source of energy that has taken on ever-increasing importance. The needs of North America's sprawling urban areas have created what seem to be endless markets for energy. As a result, hydro-electric projects have been some of the most spectacular and controversial examples of economic growth in modern Canada.

Following the ' "Pipeline Debate" of 1956, and the election of the Diefenbaker government, a royal commission on energy was appointed. One of the main recommendations, implemented in 1959, was the creation of the National Energy Board. Among its powers, is the regulation of the construction and operation of oil and gas pipelines and hydro lines on Canadian territory, and the setting of limits on quantities of oil and gas imports. The Board also reports to Parliament, through the Minister of Energy, Mines and Resources on many issues relating to energy.

The Columbia River project has made energy available not only to British Columbia, but to neighbouring states in the United States. To be sure, this energy has been abundant and inexpensive. On the other hand, the development of the facilities has caused changes in the landscape and has had harmful effects on the lives of people whose property was involved.

The same dilemma is repeated over and over. In the 1970s, projects involving the Nelson River in northern Manitoba and rivers in Quebec flowing into James Bay aroused fierce controversy. Both projects were responses to Canada's projected energy needs for industrial development and household use in the last quarter of the

Some primary resource industries

*See chapter 13 for the issue of Canada's selling nuclear reactors to other countries.

20th century. Opponents of the projects included environmentalists, who warned of the potential damage to the ecology, and native peoples whose traditional lands and way of life were threatened.

Atomic power is seen by some as a potential source of energy as the country's needs continue to expand and the traditional sources are fully exploited or depleted. Canada has been a leader in developing peaceful uses for atomic energy from the start. At the Chalk River plant not far from Ottawa, and at others, nuclear technology has been developed to the point that the CANDU nuclear reactor is now in demand in energy-poor countries.

However, atomic energy cannot be produced without raising serious issues either.* The problem of disposing of radioactive wastes is not easily solved, and there are fears that large-scale production could lead to horrible side-effects on the environment.

Energy, though it is only one example, illustrates the double-edged nature of economic growth. Though growth is needed for continued Canadian prosperity, it also produces "negative payoffs". But growth, as a goal of the Canadian economic system, is not the only concern.

Stability

While growth has been a common goal in economic systems, so has *stability*. If an economy is unstable, the potential for growth is undermined. If prices for goods and services rise sharply and quickly, the value, or buying power, of money declines. Then a person finds that his money "doesn't go as far", and any money he can save will be worth less and less in the future. The condition of rising prices, known as *inflation*, is one of the main forms of economic instability.

Another problem is unemployment. The jobless person suffers directly, but indirectly other people, and the system as a whole, are also affected. If 10% of the labour force is unemployed, the country loses the contribution of a large part of its "human resource". Furthermore, unemployed people are likely to be discontented, and their discontent may lead to political unrest.

In an unstable economy, both employers and employees suffer, since profits and buying power are diminished. The country as a whole loses, especially when dependent for its prosperity on international trade.

Because of the importance of stability to economic growth, coordination of the different parts of the system is necessary. In a free enterprise economy, part of the coordination occurs in the marketplace, through the interplay of supply and demand. If, for whatever reasons, prices begin to jump outrageously or masses of people are suddenly thrown out of work—or worse still, if both situations occur —then governments may decide they must intervene.

THE INCREASING ROLE OF GOVERNMENT

In the decade after World War II, the Canadian nation achieved higher and higher levels of prosperity. However, as the economy grew, it became more complex, and terms like *inflation* and expressions like *"The high cost of living"* became part of polite conversation.

A reminder that the economy was still subject to "ups and downs" was Canada's financial crisis of 1947. Great Britain and European countries were making their purchases from Canada on credit. But while Canadian exports were not actually bringing money into the country, Canadian consumers were sending record amounts of money out of the country. With rising wages and income from war bonds, veterans' allowances and other sources, Canadians had money to spend on imported goods, mainly from the United States, which thus enjoyed an influx of Canadian dollars. There were fears of a kind of national bankruptcy.

The federal government, its wartime authority over the economy still intact, moved swiftly to avert disaster. It introduced emergency restrictions on a wide range of imports, including household appliances, luxury goods, even fresh vegetables and fruit. Fortunately the measures seemed to have the desired effect, and Canadians only had to endure them for a short time. The foreign exchange crisis soon eased, and the restricted imports were once again admitted.

Postwar prosperity resumed and continued well into the 1950s after the crisis in 1947. But by 1957, the boom had again levelled off. Growth of the labour force outstripped job opportunities. New job seekers included women seeking fulltime employment, people moving from rural areas to cities, and a continuing flow of immigrants. Automation was reducing the need for labour in manufacturing industries. Canadian exports faced increased competition from other nations which were recovering from the war. In Canada, the demand for imports continued, but the nation's exports were having trouble finding markets. In other words, much the same situation occurred as had in 1947. And foreign investors, finding that opportunities in Canada were declining, were turning to more attractive countries.

The Diefenbaker government (1957-1962) began a number of programs designed to spark economic growth. The winter works program, in which costs were shared equally by the federal, and provincial and municipal governments, provided limited seasonal employment. The Trans-Canada Highway, built in cooperation with the provinces between 1959 and 1962, had brought short-term economic benefits by stimulating demands for goods and services during construction, and at the same time it added to the nation's physical unity. The "roads to resources" project was intended to open up the North and create jobs, although it fell short of expectations.

The nation as a whole, to which economic growth was so important, was stagnating. The Canadian government, spending far more than it was taking in, was building up large annual deficits, or debts. To make matters worse, a conflict developed between the government and the Bank of Canada. The main figures were the Minister of Finance, Donald Fleming, and James Coyne, Governor of the Bank of Canada. After months of feuding, Coyne was dismissed from office, but the "Coyne affair" had weakened confidence in the stability of the Canadian economy. Drastic action was called for, and in May, 1962, the government *devalued* the Canadian dollar. This meant that the Canadian dollar was valued at 92.5 cents in relation to the American dollar. Since it was now easier for foreigners to buy Canadian products, and Canadians had to spend more dollars to buy imports, exports increased and the flow of Canadian dollars out of the country decreased.

The bank of Canada, created in 1939, is the central bank — the "banks' bank." Commercial banks where the public keeps savings and obtains loans must maintain a certain amount of money on deposit at the Bank of Canada. The purpose is to protect against a bank's going bankrupt. In this and other ways, the Bank of Canada has a large responsibility for keeping the country's money system strong.

"THE DIEFENDOLLAR," 1962

The "Diefendollar" had no monetary value, of course, but when it was circulated during the 1962 election campaign it was enjoyed by critics of the Conservative government. What specific things and people is the "Diefendollar" poking fun at?

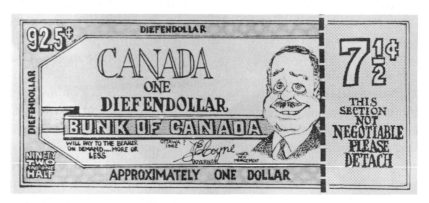

An important reason for the growing prosperity was an influx of American investment. One effect was to heighten the concern in Canada about the dangers of American domination of the economy. Note the account in Chapter 13 of the "foreign ownership" dilemma.

The economy entered a new period of growth. Not only did exports increase, but Canadians were spending more on home-produced products. The country enjoyed an "economic party" until late in the decade. However, a serious side-effect began to develop — *inflation*. In December, 1969, the Trudeau government declared "war on inflation".

Canada's choice: pay-as-you-go or bank on the future?

Governments, like individual persons or organizations, can either try to "balance their budgets" or "buy on credit". If an individual allows his debts to grow indefinitely, he may find his "credit rating" suffers. In fact, he may be forced into bankruptcy by those to whom he owes money.

The government of Canada went deeply into debt in order to pay for its war effort. Much of this debt took the form of war bonds sold to persons and companies in Canada, who would get their money back, with interest, in the future. There seemed to be two alternatives for the government at the end of the war: to spend as little as possible and try to reduce the national debt, or to spend generously to encourage economic growth which would result in larger amounts of government income through taxes. Such income could be used to reduce the national debt.

Look at the figures given below. What choices have governments made? Since governments cannot go bankrupt in the way individuals can, they can allow the national debt to continue to grow. What would be wise or unwise about this decision? How might a country's "credit rating" be affected?

THE NATIONAL DEBT: SELECTED YEARS[7]

Year	Gross Debt ($ millions)	Assets ($ millions)	Net Debt ($millions)	Interest Paid on Debt ($millions)	Interest paid per capita ($)
1905	378	111	266	11	1.77
1915	700	251	449	16	1.97
1925	2 818	401	2 417	135	14.50
1930	2 545	367	2 178	122	11.91
1935	3 206	360	2 846	139	12.77
1940	4 029	757	3 271	129	11.36
1945	15 712	4 414	11 298	319	26.32
1950	16 751	5 106	11 645	440	31.77
1955	17 951	6 688	11 263	478	31.26
1962	22 908	9 680	13 228	803	44.02
1967	30 340	14 375	15 965	1 156	57.76
1971	42 976	25 653	17 322	1 780	83.25
1973	51 718	34 262	17 456	2 105	96.43

Q Your battle against inflation: who is that battle to benefit, the sort of comfortable middle class of the country or is it to benefit the poor of the country?

A If you want to know the answer, ask yourself whom inflation hurts most. Inflation hurts most those people who are less able to defend themselves against the consequences of inflation: those people who are on fixed incomes, that is the pensioners, the retired, the aged people or those who are infirm in one way or another, those who are not members of a strong economic group; companies or owners ... can always get around inflation by increasing their rents or their professional fees or the price of their products. Even the workers in strong trade unions can protect themselves quite easily against inflation by banding together as they do and bargaining very toughly with the big companies and making sure they are as far ahead of the game as they can be. So whom does inflation hurt most? It hurts the little people, the people who don't belong to big unions, who don't belong to big corporations, who are on fixed incomes, or who are workers in either weak unions or ununionized sections of the society. These are the people who are hurt by inflation and these are the people also who will be hit hardest by unemployment if as a result of inflation the Canadian economy loses its grip on some of its foreign market.

Q Sir, ... you stated that you are willing to accept 6 per cent unemployment and that's falling right into all these terrible conditions which you have just elucidated on.

A But you see the choice isn't between inflation or unemployment. The choice is that if you have inflation you have, as I said, increasing unemployment and you have the weakening of the whole society, of the whole value of your dollar. Therefore, the choice is between: fighting inflation and eventually strengthening, not only the little man, the unprotected, but the economy to boot; or not fighting inflation and then let everyone who can run faster than inflation, those who are strong and able and who can defend themselves, keep ahead of the game, to the eventual result that the little poor people will be left further and further behind. That is the choice.[8]

Unfortunately, the policy of "wrestling inflation to the ground" did not prevent what became known as *stagflation* which means that prices increase sharply while unemployment is also rising.

In the mid-1970s, the introduction of *wage and price controls* showed how serious the problem of instability had become. The Canadian government, in October, 1975, announced a program which set out ceilings on price increases and wage settlements. The Anti-Inflation Board (AIB) was created to supervise the program. The hope was to "dampen the fires of inflation"; Canadians agreed

EQUIPMENT BY HOUSEHOLDS FOR CANADA, SELECTED YEARS MAY
1961 TO APRIL 1973[9]
(THOUSANDS)

| | May 1961 | May 1965 | May 1970 | May 1971 | May 1972 | April 1973 | Per Cent Increase 1961-73 | Percentage of Households Owning Equipment | | | | | |
								1961	1965	1970	1971	1972	1973
Cooking Stoves, gas & electric	3 388	4 035	5 110	5 370	5 738	5 919	74.7	75.5	83.1	90.5	92.9	93.9	94.5
Electric Refrigerators	4 123	4 648	5 557	5 677	6 026	6 181	49.9	91.8	96.0	98.4	98.2	98.7	98.6
Home Freezers	592	1 099	1 879	1 971	2 172	2 344	295.9	13.2	22.6	33.3	34.1	35.6	37.4
Electric Washing Machines	3 856	4 184	4 724	4 623	4 814	4 838	25.5	85.9	86.2	83.7	80.0	78.9	77.2
Clothes Dryers (Electric and gas)	657	1 331	2 502	2 491	2 781	2 990	355.1	14.6	27.4	44.3	43.1	45.5	47.7
Automatic Dishwashers	66	133	426	498	564	670	915.2	1.5	2.7	7.5	8.6	9.2	10.7
Radios	4 322	4 663	5 489	5 622	5 961	6 124	41.7	96.3	96.1	97.2	97.3	97.6	97.7
Television	3 659	4 495	5 419	5 554	5 850	6 017	64.4	81.5	92.6	96.0	96.1	95.8	96.0
Colour T.V.			686	1 065	1 478	2 080	203.2*			12.2	18.4	24.2	33.2
Phonographs & record players	2 124	2 868	3 932	4 049	4 332	4 532	113.4	47.3	59.1	69.6	70.1	70.1	72.3
Automobiles	3 087	3 638	4 388	4 481	4 720	4 885	58.2	68.8	75.0	77.7	77.5	77.3	78.0
One automobile per household	2 725	3 034	3 438	3 437	3 590	3 592	31.8	60.7	62.5	60.9	59.5	58.8	57.3
Two or more automobiles per household	362	604	950	1 044	1 130	1 294	257.5	8.1	12.4	16.8	18.1	18.5	20.7

* 1970-1973.

1. Which items show the sharpest increase?
2. Do you find the figures for any of the items surprising? If so, which ones?
3. What do the figures suggest about Canadian values?

this was a desirable goal, but many questioned the government's methods. Not since World War II had the government resorted to so drastic an approach.

OPPOSITION TO WAGE AND PRICE CONTROLS

The Canadian Labour Congress was one of the first to denounce the Trudeau government's wage and price controls. The following are excerpts from the CLCs first public reaction:

The Canadian Labour Congress, after having thoroughly considered the federal government's Wage and Price Control Programme, rejects it on the grounds that it is highly inequitable [unfair]. . . .

———————

. . . [this] government is no longer concerned about unemployment. Rather, it has opted for a policy which, in its impact, will lead only to higher rates of unemployment while at the same time failing to treat the root causes of inflation. As such, the Congress adamantly opposes this cold, calculated move by the government to fight inflation on the backs of all working men and women in Canada.

———————

It is an easy job to police the controls on wages. They are set out in black and white in collective agreements. Collective bargaining is also conducted in the glare of the public spotlight while price increases take place behind the closed doors of the corporate boardrooms. It will be impossible to provide any meaningful surveillance of the practices of 1,500 large corporations with an Anti-Inflation Board limited to a staff of 200. . . . [10]

1. What objections to the price and wage guidelines are mentioned by the CLC?
2. If you were a wage earner and your salary increase were limited by the government's guidelines to a small amount, say 3%, what would your attitude be? How would the following influence your attitude:
(a) cost of living?
(b) reports of salary increases in other industries?
(c) feelings about growing government influence?
(d) the hope that inflation can be checked?
(e) your view of "the good life"?
(f) warnings from some people that overconsumption now may deny future Canadians a decent standard of living?

FEDERAL-PROVINCIAL RELATIONS IN MATTERS OF MONEY

Though one effect of World War II was to create "Big Government", one outstanding feature of present government in Canada is the "tug o' war" between the federal government and the provincial govern-

How governments tackle economic instability

Fifty years ago, governments in Canada played a much smaller role in the economy than they do now. Canadians accepted the *business cycle*; that is, the alternation of "booms"—when business was good—and "busts"—when business was slow. During a depression, businesses reduced spending and borrowing and laid off employees. Banks, therefore, built up reserves of money and could lower interest rates. Once money was cheaper to obtain, businesses would once again begin to borrow and expand. More men would be hired, incomes would rise, the demand for products would increase and another "boom" would follow. In other words, when economic times were poor, unemployment was the threat to stability, but inflation was not. When times were good, inflation was a problem, but there was little unemployment. In any event, governments were reluctant to interfere with the business cycle.

Two developments changed the view that governments should stay aloof from the workings of the economic system. One was the Depression of the 1930s, when business stagnated year after year and unemployment stayed at record levels. The creation of the Bank of Canada in 1934 gave the federal government the means of influencing interest rates, even though manipulating the money supply was not enough to break the depression. The second was World War II, which, although it helped end the depression, also demonstrated the greatly expanded role that government might need to play in Canada's economic life. During the war, the Canadian government implemented *price and wage controls* to ensure stability during the conduct of the war effort.

Once the war ended, the government removed price and wage controls, but there were indications that "Big Government" was a permanent fixture in Canadian life. As announced in its White Paper on Employment and Income, released in April, 1945, the federal government planned to use its authority as a means of managing the national economy and improving the level of prosperity for all Canadians. To do so, borrowing from the ideas of economist John Maynard Keynes,* would mean the use of government spending to forestall depression, and the increase of taxes in "boom" times to build up funds in the federal treasury.

This simple illustration shows that economic stability in the past was threatened *either* by inflation *or* by unemployment. In good times, inflation was the danger; in bad times, it was unemployment. Governments had little direct involvement; the challenge of maintaining some kind of balance, so that neither inflation nor unemployment occurred in extreme form for very long was handled by

*John Maynard Keynes, the British economist, published his book *The General Theory of Employment, Interest and Money* in the mid-1930s. His theme was that a government should spend—not save—in times of depression or economic slowdown. By putting money into socially useful public works, such as hospitals, highways and schools, governments could stimulate the economy in general without competing with private companies.

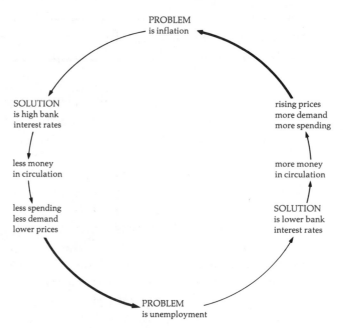

PROBLEM
is inflation

rising prices
more demand
more spending

more money
in circulation

SOLUTION
is lower bank
interest rates

PROBLEM
is unemployment

less spending
less demand
lower prices

less money
in circulation

SOLUTION
is high bank
interest rates

The Consumer Price Index

In the 1970s, Canadians as never before were anxious about the continual rise in prices. Watching the Consumer Price Index became a nation-wide activity.

The consumer price index measures the movement from month to month in retail prices of goods and services bought by a representative cross-section of the Canadian urban population. . . .

Since April 1973, the index has been based on expenditures in 1967 of families ranging in size from two to six persons, with annual incomes of $4,000 to $12,000, living in urban centres with metropolitan populations exceeding 30,000. . . .

Between 1972 and 1973 the rate of change in the CPI, as measured by calculating the difference between annual average indexes, accelerated to 7.6% compared to an average year-to-year change in the previous five years of 3.9%. On the basis of this movement in consumer prices the purchasing power of the consumer dollar declined from 72 cents in 1972 to 66 cents in 1973 relative to $1.00 in 1961.

The acceleration in the rate of price change was mainly attributable to a sharp rise in the rate of advance of food prices although notable price increases were also recorded for housing and clothing. Food prices, rising over 14% between 1972 and 1973, were responsible for almost half of the rise in the CPI between these two years. The major contributors to this largest year-to-year food price increase since 1951 were meat, fresh produce and eggs. [12]

supply and demand. Banks and other businesses made the key decisions.

Since the 1930s, governments have had to devise more and more ways of keeping the private enterprise system stable. They have intervened more and more through *monetary* policies, such as "tight money"—restricting the money supply—and changing the value of Canadian money in relation to money in other countries (for example, devaluation of the dollar).

Even more important have been *fiscal* policies. For example, by increasing or decreasing personal and corporation income taxes, governments have endeavoured to dampen or increase consumer and business demands on the economy.

In the 1970s, the Trudeau government found that the usual ways of influencing the economy were inadequate. Faced with mounting inflation, the government resorted to *wage and price controls* in 1975.

What were the arguments for, and the criticisms of, the government's policy of wage and price controls?

---

ments. This is, of course, one of the oldest themes in Canadian history, but World War II complicated things considerably. The federal government had assumed wide powers of taxation as part of the generally increased powers needed to conduct the war effort. The provinces, some more grudgingly than others, conceded that this centralization of power was necessary during the wartime emergency.

With the end of the war, however, the federal government was not prepared to give up its position of strength. The more it kept its wartime authority, the more effectively it could influence the economy in the future.*

The provinces, particularly Ontario and Quebec, were anxious to recover some of their former powers and to enlarge their shares of government revenue. A serious clash was unavoidable. When Ottawa proposed in 1945, to take control of **succession duties**, in addition to its control over income and corporation taxes, hard bargaining followed. No plan that would satisfy all the provinces could be devised. Therefore the federal government made separate, yearly agreements with each province.

The need to constantly discuss plans for dealing with the many issues involving both levels of government, led to regular meetings of many different kinds of officials. This need increased with the growth in provincial responsibilities, especially in the 1960s and 1970s, and with the corresponding explosion of provincial-municipal costs. Education, health and welfare and public works were particular fields in which costs soared.

*See page 26.

inheritance tax; that is, tax that is collected on possessions, property, money and other assets that a deceased person leaves to others.

The issue of equity: are we our brothers' keepers?

One of the measures of a democratic society is the extent to which it achieves *equity* for its population as a whole. The goal of achieving a fair distribution of a society's goods and services, of equalizing opportunity for all, involves many individuals, groups and institutions. In the final analysis, governments play a key role in the process, sometimes taking the lead, sometimes reacting to pressures applied by business organizations, unions, and the other interest groups in society.

Social security is the term used to describe government programs which provide supplementary income for those who cannot manage entirely on their own. Other forms of government action include setting improved health standards, and providing for better education, manpower training, improved housing and working conditions, and *affirmative action** on behalf of those groups that would otherwise be denied equality of opportunity.

From a practical point of view, the whole society gains when its human resources are fully developed. From a human point of view, a society is healthier when suffering and privation are minimized and a decent standard of living is recognized as the right of all rather than the privilege of a minority.

These pictures show in a simple way the contrast between Canada's economic system approximately a half century ago and now.

The Rowell-Sirois Report of 1940 was the result of a royal commission appointed by the Canadian government during the Depression. The Report, the first since Confederation was a thorough study of the Canadian system of government. One of the main concerns was federal-provincial relations—and the need to redefine the powers and responsibilities of each level of government. Because of the war, the Report was put on the shelf. Yet its findings were still very true for the postwar situation.

*Affirmative action implies the intention to equalize opportunities for disadvantaged persons, rather than merely to give them token support.

The Federal-Provincial Conference, a distinctly Canadian institution, developed over the years. Such conferences are held annually by the prime minister and premiers and also by the various cabinet ministers and senior civil servants. Though a federal-provincial conference does not have the power to pass laws, it often makes decisions that are put into effect based on the negotiations among governments. Once a federal provincial plan, in which the federal government is contributing money, is worked out, it is difficult for an individual province to opt out. If it does, it may be passing up the chance to receive a particular grant of federal funds.

1. In what ways might the federal-provincial conference be thought of as a *fourth* level of government (besides municipal, provincial and federal)?
2. What kinds of threats may it pose to "responsible government"?

What differences can you observe about the size of each part, and the relationship between the parts?

INCOME MAINTENANCE (WELFARE)

Although old age pensions were first introduced in 1927, government responsibility for welfare in Canada really began in the 1940s, after the Depression had demonstrated the need for such a program. In 1940, the federal government made arrangements with the provinces and passed an act to provide unemployment insurance. Then the Marsh Report, submitted to the cabinet early in 1943, advocated a complete program of social insurance. One of the recommendations, family allowances, was implemented in the following year.

The old age pension scheme was altered in 1951. The new act brought in payments, without any means test, to all persons over the age of seventy who had lived in Canada for ten years. Since then, the monthly payments have been increased and the age for receiving benefits reduced to sixty-five. An added feature is the guaranteed income supplement, available to pensioners who lack another source of income. The Canada Pension Plan and the associated plan in Quebec were initiated in 1965 to provide further retirement benefits, disability allowances and survivors' benefits.

Like the Canada Pension Plan, the Canada Assistance Plan was set up in the 1960s.This comprehensive program eventually brought together many schemes that had grown up piece-meal over recent years. Also a product of federal-provincial cooperation, it is designed to cover mothers' allowances, blind and disabled persons' benefits, child welfare, community development services and a range of other projects.

OTHER PROGRAMS

There are many examples of developments in recent years which have been aimed at improving life for greater numbers of Canadians.

Labour standards legislation: Once concerned mainly with minimum wages, hours of work, and protection against loss of livelihood through injury, laws about labour standards have expanded to include holidays with pay, maternity leave, non-discrimination in hiring practices, and laws requiring employers to give advance notice of large-scale dismissals (such as those that might result from automation).

Housing laws: As the scarcity and rising costs of housing have become more critical, the provision of low-cost houses has become a pressing need. There is also greater recognition that people who rent their homes can benefit from rent review boards which examine rent increases.

Human rights commissions: Provincial governments have established such bodies to investigate grievances of disadvantaged groups and supervise compensation for them. Many studies have been conducted into cases where human rights have been denied the poor, immigrants, native peoples and female wage-earners. There is a greater awareness of the problems of bias and prejudice in the media, textbooks and so on. Several provinces have appointed *ombudsmen*, to whom people can appeal directly for assistance.

Consumer protection: All Canadians, in whatever part of society, are consumers. A great deal of attention has been drawn in recent years to such issues as rising costs of goods, faulty merchandise and other problems facing the Canadian consumer.*

*See Chapter 14.

ORGANIZED LABOUR IN CANADA: EQUITY FOR THE WAGE-EARNER

Canada's earliest labour organizations pre-date Confederation, and unions were legally recognized more than a hundred years ago, in 1872. By World War I, however, only a small minority of wage-earners were members of unions. Although the Winnipeg General

Strike (1919) demonstrated both the strength of anti-labour feeling and the potential influence of organized labour, the labour movement remained weak well into the 1930s.

On the eve of World War II, the picture was beginning to change, and in the past 30-40 years the power of organized labour has grown considerably.

MILESTONES

1937:   The strike at the General Motors plant in Oshawa, Ontario. The strike by a local of the United Auto Workers of America (U.A.W.) was met with militant opposition, including that of the provincial government led by Mitchell Hepburn. Although the union did not gain formal recognition as the workers' bargaining agent, it did succeed in negotiating a contract.

1940:   Canadian Congress of Labour (CCL) formed to represent industrial workers.

1945:   Strike at the Ford plant in Windsor, Ontario. The result was the acceptance of the "Rand formula", whereby every employee affected by the bargaining, whether union member or not, had the equivalent of his union dues collected by the company and turned over to the union. This "check off" procedure was subsequently to become a common feature of union contracts.

1949:   Asbestos strike at Thetford Mines, Quebec. The result of this bitter strike was improved status in Quebec for the Canadian and Catholic Confederation of Labour (now the Confederation of National Trade Unions, or CNTU).

1956:   The Canadian Labour Congress (CLC) was formed, by a merger of the Canadian Congress of Labour (CCL) and the Trades and Labour Congress (TLC).
         The CLC became the dominant labour organization in Canada, with more than 7 500 affiliated locals by the mid-1970s. Three out of every four union members were associated with the CLC.

1961:   Formation of the New Democratic Party, successor to the CCF Party, with official backing from the CLC.

1964:   Formation of CUPE (Canadian Union of Public Employees) as a result of a merger of unions representing government employees.

1967:   The Public Service Staff Relations Act granted the right to strike to federal civil servants, except those essential to "safety and security".

1976:   The Canadian Labour Congress called for a nation-wide day of protest against the federal government's price and wage guidelines.

TOP: *Voting on the first negotiated contract with G.M., 1937.* BOTTOM: *The Asbestos Strike, Thetford Mines, Quebec, 1949*

A vegetable farmer in Ontario housed a family of eleven in a ramshackle barn while they picked his cucumbers alongside a crew of Caribbean farm workers. A team of investigators sent by the Minister of Manpower and Immigration commented: "We saw the inside of this filthy, drafty barn . . . The French-Canadian family would not speak to us, probably because the owner was present." The investigators went on to uncover poverty, sickness, and, at times, subhuman working and living conditions among the seasonal farm workers in Southwestern Ontario. Their recommendations, published in August 1973, suggested that Ontario farmers" . . . take a closer look at working conditions and wages paid to their seasonal help and cease the exploitation of—in many cases—defenceless workers and their families . . ." The investigators, interestingly enough, did not recommend that farm workers be included under the protection of the Ontario Labour Relations Act. They continued the damaging myth that farm workers are a special breed of workers, entitled to public pity and the paternalism of farmers but not ready for safeguarding under the law.[14]

TEN LARGEST UNIONS—10 YEAR COMPARISON 1963-1972[13]

1963	Membership	1972	Membership
1. United Steelworkers of America (AFL-CIO-CLC)	90 000	1. United Steelworkers of America (AFL-CIO-CLC)	165 055
2. United Automobile, Aerospace and Agricultural Implement Workers (AFL-CIO-CLC)	61 000	2. Canadian Union of Public Employees (CLC)	157 919
3. United Brotherhood of Carpenters and Joiners (AFL-CIO-CLC)	60 200	3. Public Service Alliance of Canada (CLC)	129 652
4. National Union of Public Employees (CLC)	52 900	4. United Automobile, Aerospace and Agricultural Implement Workers (CLC)	102 933
5. International Association of Machinists (AFL-CIO-CLC)	40 400	5. United Brotherhood of Carpenters and Joiners (AFL-CIO-CLC)	74 362
6. International Woodworkers of America (AFL-CIO-CLC)	37 900	6. Quebec Teachers' Corporation (Ind.)	70 000
7. International Bro. of Teamsters (Ind.)	37 300	7. International Bro. of Teamsters (Ind.)	60 560
8. International Bro. of Pulp, Sulphite and Paper Mill Workers (AFL-CIO-CLC)	36 600	8. Service Employees' National Federation (CNTU)	56 603
9. International Brotherhood of Electrical Workers (AFL-CIO-CLC)	35 500	9. International Brotherhood of Electrical Workers (AFL-CIO-CLC)	56 026
10. Canadian Brotherhood of Railway, Transport and General Workers (CLC)	32 200	10. International Woodworkers of America (AFL-CIO-CLC)	53 158

The History and Development of the Canadian Labour Movement [15]

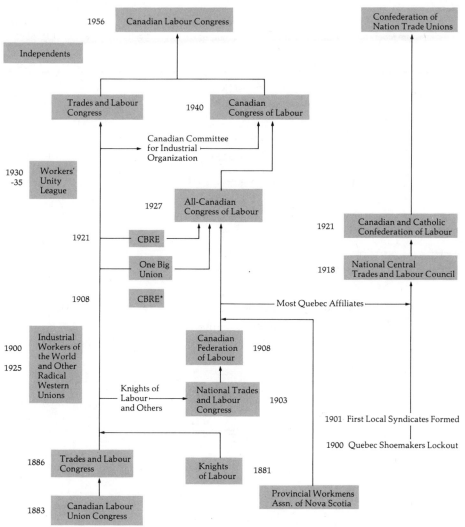

1956   Canadian Labour Congress

Independents

Trades and Labour Congress

1940   Canadian Congress of Labour

Confederation of Nation Trade Unions

Canadian Committee for Industrial Organization

1930 -35   Workers' Unity League

1927   All-Canadian Congress of Labour

1921   CBRE

One Big Union

1908   CBRE*

1921   Canadian and Catholic Confederation of Labour

1918   National Central Trades and Labour Council

Most Quebec Affiliates

1900 / 1925   Industrial Workers of the World and Other Radical Western Unions

Canadian Federation of Labour   1908

Knights of Labour and Others

National Trades and Labour Congress   1903

1901 First Local Syndicates Formed

1900 Quebec Shoemakers Lockout

1886   Trades and Labour Congress

Knights of Labour   1881

1883   Canadian Labour Union Congress

Provincial Workmens Assn. of Nova Scotia

1873-1877 Canadian Labour Union
1871 Local Trade Assemblies Begin to Emerge
1867 Knights of St. Crispin
1825-1860 Numerous Weak and Isolated Locals
1800-1825 Scattered Friendly Societies and Labour Circles

*Canadian Brotherhood of Railway Employees

447

THE EXTENT OF UNIONIZATION[16]

Industry	Women			Men		
	Paid workers	Union members	Union members as percentage of paid workers %	Paid workers	Union members	Union members as percentage of paid workers %
Agriculture	18,000	46	0.3	81,000	131	0.2
Manufacturing	485,000	148,559	30.6	1,501,000	629,997	42.0
Construction	28,000	1,102	3.9	462,000	259,906	56.3
Transportation, communications & other utilities	131,000	55,234	42.2	614,000	302,611	49.3
Trade	536,000	31,399	5.9	839,000	63,240	7.5
Services	1,320,000	251,135	19.0	847,000	178,687	21.1
Public Administration	177,000	84,202	47.6	436,000	252,958	58.0
Finance, insurance & real estate	240,000	1,719	0.7	184,000	2,766	1.5
All industries	2,945,000	575,584	19.5	5,160,000	1,801,617	34.9

CANADA'S CHANGING LABOUR FORCE[17]

Among the predominant trends in Canadian society today are the change in the size of the labour force, and the change in the types of jobs which employ the largest numbers of Canadians.

	Share of Total Employment		
	1960	1970	1980
Agriculture	11.4	6.5	4.1
Forestry	1.6	0.9	0.8
Fishing	0.3	0.3	—[2]
Mining, Oil, and Gas	1.6	1.6	1.5
Manufacturing	23.8	22.7	17.1
Construction	6.5	6.0	6.3
Electric, Water, and Gas Utilities	1.2	1.1	0.8
Transportation, Storage, and Communication	8.4	7.7	7.1
Wholesale and Retail Trade	17.1	16.8	16.5
Finance, Insurance, and Real Estate	3.8	4.6	4.9
Community, Business, and Personal Services	18.6	25.7	34.4
Public Administration	5.8	6.2	6.5
Total Economy	100.0	100.0	100.0

1. Which of the occupations listed are primarily rural? Which ones are primarily urban?

2. Which occupation shows the largest increase in its "share of total employment"?

Ideas from the social sciences: labour economics

For many Canadians, the concepts involved in the history of organized labour are unfamiliar. Yet a great part of the population are, or will be, affected by organized labour, unions, union dues, strikes, and collective bargaining.

Consider the following situations.

The case of Theodore B.

Theodore B. finishes high school and takes a job working as a stock boy in a small warehouse. Theodore's boss is a friend of the family. He pays Theodore a good salary, besides such "fringe benefits" as safe working conditions, satisfactory hours of work and a company pension plan. Theodore enjoys his relationship with his boss.

1. If Theodore has some grievance on the job, what courses of action are open to him?
2. If business slows down and Theodore's boss has to lay Theodore off, how do you think he would let Theodore know?

As an individual, Theodore seems well situated in his job and able to deal with any problems that may arise. The company is small, and the relationship between employer and employee is good. There would seem to be little, if any, need for a workers' organization.

Consider the following possibilities, however. What if:

—the warehouse is sold to a new owner who lives in a different city and employs a manager who is expected to improve the company's profits?

—it is decided that all salaries are to be frozen for at least six months, in spite of the rapidly rising cost of living?

—it is decided that hours of work are to be reorganized, so that employees will start work an hour earlier and have a shorter lunch break?

The Case of Isadora K.

Isadora K. works in a large factory that produces small household items. An immigrant, she speaks very little English and has no friends at work. She works the 4 p.m. to midnight shift, five days a week, but is often required to stay overtime. Isadora is allowed a half-hour lunch break and one 15-minute coffee break a day, the beginning and end of which are signalled by bells.

On a summer day, the temperature in the factory often reaches unbearable heights, but the women must keep their machines running. If they take extra breaks, they are docked time. This week Isadora's child was home ill, and Isadora left her machine twice to telephone the girl. Each time she had to go a block away to use a pay phone, because the office phone was "for business calls only". Because she had to leave the building, she had to punch out and lose pay. Isadora would like to explain her dilemma to someone, but her supervisor never talks to the women unless they are making mistakes or not working fast enough; otherwise, he is not around.

1. If Isadora has some grievance on the job, what courses of action are open to her?

2. If the work slows down and Isadora is laid off or fired, what can she do?

Isadora's situation is already difficult. She is just managing to keep her job and to endure the conditions of work.

Consider the following possibilities, however. What if:

—the supervisor tries to fire Isadora because she cannot speak English?

—Isadora decides to argue with her supervisor over the loss of time incurred while she makes her phone calls?

—a union were to organize the workers into a group so there could be a procedure for dealing with their grievances?

Unions, which are associations of workers, are organized to advance the interests of their members in terms of wages, working conditions and so on. By acting collectively, rather than individually, workers can exert more influence on employers.

In *collective bargaining*—direct negotiation with management by union representatives on behalf of all union members—the parties may reach agreement through discussion and compromise. If not, they can try *conciliation*, whereby a neutral third party is called in to try to find a solution. If disagreement continues, the next step may be *binding arbitration*; both parties agree to accept the decision that is drawn up by a third party after hearing the arguments from both sides.

If negotiations break down at any point, the union may be able to call a *strike*. Strikes are supposed to be the last resort in collective bargaining, and they often enable the union to put strong pressure on an employer. On the other hand, employers (management) can resort to *lockouts*, refusing to allow employees to return to work until the union has agreed to a settlement.

(April 20, 1972)

". . . to speed up the routine, I wondered if we could get our work to rule, mutual accusations of impossible demands and not negotiating in good faith over by lunch, and do the confrontation, strike, lockout and final settlement bit in time for supper . . ."

1. You are the editor of a magazine published by a union. Write an editorial in which you state reasons why unions are beneficial.

2. You are the manager of the public relations department of a company. Write an editorial in which you state reasons why unions are harmful.

3. You are a free-lance writer who does not belong to a union and who depends on businesses to buy your material. Write a letter to the editor of your local paper in which you explain the effects on people like you of the rising prices and wages resulting from costly contract settlements.

As long ago as 1967, the Economic Council of Canada pointed out that more people are expected to enter the Canadian labour force between 1965 and 1980 than will enter the labour forces of Britain, West Germany, and Italy combined, despite the fact that the 1965 population of these three countries was 155 million, in Canada only 20 million. This growth is of course in part due to net immigration, but more to natural increase—the "baby boom" of the 1950s—and to an anticipated rise in the number of working women.[18]

3. What are the possible consequences of the trends concerning the size and make-up of the labour force for each of the following:

   (a) the trend toward urbanization?

   (b) the future of rural areas?

   (c) the quality of life, for example, education, social services, housing?

What is progress? Choices for the future

Growth, stability, equity—the broad goals of our economic system. But what do these terms mean to you as an individual, both now and in the future?

Does growth mean being able to accumulate as much wealth and power as your potential allows, or does it mean progress which will benefit not only yourself but others too? Does stability mean "marking time" or even a return to a 1950s standard of living, or does it mean controlling the *rate* of growth so we do not overburden the economic system with inflation and excessive spending? Does equity mean "welfare" for those people who seem unwilling to work as you do and who can be a burden to others, or is it a sharing by the more fortunate with the less fortunate?

Some people listened to or read Prime Minister Trudeau's speeches and heard in them threats to do away with the free enterprise system. Businessmen and labour leaders, in particular, interpreted Trudeau's remarks as a prelude to increased government intervention and controls on the system. Rather than a cooperative venture between big business, labour and government—in the true sense of a mixed economy—they saw Trudeau's message as undisguised government control over the economy.

Whatever your answers to these questions are, a growing number of people the world over are questioning the very meaning of the word "progress". Prime Minister Pierre Trudeau, in an interview broadcast over CTV on December 27, 1975 and again in a speech to the Canadian Club in Ottawa on January 19, 1976, tried to describe a "new society" for the future. In his remarks, Prime Minister Trudeau said that our free market system seems out of joint. Our world has changed, and with that change must come changes in our institutions and values. He called for "a different society, a new society, one where the net human benefit would be the important thing rather than gross national product; where the good life would replace the life of more; where the value of people would be judged not by what they owned but what they are and what they do. . . ."

Mr. Trudeau's speeches pointed out to Canadians that we have

452

choices to make about our future, and we are responsible for making those choices which, made now, could determine the quality of life in Canada for years to come.

1. (a) If you were told that by reducing your present level of consumption (from the amount of money you spend on luxuries, to the kind and amount of food you eat, to the amount of electricity you use) you would ensure an adequate supply of these things for future generations of Canadians, would you agree to cut back?
(b) If you had to cut back in two areas, what would you give up and why?
2. How do you think Canadians on the whole could be convinced to cut back on the things they buy or consume?
3. Do you think people should reduce consumption just as a precautionary measure for the future? Why or why not?
4. In seeking to achieve growth, stability and equity in our economic system, what are the roles of (a) the individual, (b) business, (c) organized labour,(d) governments, (e) other organizations?

13

Canada in a changing world

There is no natural, immutable or permanent role for Canada in today's world. . . . To be liked and to be regarded as good fellows are not ends in themselves.[1]

Canadians have become accustomed to thinking themselves some of the most fortunate people in the world. Particularly since World War II, the nation has enjoyed a high standard of wealth, health and opportunity. In school we learn about our vast storehouses of resources, stable institutions and responsible leaders. Even past wars have brought economic growth rather than the destruction of our landscape.

Indeed, Canada's war service and postwar efforts to help less developed nations through the United Nations and other agencies have been a source of pride to Canadians. Other countries tended to regard Canada as a well-meaning nation which stood for justice, decency and fair play. In a world of "good guys" and "not-so-good guys", Canadians had reason to believe they were on the side of right, the side of democracy and freedom.

Yet there are signs that the future may not be as easy as the past has been, that separating the "good guys" from the "bad guys" will be much more difficult. The enemies, like Germany and Japan, are now allies, and the friends of World War II, like the Soviet Union and China, are part of the Communist world. Furthermore, the number and variety of nations has increased dramatically. Since 1945, the membership of the United Nations* has grown from 51 to more than 140.

*The United Nations is discussed on p. 447 ff.

Of more immediate significance to the average Canadian have been developments like the "energy crisis" of the mid-1970s and the persistent problem of inflation. As the costs of gasoline, heating fuel and groceries shot up, Canadians began to wonder about their assumptions of inevitable progress. Basic needs, including food, shelter and clothing, took on new importance. Moreover, Canada's "inexhaustible" supplies of petroleum, nickel and pulp and paper were being consumed at an unprecedented rate. Other nations began to have "rising expectations" of material progress and to question the privileged position of countries like Canada.

Suddenly the world had become a much more complex place. Canada could no longer take for granted its relations with the rest of the world. The clear-cut associations of the past, with the British Empire, the dominant western nations, the winners of World War II, became blurred. The Empire, of which Canada had been a leading member, was shattered; in its place stood the Commonwealth with all its tensions between the "have" nations like Canada, and the "have not" nations like the former British colonies in Africa. The major forces in world affairs were now the "super powers", the United States, the USSR and China, the latter often under leaders hostile to the West*. The many new nations in Asia, Africa and the Middle East were a new factor on the international scene.

*The term commonly used for North America and Western Europe; the United States and countries with close ties to it.

By the 1970s, the once apparently clear separation of countries into Communist or capitalist, totalitarian or democratic, rich or poor, had been thrown into confusion. The Communist bloc, dominated by the Soviet Union in the 1950s had been fragmented, and Russia competed with China for influence. The economic systems of the Soviet Union and the United States, once so different, were beginning to develop some common characteristics such as government planning and regulation. Rich countries like the United States suffered from recession, while some poor countries, especially if they possessed commodities like oil, attained new levels of wealth and power.

Canada and the United States

In foreign affairs, Canada has more to do with the United States than with any other nation. Sharing a continent with so powerful and prosperous a neighbour, Canada has been exposed to outside influences as have few nations in modern history. Generally the relations between the two countries have been harmonious, and although there have been times of misunderstanding, the two have been friends and allies since before the beginning of the twentieth century. Circumstances of the last few years have, if anything, increased the trend toward interdependence. On the other hand, the easy relationship of the decades since World War II is being tested as world conditions change and Canadians examine their feelings about United States' influence in their country.

ISSUES OF ECONOMICS (FOREIGN OWNERSHIP)

The Issue

Canada has always depended heavily on foreign investment—at first from Britain, and since World War I, from the United States. The latter is, at present, the source of more than 75% of all foreign investment in Canada. For many years the U.S. has invested heavily in Canada's *primary* resource industries such as mining, but since 1945, the interest has been extended to many other kinds of business. Canadian subsidiaries—"branch plants"—of some firms whose head offices are in the United States, have been established to satisfy and benefit from the expanding Canadian market.

With investment from the United States came an increase in industrial technology, influence on Canadian economic decisions,

Lester Pearson at the Joint U.S.-Canada Committee on Trade and Economic Affairs, 1954.

456

and initially management personnel. Such investment also led to a greater number of jobs for Canadians, and although the ownership, in principle, lay in the United States, the staff and management have been increasingly Canadian. A prosperous firm could expand, sometimes taking over a Canadian business with the help of loans from banks and other financial institutions.

Foreign ownership is not a problem in all *sectors* of the Canadian economy. The Canadian government has acted to protect "key sectors" against takeover, for example, banks, radio and television, newspapers and magazines, and to some extent the transportation industry. *Public ownership* has been used to protect the Canadian Broadcasting Corporation, Air Canada and the Bank of Canada. Government regulations concerning standards, methods of production, prices and the volume of exports permitted apply to such "key sectors" as energy, although the oil and gas industry is dominated by firms from the United States.

Yet a large part of Canada's economy is not protected against "non-resident" or "foreign" ownership. Such vital natural resource industries as petroleum, mining, and pulp and paper are largely foreign-owned. The same is true of manufacturing industries: automobiles, rubber products, electrical appliances, industrial equipment, fertilizers, drugs, synthetic textiles, and many more are produced by firms which are largely or wholly owned outside Canada.

Canadian Attitudes

Though Canadians have many different views about foreign ownership, four broad categories of opinion may be identified. These range from strongly hostile to openly favourable.

Radical nationalist: At one end of the spectrum, radical nationalists consider foreign ownership an inevitable product of free enterprise. Although few in number, they are generally well-educated and outspoken in arguing that the only solution is government takeover, or *nationalization*, of foreign-owned companies.

Liberal nationalist: Although rejecting government ownership, which the radicals recommend, the liberal nationalists believe in government action to limit foreign ownership and to promote Canadian companies. Groups like the Committee for an Independent Canada (CIC) advocate regulations, tax arrangements and financial support to benefit Canadian enterprise. Walter Gordon, former cabinet minister, Jack McClelland and Mel Hurtig, publishers, and many writers and academics have been prominent spokespersons for this viewpoint.

Laissez-faire: Those who favour a "hands off' role for government, either through distaste for nationalistic policies or through indifference, prefer an open economy. They believe that businesses, whether foreign-owned or Canadian, should be allowed to succeed or fail according to their ability to compete in the marketplace.

Continentalist: At the opposite end of the spectrum from the radical nationalists, the continentalist prefers some kind of common market with the United States. Rather than fearing that close economic ties would lead to domination by the United States, the continentalist believes they would provide opportunities for Canadian businessmen and strengthen the Canadian economy.

The role of government

Although Canadian attitudes to foreign ownership are diverse, there has been a marked increase in public awareness and concern. This has led to pressures on governments to take actions that would at least slow down the rate of foreign influence in the economy. However, it is not easy to describe the *political* effects of public pressure.

The foreign ownership issue is really a double-edged one. Foreign money, or capital, may enter a country in two ways: through *loans* to Canadian companies and governments (indirect investment), which may eventually be paid off, leaving ownership in Canadian hands; or through *purchase* of Canadian companies or the creation of "branch plants" of foreign firms (direct investment), which means foreign ownership. Broadly speaking, the problem is how to limit direct investment which may threaten Canada's control of its own economy, without discouraging indirect investment which is considered necessary to growth and prosperity.

The federal government has been hard-pressed to come up with a policy that would be widely accepted by Canadians. Provincial governments often seem to be more worried about attracting foreign investment than controlling it. A province in the West or the Maritimes may be as worried about controlling investment from "big business" in Toronto or Montreal as from foreign countries. Nevertheless the provinces from time to time have shown concern about foreign ownership of recreational land or non-renewable resources.

Thus faced with the lack of consensus among Canadian interest groups and governments, the federal government has wrestled with the issue of foreign ownership over the past several years. Several studies have been conducted: a task force produced the Watkins Report (1968), so called because of the prominence of economist Melville Watkins; a parliamentary committee produced another report (1970). The most significant study was the one carried out under Herb Gray, the Minister of Revenue. The so-called "Gray Report" became public knowledge in November, 1970 when the journal, *Canadian Forum*, printed what it claimed to be the text of the Report. How the editors obtained the material was not revealed, and for a time the Government declined comment. One reason seemed to be the mixed reaction among Canadians to it, in particular, to its recommendation that the best policy would be to set up a screening agency. Such an agency would oversee the inflow of foreign capital.

Eventually the Government unveiled its policy and Parliament approved an act setting up the Foreign Investment Review Agency. Part 1 of the Act, put into effect in April, 1974, was concerned with foreign takeovers of Canadian companies. The regulations required that foreign takeovers of Canadian businesses worth $250 000 or having a gross income of $3 000 000 must be submitted to the Review Agency.

The second part of the act was delayed until October, 1975, when regulations were implemented concerning investments by companies "in unrelated areas". As with Part 1, regulations were intended to ensure that foreign investment would be of "significant benefit" to Canada. In other words, if an auto manufacturer were to propose taking over a supermarket chain, the company would have to convince the Review Agency that the move would not be harmful to Canadian business, take advantage of Canadian resources, or increase regional disparity.

INCREASING CANADIAN CONTROL

The Foreign Investment Review Agency in its first year of operation (1974-75) claimed substantial benefits for Canada. The following excerpts are taken from the first annual report:

The screening process is providing Canadians with greater opportunities to participate in the direction and management of Canadian industry. For example, roughly two-thirds of the assets transferred to foreign owners were already foreign controlled. In the great majority of these cases the new owners undertook to provide a significant net increase in Canadian participation as shareholders, directors, and/or managers. Only one-third of the assets transferred to foreign owners were accounted for by Canadian controlled firms.

Of the 150 reviewable cases, 92 had been resolved and 58 were still under assessment at the end of the fiscal year. Of the 92 resolved, 63 were allowed, 12 were disallowed, and 17 were withdrawn by the applicant prior to a decision having been reached. The 63 allowed transactions included 3 that were deemed to have been allowed under section 13.

With respect to the 17 withdrawals, it appears that about half occurred because the applicant decided he would not be able to satisfy the test of significant benefit to Canada. Thus, the failure to proceed of roughly 20 of the proposed acquisitions—12 disallowances plus 8 withdrawals—can be attributed to the requirements of the Act. . . .

There were 12 disallowed cases, of which 2 involved foreign controlled vendor companies [those being purchased] and 10 involved Canadian controlled vendor companies. In the 10 disallowed cases involving Canadian controlled vendor companies, the primary reason for disallowance was most frequently a reduction in Canadian ownership without any or sufficient offsetting benefit. The prospect of a major reduction in competition was the primary reason for disallowance in other cases.[2]

ALLOWED CASES: SIGNIFICANT BENEFITS TO CANADA SUMMARIZED BY PRINCIPAL FACTORS OF ASSESSMENT[3]
Fiscal 1974/75

Type of benefit	Number of cases in which that type of benefit was obtained	
	Number	Percent
(a) Positive effect on level and nature of economic activity	54	85.7
Increased employment	43	68.3
New investment	37	58.7
Increased resource processing or use of Canadian goods and services	26	41.3
Additional exports	22	34.9
(b) Increased Canadian participation (as shareholders/directors/managers) in foreign-controlled companies (total of 27 cases)	17	63.0
(c) Improved efficiency, technology, etc.	59	93.7
Improved productivity & industrial efficiency	46	73.0
Enhanced technological development	29	46.0
Improved product variety or innovation	30	47.6
(d) Beneficial impact on competition	19	30.2
(e) Compatibility with national and provincial industrial and economic policies	63	100.0

ISSUES OF ECONOMICS (TRADE)

That 60 per cent of Canada's exports go to the United States and 70 per cent of our imports come from the United States indicate the extent of Canada's interdependence with the American economy. The fact that Canada is one of the United States' best customers, while depending heavily on selling exports on the American market is of major concern. On the surface, it would seem that Canada is particularly vulnerable to pressure from "south of the line".

In the 1960s, the prospect of American *political* pressure seemed to threaten. When Canada entered into trade agreements with Cuba, whose Communist government was anti-American, Canada's minister of trade and commerce found it necessary to assure the United States that such trade would not include strategic materials. When Canada contemplated selling automobiles to Communist China, the American State Department put pressure on the Ford Company of Canada, a subsidiary of the American parent company, to refrain from such trade. Profitable Canadian wheat sales to Communist countries, such as China, whose governments the United States did not approve of, aroused strong American resentment.

"Detente" is the word that has been used to describe the lessening of open hostility among the super powers in the 1970s. The United States officially recognized the People's Republic of China (Communist), following Canada's example (1971) and entered into prolonged negotiations on disarmament with the Soviet Union.* One result has been the beginning of American trade with countries that were once ignored as potential customers. In other words, the United States and Canada are now likely to be competitors on world markets, especially in products such as wheat.

*The Strategic Arms Limitation Talks (S.A.L.T.)

The shifts in world politics and other changes, such as the depletion of non-renewable resources in the United States, tended to alter the problem of American pressure, real or potential, on Canada. Energy supply, with the quadrupling of world petroleum prices, became a central issue of Canadian-American trade in the mid-1970s. American energy needs continued to climb annually, but Canada found that her proven oil reserves might not satisfy her own needs for many more years. Consequently, the Canadian government decided to reduce the quantity of oil exported to the United States. This action raised the possibility of American retaliation, or of pressure for a continental energy system.

HARDY IDEA

The idea of a continental energy policy is remarkably durable; it keeps cropping up despite Canadian yawns and sneers.

Not surprisingly, the advocates of this idea are usually Americans hoping for a relatively easy escape from OPEC domination of their oil supply. The latest is John Connally, who served as governor of Texas and later as secretary of the U.S. treasury. . . .

Mr. Connally proposes a "co-ordinated, co-operative" energy policy between Canada and the United States. That sounds attractive, but in practice it would likely mean co-ordinating Canadian supplies and American demand.

The question is what the U.S. has that Canada needs. There's good reason to hope that Canada can meet her own capital requirements in the next decade. As for export markets, it's true that

461

energy sales to the United States would improve Canada's balance of payments, but surely there are better ways of getting the same result. . . .

A continental energy policy would be a very different proposition from the arrangement under which Canada has so far supplied energy to the U.S. The American government would become a direct participant in what has so far been an internal Canadian matter. American firms and capital have played an important part in developing Canadian oil, but they have done so under regulation by the provincial and federal governments. By definition, a continental energy policy would give the U.S. government a voice in Canadian decisions about energy supply and demand. (Canada, granted, would have a voice in U.S. policy—the usual parity between the mouse and the elephant.)

As long as the American presence in Canadian energy consists only of U.S. firms, not the government itself, Ottawa and the provinces can readily exercise their power. When supplies for Canadian needs grew short, the federal government moved unilaterally to reduce exports. Would this sovereignty survive under an energy treaty between the Canadian and American governments?. . .[4]

CULTURAL ISSUES

Canadians, sharing the continent with such a powerful and productive neighbour are subject to—some would say overwhelmed by—the influence of the American way of life. Of course, most parts of the world, at least the non-Communist countries, have been Americanized to some degree. However, a visitor from the United States is more likely to find himself in familiar surroundings in Canada than anywhere else on the globe. From a Canadian viewpoint, Americanization raises many issues related to the central ones of Canadian "identity" and autonomy. Perhaps the electronic media have had more impact on Canada than any other form of American influence. Radio and television have flooded Canadian audiences with American programming, providing the styles which Canadian producers imitated. Entertainment, in the form of "top 40" music on radio and situation comedies or game shows on television, has tended to be American in content and style, as has the information provided by news programs. Public broadcasting has provided some defence against this process of Americanization. The Canadian Broadcasting Corporation (CBC) has been attempting to encourage and develop Canadian drama, music, variety shows and other expressions of Canadian culture for many years. But except for public affairs programs and sports broadcasts, Canadians have continued to be part of the mass North American audience tuning in to programs that originate in New York or California.

The story of American influence in radio and television is basi-

Canadian identity: the humour of it all

A humour magazine's comment about the "Canadian identity":
"Hard to tell a Canadian from an extremely boring regular . . . person unless he's dressed to go outdoors."[5]

Among the nations of the world, Canadians might be known as the people least sure of who they are. At different times in our history, but perhaps more anxiously in the past ten or twenty years, we have tried to define our national "identity". Perhaps our perennial search for a definition is one of our national characteristics; perhaps the tendency to be too serious about it is another. The following excerpts suggest, however, that the Canadian *sense of humour* is one quality that ought not be overlooked.

Canadians who make a living through humour are conspicuous among the emigrés to the American entertainment industry. In the 1970s Canadians succeeded both as performers (Rich Little, Don Harron, Ted Ziegler, David Steinberg) and behind the scenes as writers, producers and directors (Lorne Michaels, Allan Mannings, Alex Barris). Although most were attracted to television, many went into publishing as well. The staff of the irreverent magazine, *The National Lampoon*, has included both Canadian editors and writers.

DEFINING CANADA

Lister Sinclair, author, playwright and broadcaster, comments on Canada's "qualities":

Like everything else, Canada (from sea to sea) is a bundle of qualities. If we are careful and sensible and lucky, most of these qualities may turn out to be advantages. Otherwise we're in trouble. As the fellow says, we had a chance to combine British government, French culture and American know-how. Instead we're getting French government, American culture and British know-how.[6]

COULD YOU BE A CANADIAN IN DISGUISE?

The following item was included in an article about The National Lampoon, *a magazine published in the United States but known for its Canadian writers and satires about Canada:*

Here's how to find out if you, too, have latent Canadian tendencies:

1. A friend arranges to meet you in a restaurant and arrives an hour late. You say:
    a. "Nice of you to show up."
    b. "Next time I'll bring along my copy of Hawaii."
    c. "How about that! I just got here two minutes before you arrived!"
    d. "Remind me to give you a new watch for your birthday."

2. The color I like best is:
    a. red.
    b. blue.
    c. grey.
    d. white.

3. If I ever get a week off, I would:
    a. go to a luxury hotel in the Caribbean.
    b. paint the garage.
    c have my tonsils out.
    d. get in a lot of golf.

4. I would prefer to be stranded on a desert island with:
    a. a gorgeous movie star.
    b. this month's Playmate.
    c. a tree.
    d. Susan Sontag.

5. I would most like to curl up with:
    a. a racy novel.
    b. a slim volume of verse.
    c. the latest Sears, Roebuck Catalogue.
    d. a great metropolitan newspaper.

6. I would go to see a:
    a. hit musical.
    b. major sports event
    c. partial eclipse of the sun.
    d. rocket launching.

If you picked "c" every time, stop denying your Canadian birthright.[7]

CHARLIE FARQUHARSON SPEAKS

Actor, writer and humorist Don Harron is famous for his character Charlie Farquharson. As Charlie, he has had much to say about the "Canadian identity":

I used to worry 'bout us bein' yer Fifty-first State, but now I think all of 'em is granually movin' up here. I think they're gonna secede by us not really tryin'. But them Yanks aren't dumb. They know we got somethin' u-neek up here. Valeda's [Charlie's wife] allus sayin' yer Yanks has no culture and yer Birtish has too much, and that's us in the middle—smug as a bug.

It's the differnces we got what keep us together (that and everybuddy hatin' yer Air Canda cawfee). But everybuddy in this land has allus been purty pukewarm about all the other parts, sept in November when ther in ther Gray Cups. I think we'll be all right so as we keep a good gripe on arselves.[8]

CANADIAN IDENTITY THE EASY WAY

This imaginary advertisement takes a lighthearted view of the problem of becoming "more Canadian." The item appeared in a paperback book prepared by people associated with the humorous CBC radio program "Inside from the Outside":[9]

464

TORONTO AFTER SIX MONTHS: AN EXILE'S REPORT

This item appeared in the magazine Saturday Review *in 1972. The author, Henry Morgan, a well-known American humorist, had taken up residence in Toronto:*

True: The streets are clean and quite safe.

The people are friendly and only hate Americans as an abstraction.

Things cost more.

Waiters, shopkeepers, and cab drivers are polite.

Wages are low, taxes high.

There are four hundred thousand Italians here.

There are forty thousand Americans.

Most draft-dodgers are on welfare.

French-Canadians call themselves Canadiens and hate everybody.

And one another.

The salami is fake.

Policemen are called constables.

Z is pronounced zed; schedule is shedule.

All the streets are named, and it is infuriating.

Though there are 2,200,000 people, there is a fine sense of openness.

There is no newspaper on Good Friday.

Liquor stores are run by the government.

All American food products and many manufactures have labels in both French and English.

False: Canadians are a distinct people.
   Winters are terrible.
   Lorne Greene is American.
   Everything else you've always believed.[10]

1. Do you think Canadian humour differs from the humour of other nations? Why or why not? What examples can you give?
2. What are the advantages to a nation whose citizens generally have a sense of humour?
3. What other qualities do the documents suggest are part of our identity? What additional ones can you suggest?

---

cally repeated in the other media. American magazines or their Canadian editions* have captured much of the Canadian market. Canadian subsidiaries of publishing houses owned in the United States dominate the Canadian book industry both in popular publications and text books. American films have exerted as much influence on life in Canada as they have in the United States.

*See Chapter 1 for further consideration of this situation.

1. From a TV log, select any ten programs. Which are produced in the United States? in Canada? If for some reason, you were required to select *one* to watch for the rest of the season, which one would you choose? Why?
2. Who decided what television programs will be broadcast? Do you, as a viewer, have any say? Do you think the government should be able to influence the viewing habits of Canadians? Why or why not?
3. What reasons might there be for the popularity of products made in the United States, even when a Canadian product of comparable quality is available?
4. Should Canada protect her products from foreign competition? What advantages would this bring? What disadvantages?
5. What suggestions can you make to persuade people to "buy Canadian"?

WHEN NEIGHBOURS DISAGREE
Under normal circumstances, neighbours can co-exist peacefully and settle differences on mutual problems. Sometimes, however, differences occur on a serious issue and a solution that is satisfactory to both parties is hard to find. Canada and the United States are no

exception. The boundary between them, for example, has caused difficulties on many occasions since the American Revolution more than two centuries ago.

At the turn of this century, the Alaska boundary dispute almost led to a confrontation. Gold had been discovered in the 1890s in the Klondike region of Canada's Yukon. The boundary between Canada and the Alaskan Panhandle, the narrow, jagged strip of land and islands that cut northern British Columbia off from the sea, had never been clearly defined. Nobody cared very much until the question of transporting gold through the boom town of Skagway arose.

Canada clearly had the important gold fields in its territory, but it did not have a definite outlet to the Pacific. However, the sea was the only means of transportation between the Yukon and the rest of Canada.

When no solution was found through talks between officials of the governments of the United States and Great Britain, who still handled Canada's foreign affairs, the problem was submitted to a joint commission. The commission was made up of six officials, three appointed by the United States and three by Great Britain. The British government appointed Canadians as two of its representatives, and a British official as the third. The commission was to be made up of "impartial" people, but the United States named representatives determined to serve their country's interests. In the final analysis, American pressure led to a boundary settlement favourable to the United States.

Seventy-five years later in 1975, a boundary problem of a different sort arose—the *Garrison diversion* controversy. The United States proposed to divert water from the Missouri River, mainly for irrigation of farm land in North Dakota. The excess water was expected to drain into the Red and Souris Rivers. The Canadian government, as well as the government of Manitoba, concluded that the project would cause pollution and increase the dangers of flooding on the rivers flowing through Canadian territory. A disruption of the ecology of these waters was also feared. Such effects would contravene the Boundary Waters Treaty of 1909, which commits Canada and the United States not to pollute waters flowing across the international boundary.

Canada and the United States referred the issue to the International Joint Commission (IJC), formed shortly after the Alaska boundary dispute. The IJC conducted months of hearings on both sides of the border during 1976 and 1977, while work on the project continued.

1. What similarities between the Alaska boundary issue and the Garrison diversion issue can you note?

2. In what ways is Canada now in a better position to deal with the United States than it was at the time of the Alaska boundary issue? Are there ways in which Canada's position is weaker? If so, what are they?

3. Do Canada and the United States now cooperate with each other to a greater or lesser extent than they did at the turn of the century?

Issues of defence: Canada in North America: NORAD

Even before World War II began, the Canadian prime minister, Mackenzie King, recognized that Canada's defence was part of the defence of North America. In a speech on August 20, 1938, King said that Canadians "have our obligations as a good friendly neighbour [of the United States], and one of these is to see that ... our country is as immune from attack or possible invasion as we can reasonably be expected to make it, and that, should the occasion ever arise, enemy forces should not be able to pursue their way either by land, sea or air, to the United States across Canadian territory."[11]

*See p. 285.

During and after World War II, Canada entered into agreements with the United States for the mutual defence of North America.* In 1958, Canada and the United States signed the North American Air Defence agreement (NORAD), which coordinated North American defence. A joint command, headed by an American, with a Canadian officer second-in-command, was placed in charge of the system.

Over the years, various changes have been adopted in the equipment used by both countries, but the NORAD arrangement has been continued. A constant surveillance of Canadian airspace is maintained by Canadian long-range planes, to protect against the intrusion of an unfriendly nation.

The Canadian-American arrangements for defence are based on the assumption that the only direct military threat to Canada would be a confrontation between the super powers. Accordingly, Canada supports international efforts to place limits on the "arms race", and to bring about more cooperation between the super powers in dealing with world conflict.* But, Canada recognizes the existing reality of military power and the importance of maintaining a balance.

*In 1975, in Helsinki, Finland, Canada signed the "Helsinki agreement" resulting from the Conference on Security and Cooperation in Europe. The United States, the USSR and their respective allies agreed to work toward cooperation in non-military matters and a reduction in military manoeuvres that threaten world peace.

Canada and the United States have always had their problems, but Canadians seem to have become more aware of them as a nation since World War II. However, as the world situation changes, it is not only our relations with the United States that pose problems. The period since World War II has been a difficult one for all nations as they struggle to deal with world problems. Even before World War II ended the stage was set for this struggle. Between the

468

The Bomarc missile could be equipped with nuclear warheads as a safeguard against nuclear attack.

Soviet Union and the other Allies, the conflict which came to be known as the "Cold War" had begun to develop. It led to the search by some western nations for a method of protecting themselves against Communist expansion.

The defence of the Western World: NATO

THE COLD WAR AND NATO

The Cold War divided the nations of the world into two fairly solid blocs: the Western bloc, dominated by the United States, and including Canada; and the Communist bloc, dominated by the Soviet Union. Between these rival camps were the non-aligned nations—the Third World. Besides the direct confrontation between the alliances dominated by the two "super powers", the indirect rivalry increased as both sides frequently became involved in the conflicts of the Third World.*

To understand how the Cold War began, we need to look at the situation at the end of the Second World War. In defeating Germany, the combined Allied armies of the United States, Britain and France, along with those of Canada and other allies, had driven the Germans from western Europe and converged on Germany itself. Meanwhile, Soviet armies had not only pushed through eastern Europe and occupied part of Germany, but had also left forces in Bulgaria, Rumania, Hungary and Poland to support Communist-led governments. In 1948, a coup in Czechoslovakia brought that country under a Communist government. This bloc of "satellite states" within the Soviet sphere of influence was what Britain's Winston Churchill referred to when he said that an "Iron Curtain" had been drawn between East and West.

In the West, leadership had fallen to the United States. The former imperial powers like Britain and France had been exhausted by the war, and their many colonies were taking the road to independence.* The Soviet Union was unchallenged as the leader of the Communist world, which included China, after 1949, with the revolution led by Mao Tse-Tung.

*The number of nations in the Third World increased spectacularly in a few years, as former colonies gained their independence.

*As early as 1947, India and the newly created nation of Pakistan gained independence from Britain.

SPIES IN CANADA

An important weapon in the Cold War was espionage. Canada was the scene of one of the early incidents. In September, 1945, Igor Gouzenko, a clerk in the Soviet embassy in Ottawa, turned over to the Canadian government evidence of an elaborate spy ring operating against Canada, the United States and other Western countries formerly allied with the U.S.S.R. The Western democracies viewed the advance of Soviet-directed Communism as a threat to their security.[12]

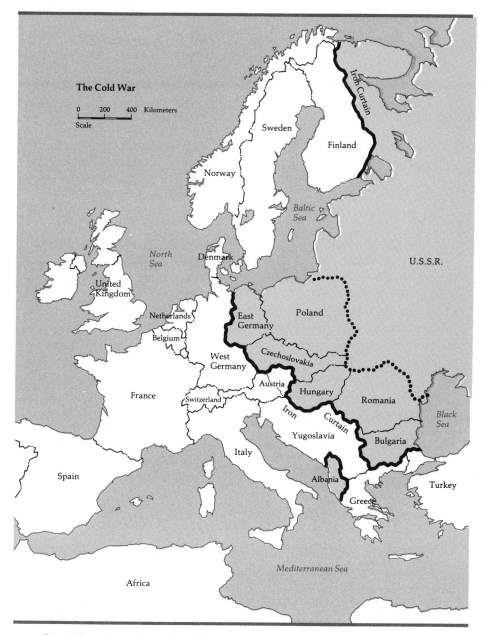

The Cold War

Scale: 0 — 200 — 400 Kilometers

Labels on map: Sweden, Finland, Norway, Iron Curtain, Baltic Sea, Denmark, North Sea, United Kingdom, Netherlands, Belgium, East Germany, Poland, West Germany, Czechoslovakia, Austria, Hungary, Romania, France, Switzerland, Iron Curtain, Yugoslavia, Italy, Bulgaria, Black Sea, Spain, Albania, Greece, Turkey, U.S.S.R., Mediterranean Sea, Africa

In 1945 Canada's armed forces of more than 750 000 were one of the world's largest. Hopeful for peace, Canada reduced that number to approximately 35 000 in all services by 1948. The air force, with a strength of more than 160 000 at the end of the war, was reduced to fewer than 15 000. Much of the equipment of army, navy and air force was sold at bargain prices as "war surplus". Then the realities of the Cold War, signalled by the Korean conflict, forced a drastic reversal of policy, and the 1950s was a decade of rebuilding the military.

Canada shared with other Western countries a concern about Communist expansion. As early as 1947, the minister of external affairs spoke about the need for a military alliance. When the North Atlantic Treaty Organization (NATO) was formed in Washington in April 1949, Canada was a founding member with the United States, Belgium, Denmark, France, Iceland, Italy, Luxembourg, Holland, Norway, Portugal and Great Britain. Greece and Turkey were admitted in 1952. Then, indicating how times had changed, the Federal Republic of Germany* (West Germany) joined in 1955. This was just ten years after her defeat in World War II, and many of her new allies had participated in her defeat.

*Germany had been divided into West Germany, with Bonn as its capital, and East Germany, the latter "behind the Iron Curtain". The city of Berlin, wholly within East Germany was also divided into Communist and non-Communist zones.

Canada, though a founder and strong supporter of the United Nations, did not believe it realistic to "put all its eggs in one basket." The United Nations had not eliminated competition and conflict among nations. Thus Canada's minister for external affairs, Louis St. Laurent, spoke in the House of Commons (April 29, 1948) of the need for a "collective security league," i.e., a military alliance of non-communist countries:

.... We are fully aware...of the inadequacy of the United Nations at the present moment to provide the nations of the world with the security which they require. The realities of this situation must be faced, and the policy of the government in respect of it may be summarized very briefly.[13]

...when I spoke seven months ago at the General Assembly, I stated then that ... it is possible for the free nations of the world to form their own closer association for collective self-defence under article 51 of the charter of the United Nations....

It may be that the free states, or some of them, will soon find it necessary to consult together on how best to establish such a collective security league.... Its purpose...would not be merely negative; it would create a dynamic counter-attraction to communism...the free democracies...would organize so as to confront the forces of communist expansionism with an overwhelming preponderance of moral, economic and military force and with sufficient degree of unity to ensure that ... the free nations cannot be defeated one by one.... We must at all costs avoid the fatal repetition of the history of the pre-war years when the nazi aggressor picked off its victims one by one. Such a process does not end at the Atlantic.... [14]

The NATO charter committed members to collective security. An attack on any one member would be regarded as an attack on all, and all would be obligated to contribute to a war of defence. Canada, in fulfillment of her obligations, stationed an army brigade in Germany and an air division in France.

In the tense atmosphere of the time, support in Canada for NATO was widespread. Fresh in the minds of Canadians was the "Berlin blockade" of 1948, when the Soviet Union tried cutting off contact with Berlin in the hope of forcing the Western powers to abandon the city. An Allied airlift maintained a flow of supplies to Berlin until the blockade was lifted, but the Berlin problem continued into the 1960s, when the construction of the "Berlin wall" dramatized the tension in Europe.

The Warsaw Pact is the term applied to the Soviet Union and her Eastern European allies.

Meanwhile, the Soviet Union organized its Eastern European neighbours into a rival military alliance. When a revolution in Hungary in 1956 threatened the solidarity of the **Warsaw Pact**, Soviet

Foreign policy review

In response to a rapidly changing international situation, the Trudeau government conducted a review of Canada's foreign policy. Shortly after its election in June 1968, the government set up committees to examine the goals, values and methods of Canada's relations with other countries. For nearly two years, interested Canadians, including politicians, political scientists, journalists, business people, labour leaders, financial experts and church leaders, expressed their opinions. The eventual result was the publication, in 1970, of a package of six booklets entitled *Foreign Policy for Canadians*. As a "white paper", the label by which such government publications are known, these booklets set out the guidelines for future decisions about Canada's behaviour in a changing world.

The Canadian Department of National Defence [15]

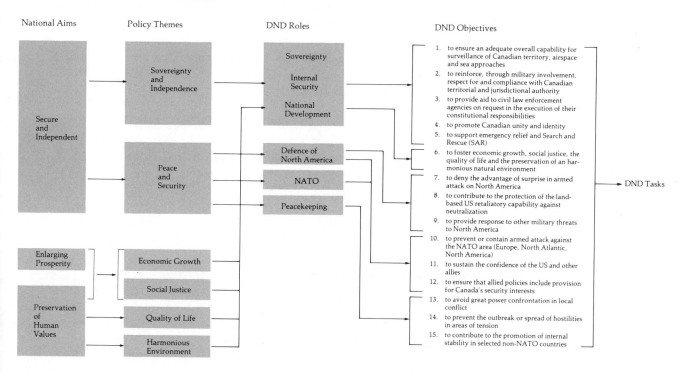

Six policy themes were identified and ranked in order of importance: economic growth, social justice, quality of life, peace and security, and sovereignty and independence. The sixth—harmonious natural environment—was judged to be part and parcel of "quality of life". This order, the government said, reflected those things which "Canada can do best in order to promote its objectives abroad."

473

The *Canadian Annual Review* (1970) presented the following comment and survey of public reaction:

What was most striking in the white paper was the government's evident willingness to abandon the past. Canada's "national interest" was defined as the touchstone of policy, and there was a distinct de-emphasis on playing the role of international "fixer." What was best for Number One, the message seemed to be, was going to be policy. This was most evident, for example, in the high priority given to economic growth. The purpose of Canadian foreign policy now apparently was to serve the interests of Canadian investors and businessmen abroad. Still there was some idealism to be found in the stress on quality of life and social justice, although even this could be interpreted as keeping the natives in their place and the developed countries from drowning in their effluents while the entrepreneurs made money.

The reaction to the results of the reviews of foreign policy, then, was mixed. The *Winnipeg Free Press* on June 26 was disturbed at the de-emphasizing of peace and security in a thermonuclear age. Without this, the newspaper asked, "how can we have much hope in other fields?" The Vancouver *Province* (June 26), relieved that the government "has formally abandoned Lester Pearson's brave attempt to make Canada the boy scout of the world, rushing about the world to do good deeds wherever countries quarrelled," was not at all displeased with the new stress on "dollar signs." The *Montreal Star* was more critical on June 26, correctly noting that "The platitudes flow like wine. We learn that Canada stands four-square for independence, economic growth . . . a posture which is undoubtedly worthy but hardly original." Claude Ryan in *Le Devoir* (June 27) was not amused by the exercise, noting that if the white paper reflected the real concerns of Canadians "ce serait à déspérer non seulement de la future politique étrangère de ce pays, mais aussi de son avenir." In the *Montreal Star* on June 29 James Eayrs was as usual sardonic, witty, nasty, and very much to the point. "Is this the kind of Canada we want?" Eayrs asked, referring to the emphasis on economic growth above all. "This is not foreign policy for Canadians, it is foreign policy for beavers." But even Professor Eayrs was not entirely displeased with the whole message, particularly in its stress on the end of "Canada—the helpful fixer." This, Eayrs said, "is more than the beginning of wisdom, it is a great leap forward."

On balance the Trudeau Doctrine, as Professor Peyton Lyon called it, was a mixed blessing, something for everyone, all things to all men. For the businessmen there was the promise of expanded trade and greater government efforts to increase private investment abroad. For those interested in foreign aid there were warm words —if little cold cash. For those concerned with the destruction of the world's ecological systems there was promise of new efforts by

Canada. For those interested in alliances and military strength, there were no pledges of bigger armies, but at least NATO remained. Not as bad as some had feared. Not as good as some had hoped. How it would all work out in practice over the 1970s remained to be seen.[16]

---

troops moved in quickly to restore a Communist regime. The same was true in Czechoslovakia in 1968.

When the Soviet Union exploded its first atomic bomb in 1949, the bonds of NATO were clearly vital. The same was true in the 1962 Cuban missile crisis.* At that time, President John F. Kennedy of the United States, and Premier Nikita Krushchev of the USSR engaged in a war of nerves brought about by the apparent intention of the Russians to place nuclear missiles on Cuba. In response, the United States effected a naval blockade of the island. In the end, the Soviets decided not to risk American retaliation and the missiles were not installed. Yet the Soviet policy of "peaceful co-existence", declared in 1958, had not apparently removed the danger of nuclear war.

*In 1959, Fidel Castro had engineered a Communist revolution in a country less than 180 km from North America.

More significant was the development by both the United States and the Soviet Union of anti-ballistic missile systems. The effect was a nuclear stalemate, in which neither side seemed capable of aggression against the other without risking massive and instantaneous retaliation.

By the time of the Canadian election of 1968, Canadians were less clear about their military role in NATO, and its value was being questioned. France, where General Charles De Gaulle was leader, doubted whether the United States would actively come to the aid of Europe in the event of a non-nuclear war. In Canada, the cost of maintaining our commitment to NATO was under attack. Prime Minister Trudeau declared that Canada might need to review her role. He noted the changes in world conditions since NATO had been formed twenty years earlier, and questioned the value of Canada's continued commitment of conventional forces in a nuclear age.

After a thorough review of the international situation, her duties to her allies, and her own military capabilities, Canada reaffirmed her commitment to NATO in the mid-1970s. In central Europe the forces of NATO are ranged against the forces of the Warsaw Pact. The weakening of NATO could endanger the security of Canada's allies in Western Europe. The outbreak of war in Europe could grow into a showdown between the super powers, the United States and the USSR, who dominate the rival alliances. As her contribution to preserving the "balance of power", Canada maintains land and air forces in West Germany and mobile support units in Canada.

The United Nations and Related Agencies

The United Nations

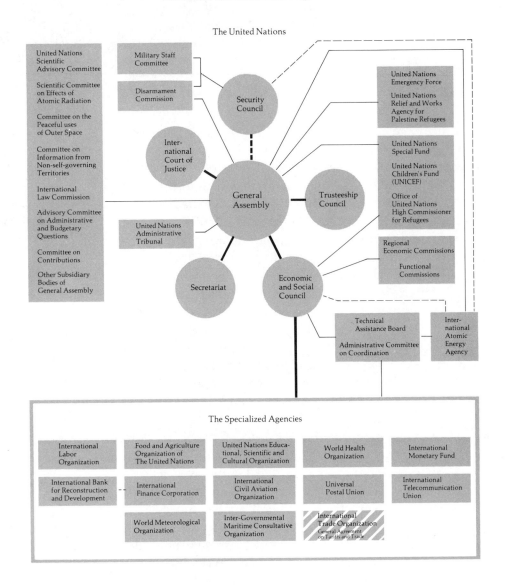

International Labor Organization	Food and Agriculture Organization of The United Nations	United Nations Educational, Scientific and Cultural Organization	World Health Organization	International Monetary Fund
International Bank for Reconstruction and Development	International Finance Corporation	International Civil Aviation Organization	Universal Postal Union	International Telecommunication Union
	World Meteorological Organization	Inter-Governmental Maritime Consultative Organization	International Trade Organization — General Agreement on Tariffs and Trade	

United Nations Scientific Advisory Committee

Scientific Committee on Effects of Atomic Radiation

Committee on the Peaceful uses of Outer Space

Committee on Information from Non-self-governing Territories

International Law Commission

Advisory Committee on Administrative and Budgetary Questions

Committee on Contributions

Other Subsidiary Bodies of General Assembly

Military Staff Committee

Disarmament Commission

Security Council

International Court of Justice

General Assembly

United Nations Administrative Tribunal

Trusteeship Council

Secretariat

Economic and Social Council

United Nations Emergency Force

United Nations Relief and Works Agency for Palestine Refugees

United Nations Special Fund

United Nations Children's Fund (UNICEF)

Office of United Nations High Commissioner for Refugees

Regional Economic Commissions

Functional Commissions

Technical Assistance Board

Administrative Committee on Coordination

International Atomic Energy Agency

The Specialized Agencies

Canada and the United Nations

The experience of World War II had shocked Canada out of her isolationism of the 1930s and made Canadians determined to work actively for a better world. On the one hand, they owed a debt to the 40 000 countrymen who had sacrificed their lives; on the other, the country had escaped the devastation of direct military attack. In fact, Canada had emerged from the war with an immensely strengthened economy and military force.

A former colony, Canada had "come of age". She was widely trusted; unlike many other countries, Canada was not suspected of wanting to acquire territories or dominate other nations. All things considered, Canada seemed uniquely qualified to assume a role as a *middle power* in world affairs. Although she could not hope to be as influential as the United States or the Soviet Union, Canada had the wealth, power and status to serve as a "helping" nation.

In San Francisco in 1945, Canada took an active part in the founding of the United Nations. Thus we were one of the 51 original members to approve the United Nations Charter, which stated in part:

WE THE PEOPLES OF THE UNITED NATIONS DETERMINED

to save succeeding generations from the scourge of war, which twice in our lifetime has brought untold sorrow to mankind, and

to reaffirm faith in fundamental human rights, in the dignity and worth of the human person, in the equal rights of men and women and of nations large and small, and

to establish conditions under which justice and respect for the obligations arising from treaties and other sources of international law can be maintained, and

to promote social progress and better standards of life in larger freedom,

AND FOR THESE ENDS

to practice tolerance and live together in peace with one another as good neighbors, and

to unite our strength to maintain international peace and security, and

to ensure, by the acceptance of principles and the institution of methods, that armed force shall not be used, save in the common interest, and

to employ international machinery for the promotion of the economic and social advancement of all peoples,

HAVE RESOLVED TO COMBINE OUR EFFORTS TO ACCOMPLISH THESE
AIMS.

Accordingly, our respective Governments, through representatives assembled in the city of San Francisco, who have exhibited their full powers found to be in good and due form, have agreed to the present Charter of the United Nations and do hereby establish an international organization to be known as the United Nations.[17]

*See page 190.

Like its goals, the organization of the United Nations bore considerable resemblance to the League of Nations.* The *General Assembly* is in many respects the central body of the U.N. Every member of the organization has a vote on proceedings, which include electing the Secretary-General (the chief officer of the U.N.), approving budgets, and appointing members to the many affiliated organizations. The peacekeeping operations of the UNEF (United Nations Emergency Force) are the responsibility of the General Assembly.

The *Security Council* was originally created as the part mainly responsible for preserving world peace. The "great powers"—the United States, the Soviet Union, the United Kingdom (Britain), France and China—reserved permanent seats for themselves in the Security Council. In contrast to the situation in the League, the permanent members of the Security Council decided that each

The first meeting of the United Nations at Flushing Meadows, New York, 1946.

would have the power to veto a decision of which it did not approve or which was not in its national interest. In recognition of the demands of the smaller nations for a decision-making voice in the United Nations, six non-permanent members—later increased to ten —were to be part of the Security Council. They were to be elected for two-year terms from the General Assembly, but would not have the right to veto.

Canada has served four terms as a non-permanent member of the Security Council, having been elected in 1948, 1958, 1967 and 1976. In 1952, Canada's Lester B. Pearson, secretary of state for external affairs, was named president of the General Assembly. But important as these political contributions have been, Canada is better known for her military and economic activities.

The peace-keeping role of the United Nations has not been an easy one to fill. The super powers have almost always opposed each other in international disputes, regardless of who else was involved. Almost from its beginning, the United Nations has been called upon to mediate international disputes, and Canada has been instrumental in the success the organization has had.

RECORD OF CANADA'S UNITED NATIONS SERVICE

1949 -	Kashmir
1950 -1954	Korea
1954 -	Palestine (Middle East)
1954 -	Vietnam, Laos, Cambodia
1956 - 1967	Egypt
1958 - 1959	Lebanon
1960 - 1964	Congo
1962 - 1963	West New Guinea
1963 - 1964	Yemen
1964 -	Cyprus
1965 - 1966	India - Pakistan

The United Nations has fielded observer groups or military forces in each of these situations. Perhaps a look at two of them will clarify the role of the UN and shed some light on Canada's function as a "helping" nation.

KOREA

In the Korean War (1950 - 1953), Canada provided 8 000 troops to the United Nations force. Following the defeat of Japan in World War II and her withdrawal from Korea, Korea was occupied by Soviet troops in the north and the Americans in the south. North Korea continued as a Soviet-dominated territory and South Korea,

The Security Council can only be effective if the "great powers" agree unanimously on a course of action. Since the Soviet Union and China are generally at odds with each other and with the "Western" powers—the United States, Britain and France—in international disputes regardless of whoever else is involved, the Security Council has not had much success in stopping wars.

The law of the sea

Canada is one of the world's many maritime nations concerned with the uses of the sea and sovereignty of the waters off her coasts. The threat to her fishing industry, especially in Newfoundland, was the first problem. In order to regulate the fishing industry from whose grounds so many foreign fishing boats were operating, Canada declared her sovereignty over a 360 km coastal fishing zone.

Other issues about the control of international waters are also cause for concern. The ocean floor contains vast resources of minerals such as nickel, copper and iron. Who should own them? Should the benefits of these resources be shared? How might the sharing be handled?

The United Nations annual "law of the sea" conference is working toward solutions for some of these problems.

Troops of the Princess Patricia Canadian Light Infantry on patrol in Korea, 1951.

formed with American military support, was recognized as a country by the United Nations.

On June 25, 1950, troops from the north crossed the border into South Korea. The United States moved quickly. Troops were transferred from their occupation duties in Japan, and the United States urged the United Nations to take action against North Korea as an aggressor. With the representatives from the U.S.S.R. absent from the Security Council meetings in protest, the United Nations followed the American lead.

Although the army in Korea was mainly American and commanded by World War II hero, General Douglas MacArthur, military forces from sixteen members of the United Nations took part in the fighting. At first the North Koreans were driven well back into their own territory, but the war turned into a stalemate when the USSR and China increased support to their Communist ally. An uneasy truce was arranged, and a demilitarized zone set up, although it was destined to remain an area of tension indefinitely.

Canada's contribution to the United Nations' effort in Korea was second only to that of the United States and Great Britain. In her first major challenge since World War II, Canada demonstrated her acceptance of international responsibility. And her greatest period of service still lay ahead. In the Suez Crisis of 1956, one of a series of wars in the Middle East, what Canada's role as a middle power would be was brought clearly into focus.

SUEZ 1956

The trouble in the Middle East stemmed from the creation of Israel by the United Nations in 1948. That event was accompanied by a bitter struggle in which Israel successfully repelled attacks by surrounding Arab countries. Though an armistice was arranged by the United Nations, the Arab states refused to accept the existence of Israel. Thus a state of war, marked by persistent border raids, continued into the 1950s.

Then in July 1956, Egypt's head of state, Colonel Gamal Nasser, nationalized the Suez Canal, a vital trade route in the Middle East. The takeover by the Egyptian government of the once internationally controlled canal was a shock to Israel—and to Britain and France, the major investors. When Israel launched an attack on Egypt, Britain and France offered support in the form of bombing attacks on Cairo and the landing of paratroopers at strategic positions along the canal. The Israelis, meanwhile, swept over the Sinai Desert, and also dislodged the Egyptians from the strategic Gulf of Aqaba.

At the United Nations, the USSR demanded immediate withdrawal of the forces invading Egypt, and appeared ready to inter-

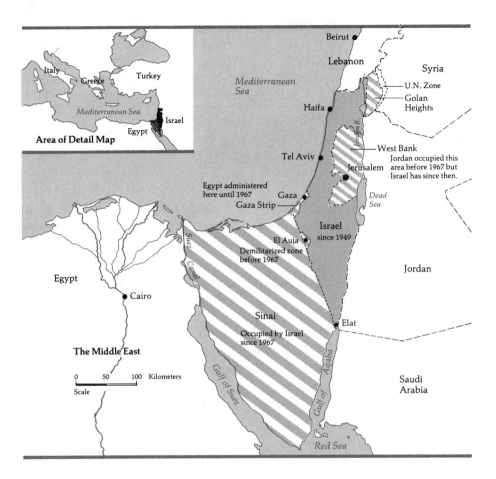

The Middle East

0 50 100 Kilometers
Scale

Area of Detail Map

vene. The United States, anxious to avoid Soviet involvement, joined the USSR in branding the combined action in the canal zone as aggression. The crisis threatened the United Nations, but the potential danger was even more widespread. With the United States and its allies, Britain and France, on "opposite sides of the fence", the NATO alliance, the Commonwealth and the unity of the non-Communist world were all threatened.

Frantic activity at the United Nations was marked by the diplomacy of Lester Pearson. As a first step, he called for an immediate ceasefire and withdrawal of foreign troops from Egypt. Then he initiated the idea of creating a multi-national United Nations Emergency Force to be stationed between the belligerent Egyptian and Israeli forces.

CANADA AND THE SUEZ CRISIS

An adviser to Pearson at the U.N. described some of the diplomatic footwork done by Pearson:

....Mike had always been interested in the idea of an international force. It would be foolish to say it was a unique Canadian idea, but we had been thinking along those lines, and so had the U.S. Someone had to take the initiative. The whole Assembly wanted something done, even the British and French. It was necessary to get the maximum support. Dulles [the U.S. Secretary of State] knew that if the U.S. proposed it, it would become a cold-war issue. Mike was able to do it because he was well thought of by the Israelis, he had been President of the Assembly, he knew half of the Foreign Ministers by their first names, he had the support of the U.S., and the Egyptian Minister, Fawzi, could talk to him rationally.

He had to play a double game. To get the Arabs and Asians to support it he had to make it seem that the UN was 'driving out' the British and French. At the same time he had to give the British and French a satisfactory reason for backing out: the reason that the UN was 'taking over. . . .'[18]

The Canadian plan was adopted, and the United Nations Emergency Force (UNEF) was formed. Several countries contributed troops, but the largest number came from Canada. The force, commanded by a Canadian, Major-General E. M. Burns, was stationed on Egyptian territory in the Gaza Strip. In spite of the continuation of tension, border raids by both sides and mutual accusations, the UNEF supervised the truce for a decade.

Canadian troops purchase camels for their duties on the Gaza Strip.

Canada: the "helpful fixer"

Historically Canadians have not been particularly pro-military even though Canada made substantial contributions in both World War I and World War II. Yet during the periods preceding both wars successive governments expressed little interest in developing or maintaining military establishments of any significance. Furthermore, there was a tendency first to rely upon the United Kingdom and then, after 1945, to draw increasingly upon the American military experience. In the process, no distinctly Canadian military tradition or basis of professionalism emerged and for most of the post-1945 period the military has been assigned roles and commitments which were difficult to relate directly to the interests of most Canadians. Consequently to be asked if Canada had a defence policy was not an uncommon occurrence. In other words, the tendency to relegate things military to a low priority within Canadian society has been the norm, and generally Canadians have not comprehended the changes in military strategy, tactics, equipment, and technology which demand a professional core of experts if a military capability is to be maintained. Unfortunately, but not entirely unexpectedly, Canadian politicians have often shared the values and opinions of the general public. In varying degrees this has been reflected by the lack of interest and/or understanding of military issues shown by successive cabinets since the beginning of the 1960s.[12]

A major military power for a brief period during World War II, Canada reduced its forces sharply in the postwar years. Since then, Canada has earned a specialized military image: provider of highly-trained troops for peace-keeping duties. The origin of this reputation was the Suez crisis, when the United Nations Emergency Force (UNEF) to which Canada was a major contributor, was created.

The person behind the idea was the then Canadian minister of external affairs, Lester B. Pearson. For his efforts during the hectic days of the Suez crisis, Mr. Pearson was awarded the Nobel Peace Prize in 1957.

Canadian forces have served with distinction on behalf of the United Nations many times since. Besides participating in peace-keeping operations in the Middle East, Canadians have seen duty along the cease-fire line between India and Pakistan, in the Congo in the early 1960s and since 1964 on the island of Cyprus, where tension between Turks and Greeks continuously threatens.

The role of "helpful fixer" may have been played up beyond reality in the 1960s. Some Canadians, including people in the Canadian government, began to wonder if Canada was getting carried

Canadian troops patrolling in Nicosia

away by her willingness to serve in troubled areas around the world. Perhaps she should be more modest and selective, undertaking only those tasks that were clearly related to the country's "national interest". Yet the feeling persisted that Canada must maintain an international outlook and be prepared to commit increasing amounts of effort and resources, both military and non-military, to solutions for problems that threaten "spaceship earth."

PEACEKEEPING IN CANADA'S FUTURE

The peace-keeping role can be a dangerous one for Canadian forces and a thankless one for the country. In the Middle East, for instance, renewed warfare is a constant threat. In May 1967, the Canadians and their United Nations comrades were doing their best to supervise the "no man's land" and to report violations of the truce by each side. Israel and Egypt were nevertheless moving toward all-out war.

Suddenly the Egyptian leader, Colonel Nasser, insisted that the UNEF, including the Canadian contingent, be withdrawn. During and after the "Six Day War,"* Canada had no influence on the situation in sharp contrast to the Suez crisis of 1956. The Canadian public was shocked and so was their government, by the apparent end of the UNEF, the setback to United Nations peacekeeping in general, and the loss of a role in which they had taken great pride.

The Canadian commitment to peace-keeping remained strong nevertheless. The government's white papers on foreign policy in 1970 and defence in 1971 both underlined Canada's continued support for the idea. Canadian forces remained on duty in Cyprus, and with the restoration of the UNEF to the Middle East following the war of October, 1973, Canada reinstalled more than 1 000 armed forces personnel.

*In early June, 1967, Israel launched a stunning attack on its Arab neighbours. Claiming that its survival as a nation depended on defensible frontiers, Israel occupied strategic territories formerly held by Egypt, Syria and Jordan.

Canada and the Third World

After World War II the colonial powers of Europe had to relinquish their hold on possessions in other parts of the world. In Africa and Asia especially, people were moved by a spirit of nationalism to seek their independence. In some cases the change from colony to nation was relatively gradual and peaceful. However, in most cases "wars of liberation" were fought, often with outside assistance from the Soviet Union or other Communist countries. Civil wars among competing groups or tribes frequently began during the struggle for independence, and ended only when a "strong man" succeeded in imposing one-party rule. Once a kind of stability had been achieved,

Women have played important political roles in several developing nations. Sirimavo Bandaranaike of Sri Lanka (Ceylon), for example was the first woman to head a democratic government in modern time. When her husband was assassinated in 1959, she decided to carry on with his reform policies and in 1960 was elected prime minister of her country.

Indira Gandhi began her political career early by serving as her father's first lady (he was India's first prime minister) since her mother had died several years earlier. In 1959 she was elected president of the National Congress party and in 1966 prime minister of India.

Angie Brooks, the second woman to serve as president of the United Nations General Assembly has had one of the most unconventional careers of any woman in the world. Determined to become a lawyer when law schools in Liberia, her home, were non-existent, and a strong prejudice against female lawyers was a reality, Mrs. Brooks won a scholarship to study law at the University of Wisconsin Law School. Afterward she worked in Liberia's Justice Department and as a professor of law at Liberia University. Before being elected to the prestigious post of president of the General Assembly, she was appointed as a delegate to the U.N. from Liberia.[19]

*Ceylon was renamed Sri Lanka in 1972.

there remained the awesome challenges of setting up workable systems of government, organizing economic systems, creating school systems, and generally establishing the institutions necessary to a national life.

The new countries that have come into existence since World War II are often known as the Third World. Many different races and cultures belong to the Third World, and specific needs and problems vary from country to country. But the fundamental problems are generally the same: the population explosion, food shortages, and how to provide education, medical care and other essential services. Many countries lack the technology and trained personnel so vital to economic growth. In some cases, political instability has meant hardship and suffering. Overdependence on outsiders, mainly from Europe and North America, for development and export markets has often meant that Third World nations are exploited.

The problems of the Third World are important to Canada for many reasons. A growing number of Canadians believe that a country with so many advantages and one of the world's highest living standards bears a social and humanitarian responsibility to those less fortunate. As Canadians strive to create a more just society within their own borders, so they must support the principle of greater justice for people elsewhere.

Canada is not, however, moved solely by idealism in her sense of international responsibility. In the last quarter of the twentieth century, a major trend is the growing interdependence of all regions of the world. What happens in one part can affect another with a swiftness that would have been unimaginable a few years ago. Is it, then, in Canada's self-interest to be known to other countries as a nation concerned for the well-being of others?

Historic ties are of great significance in Canada's relations with the Third World. Canada is a member of the Commonwealth, a voluntary, multi-racial and multi-cultural association of nations, all of which were formerly part of the British Empire. Members share many traditions as well as language and experiences. Because the Commonwealth includes some of the world's poorest as well as some of the richest nations, it continues to give hope for international cooperation.

Canada has played a major role in trying to convert the Commonwealth into an association for overcoming the problems and differences that divide nations in the present day. In 1950 Canada was one of the developed nations meeting in Colombo, Ceylon* that inaugurated the so-called *Colombo Plan*. The essence of the plan was that developed members would provide assistance to "developing," newly independent members in Asia. Aid was to take the form of technical assistance in agriculture, health, industry, education and other concerns.

486

Light on the dark continent

CIDA, The Canadian International Development Agency, has prepared a comic book, entitled *Shake-Em-Up Comics: The Adventures of Billy Buyer in Africa*,[20] for use in Canadian schools. The purpose of CIDA is to give development assistance to enable people in poorer countries to help themselves. The aim of the comic book is to get Canadian school pupils thinking about other countries and Canadians' responsibilities to the people of these poorer nations.

In the comic book, a typical Canadian teenager, Billy Buyer, is visited by a genie who grants Billy three wishes. Without a second thought, Billy wishes for a car, freedom to do what he wants without having to ask his parents, and a trip to Africa. The genie grants Billy's wishes, and the rest of the comic book is devoted to Billy's desire to get home from Africa as well as his awakening to the plight of the people in less fortunate countries. In the course of his visit, Billy learns about cultural differences between Canadians and Africans as well as the meaning of necessities, luxuries and sharing.

In this excerpt, Billy tries to find an African who will accept three wishes, the secret to Billy's passage home. Billy finds it is not as easy for his African friend or even his family to decide upon three wishes as it was for Billy.

1. How do the wishes of the Africans differ from Billy's?
2. What differences between Canadian and African values and culture can you deduce from this short excerpt?
3. Do you think CIDA's idea in producing a comic book for educational use is a good one? Why or why not?
4. Do you think Canadian school pupils should be concerned with the problems of "Third and Fourth World" countries? Why or why not? If your answer is yes, what can school pupils do to benefit people in these lands?

Between the world wars, the so-called "white dominions", including Canada, achieved full independence. Since World War II, the non-white colonies of Britain have become nations in their own right. Almost annually since India and Pakistan did so in 1947, one or more former British "possessions" has taken control of its own affairs.

Eventually Canada's international aid program was expanded to include both Commonwealth and non-Commonwealth countries in other parts of the Third World. The Canadian International Development Agency (CIDA) was established as a coordinating agency. Now CIDA coordinates and helps to finance the work of both governmental and private organizations.

The Canadian government gives the majority of its development aid bilaterally; that is, from government to government. Receiving the largest portions in recent years have been members of the Commonwealth, particularly in Asia and Africa, although French-speaking countries in the Third World have been receiving increasing amounts. The form of assistance includes technical and financial aid for projects such as dams, schools, roads and public health services, as well as shipments of food and other commodities. Canadian advisers serve in the developing countries, and scholarships are given to foreign students for study in Canada.

Multilateral assistance is that which goes to organizations, and a growing portion of such assistance from Canada has been in contributions to international financial institutions. The Asian, Caribbean,

Some of the aspects of life which are of concern to UNESCO

Inter-American and African Development Banks make loans available to developing countries. Through the United Nations, Canada also makes contributions; the UN Development Program (UNDP), the United Nations Children's Fund (UNICEF) and the World Food Program are important recipients.

CIDA also provides assistance to private, or non-governmental, organizations (NGOs). These include voluntary agencies, churches and universities. The Canadian University Service Overseas (CUSO) receives half its budget from the Canadian government; the remainder comes from private sources and from employers in the host countries where CUSO volunteers serve. Several hundred Canadians each year work in developing countries, receiving the same salaries as their local counterparts, in jobs such as teaching, medicine, agriculture and various trades.

AID TO DEVELOPING COUNTRIES: HOW AND HOW MUCH?

Cooperation between developed countries and developing countries is complicated to say the least. The following documents suggest some of the dilemmas: Actual and estimated payment of Canadian Official Development Assistance as percentage of G.N.P. [21]

Year	% of G.N.P.
1967-68	.28%
1968-69	.28%
1969-70	.34%
1970-71	.40%
1971-72	.41%
1972-73	.48%
1973-74	.48%
1974-75	.52%
1975-76	.57% (estimated)

Dr. John Holmes, foreign affairs specialist, comments on the paradox of foreign aid:

The so-called Third World is far less monolithic than we tend to assume. We have witnessed of late, for example, the differentiation of what is called the "Fourth World," those developing countries who don't possess oil or other resources with which they can bargain. The developing countries, paradoxically perhaps, insist vehemently on utter sovereignty over their own resources while they seem to be suggesting that the policies of the developed countries must be subject to some higher law.... the subject is vastly confusing. What we have to note, however, is that the thrust is towards a principle of international sharing and it is directed against those countries which have the most resources and space per capita.

490

When you get down to the ways and means of it, the noble principle of sharing resources for the benefit of mankind is somewhat difficult to implement and is full of ambiguities. It is inequitable that I should pay so little for hydro-electric power compared with a Bengali, but I don't quite know how I share the Ontario Hydro-Electric Power Commission with him. I could, of course, give up driving my car so that he could have more fuel and fertilizer, but I for one don't know how that is worked out. I could invite ten Bengalis to come and share my small heated apartment. But if every household in Canada took ten Bengalis, the population of the Asian sub-continent would be little affected. The easiest thing for the government to do is to quadruple its foreign aid spending, but even quadruple amounts remain marginal to the problem.[22]

Max Saltsman, a New Democrat M.P. who has represented Canada at many international conferences, comments on Canadian public opinion:

The first thing that strikes me about the state of public opinion in this country, and it's very important, is that we no longer feel *guilty* about the Third World (or about the poor, or even about our own Indians). I don't know why this is. There are still some people who still feel terribly guilty, who are carrying "the white man's burden" on their shoulders. But increasingly the people say: "Look, I'm not going to be blamed for everything that goes wrong in the world. I'm not going to be blamed for everybody who is poor. I have some responsibility, and I'm going to try to live up to it since I think of myself as a reasonably decent person. But don't you blame me for everything that goes wrong. I didn't do it." They look at the peoples who have become independent and what do they see? They may be black, they may be brown, but they're not behaving one whit better than the white man behaves. It turns out you have good white people and bad white people, good blacks and bad blacks, good browns and bad browns. It isn't as clear cut as it once was, when the well intentioned white felt that everything whites did was bad and everything blacks did was good; everything the rich did was bad and everything the poor did was good. People no longer accept that kind of a thing.

... People in this country are limiting population growth and saying: "We are doing it because the world can only sustain certain numbers."

Then they say: "We are limiting ourselves; others should do the same." And when the others don't a kind of despair sets in. They ask: "How are we going to help in this bottomless pit? Whatever aid we give doesn't change things." The population explosion is frightening people. They don't know how to cope with it. They don't know what's going to happen to their world. They don't see how resources they consider finite can go on being stretched to an infinite population growth.[23]

A Canadian born and educated in the Third World describes problems that originate in developing countries:

Nor is the Third World entirely free from blame. . . .

In country after country, elected governments were toppled and dictatorships installed by force. What happened, in effect, was that the white man's colonialism gave way to the black man's or the brown man's colonialism. As far as the masses were concerned instead of being governed from London or Paris they were now governed from their own capital cities by rulers who respected human rights even less. Political opponents were arrested without charge, kept for long years in jail, and in many cases murdered. Nor is racialism a white man's disease; Africans have complained of racial discrimination against them in countries of Asia, while Asians in many parts of Africa have suffered discrimination based on race.

If the Third World is in a mess today this is partly because of the Western countries that refuse to trade with them on equal terms. But it is also because of the incredible corruption based on force that prevails in some of these countries. If your dictator is corrupt, anybody who speaks against him or his family is shot or arrested.

The Third World is also in a great deal of trouble because some of the countries have their own colonial designs and are spending billions and billions on arms while other people are starving.

Then there is the problem of creating white elephants. When you look at development undertaken in some developing countries, priority has not always been given to projects which would do the most good to the most people. Instead priority often went to visible monuments to enhance the popularity or sex appeal of a particular dictator.[24]

A Third World diplomat explains the views of people in countries needing development aid:

Most developing countries have such bitter memories of colonial exploitation or racial and other forms of discrimination that deep underneath the desire for economic progress lies the psychological need to put the hurt and the humiliation behind them once and for all. The peoples of the developing countries undoubtedly want to regain their sense of dignity and self-respect, which they enjoyed for long centuries and which they lost only during the brief period of Western domination, a domination based essentially on industrial or technological revolution which is hardly two centuries old. The fact that country after country in all parts of the world has successively mastered modern technology in ever shorter timespans is also not overlooked by those who are still left behind. Against this background, it would not be too much of an exaggeration to say that the goals of the developing world today are psychological rather than economic; that they cherish their independence even

492

Canada's nuclear dilemmas

By the 1970s atomic power was taking on importance as a source of energy. Traditional sources, such as hydro and natural gas, seemed unlikely to be adequate for expanding needs. As with other forms of energy, however, atomic energy cannot be produced without raising issues about its side effects. For example, the problem of disposing of radioactive wastes is not easily solved, and there are fears that large-scale production could lead to horrible consequences for the environment, and people.

Since the beginning of the "atomic age" Canada has been involved in the development of peaceful uses for atomic energy. At the Chalk River plant not far from Ottawa, and at other plants since, Canada's nuclear technology has reached a high level of sophistication. The arguments in favour of utilizing atomic, or nuclear, power for Canadian needs are persuasive; the opposing arguments, on the other hand, are a serious cause for concern.

ARGUMENTS IN FAVOUR	ARGUMENTS AGAINST
growing need for energy	risk of accidental explosions
available "know-how" (technology)	danger of accidental release or leakage of radioactive materials
relatively low cost	
conservation of fossil fuels	possibility of sabotage against nuclear plants or the use of nuclear materials to make weapons
less pollution danger from super-tankers (oil)	
	problems disposing of radioactive waste
	long-term environmental damage and pollution harmful to future generations

1. Is it unfair for a developed country like Canada to refuse to share its nuclear technology with a developing country? Why or why not?
2. Canada signed the *nuclear non-proliferation treaty* (1968) by which countries already having nuclear technology agreed not to help other countries acquire nuclear weapons. The treaty did *not* forbid the export of equipment and materials—destined for "peaceful" uses only—which could enable more countries to build bombs. Assuming the governments of Third World countries buying CANDU reactors

commit themselves to peaceful uses only, what dangers might still remain if Canada sold such nations CANDU reactors?

Ideas from the social sciences: Which one's the foreigner? A look at cultural anthropology

---

When people in underdeveloped or developing countries resist the introduction of western technology, we often consider these people backward or somehow "uncivilized". What we fail to consider is that they are living in a culture which is far different from ours.

"Culture" means the way of life of a people. Children become part of their culture as they learn to do things the way others of their culture do. Speech, mannerisms, clothing styles, attitudes of all sorts—these and many other kinds of behaviours are learned from one's cultural surroundings.

One of the social scientists most interested in the study of culture is the *anthropologist*. *Anthropology* may be defined as the study of human differences and similarities. As a discipline, or organized form of studying human behaviour, anthropology is a fairly new subject—like the other social sciences. Yet it has come a long way from being regarded, a century ago, as the activity of eccentrics interested in strange and exotic practices.

Anthropology came into being as an attempt to blend the sciences and the arts in an objective study of human nature. Philosophers and historians had long been interested in why people acted in certain ways, but the investigation of human origins required the study of physical evidence, such as the remains of skeletons, tools, and dwellings. This required the use of procedures not normally available to "established" experts.

In trying to identify the basic characteristics of man as a species, anthropologists focused on primitive cultures. Only by studying the Samoans of the South Pacific or the Kwakiutls of British Columbia could they be satisfied they were dealing with people unaffected by modern civilization.

Yet anthropology is more than the inquiry into cultures of the pre-industrial past. For Canadians, anthropology can provide clues into the origins of their country. The first people—or aborigines— may have arrived in Canada as far back as 25 000 years ago, and anthropology is a means of reconstructing evidence about the earliest Canadians and how they lived. The *physical anthropologist* can examine artifacts that tell us about the appearance and size of people who once inhabited the country, and the environment they had to cope with. The *cultural anthropologist* can reconstruct the ways of life of simpler cultures and study basic human relationships.

494

Working with fragments of evidence, anthropologists must first make sense of the pieces. Even if they are quite successful in getting the "picture" of a culture together, they face difficulties in interpreting its meaning. They are themselves products of their own cultures and inclined to think of them as "normal" and other cultures as "strange". To understand another culture, especially one that is very different from theirs, they must try to see it through the eyes of a member of that culture.

Often in dealing with "Third or Fourth World" cultures, we experience what is known as "culture shock"—a removal or distortion of the cues in peoples' behaviour which one encounters "at home" and the substitution of other cues which are strange. "Foreigners" don't act as we expect them to, and we do not know what to expect of them. To us they are foreign, but to them and others of their culture, we are the foreigners.

Anthropologist Edward T. Hall, in his book *The Silent Language*, has advice for those who will be working in foreign countries for both government and business. He explains that they must know more about communication in other countries, and his comments about space and time are particularly interesting.

One doesn't have to go to a different country to experience "culture shock". Within every large culture—Canadian culture, for example—there are many *sub-cultures* or smaller divisions. Each sub-culture may have its own variations in attitudes, values and behaviour, making it distinct from other sub-cultures. If, for example, you are an Anglo-Saxon Canadian, you have certain "acceptable" methods of greeting strangers—perhaps a friendly handshake, or a nod of the head. If you meet someone who belongs to a sub-culture where strangers are greeted with an embrace, you might experience "culture shock". To you that form of greeting may seem odd; to the other person a handshake might seem unfriendly.

In the United States [and Canada as well], . . . propinquity [nearness] is the basis of a good many relationships. To us the neighbor is actually quite close. Being a neighbor endows one with certain rights and privileges, also responsibilities. You can borrow things, including food and drink, but you also have to take your neighbor to the hospital in an emergency. In this regard he has almost as much claim on you as a cousin. For these and other reasons the [North] American tries to pick his neighborhood carefully, because he knows that he is going to be thrown into intimate contact with people. We do not understand why it is that when we live next to people abroad the sharing of adjacent space does not always conform to our own pattern. If France and England, for instance, the relations between neighbors are apt to be cooler than in the United States. Mere propinquity does not tie people together. In England neighbor children do not play as they do in our neighborhoods. When they do play, arrangements are sometimes made a month in advance as though they were coming from the other side of town!

As for punctuality no right-minded American would think of keeping a business associate waiting for an hour; it would be too insulting. No matter what is said in an apology, there is little that can remove the impact of an hour's heel-cooling in an outer office.

Even the five-minute period has its significant subdivisions. When equals meet, one will generally be aware of being two minutes early or late but will say nothing, since the time in this case is not significant. At three minutes a person will still not apologize or feel that it is necessary to say anything (three is the first significant number in the one-to-five series); at five minutes there is usually a short apology; and at four minutes before or after the hour the person will mutter something, although he will seldom complete the muttered sentence. The importance of making detailed observations on these aspects of informal culture is driven home if one pictures an actual situation. An American ambassador in an unnamed country interpreted incorrectly the significance of time as it was used in visits by local diplomats. An hour's tardiness in their system is equivalent to five minutes by ours, fifty to fifty-five minutes to four minutes, forty-five minutes to three minutes, and so on for daytime official visits. By their standards the local diplomats felt they couldn't arrive exactly on time; this punctuality might be interpreted locally as an act relinquishing their freedom of action to the United States. But they didn't want to be insulting —an hour late would be too late—so they arrived fifty minutes late. As a consequence the ambassador said, 'How can you depend on these people when they arrive an hour late for an appointment and then just mutter something? They don't even give you a full sentence of apology!' He couldn't help feeling this way, because in American time fifty to fifty-five minutes late is the insult period, at the extreme end of the duration scale; yet in the country we are speaking of it's just right.[27]

1. Can you describe a situation in which you have experienced some form of "culture shock"?
2. Of what significance is this concept of cultural variation to Canadians visiting other countries? Canadian teachers, business people or diplomats living in other countries?
3. How would it be a reflection of your values if you say of your European neighbours, "They treat their children poorly" or "Those children have no respect for their elderly grandparents"?
4. To what extent should people who belong to sub-cultures within our Canadian society conform to the behaviour pattern of the dominant culture?

more than economic progress; that, while they know they need the assistance of those who can well afford it, they would prefer to be rid of such assistance sooner rather than later; that, while they emphasize international cooperation, they are as zealous of their national sovereignty as anyone else, perhaps more than many others.

Here then is the rub, an internal contradiction, which needs to be understood if not resolved. While the developing countries proclaim the rhetoric of one world and advocate the language of international cooperation, they want to develop primarily on their own steam and would not accept a position of prolonged dependence on others no matter what the cost in economic terms. The fact that, for the smaller and poorer among them, international cooperation or interdependence is a stark economic necessity rather than an ideological nicety, does not in any way reduce their sense of discomfort at having to demand things from a position of weakness.[25]

1. Which of the arguments involve *scientific* matters only?
2. Which involve *political* questions? *Social* and *ethical* questions?
3. As a Canadian, do you think you should have some say about whether Canada becomes a "nuclear society"? If so, how can you try to influence decisions about nuclear energy that might affect your community?

The CANDU nuclear reactor, the key to Canada's plans for the use of nuclear power to meet rising needs for electricity, is also in demand overseas in energy-poor countries. The result has been another controversy, with grave political and security complications. The sale of CANDU reactors is a boon to Canada's export trade and, at the same time, a way in which Canada can provide aid to "Third World" countries, including Commonwealth partners. However, adequate safeguards against "nuclear proliferation"—the spread of nuclear weapons—are extremely difficult to guarantee.

Canadian foreign policy today: participant or bystander?

In the 1970s, Canada has had great difficulty in defining her role, or roles, in the "family of nations." Changing world conditions have necessitated a re-examination of her participation. How should Canada approach foreign affairs in the future?

MORALITY IN INTERNATIONAL AFFAIRS

Between realism on the one hand . . . and idealism on the other . . . is no easy choice. . . .

Still, I would not be the good Canadian I like to think I am if I did not try to open up a middle way. Let us call it practical idealism.

The practical idealist knows the ways of statecraft well. He knows their deceptions, their betrayals, their cruelties. He knows how pitiless are their laws. He cannot hope to do away with them. He cannot, accordingly, share the outlook of the liberal idealist. He cannot hope to be exempt from them. He cannot, accordingly, share the outlook of the pharisean idealist.

But the practical idealist knows just as well how much wrong-

Nuclear power made simple

In essence, a nuclear reactor is a reasonably simple affair. It consists of a large cement or steel casing into which uranium rods are positioned close enough to each other to enable the radioactive uranium to cause a nuclear chain reaction, which in turn releases energy in the form of heat. The heat boils water, which releases steam, which forces turbines in the massive generator to rotate and produce the electrical energy. The major variable differentiating various reactor technologies is the substance used in controlling the nuclear chain reactor, technically known as the moderator. American reactors, which stem from the light-weight military reactors originally developed for submarines, use ordinary water; the British use graphite (also used in pencils); and the Canadian CANDU (for Canadian deuterium and uranium reactor) uses heavy water (the hydrogen component of which has a different atomic make-up than is found in ordinary water). Heavy water reactors, for a number of technical reasons, are more efficient (not requiring the enrichment of uranium fuel) and more flexible than other designs although the development effort required was certainly as great as that for any other design.[26]

doing may be done by statesmen whose moral mandate is too permissive. He will on this account refuse to allow *raison d'état* to be their guide. They are not to be trusted with so dangerous a doctrine. It leads straight to massacre and genocide, to total war with terrible weapons.

And so the practical idealist, his idealism at once prompted and tempered by his realism, clings to a more stringent ethic in international life than may be warranted by the facts of international life. If international morality did not exist, he would find it necessary to invent it; for he knows that if international morality did not exist, people might not exist.

———————————

Imagine, then, a meeting of the Cabinet. A crucial foreign policy decision is to be taken—whether or not to run the blockade of Berlin, send troops to Korea, send troops to Vietnam. Various divisions of labour take place. The Prime Minister worries about national unity. The Finance Minister is concerned at the cost. The Defence Minister is anxious about logistics. The Secretary of State for External Affairs frets about effects on friends and foes. But there is no Secretary of State for Conscience to speak up to ask two crucial questions: Is it good? Is it right?

Lacking a Secretary of State for Conscience in the organization of our government, we should, as practical idealists, insist that his function be performed by statesmen whose portfolios bear more prosaic titles. Otherwise we are in trouble.[28]

1. As described in the article, how does the "practical idealist" differ from the idealist? From the realist?
2. Why, in the view of the author, is international morality necessary?
3. Why would the practical idealist not be easy prey for the scheming, ruthless diplomat?
4. Is a Secretary of State for Conscience ever likely to be a part of the Canadian Cabinet? If not in what ways can practical idealists "insist" that other Ministers perform such a function?

As you reflect on the history of Canada's dealings with other countries since World War II, try to decide which of the following would be the most suitable course for Canada to pursue *in the future*:

1. MIDDLE POWER

While realizing that she lacked the resources to take on a "super power", like the United States or the Soviet Union, Canada would assert her power to the limit. Through international organizations, like the United Nations, and alliances, such as NATO, Canada would make her military forces available for peace-keeping and other support roles. She would be aggressive in trade and diplomacy, in order to persuade her allies to support Canadian interests.

2. SATELLITE

Canada would recognize that her security, and thus her continued material prosperity, depends on the goodwill of the United States. Thus Canada would abandon any pretext of having an independent foreign policy. At times she would act as a second voice for American ideas and wishes; at other times she would act as a go-between in smoothing relations between the United States and another nation or bloc of nations. On other occasions, Canada would be a silent partner, providing the United States with military, scientific, technical and other forms of support.

3. MORAL LEADER

Taking a stand on controversial issues, Canada would declare clear positions in the event of conflicts, even wars, among nations. She would speak out for justice in cases where minorities were being mistreated, refugees were suffering, individuals were denied civil rights. Canada would recommend action to governments on social issues like population control, the uses of technology or the economic exploitation of groups in other countries. The main concern would be the well-being of mankind as a whole, rather than the advancement of Canadian interests at the possible expense of others.

4. ISOLATIONIST

Feeling alienated from the "family of nations", Canada would withdraw from most international organizations, except for those beneficial to trade. The attitude would be that Canada has no responsibility for the problems of other countries, whether these be related to poverty in developing areas or to environmental difficulties in industrialized areas. Avoiding foreign entanglements that may lead to involvement in wars or helping nations with internal problems, Canada would concentrate on improving conditions at home.

1. What are the probable consequences for Canada of each alternative?
2. Which alternative is closest to Canada's *actual* role at the present time?
3. Are there other alternatives besides the ones described?
4. How may Canadians, either as individuals or as groups, influence the choices Canada makes in foreign policy?

14: The Latest Challenges to Canada and the World

This final chapter of *In Search of Canada* is different from the others. In "The Latest Challenges" you will be confronted by some of the most urgent, and difficult, issues of our time. Be prepared to be bombarded by ideas, images and dilemmas.

Since all the issues presented are controversial, they raise many questions. Few of the questions have simple, clear-cut answers. The answers generally involve choices which could affect you, and probably most other people in a world that has been described as a "global village" — where modern transportation and communication have led to the increasing interdependence of all regions and peoples.

Remember, controversial issues arouse emotions. If you are tempted to make snap judgements on some of the issues, stop and think. Have you closed your mind before looking at the different sides? Are you reacting on the basis of past experience, rumour, habit or some "hand-me-down" viewpoint, without examining relevant data? Are you assuming a particular explanation as the only one, when there may be alternatives? Even if you reach a conclusion on any of the issues, it may be tentative, and subject to change upon further reflection, research and analysis.

How well will Canada and the world meet these challenges? . . .

Biculturalism:

What does the future hold for the relationship between Anglophones and Francophones?
Which one do you think is *preferable*?

A. ONE CANADA

If Canada remains intact, it will do so either democratically, by the consent of all parts, or arbitrarily, through the use of force by the Canadian government:

Democratic

The governments of Canada, Quebec and the other provinces will continue to negotiate relationships that are more satisfying to all parties than any "parting of the ways." Frustration and conflict will continue but representatives of the various regions will bargain with each other in a spirit of cooperation and the national good.

Canadians will accept the reality that the population is made up of many different cultures, but that the two major groups are the Anglophones and Francophones. Quebec will be recognized by English Canada as the home of French-Canadian culture, and will offer its Anglophone minority the same rights as French Canadians enjoy in the rest of Canada. Quebeckers and Canadians of other provinces will identify with the idea of a bicultural nation.

The bicultural flavour of Canada will be enhanced by the provision of such services as radio and television in both languages, bilingual signs and markings, and increased bilingual education. In its dealings with other nations, Canada will strive for a bicultural image.

Forced

The Government of Canada will impose the power of the state, through the armed forces if necessary, on all parts of the country. Under the War Measures Act, the central government will assume "emergency" powers over all provincial governments, other institutions and groups. Civil liberties will be suspended across Canada for as long as the government sees the need.

To preserve the Canada in which they were born and raised, the majority of Canadians will accept and support a "law and order" regime. The army will be a familiar presence in the streets of the larger cities, and particularly in the capitals. Acts of sabotage will occur from time to time; bombs will explode in public places, injuring or killing small numbers of people. Suspected individuals and groups will be rounded up and detained as political prisoners. The abolition of capital punishment will be reconsidered by Parliament, an institution now used by the government to give a stamp of approval to decisions by the ruling party.

One nation or two?

Which of the following do you think is *most likely? Why?* For what reasons?

B. SEPARATION: CANADA AND QUEBEC
If separation occurs, it may do so in either of two ways:

Violent

Declaration of Quebec independence by a radical separatist group, having seized power in Quebec City. After a brief power struggle among rival leaders, the victors will form a revolutionary council, probably backed by agents from outside the country. The revolutionary government will then suppress opposition to the new regime, and place the media, police, schools and other institutions under its direction.

Quebec will be offered support from countries unfriendly to Canada and its allies. The United States' attitude toward Quebec may, nevertheless, be the crucial factor. If the United States decides to step in, in the interests of North American defence, a confrontation with other "super powers" could ensue. If, on the other hand, the United States decides to allow the Quebec revolution to run its course, many other possibilities exist.

Relations with Canada will likely be hostile, at least in the first phase after the revolution. Canadian public opinion will be aroused. The government will have to decide whether to consider talks with the new Quebec leaders—or to employ the Canadian armed forces in an attempt to establish control over Quebec, and maintain a single nation "from sea to sea."

Peaceful

Negotiation between an elected party, such as the Parti Québécois, in Quebec and the Government of Canada.

Following its election, the Quebec separatist government would hold a referendum. *Québécois* would be given the choice of approving or rejecting the creation of a separate Quebec. Should the choice be "no," the government would initiate a program of persuasion, with the idea of securing a favourable vote in a follow-up referendum. If "yes," the Quebec government would initiate talks with Canada on such points as: protection for the rights of English-Canadian minorities in Quebec and French-Canadian minorities in Canada, English-owned businesses in Quebec, trade relations, arrangements for the use of transportation systems as the St.Lawrence Seaway, facilities in Quebec owned by the Canadian government.

IMMIGRATION

What Can We Lose? What Can We Gain?

The Green Paper on Immigration and Population Tabled in the House of Commons on February 3, 1975

"The aim of the Green Paper is to furnish Canadians with a foundation for constructive discussion of the role immigration policy should play in creating the sort of society they wish for themselves and their children . . . to help Canadians to think together about the many positive purposes immigration policy is designed to serve, and to explore the complex problems that need to be resolved in establishing policies that will best support these purposes.

. . .

The Green Paper does not make firm recommendations or propose solutions. It explores problems and discusses choices which Canadians may wish to consider in relation to Canada's population future, and immigration's contribution to that future.

. . .

Through much of Canada's history, the arguments supporting rapid population expansion seemed compelling, and coloured national attitudes towards immigration. Forcible [sic] as they were in the past, and although they still have support from many, the validity of these arguments in contemporary circumstances is now being questioned. . . .

. . .

Montreal, Toronto and Vancouver are the destinations preferred by an increasing number of migrants from all parts of Canada, and it is also in these areas that foreign migrants are particularly concentrated. A more dispersed pattern of immigrant settlement might help to alleviate some of the difficulties that plague these congested and rapidly-expanding areas.

. . .

. . . future immigration policies will need to be formulated with particular attention to their effects on the quality of life Canadian city dwellers seek.

. . .

Projections show that during the next decade, the Canadian labour force will continue to grow at a very rapid rate, posing a continuing and substantial challenge to the Canadian economy in terms of the number of new jobs that will have to be created each year. As a result, there are reasons to question the wisdom of the 'expansionist' immigration philosophy that has traditionally influenced Canada's outlook.

. . .

POLICY OPTIONS

Option #1

"Retain the present 'responsive' system of immigration management abroad—a system that does not fix, in advance, the numbers of visas to be issued over a given time span."

Option #2

"Gear the immigration program even more closely than at present to meet economic and labour market objectives. This would entail drawing a very clear line between the class of immigrants Canada admits because the labour market needs them, and those who are accepted for other reasons."

Option #3

"Develop and announce explicit targets for the number of visas to be issued annually on a global, regional and possibly post-by-post basis. This option could enable the immigration program to be deliberately related to national demographic/population growth policies as these are developed. It also would mean a major innovation in Canadian immigration policy—the establishment of quotas on the number of immigrants Canada is prepared to admit each year."

Option #4

"Establish an annual global ceiling for the total immigration movement, specifying the priorities to be observed in the issuance of visas to different categories of immigrants within that ceiling. . . . With the overall ceiling and priorities established, a forecast would then be made of the number of applicants in each priority group from each source country and area of the world."[1]

1. What kinds of immigrants does this favour? Explain your answer.

2. For one of options #2, #3, or #4 design a chart showing what new selection criteria may be needed.

3. For one of the options, describe the model immigrant, the one who would best fit the selection criteria.

GLOBAL PROCESSING PRIORITIES

1. Sponsored Dependents (NEED ONLY BE OF GOOD HEALTH & CHARACTER TO BE
         ADMISSIBLE. POINT SYSTEM IS NOT APPLICABLE.)

2. Independent Applicants and
    Nominated Relatives
    - destined to arrange employment or
    - destined to a designated occupation or
    - Occupational Demand 8 - 15 units

3. Persons whose presence in Canada would create employment (entrepreneurs)

4. Nominated Relatives and Independent Applicants who do not comply
    with any of the requirements of categories 2 or 3.

NOTE: Refugees are dealt with according to the individual need.

DECISIVE FACTORS IN SELECTION - NOMINATED RELATIVES AND INDEPENDENT APPLICANTS

Units of Assessment Obtained	Occupational Demand	Arranged Employment or Designated Occupation	Selection Result *
49 or less	not necessarily relevant	not necessarily relevant	refused
50 or more	0	NO	refused
50 or more	0	YES	passed
50 or more	1 to 15	not necessarily relevant	passed

* Applicants who meet the selection criteria must also be of good
   health and good character before admission as an immigrant is
   granted.

IMMIGRATION SELECTION CRITERIA (showing maximum units)		Nominated	Independent
(a)	EDUCATION & TRAINING	20	20
(b)	PERSONAL ASSESSMENT	15	15
(c)	OCCUPATIONAL DEMAND (if "O" occupational demand, the application is refused unless the applicant has "Arranged Employment" or is in a "Designated Occupation")	15	15
(d)	OCCUPATIONAL SKILL	10	10
(e)	AGE	10	10
(f)	ARRANGED EMPLOYMENT or DESIGNATED OCCUPATION		10
(g)	LANGUAGE English ------- 5 French -------- 5		10
(h)	RELATIVE		5
(i)	AREA DEMAND		5
	*Approved Application by Relative in Canada	15 to 30	
TOTALS	Reduce by 10 units where there is not Arranged Emp. or Designated Occupation	85 to 100	100

Nominator is Permanent Resident
Nominator is Canadian Citizen

	Permanent Resident	Canadian Citizen
* SON OR DAUGHTER 21 OR OVER	30	25
MARRIED SON OR DAUGHTER UNDER 21	30	25
BROTHER OR SISTER	30	25
PARENTS OR GRANDPARENTS UNDER 60	30	25
UNMARRIED NEPHEW OR NIECE UNDER 21	30	25
NEPHEW OR NIECE 21 OR UNDER	20	15
MARRIED NEPHEW OR NIECE UNDER 21	20	15
UNCLE, AUNT, GRANDSON OR GRANDDAUGHTER	20	15

NOTE: An immigration officer may approve or reject the admission
       of an immigrant regardless of units of assessment obtained
       if in his opinion the units obtained do not accurately
       reflect the applicant's chances of successfully establishing
       himself in Canada

Multiculturalism: Myth or Reality?

1. Canada is a country known for its many cultures.
2. Canada is a land with British-American traditions.

1. Canada is an ethnic mosaic.
2. Canada is striving for a uniform Canadian identity.

1. We are all immigrants here.
2. Canada is multilingual in theory but bilingual by law.

1. Europeans took over the country and turned the "natives" into an "ethnic group".
2. The native peoples are the "first Canadians".

1. Canadian history reveals the importance of immigrants in building an interesting and prosperous country.
2. Canadian history has many examples of immigrants being exploited and victimized by discrimination.

1. Canadians should encourage tolerance for different customs and values.
2. Canadians admire the person who works hard and has the goods to prove it.

1. For each pair of statements, tell whether you think #1 or #2 is most true. Why do you feel as you do?
2. Select one pair of statements and suggest the possible value assumptions in each.
3. If multiculturalism means that ethnic groups have the opportunity to be separate but equal, is Canada truly multicultural? If Canada is not, should she be? How can multiculturalism best be achieved?

When we think of the theory behind our free enterprise system, we often think that the consumer is king—that whatever we demand, producers will supply. Unfortunately, the system does not always work according to a simple theory. As Ellen Roseman points out in her book, *Consumer, Beware!,* the unwise consumer often becomes a pawn of the system.

Every day, Canadians buy shirts that shrink, toys that injure and roofs that leak. We sign contracts we don't understand for magazine subscriptions, home repairs and correspondence courses we don't really want. We answer ads for "first-quality" carpets that are actually sub-standard, "12,000-mile" used cars with odometers that the dealers have rolled back, washing machines "reduced from $350" that never sold anywhere near that price at all.

Consumers in CANADA:
You *Can* Fight Big Business!

... We shop in large impersonal department stores with no one to help us. Our grocery stores, which used to stock 1,500 items on their shelves twenty-five years ago, now carry close to 8,000 (of which a thousand a year are new). A barrage of advertising moulds our needs and instant credit satisfies them. Instead of the kings of the marketplace we're supposed to be, we usually feel much more like its pawns.

Our standard of living has never been higher, yet we've never been so dissatisfied. Nothing we buy ever seems to work properly, or to live up to its advertising. So we start to complain. . . .

What's mirrored in the complaints is our resentment against a new 1970's phenomenon—double whammy inflation. The prices go up and the quality goes down. . . . [1]

There are, however, things we can do to "fight Big Business". One of them is to become informed, concerned consumers. We spend hundreds of hours a year earning enough money to buy food, clothing, housing and luxury items and yet we are not conscientious consumers. Often we buy something for pretty unsound reasons: we saw it advertised on TV; it was on the "specials" table in an aisle of the supermarket; our friends are wearing it; we think we should have it for some unknown reason.

If we are operating on a budget, perhaps we are not as prone to buy on impulse as we would be if we were millionaires. But especially in times of inflation, wise money management is only the first step toward becoming a conscientious consumer. Other steps we could take might include the following.

1. Practice comparison shopping; compare prices on the same item at different stores before buying.
2. Look at items in terms of unit pricing. Food stores in particular list the price of an item individually or as 2/47¢. In order to know which size can is really cheaper, the price must be converted to price per ounce, pound, etc. Sometimes, the giant economy size or the one on special at 2/47¢ is *not* the cheapest one.
3. Watch newspapers for mid-week grocery specials and shop at more than one store if the savings are not eaten up in extra gas mileage or time.
4. Remember that "convenience foods" such as TV dinners, frozen fish and chips and so forth are more costly than those made from scratch.
5. When buying prescription drugs, ask the druggist to fill the prescription with the generic drug unless your doctor specifies differently. Brand name drugs are often more expensive than their generic counterparts and yet contain the same ingredients. For example, Bayer aspirin contains acetylsalicylic and yet is more expensive than acetylsalicylic acid tablets (the generic name for aspirin).

6. Investigate credit purchases. It is much cheaper in the long run to pay cash for an item, but we are not in the habit of doing this. If you buy on credit, you will be paying monthly interest charges on the unpaid balance of your account.
7. Beware of telephone sales or door-to-door sales gimmicks. Often, people are caught off guard when this type of salesperson greets them, and their sales pitches are often quite inviting. But even after signing a contract, Canadian law does provide for a brief period of time during which the consumer can void the contract.
8. Most important, be aware of the consumer protection and complaint bureaus in your town or city and do not fail to take advantage of them.

Government Aid

Although Canada has no Ralph Nader (the American, self-styled consumers' aid who first investigated car safety and later formed a group of young adults, who called themselves Nader's Raiders, to expand his work) she does have several government consumer agencies organized to help consumers.

The Consumers' Association of Canada (C.A.C.) gives Canadians a voice in consumer affairs by presenting briefs to all levels of government and business as well. It can report complaints and/or suggest improvements in products, manufacturing, advertising, retailing and so forth. Six times a year, it publishes the magazine *Canadian Consumer* which gives product testing results, buying tips and other information.

The federal Department of Consumer and Corporate Affairs has three main divisions:

1. Combines Investigation which promotes business competition; guards consumers against deceptive business practices such as price discrimination, price fixing, pricing to eliminate competition and price misrepresentation;
2. Corporate Affairs which deals with bankruptcy, corporations, patents and so forth;
3. Consumer Affairs which protects the consumer in the marketplace and is divided into four branches:
a. Research which investigates consumer safety, packaging, labelling, consumer credit, etc.;

b. Standards which develops product standards as provided by law;
c. Operations which carries out retail investigation and enforcement of the Food and Drug Act, Hazardous Product Act, True Labelling Act;
d. Consumer Service and Information which provides a central agency for consumer complaints and inquiries; distributes consumer information such as booklets on consumer credit, metrication, hazardous products and so on. You can write The Consumer, Box 99, Ottawa, Ontario, regarding any complaint or inquiry you might have as a consumer. There are also five regional offices.

All ten provinces have Consumer Protection Bureaus whose power and influence vary from province to province.

Better Business Bureaus and Chambers of Commerce in cities and towns across Canada also help in the fight to establish fair business-consumer relationships and practices. In the long run, however, it is up to the consumer to shop wisely, to be aware of unfair business practices, of where to go if a product or service is unsatisfactory, and to be prepared to take action to remedy the problem.

> **CAVEAT EMPTOR: Let the buyer beware!**

Poverty in the midst of plenty

Case # 1

The Person

Reginald Vance: lives in Alpine Valley
41 years old; vice-president, marketing, for a large firm
married; three children

The Situation

Mr. Vance has tried to give his family everything. He thinks of himself as a "good provider" and is respected as such by his colleagues and his friends. Because of his long hours of work and work-related entertaining, he spends little time with his family except on Sundays. On Saturdays, the children receive their generous allowances; often they go shopping with their mother, or in the case of Johnny, 14, with friends. Mrs. Vance has her own bank account, and can pay cash for her new car, fashionable clothes and other possessions. Although she has her hands full raising the children, she can afford to have a lady come in to do housework and prepare meals. Thus Mrs. Vance is able to spend extended periods at her club and dine with friends if she chooses.

One Friday night, Mr. Vance is surprised to be confronted by his wife who tells him that she cannot take their lifestyle any longer and that their eldest son, Johnny, has run away from home.

1. If poverty is deprivation or doing without, in what way can Mr. Vance be said to be poor? Mrs. Vance? The children?
2. Before the Friday night incident, what might Mr. Vance have said if he were asked if the Vances were poor?

Case # 2

The Person

Mrs. Jane Donne: lives in a racially mixed neighbourhood of Central City
33 years old; 4 children
grade 9 education; no special skills

The Situation:

Jane Donne lives with her husband James in the core of Central City. Since James had an accident a year ago, he has been generally unemployed and the family has had to live on any income Jane could make. This has meant that the Donnes and their four children have to live in low-income hous-

ing which they consider inadequate for their needs. Their two-bedroom apartment is in the basement of the oldest building, and the owner does not maintain it adequately. There are no playgrounds near their home, and so the children play on side streets which sometimes worries Mrs. Donne.

Money is always a problem. Mrs. Donne takes domestic jobs when Manpower can find them for her, but when she works, she worries about her two youngest children who never seem to listen to their father. In addition, when Mrs. Donne works, she must pay for her transportation to and from work, and she often resents having to clean other people's homes and offices when she has little time or energy to clean her own home.

All in all, Mrs. Donne tries to make ends meet as best she can, and tries to be a good mother to her children, all things considered.

1. If poverty means not having enough money to maintain an adequate standard of living, to what degree is the Donne family poor?
2. In what ways might the Donnes *not* consider themselves poor?

Case # 3

The Person

Brian Bruce: lives in Grayville, a town of fewer than 1 000 people
13 years old; eldest of five children
Brian's father is a merchant

The Situation

Brian is a grade nine student with excellent grades, and is described by teachers as creative. Small compared to his mates, he does not achieve well in hockey or baseball—the only team sports available in town, other than hubcap stealing. Besides schoolwork, Brian enjoys drawing and painting, listening to classical music and swimming.

On a visit to his cousin in the capital city, Brian is able to meet other young people his age, visit places and enjoy experiences he has only read about. He returns home, comparing and contrasting his life in Grayville with that of his cousin.

1. What opportunities do you think Brian has for self-fulfillment in Grayville?
2. What different opportunities might there be if he lived in the city as his cousin does?
3. Is Brian a victim of poverty? If so, how would you describe his poverty?

THE FOOD AND PEOPLE DILEMMA:

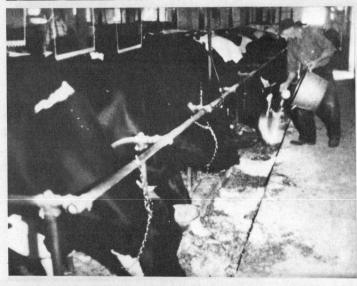

. . . Universal concern at the rapid increases in the earth's population in relation to the earth's resources is a product of this day and age. It is based on the ever-accelerating speed-up in the rate of population growth since 1900.

At the beginning of the century, the recorded world population was some 1.7 billion. By 1950, it had risen to 2.5 billion. Between 1950 and 1970 it leaped to 3.6 billion. Some 2.5 billion are recorded as living in low-income areas.

Today's picture is alarming enough. Worse is ahead. The United Nations has made two telling projections. The first reveals that, if the present levels of human fertility continue, some 8 billion people will be on this earth in less than thirty years. The second, a more moderate projection which assumes substantial fertility declines, places the world population figure in the year 2000 at approximately 6.5 billion of which 5 billion would inhabit the developing regions.

The Dilemma

The predicted doubling of the population by the end of the century underlines the dilemma of developing countries, whose economic and social development processes have not yet caught up with the basic essentials of decent living. In view of the present situation, where millions are under-fed, where educational and medical facilities are inadequate, and unemployment rampant, the prospect of a future with twice as many people to feed, house, educate and give job opportunities is hardly reassuring.[1]

Currently, one-third of the world's population is satiated by consuming three-quarters of the earth's harvested crops. Ironically, the greatest increases in food production in the past decades have occurred in the Satisfied World (SW), not the Hungry World (HW). Agricultural science and technology flourish among the well-fed and languish among the hungry. As a result, the satiated are threatened with obesity, the hungry with starvation.[2]

Metaphorically, each rich nation amounts to a lifeboat full of comparatively rich people. The poor of the world are in the other, much more crowded lifeboats. Continuously, so to speak, the poor fall out of their lifeboats and swim for a while in the water outside hoping to be admitted to the rich lifeboat. . . . What should the passengers on the rich lifeboats do? . . . (If they let the poor in) the boat is swamped and everyone drowns. Complete justice, complete catastrophe.[3]

In most poor countries, large-scale fertility declines cannot be expected until the living conditions of the majority of the population improve enough so that they no longer consider large families necessary for *economic* reasons and are therefore more likely to want fewer children.[4]

Whereas population growth in the poorer countries operates to keep people so impoverished that life itself is endangered, the most widespread consequence of population growth in the richer countries is to place restraints on personal freedoms and pleasures. When the statesmen of Asia, Africa, and Latin America talk of overpopulation, their emphasis is necessarily on economic development and the provision of bare essentials. But when we speak of overpopulation in an affluent country like the United States, it is mainly in terms of *quality of life*. It's not that we're threatened by a condition of "standing room only." Quite obviously, we're a long way from being extinguished as a people by the burden of sheer numbers. Nor, for a while at least, does our population growth present us with the prospect of becoming inadequately fed or of losing the world's highest material level of living. What most Americans stand to lose—and what to some extent they have already lost—is to be reckoned essentially in *qualitative* terms.

Population growth in the United States has already meant increasing control from external sources, less flexibility permitted in individual behaviour, greater centralization in government,

WHO WILL DECIDE?

crowded schools and recreation areas, vanishing countryside, air and water pollution, endless traffic jams, and a steady loss in time, solitude, quiet, beauty, and peace of mind.[5]

The fertility rate, defined as the number of babies born per year to 1,000 women in potentially procreative age brackets, has been declining almost everywhere. But the death rate has been descending even more drastically, resulting in larger gains in net growth. This is the least understood phenomenon. The rapid gains are predominantly due to reduced infant mortality. Few realize that among the 2.5 billion who constitute the Hungry World (HW), more than half are below 18 years of age. Yet more than half of all infants die before the age of five. The HW currently counts around 1 billion children, 650 million of whom will never reach adulthood. To all these children life is nothing more than a Vigil of Death.[6]

Currently (1973) the world is growing by almost a billion per decade. Man added 76 million in 1972, but the annual figure will be 80 million in the late 1970's and 100 million in the 1980's.[7]

Equally important to the food-and-people issue is the realization that even with zero population growth (ZPG) the amount of food needed will increase considerably, mainly because of the over-representation of young age-classes. When the 0-5 year olds reach the 10-15 year bracket, they will require a far greater daily intake per individual. For example, if ZPG became a reality in India today, 25-30 per cent more food would still be needed within a decade.[8]

Are there enough resources to allow the economic development of the 7 billion people expected by the year 2000 to a reasonably high standard of living? . . .

It depends on how the major resource-consuming societies handle some important decisions ahead. They might continue to increase resource consumption according to the present pattern. They might learn to reclaim and recycle discarded materials. They might develop new designs to increase the durability of products made from scarce resources. They might encourage social and economic patterns that would satisfy the needs of a person while minimizing, rather than maximizing, the irreplaceable substances he possesses and disperses.

All of these possible courses involve trade-offs. The trade-offs are particularly difficult in this case because they involve choosing between present benefits and future benefits.[10]

Gandhi said, "Earth provides enough for every man's need but not for every man's greed."

Should Canadians consume less? If they did, would other people have more?

What did you have for dinner Sunday? What might you have had if you lived in Peru?

Does "charity begin at home"? Should Canadians ignore the "hungry world" abroad until poverty is wiped out in Canada? Will the "hungry world" wait?

Are you cheating yourselves?

Millions Need Not Starve

Must millions starve in the coming years?

Not if the nations of the world give the effort to feed the hungry a higher priority and refuse to accept prophecies of doom which are so prevalent these days, say some food experts.

These people believe that man's inventiveness is equal to the task if the people and politicians of the world stand behind their researchers and learn from past mistakes.

In the past few years there have been repeated claims that the attempt by scientists and

technologists to produce a green revolution have failed. But people who have been involved in the attempts don't agree. Although the ''miracle grains'' developed by scientists need intensive irrigation, fertilizers and pesticides, and depend to a great extent for these on expensive petroleum, some scientists still feel that these problems can be overcome.

They suggest that we set up agricultural research centres in the third world. This is now being done in connection with high-protein corn which some claim is more nutritious than milk. There have also been suggestions that cereals be tailored to have the bean's ability to get nitrogen from the air instead of from expensive fertilizer, that trash fish be processed into a form acceptable to the public and that microbes be grown on various agricultural and industrial wastes to use for animal feed.[11]

Millions of people in Asia, Africa, and Latin America go to bed every night wondering if they will have enough food the next day to keep them alive. Millions of people in the United States go to bed every night wondering if they will have enough will power the next day to keep them on their low-calorie diets.[12]

We in the affluent world annually feed our livestock as much grain as all the people in China and India eat in a year.[13]

How did you decide what to have for lunch the other day? If the choice was yours alone to make and you had enough money, the possibilities were probably endless. But what if your finances wouldn't let you buy the food of your choice? If what you wanted wasn't available to you? If you had to buy something to share with five others? If you can imagine situations like these, you may be able to begin to realise what the food and people dilemma is all about.

Many Canadians are fortunate enough to be able to buy and eat delicious and nutritious food.

Other Canadians, however, are not so fortunate. Because of shortages in certain kinds of foods, distances to remote areas, and often low income levels, many of us are not able to eat the kinds of food we need to stay healthy. Children from some families may come to school not even having had a glass of milk to break the fast from their last meal. In northern areas, the cost of food is much higher than it would be in a southern Canadian city. Some families are unable to budget wisely and spend all their money on luxury items and convenience foods which are repeatedly advertised on TV.

Nevertheless, a visitor to Canada from Asia, Africa or Latin America would not believe that Canada had a food problem. The general level of prosperity here is so much higher than what we would find in the ''have not'' countries. For example, look at the following facts:

The U.N. estimates that in Africa and the Far East, 25 to 30 percent of the population suffers from significant malnutrition.

460 million people around the world are severely affected by malnutrition.

These countries require dramatic increases in farm productivity and effective population controls. They also need improved storage, processing and marketing facilities and nutrition education for everyone.

The question is one of people and food. What Canada's role should be in sharing the blessings she has received in terms of distribution of resources is the question we all must answer.

ARE WE OUR BROTHER'S KEEPER?

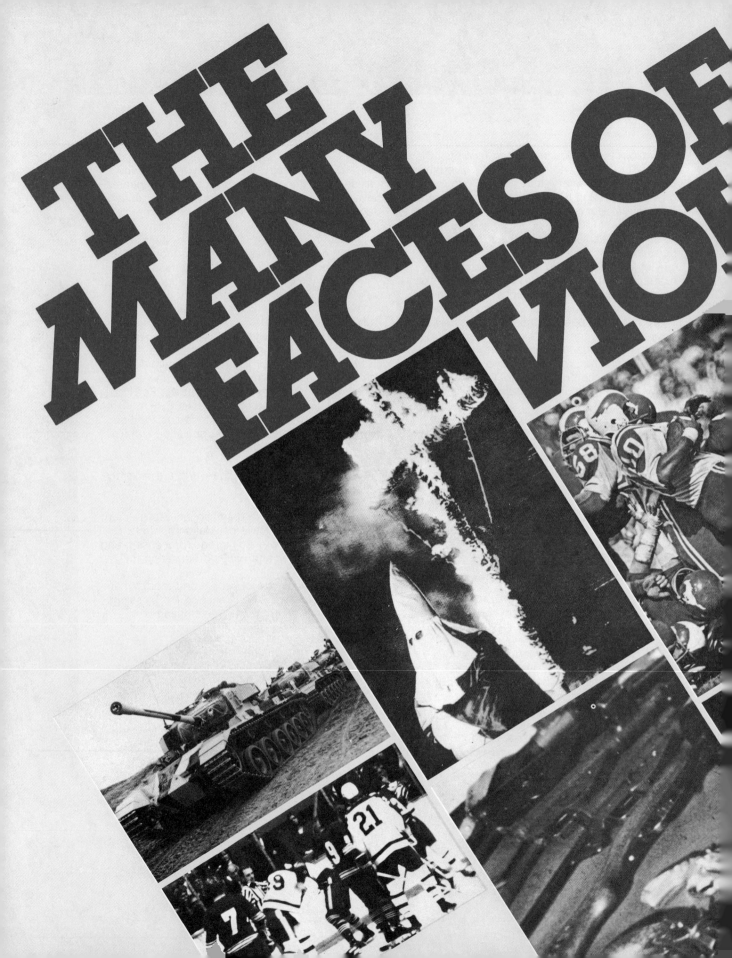

THE MANY FACES OF VIO

...ENCE

Kids can wind up in trouble or kids can wind up angels. But you have got to work on them, because it is easier to learn to be a murderer than it is to be a peace-maker.... We must not applaud the violent. We must even think twice before we applaud the motives of the violent. Successful violence merely breeds more violence.[1]

Will people learn to curb the age-old tendency toward violence, or will we have to move toward societal control through brain manipulation (mass hypnosis, drugs, surgery) either for individuals or whole cultures?

How is violence defined? Who decides about violence on TV and in the movies? When sports get violent, who is most responsible—the athletes or the spectators?

Vancouver is not the only Canadian city where organized crime has gained a foothold. In Toronto, a millionaire developer hires a man to murder his wife, a bookie is blown up in his car, a Winnipeg businessman has his legs broken with a baseball bat. Evidence of organized crime is surfacing everywhere. There has never been a federal investigation. I wonder why.[2]

MURDER-TERROR TACTICS

IRELAND

MIDEAST

The Christian Science Monitor

Technology the Good:

Wondrous as are the things computers have been taught to do, strictly they cannot think, but can only learn what men enable them to learn. They are far from infallible because they lack all judgment, and so can transform slight errors by their programmers into whopping errors. . . . Man remains the god that created them, only up to a point in his own image. They cannot go on to make up questions on their own, talk back independently, imagine, dream, aspire, create, or conspire to become Frankensteins. . . . They can process only quantitative or factual information, not qualitative judgments or social values. The real challenge is to the brains of the men who design and use the computers. . . . And the real danger is that man will abdicate his own responsibility, think only of problems of economy and efficiency that his mechanical creature can handle so swiftly and surely, and evade the value judgments that it cannot make.[1]

Modern technology may be broadly defined as the elaborate development of standardized, efficient means to practical ends. A comparable definition is Kenneth Galbraith's, "the systematic application of scientific or other organized knowledge to practical tasks." Jacques Ellul prefers to call this simply "technique". In any case, it is well to keep in mind that the term is not so precise or "scientific" as it may sound.[2]

Uses

Just what has modern technology done *to* as well as for people? For it has profoundly influenced all the major interests and activities of our society, affected people in innumerable ways. . . . [3]

What is technology? Is it just machines and tools—or is it a system, even a way of life?

What five inventions do you think have had the greatest effect on the way you live?

"Necessity is the mother of invention." What does this statement mean? Can you think of inventions that were not necessary? How do you decide?

Can an invention have both positive and negative effects?

Medical science can preserve health and life itself in ways that would have seemed incredible a few years ago. Wonderful as this is, advances in medical technology are creating new problems.

How should a hospital decide who gets the use of a kidney machine when there are fewer machines than patients? Who decides whether a patient being kept alive by a machine is more "dead" than "alive"?

What new kinds of technology are most needed now? Solar energy? Cyrogenics? Pollution controls? Farm equipment?

How are the uses of technology decided? Do you, and others like you, have a say? Should you? Do we have too much faith in technology as the way to solve human problems?

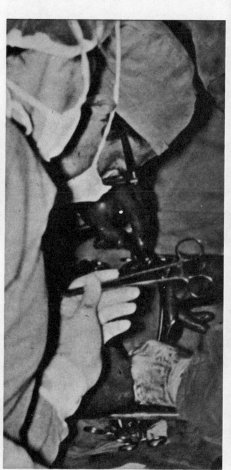

Technology the Bad:

Are the oceans habitable? Are they an alternative to life on a satellite or another planet? Will they escape the damage being done to the earth's land surface?

To get to the crux of the matter, we do well to ask why it is that all these terms—pollution, environment, ecology, etc.—have *so suddenly* come into prominence. . . .

We have indeed been living on the capital of living nature for some time but at a fairly modest rate. . . . In comparison with what is going on now and what has been going on, progressively, during the last quarter of a century, all the industrial activities of mankind up to, and including, World War II are as nothing. The next four of five years are likely to see more industrial production, taking the world as a whole, than all of mankind accomplished up to 1945.[1]

Industrialized nations have tended to rely on fossil fuels —such as coal and petroleum—for energy. What new forms of energy are being developed? What are some of the limitations? Must we learn to reduce our energy demands while waiting for new technology to come to the rescue? Do we need to change our values so that we are less dependent on technology?

. . . . The present-day economic system, based on impairment of the natural environment, is driving modern man to self-destruction. . . .

The bills must come in eventually. The growing damage to our natural environment capital which is resulting from the same processes that produce the wealth of our societies should make it clear to us that we cannot continue to grow as we have in the past.[2]

Pollution Dilemma

Main Factor Co. Ltd. in southern Manitoba has been dumping both solid and liquid wastes into a stream and has a small smokestack which creates some air pollution. The Clean Environment Commission has found the amount of pollutants from the factory to be almost double the legal levels. A hearing has been scheduled to hear from different groups involved with the Main Factor operation.

Factorville is the small town that has grown up around Main Factor. About 500 of the town's 2 000 residents work for the company and the rest depend on it to make a living. (Tom Brown, who operates the general store, would have to close if the people working at Main Factor and their families moved.) Harry Main built the Factorville and District School which serves 500 children at or below the Grade 9 level. In the centre of the town is the Ben E. Factor Park, built by Ben Factor in 1950. It has a large green area and a man-made lake for swimming, and is the town's largest recreational area.

Harry Main and Ben E. Factor are both close to being millionaires. They own and operate Main Factor Co. Ltd. and have worked hard to make it successful. They are both generous and try to keep their employees happy, because it's hard for small businesses and small towns to survive. As the wealthiest people in Factorville, they pay a large portion of the municipal taxes. This tax burden, their generosity and their seats on town council make them very powerful.

Rosey Thorne is head of Pollution Probe in the district. When her small son became ill recently, and doctors said the cause was poisoning from fish which had been caught in the stream, Rosie increased her cam-

Misuses

paign for pollution controls at Main Factor. Many other residents reported ill effects from the smoke and smells of the Main Factor plant. Rosie organized and distributed a petition demanding that Main Factor do something about the problem. She was also allowed to write three paragraphs on the editorial page of the *Factorville Town Crier*, the local newspaper, attacking Main Factor. The following edition carried a half-page rebuttal of her complaints. It explained that Main Factor operated with equipment that was outdated in 1960, but allowed Main Factor to continue to employ a large work force. It would require a large amount of money, the article said, to install new machinery required to cut down emissions, and this would mean a 40% reduction in staff. The arguments to be presented at the hearing were starting to take form.

Joe Worker, father of four, is a Main Factor employee. Reading these editorials, Joe realized that he was in a difficult position. He worked only with his hands, using a skill he had learned from his father. Main Factor was the only operation of its kind that Joe knew of that still had use for a man with his skill. The others had mechanized. He is living modestly in low-cost housing built by Main Factor. Joe is like almost everybody else in town. Sure he'd like to see Main Factor cleaned up, but not if it means losing his job.

Main Factor also affects other people in the town. Tom Brown, for instance, would suffer badly if he lost 40% of his customers and so would the other service industries.

Harry Main and Ben E. Factor have other things to consider. Such a large capital input into a product for which the demand was stable, but not rising, was a gamble. If the market suddenly dropped and Main Factor shut down, Harry and Ben would be nearly broke unless they could sell their industry to government, which is unlikely.

Rosie Thorne is prepared to fight. So are Messrs. Main and Factor.

Rosie Thorne
— Freelance writer and owner of small farm
— 39 years old, mother of a 12-year-old son
— active in community; member of school board

Harry Main and Ben E. Factor
— resourceful, aggressive, community-minded businessmen
— well-to-do, but much of their money is tied up in business
— powerful in politics, both local and provincial

Joe Worker
— in his thirties, with Main Factor for 14 years
— Grade 9 education, no skills except for those needed for his job
— curls, plays golf, belongs to the Golden Gopher lodge; otherwise uninvolved with community affairs unless directly affected or threatened

Hank Scoop
— editor of the *Factorville Town Crier*
— left large industrial city to live in the rural setting of Factorville
— town booster, member of Chamber of Commerce, coaches minor sports
— favourite hobby: fishing in stream

1. What do you think would be the main arguments presented by each of these people at the hearing?
2. Is the issue a clear-cut one between economy and ecology?
3. What values are in conflict?
4. Can you suggest a solution?

The family and sex roles: new perspectives

.... To most Canadians, the word "family" brings to mind the image of a group made up of a father, a mother and one or more children. This type of family is described as a "nuclear" family by sociologists and family experts. It is the typical family in Canada today. This has not always been true, however.

Before 1900, many families were "extended" families. This means simply that parents and children lived with, or near to, their relatives. .... Everybody worked together to make life easier. ...

In Canada, however, times changed, and with change came a better living standard. Society shifted from the country to the city. Agriculture gave way to industry. People moved from the country to the city in search of this better living standard. Relatives were slowly left behind.

The extended family was replaced by the nuclear family because of these changes in society. Change today continues at a fast rate. It seems certain that the family, faced with many pressures (including the women's liberation movement, the youthful "counter culture" and its "hang loose" philosophy, and the relaxation of sexual taboos) will force the nuclear family to change, perhaps a little, perhaps a lot.

Margaret Mead, the famous anthropologist, puts it like this:

"Students in rebellion, the young people living in communes, unmarried couples living together call into question the very meaning and structure of the stable family unit as our society has known it."[1]

Don't Limit Liberation
John Nichol

I have a wife and three daughters. They are all stronger, louder, meaner, more aggressive, less forgiving, better looking, nicer and more rested than I am. Therefore I concluded long ago that I would never write a column about the women's liberation movement. I knew that the din at home would be unbearable.

However, things have changed. Our federal government has said the magic words. **Why not**?

I believe that our whole society, going back to the time when the first ape man hit the first ape woman behind the ear with a mastodon bone, has a built in psychological bias which denies the competence of women.

I know what I am talking about. Being a woman is like being a husband or father. For as far back as anyone can remember husbands and fathers have been the subject of constant scorn and laughter in all the media.

Who is the idiot in all the comic strips? That's right—old dad! ...

On television today we have the hit show—All in the Family. Here we see the popular husband and father image at its clearest. Edith Bunker is not overly bright, but she is tolerant, smiling, warm, and above all else, forgiving. The daughter is beautiful and young—and forgiving. But Archie is stupid, bigoted, loud, fat, bald, and sloppy. . . .

And in the world of advertising the father/husband is the idiot to whom all things need explaining.

He has a cold but doesn't know how to cure it. He has an aching back but doesn't know where to rub. His garbage bags rip open. His dentures don't fit. He can't figure out his income tax. He has never tasted coffee like this before. Or tea. Or milk. He is a dolt. And a sucker.

And one day each year they have Father's Day. Tradition declares that each father will receive either a pair of carpet slippers or a necktie. These gifts are the eternal symbols of passive old age, and of slow strangulation, respectively.

So I agree that women should be released from the psychological corsets in which they struggle. And I have only one request. Women—if you do open the magic door to freedom and fulfillment, don't throw away the key. Pass it to the boys in the back room. Here—have a cigar![2]

How do the media reinforce sex role stereotyping?

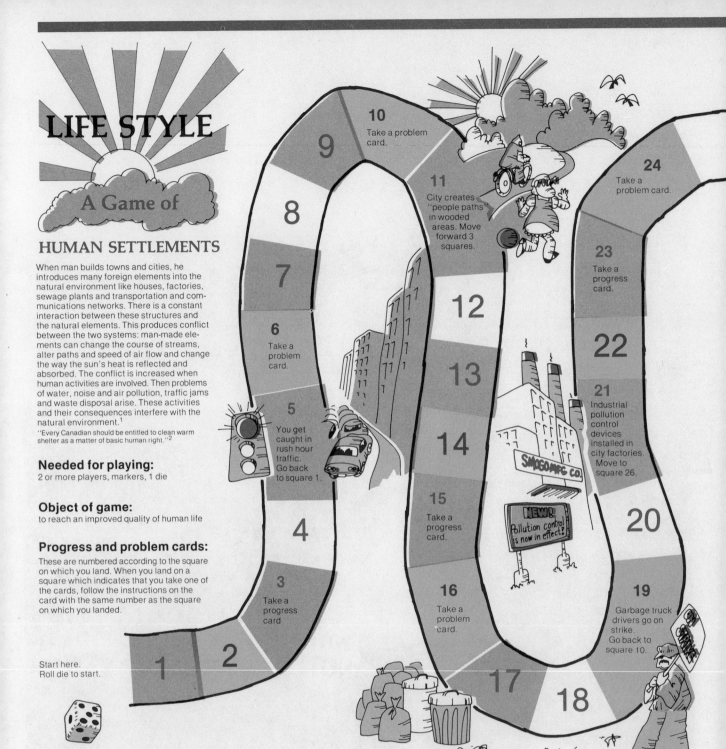

LIFE STYLE

A Game of

HUMAN SETTLEMENTS

When man builds towns and cities, he introduces many foreign elements into the natural environment like houses, factories, sewage plants and transportation and communications networks. There is a constant interaction between these structures and the natural elements. This produces conflict between the two systems: man-made elements can change the course of streams, alter paths and speed of air flow and change the way the sun's heat is reflected and absorbed. The conflict is increased when human activities are involved. Then problems of water, noise and air pollution, traffic jams and waste disposal arise. These activities and their consequences interfere with the natural environment.[1]

"Every Canadian should be entitled to clean warm shelter as a matter of basic human right."[2]

Needed for playing:
2 or more players, markers, 1 die

Object of game:
to reach an improved quality of human life

Progress and problem cards:
These are numbered according to the square on which you land. When you land on a square which indicates that you take one of the cards, follow the instructions on the card with the same number as the square on which you landed.

Start here.
Roll die to start.

1   **2**

3 Take a progress card

4

5 You get caught in rush hour traffic. Go back to square 1.

6 Take a problem card.

7

8

9

10 Take a problem card.

11 City creates "people paths" in wooded areas. Move forward 3 squares.

12

13

14

15 Take a progress card.

16 Take a problem card.

17

18

19 Garbage truck drivers go on strike. Go back to square 10.

20

21 Industrial pollution control devices installed in city factories. Move to square 26.

22

23 Take a progress card.

24 Take a problem card.

SMOGO MFG. CO.

NEW! Pollution control is now in effect!

Progress cards

3 Your town council has just decided to build a new library. Move ahead 4 spaces.

15 The town has raised enough money to build a new skating rink. Take an extra turn.

23 The city has set aside a large portion of its undeveloped land for green space. Move ahead 3 spaces.

27 Smoking has just been banned at city council meetings. Move ahead 2 spaces.

35 Your city starts free rapid transit to try to cut down on single-car traffic in the city core. Move ahead 2 spaces.

47 More low-cost housing is to be built throughout your city. Move ahead 2 spaces.

25

26 Enclosed pedestrian mall built in the downtown area of your city. Move to square 29.

27 Take a progress card.

28 Pollution count at danger level. Lose next turn.

29

30 United Way campaign in your area surpasses its goal. Move ahead 2 squares.

31

32 Unemployment in your town has been reduced by the building of a manufacturing plant. Take another turn.

33 Crime rate on the rise. Lose one turn.

34

35 Take a progress card.

36 You have been evicted from your apartment for not paying your rent. Move back 3 squares.

37

38 Your province has banned highway billboard advertising. Take another turn.

39

40

41 Federal government orders more aid for prospective home owners. Move ahead 1 square.

42 You have sold your city house and bought a farm. Take another turn.

43

44 Lose 1 turn.

45

46 Take a problem card.

47 Take a progress card.

48 The university in your city offers free tuition for senior citizens. Move forward 2 squares.

49

HOME: Improved quality of human life.

50

Problem cards

6	**10**	**16**	**24**	**43**	**46**
Sandbagging against the flood fails. Your house is badly damaged. Move back 5 spaces.	A new airport is to be constructed. Your house is on the no. 1 flight path. Lose your next turn.	A high-rise apartment is to be built across the street from your house. It will block your view. Move back 3 spaces.	The septic tank on your farm backed up. You have to pay $300 for repairs. Move back 4 spaces.	Industrial pollution has made the lake in your town unfit for swimming. Move back 2 spaces.	Because of a natural gas shortage, you decide to convert your furnace to oil at a large cost. Lose 1 turn.

Conclusion

There are some serious problems facing Canada today, many of which may seem remote to you. Perhaps you see these issues as the responsibility of those who formally hold power in Canada. But have you ever thought about what role you, as an individual, can play in this situation? What influence can you and thousands of others like you have on Canada's future? In addition to specific action like writing to your M.P. or working for local improvements in your neighbourhood, you can also influence the future of Canada by acting on the attitudes and values you hold. If you think now about what you want for Canada in the future, you can make some fundamental decisions in your own life which will help shape our future.

Suppose you had the power right now to suggest three changes to meet the challenges that are with us today. What things might you suggest? If your suggestions were adopted, how would they affect you and your lifestyle at present? How would they affect the future of Canada? What can you do now to make these suggestions happen? Are you willing to try?

End Notes

CHAPTER 1

1. Eric Nicol, "Never Mind the Act—Rehearse Your Encore", in *100 Years of What?*, pp. 8-9. Toronto: McGraw-Hill Ryerson, Ltd., 1966.
2. James Eayrs, cited in R. Reid, *The Canadian Style*, p. 233. Toronto: Fitzhenry & Whiteside, 1973.
3. From the *Organization of the Government of Canada*, 1974.
4. From Mackay, *The Unreformed Senate*, p. 1. London: Oxford University Press, 1926.
5. From "Meet the Real Quentin Durgens!" by Audrey Gill, *"Dialogue"*, a magazine of the Liberal Party of Canada. Vol. 1, No. 1, Summer 1975.
6. Sandra Gwyn, "Ottawa's Incredible Bureaucratic Explosion", *Saturday Night*, July/August, 1975.
7. From John Porter, *Vertical Mosaic*, p. 384. Toronto: University of Toronto Press, 1965.
8. The *Toronto Star*, 1972, cited in R. Reid, *op. cit.*, p. 233.
9. From P. E. Trudeau, "Constitutional Conference, June 14, 1971", *Conversations with Canadians*. Toronto: University of Toronto Press. Copyright 1972 by University of Toronto Press. Reprinted by permission of the University of Toronto Press.
9a. From the *Report of the Royal Commission on Bilingualism and Biculturalism, 1967*. Reprinted by permission of the Ministry of Supply and Services, Ottawa.
10. "Young Voters", *Winnipeg Free Press*, October 25, 1972.
11. From P. E. Trudeau, 1969, *op. cit.*, p. 13.
12. "The Heckler", *Saturday Night*, June 9, 1962.
13. Excerpted from "Franchise," copyright © 1955 by Quinn Publishing Co., Inc. which appears in the book *Earth is Room Enough* by Isaac Asimov. Reprinted by permission of Doubleday and Company, Inc.
14. From *Renegade in Power* by P. C. Newman, p. 81. Toronto: McClelland & Stewart Ltd., 1963. Reprinted by permission of The Canadian Publishers, McClelland & Stewart Ltd., Toronto.

CHAPTER 2

1. From C. Harris and J. Warkentin, *Pre-Confederation Canada*, p. 329. Toronto: Oxford University Press, 1974.
2. For a fuller account and bibliography see the article by Roy St. George Stubbs, in *Transactions*, Series III, No. 25, 1968-1969. (Manitoba: Historical and Scientific Society of Manitoba).
3. From *The National Dream: The Great Railway, 1871-1881* by Pierre Berton, pp. 184-185. Toronto: McClelland & Stewart Ltd., 1970. Reprinted by permission of The Canadian Publishers, McClelland & Stewart Ltd., Toronto.
4. From *Ideas in Exile: A History of Canadian Inventions* by J. J. Brown, p. 165. Toronto: McClelland & Stewart Ltd., 1967. Reprinted by permission of The Canadian Publishers, McClelland & Stewart Ltd., Toronto.
5. Sanford Fleming, "The Canadian Alpine Journal 1899", quoted in John Murray Gibbon, *The Romantic History of the Canadian Pacific*, p. 296. New York: Tudor Publishing Company, 1937.

6. From O. D. Skelton, *The Railway Builders*, pp. 167-168. Toronto: McGraw-Hill Ryerson Ltd., 1965.

7. From John Murray Gibbon, *op. cit.*, p. 241.

8. From *The Last Spike: The Great Railway 1881-1885* by Pierre Berton, pp. 108-109. Toronto: McClelland & Stewart Ltd., 1971. Reprinted by permission of The Canadian Publishers, McClelland & Stewart Ltd., Toronto.

9. *Ibid.*, p. 109.

10. From Joseph Pope, *Memoirs of the Right Honourable Sir John Alexander Macdonald, G.C.B.*, pp. 332-333. Ottawa: J. Durie & Son, 1894.

11. From Goldwin Smith, *Canada and the Canadian Question*. Toronto: University of Toronto Press. Copyright 1971 by University of Toronto Press. Reprinted by permission of the University of Toronto Press.

12. From George R. Parkin, "The Reorganization of the British Empire", *The Century*, Vol. XXXVII, December 1888, pp. 188-191.

13. John T. Saywell, "The 1890's", in Careless and Brown (eds.), *The Canadians, 1867-1967*, p. 110. Toronto: Macmillan Company of Canada, Ltd., 1967.

14. From Paul F. Sharp, *Whoop-Up Country: The Canadian American West, 1867-1967*, pp. 204-205. Minneapolis: University of Minnesota Press, 1955.

15. From J. K. Howard, *Strange Empire*, p. 264. Toronto: Swan Publishing Co., 1965.

16. From G. H. Needler, *Louis Riel*, p. 55. Toronto: Burns & MacEachern Ltd., 1965.

17. From G. Stanley, *The Birth of Western Canada*, p. 281. Toronto: University of Toronto Press. Copyright 1960 by University of Toronto Press. Reprinted by permission of University of Toronto Press.

18. *Ibid.*, p. 378.

19. From *The Queen vs. Louis Riel*, pp. 147-152. Ottawa: Queen's Printer, 1886.

20. *Toronto Evening News*, April 22, 1885, cited in J. M. Bliss (ed.), *Canadian History in Documents, 1763-1966*, pp. 195-196. Toronto: McGraw-Hill Ryerson Ltd., 1966.

21. Canada 70 Team, *The Toronto Telegram*, quoted in *Alienation and Anger (The Prairies)* by F. Kelly and J. Marshall, pp. 3-6. Toronto: McClelland & Stewart Ltd., 1969. Reprinted by permission of The Canadian Publishers, McClelland & Stewart Ltd., Toronto.

22. *Brandon Sun*, May, 1889. Manitoba: Manitoba Archives.

23. Father Lacombe to Laurier, quoted in O. D. Skelton, *Life and Letters of Sir Wilfrid Laurier*, Vol. 1, pp. 470-471. Toronto: Oxford University Press, 1922.

24. From *House of Commons Debates*, March 3, 1896, pp. 2758-2759.

25. *Ibid.*, pp. 2734-2736.

26. *Laurier Papers*, PAC, Series A, No. 5, pp. 3739-3743, cited in Reid *et al*, *A Sourcebook of Canadian History*, p. 353. Toronto: Longmans, Green & Co., 1959.

27. P. E. Trudeau to Mr. K. Douglas Sheldrick, President, Quebec Association of Protestant School Board. Courtesy of Mr. R. A. A. Zimmer, Special Assistant to the Minister of National Defence (Honourable James Richardson), Winnipeg. Copy of letter sent to R. Kirbyson on his request.

28. From E. C. Guillet, *You'll Never Die, John A!*, p. 52. Toronto: Macmillan Company of Canada, Ltd., 1957.

29. From J. Pope, *op. cit.*, V. 2, pp. 253, 273-274.

CHAPTER 3

1. From J. W. Dafoe, *Laurier: A Study in Canadian Politics*, p. 62. Toronto: Thomas Allen & Son, Ltd., 1922.

2. From Arthur Lower, *Canadians in the Making*, p. 350. Toronto: Longman Canada Ltd., 1958.

3. "1899/Wordly Pleasures", *Canadian Churchmen*, June, 1975.

4. From *A Living Profit, Studies in the Social History of Canadian Business: 1883-1911* by Michael Bliss, p. 5. Toronto: McClelland & Stewart Ltd. (The Canadian Social History Series), 1974. Reprinted by permission of The Canadian Publishers, McClelland & Stewart Ltd., Toronto.

5. Arthur Lower, "Canada at the Turn of the Century, 1900", in Wm. J. Megill, *Patterns of Canada*, p. 146. Toronto: McGraw-Hill Ryerson Ltd., 1966.

6. Rupert Brooke, "Letters from America", cited in Wm. Toye (ed.), *A Book of Canada*, pp. 226-228. London: William Collins & Sons & Co., Ltd., 1968.

7. From *The Anatomy of Poverty: The Condition of the Working Class in Montreal, 1897-1929* by Terry Copp. pp. 29, 31. Toronto: McClelland & Stewart Ltd., 1974. Reprinted by permission of The Canadian Publishers, McClelland & Stewart Ltd., Toronto.

8. From C. W. Gordon, *Postscript to Adventure: The Autobiography of Ralph Connor*, p. 138. New York: Holt, Rinehart & Winston, 1938.

9. From *Canada, 1896-1921* by R. Cook and Brown, p. 167. Toronto: McClelland & Stewart Ltd., 1973. Reprinted by permission of The Canadian Publishers, McClelland & Stewart Ltd., Toronto.

10. Tom MacInnes, "The Port of Vancouver", quoted in William J. Megill (ed.), *op. cit.*, p. 110.

11. Judith McErvel, "Wages and Prices", quoted in G.P. de T. Glazerbrook *et al*, *A Shopper's View of Canada's Past; Pages from Eaton's Catalogue*, p. xv. Toronto: University of Toronto Press. Copyright 1969 by University of Toronto Press. Reprinted by permission of the University of Toronto Press.

12. Katherine B. Brett, "Notes on Fashion in Costume", quoted in G.P. de T. Glazerbrook *et al*, *op. cit.*, pp. x-xi.

13. Ralph Allen, "Peace River Country", quoted in William Toye (ed.), *op. cit.*, p. 243.

14. From Andrew King, *Pen, Paper and Printing Ink*, pp. 42-43. Saskatoon: Western Producer Prairie Books, 1970.

15. From Nancy and Maxwell L. Howell, *Sports and Games in Canadian Life, 1700 to the Present*, pp. 142-143. Toronto: Macmillan Company of Canada, Ltd., 1969.

16. From *Janey Canuck in the West* by Emily Murphy, p. 188. Toronto: McClelland & Stewart Ltd., 1975. Reprinted by permission of The Canadian Publishers, McClelland & Stewart Ltd., Toronto.

17. *Ibid.*, pp. 23-24.

18. From Andrew King, *op. cit.*, pp. 86-87.

19. *Ibid.*, p. 88.

20. From Nancy and Maxwell L. Howell, *op. cit.*, p. 166.

21. *Ibid.*, pp. 171-172.

22. *Ibid.*, pp. 176-177.

23. *Ibid.*, pp. 188-189.

24. From Henry J. Morgan and Lawrence J. Burpee, *Canadian Life in Town and Country*, p. 106. London: George Newness Ltd., 1905.

25. Archibald Lampman, quoted in A. J. M. Smith (ed.), *Two Canadian Poets*, p. 30. Toronto: A. J. M. Smith, 1962.

26. Charles Mair, quoted in Douglas Lochhead (ed.), *Dreamland and Other Poems, Tecumseh: A Drama*, pp. 139, 141. Toronto: University of Toronto Press, 1974.

27. From Sara Jeannette Duncan, *A Social History: How Orthodicia and I Went Round the World by Ourselves*, p. 7. New York: A. L. Burt, 1890.

28. From Ralph Connor, *Glengarry School Days: A Story of the Early Days in Glengarry*, pp. 14-21. Toronto: The Westminister Co., Ltd., 1902.

29. Nellie McClung, quoted in M. Bliss (ed.), *In Times Like These*, pp. 40, 47-48. Toronto: University of Toronto Press (The Social History of Canada Series). Copyright 1972 by University of Toronto Press. Reprinted by permission of the University of Toronto Press.

30. "My Financial Career" by Stephen Leacock, quoted in J. B. Priestly (ed.), *The Best of Leacock*, pp. 23-25. Toronto: McClelland & Stewart Ltd., 1957. Reprinted by permission of The Canadian Publishers, McClelland & Stewart Ltd., Toronto.

CHAPTER 4

1. From H. J. Morgan and L. J. Burpee, *Canadian Life in Town and Country*, p. 238. London: George Newness Ltd., 1905.

2. From G. P. de T. Glazerbrook, *A History of Transportation in Canada*, p. 316. Toronto: Ryerson Press, 1938.

3. From *The Foreigner: A Tale of Saskatchewan* by Ralph Connor, pp. 14-15. Toronto: McClelland & Stewart Ltd. (The Westminister Co.), 1909. Reprinted by permission of The Canadian Publishers, McClelland & Stewart Ltd., Toronto.

4. From John W. Dafoe, *Clifford Sifton in Relation to His Times*, p. 142n. Toronto: The Macmillan Company of Canada, Ltd., 1931.

5. From *Under the Ribs of Death* by John Marlyn, pp. 23-24. Toronto: McClelland & Stewart Ltd. (New Canadian Library Edition), 1971. Reprinted by permission of The Canadian Publishers, McClelland & Stewart Ltd., Toronto.

6. From Ralph Connor, *op. cit.*, pp. 85-86.

7. W. O. Mitchell, quoted in *Historic Headlines* by Pierre Berton, p. 58. Toronto: McClelland & Stewart Ltd., 1967. Reprinted by permission of The Canadian Publishers, McClelland & Stewart Ltd., Toronto.

8. From Nellie McClung, *Clearing in the West*, pp. 370-371. Toronto: Thomas Allen & Son Ltd., 1935.

9. Margaret Atwood, "Afterword" in "The Journals of Susanna Moodie", quoted in John Columbo (ed.), *Columbo's Canadian Quotations*, p. 28b. Edmonton: M. G. Hurtig Ltd., 1974.

10. J. W. Sparling, "Introduction", to James S. Woodsworth, *Strangers Within Our Gates or Coming Canadians*, pp. 3-4. Toronto: The Missionary Society of the Methodist Church, 1909.

11. From Jim MacGregor, *North-West of Sixteen*, pp. 155-156. Edmonton: M. G. Hurtig Ltd., 1968.

12. Bernard Slade, "The Canadian", Winnipeg Tribune, July 26, 1975.

13. From Careless and Brown (eds.), *The Canadians, 1867-1967*, pp. 146-147. Toronto: The Macmillan Company of Canada, Ltd., 1967.

14. From Tony J. Kuz (ed.), *Winnipeg, 1874-1974: Progress and Prospects*, pp. 10-11. Winnipeg: Manitoba Department of Industry and Commerce, 1974.

15. From W. A. Mackintosh, *The Economic Background of Dominion-Provincial Relations*, Appendix III, p. 51. Ottawa: Royal Commission Report on Dominion-Provincial Relations. Reproduced by permission of the Department of Supply and Services, Ottawa.

16. From *The Opening of the Canadian North, 1870-1914* by Morris Zaslow, p. 104. Toronto: McClelland & Stewart Ltd., 1971. Reprinted by permission of The Canadian Publishers, McClelland & Stewart Ltd., Toronto.

17. From William Kilbourne, *The Elements Combined: A History of the Steel Company of Canada*, pp. 65-66. Toronto: Clarke, Irwin and Co., Ltd., 1960.

18. From A. J. T. Taylor, *Beaverbrook*, p. 33. New York: Simon and Schuster, 1972. Reprinted by permission of Harold Ober Associates Inc., © 1972 by A. J. P. Taylor.

19. From Don Aiken, "Unbelievable for those who remember rural life", *Winnipeg Tribune*, January 14, 1976, pp. 1, 5.

CHAPTER 5

1. "Waiting for the War Signal in Europe", *New York Tribune*, August 1, 1914.

2. From Bruce Bairnsfather, *Bullets and Billets*, pp. 86-89. London: Grant Richards Ltd., 1916.

3. L. O. Davis, "Le Canada", August 1914, quoted in Raymond Reid, *The Canadian Style*, p. 273. Toronto: Fitzhenry & Whiteside Ltd., 1973.

4. "Ypres—1915" by Alden Nowlan is reprinted from Andy Wainwright (ed.), *Notes for a Native Land* by permission of Oberon Press, p. 101-102. Toronto: Oberon Press, 1969.

5. William Orpen, "An Onlooker in France", quoted in Christopher Martin, *Battle of the Somme*, p. 110. London: Wayland Publishers, 1973.

6. F. Scott Fitzgerald, "Tender is the Night", quoted in C. Martin, *op. cit.*, p. 111. Reprinted by permission of Charles Scribner's and Sons, New York, 1960.

7. From Sheldon Williams, *The Canadian Front in France and Flanders*, pp. 44-45. London: A & C Black Ltd., 1920.

8. From Sholto Douglas, *Years of Conflict: A Personal Story of the First World War in the Air*, p. 304. London: William Collins & Sons, Ltd., 1963. Reprinted by permission of A. D. Peters & Co. Ltd.

9. From Lt. Col. George A. Drew, *Canada's Fighting Airmen*, p. 52. Toronto: McLean Publishing Company, 1930.

10. W. A. Willison, "In Winter Quarters, 1917-1918", quoted in *Canada in the Great World War*, Vol. V., pp. 13-16. Toronto: United Publishers of Canada, Ltd., 1920.

11. *Ibid.*, pp. 27-28.

12. "Two Years of War; As Viewed from Ottawa", p. 35. Ottawa. *The Civilian*, 1916.

13. "The White Feather" quoted in *The Canadian Annual Review*, p. 423. Ottawa: Queen's Printer, 1916.

14. From *Bethune* by Roderick Stewart, p. 8. Copyright 1973 by Roderick Stewart. Reprinted by permission of the Author and New Press, Don Mills, Ontario.

15. From *Grain* by Robert J. C. Stead, pp. 106-107. Toronto: McClelland & Stewart Ltd. (New Canadian Library Edition), 1969. Reprinted by permission of The Canadian Publishers, McClelland & Stewart Ltd., Toronto.

16. From Leslie M. Frost, *Fighting Men*, p. 54. Toronto: Clarke, Irwin and Company, Ltd., 1967.

17. From George F. G. Stanley, *Canada's Soldiers: The Military History of an Unmilitary People* (3rd ed.), p. 137. Toronto: Macmillan Company of Canada, Ltd., 1974.

18. From J. T. Copp and T. D. Tait, *The Canadian Response to War 1914-1917*, p. 41. Toronto: Copp Clark Publishing (Canada) Ltd., 1971.

19. From *House of Commons Debates*, Vol. III, pp. 2547-2548, 1917.

20. Rev. S. D. Chown, quoted in J. M. Bliss, *Canadian History in Documents, 1763-1966*, pp. 250-252. Toronto: McGraw-Hill Ryerson Ltd., 1966.

21. Bourassa, "La Conscription" (trans. Larry M. Herstein), quoted in *Canadian Annual Review*, pp. 11, 16, 17, 23, 1917.

22. Laurier, *House of Commons Debates*, June 18, 1917.

23. *Ibid.*, November 4, 1917.

24. Villeneuve, quoted in *Canadian Annual Review*, pp. 493, 495, 1917.

25. Brewster, quoted in Brown and Prang *Confederation to 1949*, Vol. III, p. 174. Scarborough, Ontario: Prentice-Hall of Canada, Ltd., 1966.

26. *Grain Growers Guide*, p. 9, October 14, 1914.

27. From David Carnegie, *The History of Munitions Supply in Canada, 1914-1918*, Appendix. Toronto: Longman's Green and Company, 1925.

28. From Morden Lazarus, *Years of Hard Labour—An Account of the Canadian Workingman His Organizations and Tribulations over a Period of more than a Hundred Years*, p. 15. Don Mills, Ontario: Ontario Federation of Labour, 1974.

29. Based on Mary Lile Benham, *Nellie McClung*. Don Mills: Fitzhenry & Whiteside, 1975.

30. From *Canada 1896-1921: A Nation Transformed* by R. C. Brown and R. Cook, Toronto: McClelland & Stewart Ltd. (The Canadian Centenary Series), 1974. Reprinted by permission of The Canadian Publishers, McClelland & Stewart Ltd., Toronto.

CHAPTER 6

1. James Eayrs, "Canadianism: Back and Forth on the National Swing", quoted in *Between Friends*, p. 200. Toronto: McClelland & Stewart Ltd., 1976.

2. From *Janey Canuck in the West* by Emily Murphy, pp. 136-137. Toronto: McClelland & Stewart Ltd., 1975. Reprinted by permission of The Canadian Publishers, McClelland & Stewart Ltd., Toronto.

3. From Brown and Prang, *Confederation to 1949*, Vol. III, p. 111. Scarborough, Ontario: Prentice-Hall of Canada, Ltd., 1966.

4. From O. D. Skelton, *Life and Letters of Sir Wilfred Laurier*, Vol. II, p. 107. London: Oxford University Press, 1922.

5. From W. A. Riddell (ed.), *Documents of Canadian Foreign Policy, 1917-1939*, p. 60. Toronto: Oxford University Press, 1962.

6. As quoted in Robert MacGregor Dawson, *William Lyon Mackenzie King: A Political Biography*, pp. 456, 477. Toronto: University of Toronto Press, 1958.

7. From A. R. M. Lower, *Colony to Nation*, rev. ed., pp. 483-485. Toronto: Longman's Green and Company, 1964.

8. From *House of Commons Debates*, p. 93, February 11, 1936.

9. From *House of Commons Debates*, p. 251, January 25, 1937.

10. From W. A. Riddell, *op. cit.*, p. 159.

11. Anne Marriott, "The Wind Our Enemy", quoted in Lorne Pierce (ed.), *The Ryerson Poetry Chap-Books*. Toronto: McGraw-Hill Ryerson Ltd. Reprinted by permission of the Author.

12. From Hugh MacLennan, *Barometer Rising*, pp. 248-249. Toronto: Macmillan Company of Canada, Ltd., 1948.

CHAPTER 7

1. From *Ordeal By Fire*, copyright © 1961 by Ralph Allen, pp. 293-294. Reprinted by permission of Doubleday & Company, Inc.

2. From O. J. Firestone, *Industry and Education*, pp. 59-60. Ottawa: University of Ottawa Press 1969.

3. D. G. Creighton, quoted in the *Canadian Annual Review 1924-1925*, pp. 676-679.

4. From G. R. Stevens, *History of the Canadian National Railways*, p. 326. New York: Macmillan Publishing Company, Inc., 1973.

5. Reprinted from *Canada On Wheels* by John de Bondt by permission of Oberon Press, p. 8. Ottawa: Oberon Press, 1970.

6. *Ibid.*, p. 46.

7. From André Sigfried, *The Race Question in Canada*, pp. 222-224. London: Eveleigh Nash, 1907.

8. From Brown and Prang, *Confederation to 1949*, pp. 177-178. Scarborough, Ontario: Prentice-Hall of Canada, Ltd., 1966.

9. From Jack Gray, *Striker Schneiderman*, pp. 33-34, 61. Toronto: University of Toronto Press. Copyright 1973 by University of Toronto Press. Reprinted by permission of University of Toronto Press.

10. From *The Kingdom of Canada* by W. L. Morton, p. 443. Toronto: McClelland & Stewart Ltd., 1969. Reprinted by permission of The Canadian Publishers, McClelland & Stewart Ltd., Toronto.

11. J. S. Woodsworth, "The Western Labour News", June 12, 1919, quoted in Grace MacInnis, *J. S. Woodsworth, A Man To Remember*, pp. 134-135. Toronto: Macmillan Company of Canada, Ltd., 1953.

12. J. S. Woodsworth, quoted in Grace MacInnis, *op. cit.*, pp. 134-135.

13. John Maclean, as quoted in Kenneth McNaught, *A Prophet on Politics, A Biography of J. S. Woodsworth*, p. 111. Toronto: University of Toronto Press, 1959.

14. *The Winnipeg Citizen*, May 19, 1919, quoted in J. E. Rea, *The Winnipeg General Strike*, p. 32. Toronto: Holt, Rinehart and Winston of Canada, Ltd., 1973.

15. *Toronto Star*, May 23, 1919, quoted in J. E. Rea, *op. cit.*, pp. 46-47.

16. Justice H. C. Robson, as quoted in D. C. Masters, *The Winnipeg General Strike*, p. 132. Toronto: University of Toronto Press, 1950.

17. *Ibid.*, p. 137.

18. From Kenneth McNaught and D. J. Bercuson, *The Winnipeg Strike, 1919*, pp. 112-113. Don Mills, Ontario: Longman Canada Ltd., 1974.

19. K. McNaught, "The Future of the Winnipeg General Strike", quoted in S. Clarkson (ed.), *Visions 2020*, pp. 253-254. Edmonton: Hurtig Publishers, 1970.

20. From Brown and Prang, *op. cit.*, pp. 100, 89-90.

21. From Ralph Allen, *op. cit.*, pp. 221-222.

22. From A. R. M. Lower, *Canadians in the Making: A Social History of Canada*, pp. 424-425. Toronto: Longman Canada Ltd., 1958.

23. From *A Treasury of Canadian Humour* by Robert T. Allen, p. 57. Toronto: McClelland & Stewart Ltd., 1967. Reprinted by permission of The Canadian Publishers, McClelland & Stewart Ltd., Toronto.

24. From H. J. Boyle, *Mostly in Clover*, pp. 23-24, 178-179, 180-181. Toronto: Clarke, Irwin & Co., Ltd., 1961.

25. From Andrew King, *Pen, Paper and Printing Ink*, pp. 93, 98. Saskatoon: Western Producer Prairie Books, 1970.

26. From Brian McFarlane, *Fifty Years of Hockey*, pp. 40-41. Toronto: Pagurian Press Ltd., 1967. © Pagurian Press Limited, re-printed by permission.

27. From Frank Boucher, *When The Rangers Were Young*, p. 58. New York: Dodd, Mead & Co., 1973.

28. W. D. Euler, *House of Commons Debates*, quoted in Ralph Allen, *op. cit.*, pp. 289-290.

29. From James Gray, *Booze* pp. 169-170. Toronto: Macmillan Company of Canada, Ltd., 1972.

30. From *Flame of Power, The Story of Canada's Greatest Businessmen* by P. C. Newman, pp. 22-23. Toronto: McClelland & Stewart Ltd., 1959. Reprinted by permission of The Canadian Publishers, McClelland & Stewart Ltd., Toronto.

31. From D. M. LeBourdais, *Nation of the North, Canada Since Confederation*, p. 201. London: Methuen and Company, 1953.

CHAPTER 8

1. From V. Hoar, *The Great Depression—Essays and Memoirs From Canada and the U.S.*, p. iv. Toronto: Copp Clark Publishing (Canada) Ltd., 1969.

2. F. R. Scott and H. M. Cassidy, "Labour Conditions in the Men's Clothing Industry", quoted in M. Horn (ed.), *The Dirty Thirties*, pp. 119-120. Toronto: Copp Clark Publishing (Canada) Ltd., 1972.

3. From *Rowell-Sirois Report*, Book I, p. 150. Ottawa: Commission on Dominion-Provincial Relations. Reproduced by permission of the Department of Supply & Services, Ottawa.

4. Sir Henry Thornton, quoted in M. Horn (ed.), *op. cit.*, pp. 46-47.

5. *Toronto Star*, May 11, 1932, quoted in M. Horn (ed.), *op. cit.*, p. 142.

6. From Brown and Prang, *Confederation to 1949*, pp. 243, 244, 246. Scarborough, Ontario: Prentice-Hall of Canada, Ltd., 1966.

7. From H. B. Neatby, *The Politics of Chaos, Canada in the Thirties*, p. 49. Toronto: Macmillan Company of Canada, Ltd., 1972.

8. "Regina Manifesto", as quoted in Kenneth McNaught, *A Prophet in Politics, A Biography of J. S. Woodsworth*, pp. 321-330. Toronto: University of Toronto Press, 1959. Our thanks to the New Democratic Party of Canada for their permission to reprint.

9. From the book *Ten Lost Years: 1929-1939* by Barry Broadfoot, p. 387. Copyright © 1973 by Barry Broadfoot. Used by permission of Doubleday & Company, Inc.

10. Anne Marriott, from *The Wind Our Enemy*, quoted in Lorne Pierce (ed.), *The Ryerson Poetry Chap-Books*. Toronto: McGraw-Hill Ryerson Ltd. Reprinted by permission of the Author.

11. R. Ross Annett, "It's Gotta Rain Sometime", quoted in Green *et al*, *A Century of Canadian Literature*, pp. 196-197. Toronto: McGraw-Hill Ryerson Ltd., 1967.

12. "What happened to all the Pianos?", in Barry Broadfoot, *op. cit.*, pp. 242, 246-247.

13. From J. H. Gray, *The Winter Years*, pp. 50-52. Toronto: Macmillan Company of Canada, Ltd., 1966.

14. From *This Was Radio: A Personal Memoir* by Joseph Julian. Copyright © 1975 by Joseph Julian. Reprinted by permission of The Viking Press.

15. Roy Daniells, "All Through the Thirties", quoted in *The Poet's Record: Verses on Canadian History* by K. Wilson and E. Motheral, p. 81. Toronto: McClelland & Stewart Ltd., 1975. Reprinted by permission of The Canadian Publishers, McClelland & Stewart Ltd., Toronto.

16. From J. H. Gray, *op. cit.*, pp. 148-149.

17. From Barry Broadfoot, *op. cit.*, p. 97.

18. From J. H. Gray, *op. cit.*, pp. 144-145.

19. From Ernest Watkins, *R. B. Bennett*, p. 168. London: Martin, Secker & Warburg Ltd., 1963.

20. From H. B. Neatby, *op. cit.*, p. 32.

21. From *The Making of a Nation* by William Kilbourne, p. 69. Toronto: McClelland & Stewart Ltd., (Canadian Centennial Publishing Co.), 1965. Reprinted by permission of The Canadian Publishers, McClelland & Stewart Ltd., Toronto.

22. "Pompous, Smug and Rich", in Barry Broadfoot, *op. cit.*, pp. 310, 311.

23. "The Regina Riot—A Snow Job?", in Barry Broadfoot, *op. cit.*, pp. 366-367.

24. *Ibid.*, pp. 125-126.

25. "Hard Times Killed My Man", in Barry Broadfoot, *op. cit.*, pp. 320-321.

26. As quoted in L. Grayson and M. Bliss (eds.), *The Wretched of Canada, Letters to R. B. Bennett 1930-1935.* Toronto: University of Toronto Press, 1971.

27. *Ibid.*

28. From N. E. Hoopes (ed.), *Who Am I? Essays on the Alienated.* New York: Dell Publishing Company, 1969.

29. From *One Damn Thing After Another* by H. Garner, pp. 26-31. Copyright © 1973 Hugh Garner. Reprinted by permission of McGraw-Hill Ryerson Ltd.

30. "Not a Hobo, Just a Wanderer", in Barry Broadfoot, *op. cit.*, p. 18.

31. *Ibid.*, p. 316.

CHAPTER 9

1. From Ross Munro, *Gauntlet to Overlord: The Story of the Canadian Army*, p. ix. Edmonton: Hurtig Publishers, 1972.

2. From Nicholas Bethell, *The War Hitler Won: The Fall of Poland, September 1939*, pp. 30-31, 27. New York: Holt, Rinehart & Winston Ltd., 1972.

3. Buckminister Fuller, quoted in A. Cotterell and N. Collins (eds.), *Futureprobe*, p. 41. London: Heinemann Educational Books, 1974.

4. Senator Hiram Johnson, 1917.

5. From P. K. Knightley, *The First Casualty: From the Crimea to Vietnam: The War Correspondant as Hero, Propagandist, and Myth Maker*, p. 236. New York: Harcourt Brace Jovanovich, Inc., 1975.

6. Mackenzie King, *House of Commons Debates*, September 1939.

7. R. J. Manion, *House of Commons Debates*, September 1939.

8. M. J. Coldwell, *House of Commons Debates*, September 1939.

9. J. S. Woodsworth, *House of Commons Debates,*, September 1939.

10. From Col. C. P. Stacey, *Six Years of War*, p. 3. Ottawa: Queen's Printer, 1966. Reproduced by permission of the Department of Supply and Services, Ottawa.

12. From *The Tools of War 1939/45*. © 1969 The Reader's Digest Association (Canada) Ltd., Montreal.

13. As quoted in J. W. Pickersgill (ed.), *The Mackenzie King Record, Vol. I, 1939-1944*, p. 417. Toronto: University of Toronto Press, 1960.

14. J. L. Ralston, *House of Commons Debates*, 1943, Vol. III, pp. 2688-2691.

15. Mona Gould, "This Was My Brother", quoted in *The Poet's Record: Verses on Canadian History* by K. Wilson and E. Motheral. Toronto: McClelland & Stewart Ltd., 1975.

16. Matthew Halton, September 3, 1943. Printed by permission of the Canadian Broadcasting Corporation from the book *The Coming of Age* by D. C. Masters, D. Phil., F.R.C.S., pp. 83-84. Published in 1967.

17. From G. F. G. Stanley, *Canada's Soldiers: The Military History of An Unmilitary People*, pp. 367-368. Toronto: Macmillan Company of Canada, Ltd., 1974.

18. From *Ordeal By Fire*, copyright © 1961 by Ralph Allen, p. 443. Reprinted by permission of Doubleday and Company, Inc.

19. From Ross Munro, *op. cit.*, p. 90.

20. From *The Tools of War, 1939/45, op. cit.*

21. *Ibid.*

22. *Ibid.*

23. C. D. Howe, *House of Commons Debates*, Vol. I, 1910, p. 840.

24. C. D. Howe, *House of Commons Debates*, Vol. II, 1945, pp. 2243-2244.

25. From Alan Walker, *How Johnny Canuck Won the Second World War.* Toronto: The Canadian.

26. "Helping the War Effort" from the book *Six War Years, 1939-1945* by Barry Broadfoot, p. 129. Copyright © 1974 by Barry Broadfoot. Reprinted by permission of Doubleday and Company, Inc.

27. P. J. A. Cardin, *House of Commons Debates*, November 30, 1944, p. 6708.

28. Louis St. Laurent, *House of Commons Debates*, November 30, 1944, p. 6860.

29. "If Only They Knew", in Barry Broadfoot, *op. cit.*, p. 397.

CHAPTER 10

1. From "W.L.M.K.", by F. M. Scott in *Poets Between The Wars* by Milton Wilson (ed.), p. 97. Toronto: McClelland & Stewart Ltd., 1967.

2. As quoted in J. W. Pickersgill and D. F. Forster (eds.), *The Mackenzie King Record, Vol. IV, 1947-1948*, pp. 211, 212. Toronto: University of Toronto Press, 1970.

3. *Ibid.*, 212-213.

4. Reverend B. Fish Austin, 1890.

5. From *Smallwood, The Unlikely Revolutionary* by Richard Gwyn, p. 81. Toronto: McClelland & Stewart Ltd., 1968. Reprinted by permission of The Canadian Publishers, McClelland & Stewart Ltd., Toronto.

6. From Bruce Hutchison, *Mr. Prime Minister, 1867-1964*, p. 297. Toronto: Longman Canada Ltd., 1964.

7. From Dale Thomson, *Louis St. Laurent, Canadian*, p. 265. Toronto: Macmillan Company of Canada Ltd., 1967.

8. From *House of Commons Debates*, June 1, 1956, p. 4553.

9. From William Kilbourne, *Pipeline Transcanada and The Great Debate: A History Of Business and Politics*, p. 23. Toronto: Clarke, Irwin & Co., Ltd., 1970.

10. From *House of Commons Debates*, September 18, 1968.

11. *Ibid.*, March 26, 1965.

12. *Ibid.*, April 25, 1975.

13. *Ibid.*, March 24, 1955.

14. From an address given April 30, 1957 in New Glasgow, New Brunswick.

15. From J. M. Bliss (ed.), *Canadian History in Documents*, pp. 332-333. Toronto: McGraw-Hill Ryerson Ltd., 1966. Reprinted by permission of the Rt. Hon. J. G. Diefenbaker.

16. From *Renegade in Power: The Diefenbaker Years* by P. C. Newman, p. 71. Toronto: McClelland & Stewart Ltd., 1963. Reprinted by permission of The Canadian Publishers, McClelland & Stewart Ltd., Toronto.

17. From Bruce Hutchison, *op. cit.*, p. 315.

18. David Helwig, quoted in *Storm Warning, The New Canadian Poets* by A. Purdy (ed.), pp. 74-75. Toronto: McClelland & Stewart Ltd., 1971.

19. From *The Search For Identity* by Blair Fraser, pp. 244-245. Copyright © 1967 by Blair Fraser. Used by permission of Doubleday & Company, Inc.

20. *Ibid.*, p. 243.

21. *Ibid.*, p. 246.

22. From B. Thordarson, *Lester Pearson, Diplomat and Politician*, p. ix. Toronto: Oxford University Press, 1974.

23. From *The Distemper of Our Times, Canadian Politics in Transition: 1963-1968* by P. C. Newman, pp. 37, 42, 47. Toronto: McClelland & Stewart Ltd., 1968. Reprinted by permission of The Canadian Publishers, McClelland & Stewart Ltd., Toronto.

24. From *Stanfield* by G. Stevens, pp. 5, 5-6. Toronto: McClelland & Stewart Ltd., 1973. Reprinted by permission of The Canadian Publishers, McClelland & Stewart Ltd., Toronto.

25. Charles Lynch, *Winnipeg Tribune*, June 29, 1968.

26. From J. M. Beck, *Pendulum of Power*, pp. 416-417. Scarborough, Ontario: Prentice-Hall of Canada, Ltd., 1968.

27. G. Radwanski, "Bilingualism Battle Shows How Little We Have Learned", *Financial Times*, September 27, 1976, p. 2.

28. From "What is Canada Doing?", June 1974 Bulletin of the Canadian Commission for Unesco.

29. D. Anderson (ed.), "International Women's Year: Will Canadian Women Get Their $5 Millions Worth?", *Chatelaine*, February 1975.

30. Michele Landsberg, "IWY", *Chatelaine*, November 1975.

31. René Levesque, "For An Independent Quebec", *Foreign Affairs*. Reprinted by permission from *Foreign Affairs*, July 1976. Copyright 1976 by Council on Foreign Relations, Inc.

32. E. Birney, quoted in A. Purdy, *Fifteen Winds, A Selection of Modern Canadian Poets*, p. 15. Toronto: McGraw-Hill Ryerson Ltd., 1969. Reprinted by permission of The Canadian Publishers, McClelland & Stewart Ltd., Toronto.

33. Alden Nowlan, quoted in Weaver and Toye (eds.), *The Oxford Anthology of Canadian Literature*, pp. 377-378. Toronto: Oxford University Press, 1973.

34. Irving Layton, quoted in *Poetry of Mid-Century 1940-1960* by M. Wilson (ed.), p. 83. Toronto: McClelland & Stewart Ltd., 1964. Reprinted by permission of The Canadian Publishers, McClelland & Stewart Ltd., Toronto.

35. P. Desjardin, quoted in *Storm Warning, The New Canadian Poets* by A. Purdy, *op. cit.*, p. 47.

36. D. Zieroth, quoted in *Storm Warning, The New Canadian Poets* by A. Purdy, *op. cit.*, p. 151.

37. From M. Waddington, *Driving Home: Poems New and Selected*, pp. 175-176. Toronto: Oxford University Press, 1972.

38. From W. O. Mitchell, *Who Has Seen The Wind*, pp. 32-33, 191. Toronto: Macmillan Company of Canada, Ltd., 1947.

39. From *Stone Angel* by Margaret Laurence, pp. 209-302. Toronto: McClelland & Stewart Ltd., 1964. Reprinted by permission of The Canadian Publishers, McClelland & Stewart Ltd., Toronto.

40. From *The Edible Woman* by Margaret Atwood, pp. 269-271. Toronto: McClelland & Stewart Ltd., 1969. Reprinted by permission of The Canadian Publishers, McClelland & Stewart Ltd., Toronto.

41. From M. Richler, *The Apprenticeship of Duddy Kravitz*, p. 56. Markham, Ontario: Penguin Books of Canada Ltd., 1964.

42. From *Lives of Girls and Women* by Alice Munro, pp. 372-374. Copyright © 1971. Reprinted by permission of McGraw-Hill Ryerson Ltd.

43. From *The Tin Flute* by Gabrielle Roy, pp. 82-83. Toronto: McClelland & Stewart Ltd., 1969. Reprinted by permission of The Canadian Publishers, McClelland & Stewart Ltd., Toronto.

CHAPTER 11

1. From *A Leisure Study—Canada 1972*. Ottawa: Federal Department of Secretary of State, Arts & Culture Branch. Reproduced by permission of the Department of Supply & Services, Ottawa.

2. J. Batten, "About the CRTC", *Saturday Night*, April 1972.

3. R. Mercer, "COC a 150-Year History", *Opera Canada*, Vol. XIV, No. 3, Fall 1973, p. 45.

4. From *Inner Views: Ten Canadian Filmmakers* by J. Hofsess, pp. 11-12. Copyright © 1975. Reprinted by permission of McGraw-Hill Ryerson Ltd.

5. *Ibid.*, pp. 13-14, 21-22.

6. C. Jutra, "How Not to Make a Canadian Film", quoted in A. Pâquet (ed.), *How To Make Or Not To Make A Canadian Film*, p. 19. Montreal: La Cinémathèque Québécoise, 1967.

7. J. Foley, "Canlit", *Canadian Literature*, No. 64, Spring 1975, p. 127.

8. G. Russell, "Cultural Chain Gang", *Time Canada*, January 19, 1976, p. 8. Copyright © 1976 by The New York Times Company. Reprinted by permission.

9. R. MacMillan, "Yes! There IS a Canadian Opera", Opera Canada, Vol. XVII, No. 3, Fall 1973, p. 12.

10. R. Mercer, *op. cit.*, pp. 48-49.

11. Applebaum, *The Canadian Composer/Le Compositeur Canadien*, January 1974.

12. From James F. Murphy, *Concepts of Leisure, Philosophical Implications*, p. 237. Copyright © 1974. Reprinted by permission of Prentice-Hall Inc., Englewood Cliffs, New Jersey.
13. *Ibid.*, p. 15.

CHAPTER 12

1. "Quality of Life in Canada", cited in *Perspective Canada: A Compendium of Social Statistics*, p. xxi. Ottawa: Ministry of Industry, Trade & Commerce, 1974. Reproduced by permission of the Department of Supply and Services, Ottawa.
2. Scott Young, "Pay-off In Oil", *Maclean's Magazine*, June 15, 1947, pp. 7-8.
3. From *An Energy Strategy for Canada*, p. 90. Ottawa: Department of Energy, Mines and Resources, 1971. Reproduced by permission of the Department of Supply and Services, Ottawa.
4. *Ibid.*, p. 91.
5. *Ibid.*, pp. 92-93.
6. D. Johnson, "Miles and miles of pipeline to bring gas and oil south to markets", *Financial Times*, Vol. 65, No. 9, August 2, 1976.
7. "The National Debt: Selected Years", cited in the *Canada Year Book*, 1945, 1951, 1959, 1972, 1974. Reproduced by permission of the Department of Supply and Services, Ottawa.
8. From P. E. Trudeau, *Conversations with Canadians*, pp. 103-104. Toronto: University of Toronto Press, 1972. Reprinted by permission of the Canadian Broadcasting Corporation.
9. "Equipment by Households for Canada, Selected Years May 1961 to April 1973", cited in *Canadian Consumer Credit Fact Book*, p. 71. Toronto: Association of Canadian Financial Corporations, 1974.
10. *Canadian Labour*, December 1975, pp. 25, 27. Ottawa: Canadian Labour Congress, 1975.
11. *The Bulletin*, quoted in *Labour Gazette*, February 1975. Ottawa: Canadian Department of Labour.
12. "Sign of the Times: Watching the C.P.I.", cited in the *Canada Year Book*, 1974, p. 800. Reproduced by permission of the Department of Supply and Services, Ottawa.
13. From M. Lazarus, *Years Of Hard Labour*, p. 94. Toronto: Co-operative Press Associates, 1974.
14. *Labour Gazette*, June 1975, p. 362. Ottawa: Canadian Department of Labour.
15. From M. Lazarus, *op. cit.*, p. 70.
16. "The Extent of Unionization", *Labour Gazette*, June 1975, p. 350. Ottawa: Canadian Department of Labour.
17. From C. I. Jackson (ed.) *Canadian Settlements—Perspectives*, p. 47. Ottawa: Ministry of State for Urban Affairs, 1975. Reproduced by permission of the Department of Supply and Services, Ottawa.
18. *Ibid.*, pp. 48-49.

CHAPTER 13

1. From *Foreign Policy For Canadians*, p. 8. Ottawa: Information Canada, 1970. Reproduced by permission of the Department of Supply and Services, Ottawa.
2. From *Foreign Investment Review Act—Annual Report 1974-1975*, pp. 1, 6, 10, 11, 36. Ottawa: Foreign Investment Review Agency, 1975. Reproduced by permission of the Minister of Supply and Services Canada.
3. From "Allowed Cases: Significant Benefits to Canada Summarized by Principal Factors of Assessment—Fiscal 1974-1975". Reproduced by permission of the Minister of Supply and Services Canada.
4. "Hardy Idea", *The Calgary Herald*, October 20, 1975.
5. "Canadian Identity", *The National Lampoon*. Reprinted by permission of The National Lampoon, Inc. from the May, 1976 issue.

6. "Defining Canada" by Lister Sinclair is reprinted from *Notes for a Native Land*, p. 143 by permission of Oberon Press, 1969.

7. "Could You Be A Canadian in Disguise?", *The Canadian*, December 29, 1973. Reprinted by permission of the National Lampoon, Inc.

8. From *Charlie Farquharson's History of Canada*. Copyright © Don Harron 1972. Reprinted by permission of McGraw-Hill Ryerson Ltd.

9. From Murray Soupcoff & Gary Dunford (eds.), *Inside From The Outside: Good Buy Canada!* Toronto: James Lorimer & Co., Publishers, 1975.

10. Henry Morgan, "Toronto After Six Months: An Exile's Report", *Saturday Review*, April 22, 1972.

11. Mackenzie King, August 20, 1938.

12. R. B. Byers, "The Canadian military and the use of force: the end of an era", *International Journal 1974-1975*, pp. 289-290.

13. From the *House of Commons Debates*, April 29, 1948, p. 3443.

14. *Ibid.*, pp. 3449-3450.

15. From *Defence 1975*. Ottawa: Department of National Defence, 1976. Reproduced by permission of the Minister of Supply and Services Canada.

16. J. L. Granatstein, "External Affairs and Defense", *Canadian Annual Review*, pp. 314-315. Toronto: University of Toronto Press. Copyright 1970 by University of Toronto Press. Reprinted by permission of the University of Toronto Press.

17. From the *United Nations Charter*, 1945.

18. From J. R. Beal, *The Pearson Phenomenon*, pp. 116-117. Toronto: Longman Canada Ltd., 1964.

19. Based on Barbara Stanford (ed.), *On Being Female, An Anthology*. New York: Simon & Schuster Inc. (Washington Square Press ed.), 1974.

20. From "The Adventures of Billy Buyer in Africa: Shake-Em-Up Comics", p. 6. Ottawa: CIDA (Canadian International Development Agency).

21. Based on *Canada: Strategy for International Development Cooperation, 1975-1980*, Appendix VIII, p. 48. Ottawa: Information Canada, 1975. Reproduced by permission of the Ministry of Supply and Services Canada.

22. From *Canada: A Middle Aged Power* by John Holmes, pp. 3-4, 4. Toronto: McClelland & Stewart Ltd., 1976. Reprinted by permission of The Canadian Publishers, McClelland & Stewart Ltd., Toronto.

23. Max Saltsman, quoted in Dean Walker (ed.), *Canada and the Third World, What are the Choices?*, pp. 181-182. Toronto: Canadian Institute on Public Affairs, 1975.

24. Mohammed Azhar Ali Khan, quoted in Dean Walker, *op. cit.*, pp. 132-133.

25. I. G. Patel, quoted in Dean Walker, *op. cit.*, p. 92.

26. "Nuclear Power Made Simple", *Canadian Review*, July 1976.

27. From *The Silent Language* by E. T. Hall, p. 175. Copyright © 1973 by E. T. Hall. Used by permission of Doubleday and Company, Inc.

28. From James Eayrs, *Right and Wrong in Foreign Policy*, pp. 31-32. Toronto: University of Toronto Press. Copyright 1966 by University of Toronto Press. Reprinted by permission of the University of Toronto Press.

CHAPTER 14

Immigration

1. From the *Green Paper on Immigration and Population* tabled in the House of Commons on February 3, 1975.

Consumers in Canada

1. Ellen Roseman. *Consumer, Beware!*, Toronto: New Press, 1974.

The Food and People Dilemma

1. *United Nations Population Fund*. New York: United Nations.

2. Georg Borgstrom. *The Food and People Dilemma*. North Scituate, Mass.: Duxbury Press, 1973. p. 27.
3. *Population Issues*, C.U.S.O.
4. William Rich. *Smaller Families through Social and Economic Progress*. Washington, D.C.: Overseas Development Council, 1973. p. 2.
5. Lincoln H. Day and Alice Taylor Day, *Too Many Americans*. Houghton-Mifflin, 1964. c The American Sociological Association.
6. Borgstrom, *op. cit.*, p. 16.
7. *Ibid.*, p. 15.
8. *Ibid.*, p. 17.
10. Donella H. Meadows *et al. Limits to Growth*. New York: Universe Books, 1974. pp. 67-68.

The Many Faces of Violence

1. Robert Ardrey. "Man the Killer". *Psychology Today*, September, 1972. pp. 85.
2. Heather Robertson. *Maclean's*. March, 1973.

Technology the Good: Uses

1. Herbert J. Muller. *The Children of Frankenstein: A Primer on Modern Technology and Human Values*. Bloomington, Indiana: Indiana University Press, 1970. pp. 91-92.
2. *Ibid.*, p. 3.
3. *Ibid.*, p. x.

Technology the Bad: Misuses

1. E. F. Schumacher. *Small is Beautiful, Economics as if People Mattered*. New York: Harper & Row Perennial Library, 1973. pp. 17-18.
2. *Winnipeg Free Press*, November 13, 1975. (CP)

The Family and Sex Roles: New Perspectives

1. From *Canada and the World*. "What Kind of a Family Would you like to have in the Future?", October, 1973.
2. John Nichol in the *Winnipeg Tribune*, February 3, 1975.

Lifestyle: A Game of Human Settlements

1. Based on material from *Human Settlements: The Environmental Challenge*. A compendium of U.N. papers for the Stockholm Conference on the Environment.

Index